CW01307459

THE AUSTRALIAN ARMY

The Australian Army History series

(General Editor: David Horner)

Janette Bomford	*Soldiers of the Queen: Women in the Australian Army*
John Coates	*Bravery above Blunder: The 9th Australian Division at Finschhafen, Sattelberg, and Sio*
David Coombes	*Morshead: Hero of Tobruk and El Alamein*
C.D. Coulthard-Clark	*Australia's Military Map-makers: The Royal Australian Survey Corps 1915–96*
Peter S. Sadler	*The Paladin: A Life of Major-General Sir John Gellibrand*
Michael B. Tyquin	*Neville Howse: Australia's First Victoria Cross Winner*
Glenn Wahlert	*The Other Enemy? Australian Soldiers and the Military Police*

THE AUSTRALIAN ARMY

A History of its Organisation 1901–2001

Albert Palazzo

OXFORD
UNIVERSITY PRESS

OXFORD
UNIVERSITY PRESS

253 Normanby Road, South Melbourne, Victoria, Australia
Oxford University Press is a department of the University of Oxford.
It furthers the University's objective of excellence in research, scholarship,
and education by publishing worldwide in

Oxford New York

Athens Auckland Bangkok Bogotá Buenos Aires Cape Town
Chennai Dar es Salaam Delhi Florence Hong Kong Istanbul Karachi
Kolkata Kuala Lumpur Madrid Melbourne Mexico City Mumbai Nairobi
Paris São Paulo Shanghai Singapore Taipei Tokyo Toronto Warsaw
with associated companies in Berlin Ibadan

OXFORD is a trade mark of Oxford University Press

Copyright © 2001 Commonwealth of Australia

First published 2001
Reprinted 2002

This book is copyright. Apart from any fair dealing for the purposes
of private study, research, criticism or review as permitted under the
Copyright Act, no part may be reproduced, stored in a retrieval system,
or transmitted, in any form or by any means, electronic, mechanical,
photocopying, recording or otherwise, without prior written permission.
Enquiries to be made to Oxford University Press.

Copying for educational purposes
Where copies of part or the whole of the book are made under Part VB
of the Copyright Act, the law requires that prescribed procedures be
followed. For information, contact the Copyright Agency Limited.

National Library of Australia
Cataloguing-in-publication data:

> Palazzo, Albert, 1957- .
> The Australian Army: a history of its organisation 1901–2001
> Bibliography.
> Includes index.
> ISBN 0 19 551507 2 (slipcase).
> ISBN 0 19 551506 4 (hbk).
>
> 1. Australia. Army—History. 2. Australia—History,
> Military. I. Title. (Series: Australian Army History series.)
> 355.30994

Edited by Bruce Gillespie
Indexed by Geraldine Suter
Text designed by Jason Phillips
Cover designed by Jason Phillips at Polar Design Pty Ltd
Typeset by Polar Design Pty Ltd
Printed in China through The Bookmaker International Ltd

Oxford University Press and the Australian Army would like to thank the staff of the
Australian War Memorial, Canberra, for their assistance in locating, and
permission to reproduce, many of the photographs.

To the men and women of the Australian Army

Contents

Illustrations	viii
Tables	x
Maps	xiv
Charts	xv
Acknowledgments	xvi
1 The origins of army organisation	1
2 From Federation to World War I	14
3 World War I	62
4 The interwar years	81
5 World War II	135
6 Post-war reorganisation and the Korean War	192
7 The rise of the Australian Regular Army	229
8 The defence of Australia	309
9 The future of army organisation	373
Abbreviations	388
Notes	395
Bibliography	436
Index	447

Illustrations

General Sir Edward Hutton	18
Agricultural High School Cadets, Sale, Vic, 1909	45
No. 5 Battery, Australian Field Artillery, 1908	49
Staff cadets on parade at Royal Military College, Duntroon, 1913	58
Major-General Sir William T. Bridges	64
Mena Army Camp, Egypt, 1915	66
Brigadier-General C. B. B. White	69
Brigadier-General T. H. Dodds	73
Major-General J. G. Legge	86
Lieutenant-General Sir John Monash	89
Lieutenant-General Sir J. J. T. Hobbs and staff	90
Lieutenant-General Sir Harry Chauvel	94
Lieutenant-General J. D. Lavarack	116
Major-General Sir Julius Bruche	120
Lieutenant-General Ernest Squires	124
1st Armoured Division at Puckapunyal, 1942	145
General Sir Thomas Blamey	149
Coastal Artillery gunners	155
Darwin Mobile Force during anti-gas drill	160
Army Boat 442 *Frances Peat* at Lae, New Guinea	161

ILLUSTRATIONS

Lieutenant-General Sir Iven Mackay	164
General Douglas MacArthur	173
Lieutenant-General John Northcott	176
Lieutenant-General J. Northcott inspecting Australian troops	199
Lieutenant-Colonel F. S. Walsh (3 RAR, BCOF) receives the Gloucester Cup	200
Lieutenant-General S. Rowell	204
Lieutenant-General V. A. H. Sturdee	222
Major-General George F. Wootten	227
Lieutenant-General Sir John Wilton	269
Russell Office Complex	314
Lieutenant-General Sir Leslie Morshead	315
Lieutenant-General Peter Gration	323
Armoured Personnel Carrier of 5/7 RAR	329
Members of a Regional Force Surveillance unit	332
The campus of the Australian Defence Force Academy	335
Army aviation: a Blackhawk helicopter	339
The SAS on patrol	340
Major-General John Sanderson	363
Australian light armoured vehicles	365
An armoured personnel carrier on Exercise K95	375
Lieutenant-General Peter Cosgrove	376

Tables

1.1	Population of Australia, 1905–95	5
2.1	Strength of the Australian Army at Federation, by State	16
2.2	Establishment of cadet corps and rifle clubs, 1901	17
2.3	Distribution of garrison force formations	28
2.4	Composition of typical infantry brigade	29
2.5	Composition of typical light horse brigade	30
2.6	Distribution of field force brigades	31
2.7	Composition and distribution of 5th Light Horse Brigade, 1904–05	31
2.8	Expansion of the army under the Universal Training Scheme, 1911–14	54
3.1	Recruitment of AIF, 1st Contingent	65
3.2	Organisation of the 1st AIF, 1918	68
4.1	Proposed post-war army, 1919	85
4.2	Training program recommended by the Swinburne Committee	87
4.3	Major formations and catchments for the post-World War I army	91
4.4	Field army personnel requirements	92
4.5	Organisation of the army, 1928: major formations and units	102

TABLES

4.6	COMPARISON OF DEFENCE FORCE STRENGTH, 1921–22 AND 1922–23	104
4.7	REDUCTION IN PERMANENT FORCE PERSONNEL, 1922	105
4.8	AUSTRALIAN COASTAL DEFENCES, AUGUST 1939	117
4.9	AUSTRALIAN ANTI-AIRCRAFT DEFENCES, AUGUST 1939	118
5.1	DISTRIBUTION AND STRENGTH OF GARRISON BATTALIONS, OCTOBER 1939	137
5.2	DISPOSITION AND STRENGTH OF GARRISON BATTALIONS, EARLY 1942	138
5.3	ORGANISATION OF THE 2ND AIF: MAJOR FORMATIONS, 1941	142
5.4	COMPARISON OF AUSTRALIAN AND BRITISH DIVISIONAL STRUCTURES FOR THE 6TH DIVISION	143
5.5	COMPARISON OF CMF FIELD FORCE WAR ESTABLISHMENT AND AVAILABLE STRENGTH, EARLY 1942	147
5.6	ORGANISATION OF THE 3RD DIVISION, SEPTEMBER 1939	151
5.7	ORGANISATION OF THE ARMY'S SCHOOL SYSTEM, FEBRUARY 1944	154
5.8	ANTI-AIRCRAFT ORGANISATION, LATE 1942	158
5.9	WAR ESTABLISHMENT REQUIREMENTS OF THE ARMY, SEPTEMBER 1943	175
5.10	COMPARISON OF JUNGLE AND STANDARD DIVISION ORGANISATIONS	185
5.11	ORGANISATION OF VOLUNTEER DEFENCE CORPS, 1944	189
6.1	DISTRIBUTION OF FIELD FORCE PERSONNEL IN THE POST-WAR ARMY, 1947	207
6.2	DISTRIBUTION OF FIXED ESTABLISHMENT PERSONNEL IN THE POST-WAR ARMY, 1947	207
6.3	ORDER OF BATTLE OF PMF FIELD FORCE UNITS	208
6.4	ORDER OF BATTLE OF THE CMF FIELD FORCE	209
6.5	ORGANISATION OF FIXED DEFENCES	211
6.6	ORDER OF BATTLE, CMF SUPPLEMENTARY RESERVE	215
6.7	CADET CORPS ORDER OF BATTLE, 1948	217
7.1	DISTRIBUTION OF MAJOR CMF COMBAT FORMATIONS, APRIL 1953	238
7.2	ESTABLISHMENT OF PLAN A FIELD FORCE	242
7.3	COMPOSITION OF THE ARMY: PLAN A	244
7.4	COMPOSITION OF THE ARMY: PLAN B	245

TABLES

7.5	Organisation of ARA brigade group, 1957	246
7.6	Organisation of ARA battalion group, 1957	246
7.7	Organisation of ARA brigade group: logistical support force	247
7.8	Organisation of ARA battalion group: logistical support force	247
7.9	Composition of regular army, 1956–57	248
7.10	Manpower deficiency in ARA brigade group, 31 July 1958	250
7.11	Comparison of existing order of battle with proposed pentropic order of battle: ARA formations	253
7.12	Comparison of existing order of battle with proposed pentropic order of battle: CMF formations	254
7.13	Current and planned allocation of strength in the ARA	256
7.14	Redesignation of CMF battalions as pentropic companies	259
7.15	Main elements of 1st Division (pentropic)	261
7.16	Main elements of 3rd Division (pentropic)	262
7.17	Main elements of combat support group for 1st Division (pentropic)	262
7.18	Main elements of combat support group for 3rd Division (pentropic)	263
7.19	Australian Task Force order of battle, 1970: main units	281
7.20	Comparison of 1964 army manpower allocation with estimated post-Vietnam requirements	283
7.21	Allocation of field force strength in June 1973 compared with 1976 goal	286
7.22	CMF strength, March 1970	294
7.23	Amalgamation and disbandment of CMF units, 1974: major units	300
7.24	Units transferred to the Papua New Guinea Defence Force upon independence of PNG	303
7.25	Australian army units remaining in Papua New Guinea upon independence of PNG	303
8.1	Movement plan for the increased army presence in northern Australia, 1991–92 to 2000–01	342

TABLES

8.2	Projected share of combat force soldiers in the north of Australia, 1991–92 to 2000–01	343
8.3	Logistic Command order of battle, 1991	345
8.4	Force element groups: levels of personnel and preparedness, 1990–91	346
8.5	Planned distribution of personnel in Land Command after implementation of force structure review	350
8.6	Land Command order of battle, June 1991	351
8.7	Raising of brigade administrative support battalions	356
8.8	Army personnel levels, 1990s	360
9.1	Army's combat order of battle, 1999: major elements	379

Maps

1	Australia and its neighbours	2
2	Australian territory at Federation	15
3	Kitchener Plan of the regional distribution of Australian Army	52
4	Regional organisation of army administration, 1911	55
5	Australian territory, 1919	82
6	South-West Pacific Area service boundary	152
7	Coastal defence at its peak, 1944	157
8	Regional organisation of army administration, 1939	163
9	Regional organisation of army administration, 1944	168
10	Japanese occupation zone	202
11	Regional organisation of army administration, 1946	223
12	Regional organisation of army administration, 1950	224
13	Australian territory, 1975	308

Charts

1	Composition and duties of the Military Board, 1909	36
2	Office of the Chief of the General Staff (CGS), 1909	47
3	Post-war chain of command, 1920	100
4	Squires' proposal to reform the geographic control of the army	129
5	The army's higher direction, 1941	165
6	The army's higher direction within Australia after Japan's entry, 1942	166
7	The army's higher direction: organisation of Land Headquarters, 1944	169
8A	Distribution of the Australian Army, May 1942	170
8B	Distribution of the Australian Army, September 1943	179
8C	Distribution of the Australian Army, February 1944	180
8D	Distribution of the Australian Army, August 1945	181
9	Organisation chart of Army Headquarters	226
10	Army post-pentropic organisation, 1965	276
11	Army higher direction, Hassett reforms, 1973	293
12	Defence higher organisation, 1976	319
13	Defence higher organisation, 1988	322
14	Defence higher organisation, 1999	382

Acknowledgments

In preparing this manuscript, I have incurred a great number of debts. It was written during my tenure as a Research Associate in the School of History, University College, Australian Defence Force Academy, University of New South Wales. The School of History has been fundamentally involved in this project and, in particular, I would like to express my thanks to Professor Peter Dennis and Associate Professor Robin Prior. Also of the School of History, I must express my great thanks to John Connor for all his assistance. In addition, I would like to extend my gratitude to Roger Lee, the Head of the Army History Unit, for the opportunity to undertake this study.

The problems of this manuscript's research were greatly eased by the professionalism of the staffs of a number of repositories. I would like to thank the staffs of the National Archives of Australia—Victorian, Australian Capital Territory, and New South Wales branches, the Australian War Memorial, the Manuscript Room of the National Library of Australia, the Special Collections section of the Library of the Australian Defence Force Academy, and the staff of the Department of Defence Central Registry.

1

THE ORIGINS OF ARMY ORGANISATION

The geographical position of Australia and its now considerable population render it comparatively little liable to aggression from any Foreign Power. In view of the Military Force now in existence, and the strong spirit which animates it, territorial aggression, except upon a large scale, would be impossible.[1]

Upon Federation, the new state of Australia, formed by the union of six former colonies, assumed control over many of the prerogatives reserved to sovereign states. Among the myriad new responsibilities, that of the defence of its territories, subjects, and interests, along with the merger of the colonial forces into the first Australian Army, were among the most critical. Although Australia would at first defer to Britain certain important national responsibilities, such as foreign policy, and while it would remain for the immediate future under the defence umbrella provided by the imperial army and navy, international security and the organisation of the country's military forces would emerge as central questions in the development of the nation state and its character.

The term 'first Australian Army' is employed deliberately. Although there has been continuity in the provision of a military force, during its hundred-year history the Australian Army has had structures of such differing composition as to suggest the existence of a series of distinct military bodies. However, while the organisation of the army has frequently and sometimes dramatically changed, tradition, culture, and a common national purpose have provided enduring constants that have linked the structure into a continuous institution. Moreover, these changes are part of a natural and essential process. All armies must, under the stress of ever-advancing technologies, shifting national priorities and diplomatic initiatives, and adjustments to relative power relationships, to mention just a few potential security variables, periodically reinterpret their organisation. Therefore, the relationship between an army and its

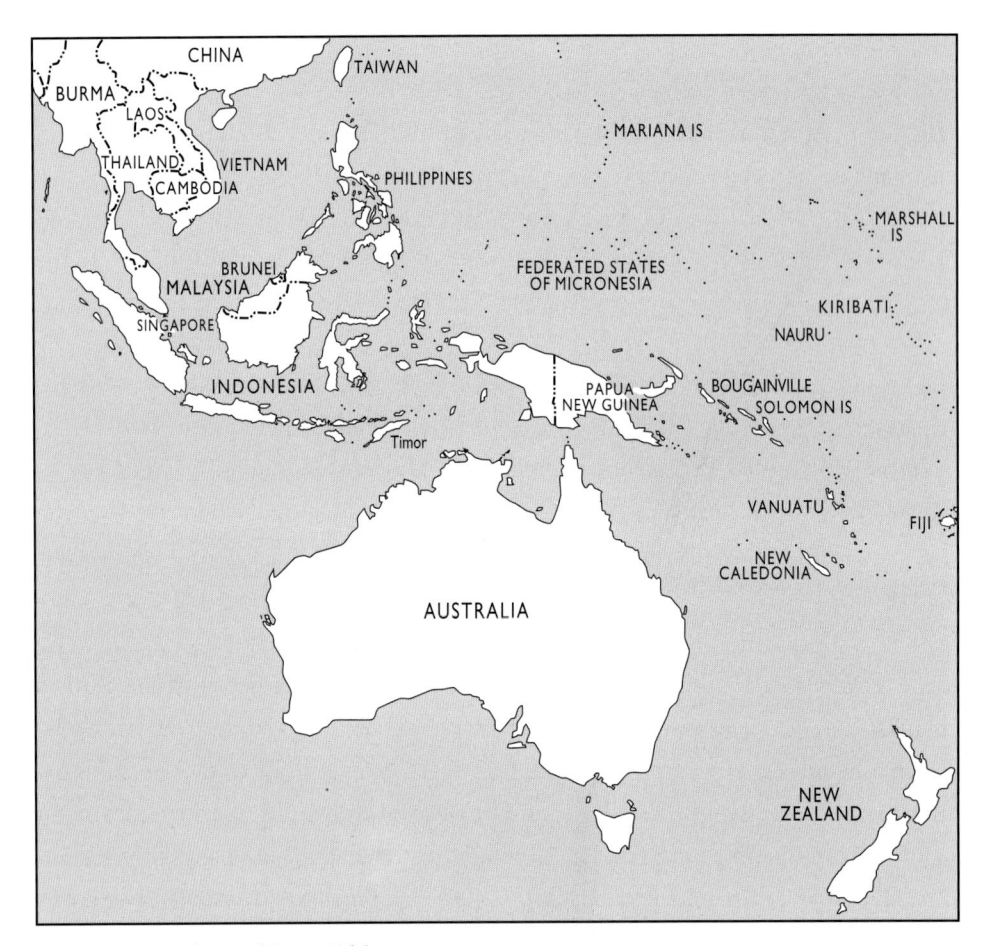

Map 1 Australia and its neighbours

parent society should be a dynamic one. As the national polity interprets its security needs and responsibilities, the Australian Army must respond in a manner that best, and most efficiently, meets the requirements of the nation.

This work is a history of the Australian Army in its most basic form. It is neither an account of battle nor a saga of heroism, although these factors do play a part in defining the army. Rather, it is a study of the institutional make-up of the army and, in particular, the organisation of its forces, both the field force and the support elements, in peace and war. It will discuss the army's organisation, in its many permutations, from the attainment of Federation through to the present. It will also attempt to peer into the near future, as the army of the twenty-first century takes shape.

The interpretation of this brief will be in the broadest possible context. This work recognises that the organisation of an army is determined by a number of interdependent conflicting and variable issues. Therefore, it will discuss not only the actual organisation of the Australian Army but also the influences that acted upon the military and political leadership as they determined the shape of the force. These influences are many, and include political requirements such as the budgetary imperative, civil–military relations, conscription versus voluntarism, and alliance responsibilities. Other factors of a strategic nature include the perception and reality of threat and the desired level of power projection. Another set of determinants include those pertaining to the military services themselves, such as inter-service conflicts and intra-army rivalry over the allocation of resources and missions, and the tensions that might exist between regular and reserve (citizen and militia) components.

Having identified the army's organisation and explained the factors that guided the judgment of decision-makers, this work will also analyse whether the resulting force and its capabilities were in actuality appropriate for the force's mission requirements. As this study will demonstrate, even after careful reflection by the army's leaders, the resulting organisation was sometimes poorly designed to fulfil the role expected of it by the political heads of the country. The final objective of this work is its most difficult. It is also, however, potentially its most important. The process by which a country designs or reorganises its military forces is one of the most important decisions it can make. As such, it cannot be taken too lightly. The formation of an army is one of the most difficult and expensive tasks a nation can undertake, but also one of such vital importance that failure risks the very survival of a people. Therefore, an understanding of this process in the Australian context is critical, not only for the development of the army but also, possibly, for the future of the nation.

The parameters of army organisation

The intellectual processes by which decision-makers determine the organisation of an army occur within a framework of certain definable parameters. These parameters might be constants, such as geography, which does not effectively change, or they can be variables, such as culture. However, while the latter are variable, the rate of change tends to be slow. Thus the forces affecting the selection of an army's organisation are fairly inflexible, especially over the relatively brief period of time under consideration in this work. Since these conditions are generally present throughout the period under discussion, it will be beneficial to identify them here in order to avoid repetition in subsequent chapters.

Geographic parameter

Australia's geographic position has had a profound effect upon the development of its national security requirements and the nature of its military force. Foremost, the nation occupies an island continent that would require any potential opponent to obtain, at a minimum, local naval superiority before attempting an invasion. The sea has provided the nation with a defensive moat, an advantage unavailable to countries that share a land border with a potentially hostile neighbour. Furthermore, the continent is isolated. Its position, with wide oceans on three sides and with nearby landmasses only off the northern perimeter, has served to increase the buffering effect of the sea. Certain technological innovations, such as the aeroplane, the cruise missile, and the intercontinental ballistic missile, have weakened the sea's protective mantle, but it still remains a formidable barrier to any attempt to invade Australia.

Despite the advantages the sea confers, Australia's lengthy oceanic lines of communication also represent a potential weakness. The Australian economy is highly dependent upon the security of its seaborne commerce, and the nation's shipping is vulnerable to attack by hostile forces at great distances from Commonwealth territory.

While Australia is the smallest continent, it is still a considerable landmass. Including Tasmania, it encompasses nearly 7.7 million square kilometres, or 5.7 per cent of the earth's total land surface. The coastline is also considerable, and measures over 36,700 kilometres. In addition, until World War I Australia maintained southeastern New Guinea as a colony. After the war it added the former German colony of north-east New Guinea as well as the adjacent Bismarck, Admiralty, and Solomon Island groups to its territory under a League of Nations (later United Nations) mandate. These areas obtained independence in 1975.

The Australian defensive perimeter is further affected by its sovereignty over a number of small offshore islands. These include Norfolk and Lord Howe Islands off the east coast, the Cocos, Christmas, McDonald, and Heard Islands in the Indian Ocean, Macquarie Island in the Southern Ocean, the Coral Seas Island Territory off Queensland, as well as various islets and reefs in the Arafura Sea. Although at present these islands do not contain significant known resources of commercial value, they represent potential assets. If, for example, improvements in seabed mining reveal recoverable mineral resources, the value of these territories may increase significantly. The Australian Government recently recognised the potential of these islands when it settled a boundary dispute with Indonesia in 1997 over the Arafura Sea, thereby eliminating an impasse to seabed mineral exploration. East Timor's recent emergence as an independent country, however, adds a new complication to the region. In addition to mining, Australia also needs to maintain its fishing interests in these waters. Finally, Australia has responsibility for a large section of Antarctica.

Demographic parameter

Despite its large territorial responsibilities, Australia's population has always been sparse, especially when compared to the much more heavily and densely populated regions to the north. Table 1.1 summarises the population of Australia at various points in time.

Table 1.1 Population of Australia, 1905–95 (in thousands)[2]

State	1905	1935	1945	1995
NSW	1,470	2,145	2,918	6,115
VIC	1,205	1,837	2,007	4,502
QLD	529	968	1,007	3,277
SA	359	585	627	1,474
WA	248	447	488	1,732
TAS	183	229	249	473
NT	4	5	11	174
ACT	0	10	15	304
National total	*3,998*	*6,226*	*7,322*	*18,051*

Furthermore, the population has remained concentrated in a fairly narrow coastal arc from Brisbane in the north to Adelaide in the south, with an isolated population cluster centred on Perth in Western Australia. The largest inland centre is Canberra, with approximately 300,000 people; however, it is situated less than 200 kilometres from the sea. Despite the recent growth of the Northern Territory, the population catchments of Melbourne, Sydney, and Brisbane/Gold Coast have increasingly come to dominate the national settlement distribution.

Another consistent demographic trend is the nation's growing preference for urban concentration. Census reports for 1911 described 43 per cent of the population as rural, a figure that has since steadily contracted, to reach a mere 15 per cent in 1991.

Infrastructure parameter

The combination of a large landmass with a relatively small and concentrated population has resulted in a fairly poor transportation infrastructure over much of the country. Except near major population centres, roads tend to be infrequent, narrow, poorly designed for heavy traffic, and, until recently, unsealed. Railways connect most of the major centres, but there are major gaps in the network. The principal rail routes are in the eastern and southern parts of the country, with another cluster in the south-western corner of Western Australia. A transcontinental railway connecting Western Australia with the rest of the nation opened in 1917; however, the frequently proposed transcentral Australian line has never been completed, leaving Darwin unconnected to the national rail net. Much of the Top End remains without rail access, except for isolated lines serving the mining industry. In 1901, there were 20,200 kilometres of track in Australia. Trackage peaked in 1941, with 43,800 kilometres in use, before declining to 39,400 in 1979.

Further complicating the rail situation is that the States, following colonial practice, constructed their lines on different gauges. New South Wales adopted the British standard gauge of 4 feet 8.5 inches, Victoria and South Australia built their lines according to the Irish wide gauge of 5 feet 3 inches, whereas Queensland, Tasmania, and Western Australia constructed their lines on the basis of a narrow gauge of 3 feet 6 inches. After World War II, the government slowly adjusted the lines connecting the principal cities to standard gauge, but it wasn't until 1969 that the first freight train crossed Australia from Sydney to Perth without a break of gauge. However, many regional lines still employ non-standard track widths.

Racial parameter

The racial origins of the Australian nation also provide certain parameters that affect the organisation of the army. Initially, the white inhabitants of Australia came predominantly from the British Empire. It was not until after World War II that the government encouraged the emigration of people from eastern and southern Europe. In 1901, to prevent immigration by Asians the government established, as one of its first legislative acts, the 'white Australia policy'. Immigration by non-whites remained prohibitive for most of the twentieth century, and the government did not adopt a racially neutral immigration policy until 1974. Consequently, the population of Australia remains heavily derived from British and, to a lesser extent, European stock while races of non-Western origins are represented by small minorities.

Cultural parameter

Australia's founding as a group of British colonies and its settlement principally by British subjects has resulted in an enduring relationship with the 'mother country' that affected the development of an Australia-centred national security policy.

Although Australians developed their own national character, they continued to regard Britain's armed forces as the nation's first line of defence. The familial association between the two countries was also responsible for the willingness of Australians to come to the empire's assistance in both world wars, the Malayan Emergency, and Confrontation. The practice of looking to Britain in defence matters created a cycle of security dependency upon the empire that did not fully come to an end until the conclusion of the Vietnam War.

The principles of defence planning

The principles of defence planning, at its most fundamental conception, consist of two interrelated points. First, it is essential to identify a threat against one's country and interests; and second, it is necessary to determine what resources the state will employ to counter the said threat. Although seemingly simple, defence planning is perhaps the most difficult and complex task a government can undertake. Furthermore, the failure to get it right can have catastrophic results for the nation, including the demise of its existence as an independent polity and its citizens as a free people. It is, therefore, understandable that defence planning is an essential duty of all responsible governments.

What makes the process of defence planning complex is the multitude of inputs that exist, and for which there may be incomplete or even nonexistent information upon which to make a judgment. The state must correctly identify a potential adversary, analyse its offensive and defensive potential, measure its economic and industrial resources and its ability to produce military equipment, determine the strategic balance and attitude of other interested parties, and factor in the potential for an opponent to act. Additionally, defence planning is always relative and subject to change with the passage of time. An assessment that limits itself to current capabilities is useless, as the situation might have progressed before the government can finalise its plans, based upon the provided information. Therefore, national security planning requires defence thinkers to project defensive requirements into the future. Finally, no nation can consider any defence plan definitive. Instead, a finding is merely the latest draft of a never-ending process.

The identification of a threat and the extrapolation of the degree of risk is only one stage of defence planning. National security reviews must balance the estimated level of resources required to meet the threat with the level of resources that the state is willing to provide to counter the threat. Ideally, resource requirement and allocation should be the same, but this is rarely the case. Despite its vast territory, Australia is a small to middle size power, and it does not have the ability to meet a threat from a major power on its own. However, even when conducting a security review of a power of equivalent or smaller size, the process of defence planning remains difficult. This is because proper defence planning has as a prerequisite the absolute requirement that political leaders and their military advisers honestly assess the nation's strengths and weaknesses and recognise the need to set aside, or at least minimise, the influence of party politics and service rivalry. This may require policymakers to confront uncomfortable political realities, including a public that is unconvinced of the need to maintain the armed services at the projected level of defence spending.

One example should suffice to illustrate the consequences of the failure of the political leadership to fulfil its defence planning obligation. T.B. Millar has rightly criticised the Nationalist and United Australia Party governments of the late-interwar period for their refusal to deal with the growing threat of Germany and Japan. He wrote that these governments displayed 'little determination to think through and come to grips with the military situation'. Millar continues that they abdicated their defence responsibilities by basing their ideas upon the worn-out ideas of the colonial period and relied upon the empire for Australia's defence. The result was an army that was completely unprepared for war.[3]

National characteristics of army organisation

If the above described parameters set limits on army organisation, and if defence planning principles provide the framework of decision-making, there remains one other major factor that defines the organisation of a nation's military forces. Each country possesses national characteristics that help to shape the organisation of its army according to the requirements of its individual situation. Like some parameters listed above, these characteristics tend to be inflexible and exert their influence over considerable lengths of time. Three major national characteristics appear to have helped shape the organisation of the Australian Army. They are:
- the government's frequent change in the direction of national security policy
- the periodic resistance of army leaders to conforming to strategic guidance
- the nation's dependence on a major ally for its ultimate defence.

National security planning plays an important role in how decision-makers determine an army's organisation. The perception of threat and the defence response to counter a threat are directly linked. In Australia, the most influential of its particular national characteristics is the government's direction of security policy. Unfortunately, all too frequently, the government has failed to make consistent and long-lasting policy, even in periods when the threat environment was relatively stable or easily identifiable. Moreover, the government has frequently failed to provide adequate warning or even consultation with military leaders regarding a change in strategic direction. Last, when making security decisions the Australian Government has historically tended to place a higher priority on fiscal matters, rather than strategic requirements.

The result of these tendencies on the part of the government is that the army has had to undergo frequent reorganisation, including hurried expansion, which has been followed by painful contraction, and which ultimately diverted resources from the achievement of military effectiveness. Furthermore, as the example above suggests, government decision-makers have sometimes failed to undertake realistic defence reviews or have failed to apply the findings of their studies in an appropriate manner.

The leaders of the Australian Army, for their part, have occasionally failed to conform the force's organisation to the requirements of the government's security policy. In fact, on some occasions, senior officers have actively sought to undermine or replace the established strategic policy. When this has occurred, civilian decision-makers are sometimes also at fault for failing to define the government's directives adequately or for not insisting that the army conform its organisation to the strategic guidelines. This national characteristic has not been as major a factor as the government's inconsistency in direction, but during its history the army's organisation has sometimes borne little relation to the official appreciation of the threat environment and the desired capability response.

The final national characteristic that has helped shaped the army's organisation is Australia's traditional reliance on a major power for its ultimate defence. As the parameters listed above suggest, it would be virtually impossible for Australia to defend itself against an assault by a great power. Australian political and military leaders have rightly recognised that the nation's resources are simply too limited to defend its vast territorial obligations on its own. At first, Britain served as the guarantor of Australian security. During World War II, the United States took over this duty, and the American alliance remains Australia's most important security arrangement to the present. However, Britain and the United States did not provide this security without a price. More importantly, this dependency has influenced, if not at times dictated, the army's organisation.

The colonial legacy

Although the Australian Army was a new institution in 1901, the method of its creation assured that it did not begin with a blank slate. Upon Federation, the constitution merged the military forces of the former colonies into a national army. This process not only brought with it the problem of standardisation but also meant that the Australian Army would initially inherit the organisation, tradition, and ideas of its colonial antecedents. The most important aspects of this legacy were a dependence upon a strong ally and a preference for voluntarism. These factors would prove resilient, and would affect the basis of Australian military planning until well into the twentieth century.

The new nation inherited a defence policy that perceived Australia as part of an imperial fraternity. Many early defence assessments were conducted either by British officers in Australia or by the Colonial Defence Committee (and it successor agency, the Committee of Imperial Defence) in London. Naturally, their recommendations tended to contain an imperial bias. The primary objective of imperial decision-makers during the years immediately before and after Federation was to have the colonies agree to play a greater role in the empire's defence.

Initially, British defence planners sought a commitment from the self-governing colonies that they would dedicate a body of troops for imperial requirements. These forces would come under the direct command of the War Office in time of emergency, and they would be liable for service anywhere in the empire. Major-General Alexander Tulloch, the military commandant of Victoria, supported this concept with the observation that 'the defence of Australia commences in India'. He also advocated the idea that it was not possible to separate Australian defence from that of imperial defence.[4]

At the 1897 Imperial Conference, Joseph Chamberlain, the Secretary of State for the Colonies, suggested that the colonies exchange military units with the British Army for joint training exercises, and noted that colonial troops could participate on imperial expeditions. However, Chamberlain's long-term goal was more than just British access to colonial military resources. He actually sought the creation of an imperial federation, in which the mother country and her offspring would jointly make policy, a forum that Britain would dominate. At the same meeting, Lord Wolseley, the British Army's commander-in-chief, proposed the raising of an Australian Regiment whose battalion(s) would be under the control of the War Office.[5] Major-General Edward Hutton, the future commander of the Australian Army, shared these goals. He argued for the creation of an Imperial Council of

Defence, which would have under its control an imperial body of troops. The Council would allocate its force structure on the basis of population, and Australia's share, he estimated, would be about 12,000 men.[6]

Consistently throughout this period, Australian leaders gave British advances on the issue of imperial defence a poor reception. George Reid, then the Premier of New South Wales, summed up antipodean opinion at the 1897 Imperial Conference, at which he stated that the Australian colonies would come to Britain's need in a crisis, but during peace Australia would consider its military requirements solely from the perspective of local defence.[7]

Continually rebuffed, British defence planners gave up on the creation of an imperial army, and instead directed their efforts towards having the colonial armies adopt the British Army's standards regarding organisation, administration, code of justice, and equipment. In this way, if colonial governments did decide to participate in an overseas conflict, the War Office could quickly integrate their contributions into the British Army's force structure and maintain them easily from imperial sources.

Reinforcing the imperial connection was the widely accepted idea that naval superiority was the first line of defence. A distant second, the army's primary purpose was to safeguard ports, installations, and strategic passages that the fleet might require. The Duke of Devonshire outlined the basis of this principle in a speech in 1896. He stated: 'Maintenance of sea supremacy has been assured as the basis of the system of Imperial defence against attack by sea. That is the determining factor in shaping the whole defensive policy of the empire.'[8]

These sentiments had found local expression at the Federal Military Conference, which met in 1894 to consider the creation of a mechanism for federal control of the colonial military forces in time of emergency. The conference concluded that the most 'probable form of attack on the Australian littoral would be by means of raids of an enemy's cruisers ...'. It reached this judgment as a result of the determination that an enemy that intended to invade Australia would have to organise a fleet of such size that it could avoid neither detection while assembling in port nor interception by the imperial fleet once at sea. Moreover, the conference concluded that an opponent could not dispatch its transports until after its battle fleet had bested the Royal Navy, a feat that at the time was beyond consideration. The conference representatives saw the threat of invasion as so remote that they did not even identify the prevention of enemy landings as the major objective of Australian military forces. Instead, they focused upon the place of garrisons and local troops in safeguarding the continent's seaborne trade. To this end, they believed that Australian military forces could best support the supremacy of the Royal Navy by the protection of commercial centres, naval bases, and strategic positions, thereby assuring the fleet its freedom of operations.[9]

This conclusion was not a new development in Australian security policy, but rested upon a firm foundation of earlier assessments, both in London and in the colonies. In the late 1870s, the British Government established the Colonial Defence Committee as a forum to review the state of colonial defences. This organisation consistently advanced the primacy of the Royal Navy as the bulwark of imperial defence.[10] In the 1901 review it prepared for the new Australian Government, the Colonial Defence Committee declared:

> The maintenance of British supremacy at sea is the first condition of the security of Australian territory and trade in war. Such supremacy implies that no organised attack will be directed against any part of Australia, and that the maritime communications between Australian ports and the rest of the world will be kept free from sustained interruption.[11]

Earlier colonial defence reviews had come to similar conclusions. In 1877 and 1878, Colonel Sir William Jervois and Lieutenant-Colonel Peter Scratchley conducted the first multicolony defence review during their inspection of the defensive arrangements of New South Wales, Victoria, Queensland, and South Australia. They believed that the only realistic threat was small-scale naval raids consisting of one or, at most, several enemy vessels, which would raid shipping, bombard towns, or extort payments or services from coastal communities. They recommended that the first line of defence for the colonies should be naval, with a secondary defence provided by small mobile forces and fortifications placed at the entrances of the principal cities and harbours. The military forces would consist of a paid, part-time militia and a small number of permanent soldiers.[12]

An even earlier review of South Australian defence needs in 1858 presented similar findings. It identified the colony's first line of defence as the Royal Navy, and noted that the only requirement for local military forces would be to repel a single raider or, at most, a small flotilla of enemy vessels that had eluded the imperial navy.[13]

The other aspect of the colonial period that would have repercussions for later army organisations was the widespread preference in Australia for military service on a voluntary basis. Such a condition of service made great sense for the colonies that did not have sufficient wealth, population, or desire to maintain a standing army. Militia organisations had existed from as early as 1792, when the commandant of Norfolk Island organised 44 of his free male settlers into a local body. Most militia organisations were short lived. They came into enthusiastic existence when the colonies felt threatened, such as during the Crimean War, then dissolved from lack of interest when the threat abated. Volunteer organisations gained a more permanent existence after the British withdrew their regiments in 1870, thus forcing the colonies to rely upon their own resources for local defence. In 1874, New South Wales introduced partial payment for citizen soldiers, a step subsequently taken by Victoria and Queensland in 1884. The colonies also raised small numbers of permanent troops. These consisted largely of gunners and engineers, which the colonies required to staff their coastal defences. They did not have any field-force capability.

As the Australian Government began the process of organising its army in 1901, it could not escape its colonial legacy. Australian defence planning continued to be influenced by, to use Hutton's words, 'sentiment and self-interest'.[14] The ties to the mother country and the national preference for voluntarism became incorporated into the very structure of the new army.[15] Furthermore, the consequence of its reliance upon the Royal Navy, and its related deference to Britain, was the creation of a mentality of dependence on the empire to secure antipodean interests. While perhaps a legitimate factor of the colonial period, this policy failed to recognise that the interests of Britain and Australia were not necessarily the same.[16] However, defence planners would continue to reiterate the theme of naval supremacy as the ultimate protector of Australia until the sinking of the *Prince of Wales* and the *Repulse* on 10 December 1941 revealed the fragility of this relationship.

2
FROM FEDERATION TO WORLD WAR I

The most essential element in the organisation of the future is to provide a Military System which shall be elastic, capable of expansion, and which shall form a carefully constructed framework into which the fighting material can be fitted when the emergency arises.

Edward Hutton[1]

On 1 March 1901, in accordance with the terms of the Commonwealth's Constitution, the Governor-General transferred control of the nation's military forces from the States to the Federal Government. By this action the Australian Army came into existence. Technically, the new Australian nation, whose creation predated the federalisation of the army by two months, was in a state of war, as it also inherited the military commitments of the colonial governments that had dispatched troops to South Africa and China. However, these troops were not Australia's real army. They were volunteers who had answered Britain's call, and had come to the aid of the Empire, as others before them had assisted the mother country in Sudan and New Zealand. The proper Australian Army, composed of permanent forces, militia, and volunteers, who had remained behind to guard the continent, were soldiers of the former colonies, and they too passed under federal control. Reflecting their disparate origins, these forces were a mix of units represented by different organisations, terms of engagement, levels of efficiency, and standards of equipment.

With its assumption of military responsibility, the Commonwealth Government needed to 'provide for a continuous defence policy, the efficient control of the military forces, and to introduce homogeneous organisation and training'.[2] The value in reaching these goals was simple; a nation's possession of a properly organised military force in peace would greatly ease the attainment of the army's objectives in war. Furthermore, an efficiently trained army would free commanders from the necessity of devoting their energies upon mobilisation towards organisation, in lieu of the planning and conduct of operations. Therefore, a nation with an army that was ready for war would have a great advantage over an opponent that still had to organise its units.[3] During the period from Federation until the outbreak of World War I, the government, along with the army's leaders, would establish the policies and structures that would determine the Commonwealth's ability to utilise military force until well into the post-World War II period. However, these years would also reveal a number of enduring impediments to the development of an efficient force, impediments that would also have a considerable impact on the future well-being of the army. This era, therefore, represents a crucial period in the development of the Australian Army.

The inheritance

It fell to John Forrest, hastily appointed by Prime Minister Edmund Barton as the Commonwealth's second Minister for Defence upon the death of his predecessor after

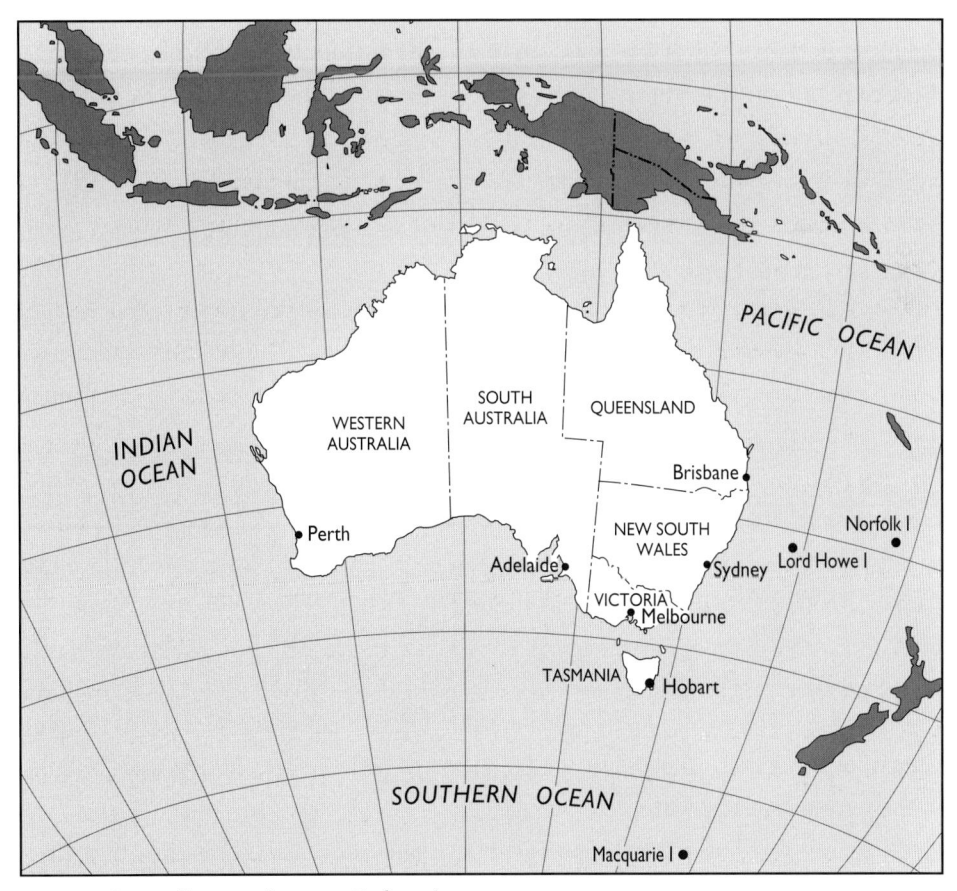

Map 2 Australian territory at Federation

only nine days in office, to begin the work of creating an efficient military force. Complicating his task was the absence of a commander-in-chief and the lack of federal legislation to govern the defence forces. Forrest did not appoint a General Officer Commanding until the next year, and Parliament did not pass a Defence Act until 1903. In the meantime the troops remained subject to the different defence codes of their respective states, themselves hold-overs of colonial statutes. The army also subdivided the nation into six administrative regions called military districts, one for each State, under the command of a commandant. Each military district was named after the State in which it was located. These regional commands were simply a federalised version of the former headquarters of the colonial armies. Each military district was responsible for the command and administration of the units within its region. With the arrival of a General Officer Commanding, the commandants of the military districts became subordinate to his authority.

At the time of transfer, the Australian Army had a strength of just over 29,000. The colonies had divided their forces into three categories—Permanent, Militia, and Volunteers—a distinction that the Commonwealth maintained. Table 2.1 outlines the establishment and strength of the army at Federation by State.

Table 2.1 Strength of the Australian Army at Federation, by State[4]

State	Permanent	Militia	Volunteers	Total
NSW	669	5,549	3,493	9,711
VIC	443	3,554	2,602	6,599
QLD	301	4,053	654	5,008
SA	51	2,949	nil	3,000
WA	50	nil	2,235	2,285
TAS	30	nil	2,377	2,407
Total	*1,544*	*16,105*	*11,361*	*29,010*

The nation had, as well as these troops, a potential reserve in the form of the rifle clubs and the school cadet corps. Although they were not an official part of the defence forces at takeover, they did formally join the army's establishment with the passage of the *Defence Act 1903*. At Federation, the rifle clubs and cadets had a membership of more than 30,000 and 10,000 respectively. Table 2.2 outlines the strengths of these formations by States.[5]

While not forming a part of the army's organisation, thousands of other Australians were on active duty with the British Army in South Africa. The majority of these soldiers had enlisted in units raised by the colonial governments, and only the final contingent was a federal matter. In late 1901, Joseph Chamberlain, Britain's Secretary of State for the Colonies, asked Barton if Australia could provide further drafts for the empire's war effort. Within five months, Australia enlisted and embarked over 4,200 volunteers, organised into eight battalions of mounted infantry called the Australian Commonwealth Horse. However, half of the battalions arrived in Africa after the conclusion of hostilities, and only two of the eight saw any action. Thus, while the Commonwealth Horse were the nation's first truly Australian military units to serve overseas, their limited experience left only a minimal mark on the army's history and tradition.[6]

Table 2.2 Establishment of cadet corps and rifle clubs, 1901[7]

States	Senior cadets	Junior cadets	Rifle clubs
NSW	109	4,242	1,908
VIC	483	5,259	21,570
QLD	101	916	4,352
SA	155	nil	2,180
WA	180	240	nil
TAS	nil	216	nil
Total	*1,028*	*10,873*	*30,010*

Although Australia possessed a large military establishment, its quality, particularly its degree of training and standard of equipment, was poor. As one of his first acts as Minister for Defence, Forrest appointed a Federal Military Committee, composed of the commandants of the military districts, to undertake an appreciation of Australian defence infrastructure. Their report revealed severe problems. Of particular concern was the low stock of ammunition held by the States, of which the worst case was Victoria, which had reserves of only 17 rounds per rifle. By comparison, the Colonial Defence Committee in London recommended a minimum reserve of 1,000 rounds per rifle. The field artillery, the military commandants noted, had in its inventory unserviceable guns, guns without carriages, and carriages without guns, as well as obsolete ammunition. The supply of submarine mining stores was out of date, and over the years the States had followed a haphazard procurement policy, so that there were few replacement parts.

The organisation of the services also came under scrutiny. New South Wales was the only state with an ordnance store depot and a medical department set up as military

General Sir Edward Hutton. (AWM A03735)

units. In Queensland, South Australia, and Western Australia the local governments had made no provision for an army service corps, and the last two States did not have an engineering corps. Last, despite the army's reliance upon horses for transport, none of the states had a veterinary department.[8]

In 1902, Forrest appointed Major-General Edward Hutton as the army's first, and only, General Officer Commanding. Hutton, an imperial officer, had considerable experience with colonial troops, including having served as the commander of the

New South Wales military forces from 1893 to 1896. One of his first tasks was to assess the equipment held by the army. While he found the materials available to the garrison force sufficient for static troops, he observed that what was available for the field force 'leaves much to be desired'. He wrote that in all the States there was a nearly complete absence of modern infantry equipment, including the supply of magazine rifles, and that the ammunition stores were in a seriously defective condition. Hutton described the materials for the mounted troops and field artillery as incomplete and unequal to modern demands. Last, he considered the quantity of supplies available to the field engineers and field hospital as inadequate. Hutton concluded his assessment with the warning that 'troops without efficient and sufficient arms, ammunition, and equipment are useless for the purpose for which they exist, and are therefore a mischievous delusion'.[9]

The coast defence system also suffered from grave equipment and infrastructure deficiencies. Between the six States there were five different fire-control systems, including two types in New South Wales. Guns and equipment were in poor condition, and included unserviceable pieces. A report on the defences at Albany by Major V.L. Beer, the Commanding Officer Western Australian Artillery, highlighted the gravity of the deficiencies. While he complimented the garrison on its efficiency, he noted that the current staff of 40 gunners was only sufficient to man two of the fort's guns, leaving a further five pieces and two machine-guns unattended. Furthermore, he observed that the fort's two Hotchkiss 6-pounders were not yet on permanent mounts, even though they had been on site for five years. He also noted that the reserves of ammunition were inadequate. The government provided for only 200 rounds for the 6-inch breech loader, and it was necessary to order replacements from England. Beer also complained about insufficient uniforms and the unavailability of cloth to make them. The medical officer submitted a companion report that highlighted the paucity of the base's reserves of water. He observed that the capacity of the establishment's storage tanks was insufficient for the dry season, and that if a large body of troops were to man the defences, they would quickly exhaust the water supply.[10]

The Colonial Defence Committee also evaluated the coastal defences of Australia in 1901. It concluded that there was far too great a variety of weapons and mountings, and that in some cases certain guns were peculiar to individual States, with only two or three pieces in existence throughout the empire. It went on to observe that many of the Commonwealth's guns were obsolete, and that they lacked the range and power to deal with the improved armour and weaponry of modern cruisers. The report further pointed out that the Commonwealth's great number of calibres was a financial liability, and that it could lower the overall cost of its ammunition purchases by replacing its non-standard gun types. Finally, the Colonial Defence Committee also recommended that the Australian Government construct an arsenal for the local manufacture of ammunition, and stores to alleviate the difficulty of obtaining supplies from abroad, especially in time of war.[11]

In 1902, Hutton undertook his own study of the garrison artillery, which confirmed the Colonial Defence Committee conclusions. Hutton found that of the 185 weapons assigned to coastal defence, including machine-guns, there were 25 different types. Some were quite rare, such as the two 10-inch breech loaders in Victoria and the two 7-inch rifled muzzle loaders in Tasmania.[12] In a related assessment, Hutton also recommended that Australia create its own manufacturing department for its defence forces. He believed it necessary for the Commonwealth to have the ability to produce its own small arms, guns, and ammunition. He also thought that such a facility could meet the needs of the Royal Navy and the future Australian Navy.

The establishment of the field artillery displayed a similar degree of variety and antiquity as had the garrison batteries. A 1904 assessment found that Australia possessed 84 field guns. However, of these, only the 28 15-pounders and the four 5-inch howitzers were modern, while the rest consisted of obsolete breech loaders or even older muzzle loaders. The colonies had made no attempt to standardise their armaments, and the army inherited eight kinds of calibres, including some of which there were only two in the nation. By 1904, under Hutton's initiative, the army had taken some steps to improve the field artillery, and six of the twelve 12.5-pounders that had belonged to Victoria were in England for conversion to up-to-date 15-pounders.[14]

Threat assessment and defence policy

Soon after taking office, Edmund Barton, the Commonwealth's first Prime Minister, declared, 'Australia could have no foreign policy of her own.' This statement was more than just a recognition of the Commonwealth's abdication of responsibility for the conduct of its foreign affairs in favour of the Foreign Office in London. As Neville Meaney points out, Barton was also making a reference to his belief that it was necessary for a single voice to speak for the empire and that Australia would consequently rely upon Britain to represent its external policy interests. With hindsight, Barton could also have stated that Australia could have no defence policy of her own, as, until after World War II, the Commonwealth would rely upon Britain for the provision of its defence nearly as much as it did for the conduct of its foreign relations.[15]

For the first few years of nationhood this did not matter, as Australia existed in an environment in which a credible threat was virtually unimaginable. The Colonial Defence Committee was correct when it noted that 'on account of its insular character and its geographical position there is no British territory so little liable to aggression ... as that of Australasia'. Geography had been particularly favourable to Australia, but, as the Colonial Defence Committee report observed, it would remain invulnerable only 'so long as British naval supremacy is maintained in Eastern waters'.[16] The Australian Government shared the Colonial Defence Committee's opinion, not perceiving any dangers during the years immediately following Federation. In the Parliamentary debate over the 1903 Naval Agreement with Britain, the Australian Government accepted that, while France, Germany, Japan, and Russia were potential enemies, it did not foresee any immediate challenge to the integrity of the country.[17]

The Royal Navy had long served as Australia's primary defence, and reliance upon the imperial fleet would remain unchecked until Pearl Harbor. Since 1887, the Australian colonies had paid a subsidy to the Admiralty for the maintenance of a small squadron of warships in local waters. The Commonwealth renewed the agreement in 1903, and increased the payment from £106,000 to £200,000, a figure, however, that did not recoup all of the Admiralty's costs. Several of the colonies also had small navies of their own. These would become the basis of the Royal Australian Navy (RAN). However, the ships of the Royal Navy squadron, and especially the colonial vessels, tended to be small and out of date, and for some, for example HMS *Phoebe*, *Archer*, and *Katoomba*, Australia was the last posting before the wrecker's yard.[18]

The real protection that the imperial fleet provided to the Commonwealth was Britain's reassurance that it would dispatch its battle squadrons to the Far East if an enemy attempted to sever Australia's maritime lines of communication or invade the continent with an army intent upon conquest. The Colonial Defence Committee enunciated this principle in a 1901 memorandum on Australian defence. It wrote:

> The maintenance of British supremacy at sea is the first condition of the security of Australian territory and trade in war. Such supremacy implies that no organized attack will be directed against any part of Australia and that the maritime communication between Australian ports and the rest of the world will be kept free from sustained interruption.[19]

It was the Royal Navy that provided the sea power that sustained the empire as a whole. Through its control of the seas, it provided Australia with protection from invasion and safeguarded the nation's commerce from interference.

The imperial fleet could assure this degree of protection because the Admiralty believed that the Royal Navy would lose control of the seas only if an opponent bested it in a decisive battle, an improbable result in 1901, given the superiority of its ships. Australia did not have to worry about a defence against an enemy armada, since that was the responsibility of the Admiralty. Naval doctrine of the time insisted that the only vessels that a rival could consider dispatching on an independent operation, such as the shelling of an Australian port, were units it could spare from the main battle fleet. Defence planners believed that this would consist of, at most, a small squadron of unarmoured cruisers or possibly small torpedo boats that the enemy could launch from a larger ship. Another report further narrowed the field of potential opposition by noting that, because of the range limitations of the ships, only ports within 300 miles of an enemy base needed to take precautions against destroyers or first-class torpedo boats. Thus the Commonwealth could expect, at worst, a raid by a few second-class enemy cruisers and landings of small bodies of troops of not more than a thousand sailors drawn from the warship's crews.[20]

Although Australian political leaders gladly accepted the protection of the Royal Navy, they remained adamant in their opposition to any suggestion that the Commonwealth make a formal commitment of troops to an imperial reserve. Britain had throughout the 1890s attempted without success to obtain such an agreement from the colonies. The new Commonwealth would prove equally obdurate. The British position was simple and quite reasonable. London believed that as the self-governing colonies, and later independent states, increased in wealth, they should take up a greater burden of the empire's defence. However, the Australian governments perceived such expectations by the central authority as an infringement upon their independence, and steadfastly refused the suggestion.

In its 1901 memorandum the Colonial Defence Committee again raised the question of an imperial contribution. While it conceded that the prerogative of providing support belonged to the Commonwealth, it also made clear that it hoped Australia would dedicate a force for the defence of the empire. The committee advanced the idea that, after the demonstrated success of its mounted infantry in South Africa, Australia should strengthen this arm and establish it as a source of troops for overseas service in time of war. Joseph Chamberlain, at the Colonial Office, also wanted Australia to take on greater responsibilities in the defence of the empire. He was encouraged by favourable, though misleading, statements by Hutton regarding the Australian environment and by the submission to the Colonial Office by New Zealand of a proposal that the colonies should maintain military reserves for imperial operations. At the 1902

Imperial Conference, Chamberlain urged the former colonies to maintain complete units trained on British Army principles and ready for overseas duty.[21] Once again, however, Australia rebuffed his overtures. Barton, who represented Australia at the conference, replied to Britain's demand for a commitment with the statement that 'to establish a special force, set aside for absolute control of the Imperial government, was objectionable in principle as derogating from the power of self-government enjoyed by them'. He went on to concede that Australia would agree to uniformity of equipment and organisation with the British Army, but the Commonwealth would reserve the right to decide upon military assistance when the need arose.[22]

The refusal to guarantee a commitment to imperial defence, however, did not signify an abdication of intention to come to the aid of other members in the empire. Australia, after all, had already made a significant contribution to the war in South Africa. Barton made the Commonwealth's position clear at the 1902 Imperial Conference. Although he would not commit the Commonwealth in advance, he did say that Australia could be counted upon when the empire was in danger. Australia's participation would have to be left to the spontaneous response, tendered freely, of its people.[23]

Within this environment, no clearly defined and self-formed defence policy emerged, a criticism which Meaney has correctly levelled against the Barton administration. On one hand Barton suggested that Australia stood ready to take on its share of imperial defence but, with the exception of the increase in the naval subsidy, he rejected any proposals for a contribution to an intra-empire reserve. Instead, the most intense area of defence planning was directed towards the goal of reducing the military estimate to the lowest level possible. Ronald Norris believes that to the nation's early political leaders the benefit of Federation for defence was the opportunity not only to create a larger military force but also to achieve efficiency and economy of central command. A single federal army, they thought, would be cheaper than six colonial forces. Forrest's performance as Minister for Defence certainly reflected this attitude, as he perceived his primary duty as the containment of costs. In his address to the first parliament, the Governor-General of Australia, the Earl of Hopetoun, summed up the government's attitude towards defence expenditure. He stated that 'extravagant expenditure will be avoided, and reliance placed, to the fullest reasonable extent, in our citizen soldiery'.[24]

Australian defence planners in 1901 found themselves in an enviable position. Geographic isolation would increase an invader's logistical difficulties and provide the Admiralty with considerable advance warning, allowing the Royal Navy the opportunity to deploy its strength to the east. The only threat of any concern was the possibility of a raid by a few minor enemy ships and landings by small parties of hostile troops or sailors. Even this threat was temporary, as once the Royal Navy had destroyed the enemy's battle fleet it would deploy its vast resources to sweep the ocean clean of the enemy's remaining warships. However, while imperial membership and the guarantee of maritime supremacy was comforting, it did have serious implications for the role of the army in the nation's defence. Confronted with such assurances, the Australian Army would see its role in the Commonwealth's defence confined to a secondary position, and to a certain extent, as an instrument to help facilitate the success of the fleet through its garrison of ports, harbour defences, and strategic points.

The Defence Act

The concerns of Australia's defence planners were reflected in the terms of the Defence Act, which was finally passed in 1903. This statute was actually the second attempt by the government to establish the legislative basis of the nation's armed forces, as Parliament had rebuffed a first attempt in 1901. For the first effort, Forrest had relied on a committee of officers to write the bill. However, their draft contained numerous clauses that Forrest found objectionable, and which he rewrote. These included the officers' desire to create an army independent of government control by designating the Governor-General as Commander-in-Chief. The senior officer would report to him, not to the Minister for Defence. Moreover, the committee intended that soldiers would take an oath to the monarch and be subject to the provisions of the British Army Act. The officers' draft also included a mechanism for the deployment of Australian units on imperial operations, and a requirement that the force's leaders be drawn from the British Army.[25]

Forrest changed the bill in order to make the army subservient to government control and subject to the Minister for Defence. He also limited the government's power to force soldiers to serve overseas, deleted the requirement that the army recruit its leaders from Britain, and opened the senior ranks to part-time soldiers in order to prevent the creation of a military elite. However, Forrest had done a poor job in drafting the language, and it still contained a number of objectionable points. The reception it received by parliament was so hostile that Forrest withdrew it for reconsideration. The government then decided to defer the presentation of another defence bill until after the appointment of a General Officer Commanding. In the interim, soldiers continued to serve under the defence acts of the various States.[26]

After Hutton's arrival in 1902, Forrest again took up the issue of a Defence Act. Hutton renewed the army's efforts to include a recognition of imperial responsibility and control in the act. Writing to Forrest, he explained his rationale for an army that the government could deploy outside of Australia in terms of the defence needs of Australia. Hutton argued that since the militia filled the function of a regular army, it was the only force available to go on overseas operations. The permanent forces were too small to fulfil that mission. He explained that it was militarily unsound to rely upon a passive defence, and that one of the first principles of success in war was the ability to assume the offence. Hutton continued that it was unwise for the government to give up the means to employ its armed forces wherever opponents threatened the Commonwealth's interests. He also employed an organisational argument, which noted that to depend upon voluntarism would result in the complete disorganisation of the peacetime militia system. Instead of relying upon established units, at the moment of danger the nation would have to create a completely new force to meet a threat.[27] He concluded that the Commonwealth could best protect its interests if it had already in existence units that could undertake offensive operations against an opponent instead of passively awaiting the enemy's attack.[28]

Hutton had other objections to the bill, including the proposal to create a Council of Defence, which he believed would degrade the authority of the General Officer Commanding, and a clause that would give preference for commissions to those who had served in the ranks for three years. Hutton also wanted the government to give itself the power to place its military forces under the command of British authorities. Forrest resisted Hutton's entreaties, but did include a clause that allowed the dispatch of the permanent force overseas, although not the militia. However, parliament objected to even this modest concession to imperial commitment, and the bill's final form allowed for overseas service only on a voluntary basis. Furthermore, to prevent the development of militarism, parliament statutorily limited the role of the permanent forces to administration, instruction, and garrison functions. Australia would not have any standing field force units.[29]

The Defence Act went into effect on 1 March 1904, and set the structure of the Australian Army. The sections that were to have the greatest effect upon the organisation of the army were:

> 30. The Defence Force shall consist of the Naval and Military Forces of the Commonwealth and they shall be divided into two branches called the Permanent Forces and the Citizen Forces.
>
> 31 (1). The Permanent Forces shall consist of officers who are appointed officers of those Forces, and of soldiers, petty officers, and sailors who are bound to continuous naval and military service for a term.

31 (2). No Permanent Military Forces shall be raised, maintained or organized except for Administrative and Instructional Staffs, including Army Service, Medical and Ordnance Staffs, Garrison Artillery, Fortress Engineers, and Submarine Mining Engineers.

32 (1). The Citizen Forces shall be divided into Militia Forces, Volunteer Forces and Reserve Forces.

32 (2). The Militia Forces shall consist of officers, soldiers, petty officers, and sailors who are not bound to a continuous naval or military service and who are paid for their services as prescribed.

32 (3). The Volunteer Forces shall consist of officers, soldiers, petty officers, and sailors who are not bound to a continuous naval or military service and who are not ordinarily paid for their services in times of peace.

32 (4). The Reserve Forces shall consist of—
    a Members of Rifle Clubs …
    b Persons who, having served in the Active Forces … are enrolled as members of the Reserve Forces.

49. Members of the Defence Force who are members of the Military Forces shall not be required, unless they voluntarily agree to do so, to serve beyond the limits of the Commonwealth and those of any Territory under the authority of the Commonwealth.[30]

The passage of the Defence Act established the citizen–soldier as the basis of the Australian Army. It mandated that the Commonwealth defence would consist of a part-time militia and volunteer forces, supported by a small permanent force that the government limited to staff, training, and garrison duties. Furthermore, if the nation were to participate in imperial wars it could do so only on the basis of voluntarism.[31]

The bill's final form was not surprising, despite the entreaties of Hutton and others. It drew upon an established tradition of part-time soldiering and voluntarism that had already served Australia and the empire well. Its frugality also appealed to a government that desired defence at the lowest possible price. An additional consequence was that it also assured the army's subordinate position in the defence hierarchy. It placed the army below the imperial fleet in importance to national survival. By not permitting the creation of a standing field force, it recognised that Australia's first line of defence was the Royal Navy. Finally, from the perspective of the level of risk which the country faced, the Defence Act was a reasonable attempt to provide effective and efficient national security. However, it was a minimalist approach, and the real test lay in the future, when Australia would discover whether the system had the ability to respond to increases in the threat environment.

Hutton and the army's organisation

The organisation of the States' military units into an efficient national military force fell to Hutton, who took up the mantle of General Officer Commanding on 29 January 1902. He had not been the government's first choice, as other more senior officers had rejected the Commonwealth's offer, but he was a wise selection because of his experience with citizen soldiers in Australia, Canada, and South Africa. Although Hutton would largely succeed in laying the foundation of a modern military organisation, his tenure as General Officer Commanding was not without controversy, and he would come into conflict with the government on issues of expenditure and the contribution of troops to an imperial reserve.

In his memorandum of 23 April 1902, Hutton outlined the strategic factors that governed his conception of the organisation of the Australian Army. As an imperial officer, he not surprisingly interpreted Australian national security needs from the perspective of membership in an empire. Hutton saw the nation's defence in its broadest terms, and consequently divided its requirements into two spheres, 'the defence of Australian soil' and 'the defence of Australian interests wherever they may be threatened'.[32] Hutton rightly believed that Australian prosperity was dependent not only on its maritime communications but also on the ability of its commerce to find markets within the imperial system. Because of this, Hutton postulated that Australia had overseas defence concerns that were as vital to the nation's economic well-being and political future as was the inviolability of its shores.

Hutton accepted that the primary bulwark of Australian defence was the Royal Navy, and he agreed with the assessment of the Colonial Defence Committee that the only probable threat was that of a raid by a small cruiser squadron. However, within the context of maritime defence he demonstrated that the Australian Army still had a central role. In order to operate effectively in local waters, the fleet would require secure installations, such as Sydney, King George's Sound, and Thursday Island, on which to base its operations. Moreover, the army would also have to guard the many coastal commercial centres, from which the nation's overseas trade originated, against seizure by landing parties or bombardment by raiding warships. Despite the unlikelihood of invasion, Hutton asserted that the Commonwealth still required a body of troops that it could concentrate in support of the nation's scattered garrisons, which would have the strength to expel an incursion anywhere within Australian territory. Additionally, he believed the nation needed a military force that was capable of operations in any part of the world. Last, Hutton also saw the military as having an internal security role in the countering of domestic unrest.[33]

To provide for these multiple objectives, Hutton divided the army into two distinct structures, the garrison force and the field force, in addition to the permanent force.

The garrison forces were to serve as local defence troops for strategic centres. The army enlisted the majority of its members on the basis of unpaid volunteers. They had limited mobility and were unable to maintain themselves away from their appointed localities. Their primary purpose was to bring nearby defensive works to war establishment, complement the permanent force gunners in manning the coastal batteries, and provide a local reaction force to respond to nearby enemy landings. Into this structure Hutton planned to absorb the existing garrison units left over from the States. He had hoped to maintain the garrison force's establishment at over 15,000, but by 1906 manpower cutbacks had reduced it to only 9,591 personnel.[35] Table 2.3 outlines the distribution of the garrison force.

Each formation contained a mixture of infantry, field artillery, garrison artillery, engineers, and support troops as required by the local situation. For example, the composition of the Wollongong Garrison was No. 6 Squadron (2nd Australian Light Horse Regiment), No. 4 Company Australian Garrison Artillery, No. 4 Field Company (detachment), No. 1 Electrical Company (detachment), St George's English Rifle Regiment (two companies), and detachments of Army Service Corps and Army Medical Corps troops.[36]

Table 2.3 Distribution of garrison force formations[37]

State	Formations
NSW	District Reserve, Sydney Fortress (Port Jackson and Botany Bay), Wollongong, Newcastle, Lismore
VIC	District Reserve, Port Phillip Fortress
QLD	District Reserve, Brisbane, Rockhampton, Townsville, Thursday Island
SA	District Reserve, Adelaide
WA	District Reserve, Albany
TAS	Hobart, Southern Reserve, Northern Reserve

Hutton saw the field force as the army's mobile troops. They were to have the capacity to respond to a military threat or social unrest anywhere in Australia, or even overseas, he hoped, if the government so desired. The field force would be drawn either from the permanent force or the militia, and would therefore contain only paid soldiers, unlike the members of the garrison force. Hutton envisaged a field force composed of six light horse brigades and three infantry brigades, along with a suitable establishment of field artillery, engineers, and specialist troops. In peacetime, its establishment was to be 14,101, and it was to have the capability to expand to a war footing of nearly 29,000. In peacetime, the units would contain a nearly full complement of officers and non-commissioned officers, but only about half of their war establishment of enlisted personnel. Hutton based the composition of each brigade on the basis of a mixed force so that each formation would be capable of independent operations.[38] Table 2.4 outlines the composition of a typical infantry brigade, and Table 2.5 (p. 30) outlines the organisation of a typical light horse brigade, which had a similar composition to that of the infantry.

Table 2.4 Composition of typical infantry brigade[39]

Type	Number
Headquarters	Brigadier and brigade staff
Infantry	4 battalions
Light Horse	1 light horse squadron
Artillery	1 field artillery brigade (2 18-pr btys and 1 heavy bty)
	1 ammunition column
Engineers	1 field company
Signallers	Half company
Support	1 infantry transport and supply column
Medical	1 field ambulance

The rationale behind Hutton's scheme was to provide Australia with a military system that was 'elastic, capable of expansion, and which shall form a carefully constructed framework into which the fighting material can be fitted when an emergency arises'.[40]

Hutton placed the emphasis upon mounted troops because he believed that they best fitted the Australian ethos and that the Anglo-Boer War had proved the value of mobile firepower. Additionally, because of the country's poor transportation infrastructure, mounted troops would be better able to respond to enemy landings in remote areas than would infantry. However, the organisation that the Commonwealth inherited from the States had favoured the infantry over mounted troops. Hutton's reorganisation, therefore, would prove highly traumatic for many regions as the army disbanded established community-based infantry units in favour of creating new mounted squadrons. Furthermore, even if a town did secure a reformulated unit, many former soldiers were unable to continue their affiliation on financial grounds. The government required a trooper to supply his own horse, which was a financially prohibitive undertaking for many recruits.[41]

Table 2.5 Composition of typical light horse brigade[42]

Type	Number
Headquarters	Brigadier and brigade staff
Light Horse	3 light horse regiments
Artillery	1 field bty (15-pr)
	1 ammunition column
Engineers	1 field troop
Signallers	Half company
Support	1 light horse transport and supply column
Medical	1 light horse field ambulance

Through his scheme, Hutton demarcated the boundary between those who would command and those who would administer. He proposed that the army should appoint the brigadiers and staff allotted to the field force brigades from the militia. Similarly, the militia and volunteers would provide the leaders for the regiments and the department staffs. Hutton restricted the permanent force members to administrative and instructional duties and as a stiffener in wartime. His rationale was that 'in time of peace the responsibility of command and administration shall, as far as possible, be placed in the hands of those militia and volunteer officers who would inevitably have those responsibilities thrust upon them in time of war'.[43] Through this policy, Hutton hoped to make the militia and volunteer organisations complete so that their leaders could prepare in peace for a predefined role in war, and thereby lessen the confusion of responsibilities upon mobilisation.

Hutton allocated the brigades on the basis of State population. Table 2.6 summarises the distribution of the field force, and Table 2.7 illustrates the composition and distribution of a typical formation, 5th Light Horse Brigade.

Table 2.6 Distribution of field force brigades[44]

Brigade	Catchment
1st Light Horse Bde	Southern and Western NSW
2nd Light Horse Bde	Northern NSW
3rd Light Horse Bde	Northern VIC
4th Light Horse Bde	Southern VIC and TAS
5th Light Horse Bde	QLD
6th Light Horse Bde	SA and WA
1st Infantry Bde	NSW
2nd Infantry Bde	VIC
3rd Infantry Bde	QLD, SA, WA, TAS

Table 2.7 Composition and distribution of 5th Light Horse Brigade, 1904–05[45]

Unit	Peace establishment	War establishment	Provided for on estimate	Headquarters location
Headquarters	10	23	1	Not given
13th Australian LH Regt	294	581	222	Brisbane
14th Australian LH Regt	294	581	262	Toowoomba
15th Australian LH Regt	294	581	262	Rockhampton
No. 1 Queensland Bty	76	181	76	Brisbane
No. 3 Fd Coy	29	55	0	Not raised
No. 5 LH Supply Column	44	77	0	Not raised
No. 5 Mounted Bearer Coy	25	50	25	Warwick
No. 5 Fd Hospital (half)	15	30	15	Brisbane
Veterinary Department	3	3	3	
Attached Officers	4	4	4	
Total	1,088	2,166	870	

Hutton did not anticipate a need to increase the size of the permanent forces or change their role in the army. They constituted a relatively small part of the nation's military forces, and numbered approximately 1,500 at Federation. Under Hutton's scheme, the permanent forces would include an Administrative and Instructional Staff, the Royal Australian Artillery Regiment, and detachments of engineers, Army Medical Corps, Army Service Corps, and other specialist troops. The army would draw from their ranks the skilled personnel needed for the staffing of coastal guns, forts, and submarine mine defences, the maintenance of stores, and the garrison of isolated posts, such as at Thursday Island and King George's Sound.

In addition to providing staff officers for administrative purposes, Hutton believed that the permanent forces would play a vital role in the training of the militia and volunteers. Accordingly, he created the Instructional Staff (a precursor to the Australian Instructional Corps), whose members would serve as instructors and who would organise training schools in each State. The Royal Australian Artillery, itself only recently formed as a result of Hutton's amalgamation of all the permanent artillery units of the states, would fulfil most of the required instructional duties, in addition to their other responsibilities as gunners. The Royal Australian Artillery organised schools of instruction for the light horse, field and garrison artillery, and the infantry. The Corps of Australian Engineers, the Australian Medical Corps, and the Army Service Corps provided instruction in their respective fields.[46]

Hutton placed such emphasis on the need for well-trained instructional and staff officers that he advocated the establishment of a military college. He reiterated this plea in each of his annual reports, but it would not see fruition until 1911. Hutton also believed that the government should further the education of its officers by sending select permanent force members overseas for study in England or India. He also instituted a system of staff rides, and in 1905 the Commonwealth entered into an agreement with Britain for the exchange of officers.[47]

Despite his declarations that Australia's defence required the ability to 'concentrate on any threatened point as many available field troops as circumstances may render necessary', Hutton encountered difficulty in justifying the need for a field force.[48] First, he had to reassure the government that its raising did not imply agreement to provide the mother country with troops for imperial expeditions. In actuality, Hutton was playing a double game, and he did hope to deliver to London that very commitment. However, local politics made such a suggestion impossible, and Hutton had to include in his minutes a statement that made it absolutely clear that 'the utilisation of the Military Forces of the Commonwealth would rest entirely with the Commonwealth government'.[49] Furthermore, with the passage of the Defence Act, the government explicitly denied for any part of the Australian Military Forces an imperial role, and assured that the nation's soldiers served only in the defence of Australian territory. While this was the government's formal policy, it was not, however, an abdication of imperial responsibility but rather an example of a new nation protecting its prerogatives. To parliament, Forrest restated the importance of the Commonwealth's ties to

Britain and declared, 'if the British nation is at war; so are we', and that Australia would respond to the mother country's call if needed.[50]

Hutton also had to overcome resistance to his organisation from London. The Colonial Defence Committee was critical, and thought that the field force was twice as large as necessary. It stridently maintained that Australia's protection was guaranteed by the fleet, and it would not accept that any alternative defence arrangement was necessary. Since the garrison force was more than adequate to protect against the possibility of raids, the Colonial Defence Committee interpreted the field force's role as being for the benefit of the empire. In which case, the Colonial Defence Committee's report continued, it preferred a smaller force with a higher level of readiness.

London's response made Hutton's task more difficult. When Forrest received this opinion, he concluded that the entire field force was in excess of requirements, an expense that the government need not bear. He then requested the General Officer Commanding's response to the Colonial Defence Committee's review. Hutton defended the need for a field force in terms of the defence of the Commonwealth as a whole and as a support for the garrison force. He also insisted that the proposed establishment was the minimum size consistent with the defence of the Commonwealth. The government relented and gave the organisation its approval in June 1903.[51]

To improve the efficiency of the army, Hutton also sought to modernise its equipment. In his 1903 report, he summarised the standard of the equipment thus:

> The military stores and equipment are in a most unsatisfactory condition throughout the Commonwealth, and the situation can only be viewed with the gravest concern. Modern equipment for Cavalry, Artillery, and Infantry (a proportion of rifles ... [and some] field guns excepted) may be regarded as non-existent.[52]

He also complained privately to the minister that none of the infantry accoutrements (such as belts, bandoliers, pouches, and waterbottles) were of a more recent vintage than 1882. Although the fixed defences were somewhat modern, many guns of the field artillery were obsolete, and the army needed to replace them with quick-firing pieces. To rectify the condition he requested £486,283 over four years, allocating £357,384 for the field force and £128,899 for the garrison force. Hutton estimated that expenditure at this level would see the army fully equipped by 1908 at its war establishment level. Hutton's requisition, however, fell victim to demands by the Labor and Free Trade parties for a massive reduction in the military estimate. Consequently, the Minister for Defence informed his subordinate, 'it is pointless to submit any requisitions in excess of £50,000 for the fiscal year' and Hutton had to redefine his priorities. His new requisition now asked for £32,000 for the field force and £18,000 for the coastal defences, but he also noted that he was no longer able to estimate a date by which the army would be effectively equipped.[53] During 1903–04 Parliament demanded further reductions from the army's establishment, especially from Hutton's headquarters staff and the permanent artillery. Hutton strenuously objected, but in the end he had to capitulate. His response, however, bordered on insubordination, and he questioned whether the government intended to reduce the efficiency of the army to the poor levels which existed before Federation.[54]

Administrative reforms: the Military Board, the Council of Defence, and the General Staff

As Hutton's appointment grew to a close, it became apparent that the government was dissatisfied with the existing system of oversight it wielded over its military forces. The General Officer Commanding had been responsible for all military matters, within the financial limits set by the government, and only referred to the Minister for Defence items that affected policy. He had also served as the exclusive military adviser to the government. In 1904, the government proposed to replace the office of the General Officer Commanding with a Military Board, as well as establish a Naval Board, a Council of Defence, and an Inspector-General of the Military Forces. Part of the reason for these changes lay in the government's annoyance at Hutton's sometimes arrogant attitude towards civilian authority. However, the new arrangement also represented an effort to improve the standard of military oversight by the government and its access to professional advice in the formulation of security policy. The Minister for Defence would hold final administrative authority on all matters, rather than merely on policy concerns, as under the General Officer Commanding system. These reforms, therefore, guaranteed the government's position as the ultimate arbiter of all military decision-making. Furthermore, the reforms corresponded with the efforts of Lord Haldane to modernise the administration of the British Army. Britain would abolish its equivalent position, the Commander-in-Chief, and replace it with a board. The Military Board met for the first time in January 1905.[55]

The Minister for Defence, J.W. McCay, outlined the goals for the new system as:

1 The establishment of continuity in Defence Policy, and of a continuous connection between Parliamentary responsibility and the control and development of the Defence Forces.

2   Effective touch between the Minister and the Department for which he is responsible to Parliament.
3   The separation of administration from executive command …
4   Continuity of administrative methods by the establishment of a continuous Board.
5   The maintenance of uniformity and of efficiency by continuous and searching inspection by, and independent report from, an Inspector-General.[56]

These reforms also created a degree of decentralisation, as the government would vest responsibility for army administration in the several military members of the Military Board, each answerable to the minister, rather than just the General Officer Commanding. For example, the Deputy Adjutant-General would be responsible for all issues of personnel and transport, while the Chief of Ordnance would oversee all matters involving supply and armament. Under the new system, the commandants of the military districts would remain, and continue to command, train, and administer units within their districts. However, they would now be subject to the Military Board, as they had been formerly to the General Officer Commanding.

The mandate of the Military Board was the management of the military forces and the resolution of administrative questions that did not involve policy decisions. It would also issue orders to put into effect government directives. The military members of the board would be responsible for the portion of administration subject to their portfolio. The initial members of the Military Board were the Minister for Defence (McCay), a finance member (J.T. Thompson), and three representatives for the army: the Chief of Intelligence (Lieutenant-Colonel W. T. Bridges), the Deputy Adjutant-General (Colonel J.C. Hoad), and the Chief of Ordnance (Major Havilland de Mesurier). The government would soon add a fourth officer to represent quartermaster interests. In April 1905, the government further modified the roster to include two militia officers, one volunteer officer, a representative of the rifle clubs, and one civilian as consultative members. Chart 1 outlines the responsibilities of the principal members of the Military Board as it was composed in 1909.[57]

The creation of an office of an Inspector-General was the result of a decision to separate the executive function of army administration from that of evaluation of military effectiveness. The duties of the Inspector-General were to provide an annual report that commented on 'the results of the policy and administration of the forces, on the efficiency of the troops, the system of training, the suitability of equipment and the readiness of the forces for war'.[58] In time of war, the Inspector-General was to become the Commander-in-Chief; however, this responsibility passed to the Chief

THE AUSTRALIAN ARMY

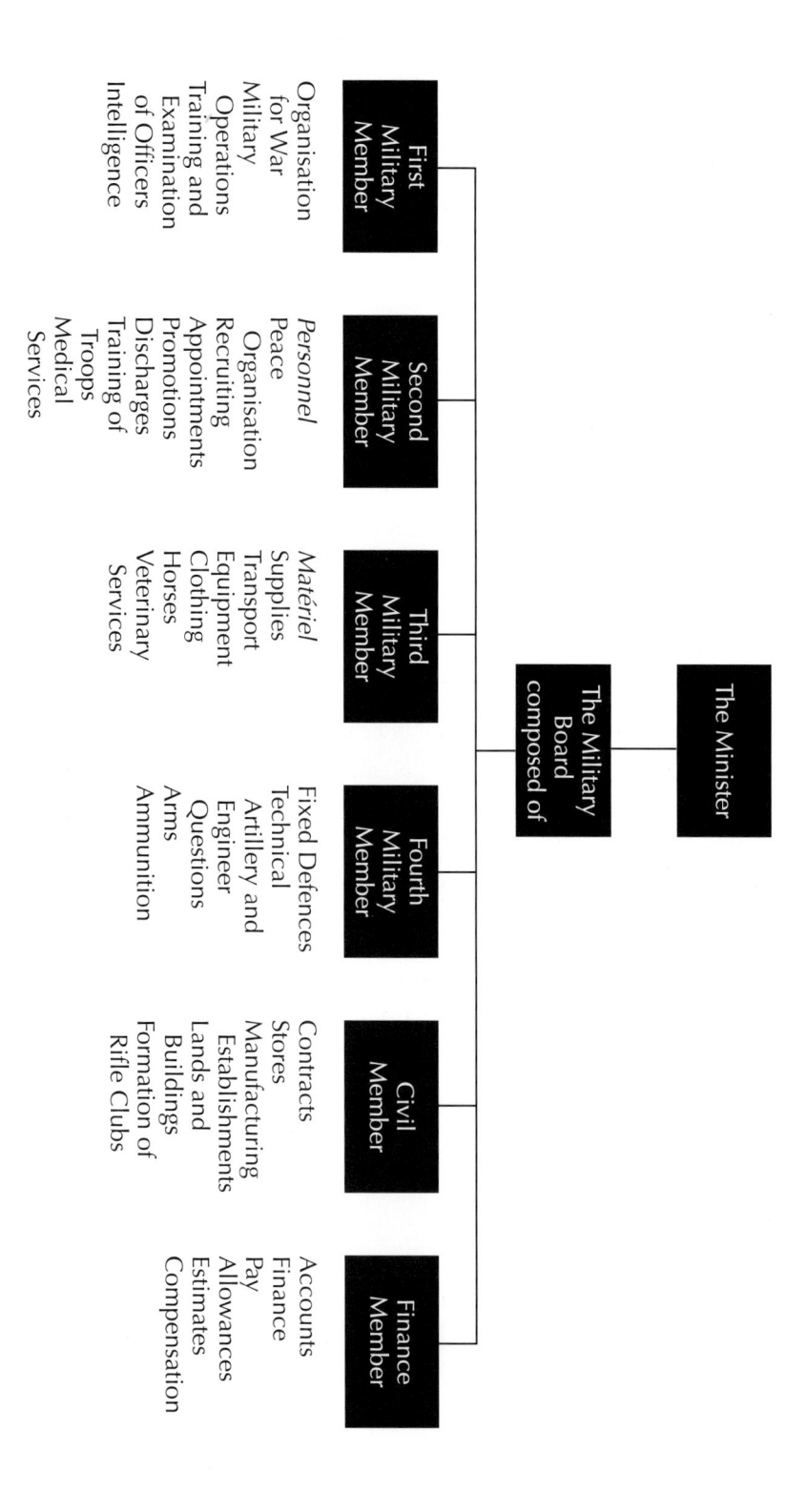

```
                                    The Minister
                                         |
                              The Military Board
                                  composed of
    ┌──────────┬──────────┬──────────┼──────────┬──────────┐
  First      Second      Third     Fourth     Civil      Finance
 Military   Military   Military   Military   Member      Member
  Member     Member     Member     Member
```

First Military Member
Organisation for War
Military Operations
Training and Examination of Officers
Intelligence

Second Military Member
Personnel
Peace Organisation
Recruiting
Appointments
Promotions
Discharges
Training of Troops
Medical Services

Third Military Member
Matériel
Supplies
Transport
Equipment
Clothing
Horses
Veterinary Services

Fourth Military Member
Fixed Defences
Technical Artillery and Engineer Questions
Arms
Ammunition

Civil Member
Contracts
Stores
Manufacturing Establishments
Lands and Buildings
Formation of Rifle Clubs

Finance Member
Accounts
Finance
Pay
Allowances
Estimates
Compensation

Chart 1 Composition and duties of the Military Board, 1909.
(Source: *Memorandum on Australian Military Defence and its Progress Since Federation*, Govt Printer, Melbourne, 1909)

of the General Staff (CGS) when the government created that office in 1909. The Inspector-General's responsibilities were simply stated as to 'report upon the condition of the Military Forces, their equipment, and the armament'. The reforms deliberately excluded the Inspector-General from the Military Board in order to distance the office from administrative decisions and to further ensure the office's independence. The first Inspector-General was Major-General H. Finn.[59]

The last of the 1905 reforms was the formation of a Council of Defence. The purpose of this body was to advise the government on questions of policy. Its mandate included advice on issues such as the steps to be taken in a national emergency, the development of defence schemes, the allocation of troops, and the review of the defence estimate. The original members of the council were the Minister for Defence as president, the Treasurer, the Inspector-General, the Director of Naval Forces, and the Chief of Intelligence. The Council of Defence, however, generally did not function as planned, and had a tendency to involve itself in matters that did not affect policy. The Council of Defence also had an intermittent history, and there were long periods when it did not sit.[60]

Meeting for the first time on 12 May 1905, the Council of Defence attempted to fulfil its role, as McCay sought, to define a middle ground for Australian defence policy. While he was cognisant of the importance of the Royal Navy and its role as the first line of defence for the Commonwealth, McCay also wanted to stress the function of land forces in the defence of population and industrial centres. He also noted that the army would provide the troops necessary to secure the defence of the ports from which the fleet would operate. Furthermore, he observed that the nation was justified in maintaining what some might consider a larger than necessary field force because of the difficulty in concentrating troops from adjacent states at the threatened point. In the current environment the Minister believed that Australia could postpone the development of an indigenous maritime force. McCay concluded that Australia would maintain its policy of subsidising the Admiralty for the maintenance of warships on the Australian station and continue to support an army for the defence of the Commonwealth's territory.[61]

McCay's memorandum brought forth a strong protest from Captain W.R. Creswell, the Director of Naval Forces, who since Federation had advocated the termination of the naval subsidy to the Admiralty and the creation of an Australian fleet.[62] Creswell provided the meeting with a detailed, prepared objection to the minister's minute. His motivation, he noted, as this was the first meeting of the Council of Defence, was to establish defence policy upon correct principles. These, he continued, had to be in accordance with the nation's natural conditions, its place in the empire—geographically and strategically—and within the means and conditions of the Commonwealth. He defined the principles of Australian defence as:

1   That Australia forms an integral part of the British Empire.
2   … that this compels a form of defence that shall be an integral part of the British Imperial defence, and in accord with the British Imperial method and policy.
3   That victory depends, in every great war, upon the maintenance of supremacy at sea.
4   … that the defence of Australia is the British fleet and that the best policy for Australia would be to increase the strength of the Royal Navy.[63]

Creswell proposed to fortify the capability of the Royal Navy through the modernisation and expansion of Australia's fleet. He recommended, at first, the laying down of three cruiser-destroyers, 16 torpedo-boat destroyers, and 15 torpedo boats.[64] The Director of Naval Forces also opined that the government should limit the military forces to the absolute minimal level necessary for the protection of naval bases and commercial centres and no more. He concluded that 'every increment in force added by Australia to sea power of the Empire makes directly for Australian defence and security in a manner more direct than can be achieved by any other form of contribution'.[65]

When asked how he would pay for the expansion of the RAN, Creswell replied that it would be through the abolition of the field force. He would sweep away the organisation that Hutton had carefully built up, and Australian defensive capability would consist of the battle fleet of the Royal Navy, an Australian coastal squadron, and the virtually static garrison force. Creswell was correct in his assessment that Australia's present vessels were obsolete and in need of replacement. However, his plan derived more from an ideological loyalty to Mahanian naval doctrine, a blind faith in the Royal Navy's ability to deter aggression, and a desire to develop the maritime spirit of the Australian people than to a realistic assessment of a defence policy. Among the defects in his plan was his failure to suggest how the Commonwealth would repel landings from enemy vessels that took place away from the proximity of the garrison force, and who would relieve an attack upon an isolated garrison such as King George's Sound. The plan also created a naval force capable only of coastal patrolling, which duplicated the defensive capability of the Commonwealth's fortifications. Finally, the demand for cruiser-destroyers created confusion, as no such class of vessels existed, and Creswell did not include a description of their size or armament. Consequently the government, no doubt motivated in part by a desire to avoid the expense of such a naval expansion, failed to take up Creswell's scheme. Although the Naval Director did not achieve his ambitions, at least in 1905, the presentation of the plan was significant because it represented the first time that one service attempted to advance its own interests at the expense of another. Moreover, Creswell's willingness to base Australian defence almost solely on naval power suggested an unreasoning belief in the veracity of maritime defence principles and an unwillingness to appreciate other forms of defence, a problem that would become more apparent in the period between the world wars.[66]

The system outlined by McCay went into effect on 9 December 1904. Hutton had already left for England in November at the expiration of his contract. Brigadier-General H. Finn filled in as General Officer Commanding in the position's final days, until his appointment as Inspector-General of the Australian Military Forces on 24 December 1904.[67] Before the end of his tenure, Hutton provided an assessment of the organisation he left behind. He noted:

> The changes thus effected are of a most far-reaching character. A complete military organisation has been created, which while capable of expansion, forms a carefully constructed frame-work into which additional and necessary fighting material can be fitted when the time of action arrives.[68]

Hutton's legacy, in combination with McCay's reforms of 1905, gave the Commonwealth the foundation for a modern military organisation. Although the military forces remained poorly equipped and lacked sufficient training to gain a high degree of efficiency, the institution did have the structure for the raising of a sizeable field force, as well as a useful supplement to naval power, in the form of the garrison force. Finally, the Commonwealth had in place an administrative hierarchy for the conduct of business and the development of policy. While problems remained, considerable advances had occurred in the development of the nation's ability to formulate security policy and shape defence requirements.

Threat and response: the rise of Japan, universal training, and fleet expansion

With its defeat of Russia in 1905, Japan confirmed its status as a rising power in the Pacific region. Despite its alliance with Britain since the signing of the 1902 Anglo-Japanese Pact, the growth of Japan's military capability and its emergence as a first-rate naval power alarmed Australian military planners, who identified Japan as the most likely threat to the nation. Complicating the situation was the perception in

Australia that the Anglo-Japanese Alliance actually weakened the Commonwealth's security, as it allowed Britain to reduce its naval presence in the Far East.

Events in Europe also raised concern. Germany's determination to dominate the affairs of the Old World and establish itself as a major factor on the world scene exacerbated the level of tension between the two empires and started Europe on the path to war. The expansion of the German fleet, heightened by the Dreadnought Crisis of 1909, suggested a direct threat to the maritime security of the empire. Furthermore, Germany held colonies in near proximity to Australian territory—in New Guinea— and maintained a powerful cruiser squadron in China.

Japan's victory over Russia in 1905 made it clear that Australia's period of tranquillity, including the absence of a definable threat, was about to come to an end. The Russo-Japanese War and the coming conflict with Germany would awaken public attitudes towards changes in the security environment and encourage the government to increase expenditure on the army and navy. The result would be the Commonwealth's first foray into 'self-reliance', as the government would attempt to counter these threats by creating a broadbased militia army and laying the foundation for a modern fleet. These changes in policy would simultaneously demonstrate the potential for schism within the imperial security network. While continuing to serve as the bulwark for an empire, Britain had signalled an intention to concentrate its efforts on protecting the heart of its territories, the United Kingdom, rather than the periphery, thereby forcing Australia to look to its own interests.[69]

The worsening threat environment coincided with Alfred Deakin's second ministry. Deakin was an Australian nationalist, and under his prodding the government increasingly focused its attention on defence issues. In June 1905, Deakin issued a statement that outlined his intentions regarding national security. The Prime Minister asserted that, as a result of the recent emergence of new naval powers, the defensive situation of Australia had changed. The Japanese destruction of the Russian fleet at Port Arthur demonstrated, he believed, the rapidity with which a rival could alter the strategic balance. Deakin did not believe that Australia could resist a similar onslaught, and even doubted the Commonwealth's ability to repel an attack by two or three fast cruisers on a weak spot. The Hutton era, he continued, had successfully laid the foundation for the organisation of the army, but the efficiency of the nation's military power remained neglected. Deakin noted that the Commonwealth's armed forces remained 'inadequate in number, imperfectly supplied with war material, and exceptionally weak on the naval side'.[70] He observed that Australia's warships were out of date, the coastal guns were generally old or even obsolete, manpower was below establishment, and the field force had only a handful of modern artillery pieces and inadequately trained gunners. The Commonwealth's dependency upon overseas factories for its munitions also worried Deakin, as it might prove impossible to obtain quick replenishment in time of war. Strategically, Deakin pointed out that while Australia could rely upon the Royal Navy's Australian squadron for its protection, there was no guarantee that these vessels would be in local waters when the enemy struck. According to the terms of the 1903 Naval Agreement, the Admiralty could move these vessels off station if it believed it needed them elsewhere.[71]

Deakin shared with officials in London his concerns over Australian defence readiness. Writing to Sir G. Sydenham Clarke, Secretary of the Committee of Imperial Defence, Deakin noted that the current system of voluntarism was inadequate, and advocated conscription as the basis of militia training.[72] The Prime Minister also expressed his doubts on the continuing acceptability of the naval subsidy. Deakin believed its payment was unpopular because it was not visibly Australian, and because it principally provided for imperial needs. The government was also in receipt of a number of studies from London that questioned the basis of the Commonwealth's military organisation. In answer to an Australian query on fixed defences, the Colonial Defence Committee reaffirmed that Australian defence relied on the maintenance of sea supremacy, and highlighted the importance of the Naval Agreement of 1903 in securing this goal. Elsewhere, the Colonial Defence Committee stated that the scheme for the Australian Military Force 'answers to no definite war requirement'. It also argued that the field force was not needed because the Royal Navy would make it too risky for any foe to attempt an invasion. Instead, all Australia required was coastal defences and garrisons for its major centres. Rather than a nationally organised field force, the Colonial Defence Committee recommended its replacement should be a State-based scheme that would only respond to local incursions.[73]

Underlying the government's concerns was the belief by some Australian officers that an imbalance existed between the army's force structure and the needs of the strategic environment. In 1905, Colonel J.C. Hoad voiced such concerns to the Military Board regarding the organisation of the field and garrison forces. After his appointment as Inspector-General, Hoad expanded on this point in his 1907 report. He wrote that Australia still did not have a scheme of defence based upon strategic considerations, and that the current policy of force planning was based on the availability of funds. Hoad went on to suggest the importance of first identifying the nature of the threat facing Australia, then settling on the types and scale of forces required to meet such an attack.

W.T. Bridges, the Chief of Intelligence, made a similar complaint to the Minister for Defence when he opined that it was impossible to make any defensive plans until the government established a clear policy on whether the army should prepare to repel an invasion or focus on the prevention of raids.[74] Bridges' concern suggested his awareness of the inherent flaw within Australian defence planning. The question was whether the army's primary function was to protect the integrity of the Commonwealth's territory or to safeguard the ports and installations needed for maritime supremacy. Additionally, despite the conditions of the Defence Act, which prohibited overseas service by troops unless they volunteered, the government had merely obscured rather than definitely answered the question of military participation in imperial expeditions.

To clarify the matter, Deakin wrote to the Imperial Defence Committee in London in late 1905 to ask it to prepare a scheme of defence for Australia.[75] The review, which the committee presented in August 1906, contained few new recommendations, and was mainly a reaffirmation of existing defence principles. The Committee of Imperial Defence continued to maintain that the primary line of Australian defence was the imperial fleet, supported by the garrison force's protection of naval installations, and backed up by the field force. Under this defensive umbrella, the Committee of Imperial Defence concluded, Australia needed to prepare only for raids by cruisers and landings of not greater than a thousand troops. The report acknowledged the correctness of the army's organisation into field and garrison forces, but recommended that the further distinction between static garrison troops and local reserves was unnecessary. It suggested that any troops within the garrison command who were not assigned to fixed point defences should be added to the field force. The Committee of Imperial Defence also suggested that the subunits of the field force brigades should not be drawn from multiple states, as was the case for the 4th and 6th Light Horse Brigades and 3rd Infantry Brigade. The Committee of Imperial Defence then made a point of condemning Creswell's 1905 suggestion to establish a Commonwealth naval force for coastal defence. It asserted that there was no strategic justification for such a force, that its maintenance would be more expensive than current arrangements, and that the existence of such a fleet would violate the principle of unified naval command.[76]

Of greater interest was the Committee of Imperial Defence's interpretation of the purpose of the field force. With the Royal Navy's assurance of maritime supremacy and the adequacy of garrison troops for local defence, the Committee of Imperial Defence did not see a vital domestic role for the field force. As the situation worsened in Europe, it became clear that the Committee of Imperial Defence was conscious of the potential outbreak of what it termed a 'war of national existence'. It was within the context of such a struggle that it defined a function for the field force. Instead of being an organisation designed to respond to incursion of Australian territory, the Committee of Imperial Defence saw the field force as little more than a training establishment, suitable for expansion into a militia army. Furthermore, the Committee of Imperial Defence suggested that in a great war, Australia might move its field force overseas in order to participate in a decisive struggle on foreign soil.[77]

At the 1907 Imperial Conference, the British Government continued its attempts to get the Dominions to accept its interpretation of colonial forces as part of an imperial army. The British proposed the establishment of an imperial general staff, whose purpose was to coordinate the military power of the entire empire in time of war. In this scheme, the colonial troops would be placed under the control of the Imperial General Staff which, of course, was effectively placing them under the command of the War Office. The British General Staff also distributed a paper at the conference, advancing the benefits of mutual support in time of crisis and the importance of standardisation of force structure, equipment, and other aspects of military preparation throughout the empire.[78]

The British only partially succeeded in their agenda, because their interpretation of the strategic environment differed significantly from that of Australia. Deakin did see the benefit in standardisation of equipment and establishment throughout the empire, and the Australian Army modified its organisation to adopt the British Army force structure. However, he strongly rebuffed the British desire for the former colonies to consider their field forces as part of an imperial reserve. Deakin also refused to accept the Committee of Imperial Defence's interpretation of the empire's strategic balance, and instead believed that the rise of Japan had changed the situation, particularly in the Pacific. Whereas London insisted that Japan was an ally, Australia saw it as a major threat, and rather than perceiving the location of a war of national existence in Europe, it was the Pacific that held Deakin's attention. Instead of simply accepting the assurances of the Committee of Imperial Defence, he referred their findings to a committee of Australian officers for comment.

In September 1906 the committee, under the direction of Hoad as Inspector-General, presented its findings to Thomas Playford, the Minister for Defence. While accepting most of the minor recommendations of the Committee of Imperial Defence, the officers objected to the review's strategic considerations. Their report noted that it was essential to plan to repel enemy landings in excess of the thousand-man maximum that the Committee of Imperial Defence predicted. The officers believed that under certain conditions Australia was vulnerable to threats greater than raids from a few enemy cruisers, and concluded that it would be 'unwise not to provide for the possibility of the supremacy of the sea being temporarily lost'. The officers pointed out that the events of the Russo-Japanese War demonstrated the impossibility of anticipating the outcome of naval warfare in the future. Their report stated that Australia should be prepared for the temporary loss of maritime control by the Royal Navy and the subsequent vulnerability of the continent to invasion by a large and highly trained force.[79]

The central question that the officer's report thus posed concerned the steps that the Commonwealth should take to prepare for a possible loss of maritime supremacy by the Royal Navy in order to safeguard the nation's territory from invasion. Australia's response would be to undertake the broadening of the military experience of the nation's able-bodied men through a universal training scheme and through the laying down of warships to provide for local maritime defence.

In 1907, Deakin sent Bridges to Switzerland to study that country's universal training scheme and determine its application to Australia.[80] However, because of political factionalism the government was unable to proceed until September 1908, when it introduced a bill for universal military training. Thomas Ewing, the Minister for Defence at this time, explained the objectives of the bill. He believed that it was not possible to establish the defence of the Commonwealth on a satisfactory basis until the men of Australia accepted that 'times of peace must be utilised in preparation, in order that in time of war those duties may be intelligently performed'. He continued that 'valour, which would not be wanting in time of trial, is not sufficient in itself, but must be sustained by preparation and forethought'.[81] Ewing saw military training as an obligation the members of a society owed to the state, and he believed it was a duty of the government to assure that all able-bodied men were prepared for its competent discharge. Finally, the Minister noted that the current system of voluntary enlistment did not provide a large enough force for the expenditure involved, the standard of training was unequal, and too many recruits resigned before they obtained a sufficient degree of proficiency. The Military Board supported this argument when it advised the government that the present conditions of service provided an inadequate period for the proper training of the troops.[82]

The Deakin ministry did submit to parliament an amendment to the Defence Act for the introduction of universal service; however, the government fell before it could secure any substantive changes in the army's organisation. The Fisher Government also made an attempt to pass a conscription bill but it, too, failed. Success finally came in late 1909 when Joseph Cook, the Minister for Defence in Deakin's third ministry, succeeded in guiding a universal service scheme through parliament. The *Defence Act 1909* established terms of service as:

a 14–18 year olds to serve in the Senior Cadets and to train for the equivalent of sixteen whole days annually.

b 18–20 year olds to serve in the Citizen Forces and to train for sixteen days annually of which eight were to be in camp.[83]

Despite the passage of the legislation, however, implementation did not take place, as yet another change of government occurred. Furthermore, the new government, Fisher's second ministry, chose to await the recommendations of Lord Kitchener, whom the previous administration had invited to tour Australia. Kitchener presented his findings in February 1910. George Pearce, Fisher's Minister for Defence, then submitted a new bill for universal service, which greatly increased the obligations required in the 1909 version. In its final form the scheme called for the mandatory military service of all able-bodied males who were British subjects on the following basis:

a 12–14 years of age—service in the Junior Cadets

b 14–18 years of age—service in the Senior Cadets

c 18–26 years of age—service in the Citizen Forces.

Agricultural High School cadets, Sale, Vic, 1909. (AWM P1258/04/04)

The Act required junior cadets to perform 124 hours of service per year (subsequently reduced to 90), while senior cadets had a training responsibility of four whole days, 12 half-days, and 24 evening parades. The government obligated the members of the citizen forces to train for 16 days per year, of which at least eight were to be in a camp of continuous instruction. Members of the artillery and engineers had to train for 25 days annually, of which 17 were to be in camp. However, citizen force members in their final year of service had only to attend one unpaid muster parade.

Also in 1909, Commonwealth representatives attended an Imperial Conference in London. The meeting was principally concerned with maritime affairs, especially the naval arms race between Britain and Germany. As a result of the conference, Australia agreed to build a fleet unit of one armoured cruiser, three unarmoured cruisers, six destroyers, and three submarines. In return, Britain pledged to base at its China and East India stations fleet units of its own, which could unite, under Admiralty control, with the Australian section and a possible Canadian contribution to form a pacific fleet. As a result of this decision, the mother country had conceded the right of its former colonies to build their own fleets, and Australia also gained the naval presence it so desired. The British agreement to encourage the construction of Dominion navies, after many years of determined opposition, signalled the realisation that the Royal Navy might have to surrender local maritime control temporarily until it had stabilised the situation in home waters. To command the new fleet, the government established the RAN in 1911.[85]

The conference's attention to military matters was of less concern, but still resulted in important determinations for the Australian Army. While avoiding the issue of the creation of an imperial reserve, the British Government successfully argued for closer integration between the forces of the mother country and those of the Dominions. Britain sought widespread participation by the empire in an imperial general staff so that this body could fulfil its function as an imperial coordination agency. While the British accepted the reality that the Dominions would retain complete control over their forces, they still saw benefit in having an organisation that would prepare defence schemes based on common principles and mutual support.[86]

Australia had established its own Chief of the General Staff (CGS) only in January 1909, and Bridges received the inaugural appointment. His duties included the maintenance of the army's war organisation, the preparation of defence plans, the training and examination of officers, and the gathering and interpretation of intelligence. The CGS also served as the First Military Member of the Military Board, replacing the Chief of Intelligence. The changes of administration were actually rather modest, as

```
                    ┌─────────┐
                    │   CGS   │
                    └────┬────┘
         ┌───────────────┼───────────────┐
  ┌──────┴──────┐ ┌──────┴──────┐ ┌──────┴──────┐
  │ Director of │ │ Director of │ │ Director of │
  │   Defence   │ │   Military  │ │ Intelligence│
  │Organisation │ │   Training  │ │             │
  └─────────────┘ └─────────────┘ └─────────────┘
```

Chart 2 Office of the Chief of the General Staff (CGS), 1909.
(Source: *Memorandum by the Chief of the General Staff and of the Commonwealth Section of the Imperial General Staff*, Govt Printer, Melbourne, 1910)

the Chief of Intelligence had essentially filled the function of the CGS, and Bridges had served in that capacity from 1905 until his appointment as CGS.

Having created the position, the Commonwealth now undertook to include within its mandate participation on the Imperial General Staff. On 1 July 1909, in a reshuffle of duties, the government appointed Major-General J.C. Hoad to the dual position of CGS and Chief of the Commonwealth Section of the Imperial General Staff. Bridges instead received the appointment as Commonwealth military adviser to the 1909 Imperial Conference, and stayed on in London to serve as Australia's first representative to the Imperial General Staff headquarters. Chart 2 outlines the structure of the Office of the CGS.

Broadly defined, Hoad's responsibilities included those of the CGS, plus the task of liaising with London on matters of imperial defence. Serving directly under Hoad were officers responsible for the following duties:
- Director of Defence Organisation: responsible for the preparation of Commonwealth defence schemes and plans of concentration for war
- Director of Military Training: responsible for overseeing the training and instruction in all arms, the education and examination of officers for promotion, and the preparation of staff rides, drill books, training manuals, and courses of instruction
- Director of Intelligence: responsible for the collection of information and the preparation of maps.[87]

In a parallel development, the authorities in London also sought at the 1909 conference an agreement by the Dominions to standardise their formations, training, administrative and staff procedures, ammunition, and equipment on a British pattern. The Australian acceptance of this policy had practical affects on the army's structure. The light horse brigades were now to have three regiments instead of the existing four, although each regiment would be significantly larger. The army also had to reorganise its infantry brigades as purely infantry formations, consisting of a headquarters and four battalions in place of the existing battle-group organisation. Although Australia did not have any formations larger than the brigade, the army decided to establish its field artillery, engineers, signals, Australian Army Service Corps, and Australian Army Medical Corps according to the requirements of a division in anticipation of the creation of such formations.[88]

Despite Australia's insistence that London should not construe the Commonwealth's cooperation as a willingness to commit troops to imperial expeditions, the government signals could easily be misinterpreted. The government's protest that its forces existed solely for home defence did not prevent the Commonwealth from reorganising its army on a pattern designed to wage a war against a European opponent. As Donald C. Gordon pointed out in *The Dominion Partnership*, these decisions by Australia served to expose an inconsistency in the nation's military policy. While continuing to assert a theory of local control for local defence, the nation's military policy was increasingly one of imperial participation. John Mordike, in *An Army for a Nation*, maintains that persistent subterfuge by officials in London, aided by the army's senior officers, gradually undermined the Australian Government's resistance to imperial adventures. He suggests, that by a series of small steps, imperial planners manoeuvred the Australian Government into giving a de facto commitment of troops, despite the government's protests. Mordike is right that the government was under considerable pressure, both from Britain and from its own military advisers. However, his interpretation is overly conspiratorial and does not recognise the close affinity that existed between Australia and the mother country. Australian politicians were not outwitted, but were simply following a policy trend that they instinctively shared with imperial officials. What is clear, however, is that the debate over overseas commitments underscored a lack of clarity in defence planning that resulted in a growing difference between policy and force structure.[89]

Kitchener's organisation

At the request of the government, Lord Kitchener toured Australia in 1910 in order to conduct a review of the Commonwealth's defence requirements. In his report, Kitchener proposed sweeping changes in the organisation of the army, which the government incorporated into its universal service reforms. The result was the complete remaking of the army's force structure from the pattern that Hutton had established.

Despite conscription, the army organisation remained based on the citizen soldier. Service was mandatory, but training remained limited to brief periods of camp, supported by parades at the local drill hall. The nation's military structure continued to consist of a small permanent force for administration, training and the garrisoning of fixed defences and a much larger limited service force that provided for local defence and the field force.[90]

The division of the non-permanent forces into two categories also ceased at this time, and by mid 1911 the army had merged its militia and volunteer formations and units into a single organisation called the Citizen Forces. The Universal Service statute had foreshadowed the use of the term Citizen Forces in 1909. The title 'Citizen Forces' remained in use until the government abandoned conscription in 1930 and revived the designation 'Militia' to describe the army's volunteer non-permanent forces.

Kitchener began his report with the traditional mantra that as long as the empire maintained an efficient and adequate naval force 'no British dominion can be successfully and permanently conquered by an organised invasion from overseas'. However, he then immediately added a condition that complicated this refrain. The conduct of a great war, Kitchener noted, might require the concentration of the British naval forces in a theatre at a considerable distance from the Commonwealth. Even if the ultimate control of the sea was never in doubt, he believed that Australia

No. 5 Battery, Australian Field Artillery, training with a 12-pounder gun, 1908. (AWM P0587/52/33)

must be able to protect itself until the Royal Navy decisively asserted global maritime supremacy.[91] It was in this last capability that he found the current Australian military forces most deficient. Under the existing scheme of voluntary service he believed that 'the present forces are inadequate in numbers, training, organisation, and munitions of war, to defend Australia'. Kitchener, therefore, enthusiastically endorsed the amendments to the Defence Act regarding universal service, which was currently under the government's consideration, and he assumed its successful passage in his revisions to the army's organisation.[92]

The army that Kitchener recommended would have a peacetime strength of 80,100 men and a wartime establishment of about 135,000. This represented a 360 per cent increase in the number of citizen force personnel compared with the level in the last year before the commencement of universal service. The army would maintain in peace its infantry battalions and light horse regiments at approximately 75 per cent of the wartime establishment, while the field artillery batteries would typically be at 90 per cent of their wartime strength. Upon mobilisation for war, units would be brought up to full strength by the inclusion of soldiers in the final year of service, whom the Defence Act obliged to report only for a single muster parade, and by the incorporation into the formation of the incoming class of recruits. The rifle clubs also continued to serve as a source of reserves. Kitchener proposed an army of:

- 21 brigades of infantry with 4 battalions in each brigade for a total of 84 battalions (subsequently raised to 23 brigades and 92 battalions)
- 28 regiments of light horse
- 49 four-gun field batteries and 7 four-gun howitzer batteries
- 14 field companies of engineers and 7 communication companies
- departmental troops in proportion.[93]

Although the plan did not include any divisions (the largest formation was the brigade), it did call for the creation of divisional troops in order that the army could raise such formations in the future.[94]

For the purpose of administration and training, the scheme divided the country into 92 battalion areas, and further subdivided these into 215 (subsequently 219) training areas. Generally, each metropolitan battalion had two training areas, while country battalions had three areas from which to draw their members. The plan linked four battalions together to form a brigade area. Initially each brigade area began with a single battalion, but as trainees arrived annually from the cadet battalions, over a period of several years, the army planned to split the units until the area had obtained the required four infantry battalions. Eventually, each brigade area was also to provide a company of engineers, a company of the Army Service Corps, and a field ambulance. This training area scheme remained in effect until after World War II. Map 3 (pp. 52–3) illustrates the distribution of battalion and training areas as required under the Kitchener Plan.

Kitchener suggested that the army allocate an officer from the permanent forces to command each training area, assisted by one or two non-commissioned officers. This, however, proved impossible, as there were simply too few available officers. Instead, in many localities, the army had to assign training areas to citizen forces officers. In the scheme's first year of operation, the army had to second 171 citizen forces officers to serve as training area officers.[95] Kitchener identified the duties of the training area officer as:

a The inspection of the junior cadets training in the schools.
b The organization and training of the senior cadets.
c The enrolment, equipment, and training of the adults from eighteen to nineteen years of age.
d The equipment, organization, and training of the trained soldiers from nineteen to twenty-five years of age.
e The maintenance of records regarding the numbers, residence, and classification of the reserve men in the areas, and the organization of rifle clubs.[96]

Kitchener also suggested that when establishing the training areas the army should retain the designations and historical associations of the existing units in order to transfer the esprit de corps of the old formations into the new.[97]

Although universal training called for compulsory military service by all able-bodied males (of British ancestry), the scheme made some allowance for those whose participation would have been excessively difficult. The scheme temporarily exempted all men who resided more than five miles from a training locality, since travelling to attend a parade from such a distance would impose a considerable hardship. The plan also included a transition period. Although the scheme officially came into operation on 1 January 1911, the government did not halt access to the army on a voluntary basis until 30 June 1912. Additionally, enlisted men who were volunteers would continue in the ranks until their terms of service had expired. The army gave serving non-commissioned officers, of the rank of corporal and above, the right to re-enlist for a further three years. The government also continued to allow recruitment into the light horse on the basis of voluntarism. Partially this was because many of these units were located in country areas, and drew upon men who resided outside the radius of a training locale, but the requirement for soldiers to provide their own horses was also a factor.[98]

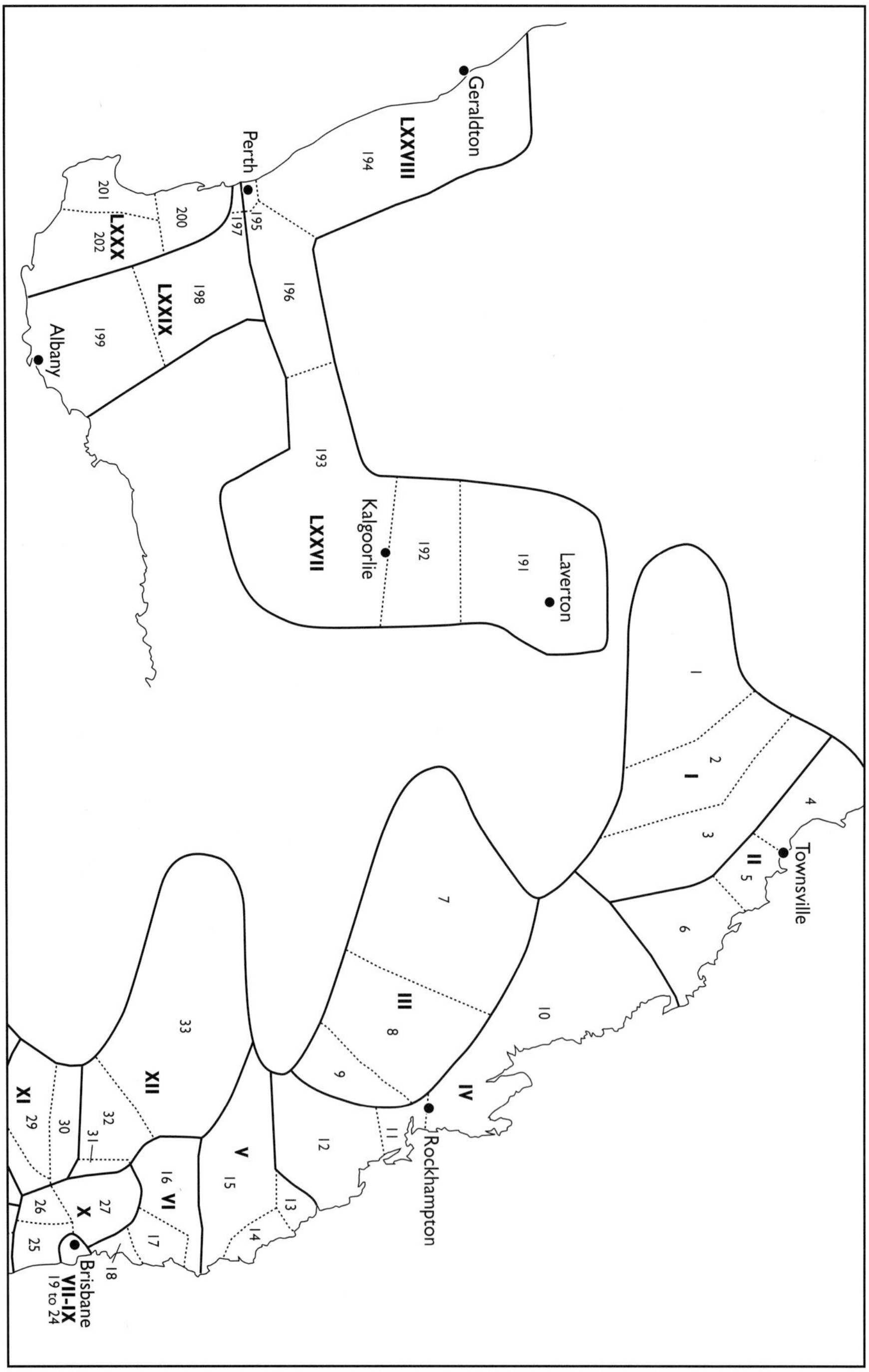

Map 3a Kitchener Plan of the regional distribution of the Australian Army

FROM FEDERATION TO WORLD WAR I

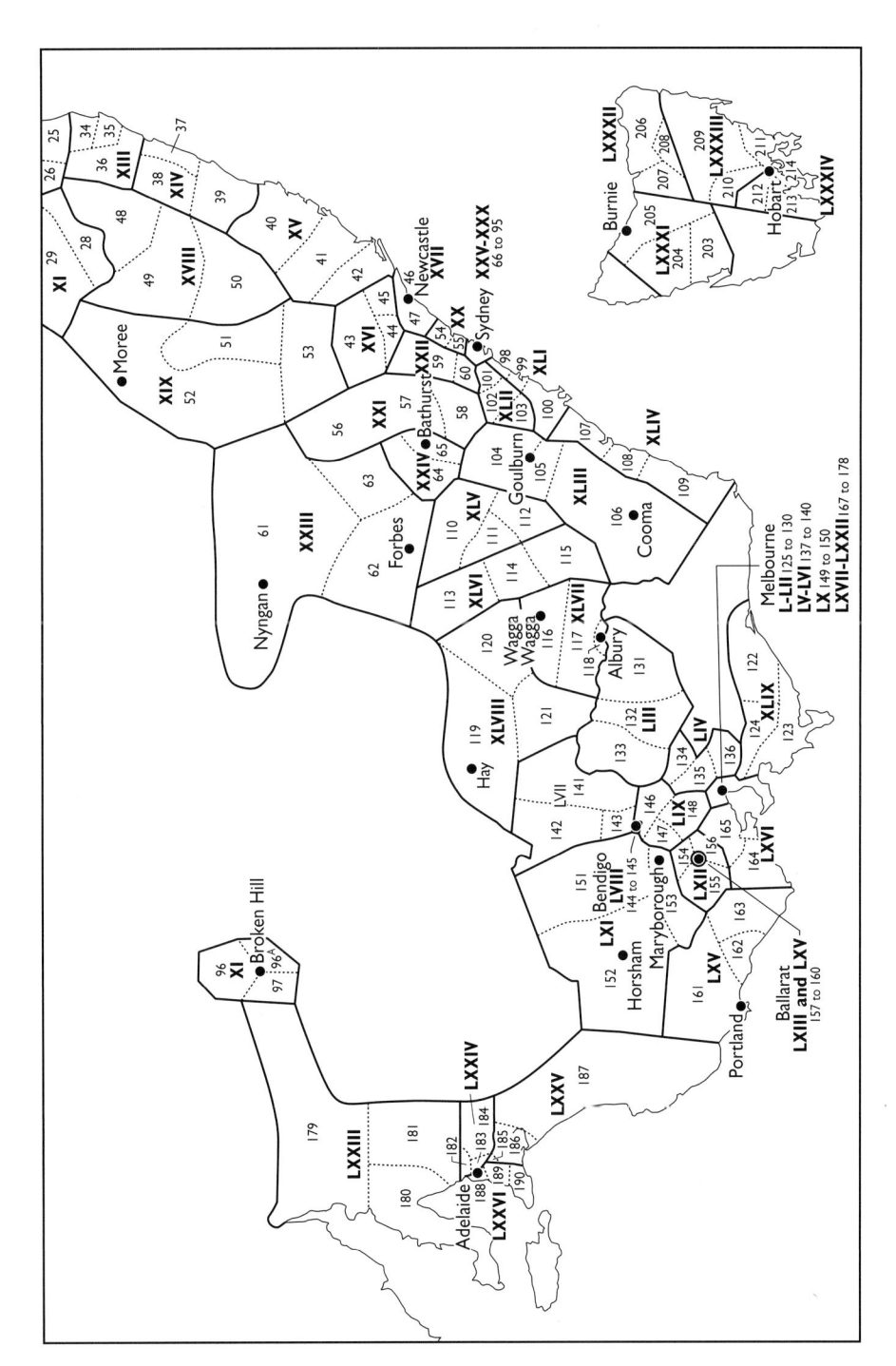

Map 3b Kitchener Plan of the regional distribution of the Australian Army

The army decided to apply the terms of the scheme gradually rather than imposing universal service immediately on all eligible classes. The inaugural intake was the first eligible year of senior cadets. In 1912, the citizen forces had reached a strength of 33,955, of which 16,211 served under universal training obligations, while for the following year the figures were 33,601 conscripts out of 45,915.[99] Each passing year would result in the expansion of the scheme by an additional class, and it would take eight years for the plan to become fully operational. Table 2.8 illustrates the gradual build-up of the army to its authorised size in the scheme's first three years of operation, until the interruption of World War I.

Table 2.8 Expansion of the army under the Universal Training Scheme, 1911–14[100]

Arm	No. of units authorised	No. of units established 1911–12	No. of units established 1912–13	No. of units established 1913–14
Light Horse	31 regiments	19	23	23
Field Artillery	56 batteries	22	26	27
Garrison Artillery	13 companies	13	13	13
Engineers	42 companies	21	29	30
Infantry	94 battalions	32	45	52

As Table 2.8 suggests, after three years the army had raised approximately 50 per cent of its authorised formations. The only exception was the garrison artillery, as these had existed previously as part of the coastal defence component of the garrison force.

The new scheme also led to a revision of the boundaries and a change in designation of the military districts. Instead of the military districts being known by their State names, the government now numbered them from one to six. They still closely conformed to, but did not exactly match, State boundaries. The new arrangements were:

- 1st Military District, based on Queensland
- 2nd Military District, based on New South Wales
- 3rd Military District, based on Victoria
- 4th Military District, based on South Australia
- 5th Military District, based on Western Australia
- 6th Military District, based on Tasmania.

Map 4 outlines the territorial responsibilities of the military districts.

Both the universal training scheme and Kitchener's report placed great emphasis upon the role of the cadets, and to a lesser degree, the rifle clubs, in the nation's security

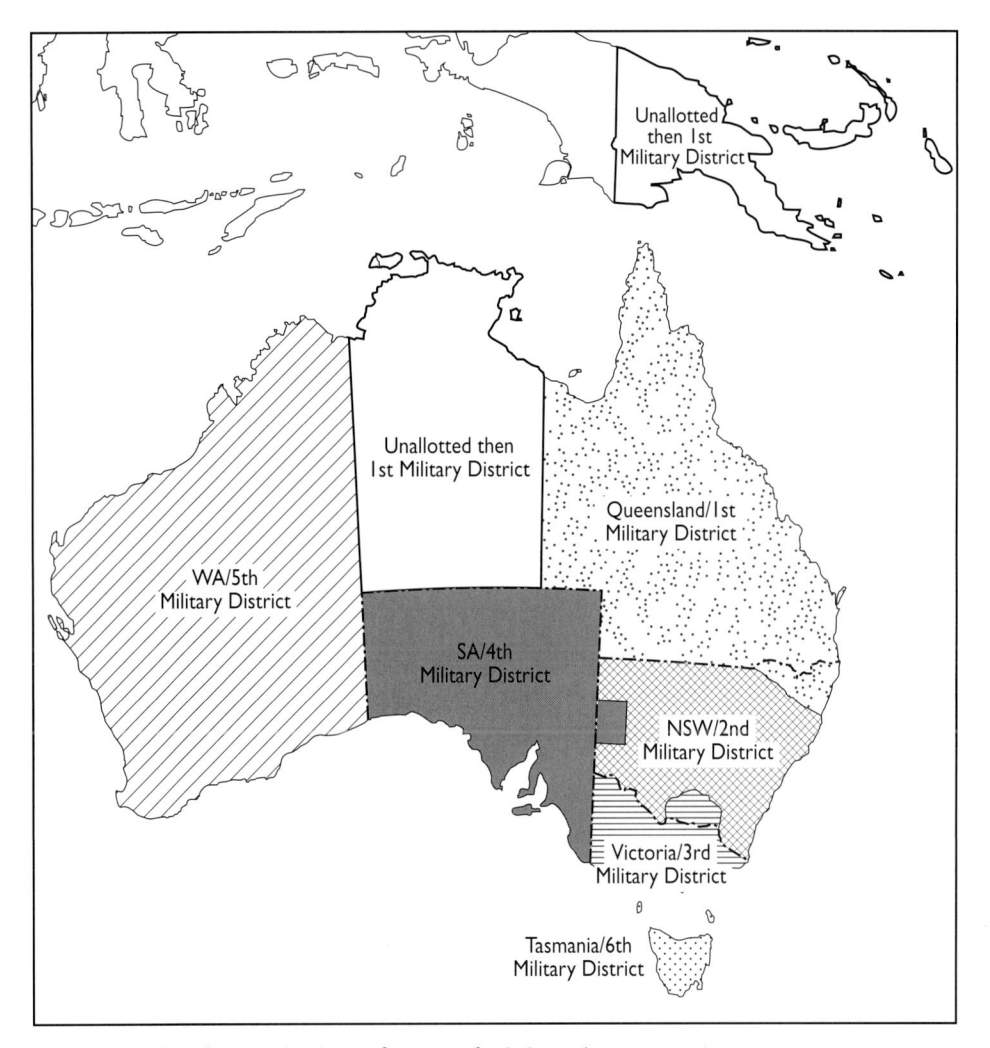

Map 4 Regional organisation of army administration, 1911

arrangements. Neither of these institutions was new. Rather, they had enjoyed a long association with the Australian military tradition. St Mark's Collegiate School in New South Wales formed Australia's first cadet unit in 1866, and Victoria in 1884 and New South Wales in 1890 passed acts regulating their cadet formations.[101] After Federation, the Commonwealth inherited cadet units from several States. Queensland had the largest system, with more than 1,200 boys enrolled. Section 62 of the *Defence Act 1903* unified the cadet forces into a single federal system; however, the lack of funds prohibited its further development. It was not until Deakin's first ministry in 1906 that the Commonwealth decided to direct resources to the development of the cadet system. In that year, the government designated the cadet system as the Commonwealth Cadet

Corps. By 1910, the final year in which cadet membership was voluntary, the system included 16 battalions of senior cadets and nine squadrons of mounted cadets, with a membership of 10,255 and 334 respectively.[102]

The Commonwealth expected the cadets to have an important place in the development of the nation's military strength. While this was in part a reflection of the worldwide youth improvement movement, it also reflected a desire by the nation's leaders to incorporate Australian boys into the Commonwealth's security arrangements. As early as 1905, the Minister for Defence, McCay, had proposed the creation of a training scheme. He identified the objectives as:

a The inculcation, in early years, of habits of obedience and discipline.
b The bringing home to the minds of our boys the knowledge of their duty . . . to take part in the defence of their country, should occasion arise, and to be properly trained before hand for the task.
c The improvement in physique consequent upon such training.[103]

Furthermore, McCay believed that the military training of youth was a key element of national defence, especially for Australia, which relied upon citizen forces.[104]

The Military Board in 1908 outlined its objectives for the cadet corps as:

a The physical improvement of all boys up to the age of 14 years, and such elementary drill as may be of use to them as citizens in later life.
b To provide elementary military training and musketry for all boys over 14 years of age, with the object of minimising the period of recruit training of those who subsequently enter the Defence Force.[105]

In addition to practical military training in activities, such as drill and rifle practice, the government and the military also saw the cadet movement as a means to instil within its members a sense of patriotism, loyalty, and obligation to defend the nation.

In the first half of 1911, the government registered, inspected, and medically examined boys of the 1894, 1895, 1896, and 1897 quotas for the senior cadets, as well as medically inspected the 1898 and 1899 cohorts of the junior cadets. More than 38,000 senior cadets reported for duty in the plan's first year of operation, a figure that grew to nearly 90,000 by 1914, with an additional 55,000 boys undergoing training as junior cadets. The army also divided the nation into 92 battalion areas for the senior cadets, each of which would become the catchment for a citizen force battalion.[106]

It is clear that both government and military leaders expected too much from the cadets. Deakin, in a letter to London in 1906, expressed his hope that the cadets would make splendid, almost efficient recruits for the citizen forces. A 1909 report on universal training echoed this theme, as well as the belief that the training a soldier received as a cadet was directly transferable to his military service, and that new recruits would begin their term of service at a higher degree of efficiency than those who had not been cadets. The government hoped that by providing military instruction to children the army would have to expend relatively little additional effort once those children had passed into the citizen forces. As one defence report noted, Australia hoped to gain the same degree of military efficiency in the brief camps and periodic parades that other nations achieved with considerably longer periods of continuous training.[107]

However, after operating for several years, the scheme was clearly not working. In 1912, the Minister for Defence complained that cadet attendance at parades was irregular, and that the system tended towards inefficiency. General Sir Ian Hamilton, in his 1914 defence review, was much more damning of the success of the Commonwealth Cadet Corps. He wrote that the training received by cadets had largely failed to produce adequate soldiers. Moreover, he noted that citizen forces officers had complained to him of instances of having received cadets who were ignorant of the rudiments of drill or, worse, so badly trained that they had to expend great effort in eradicating faults that were the result of poor initial training. Many boys also objected to their forced participation in the scheme. Between 1911 and 1914, the government prosecuted 28,000 boys, including multiple defaulters, for failing to register or complete their training obligation.[108]

To supply the officers needed to staff and train Australia's conscription army, Kitchener had proposed the creation of a military college. This was not the first time the government received such advice, as Hutton had made a similar recommendation during his tenure as the army's commander. Besides officer training, a military college had the additional benefit of providing competent officers for the recently formed general staff. The government acted on Kitchener's advice, and the Royal Military College Duntroon opened in 1911.

Final plans

In 1913, the army presented its first comprehensive defence review for the Commonwealth since the imposition of universal service. Although the 'Defence Scheme for the Commonwealth of Australia' again confirmed the axiom of the empire's reliance upon the maintenance of maritime supremacy, it also highlighted the principle of the Dominions' responsibility for their own defence that was established at the 1909 Imperial Conference. However, in addition to passive defence

Staff cadets on parade at Royal Military College Duntroon, 1913.
(AWM P02029.015)

against raids and landings, the plan identified two potential offensive overseas roles for Australian military forces. The first was the Commonwealth's participation in an imperial military operation under the control of British authorities. The second was the overseas commitment of small expeditionary forces, under Australian control, against foreign possessions that an opponent might employ as a base of operation against the Commonwealth. This implied that the army had interpreted the principle of Dominion defence responsibility to include offensive actions beyond the Australian littoral, to protect Commonwealth interest, without imperial sanction. Although the necessity of enrolling volunteers for such a deployment would hinder the dispatch of such a force, the terms of the Defence Act, as another staff study noted, did not preclude the army from considering the possibility.[109]

The CGS also believed that the strategic needs of the nation required the following military capabilities:
- garrisons for defended ports
- local field forces capable of dealing with a raiding force
- a field army capable of moving to the support of any threatened district.

He also suggested the future adoption of the division as the basis for the organisation of the army, although for the present he believed that formations higher than brigade were impractical.[110]

In 1914, General Sir Ian Hamilton, as Inspector-General of the Overseas Forces, visited Australia and conducted another major defence review of the Australian military forces. He presented his findings to the government in May of the same year. In general, he was pleased with the extent to which the army had progressed in its adoption of Kitchener's recommendations. Hamilton did, however, raise some concerns as well as offering some suggestions for improvement.

Hamilton's most serious problem was that when the army reached its planned size in 1919–20, its manpower would remain considerably short of requirements. He estimated that in 1919–20 the army would have available for its wartime establishment the following:

- Permanent forces
  — 380 officers
  — 2,800 other ranks
- Citizen forces
  — 4,000 officers
  — 86,000 trained soldiers
  — 12,500 trained soldiers in their 25th–26th year
  — 17,000 recruits in their first year of service.

These figures represented a deficit of more than 12,000 from the required amount of 135,000. Hamilton also pointed out that the army had made no provision for service troops, which he believed would require a further 62,500 men. Also, he noted that the army had made no allowance for wastage in its calculations. The only formal reserves the army possessed were the rifle clubs, wherein acceptance as a member also constituted attestment as a member of the reserve forces. Out of a membership of 47,500, there were 28,500 rifle club members fit for active service and, of these, the army had allotted nearly 20,000 to active units or to static duties such as cable guards.

However, Hamilton believed that the rifle clubs were too narrow a base upon which to rest a reserve system, and that such organisations offered only a temporary solution. In order to make up the manpower deficit, Hamilton advocated the imposition of a reserve requirement on all able-bodied males who had completed their universal training obligation. He noted that, in its current form, the Defence Act only provided for the voluntary enlistment of experienced soldiers in the reserve forces, whereas in many countries such an obligation was mandatory. In the report, Hamilton observed that from 1920–21 onwards, a quota of approximately 12,500 trained soldiers would fulfil their terms of service in the army, and that the government should impose a service obligation up to the age of 60.[111]

Hamilton's report also identified a lengthy list of units that the army still needed to organise in order to complete the requirements of the Kitchener plan. These included six light horse regiments, 33 infantry battalions, 30 batteries of artillery, 34 ammunition columns, and various companies of field engineers, signals, Army Service Corps, field ambulances, and other units. Although he did not demand the formation of divisional headquarters, Hamilton did acknowledge the possibility of such an event. If the government ever authorised this step, he anticipated that the Australian forces would support the creation of six divisions, with additional subdivisional size formations in the smaller military districts.[112]

In the 14 years between Federation and the outbreak of World War I, the military forces of Australia had developed remarkably. At the turn of the century, the continent's military resources had consisted of six separate, poorly equipped, and inconsistently trained armies. Hutton had perhaps the hardest job. It fell to him to eliminate the differences among the forces of the six States and weld them into a unified military force. Simultaneously, he also had to establish the administrative and staff organisations that would manage the army. Despite generating some degree of controversy, he largely succeeded at this task. Hutton's organisation, however, lasted only a few years. The worsening threat environment after 1905 led to a reevaluation of the nation's security requirements. In response to these developments, successive Australian governments gave greater attention to security matters and expanded both the nation's military and naval assets.

Although the government did build up the Commonwealth's armed forces and integrated the army into the imperial military system, certain critical aspects of the army's organisation remained unchanged. Clause 49 of the *Defence Act 1903* continued to prohibit overseas use of troops, except on a voluntary basis. Despite the growing threats facing the empire, the government steadfastly refused to obligate itself in advance to come to the mother country's aid. The other critical issue that remained unchallenged was the belief that the army could create an efficient military organisation on the basis of eight days of continuous camp training.

The final years before the war highlighted the fundamental problem of Australian security planning—the need to balance the requirements of the empire against the local concerns of the nation. Although members of a sovereign state, Australians still considered themselves to be also part of an imperial confederation. Despite the government's insistence upon the maintenance of its independence, imperial obligations remained, barely hidden, within the cultural commitment of the people. The pursuit of a balance between local interests and imperial responsibilities was the most significant security issue facing the Commonwealth, and its resolution was fundamental to the army's ability to formulate plans for the defence of the continent and determine the requirements of its structure. However, despite its importance, successive governments failed to confront the issue, and instead supported the maintenance of the status quo.[113]

Australia had spent considerable effort and expense since Federation in addressing the military requirements of the nation. Representatives of the government had attended a series of imperial conferences in London, while British authorities, as well as local officers, had conducted a number of reviews of the Commonwealth's military requirements. The result of this intellectual focus was an organisation for national military service and the acceptance of citizen soldiers as the basis of national defence. At the end of 1909, in an assessment of the progress of the military since Federation, the Department of Defence identified the principles upon which the nation would base its security. Among the clauses was the assertion that 'the whole of the Peace organisation of an army is worked out with reference to the requirements for War'.[114] On the battlefields of World War I, the Australian Army would shortly receive a test of this principle's correctness and the degree to which the structure of the nation's military forces conformed.

3
WORLD WAR I

When the Empire is at war, so is Australia at war.

Joseph Cook[1]

We shall pledge our last man and our last shilling.

Andrew Fisher[2]

War came to Australia on 4 August 1914 with the expiration, unfulfilled, of Britain's ultimatum to Germany demanding its withdrawal from Belgium. The Commonwealth had previously made it clear to Britain and the world that the 'mother country' could rely upon the naval and military support of Australia. If Britain were to go to war, so would Australia. London's notification of the declaration of war reached the Governor-General at midday on the 5th, and the government passed the news on to the press shortly thereafter.

Australia now faced an interesting dilemma. For years the government had steadfastly rejected suggestions by London that it identify the military resources it would make available for an imperial expedition. With the coming of war, the Commonwealth was now in exactly the situation that authorities in London had tried to prevent. Despite the existence of a respectable-sized army, the Defence Act forbade the government from dispatching its forces outside the nation's territory. Instead, Australia had to extemporise a second army, composed entirely of volunteers, who were willing to serve the empire. Australia would create the Australian Imperial Force (AIF) for overseas service, while the citizen forces would continue to provide for the defence of Commonwealth territory. In effect, the Defence Act mandated the maintenance of two Australian armies.

The AIF

On 3 August, the Australian Government cabled to London its offer to raise an expeditionary force of 20,000 men for use at the empire's discretion in the event of war. Britain's initial reply, on the 5th, was that while there was no immediate need for an

Australian contribution, it would be wise for the Commonwealth to make preparations for the rapid mobilisation of such a force if it were to become necessary. However, by the next day the War Office was ready to accept the Commonwealth's proposal, and requested Australia to dispatch the troops as soon as possible. At first, the British suggested that the contingent should contain no formations greater than the brigade level, but they soon accepted the Commonwealth's preference for an infantry division as well as a light horse brigade.[3]

On 6 August, Britain also asked Australia to dispatch an expeditionary force to capture German possessions in New Guinea and the Bismarck Archipelago. In response, the Commonwealth rapidly organised the Australian Naval and Military Expeditionary Force. This body consisted of one battalion of infantry, six companies of naval reservists organised into a naval brigade, and small bodies of attached machine-gun, signal, and medical troops under the command of Colonel William Holmes. The troops were all volunteers, and each had to attest to his willingness to serve anywhere in His Majesty's forces. Enlistment began on 11 August, and the force was underway by the 19th. The Australians soon accomplished their mission. The German governor at Rabaul surrendered on 13 September. The occupation of the other German settlements followed shortly after.[4]

The creation of the Australian Naval and Military Expeditionary Force was a hasty and improvised exercise, which succeeded only because it did not have to face any serious opposition. The formation of the AIF, however, was a much greater responsibility. It fell to Bridges, currently Inspector-General, to mobilise the Australian force. With the assistance of Major C.B.B. White, Bridges was able to present an organisational scheme to Edward Millen, the Minister for Defence, on 8 August. It was Bridges who had suggested that the Commonwealth's contribution take the form of a division so that Australians could fight as a national force rather than in smaller formations, which the British would subsume into their own order of battle.[5]

Bridges proposed to raise the AIF on a territorial basis, with each State contributing roughly in proportion to its existing military establishment. Mobilisation also utilised the existing administrative structure, as responsibility for raising the required units rested with the commandants of the military districts. Table 3.1 (p. 65) outlines the contribution by each state to the AIF's first contingent. Each State was also to provide a proportion of engineers, ammunition columns, and departmental troops. The response of the nation was immediate, and so massive that on 3 September Australia could offer Britain a further infantry brigade and light horse brigade, followed quickly by a third brigade of mounted troops. Britain readily accepted these additional contingents.[6]

Major-General Sir William T. Bridges. (AWM H15442)

It is not the place of this work to discuss the wartime performance of the AIF or the course of events of the Great War (World War I). Instead, this chapter will limit itself to those issues that affected the organisation of the AIF and the home army. Bridges' proposal established the broad pattern by which Australia raised the units of the AIF for the duration of the war. While each division drew upon the entire nation for its members, the raising of the subunits was on a territorial basis. The larger States contributed entire brigades, while the less populous regions contributed elements to composite brigades. Most subunits—battalions, regiments, or batteries—came from individual States, although in some cases it was necessary, particularly in the case of Tasmania, to have more than one region represented in a unit.

Table 3.1 Recruitment of AIF, 1st Contingent

State	Contribution
Queensland	1 light horse regiment
	1 infantry battalion
	1 field artillery regiment
Tasmania	1 squadron light horse
	Half an infantry battalion
	1 field artillery battery
New South Wales	1 light horse regiment
	1 infantry brigade
	1 artillery brigade
Victoria	1 light horse regiment
	1 infantry brigade plus one battalion
	1 artillery brigade
South Australia	2 squadrons light horse
	1 infantry battalion
Western Australia	Half an infantry battalion
	1 field artillery battery

Bridges had suggested that half of the first contingent of 20,000 men, who would make up the 1st Division and 1st Light Horse Brigade, be drawn from soldiers currently serving in the citizen forces, while the remainder would be selected from men who had prior service experience. His goal was to create a force that already had some military experience, in order to speed up training and thereby permit an early transfer to the front. When recruiting offices opened, a flood of eager volunteers flowed through their doors. The response was so overwhelming that recruiting officials were free to select only the best candidates. Among the applicants were large numbers of citizen forces personnel, veterans of the Boer War, and former members of the British Army. By the end of the year, approximately 10,000 members of the citizen forces had enlisted in the AIF, although this included those serving in the three light horse brigades and the 4th Infantry Brigade.[7]

The hasty formation of the AIF and the desire to get the troops to Europe as quickly as possible had serious consequences for the military effectiveness of the force. While the volunteers were enthusiastic, in excellent physical condition, and possessed no shortage of courage, the force was, in general, lacking in basic military skills and equipment. The first contingent left Australia essentially untrained, and would require

Mena Army Camp, Egypt, 1915, where Australian troops trained before going into action at Gallipoli. (AWM H03083)

considerable effort in Egypt to bring it up to standard. Even by the time of its commitment to Gallipoli in April 1915 much work remained, and the formation had still not reached the level of divisional manoeuvres. In the opinion of one historian, the 1st Division was 'probably the worst-trained formation ever sent from Australia's shores'.[8]

Although the lack of training and experience were problems that would be corrected by the expenditure of time and blood, the Commonwealth's difficulty in supplying the necessary equipment and support services would prove much more intractable. When the 1st Division sailed, it did so without a full complement of artillery, as the Commonwealth was unable to provide the division with its howitzer batteries or the heavy gun battery (60-pounders). The AIF would miss the howitzers when it got to Gallipoli, because the rough terrain of Anzac Cove demanded weapons with plunging fire capability. Even into 1915, small arms were in short supply and the commandant of the Third Military District complained that the lack of rifles limited the men's training. Shortages of equipment also affected the raising of additional formations. In July 1915, Britain requested that Australia combine its three independent infantry brigades in Egypt into what would become the 2nd Division. The Commonwealth replied favourably, but noted that it would be unable to provide divisional headquarters, divisional artillery, or divisional engineering officers. When the government offered another division to Britain in December 1915, the Commonwealth did so with the condition that Australia made no provision for the formation's artillery or other divisional units. These elements would have to come from Britain.[9]

These events suggest a willingness on the part of the Australian Government to emphasise combat troops over support services. The AIF was not designed, nor was it able, to fight on its own. Rather, it had to be subsumed into the organisation of another army, which would provide for the essential support services. Despite prewar objections to an imperial commitment, the force that Australia created was in fact entirely dependent upon such a relationship. As a result, the AIF had a much higher 'teeth-to-tail' ratio than forces that provided for their own support. While this increased the size of the combat elements that the nation could support, it also meant that a greater proportion of Australian soldiers were in contact with the enemy. In part, this helps to explain the AIF's relatively high mortality rate. Australia suffered nearly 59,000 dead during World War I, a casualty rate, proportionate to population, that was one of the highest of the conflict.

The organisation of the AIF would not change greatly over the course of the war. During refit in Egypt, after the evacuation from Gallipoli, the AIF expanded from two to five divisions. In the process, the army split several brigades in order to provide cadres for the units that would form the 4th and 5th Divisions. These formations were then brought up to strength from the reinforcement drafts awaiting assignment in Egypt. Simultaneously, Australia raised the 3rd Division in Australia directly from new recruits. The Commonwealth did attempt to raise the 6th Division, but the formation never took the field. The AIF broke it up to provide reinforcements for the other divisions. The divisional structure remained largely unchanged until late in the war, when the AIF disbanded a number of infantry battalions to provide replacements to other infantry units. Throughout the war, at the request of Britain, Australia also provided a number of specialist units, such as tunnelling companies. However, all these adjustments represented a change of scale rather than organisation. The AIF's establishment remained based on the British model for the entire course of the war, and consistently followed imperial initiatives regarding its organisation. Table 3.2 (p. 68) outlines the organisation of the 1st AIF in 1918.

To support the AIF, the Australian Army established an administrative system that paralleled the administrative apparatus of the home army. Initially, in addition to his command duties, Bridges was responsible for the administrative details of the expeditionary force. These included items such as record-keeping, finance, ordnance, personnel, quartermaster, and other issues that assured the smooth and efficient maintenance of military forces. However, it soon proved necessary to create an AIF

Table 3.2 *Organisation of the 1st AIF, 1918*[10]

1st Infantry Division	1st Inf. Bde (1st, 2nd, 3rd, 4th Battalions)
	2nd Inf. Bde (5th, 6th, 7th, 8th Battalions)
	3rd Inf. Bde (9th, 10th, 11th, 12th Battalions)
	1st Fd Art. Bde (1st, 2nd, 3rd, 101st Batteries)
	2nd Fd Art. Bde (4th, 5th, 6th, 102nd Batteries)
2nd Infantry Division	5th Inf. Bde (17th, 18th, 19th, 20th Battalions)
	6th Inf. Bde (21st, 22nd, 23rd, 24th Battalions)
	7th Inf. Bde (25th, 26th, 27th, 28th Battalions)
	4th Fd Art. Bde (10th, 11th, 12th, 104th Batteries)
	5th Fd Art. Bde (13th, 14th, 15th, 105th Batteries)
3rd Infantry Division	9th Inf. Bde (33rd, 34th, 35th, 36th Battalions)
	10th Inf. Bde (37th, 38th, 39th, 40th Battalions)
	11th Inf. Bde (41st, 42nd, 43rd, 44th Battalions)
	7th Fd Art. Bde (25th, 26th, 27th, 107th Batteries)
	8th Fd Art. Bde (29th, 30th, 31st, 108th Batteries)
4th Infantry Division	4th Inf. Bde (13th, 14th, 15th, 16th Battalions)
	12th Inf. Bde (45th, 46th, 47th, 48th Battalions)
	13th Inf. Bde (49th, 50th, 51st, 52nd Battalions)
	10th Fd Art. Bde (37th, 38th, 39th, 110th Batteries)
	11th Fd Art. Bde (41st, 42nd, 43rd, 111th Batteries)
5th Infantry Division	8th Inf. Bde (29th, 30th, 31st, 32nd Battalions)
	14th Inf. Bde (53rd, 54th, 55th, 56th Battalions)
	15th Inf. Bde (57th, 58th, 59th, 60th Battalions)
	13th Fd Art. Bde (49th, 50th, 51st, 113th Batteries)
	14th Fd Art. Bde (53rd, 54th, 55th, 114th Batteries)
A&NZ Mounted Division	1st LH Bde (1st, 2nd, 3rd LH Regiments)
	2nd LH Bde (5th, 6th, 7th LH Regiments)
Australian Mounted Division	3rd LH Bde (8th, 9th, 10th LH Regiments)
	4th LH Bde (4th, 11th, 12th LH Regiments)
	5th LH Bde (14th, 15th LH Regiments)
Corps troops	13th LH Regiment
	3rd Army Art. Bde (7th, 8th, 9th, 103rd Batteries)
	6th Army Art. Bde (16th, 17th, 18th, 106th Batteries)
	12th Army Art. Bde (45th, 46th, 47th, 112th Batteries)
Miscellaneous units in France	36th Heavy Artillery Bde (1st, 2nd Siege Batteries)
	1st, 2nd, 3rd General Hospitals
	2nd, 3rd, 4th Squadrons Australian Flying Corps
HQ AIF depots in England	1st Training Bde
	2nd Training Bde
	3rd Training Bde
	Australian Heavy Artillery Training Depot
	Engineer Training Depot

Administrative Headquarters to oversee all non-operational matters. Its original location was in Cairo, although after the infantry divisions moved to France, the AIF relocated its administrative headquarters to Horseferry Road in London. In addition to administrative matters, the administrative headquarters also became responsible for liaison with the War Office, as well as the Department of Defence in Melbourne, and it commanded all Australian troops in Britain. The AIF would also open a training headquarters at Salisbury. At this facility, all new troops and returning soldiers received instruction in the latest aspects of trench warfare before embarking for France.[11]

The most tumultuous event affecting the organisation of the AIF was the issue of conscription for overseas service, which dominated the Australian political scene in 1916 and 1917. The rate of enlistment in the AIF gradually declined to the point where, after the losses of the Somme, the British Army Council and the Australian headquarters in London considered the break-up of the 3rd Division. The debate over conscription was a highly emotional one, and fundamentally a question of societal obligation versus free will. Rather than risk the almost certain fall of the government,

Brigadier-General C. B. B. White at Headquarters, I Anzac Corps. (AWM E00559)

Prime Minister William Hughes opted to let the nation's voters make the decision, in the form of a plebiscite. The electorate would reject the government's plan in October 1916, and Hughes' second attempt in December 1917 met a similar fate. In both cases, the members of the AIF voted in favour of conscription, but by narrow margins.

The nation's rejection of compulsory overseas service had both immediate and long-term consequences for the army. In the short term, it meant that the AIF remained a volunteer organisation. In the broader dimension, the voters' desire reinforced the government's policy, as established by the Defence Act, that military service outside the nation's territory was solely on the basis of voluntarism. Hughes' inability to overcome this principle would have serious consequences for the organisation of the Australian Army during the lead-up and conduct of World War II.[12]

The home army

On 30 July 1914, authorities in London informed the Governor-General in Sydney that war with Germany was imminent. The telegram advised Australia to adopt the precautionary stage of mobilisation, although because of a mistranslation of the coded notice and his own hesitancy, Millen did not authorise this step until 2 August. When finally given, his instructions set in motion the mobilisation arrangements provided for by the Commonwealth's defence scheme. At this stage, it mandated the call-up of a small number of designated troops and rifle club members to guard the country's munition factories, defence installations, communication centres, and wireless stations. It also ordered the gunners and engineers of the permanent forces to their posts at the fortresses protecting Australian ports. The army next mobilised the Kennedy Regiment from Northern Queensland, and these men soon sailed from Townsville to augment the garrison at Thursday Island.

With the arrival of news of the declaration of war, Australia moved to the next stage of readiness. The government issued mobilisation orders to 10,000 citizen soldiers, bringing the fortresses up to full strength and providing local units to repel enemy landings. That day the permanent forces' gunners at Fort Nepean near Port Melbourne discharged the first and only shot fired in anger on Australian territory over the course of the war. They directed a warning shot across the bow of a German merchantman, the *Pflaz*, which was attempting to reach the high seas, and forced its return to port.[13]

The early days of August would prove the high point of the home army's role in World War I, as the decision to dispatch an expeditionary force focused national interest on the AIF. Japan's declaration of war on Germany on 23 August not only removed the possibility of a sneak landing, but also obviated the primary purpose of the citizen forces—invasion deterrence. From that point onwards, the home army entered into a period of relentless decline as the nation directed its attention, manpower, and resources to events in the Middle East and France. By the end of 1914 the government had stood down most of the guard detachments, and the garrison artillerymen served at reduced levels. In mid 1915, volunteers from the ranks of the army's permanent garrison artillery, who the government had at first refused leave to join the AIF, received permission to organise a Siege Artillery Brigade. In July, the formation sailed for France, taking with it the nation's most experienced gunners. From then on, the army manned the coastal forts on a skeleton basis. The home army would even lose responsibility for some basic guard duties to other organisations. The government raised a special corps of men rejected for service in the AIF for domestic garrison duties, and the RAN created a Naval Guard Section to protect wireless stations and ships in port.[14]

Although Australia's primary military effort was the AIF, the army's leaders at the start of the conflict had intended to maintain the citizen forces' organisation, establishment, and training regime as it had done before the war. The conflict caught the army in a period of transition from the volunteer force of Hutton to the universal service model of Kitchener, and the latter scheme would not be fully operational until the class of 1919–20 had entered service. To continue its development, the Military Board decreed that while every effort was to be made to assist the formation of the AIF, 'there must be no relaxation in the training of the Militia, Senior Cadets and Rifle Clubs'.[15]

In the early days of the struggle this objective seemed obtainable, as the demands upon the home forces were low enough that the army could even create three new battalions, as required by the organisation's growth under universal training. A statement drawn up in November 1914 showed that while there were over 41,000 men committed to overseas service, the citizen forces still had an establishment of more than 56,000 troops, not including rifle club and cadet reserves of a further 67,000. However, by the following month a similar statement revealed that over 10,000 serving soldiers had already agreed to join the AIF, a figure that was certain to grow larger, and which would have serious consequence for the welfare of the citizen forces.[16]

While the citizen forces would lose a steady stream of experienced enlisted men to the AIF, it was the transfer of its officers that proved to be the most troublesome. By 1916, one of the principal activities of the Military Board had become the approval of replacement or appointment of acting officers to command citizen forces units whose officers had joined the AIF. In many cases, the Military Board believed it had no recourse but to appoint quite junior officers to battalion commands. The Military Board also sought to fill command posts by extending the retirement age of officers nearing the end of their career.

The situation only worsened as the war progressed. In July 1917, the Adjutant-General observed to the Military Board that, currently within the citizen forces, one artillery brigade and six light horse regiments or infantry battalions were under the command of lieutenants. In taking these steps, the Military Board made it clear that it considered some of the acting officers unqualified, but there was simply no one else.[17]

Despite the debilitating effect on the citizen forces, the government eventually sought the transfer of all able officers from the home forces to the AIF. Soon the AIF became the priority organisation, and its support required a steady supply of leaders. One means of encouraging citizen forces officers to volunteer was the practice of replacing them in training or garrison establishments with returned AIF officers who were no longer fit for active duty, but still able to carry out less demanding responsibilities. When suggestion failed to convince reluctant officers that their duty lay overseas, the army undertook a policy of coercion. In a report prepared at the end of 1915, the Inspector-General of the AIF, Major-General J.W. McCay, denounced citizen forces officers who had not come forward. In particular, he thought it was highly improper and potentially injurious to morale to have citizen forces officers employed in a training capacity at AIF camps. He proposed that at these camps the army should use only officers who had volunteered for service abroad or who were certified unfit for active duty by reason of age or physical defect. The Inspector-General of the AIF also recommended that:

> any officer of the Commonwealth Militia Forces who is fit and does not volunteer be dispensed with and gazetted out of the Commonwealth Military Forces on the ground that he has not volunteered, and that, therefore, his services are no longer required.[18]

McCay went on to suggest that the army should compel all citizen forces officers under the rank of captain, who had not gone through the required course of instruction, to obtain a commission in the AIF to complete said course. Furthermore, he believed that the army should not commission any lieutenants until they had passed an AIF school of instruction for qualifying for commissions in the AIF. The report of the Inspector-General of the AIF contained a number of additional recommendations on this point, but McCay's objective is fairly obvious. If an officer wanted to remain a member of the citizen forces, he would also have to agree to serve in the AIF.[19]

Brigadier-General T. H. Dodds at the dedication of the Jerusalem War Cemetery. (AWM HI2704)

In an assessment of the report by the Inspector-General of the AIF, the Adjutant-General, Colonel T.H. Dodds, completely agreed with his colleague's recommendations. In fact, he went even further and suggested that the army should retire any citizen forces officer who had not volunteered.[20] The Adjutant-General was well aware that, if the army implemented these recommendations, it would breach the covenant in the Defence Act against compelling anyone to serve overseas. Undeterred, he wrote that he did not have any sympathy for those who did not offer their services, and that the government should amend the Defence Act to provide that all officers of the military forces were liable for service beyond Australia. This issue eventually involved the Minister for Defence, George Pearce. He returned most of these recommendations, either as merely noted or as unapproved, with the exception of those clauses requiring AIF instructional accreditation for citizen forces officers. The government would not compel officers to serve overseas and it would not, at least at this stage, sanction the forced resignation of anyone who refused to join the AIF.[21]

Later in 1916, the Inspector-General of the AIF issued the results of a survey that established that in the 1st, 2nd, 3rd, and 4th Military Districts a high percentage of citizen forces officers and senior cadet officers had refused a request to volunteer for overseas service. He reported that 39 per cent of the citizen forces and 48 per cent of the cadets would not agree to join the AIF. However, the issue remained dormant until early 1918, when the Military Board re-examined the status of officers who still refused to serve abroad. In February, the Adjutant-General presented the Military Board with a list of 80 officers, nearly all lieutenants, who continued to object to service in the AIF. He recommended that the army should inform these men that the force no longer required their services. The Military Board agreed, and referred the recommendation to the Minister, who also concurred.[22]

As a result of its secondary status, the citizen forces were allowed by the government to run down to such an extent that it was virtually worthless militarily by the conflict's end. As early as 1915, the government had to abandon its intention of maintaining the training of the citizen forces, even at the already low prewar level. On 11 September 1915, the Military Board suspended the training of the citizen forces and senior cadets for a period of six months, and stopped the issuance of clothing and equipment to these forces. As a substitute, it suggested that attendance at voluntary parades would count towards proficiency requirements. In addition, the army reduced the staffs of the training areas to the absolute minimum needed for the purposes of record-keeping and maintenance of the organisation's skeleton. Under these circumstances, the army had few officers capable of conducting citizen forces' training camps.[23]

Although originally intended as a six-month suspension, the demands of the war dislocated the training of the citizen forces and senior cadets for most of the conflict. Additionally, what little training that did occur was largely ineffective because of the shortage of qualified instructors and proper equipment. In May 1916, the Military Board decided that it would not hand over to the citizen forces the trainees of the incoming quota, the class of 1898, with the exception of those destined for the garrison artillery, because 10 per cent had already opted for the AIF, and the army expected the majority of the remainder to do likewise. Moreover, the Military Board did not recommend a resumption of citizen forces training, because the available instructors were so young and inexperienced that they would not be of any use to the trainees. Since inefficient leaders made poor instructors, the army believed that there was little point in exposing new recruits to training.[24]

The army did resume training for the 1917–18 cycle, and the infantry attended eight-day camps of continuous instruction. This was the first training undertaken in two years, but was still only half the length as required by regulations. However, military leaders were realistic, and did not expect many positive benefits for the home army. As the Inspector-General pointed out to the Military Board, not only had training seriously deteriorated but discipline was also bad. He noted that conditions in the senior cadets were even worse. However, the resumption of training was not primarily a result of the Military Board's concern over the inefficiency of the men, but grew instead from its desire to preserve the institution. In June, the Inspector-General reported to the Minister for Defence that more than 75 per cent of the officers and nearly 50 per cent of the other ranks were now serving abroad, and those who remained had had little training for three years. He suggested that it was vital to keep the units of the citizen forces in existence, even as skeletons, because as long as the structure survived it would be possible to bring the units back up to strength.[25]

The same fear is apparent in a government proposal for training for the 1918–19 cycle. Pearce wrote:

> The condition of the Citizen Forces has been giving the Government some concern for considerable time, owing to the fact that many units have approached the vanishing point and might entirely disappear if steps are not taken to preserve their organisation and identity.

He pointed out that the army had greatly reduced the establishment of many units, and that the citizen forces were composed of 'youths insufficiently officered and necessarily inadequately trained'. Pearce suggested that the citizen forces accept volunteers, from between 21 and 50 years of age, whom the army had declared medically unfit for the AIF but who were sufficiently fit for home service. While this was a sound idea for maintaining the strength of citizen forces units, it also served to highlight the difference in effectiveness between the two forces. Pearce also proposed the temporary amalgamation of citizen forces units in order to create entities that were viable. While there is no evidence that the army implemented these ideas, their presentation to parliament suggests the extent to which the citizen forces had declined.

Further affecting the organisation of the citizen forces was the Minister for Defence's decision to renumber its units with AIF designations. Pearce undertook this step because he believed that it would 'preserve the traditions and honours won by units of the Australian Imperial Force on active service, and, so far as possible, to associate the records of such units with the local tradition of old militia units …'.[27]

Although nearly two more years of hard fighting remained, the AIF had already proved itself a formidable force. Moreover, the AIF had developed its own *esprit de corps*, which distinguished it from the army that had remained in Australia. To preserve the AIF's unique identity, Pearce hoped to transfer its sense of morale and spirit to the citizen forces, so that after the war ended, the values of the AIF and its accomplishments would become a source of pride, inspiration, and determination for the future soldiers of the Commonwealth. Pearce's suggestion was not well received by the military members of the Military Board, and they pointed out numerous practical problems his scheme would create. Not the least of these was that there were more citizen forces units than AIF units, and the recruitment catchment areas of the two forces did not coincide. As minister, however, Pearce would not be deterred by procedural objections. Citizen forces units, most of whom were themselves only recently created under the universal training scheme, lost their identities and were given the number of an AIF unit that corresponded most closely with the citizen forces' recruiting district.[28]

Pearce's plan did have merit, because intangible concepts, such as morale or tradition, are of critical importance in war. However, his decision that it was the spirit of the AIF that was to live on confirmed the inferior status of the citizen forces during World War I. The citizen forces had no spirit or traditions of its own worth preserving. More importantly, however, Pearce's scheme also highlighted the deficiency of citizen forces, when compared to the AIF, and the extent of its decline during the course of the war. The redesignation was a way to salvage something of the citizen forces in order to prevent the organisation's extinction, and so that there would be something left to build upon when the war ended and the Commonwealth embarked upon army reconstruction.

Lessons of the war

Australia's experiences during the war highlighted a number of problems that the army's leaders would attempt to rectify after the Armistice. Of primary importance was the realisation that in August 1914 the Australian Army was not ready for war. Had the threat been an invasion of the continent rather than war in Europe, the Commonwealth would have been in grave danger. An assessment made in 1917 identified one of the key deficiencies as lack of training, particularly among its leaders. It noted:

> We must not have an Army in Australia whose officers need months of training before being put into the field, but they must be ready for war at short notice, if it is to be looked on as a real Army available at any time for defending this country.

> At the outbreak of this war it would not have been possible to take a Militia Regiment as it stood and put it in the field at once against an efficient enemy, without disaster.[29]

Although the questions of training would have to wait until after the war's conclusion, the government did move to address another glaring problem while the conflict still raged. In 1916, Pearce asked Colonel Kenneth Mackay to develop a scheme for the establishment of an Australian Army Reserve. As previously mentioned, there was a considerable difference between the army's peacetime and wartime establishments. To bring the citizen forces up to fighting strength, the army had planned to rely upon the rifle clubs, raw recruits, and the patriotism of former soldiers. Pearce now sought to place the army's expansion policy onto a more regular and predictable basis while also assuring the intake of a more efficient soldier than was possible under the existing *ad hoc* arrangement. Pearce wanted a reserve organisation of such size that it would allow the army to reach its war establishment without delay. He also realised that a reserve system could provide the army with an efficient means to replace wastage.[30]

Pearce also saw the reserves as a means to preserve the military experience of the AIF, as the government would encourage expeditionary force veterans to enrol. The Minister hoped that within twelve months of the war's end the reserves would contain between 150,000 and 200,000 trained soldiers.[31] Membership in the Australian Army Reserve would include men divided into the following categories:

Class A

Men who have completed their term of service under the Universal Training Scheme.

Class B

1. Men who have been on active service and are in possession of a 'good' discharge.
2. Retired members of the Permanent Military Forces.
3. Commonwealth residents who have served with other military forces of the Empire and who are in possession of a 'good' discharge and are not currently members of a reserve of another part of the Empire.

Class C

1. Those who have completed their service in Class A and desire to remain in the Reserve.
2. Members of Rifle Clubs.
3. Men who prior to the introduction of Universal Training had served at least 12 months in the Citizen Forces or Cadet Forces.

Attestment in the reserves for soldiers in Class A was compulsory, while Classes B and C were open to volunteers. For all categories, the government set the term of service at five years. Since the members of the reserve were theoretically already efficient soldiers, the scheme mandated modest periods of home training, not in excess of the equivalent of four days. For administrative and training purposes, the army linked the reserve unit with the local citizen forces unit. The scheme also called for the creation of an honorary reserve for members of the reserve who were over the age of 50 or who were physically unfit. To oversee the reserves, Pearce appointed Mackay to the position of Director-General of the Australian Army Reserve.[32]

The government announced the reserve's establishment in November 1916 and commenced its recruitment. Since no quota had yet completed its term of service under universal training, the scheme was initially open only to volunteers. Upon demobilisation of the AIF, the program underwent a period of rapid growth. In 1919, there were already 45,000 reservists enrolled, but recruitment soon reached a plateau, and the organisation's membership peaked the following year at about 48,000. Although this was well short of Pearce's goal of 150,000, it did represent a considerable body of experienced soldiers on whom the Commonwealth could rely in an emergency. However, as the next chapter will detail, this first Australian Army Reserve did not survive long, and by 1924 it had virtually ceased to exist.[33]

One consequence of the establishment of the reserves was that it effectively extended the period of military obligation that an individual owed the state. Under universal training, able-bodied men had to serve in the citizen forces until the age of 26. Now, instead of having completed their military service when they passed out of the citizen forces, regulations imposed a reserve commitment of a further five years. Furthermore, those who wished to had the option of remaining in the reserves up to the age of 50, and even longer in the honorary reserve. Another consequence of the scheme was its effect on the status of the rifle clubs. Once the army acquired a formal reserve structure, it no longer needed to maintain its relationship with these groups of enthusiastic but ill-trained shootists. Consequently, in November 1920 the army removed the rifle clubs from its organisation, although the government continued to provide support in the form of grants and ammunition.[34]

To improve the coordination of the country's defence capabilities, Pearce also proposed the reorganisation of the Council of Defence. Since its establishment in 1905, the council had largely dealt with preparations for the defence of Australia and cooperation between the army and navy. Pearce believed the present war had demonstrated that national defence was far more complex, and that it was necessary to have a mechanism to identify and coordinate all the resources of the Commonwealth. Starting in 1916, with additional undertakings in 1917 and 1918, Pearce attempted to reform the council so that it would serve as the principal mechanism for defence planning and would become the agency responsible for assuring coordination between the services as well as all other parties that had a role in the provision of national security. In August 1918, the government would reorganise the Council of Defence on the basis of Pearce's recommendations.[35] Pearce believed that a revitalised Council of Defence should fulfil the following requirements:

- a That the policy of the Government should be understood by the officers responsible for the Navy and the Army.
- b That the Government should know how far the Navy and the Army are adequate for supporting any policy.
- c That the strategy of the Navy and the Army should conform to the policy, and that the Forces should consistently co-operate.
- d That provision be made to link up all the factors in the nation which affect, or are affected by, war.[36]

To achieve these goals, Pearce proposed the formation of a series of subcommittees that would focus their attention on particular issues and also serve as the agencies for defence coordination. His suggestions for subcommittees were: Operations; Resources and Manufacture; Intelligence; Inventions; Economics; Transport; Censorship; and Legal. Finally, he also recommended the establishment of a Permanent Secretary and staff. Despite these changes, however, the Council of Defence would still continue to mire itself frequently in relatively trivial matters, and would largely fail to achieve the goals at which Pearce aimed. With the onset of the Depression in 1929, the council lapsed into disuse, and would not meet again until 1935.[37]

The outbreak of war caught the Australian Army in a period of transition. The universal training scheme had been underway for only a few years, and the development of the army was barely half-way towards its ultimate objective. Furthermore, the units that did exist were poorly trained for the conditions of modern war and were lacking in essential equipment and reserves. Ironically, none of this mattered. Except for the single shot fired by the garrison artillery at Melbourne, the home army did not play an active role in the war. Instead it performed as regulations required. Its members garrisoned forts, protected harbours, and guarded points of military significance, all the while waiting for an invader who never came. Consequently, *ennui*, the lack of training, and the loss of the most ambitious officers and enthusiastic men to the AIF took their toll, and by the war's end the citizen forces barely existed.

Instead of supporting the empire with the citizen forces, both statute and national preference forced the government to create another army, composed of volunteers, for service overseas. This became the AIF, as well as the much smaller Australian Naval and Military Expeditionary Force (AN&MEF). These bodies actually fought the war, garnered the honours, and forged what was to become known as the 'spirit of ANZAC'. However, upon demobilisation this force, too, ceased to exist. After more than four years of war Australia was left without an army.

That this should happen was not a surprise. It was an outcome of predetermined government policy. Throughout the years leading up to World War I there was a discontinuity between government policy and army organisation in regard to Australian national security arrangements. The Defence Act prohibited the dispatch of the citizen forces overseas, yet as war neared the government increasingly signalled that it would commit troops to the empire's defence. Senior officers, in the case of the citizen force itself, assumed that such a deployment would occur. However, neither body was willing to address the organisation, training, equipment, or any other element of creating an expeditionary force. With the coming of the Armistice, Australia could lay claim to an impressive war record and could demand the right to participate in the world's councils at Versailles, but the nation would have to make a new army from the debris of the AIF and the citizen forces to ensure its security in the post-war environment.

4
THE INTERWAR YEARS

The Empire of Japan remains ... in the immediate future, as the only potential and probable enemy.[1]

Although Australia celebrated a victorious conclusion to the Great War, the ending of the conflict did not lead to a simplification of the Commonwealth's national security situation. Despite the decisive defeat of Germany by the combined strength of the British Empire and its allies, the balance of power, from Australia's perspective, had worsened. Meanwhile, Germany's strategic position had actually improved, with the collapse of Russia into civil war and the creation of a weak Polish state in the east. Furthermore, German factories and mines were largely intact, unlike the infrastructure of Northern France, and Germany's ability to increase its industrial lead over its rivals remained unfettered. Conversely, the price of victory for Britain would prove ruinously high, not only in terms of the moral determination to face aggression but also in more practical matters, such as the economic and financial health of the country and the war's dislocation of imperial trade and communications. Finally, the American refusal to participate in the League of Nations left the Western democracies with the difficult, if not impossible, task of containing hostile, expansionist regimes.

It was in the Pacific, however, that the strategic balance had shifted most gravely against Australia. Japan had had a relatively easy war. It had fulfilled the letter of its treaty obligation to Britain by declaring war on Germany, in August 1914, but the Japanese military contribution to the conflict was trivial. Japanese forces attacked the German concession at Tsingtao, while its navy occupied the enemy's island colonies in the Pacific, north of the Equator. Except for the dispatch of a squadron of warships to help patrol the Mediterranean, Japan's military role had come to an end. Japanese

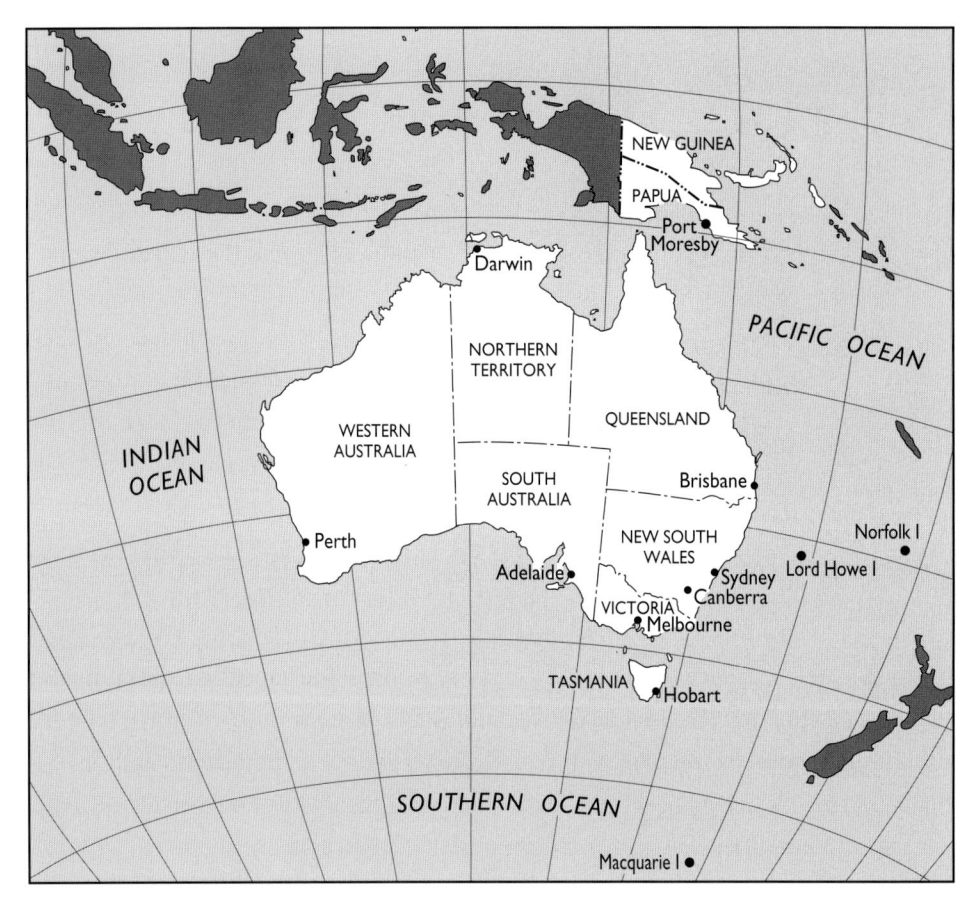

Map 5 Australian territory, 1919

industry also enjoyed a boom during the war, while the economy avoided the financial drains that would affect Britain. Japan had, therefore, substantially improved its position, and its claim to Germany's colonies brought the 'Rising Sun' considerably closer to Australia's shores.

Shortly after the end of the conflict, Australia undertook a series of reviews to consider the nation's post-war defence policy. Japan's participation in the war as an ally did little to deter planners from identifying it as the primary threat to the Commonwealth. Viscount Jellicoe made this point in the report of his 1919 naval mission to Australia. He wrote, quite openly, that Japan posed the only threat in the Pacific to the welfare of Australia, and that the empire should prepare its naval resources to counter Japanese ambition.[2] In a different security assessment, the Council of Defence suggested that it was necessary for Australia to retain the German colonies it had taken in order to provide a buffer against any attack from the north. Furthermore, it asserted that the former German islands now held by Japan would be of great use to an enemy contemplating military action against Australia.[3]

Australia's representatives would take these attitudes with them to the 1923 Imperial Conference, at which they would establish the principles of the Commonwealth's defence policy for the interwar period. The conference concluded, as imperial gatherings had so often in the past, that the defence of the empire depended primarily upon the maintenance of maritime supremacy. While the representatives did acknowledge that each territory was responsible for its own local defence, they also stressed the principle of mutual support, the importance of maritime communications, and the critical role of the fleet in safeguarding the empire.[4] These conclusions only reinforced the government's belief that sea power ultimately secured Australia's defence, and, as a corollary, that the Commonwealth's first line of defence was the Royal Navy. Australia's security would depend upon the arrival of the Royal Navy's battle fleet in Eastern waters and the ability of the imperial fleet to defeat the enemy's forces decisively. The Imperial Conference provided that Britain would establish a base at Singapore, at which it would station its fleet upon its arrival in the Pacific. Singapore, with secondary installations at Sydney, and later Darwin, would provide the Royal Navy with the facilities it required to conduct operations in the Australian–Western Pacific–Indian Ocean theatres. Hong Kong, the Admiralty assumed, could serve as a forward base.[5]

The continued reliance by Australia upon the imperial fleet had significant implications for the development of the army and for non-maritime-based defence policy. Once again it raised the still unresolved issue of whether the army should prepare against the possibility of raids or invasion. It also left unanswered the role of the army in an imperial conflict that threatened the survival of the 'mother country', and failed to identify Australian responsibilities for the garrison of the Singapore base. Yet, by agreeing to a defence policy based upon Singapore, Commonwealth politicians had actually implicitly accepted the necessity to support Britain, because if an opponent ever defeated Britain, Australia would have to face the possibility of Japanese aggression without the countervailing security of the Royal Navy. This unstated commitment to aid Britain remained in effect despite Defence Act prohibition against compelling soldiers to serve overseas. Moreover, the elevation of the Royal Navy to the primary position in the defence hierarchy assured that the army faired poorly in the struggle for its share of the military estimate, and that it would have to allocate part of the inadequate resources it did receive to the defence of facilities designated for use by the fleet. Finally, despite attempts by army planners to open a debate on whether

Britain would actually dispatch the fleet, a series of governments never wavered in the trust they placed in the Royal Navy, and they consistently refused to consider that the cornerstone of their defence preparations might prove hollow.[6]

Having established the principles of its security, Australian leaders strove to maintain the status quo throughout the period.[7] Any admission that the Singapore strategy was not sound defence policy threatened to wreck the government's conception of national security, and would have required political leaders to engage in a more realistic security assessment. The need to sustain Singapore as the basis of defence planning also helped shape Australian foreign relations with Japan, especially its reaction to Japanese aggression in Asia. Australian policy was much more interested in sending exports to Japan than in antagonising its future opponent, and instead of condemning its interventions in Manchuria and China, Australia preferred to interpret these actions as a useful diversion from any interest in movement towards the south. T.B. Millar has rightly described Australia's position over Japanese expansionism as a 'triumph of self-interest and pusillanimity over principles of any kind, of political and economic appeasement'.[8]

As World War II approached, an air of unreality pervaded Australian security considerations. Despite the obviously changing security situation, Australia's defence policy remained the same. Australia's representatives at the 1937 Imperial Conference did not question the principles of security that the 1923 meeting had established. In April 1938, Prime Minister Joseph Lyons reaffirmed that the nation's defence was related to the wider pattern of imperial defence, and that sea power and the Singapore base were its cornerstones.[9] The army repeatedly attempted to prod the government into reassessing the Singapore strategy, particularly the implications if Britain failed to send in the fleet. Instead of engagement, however, successive governments sought comfort in the blandishments of naval enthusiasts and the promises of the imperial system. Rather than seeking a re-examination of the principles of Australian security, and confronting the uncomfortable and harsh realities of the era, the nation's leaders preferred to maintain their blind faith in a fundamentally flawed strategy. As Millar has noted, Australian political leaders maintained the colonial reliance upon the Royal Navy out of a desire to reap 'the benefits of independence without the international responsibilities'.[10] The result would be the nation's fundamental unpreparedness for war.

The re-establishment of the army

In 1919, the Australian continent was virtually undefended. The AIF was in the process of demobilisation as transports gradually returned its members to Australia, while the citizen forces had decayed through necessity and neglect into an untrained and inefficient force. The only viable component that remained was the small body of professional soldiers who composed the permanent forces. Australia would once again have to build an army from the remnants of predecessor entities.

The first steps were taken in 1919 as the Commonwealth began the process of identifying its national security requirements. These initial efforts, however, were undertaken somewhat cautiously, as the government was aware that the world security situation was in a state of flux and that it would remain difficult to define the future strength and responsibilities of the army until the completion of the Versailles Conference and the finalisation of the League of Nations. Furthermore, the foreign policy of the empire would influence Australian obligations, and this too was in the process of redefinition. Last, there was some hesitancy to finalise any recommendations until the Prime Minister, William Hughes, returned from the peace talks.[11]

Despite these constraints, the army's leaders had already made assumptions on the type of force they believed Australia required. In January 1919, the officers on the Military Board requested that the Minister for Defence present their opinion to cabinet that Australia required a war establishment of 300,000 troops. They also estimated a need for a capital expenditure of over £5.3 million for equipment alone, to outfit a force of 26 regiments of light horse, 84 battalions of infantry, more than 20 brigades of field artillery, 14 field engineer companies, and numerous other support and service formations. The army's leaders had concluded from their experiences in World War I that Australia required not only a balanced field force but also one that was capable of providing its own logistical support. Table 4.1 provides a list of the desired formations.[12]

Table 4.1 Proposed post-war army, 1919[13]

Light Horse	26 regiments, 12 division squadrons
Field Artillery	20 brigades (18-pounders), 18 howitzer batteries, 6 heavy batteries, 6 ammunition columns
Infantry	84 battalions
Engineers	14 field companies, 8 signal troops, 2 divisional signal squadrons, 2 wireless companies
Service Corps	6 headquarter companies, 22 companies, 8 light horse companies
Medical Corps	22.5 field ambulance companies, 8 light horse field ambulance squadrons
Fortress Troops	13 garrison artillery companies, 8 fortress companies
Miscellaneous	3 cyclist battalions, 4 machine gun squadrons, 6 machine gun battalions, 6 pioneer battalions, 18 light trench mortar batteries, 6 heavy trench mortar batteries, 3 tunnelling companies, 1 armoured car company, 6 divisional mechanical motor transport companies, 1 signal subsection, 10 anti-aircraft batteries, 1 carrier pigeon service

Major-General J. G. Legge. (AWM 100140)

With the war over, it was naïve of the officers to expect that the government would sanction expenditure on such a grand scale simply on the request of its military advisers. The government opted instead for a more deliberative approach. Pearce, the Minister for Defence, appointed the Hon. G. Swinburne to chair a committee to advise the government on a number of defence questions. Assisting Swinburne was a delegation of army officers composed of Lieutenant-General C.B.B. White, Major-

General J.W. McCay, and Major-General J.G. Legge. The committee presented its findings in June 1919.[14]

The question of the nature of training was one of the most important issues affecting the definition of the post-war army. Because of the uncertainty of the post-war strategic situation, Swinburne recommended the continuation of the Universal Training Scheme. However, the committee recognised that the army needed to modify the type and extent of training provided to the trainee, because the degree of efficiency obtained by the army in 1914 proved grossly deficient for the prosecution of modern war. It was the unanimous opinion of the committee that

> unless the training was of a more intensified character than has hitherto been the case, and unless there was a greater concentration of troops for training, the results from a military point of view would be of little value, would not diminish appreciably the further training necessary if war broke out and the men were called up for active service, and would not justify the expenditure of large sums of public money.[15]

The committee discussed a number of training options, but recommended to the government a scheme that proposed 21 weeks of training over four years. As back-up proposals, the committee included two other schemes that included less extensive amounts of training. However, these schemes were intended as cost-saving measures, and Swinburne's report made it clear that only the recommended program contained the degree of preparation that the army believed essential for efficiency. Table 4.2 outlines the recommended training program.

Table 4.2 Training program recommended by the Swinburne Committee[16]

Year	Period of training	Character of training
First	13 weeks	10 weeks individual
		3 weeks section and platoon
Second	4 weeks	2 weeks refresher training
		2 weeks company training
Third	3 weeks	1 week refresher training
		2 weeks company and battalion training
Fourth	1 week	Battalion training
Total for first four years	*21 weeks*	
Years 5 to 8	occasional afternoons and evenings	Mustering, the trainee having passed into 'First Reserve'

If implemented, this program promised to provide an effective force within five years, an improvement upon the eight years required before the war. It accomplished this by concentrating 21 weeks of training into four years, instead of the more diffuse 32 weeks in eight years under the existing program. The committee also noted that the scattered afternoon and evening parades were of little military value, and that the results of such short periods of assembly did not justify expenditure. Instead, the army would obtain the best results if the soldier underwent training at camps of continuous instruction.

However, the committee also recommended a postponement of training until the following year. Swinburne suggested that the army should first focus on preparing its infrastructure, and that its initial priority should be the provision of an adequate training staff of officers and non-commissioned officers. Only when the army had properly readied itself should it recommence training, in order to prevent a recurrence of the inadequate citizen forces instruction that had taken place during the war. Swinburne offered the government a further inducement to delay the recommencement of training until June 1920 by pointing out that it would save over £600,000.

Swinburne's report also suggested that the Commonwealth strive for an army with an establishment of approximately 180,000 troops. These would allow the formation of a force of six infantry and two cavalry divisions, plus line-of-communication troops. The report continued that this was the minimum size of force which could ensure that the army could hold out until the arrival of assistance from overseas. However, it warned that such a force would only be able to provide for the nation's defence for the limited time until the imperial fleet had regained command of the sea.[17]

Although the Swinburne Report set the tone for Australian security reviews, it was the next analysis that was to lay the foundation for the structure of the army's organisation for the remainder of the interwar period. In one historian's opinion, the *Report on the Military Defence of Australia by a Conference of Senior Officers of the Australian Military Forces* was the army's most important strategic planning document for the next two decades.[18] It was a broadly based study, whose recommendations not only touched upon the army's organisation but also considered the principles of mobilisation and training, coastal defence, finance, equipment, and armaments. In addition, it contained an assessment of the threat Japan posed towards Australia.[19]

In establishing the conference's references, Pearce reminded the committee that 'finances were straitened, and that therefore any scheme submitted must be within reason. Proposals that were too ambitious could not be accepted; not counsels of perfection, but counsels of practicability were required.' The Defence Minister also noted that the strategic environment had not cleared, and that the creation of the League of

Nations and the scale of Britain's participation in the Pacific might yet affect the recommendations of the conference. In addition to White, McCay, and Legge, who had served on the Swinburne Committee, the conference also included Lieutenant-General Sir H.G. Chauvel as chairman and Lieutenant-General Sir J. Monash and Major-General J.J.T. Hobbs as members. The conference met in January 1920, and presented its findings to Pearce in February.

Lieutenant-General Sir John Monash. (AWM E03186)

Lieutenant-General Sir J. J. T. Hobbs (second from right) and staff. (AWM H00391)

The conference was quite emphatic that Japan was the only identifiable potential enemy of Australia, and its findings centred around which resources the army would require to oppose its threat successfully. The conference was equally clear that Australia would be unable to resist Japanese aggression on its own, and that the Commonwealth would require the assistance of a great power. While its report acknowledged the possibility of the League of Nations serving as Australia's protector, the conference recognised that for the foreseeable future the nation would continue to remain dependent upon Britain and the Royal Navy for its ultimate defence. Finally, the conference pointed out that the treaty between Britain and Japan was due to expire in 1920, and it was then possible that Japan could ally itself with powers that were hostile to Britain, thereby worsening Australia's security environment.

The senior officers made their decisions on the organisation of the army on the basis of what forces and installations the Commonwealth required either to deter a Japanese invasion or to prevent a decisive defeat before the arrival of the Royal Navy and reinforcements from the empire. They concluded that an army of 180,000 men would give the nation a 'sporting chance' to hold out until help arrived from overseas.

Anything less, they believed, would invite disaster. The conference suggested a force of four infantry divisions, two cavalry divisions, three mixed brigades that could unite to form a fifth division, and appropriate corps, army, and line-of-communication troops. Table 4.3 outlines the catchment areas for the army's main formations.

Table 4.3 Major formations and catchments for the post-World War I army [20]

Formation	Catchment
1st Cavalry Division	Queensland: 1st Cavalry Brigade
	New South Wales: 2nd and 4th Cavalry Brigades
2nd Cavalry Division	Victoria: 3rd and 5th Cavalry Brigades
	South Australia: 6th Cavalry Brigade
1st Infantry Division	New South Wales: 1st and 8th Infantry Brigades
	Queensland: 7th Infantry Brigade
2nd Infantry Division	New South Wales: 5th, 9th, and 14th Infantry Brigades
3rd Infantry Division	Victoria: 4th, 10th, and 15th Infantry Brigades
4th Infantry Division	Victoria: 2nd and 6th Infantry Brigades
	South Australia: 3rd Infantry Brigade
3 mixed brigades to form a 5th Infantry Division	Queensland: 11th Mixed Brigade
	Tasmania: 12th Mixed Brigade
	Western Australia: 13th Mixed Brigade

This establishment, as well as the members of the permanent forces, provided troops for the garrisons of the coastal defences. The conference concluded that this was the maximum effort a nation of only five million could maintain. It did not recommend the expansion of the field army in time of war, except for the creation of the required support and supply units that would not exist in peacetime.

The figure of 180,000 greatly underestimated the actual requirements of the field force, as it did not include the personnel required for the numerous support and service formations that the army would raise on the commencement of hostilities. For example, the army required considerable additional artillery assets, particularly heavy batteries, more engineers, chemical warfare troops, and other specialists if the field force could achieve its maximum battlefield capability. Additionally, many of the army's essential line of communication units existed only on paper.

Furthermore, the senior officers did not propose maintaining the organisation at its wartime establishment, but instead suggested a lower peacetime scale. Instead of keeping the enlisted ranks of its formations at war levels, the army intended to staff the cavalry divisions at less than 67 per cent of war strength and the infantry divisions at approximately 87 per cent of full strength. Table 4.4 outlines the actual manpower needs of the army in war.

Table 4.4 Field army personnel requirements

Formations	Peace scale	War scale	Expanded war scale	Non-fighting war scale
Cavalry	11,000	22,000		
Infantry divisions	80,000	92,000		
Local troops	19,000	23,000		
Extra divisional	20,000	33,000	28,000	24,000
L. of C.		12,000	13,000	25,000
Total	*130,000*	*182,000*	*41,000*	*49,000*

Notes:
- 'Cavalry' includes the two cavalry divisions plus three regiments for local duties and two corps regiments
- 'Local troops' includes the three mixed brigades
- Expanded war scale units are mainly artillery
- Many of the line-of-communication and extra divisional formations would not exist in peacetime on any scale.

As this table suggests, the actual scale, once the army raised its extra-divisional and lines-of-communication units, was more of the order of 270,000 instead of the 180,000 that the senior officers first presented. Furthermore, the report suggested the need to allocate a further 100,000 men for the replacement of wastage.

The goal of a 370,000-man army reveals some inconsistencies in the conference's projections. The senior officers did detail the sources of the required manpower for both the peacetime and wartime versions of the army. The annual intake under universal training averaged 16,000 trainees per year. Since the training obligation under the Defence Act affected men between the ages of 18 and 26—a period of eight years—this would provide a force of about 120,000 once the system was fully operational. The senior officers believed that the army could rely upon volunteers to cover the difference between the 120,000 raised through universal service and the 130,000 required for the peacetime army. They did note that under the present conditions the army enrolled 8,000 volunteers a year, and they thought it likely that this amount could be increased by a further 2,000.

The requirements to raise the army to its war footing, however, were a little more complicated. The immediate source of manpower were the reserves, which in 1920 numbered 45,000. The senior officers then estimated that in the age class of 26 to 35 there were an additional 125,000 men who had not opted to join the reserves. Combined with the reserves, this provided a pool of 170,000 men. After deducting the 50,000 needed to bring the army up to its war establishment this still left, the senior officers noted, 100,000 for replacement of wastage and 20,000 for the necessary expansion of the support and service elements. However, a deficit of approximately 70,000 unidentified men remained, leaving the field force well short of the number needed to give the nation a 'sporting chance'.

From the reasoning of the senior officers, it is clear that the units which would suffer most from this shortage of manpower would be the line-of-communication troops, whereas the army was to give priority to the field force, followed by the corps and army artillery batteries and other combat support arms. The neglect of the logistical side of the army's organisation is further troubling because of the serious deficiencies that existed in the country's distribution network. Unlike northern France, Australia was relatively poor in sealed roads, and its fragmented and underdeveloped rail system provided an inadequate transport option. Moreover, the army would be unable to rely upon coastal shipping, because the RAN was too weak to prevent the loss of control over maritime communications. During World War I, the British had compensated for Australian logistical inadequacies by subsuming the Commonwealth's requirements into its own supply system. This support would be unavailable to Australia in a war against Japan, and for a critical part of the conflict the army would have to rely upon its own inadequate resources for the sustainment of its combat element. The placing of line-of-communication troops as the lowest priority also assured that in a war of national survival, Australia would again provide an unbalanced contribution to an imperial coalition, and that its forces would once again depend on another army for their maintenance.

To prepare the army for its duties, the conference proposed the same training scheme as had the Swinburne Committee. The senior officers also included less costly options, but they, too, made it clear that only the recommended program provided the concentrated training they believed essential for the creation of efficient soldiers. The senior officers did reiterate Swinburne's condemnation of the current practice of short camps and frequent half-day or evening parades that had been the basis of universal training before the war, and they noted that the 90,000 troops currently in the citizen forces were practically untrained. In the interim, until the army had created a force developed on the lines the senior officers had proposed, Australia's defence depended upon the continued availability of former AIF soldiers. Not only did these veterans form a ready source of experienced reserves, but also the army hoped that many would continue to serve as training staff for the citizen forces.

However, the senior officers realised the importance of creating an effective ongoing training organisation to compensate for the inevitable decline in the AIF, as both age and time distanced them from current developments in military science. In 1921, the army reorganised Hutton's instructional staff into a corps that it called the Australian Instructional Corps. Its members continued to be responsible for the conduct of courses at army schools and the provision of instructors at citizen forces camps of continuous instruction. In addition, the army posted non-commissioned officers as

Lieutenant-General Sir Harry Chauvel. (AWM J00503)

specialists to citizen forces units and assisted with cadet training. In 1920, the army also established a Central Training Depot at Liverpool for the training of its instructors, and to ensure the qualifications of the Australian Instructional Corps. Unfortunately, the Central Training Depot fell victim to budget cutbacks just six months after its opening. Despite the efforts of Chauvel, it did not reopen until 1939.[21]

The provision of instructors was also related to another administrative issue that the senior officers considered essential: the provision of an adequate staff. The officers explained that the army required a staff capable of 'the bulk of peace administration, but sufficient also to furnish a nucleus for the Staffs required in war by the whole Army'.[22] The senior officers, therefore, renewed a call for the creation of a formal Staff Corps, an issue that Kitchener had raised in his 1911 report. The army possessed staff officers, of course, but their appointment and professional status remained on an *ad hoc* basis. The first corps structure that provided a source of staff officers who performed essentially a staff function was the Australian Intelligence Corps, which the army had established in 1907. It had lapsed in 1914, however. Kitchener had also recognised the importance of a staff corps in relation to his Area Training Scheme, for which he estimated a need for 350 well-trained officers. It was for the provision of this need that he had proposed the creation of a military college, and by 1920 Royal Military College Duntroon had been producing staff officers for nine years. The senior officers now sought to raise a distinct corps for staff officers. This would allow the army to maintain a separate promotional list for these officers and assure the creation of a body of skilled officers who would be available to serve in any staff position. The government agreed, and the Australian Staff Corps came into existence in October 1920.

The senior officers took the opportunity in their report to remark on the training of the senior cadets. They opined that the training provided under the Defence Act had been of relatively little value in the physical aspects of their preparation as soldiers, but that there were some psychological benefits. They therefore recommended its continuation, but with modifications. The conference suggested that senior cadets should train only for two years, commencing at 16, and that the organisation should be of a recreational, inspirational, and disciplinary character, directed by a staff specially qualified for this role. They also believed that the cadets should not wear uniforms. Regarding junior cadets, the conference accepted that, since their training costs were borne by the schools rather than the Commonwealth, the program should continue unchanged. The senior officers' evaluation of the rifle clubs was even harsher. The senior officers believed that they were not a military necessity since they no longer constituted a part of the reserves. Therefore, the report concluded, if the Commonwealth chose to continue to subsidise these organisations, it should not do so from the military vote.

The senior officers also commented on the need to provide sufficient stocks of equipment adequate for the army, including wastage. They noted that Australia was in the process of acquiring from Britain war surplus materials adequate for the equipping of the cavalry and infantry divisions at establishment levels, but without any reserves. In addition, the report pointed out that there remained the essential provision of armaments for the corps and army troops as well as the need to establish reserves of munitions. Most of the extra-divisional troops were artillery, and the senior officers provided a list of the additional ordnance that they wanted the government to purchase. This included 68 18-pounder guns, 42 4.5-inch howitzers, 42 60-pounder guns, 42 6-inch howitzers, and 24 6-inch guns. The report further identified the need to acquire the equipment required by specialist formations, such as sound ranging, gun calibration, air defence, additional machine-gun units, gas, meteorological, signals, and other technical units. The senior officers also admitted that no provision had been made for the equipping of the line of communication, and that materials for these units would also have to be found. Coastal defence posed another area of concern, and the conference concluded that it was necessary to modernise these installations. For the moment, however, the senior officers rejected the acquisition of tanks because their design had not yet evolved to the point that the staff could identify the army's requirements with any certainty that they would not become immediately obsolete.

The last major issue that the conference raised was the army's desire to modify the Defence Act regarding the prohibition on the government's ability to compel overseas service. The officers explained that one of the obvious lessons of World War I was the benefit of waging a conflict on the enemy's soil rather than having to wait until actually attacked in one's own territory. They also noted that in a future conflict the government might not have the luxury of time that it had in World War I to create another AIF, and that the defence of the nation might be most effectively served by the dispatch of existing formations. Finally, the officers argued that since Australia had acquired foreign responsibilities in the form of mandated territories, the army might have to defend these acquisitions with citizen forces units, which the Defence Act did not permit at present. While unstated, there is some suggestion that the army's leaders did not want to repeat the experience of World War I, when they had to cannibalise the existing army in order to raise a volunteer force.

The conference presented its recommendations to the government in the form of a priority list. As the report explained, it was essential that the government follow the sequence and not commence any steps unless it had already provided for the previous ones. Furthermore, the officers suggested that if financial provisions were inadequate for the scheme to be adopted completely, then it should still be approved in principle and its realisation postponed until resources permitted its full realisation. The scheme's steps can be summarised as:

1. the adoption of the army establishment of two cavalry divisions, four infantry divisions, certain troops for local defence, personnel for coastal defence, and a proper proportion of staff and auxiliary troops
2. the territorial allotment of the units of the above establishment
3. the acquisition of supplies of equipment, arms, and ammunitions and reserves of raw materials
4. the establishment of a Munitions Supply Branch
5. the modernisation of the fixed defences
6. provision for the instruction of staffs, commanders, and non-commissioned officers
7. provision for a qualified instructional staff for the training of the citizen forces
8. calling up and training of the rank and file.

As this list shows, the senior officers defined the filling-out of the army's formations, at least at the other ranks level, as their lowest priority. Instead, the officers placed greater importance on the creation of the infrastructure and the provision of sufficient materials. The officers wanted to avoid a repetition of having large numbers of troops but not the resources with which to create an effective force. This also explains the greater emphasis on the provision of instructors and the teaching of officers and non-commissioned officers in their duties over the calling up of men. Additionally, the entire system depended upon the establishment of a sound divisional structure around which to organise the field force.

The Council of Defence met in April, and recommended the adoption of the organisation as outlined by the senior officers. This was to include the continuance of the Universal Training Scheme, employing 13-week-long camps of continuous training, and the provision of an adequate supply of guns and reserves of ammunition. The Council of Defence estimated the minimum funding level for the three services at £8.25 million, and it warned that a lower expenditure would leave Australia with no chance of security in case of war. It set the military's share at £3.5 million, of which nearly a third was for capital expenditure. Additionally, the Council of Defence noted that these estimates did not include any monies for the modernisation of the coastal defences, which would require a separate allocation once the Commonwealth had decided upon its requirements.[23]

The senior officers had succeeded in identifying the detailed requirements for the creation of a modern military force. However, the government proved unwilling to provide for all of their recommendations, the principal impediment, as Pearce had warned, being finances. In June, after the Minister for Defence had informed the officers of the Military Board of the expected level of government funding, they noted that it was impossible 'within the limits prescribed to effect under the present Act the payment and training of the existing forces'.[24] Finances were again on the agenda in July when the Military Board discussed the full impact of the government's stringent proposals. The Military Board agreed that the effect of the suggested funding would mean that the level of training would permit nothing more than the bare organisation of the forces. The government also refused to lengthen the citizen forces' training obligation. Instead, the existing provisions of the Defence Act remained in effect. These called for 16 days' training, divided into eight days of camp and eight days of home instruction. However, even this would prove far too expensive, and the government allocated only enough funds for the training of one quota. For the coming year only, the 1902 quota would receive camp training, and then for only eight days, plus four days of home training. The army required the 1899 through 1901 quotas to attend only four days of home training, while for the 1896–98 years, the obligation was only a half-day parade. In addition, the Military Board noted that the funds provided would not allow the issue of ammunition to the artillery for practice.[25]

In August, the Military Board asked the Minister for Defence to place on the agenda for the general meeting of the Military Board the question of the government's failure to fund the senior officers' recommendations at the expected level. Instead of the desired £8.25 million, the government had only allocated £3.2 million to be divided between the three services. The government had also failed to make any appropriation for capital expenditures. The officers argued that the estimates currently provided permitted the organisation of the force, but would only allow for nominal training, and that the army would remain inadequately supplied with artillery and reserves of ammunition. Furthermore, the army leaders noted that at current funding levels there would be no improvements in the almost defenceless state of the coastal batteries.[26]

The officers lost this argument, and Hughes set the military estimate at a level that was considerably below that which the army's leaders considered the minimum. The government did approve the suggested organisation, however, and the army adopted the divisional system on 1 May 1921. Home training began in July, and the citizen forces numbered 127,000, with a permanent forces cadre of 3,500. In September, the Military Board issued instructions organising the nation, along AIF lines, into 15 brigade areas, 60 battalion areas, and 144 training areas, as well as the distribution of the cavalry and non-divisional units.[27]

At this time the army also changed the force's regional command and administration structure. One of the conclusions the army's leaders derived from World War I was that the existing military district organisation could not provide and sustain a mobile field force against an invader. Consequently, the Military Board decided to separate responsibility for Field Force Command from that of administration. Up to now, both functions had been a responsibility of the six headquarters military districts, each one controlling and maintaining the forces in its regions. With the raising of divisions, the Military Board vested command with the divisional headquarters. In the smaller regions, the headquarters mixed brigades took on this function. The headquarters of the divisions and mixed brigades then reported directly to Army Headquarters. To replace the military districts the army raised district bases. Their duty was to support the field force. In addition, they commanded the army's garrison element within their respective territories. In this way the army now possessed distinct machinery to command and maintain the field force, thus relieving divisional commanders of much of their administrative workload and allowing them to focus on operational matters such as training. See Chart 3 (p. 100) for an outline of the new structure.[28]

The raising of the district bases was the army's first effort to balance the tasks of command and administration of the field force within Australian territory. The most important influence in this task, however, was not under direct military control. Rather, the guiding factor was the Treasury and the army's need to manage command and administration with the limited resources provided. Hence the army's efforts in this area proved unstable, and periodically the army had to seek economies by again merging command and administration into a single office, only to separate them again once more money became available. The district base scheme itself soon underwent major revision in order to reduce expenditure. By 1927, the organisation in the 1st, 4th, 5th and 6th military districts had reverted to the original district system, while in the 2nd and 3rd districts one of the divisional commanders also had to serve as district base commandant. The recombining of the functions of command and administration in a single office had the effect of greatly increasing the administrative work of field commanders, while causing operational responsibilities to become a secondary consideration.[29]

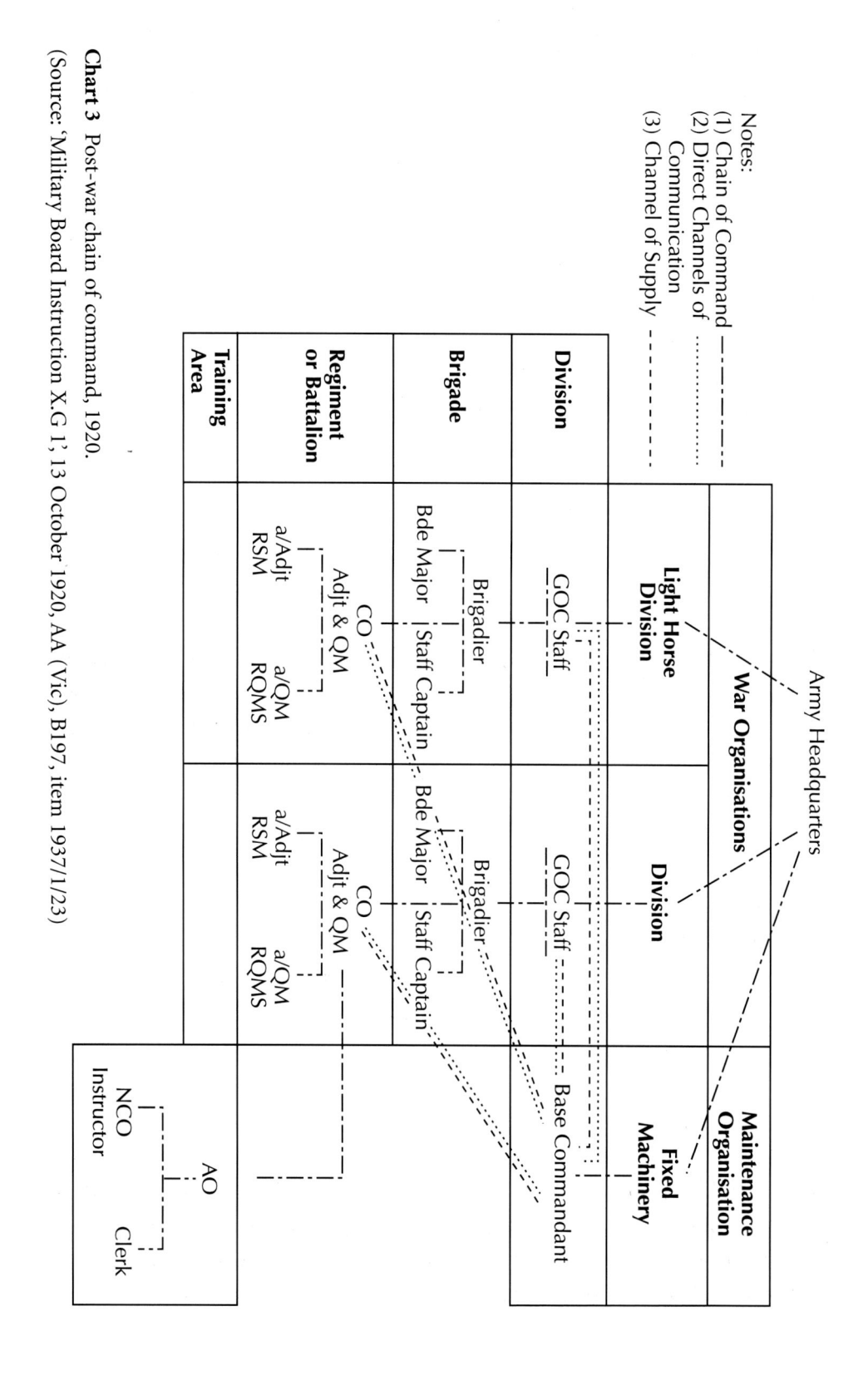

Notes:
(1) Chain of Command —·—·—
(2) Direct Channels of Communication ············
(3) Channel of Supply — — —

	War Organisations	Maintenance Organisation
Division	Light Horse Division — GOC Staff	
	Division — GOC Staff	
Brigade	Brigadier — Bde Major | Staff Captain	Base Commandant
	Brigadier — Bde Major | Staff Captain	Fixed Machinery
Regiment or Battalion	CO — Adjt & QM / a/Adjt RSM / a/QM RQMS	
	CO — Adjt & QM / a/Adjt RSM / a/QM RQMS	
Training Area		AO — NCO Instructor / Clerk

Army Headquarters

Chart 3 Post-war chain of command, 1920.
(Source: 'Military Board Instruction X.G 1', 13 October 1920, AA (Vic), B197, item 1937/1/23)

100

The government's refusal to allocate greater monies also handicapped the equipping of the armed forces. The war surplus provided by Britain, supposedly sufficient to outfit two cavalry and five infantry divisions, proved slightly deficient, and the army required a further 66 field guns. Shortages also existed in machine-guns, and stocks of artillery ammunition were only 25 per cent of war establishment. In addition, little in the way of equipment was available for the non-divisional formations. The government also refused to stockpile essential war materials. The army, therefore, could theoretically field a force of seven divisions if called out in an emergency, but it was an extremely fragile organisation, lacking depth, firepower, and mobility. Moreover, the logistical system remained overly frail, and the army would be either immobile or heavily dependent on the requisition of vehicles from the public. While the army would have a considerable paper strength, without extra resources it would be unable to direct, manoeuvre, and sustain its operations or focus its offensive power.[30]

The government also failed to modify the Defence Act requirement limiting service outside Australia to volunteers. This decision placed the army's leaders in the same situation that existed before World War I. If the nation were to honour its implied obligations to the empire, and the survival of the Singapore strategy demanded no less, it would have to create an entirely new organisation from recruits who agreed to serve overseas. The army that the senior officers had crafted was essentially a territorial defence force, just as the body that existed before World War I had been. It had no ability to intervene in operations outside the Australian littoral, and was barely capable of operations within its own territory.

Table 4.5 (p. 102) outlines the army's organisation in 1928.

The headquarters for the 1st Cavalry, and 1st and 2nd Infantry Divisions, were in New South Wales, while the headquarters for the 2nd Cavalry and 3rd and 4th Infantry Divisions were in Victoria. The headquarters for the 11th, 12th, and 13th Mixed Brigades were based in Queensland, Tasmania, and Western Australia, respectively.

The army nucleus

Although the senior officers received considerably less than they had hoped for, they did succeed in laying the foundation for the interwar military defence of Australia. Unfortunately, future government policy soon dashed any hopes that they might have held for any improvement in the army's organisation, training, or equipment. Therefore 1920 proved to be the high-water mark for the interwar institution.

Table 4.5 Organisation of the army, 1928: major formations and units[31]

Military district	Formation	Units
1st	HQ 1st Cavalry Bde	5th, 11th, 14th, 2nd Light Horse Regts
	HQ 5th Field Bde	13th, 14th, 15th, 105th Batteries
	HQ 9th Field Bde	41st, 42nd, 43rd, 111th Batteries
	HQ 7th Infantry Bde	15th, 25th, 26th, 49th Battalions
	HQ 11th Infantry Bde	9th, 31st, 42nd, 47th Battalions
2nd	HQ 2nd Cavalry Bde	12th, 15th, 16th Light Horse Regts
	HQ 4th Cavalry Bde	1st, 6th, 7th Light Horse Regts
	HQ 21st Field Bde	28th, 35th, 36th Batteries
	HQ 1st Field Bde	1st, 2nd, 3rd, 101st Batteries
	HQ 7th Field Bde	25th, 26th, 27th, 107th Batteries
	HQ 9th Field Bde	19th, 20th, 21st, 109th Batteries
	HQ 14th Field Bde	53rd, 54th, 55th, 114th Batteries
	HQ 18th Field Bde	59th, 60th, 61st, 117th Batteries
	HQ 1st Infantry Bde	13th, 33rd, 35th, 41st Battalions
	HQ 8th Infantry Bde	2nd, 17th, 18th, 30th Battalions
	HQ 5th Infantry Bde	4th, 20th, 36th, 54th Battalions
	HQ 9th Infantry Bde	1st, 19th, 34th, 45th Battalions
	HQ 14th Infantry Bde	3rd, 53rd, 55th, 56th Battalions
3rd	HQ 3rd Cavalry Bde	8th, 13th, 20th Light Horse Regts
	HQ 5th Cavalry Bde	4th, 17th, 19th Light Horse Regts
	HQ 22nd Field Bde	40th, 44th Batteries
	HQ 2nd Field Bde	4th, 5th, 6th, 102nd Batteries
	HQ 4th Field Bde	10th, 11th, 12th, 104th Batteries
	HQ 8th Field Bde	29th, 30th, 31st, 108th Batteries
	HQ 10th Field Bde	37th, 38th, 39th, 110th Batteries
	HQ 15th Field Bde	22nd, 23rd, 24th, 112th Batteries
	HQ 4th Infantry Bde	14th, 22nd, 29th, 46th Battalions
	HQ 10th Infantry Bde	24th, 37th, 39th, 52nd Battalions
	HQ 15th Infantry Bde	57th, 58th, 59th, 60th Battalions
	HQ 2nd Infantry Bde	5th, 6th, 23rd, 32nd Battalions
	HQ 6th Infantry Bde	7th, 8th, 21st, 38th Battalions
4th	HQ 6th Cavalry Bde	3rd, 9th, 23rd Light Horse Regts
	HQ 13th Field Bde	49th, 50th, 51st, 113th Batteries
	HQ 3rd Infantry Bde	10th, 27th, 43rd, 48th Battalions
5th		10th Light Horse Regt
	HQ 3rd Field Bde	7th, 8th, 9th, 103rd Batteries
	HQ 13th Infantry Bde	11th, 28th, 44th Battalions
6th		22nd Light Horse Regt
	HQ 6th Field Bde	16th, 106th Batteries
	HQ 12th Infantry Bde	12th, 40th Battalions

When Swinburne and the senior officers had begun their defence reviews, they had done so with the knowledge that Australia's post-war security concerns were still undefined. Unfortunately, once the international picture cleared, the government's assessment of the threat environment no longer conformed with the fundamental assumptions of the senior officers. The result was an ongoing difference of opinion regarding security requirements between the army's senior leadership and the nation's political masters, as well as a force structure that did not match the government's defence policy. The international initiatives that had the most effect on the army were the Limitations of Armaments Conference held in Washington and the Imperial Conference of 1923.

The Washington Conference began in 1921, and would generate three treaties. Although not present, Australia was affected by virtue of its membership in the British Empire and was, through this relationship, subject to the provisions of these treaties. They were the Four Power Pact between the United States, Britain, France, and Japan, which required consultation to resolve disputes between these nations; the Nine Power Treaty, whose signatories agreed to respect the integrity of China; and a Five Power treaty on naval disarmament. The latter set tonnage limits on capital ships that the nations could possess. It imposed levels of 500,000 tons on Britain and the United States, 300,000 tons on Japan, and 175,000 tons on France and Italy. Furthermore, no warship was to have a displacement of greater than 35,000 tons. The parties failed to reach agreement regarding cruisers, destroyers, or submarines, and the treaty did not consider limitations on air power. The agreement covered an initial period of 10 years.

Despite their intention of providing for security in the Pacific, these agreements were flawed, a fact not realised by Australia's political leaders. John McCarthy identifies the incorrect assumption at their core when he writes: 'the discussions at Washington were tinged with unreality: Japan was treated as a satiated power, and the naval and territorial provisions of the Four Power Pact were based on the false premise that she was'.[32] The treaty's prohibition on the construction by the United States of bases west of Hawaii hindered the ability of the American fleet to influence events in the Western Pacific. Without secure facilities at Wake Island, Guam, and the Philippines, the Americans would be unable to counter Japanese sea power. With the removal of American influence from these waters, the provision of security for Australian interests fell even more heavily upon the Royal Navy. However, despite Britain's exemption regarding the construction of a base at Singapore, the limitations on fleet size reduced the Royal Navy's ability to project power into eastern waters. The permitted ratios effectively lowered the British fleet to a one-power standard, thereby making it even less likely that the Admiralty would dispatch the Royal Navy to the east, especially if there was any potential for confrontation in home waters. Consequently, as some officers rightly noted, the Washington agreements left Britain, and hence Australia, in a worse position in the Pacific than before.[33]

Aggravating this situation was the fact that British and Australian political leaders saw the Washington treaties as an opportunity to reduce expenditures on defence, and their signing initiated a period of severe military cutbacks, further weakening the empire's military capabilities. In London, the Treasury became the dominant and final voice in defence matters, and it ruthlessly controlled the services through the dictates of the 'ten-year rule', the belief that Britain would not wage a great war during the next 10 years. McCarthy concludes his criticisms of the results of the Washington agreements with the observation that the treaties were 'backed simply by moral force'.[34] The signatories assumed that Japan had no further expansionist ambitions, and that as a member of the League of Nations she would respect the integrity of her neighbours and would prefer to settle disputes through peaceful means. The fallacy of these assumptions was soon revealed.[35]

The consequence for the army was the government's belief that the Washington treaties provided for the security of Australia. Like other members of the empire, the Australian Government was anxious to reduce defence expenditures to the lowest possible level. Policy-makers in Australia copied their counterparts in London and adhered to the notion of the 'ten-year rule', which provided them with a convenient rationale to restrict expenditures. The army salvaged its divisional structure but it became a mere shell, as the government denied the institution the resources it needed to create an effective military force.

The government lost no time in implementing reductions to the defence forces. Walter Massey-Greene, the Minister for Defence in 1922, outlined the effect of the scaled-back military estimate in a report to parliament in October of the same year. He explained that while the army would retain its structure, it would maintain its formations on a skeleton basis. Table 4.6 compares the strength of the defence forces for the fiscal year 1921–22 with that of 1922–23.

Table 4.6 Comparison of defence force strength, 1921–22 and 1922–23[36]

Force	Fiscal year 1921–22	Fiscal year 1922–23
Permanent forces	2,495	1,603
Citizen forces	118,400	31,000
Senior cadets	99,000	35,000
Junior cadets	50,000	nil

Table 4.7 illustrates the distribution of the cutbacks among the corps of the permanent forces, and suggests the effect of the reductions on the army's ability to train the citizen forces. The hardest hit corps was the Royal Australian Field Artillery, which declined by 78 per cent and lost two and a half of its three batteries, leaving only one section of field artillery to serve as a training establishment.[37]

Another consequence of these redundancies was that the understaffing of the staff corps became one of the intractable problems facing the army for the remainder of the interwar period. By 1937 the staff corps was still 150 officers short of the desired establishment of 400, and the CGS estimated that it would take the Royal Military College 17 years to overcome the deficiency. Consequently, the army had to appoint citizen forces officers to positions whose duties would have been better served by specially trained and full-time serving staff officers.[38]

Table 4.7 Reduction in permanent force personnel, 1922[39]

Corps	Estimate of personnel 1921–22	Estimate of personnel 1922–23	Decrease in personnel
Staff Corps	313	244	69
AIC	960	602	358
RAFA	249	56	193
RAGA	549	444	105
RAE	183	140	43
AASC	195	89	106
AAVC	7	3	4
AAMC	25	17	8
Survey Section	21	14	7
Total	2,502	1,609	893

The reduction in their strength, however, was only the most visible of a number of hardships that the government's interwar policies imposed on its permanent forces, especially the staff corps. Permanent soldiers who had prospered in the AIF returned home to take up positions at greatly reduced rank. Making matters even more dire was that when promotion did occur it did so at an extremely torpid rate, with the result that young officers remained in the junior ranks for virtually their entire careers. One officer so affected was George A. Vasey. He graduated from Royal Military College in 1915, and reached the rank of major while serving on the Western Front. However, the government did not confirm his rank, and he did not reach substantive captain until 1923. Vasey became a substantive lieutenant-colonel only after the commencement of

World War II. Another example was Horace Robertson. While already a major by 1916, he did not reach the rank of lieutenant-colonel until 1935. In addition, opportunities in the Australian force were so scarce that good officers either left the service or sought employment in the British or Indian armies. Adding to the injustice of the permanent force's promotional situation was that the government treated the citizen forces differently from the permanent forces. Most citizen forces officers retained their rank after demobilisation. Promotion in the citizen forces was effortless when compared with the permanent forces. Consequently, the military career of a part-time officer progressed far more rapidly than that of a staff corps officer. In his 1927 Inspector-General Report, Chauvel outlined the difficulties that the staff corps faced. Unfortunately, the government allowed few improvements before the commencement of World War II. As the end of the interwar period neared, Lieutenant-General E.K. Squires, in his 1938 Inspector-General Report, again found it necessary to submit a list of deficiencies regarding service in the staff corps.[40]

The army retained its divisional structure, but only at great cost. Instead of staffing divisional units at the planned rate of approximately 90 per cent for infantry and 67 per cent for cavalry, the army had to make do with barely 25 per cent of the required troops. The Department of Defence also cut back participation in the senior cadet program, and eliminated the junior cadet scheme altogether. The army continued to recruit under the Universal Training Scheme, but it restricted its intake to populous centres and to certain quotas only.

The limits on the geographic scope of recruiting meant that the army could no longer maintain its infrastructure of 144 training areas. It reduced these to 91, closing mainly those located in country centres. Lack of resources also forced the army to reduce the number of days spent in training from their already inadequate level. Consequently, the army had to limit citizen forces training to two quotas—those of 18 or 19 years of age—and finances allowed camps of only six days supported by four days of home training. Even this proved too much for an organisation in the midst of a major reduction in establishment and funding, and the army temporarily ceased all training, except on a voluntary basis, in February 1922. As partial compensation for the lost training, the army encouraged citizen force members to form regimental rifle clubs so that they could at least practise their marksmanship.[41]

At a stroke the government reduced the size of the army to a quarter of the scale that the senior officers had proposed. Furthermore, the conference's arguments over the need to provide longer periods of training were summarily discarded and the provision of equipment and ammunition suspended. With the gutting of the intentions of the Universal Training Scheme and the overturning of the Senior Officers Conference recommendations, the army entered into a period of decay and inefficiency. David Horner summarised the effect of these cutbacks on the army thus:

> The senior officers had hoped to have an army that could repel a possible invader. All that was left was a skeleton force which, with ten days' training per year, could hardly be described as a real army.[42]

Instead of military requirements and national security being the guiding forces behind its decisions regarding the army, the government made all determinations from a fiscal perspective.[43] This pattern lasted until the government began a belated rearmament on the eve of World War II.

The army was no longer a force in being, but had instead become what its leaders would term a 'nuclear structure'. This idea was that the army should keep alive a bare structure, which it could expand into a field force in case of an emergency. In its discussion of this change the Council of Defence opined that:

> in its judgement, the nucleus proposed for the Defence Forces is the definite minimum upon which the expansion which would be demanded by a change in the international situation could be made. The Council considers that the limited measures it has recommended are only justified by the satisfactory results of the Washington Conference, which contain promise of a prolonged peace in the Pacific.[44]

The army had in effect become a mothballed warship that had operational potential, but which required a lengthy refit before being able to go to sea.

As a 'nuclear' organisation, the army found that its purpose had also changed. It ceased to be a force capable of preventing or containing an invasion, and became an organisation whose primary purpose was the training of the leaders—officer and non-commissioned officers—required to staff its force structure in case of expansion. Under the nuclear scheme, the army was essentially a leadership training establishment with little integral combat capability. The army rationalised that it should focus its resources on the provision of the well-prepared officers and non-commissioned officers that it would require to convert raw recruits rapidly into an effective combat force. This shift in perception had another consequence. The longer mobilisation and training periods required to fill out the army served to increase the Commonwealth's dependence upon the Singapore strategy and the timely arrival of the Royal Navy. Without its own deterrent force, Australia's reliance on already over-extended imperial resources was total.

To have any chance of being effective, the nuclear army required the military to have access to a pool of semi-trained troops upon which the force could draw to bring its units up to strength. This should have been an ideal task for the Australian army reserve organisation. Unfortunately for the army's leaders, as the force's dependence on rapid expansion increased, its ready access to reservists actually declined. Although only a couple of years old, the reserve organisation was in a state of terminal decline, mainly, as Chauvel has suggested, from fiscal neglect. He noted that the scheme required the maintenance of an elaborate system of records in order to keep track of reservists' addresses and their allocation to units. Under present conditions, the army believed that it was no longer practical to dedicate extremely scarce resources to this task, and quickly lost administrative control over reserve membership. In 1924, Chauvel could state that the reserve force had ceased to exist.[45]

As a result of policies agreed to by Australia at the 1923 Imperial Conference, there were some minor improvements in the condition of the army, but the direction of Australia's security policy did not change. Consequently, the military establishment remained far short of the objectives identified by the Senior Officers Conference. The Imperial Conference mandated two principles as the basis of Dominion defence in the Far East. First was the obligation of each member of the empire to be responsible for its own local defence. Second was the reassertion of the idea that the defence of the empire depended upon maritime supremacy. In local waters, this took the form of a commitment by Britain and Australia, as well as New Zealand, to the Singapore Strategy.

In practical terms, the need to provide for local defence obligated the Australian Government to increase its level of defence spending, if only slightly. Unfortunately for the army, most of the additional resources went to a RAN construction program. The army did receive £250,000 for the purchase of some, albeit still inadequate, reserves of ammunition and for two additional days in camp for the quotas who were subject to training. However, the increased munition purchases were so slight that all it allowed, for the artillery for example, was for the field guns to actually take the field. Additionally, the government reached an agreement with the States for the resumption of junior cadet training in the schools, provided that most of the expense was borne locally.[46]

The Commonwealth's adherence to the Singapore Strategy at the Imperial Conference, however, had significantly greater impact on the organisational purpose of the army. Since the fleet guaranteed Australian security from invasion, the argument proceeded, the only threat which the Commonwealth had to fear was raids. Singapore was simply a restatement of the colonial and pre-World War I tenet of maritime supremacy of the Royal Navy as expressed by the Colonial Defence Committee and the Committee of Imperial Defence. In a confirmation of this strategic interpretation, in August 1923 the Overseas Defence Committee issued an analysis explaining that the most Australia had to worry about from Japan was the possibility of mining or bombardment of ports by raiders. It did not anticipate that the Commonwealth defences would have to contend even with parties of troops landed from these vessels.[47]

The government's acceptance of the principles of the 1923 Imperial Conference also widened the gap between the army's and the politicians' perception of the threat environment. The army's leaders remained convinced that they required a force capable of containing a Japanese invasion until help arrived from the empire. The government, by contrast, believed that the army's primary function was to repel raids. Therefore, the nation's political and military decision-makers not only evaluated defence policy on the basis of entirely different threat assessments, but also expected the army to meet completely different requirements.

As the decade progressed, the army was able to modify the Treasury's stringency, if only slightly. In 1925, Neville Howse, the Minister for Defence, accepted the army's argument that in order to assure adequate officer training it needed additional citizen soldiers. Accordingly, the government expanded the service obligation to a third annual quota and increased the training regime from 10 to 12 days, including eight days at a camp of continuous instruction. As partial compensation for the extra expense, the government reduced the service requirement for senior cadets from two years to one. Such largesse did not come without a warning, however. In a follow-up memorandum, the government informed the Military Board that it was to ensure that the number of citizen soldiers in service did not exceed the absolute minimum required for the training of leaders.[48]

The Great Depression

As the decade drew to a close, the condition of the army again worsened. The critical factors were the election of the Scullin Labor Government and the onset of the Great Depression, both occurring in late 1929. The effect of these events was a further weakening of the effectiveness of the military and a widening of the breach between the army and the government in their respective interpretations of the nation's security policy.

On 1 November 1929, the newly invested Labor Government of James H. Scullin acted on the party's long-standing hostility towards conscription and summarily suspended the Universal Training Scheme. Conscription had served as the main source of the army's manpower since its inauguration in 1911. At a stroke, and without any consultation with the Military Board or the Council of Defence, the government returned membership in the army to an exclusively voluntary basis. This change similarly affected the senior cadets. As a result of this sudden and unanticipated change, the army cancelled all camps of training for the rest of the fiscal year. From January to the end of June 1930, the army managed a program of just four days of home training.[49]

The effects upon the army were sudden and harsh. The Military Board had set 49,000 officers and men as the minimum required to maintain the nucleus organisation. Before the advent of the Scullin Government, the army's establishment had nearly reached achieved this objective. The army considered it doubtful, however, that it could recruit a force of such size from volunteers. The Council of Defence, meeting on 12 November 1929, therefore reset the army's establishment for its citizen forces to 35,000 plus 7,000 senior cadets. It also authorised a training obligation of eight days of camp and eight days of home training. The Council of Defence also decided to change the name of the citizen forces. Henceforth the army's non-permanent branch was to be known as the Militia. The Council of Defence's restoration of the term 'militia' was an attempt to distinguish between compulsory and voluntary terms of service in the nation's non-permanent forces. The council associated 'militia' with volunteers, whereas 'citizen' identified those who served under a universal training obligation. Enlistment into the militia commenced in January 1930.[50]

Unfortunately, it would prove impossible for the army to reach even these modest levels. In mid 1930, the army had an enrolment of over 29,000, of whom 5,300 were Senior Cadets, which meant that the army's establishment was actually more than 10,000 below the minimum level set by the Council of Defence. The permanent force also suffered, and in 1930 its membership was barely 1,500. By the next year the situation had hardly improved, and it was not until 1936 that the army would raise its establishment back to 35,000. It would not reach 70,000 until 1938. The struggle to maintain the structure of the organisation forced the army to amalgamate units. In 1930, the army linked five infantry battalions and two light horse regiments with other formations, in an attempt to preserve the unit's traditions and honours while also keeping the structure technically alive. The following year, a further nine infantry battalions disappeared, resulting in the army's decision to reorganise its brigades into a three battalion format.[51]

The crisis reached its peak in 1932, when the army considered the disbandment of all its infantry and cavalry divisions, accompanied by the mass elimination or linkage of numerous battalions, light horse regiments, and artillery batteries, as well as considerable losses in the other arms. The Adjutant-General, Major-General T.H. Dodds, noted that, with the reduction of the army to an establishment of less than 30,000, it was no longer possible to maintain units at an efficient size. He proposed to the Military Board the disbandment of all higher headquarters in the military districts and the amalgamation of the remaining units under the command of the military district commandant. He believed that in the 2nd and 3rd Military Districts the army had enough resources to provide for an infantry division and cavalry brigade, while the other areas could each sustain a mixed brigade. Dodds observed that the money the army saved through the elimination of division and brigade headquarters could provide for additional militia training. Dodds went so far as to write to all the affected staffs to inform them of the possibility of their disbandment. However, on further reflection, the army decided to salvage its organisation, and notified the military commandants that there would be no drastic reduction, at least for now. Pearce, once again the Minister for Defence, also noted that the government did not want to make any changes to the army's organisation until the outcome of the latest League of Nations disarmament initiative became known.[52]

The nation's economic condition and the collapsing world economy led to renewed demands from the government for additional savings from the military estimate. Training remained at the absolute minimum level to save on militia costs. The long-suffering permanent forces had to accept a further injustice, as the government imposed a mandatory eight week unpaid leave on its members, both officers and other ranks.[53] When Chauvel retired in 1930, the government let the position of Inspector-General remain vacant and merged its responsibilities into the office of the CGS. The government would not find the funds to reinstate the position until 1938. Financial considerations also forced the army to place even greater emphasis on voluntary activities in its training policies. The army continued to offer courses, weekend bivouacs, and military competitions, but it had to transfer more of the cost of professional instruction from the institution to the individual. In his last report, Chauvel acknowledged that under present conditions 'it will still be necessary to rely upon leaders putting in a great deal of extra time, in some instances at personal loss, in order to fit themselves for their position'.[54]

Policy review: raid versus invasion

Since 1923 the government had accepted the Singapore Strategy as the foundation of the nation's defence. This policy included the assumptions that the Royal Navy guaranteed

Australian security, and that all the military had to worry about was minor landings or coastal bombardments from enemy cruisers. The RAN also strongly supported this policy, and perceived its role as that of a unit of the imperial fleet. However, despite the government's and the RAN's adherence to this philosophy, the army's leaders continued to have significant doubts about the Singapore Strategy's validity and instead focused their attention on the prevention or containment of a Japanese invasion.

The army's doubts had existed from the beginning. At a 1923 meeting of the Council of Defence, General White questioned the ability of the Royal Navy to deter Japanese aggression with a fleet based on a one-power standard. Chauvel supported White with his prediction that Japan would attempt to destroy Sydney and Newcastle, then land elsewhere to acquire some Australian territory, so that even if eventually defeated she would still have bargaining power at peace talks. The senior officers, however, were not under any delusion that Australia could defeat a serious Japanese invasion. They simply hoped to hold out long enough for the arrival of assistance from the empire.[55] Over the following years, the army continued to produce assessments that assumed a large-scale Japanese landing, which the imperial fleet, still in home waters, would be unable to prevent.

At its core, the divergence between policy and force structure was a result of difference of interpretation of the strategic environment by the two parties. Both the army officers and political decision-makers saw Japan as a threat, but it was in their respective assessment of the empire's ability to counteract this threat that their differences lay. Through their insistence on the vitality of maritime defence and their commitment to the Singapore Strategy, the British provided a series of Australian governments with a convenient rationale for the denial of resources to the defence vote. As long as Britain continued to utter assurances, successive governments saw no need to question the appropriateness of the Singapore Strategy.

However, army leaders remained extremely sceptical of the Singapore base and of Britain's willingness to commit the fleet to the Pacific, especially if there was a distraction closer to home. The slow rate of the base's construction, including a complete suspension of work in 1924 during the government of Ramsay MacDonald, served to further undermine army faith in imperial resolve in the region. From the establishment of the strategy in 1923, all the way through to its obvious failure in 1941, senior army officers attempted to force the government to reconsider the appropriateness of the strategy for Australian interwar defence policy.

In 1932, the difference of opinion between the government and army decision-makers regarding security policy finally came to a head. On 15 February, the recently elected government of Joseph Lyons instructed the military that it was to regard raids as the sole threat against which the army was to prepare.[56] The government then divided defence policy into two spheres—imperial and local. Within the context of imperial defence, sea power would provide the principal means to protect the nation from invasion, raids, and the interdiction of its commerce. To this end the government decided that it would maintain the RAN at a strength 'which is an effective and fair contribution to Empire Naval Defence'. The Lyons administration defined a lesser imperial function for the army: the provision of an expeditionary force of one division for overseas service within three months. The purpose of the air force was even more restricted, and the government defined its function as the provision of cooperation aircraft for the other two services. The focus of local defence policy was on the protection of cities and installations, particularly ports, from raids. The army, the government noted, was to supplement the navy's protective capabilities against raids through the provision of artillery, garrisons, and military forces of sufficient strength to deal with limited incursions.[57]

In March 1932, to meet the army's responsibility of defence against raids, the Military Board proposed to Pearce a revised military organisation. Instead of the army's present establishment of two cavalry divisions, four infantry divisions, and three mixed brigades, the Military Board suggested a smaller organisation of three cavalry brigades, two infantry divisions, and four mixed brigades. This structure would have a higher degree of mobility and greater capacity for independent action. Also, since the manpower would remain the same, the formations would have higher peacetime strength and thereby be able to react more quickly to enemy actions. The government, however, did not approve this submission, and the army remained organised along the lines set by the Senior Officers Conference.[58]

Despite the decision to retain the existing structure, the government's insistence that raid defence was the army's primary responsibility would result in the creation of a two-tier force structure. Pearce required the army to identify certain formations as its first line component. These would serve as the army's reaction force against raids. These formations would receive priority for army resources and exist at a higher level of readiness. The first line component would consist of the three cavalry brigades, two infantry divisions, and four mixed brigades, which the army had already advanced in its modified organisational proposal noted above. The army did retain the rest of the field force, but the other elements would have little opportunity for improvement until the government provided the force with significantly greater funding.

Army resistance, plus problems of geography and population distribution, would make the establishment of the first line component, on anything more than a theoretical level, extremely difficult. Since the army retained its structure of two cavalry divisions, four infantry divisions, and three mixed brigades, it had to designate forces for the first line component from within the existing organisation. However, because of the concentration on population in the south-east corner of the continent, the army had to impair the efficiency of the scheme by identifying as first line component units that were actually subunits of another formation. This meant that, in case of the activation of the first line component, the army's peacetime structure would not be the same as its wartime organisation. Additionally, the field force itself would require significant modification on mobilisation, as formations that in peace had existed within a stable command structure would now shed subunits to fill out the organisation of the first line component. A few examples might help to explain these points. The 1st Mixed Brigade in the 2nd Military District (Newcastle Area) was short one battalion in its peacetime establishment but would absorb the 25th Battalion from the 1st Military District upon mobilisation. The 2nd Division (Sydney Area) lacked three battalions, but would make up the deficit by taking over the battalions belonging to the 15th Brigade in the 3rd Military District. The 2nd Division was also missing a field brigade, but would borrow one from Victoria if needed.[59]

Those formations and units that were not part of the first line component would also undergo significant modification from their peacetime composition if mobilisation occurred. Instead of being activated as field force units, they would transform themselves into training establishments in anticipation of a general mobilisation. For example, if the government called out the first line component, the 11th Light Horse Regiment, which the army had not designated as part of the scheme, would form the 1st Light Horse Training Regiment. It would become responsible for preparing the 11th Light Horse Regiment for service in case of escalation. In addition, some formations that had existed as part of the peacetime establishment might disappear if first line component mobilisation occurred. The army planned to disband the headquarters of the 10th and 15th Infantry Brigades in Victoria if other military districts required their battalions. Thus, while providing a reaction force against a small-scale enemy incursion, the scheme did so only by greatly disrupting the existing organisation and command relationships, which controlled the army during peacetime.[60]

The thrust of the government's defence policy took further shape when Pearce delivered a major address in September 1933. While he couched his speech in terms of the need for the Dominions to take a greater role in the provision of their own defence, he also clearly perceived Australia as being a junior partner within an imperial defence network in which the key institution was the Royal Navy. Employing a trade-based argument, Pearce concluded that Australian security was first based upon the sea, and that the nation must rely 'on the power of the Navy to defend her against aggression'.[61] He further concluded that, since Australia was unable to provide the degree of required naval protection, the Commonwealth's security policy had to dovetail with that of the empire. Pearce then highlighted the need for Australia to strengthen the RAN and modernise its coastal defences. He also announced the intention of providing some additional monies for the field force, but he clearly viewed this as less significant.[62]

The government then announced its intention to fund a three-year capital expenditure program. Major-General John Lavarack, who would soon become CGS, believed the priority for the army was to train commanders and staff, purchase equipment for the field force, and begin training the militia.[63] Instead, Pearce put forward a plan that gave the majority of its funds to naval rearmament. Within the army's portion, the government allocated most of the money towards the upgrade of the coastal guns, and consequently comparatively little was left over for the improvement of the field force. It is true that the guns were in a desperate condition, as nothing had been done with them since before World War I, and Australia's coastal defences were now obsolete. However, the field force was also in a dire state. Pearce's direction of funding supported the government's objective of raid prevention and took away from the army's ability to resist invasion.

The government's program of coastal defence modernisation included the installation of new guns, searchlights, anti-aircraft guns, fire control equipment, harbour booms, and anti-submarine nets at ports around Australia. Sydney, Newcastle, and Fremantle received 9.2-inch and 6-inch guns. The batteries at lesser strategic centres—Port Phillip, Hobart, and Darwin—mounted 6-inch guns. By the end of the interwar period, the nation could boast an extensive, although incomplete, coastal defence system. However, while the government quickly authorised the acquisition of the guns, the army did not receive many other key components until just before, or even after, the commencement of World War II. A 1938 report revealed that only the 6-inch guns at Newcastle were ready to 'engage the enemy under emergency conditions'. Most batteries lacked modern range-finding devices, searchlights, armour-piercing shells, and signal equipment. These deficiencies had to be made up after the war began.[64] Table 4.8 (p. 117) outlines Australia's fortress and garrison organisation on the eve of the war.

Although the field force was starved for funds, the government's allowance for it remained extremely limited, and all the army could hope for was a small increase in the reserve of artillery and small arms ammunition, some engineer, signal, and anti-gas

Lieutenant-General J. D. Lavarack, CGS 1935–39. (AWM 100129)

stores, and the purchase of a handful of light tanks and armoured cars. Such were the constraints that the CGS noted that the army would be able to import from England just ten tanks over a period of two years, and stocks of small arms ammunition stood at 60 per cent of the minimum war reserve. In 1937, the government authorised a second development program, but this also emphasised improvements in the coastal batteries. Under this latter program, all the CGS managed for the field army was a small instalment of Bren guns.[65]

Table 4.8 *Australian coastal defences, August 1939*[66]

Fortress	Garrison
HQ Brisbane Fortress	Cowan Battery Command
	1st Garrison Battalion
HQ Sydney Fortress	Banks, Signal, Hornby, South Head, North, Middle, Georges, Bradley, Broken Bay, and Kembla Battery Commands
	2nd, 7th, 13th Garrison Battalions
HQ Newcastle Fortress	Scratchley and Wallace Battery Commands
	8th Garrison Battalion
HQ Port Phillip Fortress	Queenscliff, Nepean, Pearce, and Franklin Battery Commands
	3rd, 9th Garrison Battalions
HQ Port Adelaide Fortress	Largs Battery Command
	4th Garrison Battalion
HQ Fremantle Fortress	Rottnest, Bickley, Swanbourne, and Arthur Head Battery Commands
	5th, 10th Garrison Battalions
HQ Albany Fortress	Princess Royal Battery Command
HQ Hobart Fortress	Nelson, Direction, and Pierson Battery Commands
	6th Garrison Battalion
HQ Darwin Fortress	East and Emery Battery Commands
	Darwin Mobile Force

During the final years of the interwar period, the army turned its attention to the nation's anti-aircraft defences. In 1938, the army had only four obsolete 3-inch anti-aircraft guns on its establishment. The lack of an aerial defence system meant that Australian cities were open to air bombardment, an increasingly likely possibility, given the expansion of the Imperial Japanese Navy's aircraft carrier arm. Between mid 1938 and early 1939, the government placed orders for more than 60 anti-aircraft guns, as well as the required fire control equipment and searchlights. As with the coastal defence system, the anti-aircraft defences were designed to protect the major cities and key military and industry centres. The equipment was not destined for the field force, which continued to lack an effective means of aerial defence. While Australian manufacturers could supply most of the guns, the army had to order much of the technical equipment from overseas. This impaired the efficiency of the air defence network, since Britain's own belated military build-up delayed the receipt of many key items. Still, in October 1938, the army was able to raise the 1st Anti-Aircraft Brigade.[67] Table 4.9 outlines Australia's nascent anti-aircraft defences on the eve of the war.

Table 4.9 Australian anti-aircraft defences, August 1939[68]

Fortress	Unit
HQ Anti-Aircraft Defence Sydney	1st Anti-Aircraft Battery
HQ Anti-Aircraft Defence Newcastle	3rd Anti-Aircraft Battery
HQ Anti-Aircraft Defence Port Phillip	4th Anti-Aircraft Battery
HQ Anti-Aircraft Defence Fremantle	5th Anti-Aircraft Battery
HQ Anti-Aircraft Defence Darwin	2nd Anti-Aircraft Battery

Notes:
- The army raised the 2nd Anti-Aircraft Battery in Sydney, and it would deploy to Darwin upon activation.
- By this date, the army had formed only parts of 5th Anti-Aircraft Battery. The order of battle listed most of the unit's components as either cadre status or not raised in peace.

While the army's leaders tactfully subscribed to the government's preference for an anti-raid-based defence, and while they incorporated the first line component into their organisation, they continued to make defence against invasion their primary planning and training priority. In fact, the army played a duplicitous game with the government over the focus of defence planning, and strove to reverse or undermine its instructions.

The army's primary target was the Singapore Strategy, since it was the foundation of the government's maritime defence policy. Shortly after Pearce's directive to concentrate on protection from raids, the army issued its own policy review. This paper again advanced serious concerns about the timely arrival of the imperial fleet, and highlighted the need to increase the nation's defence against invasion. Calling the paper 'Appreciation of Australia's Position in Case of War in the Pacific', the Australian Section of the Imperial General Staff wrote that 'Australia must be able to rely absolutely on the presence of the British main fleet, or a considerable portion of it, based on a completed Singapore Base and arriving in sufficiently good time'.[69] However, it continued, since treaty restrictions had reduced the British fleet to a one-power standard, a situation might arise in which the Royal Navy would be unable to sail to the east. This, it warned, would be precisely the time when the Japanese would strike. Regarding the arrival of the imperial fleet, the review continued:

> In fact there seems but little hope that the British Government and people will ever consent to the dispatch of a considerable portion of the main fleet ... to a theatre on the other side of the world. The issue is simple. Command in the Atlantic is of vital importance to the British people, command in the Far East is not.[70]

The review then concluded that, since the provision of naval security was beyond the ability of Australia to provide, the nation's primary means of defence must be based upon land and air forces.[71]

In a document presented to the Council of Defence, Lavarack expressed the view that 'grave risks are entailed in basing the Defence organisation of Australia entirely on the assumption that the Main British Fleet will be made available to move to the Far East as soon as possible after the outbreak of hostilities'.[72] Lavarack continued that such faith in the Royal Navy was no longer appropriate, and that these attitudes were a legacy of the 'palmy days of the two-power naval standard'.[73] He then concluded that the basis of Australian defence was untenable, and that the government should therefore increase its reliance on local defence so that the nation's armed forces were sufficiently strong to deter an invasion.[74]

The stridency of military leaders' efforts to have the government reconsider its commitment to the Singapore Strategy eventually exceeded the allowances of decorum and crossed over into insubordination. Major-General Julius Bruche, as the CGS, committed this offence in his review of Maurice Hankey's 1934 assessment of Australia's defence. The long-serving secretary of the Committee of Imperial Defence's assessment contained the now standard blandishments on the maritime basis of imperial defence, the Singapore Strategy, the timely transfer of the fleet to the Pacific, and the ability of the Royal Navy to defeat the Imperial Japanese Navy. Bruche revealed the fallacy of Hankey's assertions one by one, and rejected them as incompletely thought-out articles of imperial faith rather than statements which met the security requirements of a sovereign state that lay on the other side of the world from the fleet. Bruche then asserted that the government's anti-raid policy was wrong, and that it should readopt the recommendations of the Senior Officers' Conference of 1920. He concluded that if the government insisted on relying on the arrival of the Royal Navy, it should obtain from the British Government a tangible guarantee concerning the completion of the Singapore Base and the dispatch of the fleet.[75]

At 62 Bruche had reached retirement age, and this might account for his tone. However, his successor as CGS, Lavarack, continued the army's efforts, and he too criticised Hankey's report, although more discreetly.[76] Shortly after taking up his duties, he also let the government know his position on what he believed to be the correct focus of Australian security. He pointedly informed the government that he considered the defence expenditure unbalanced, and that the RAN was throttling the army and preventing the development of the air force. Lavarack suggested that the government should immediately recondition the army, expand the air force, and

Major-General Sir Julius Bruche, CGS 1931–35. (AWM 100128)

allocate to them a greater share of the responsibility for the nation's defence.[77] Under his tenure, the army then issued a major policy paper entitled 'A Common Doctrine on the Organisation and Employment of the AMF'. Its primary purpose was to convince the government of the need to redirect resources to the army in order to prepare against an invasion.[78]

Despite the government's directions, the army's leaders also continued to make protection from invasion the primary concern of their planning. In 1936, four years after Pearce's request, Lavarack would admit that he had still not finalised the selection of the first line component. Instead, Lavarack noted that he continued to hope that sufficient funds would become available to improve the whole army. He revealed that he regarded the subdivision of the field force into '1st and 2nd line components merely as a method for giving priority of expenditure of available Army funds for the next few years'.[79] Another year would pass before the army had officially distinguished between those units of the field force that were members of the first line component and those that existed at a lower priority. Only in December 1937 did the army prepare a list of first line component units and outline the fate of the rest. In this report, the army planned to disband or reform as training establishments those formations that did not mobilise as part of the first line component. For example, the 3rd Division headquarters would cease to exist and its subunits would either transfer, if needed, to commands that were a part of the first line component or disband and survive only as training centres.[80]

Oddly, in the same year, the army also prepared a non-first line component organisation. Its appearance can only call into question the army's commitment to the anti-raid scheme. In this document the army revealed a different role for many of the elements that simply disappeared in the first line component organisation. For example, the 3rd Division now played a critical role in national defence against invasion. After mobilisation, it moved to New South Wales to help defend the Sydney basin. Clearly, the army's senior officers were continuing to play the game of being seen to adhere to the directives of their political masters while in reality preparing for their preferred role, invasion defence.[81]

Another army undertaking supports this conclusion. The army designated 40 of its infantry battalions as members of the first line component. At first examination this is a legitimate action, since the two divisions and four mixed brigades equalled ten infantry brigades. Based on the World War I standard of four battalions per brigade, it required an allocation of 40 battalions. However, since the reduction in the force's establishment in 1929 the army operated on the basis of a three-battalion brigade. Thus, an assignment of 30 battalions to the first line component would have been more reasonable. Additionally, in mid 1936 the army only had 44 battalions, plus the two university regiments, on its effective order of battle. The army leaders maintained the illusion that their force still contained the 60 battalions that the Senior Officers' Conference had recommended through the series of linkages that they had implemented in the early 1930s. By assigning 40 of its 44 battalions (not including the university regiments) to the first line component, the army had effectively undercut the government's objective of creating an anti-raid reaction force.[82]

In 'A Common Doctrine', the military advanced several potential war scenarios. The report predicted that in a future war the aggressors would be Germany and Japan, and that Australia would become involved in a conflict in order to aid Britain in Europe against Germany or to assist the empire in a war in the Pacific against Japan. The worst-case situation was simultaneous involvement in both theatres. The army's planners were under no illusion that they could defeat Japan on their own and that they would manage without aid from overseas. Therefore, they saw the proper defence policy of the country as one that preserved vital national interests in order that Australia could undertake a prolonged defence. The report identified these interests as:

a   The maintenance of the morale of the majority of the population.
b   The main centres of production and distribution.
c   Industrial areas essential for war purposes.
d   Certain terminal ports, necessary for overseas military relief and commercial traffic.
e   The fleet base at Sydney, and the local ports of naval importance, on which the eventual restoration of British sea control depended.[83]

They believed that to accomplish this it was essential that the army safeguard the nation's population and industrial centres, in particular the corridor from Port Kembla to Newcastle along the New South Wales coast whose loss would assure defeat.[84]

The army then used 'A Common Doctrine' to refine its ideas on anti-invasion defence. The report stated that the Commonwealth needed a field army that was capable of resisting a large, well-trained opponent. To do this, it wanted to develop a force of overwhelming superiority in armament and an equivalent degree of training as the enemy's first contingent, as well as a high degree of strategic mobility. In addition to the field force, the army would still require local troops for the protection of ports and a coastal defence system to deter enemy landings and bombardments. It also wanted the further development of the air force in order to provide strategic and tactical reconnaissance, close air support, and interdiction of the enemy's support services. The report conceded that the requirements of the military exceeded the financial resources presently available, but it stressed the need to begin rebuilding the army. In the immediate term, the army's leaders called for the implementation of the following steps:

a   Provision of an adequate stock for the initial war requirements of armament, ammunition, and war equipment of all natures, including armoured fighting vehicles.
b   Elevation of the training and organisation of the peace establishment of personnel to a stage that would permit effective mobilisation, collective training and concentration, in the time likely to be available.
c   Institution of adequate preparations for war maintenance of the forces.[85]

Once these improvements were underway, the army would then attempt to establish a reserve, shorten mobilisation times, increase strategic mobility and ammunition stocks, and develop an anti-aircraft defence system.[86]

The report suggests that the senior officers were looking beyond the army's structure as a nuclear institution that existed primarily for the purpose of training leaders. Instead, it implies, along with the concentration plans they developed to defend the Sydney area, that they believed that the ten-year rule was no longer appropriate and that, as a result of the deteriorating international climate, the time had come to begin rebuilding the nation's military forces. However, as with their previous initiatives, this one also failed to move the government, whose defence policy focus remained unchanged. In 1936, Archdale Parkhill, Pearce's successor as Minister for Defence, in face of the worsening international climate, classified the army's function as a supplement to British sea power and reiterated that the Royal Navy was the first line of Australian defence. He continued that the defence priority for the military was to provide protection against raids, and that the government would continue to focus its spending on the requirements of coastal defence at the expense of those of the field force.[87]

The approach of war

In June 1938, the government finally appointed a new Inspector-General. The government chose to overlook Lavarack for the position, and instead selected a British officer, Lieutenant-General Ernest K. Squires. He submitted only one report before the onset of war, but his assessment had important ramifications for the organisation of the army. Squires defined two roles for the army. They were:

1. to defend certain vital and vulnerable areas and localities against attacks on a relatively small scale, which may take place with little or no warning.
2. to be able to expand, after their initial mobilisation, into an army strong enough to resist aggression on any larger scale likely to be developed against Australia.[88]

Squires' report made it clear that he considered the army's preparations to fulfil either of these tasks inadequate.

Squires believed the training of the militia to be poor. He noted that camp attendance was often low, sometimes little more than 50 per cent of a unit's strength in residence. Even if a militiaman fulfilled his entire training obligation, however, the result, Squires knew, was only a partially trained soldier who still needed several months of intense training before being capable of serving at the front. The Inspector-General

Lieutenant-General Ernest Squires, CGS 1939–40. (AWM 000283)

concluded that the expectation that the militia could be ready in a few weeks was false. Many of the army's units were also greatly under strength, some so low as to prevent useful training. In mid 1936, the largest battalion in the army was the linked 30th/51st, and it had only 412 officers and men. Many battalions had fewer than 200 members, the smallest being the 11th/16th, with a mere 156.[89]

Squires also complained that the field units lacked many essential items, and that the reserves for even the first line component were below war requirements. Furthermore, the army's stocks of equipment and munitions were inadequate to cover the period from the commencement of hostilities until expansion of production of war stores.

There was a great deal of justification behind the Inspector-General's observations. A February 1939 study of first line component requirements revealed serious deficiencies. In some categories the gulf between requirements and actual stock was vast. For example, the army anticipated a need for more than 2,700 Bren guns, but only had 36 in inventory. Of the required 262 2-pounder anti-tank guns, only 64 were on order, and none had arrived from England. Even as war approached, the need to purchase items from British factories, already at full capacity providing for their own army, made the elimination of these shortages almost impossible.[90]

Squires also believed that the first line component organisation was insufficient to defend Australia's extensive coastline, and he wanted to raise four more formations—two in New South Wales, one in Queensland, and one in Western Australia. Moreover, he thought that the militia's establishment of 35,000 was too low, both for efficient training and as a pool for expansion, and he wanted the government to raise its peacetime strength to 60,000. Also, the staff of the permanent forces could not compensate for the inadequacy of militia numbers, as they continued to be significantly under establishment. Although the government had spent considerable sums of money on the modernisation of the coastal defences, it had refused to provide staffs for these installations at even the minimum levels suggested by the army. Every fort was under strength, and some works, such as Brisbane and Newcastle, had less than half of the personnel they needed. Overall, the Royal Australian Artillery Regiment had only 470 soldiers out of a desired establishment of 804. The situation of the Royal Australian Engineers was somewhat better, but it still had a deficit of 61 out of 196.[91]

In order to improve the readiness of the army, Squires proposed the creation of combat formations for the permanent force. The Inspector-General did not believe that, with current levels of training, the militia was able to mobilise rapidly enough to repel a raid, deter an invasion, or prevent an invader from successfully gaining a lodgement on Australian territory. The Defence Act, however, explicitly limited the function of the permanent forces to administration, training, and the garrison of the coastal defences, and prohibited the creation of a regular body of infantry. The Australian tradition had always been that the militia would serve as the nation's army in time of war, while the permanent forces existed to maintain the infrastructure in a state of readiness for expansion. Squires was therefore proposing a significant variation in the traditional Australian reliance upon the militia.

Squires suggested the creation of a permanent combat force, with a peace establishment of 8,000 that would expand to 10,000 upon the commencement of hostilities. It would contain:
- two infantry brigade headquarters
- nine infantry battalions
- one machine-gun battalion
- two field brigades
- two anti-tank batteries
- two field companies
- four signal sections
- detachments of support corps.

Squires planned to locate a mixed brigade in both New South Wales and Victoria, while Queensland, South Australia, and Western Australia would each receive an infantry battalion. New South Wales would also receive the machine-gun battalion. Tasmania would only have a detachment of riflemen. The Inspector-General also noted that in peacetime these units could help train the militia, a useful supplement to the chronically understaffed Australian Instructional Corps.[92]

Surprisingly, Squires' overture received a promising response from the Lyons Government. Although the government reduced the scale of the establishment, it did approve the principle of the formation of permanent force combat units. Instead of the force of more than two mixed brigades that the Inspector-General wanted, the Minister for Defence, G.A. Street, announced the government's intention to raise a force of 1,571 men, consisting of two small infantry battalions, a field artillery brigade, a section of signallers, and detachments of Australian Army Service Corps and Australian Army Ordnance Corps personnel.[93] In May, the army received authorisation to form the new units for the 1939–40 fiscal year at a slightly higher establishment of 1,676, although the Military Board noted that the expansion was subject to the government's provision of the necessary funds.

However, the fall of the Lyons ministry provided an opportunity for the reconsideration of this expenditure. In June, the army noted that it had suspended further action pending a decision by the government. This soon arrived, and Lavarack announced the scrapping of the plan. The recently formed government of Robert G. Menzies gave financial grounds as the reason for its action. Instead, the government ordered the intensification of training for part of the militia. The government's reversal also obviated the need to amend the Defence Act.[94]

The only permanent combat troops Australia raised at this time was the Darwin Mobile Force, which the Lyons Government had also authorised, and whose formation it announced in October 1938. The defence of Darwin was proving increasingly difficult for the Commonwealth, especially after its expansion into a minor naval base. Located roughly half-way between Singapore and Sydney, Darwin could serve as a defended fleet anchorage, and it was the only port along the entire Top End at which it was possible to refuel and reprovision warships. To protect against bombardment, the army had relocated to Darwin the 6-inch guns from Thursday Island, and had made provisions for the installation of anti-aircraft weapons to safeguard against an aerial attack. However, the surrounding district did not have a sufficient number of men of British ancestry to support a militia unit, which left the city defenceless against an enemy landing. The Darwin Mobile Force was a small, combined arms unit with an establishment of just 245 officers and men. It consisted of an infantry company of 72 personnel, a battery of 18-pounders, support sections of 3-inch mortars and medium machine-guns, and intelligence, engineer, and signal elements. Since the Defence Act prohibited the enlistment of infantry in the permanent forces, the soldiers of the Darwin Mobile Force joined as members of the Royal Australian Artillery or the Royal Australian Engineers. Only by employing this ruse was it possible to get around the Defence Act's limitation on a non-militia organised field force. In March 1939, the force sailed north to take up its duties.[95]

Squires had greater success in getting the government to implement the second major recommendation of his report. The Inspector-General proposed reforming the State-based military districts into a system of regional commands. Under the current system, Army Headquarters had direct control over 13 lower headquarters: four infantry divisions, two cavalry divisions, six district bases, and the independent command at Darwin; a figure which Squires believed was far too large for the efficient management of the force. Furthermore, Army Headquarters also managed the military's educational establishments. The Inspector-General objected in particular to the situation in which the army's headquarters exerted direct control over field force formations in peace, which would fall under the command of a subsidiary headquarters in time of war, thus violating the principle that command in war should be the same as command in peace. Moreover, within a single military district, Army Headquarters might control some field force formations, while the district base commanded garrison units. Within the same region, therefore, two command structures existed, a liability if war eventuated. To remove this oddity, Squires recommended the reorganisation of the chain of command into four military districts, with two first-class districts, comprising the area of New South Wales to South Australia, including Tasmania, and two second-class districts, covering Queensland and Western Australia. The Darwin area remained an independent garrison controlled directly by Army Headquarters. Chart 4 outlines Squires' proposal.[96]

As promulgated by the government, the recommendation followed the geographic distribution which Squires had suggested, but with a slight change in the terminology, thereby removing the distinction between first- and second-class districts. The modifications were:

a   Northern Command (Queensland)
b   Eastern Command (New South Wales)
c   Southern Command (Victoria, South Australia, Tasmania)
d   Western Command (Western Australia)
e   one independent garrison (Darwin).

The name of the command element in Darwin subsequently changed and, when it was raised, the army designated it the 7th Military District. Its responsibilities included all of the Northern Territory.[97]

Under this scheme, Army Headquarters now communicated directly with only five subordinate headquarters, thereby transferring much of the management for the field force to the regional command structure. Additionally, a single command-level headquarters now controlled all combat formations within a region. While the scheme had the effect of simplifying the chain of command for operations, it complicated the force's structure for administration. In effect, the command headquarters also became responsible for the administrative needs of the forces in their region, including such tasks as recruitment and housekeeping. While Squires' scheme simplified the duties of the army's headquarters, it did so by devolving much of the force's administrative tasks onto the commands. This was an enormous burden for which they were not adequately staffed, a problem that mobilisation exacerbated. The consequence was that staff officers assigned to a command soon found themselves fully involved in administrative detail rather than operational matters. The new command structure came into effect on 13 October 1939, shortly after the start of World War II.[98]

Squires' limited success also had some effect on the government's level of funding for defence, although it is perhaps more likely that Menzies was responding to the worsening international situation in Europe. In 1938, the government increased the militia establishment to 42,000, then raised it again to 70,000. This exceeded Squires' recommendation, and represented a force level that the army had not seen since 1920. By June 1939, the militia totalled nearly 77,000 and the army had sufficient soldiers to separate most its of linked units. The expansion, of course, brought with it a new set of problems. The enormous increase of raw recruits caused havoc in the army's

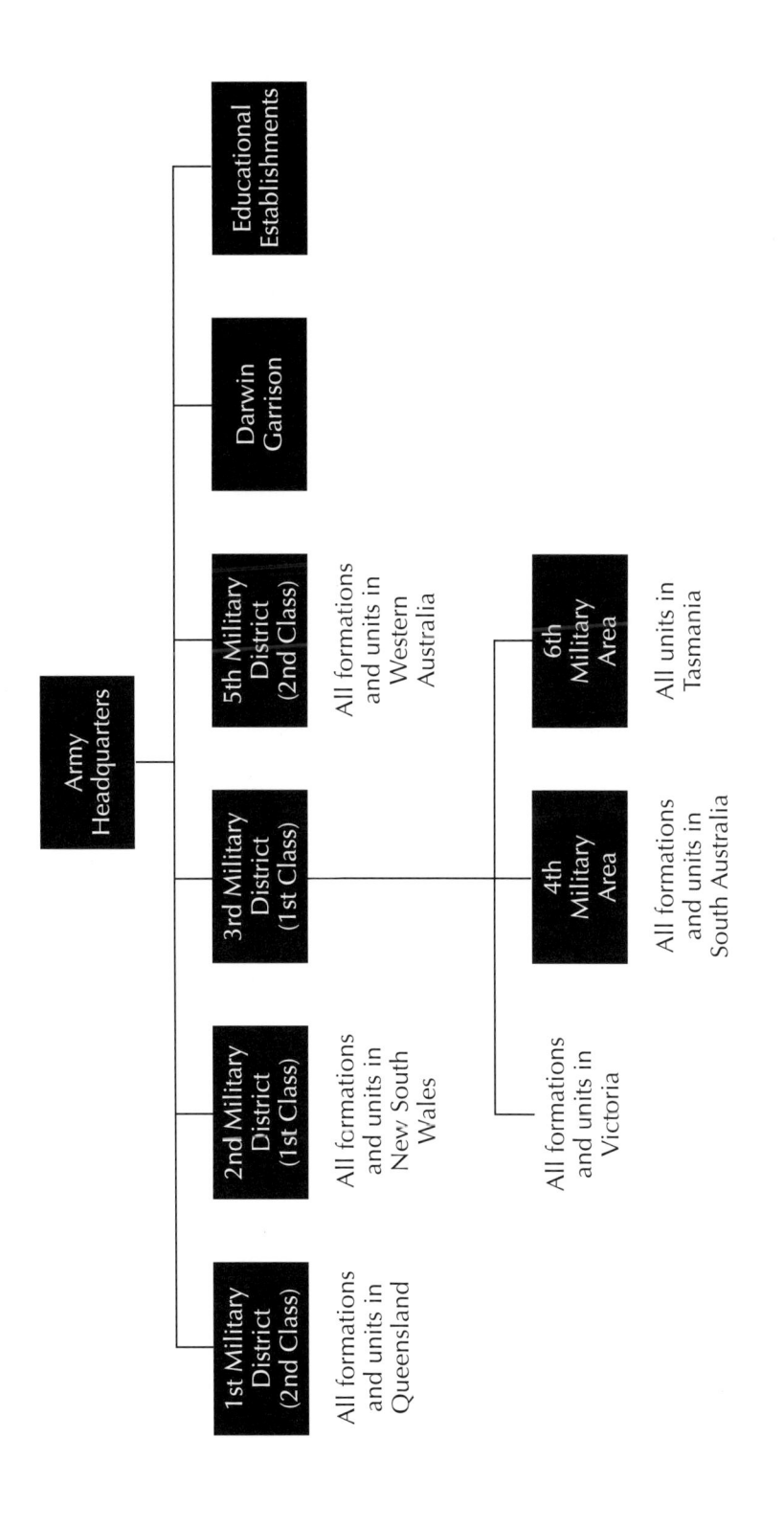

Chart 4 Squires' proposal to reform the geographic control of the army.
(Source: 'First Report by Lt.-Gen. E.K. Squires, Inspector-General of the AMF', AWM 54, item 243/6/58)

training establishment and created a severe shortage of training staff. Although the army had increased greatly in size, there was initially little improvement in the soldiers' level of skill. In mid 1939 Squires, now serving as acting CGS, noted that the state of effectiveness was not high. Despite the chaos, however, the expansion of the militia was long overdue.[99]

The sudden doubling of the militia created severe material shortages. Even for locally produced items, such as uniforms and boots, it would take time to satisfy demand. Many militiamen had to make do with World War I vintage weapons and uniforms. For example, as the government's arsenal at Lithgow had still not begun to produce Bren guns, the army had to issue obsolete Lewis guns. Technical equipment was even harder to obtain, and Menzies complained to British Prime Minister Neville Chamberlain over the delay in the delivery of critical fire-control instruments for the coastal guns and anti-aircraft batteries. Australia also depended on Britain for its tanks, modern field artillery, and anti-tank guns, as well as for much of its artillery ammunition. For example, the army reported in June 1939 that of the 64 2-pounder anti-tank guns it currently had on order, it expected to receive just four in the next few months, and could not state when it would receive any of the weapon's ammunition. The army had also ordered 350 Bren guns from Britain, but anticipated getting only 50 by the end of year, and a further unstated number in 1940.[100]

The expansion also had an effect on the size of the permanent forces, and led to a reinvigoration of the army's educational system. By mid 1939 the army had enlisted about 600 other ranks to make up most of the deficiencies in the coast and anti-aircraft establishment. It also appointed additional instructors to the Australian Instructional Corps and set up a special course at the Royal Military College to accelerate the production of officers for the staff corps. In August 1938, the army opened the Command and Staff School in Sydney for instruction of militia and permanent force officers in minor strategy, tactics, and administration. For the training of the field force, the army also reestablished its long-dormant Central Training Depot in Liverpool and reformed the Australian Army Service School on a permanent basis.[101]

Unfortunately, despite the threat of war, the primary determinant of security policy remained financial. The reaction of the government to the army's efforts to provide additional voluntary training for the militia serves as an example of the enduring influence of the Treasury. In mid September 1939, the Military Board took up a request from Squires that it remove the prohibition against militia receiving pay for attending more than two courses of instruction in any fiscal year. The government had imposed this restriction after World War I as an economy measure. The Military Board pointed out that even when it had implemented the restriction it had not been in the best interests of the citizen forces, and that 'at the present time, [Australia being in a state of war] the limitation to two schools must have a more serious effect'.[102] Street replied unfavourably two months later, noting that in order to limit expenditure he wanted the Military Board to continue to exercise its control over militia attendance at training courses.[103]

Moreover, in the face of increasingly aggressive moves by Germany and Japan, the long-term implications of Squires' comments were still not being heard in all quarters of the Australian defence hierarchy. The RAN, in particular, continued to insist upon the maintenance of maritime orthodoxy, which assured its position, through its affiliation with the Royal Navy, as Australia's first line of defence. In March 1939, the Naval Board announced that:

> the essential requirements of the Australian defence are a Navy to maintain ... the control of sea communications, an Army adequate to deal with raids, and an Air Force strong enough to co-operate with the Army and to locate and attack raiders by land and sea.[104]

To the absolute end, the complacency that dependence on Britain and the fleet offered proved an irresistible lure to some.

The major policy issue that dominated the interwar period, and which had the greatest effect upon the military's organisation, was the debate over whether the focus of army planning and structure should be on raids or invasion. The disagreement between the army's leaders and the nation's political decision-makers was more than simply a difference of opinion, however. Instead, it represented conflicting interpretations of national security policy. It therefore involved the broader subjects of the nation's reliance upon the Singapore Strategy, the ability of the empire to provide maritime security, the place of the army in the nation's defence hierarchy, and the degree of self-awareness of Australia as a sovereign state. The struggle over the need to plan against the possibility of raids or invasion also masked a broader conflict regarding whether the basis of Australian security should be external, and rest upon the empire, or if it should be internal, and rest upon self-reliance. The debate was never resolved, and the blame for its deleterious effect on the organisation and preparation of the army must be shared by both camps.

Throughout the interwar period, the only aspect of defence planning that appealed to the nation's political leaders was the containment of costs. The advancement of the Singapore Strategy at the 1923 Imperial Conference consequently held great appeal, as it provided Australia with the guise of security while at the same time transferring most of the expense to Britain. Despite the occasional small subsidy from Australia, British taxpayers bore the great expense of the Singapore base construction, as well as the maintenance of the fleet. With security seemingly guaranteed by the Royal Navy, the government believed that there was no need to keep an army on the scale that invasion defence required. Instead, it reduced the army to a skeleton establishment, a situation which the suspension of universal service only reinforced. Rather than invasion prevention, the government downgraded the army's role, and welcomed the Royal Navy as the primary defender of the nation.

Although it identified raid prevention as the army's first mission, the government's intractable determination to achieve defence on the cheap prevented the military from achieving the minimal level of efficiency required for even that relatively minor task. The government starved the army of funds to such an extent that it left the institution chronically under establishment, bereft of modern equipment, and so poor that training was impossible, except on the most basic level. From 1922 through 1938, the army consisted of skeleton formations that were so far under strength that even after linkage they more closely resembled social clubs than military units. The government's failure to provide meaningful resources to the formations of the first line component doomed that experiment to failure, even allowing for army reluctance. In the mid 1930s, the government did increase the army's vote, but nearly all the additional funds went to the modernisation of the coastal defences, and little was left over for the purchase of equipment and ammunition for the field force. The government's attitude towards its armed forces assured that military competence would decline from the high point of 1918, when Australian divisions were among the elite on the Western Front, to 1939 when, on the eve of war, the nation's army was virtually impotent.[105]

While the government's contribution to the sacrifice of Australian military effectiveness was more overt, the army's senior officers cannot escape from a share of the blame. Throughout this period, the nation's military leaders showed a consistent determination to ignore or subvert the wishes of their political masters. The government was quite clear in its policies: the army was to repel raids, and its principal effort, both in the preparation of plans and troops, was to be directed towards this task. However, the army repeatedly refused to accept this role. The officers were quite right to raise with the government their doubts about the viability of the Singapore Strategy and to question the politicians' unreasoning faith in the arrival of the Royal Navy. Yet their efforts contained a degree of obsessiveness that distracted them from their primary responsibility, that of preparing their forces as best they could with the limited resources that were available.

Furthermore, except for the initiative by Dodds in 1932, the army's leaders insisted on the retention of the seven-division structure that the Senior Officers' Conference recommended. Even after the cutbacks of 1922–23 and the abandonment of universal training in 1929, the army retained this organisation. The result was that the army's manpower was spread so thinly that nowhere in the force structure was there a unit whose strength approached its wartime establishment. The army had attempted to limit this effect by ending recruitment in the less populous areas, but even in urban Australia there were too many units for the available manpower. The military rationalised this problem by redefining the army's function away from that of preparing a field force capable of engaging an enemy to that of an institution for the training of leaders. The result was the nuclear army, in which the training of leaders received the highest priority and that of soldiers the lowest. Unfortunately, with the large number of formations and units requiring officers and the limited funds at their disposal, the army could not achieve either task with a great deal of efficiency, and the senior officers sacrificed competency for the preservation of structure.

Curiously, during the interwar period senior military leaders and political decision-makers reversed the policies to which they had held so tenaciously during the pre-World War I years. Before the Great War, politicians had adamantly denied any imperial responsibility for Australian military forces and had consistently refused to provide the British with a commitment in advance. Instead, they reserved the right to decide whether or not to assist the empire until after the commencement of hostilities. Parliament believed so strongly in this right that the Defence Act included a prohibition on compelling soldiers to serve overseas. After World War I, the nation's political leaders revised their opinion. While still honouring the intent of the Defence Act, they knowingly accepted an implied obligation to aid the empire through their adherence to the Singapore Strategy. At the 1923 Imperial Conference, Australia undertook a greater imperial duty than had existed previously. Moreover, as early as 1922, Prime Minister Hughes had required the army to develop a plan for the dispatch of a one-division expeditionary force. The army's response was Plan 401. It remained in force throughout the interwar period, and the government frequently made reference to the need for an expeditionary force in its organisational instructions to the army.[106]

On the other hand, army leaders before World War I had sought to define an imperial obligation for the field force. The officers corps welcomed participation in the Imperial General Staff, and the integration with the British Army that it brought. During the interwar period, the reverse was true. It was the officers who focused their efforts on the defence of Australia, downplayed participation in the imperial arena, and questioned the worth of Singapore. In 1936, Lavarack noted that conditions had changed since the drafting of Plan 401, particularly as a result of the dominant position Japan held in the Far East. He informed London that, while it was desirous to cooperate in imperial military operations, Australia must first assure its own defence. The CGS warned that the dispatch of a division would remove many trained officers and much of the army's equipment, though he thought it was possible for Australia to provide one or two brigades for garrison duty in the Pacific. In another communication with London, Lavarack told British leaders that Australian units might serve in the Far or Middle East but that he did not expect them to fight in Europe again. Clearly, the military approached the commitment of resources to an imperial war with some reluctance.[107]

By 1939, the government's position differed little from that which existed at Federation. In 1901, the defence scheme of New South Wales identified the maintenance of maritime supremacy as the key factor in shaping imperial security, and posited that the State need only worry about attack in the form of a raid, a policy that interwar politicians could easily have accepted.[108] Contemporary civilian defence reviewers failed to take into account that the relative power balance had changed, and if Japan had been a threat before 1914, it was an even greater danger after Versailles. The potential enemy was no longer a distant European rival but a relatively nearby Pacific power. To their discredit, the politicians appeared signally concerned with keeping the military estimate as low as possible, and for this reason they did not question the Singapore Strategy and the ability of the Royal Navy to provide maritime security. After Munich, Australian political leaders, like their opposites in London, began to emerge from a long slumber of national security indolence. However, while Australia accelerated its defence preparation efforts, they were, like Britain's, much too little and much too late. The nation would shortly become involved in a second struggle for national survival. However, as a result of its tardy rejuvenation, the army would go to war fundamentally unprepared on all levels.

5
WORLD WAR II

It is my melancholy duty to inform you officially that, in consequence of a persistence by Germany, in her invasion of Poland, Great Britain has declared war upon her and that, as a result, Australia is also at war.

Robert Menzies[1]

Upon Britain's declaration of war on Germany, Australia once again found itself supporting the 'mother country' in a struggle of survival against a European rival. Before making the above announcement, Menzies consulted neither his cabinet nor parliament, yet his action did not bring forth any criticism from the opposition. Instead, as at the beginning of World War I, the involvement of the Commonwealth was not questioned. Australia's entry, however, was more than simply a result of sentimental attachment to Britain. Throughout the interwar period, various Australian governments had linked the Commonwealth's security with the fate of the empire. Australia could neither stand alone in a great war nor stand by and allow the empire to fall.

Australian decision-makers accepted that, if Britain ever faced defeat, the well-being of the nation depended upon the consideration of Japan, an increasingly uncomfortable prospect, given Japanese expansionist ambition. On 25 August 1939, in an address to the nation, Menzies highlighted the reciprocal nature of Australia's defence relationship with Britain. He explained to the Australian people that 'we in Australia are involved because … the destruction or defeat of Great Britain would be the destruction of the British Empire and would leave us with a precarious tenure of our own independence'.[2] Australia's help against Germany was, therefore, a prerequisite for ensuring British assistance at a later date.[3] Shortly after the commencement of hostilities, Menzies summed up his nation's relationship with the 'mother country' in a speech he made to the British people. In it he stated 'your danger is our danger; your success will be our success; your peace will be our peace'.[4]

Although World War II was initially a conflict between European rivals, Australia found itself directly threatened once Japan entered the fray in December 1941. This event, followed quickly by the loss of Singapore, showed the validity of the army leadership's concerns regarding Britain's ability to come to the aid of Australia. The spread of the war to the Pacific also revealed the inadequacy of the nation's military preparations. World War II required the mobilisation of every aspect of Australian life for the defence of the nation. It also placed tremendous stress upon the army as it struggled to compensate for years of neglect and create an organisation that could defend the continent.

Mobilisation

On 24 August 1939, His Majesty's Government informed the Australian Government that it had presented a letter to Germany expressing Britain's determination to stand by its obligation to Poland. If Germany continued its hostile overtures towards Poland a European war was a certainty. On the same day, the Defence Committee met and undertook preliminary steps to increase Australia's readiness. The committee recommended the dispatch of additional troops to Darwin, the emergency installation of 6-inch guns at Port Kembla, the call-up of some militia soldiers to help the permanent garrisons of the coastal forts, and the placing of volunteer guards at vulnerable points. On the following day, the commandant at Darwin received instruction to enlist a local militia force of up to 250 men. On 1 September, Britain advised Australia to adopt the precautionary war stage against Germany. The next morning, the military districts received orders to man the coastal defences, although only with permanent troops. The announcement of the declaration of war followed on the 3rd.[5]

Despite the state of war, Australian mobilisation proceeded at a leisurely pace. Germany was a distant foe, with limited ability to project power into the Indian and Pacific Oceans. Instead, the Australian Government was much more concerned with the intentions of Japan. After Germany's swift conquest of Poland, the onset of the 'phoney war' further exacerbated an Australian preference to augment its military capabilities by steady, measured increments, all the while seeking assurances from Britain regarding its commitment to the Far East. On 3 September, the government did not call out the entire militia, but mobilised only 8,000 soldiers, and then for just 16 days. Some of these replaced the volunteer guards protecting vulnerable points, while the rest manned the coastal and anti-aircraft defences and provided internal security. The government neither considered the full mobilisation of the army necessary at this time nor was prepared to activate even the first line component.[6]

On 11 September, the Military Board secured Street's permission to activate the garrison battalions from the AIF Reserve. By 29 October, the army had raised the equivalent of eight battalions of these older soldiers. Table 5.1 shows the distribution and strength of these units.

Table 5.1 Distribution and strength of garrison battalions, October 1939[7]

Command	No. of units	Establishment: officers	Establishment: other ranks
Northern Command	1 battalion	34	617
Eastern Command	2 battalions	45	858
Southern Command	4 battalions less two companies	62	1,191
Western Command	1 battalion	23	358
7th Military District	1 company	nil	14
Total personnel		*164*	*3,038*

The army had not fixed establishments for the garrison units, and commandants varied their size according to local conditions. By mid October, the garrison formations had relieved the militia of their guard duties. For example, Southern Command raised the 3rd and 9th Garrison Battalions for the defence of the Port Phillip Fortress. Once needed, the garrison battalions also provided internal security and served as guards at prisoner-of-war and internment camps. By January, these formations had expanded to a strength of 4,967 officers and men.[8]

The army continued to raise garrison battalions, and after Japan's entry into the war there were nearly twenty of these formations. Table 5.2 (p. 138) shows the distribution and strength of the garrison battalions in early 1942.

The next step in improving the state of the army was taken on 15 September, when Menzies informed the public of the government's decision to call up the militia in batches of 40,000 for month-long periods of training. The goal was to complete as much individual training as possible while at the same time having about half of the militia under arms. In recommending this step, the Military Board made it clear that it believed the improvement of the army's home defence capability was the priority. While acknowledging the German threat, the Military Board feared Japanese intervention even more, and it sought to bring 'the Militia Forces up to the highest possible standard of efficiency'.[10] During the same speech, Menzies also revealed the government's intention to raise a special force of 20,000 for service in Australia or overseas. This would become the 2nd AIF.[11]

Table 5.2 Disposition and strength of garrison battalions, early 1942[9]

Commands	Coastal defence	Internal security	Personnel
Northern	1 battalion	2 battalions	2,821
Eastern	5 battalions	1 battalion	3,658
Southern: 3rd MD	2 battalions	1 battalion	1,369
Southern: 4th MD	1 battalion	1 battalion	1,109
Southern: 6th MD	1 battalion	1 company	694
Western	3 battalions	1 company	2,422
Total personnel	*13 battalions*	*5 battalions and 2 companies*	*12,073*

On 20 October, Menzies announced his intention to maintain the militia at a strength of approximately 75,000. However, the government realised that the militia would inevitably be depleted as soldiers became ineligible for continued service because of their work in a reserved occupation or as a result of their transfer to the 2nd AIF. By mid November, the militia's strength was approaching 60,000. To offset these losses, Menzies accepted the need to reintroduce universal service, which had been suspended since 1929. The first intake under the new scheme required all unmarried men who became 21 during the year ending 30 June 1940 to report for a three-month period of training commencing on 1 January 1940. The majority of this three-month period was spent on individual skills, but for the final 12 days the new soldiers served in militia units. At the end of the three months, the universal servicemen passed into reserve status. Their remaining obligation was to attend an annual refresher camp of 12 days and to report for 12 days of home training. The army also hoped that some men might volunteer to serve in the militia. Universal service did not apply to the cavalry because of the continuing need for a soldier to provide his own mount.[12]

Also to begin in January was another round of militia training. The training was again undertaken in batches of approximately 40,000 men, but this time for a term of three months. The objective of this period was to continue individual training, but also to advance to combined arms, brigade, and possibly divisional exercises. There was one exception to the three-month obligation. The army allowed married privates to leave camp after only one month, on hardship grounds, after which they would pass into the reserves. The army estimated that 12,000 soldiers would be eligible for this status. In March 1940, Menzies announced another round of training as the government called up two further quotas of universal trainees.[13]

The consequence of these schemes was that the army had troops simultaneously in several different training streams with different degrees of obligation. The militia were continuing to improve their efficiency through a series of one-month, then three-month, camps. The universal service trainees were receiving a foundation in individual military skills, then briefly joining their militia units. The senior officers of the 2nd AIF were organising their units and preparing for possible overseas service. None of these steps, however, brought the units that made up the field force up to war establishment. With a manpower goal of only 75,000, militia battalions remained severely understaffed. Furthermore, the universal service obligation did not directly contribute to the size of militia units because, after only a brief period of service with a battalion, these soldiers became reservists. They would provide a pool of partially trained men to fill out the field force in case of a general mobilisation but, as Australia entered 1940, the army remained part time and under strength. The only troops that were on actual operational duty were the permanent forces and the over-age soldiers of the garrison battalions.

Instead of showing the same alacrity with which the government of 1914 agreed to an expeditionary force, the Menzies Government approached the creation of the 2nd AIF with extreme caution. The Prime Minister had swiftly approved the transfer of the RAN to Admiralty control, and on 20 September he had agreed to the dispatch overseas of an Air Expeditionary Force. Then, a few weeks later, the government agreed to expand its aerial commitment to include participation in the Empire Air Training Scheme. However, Menzies and his military advisers proved reluctant to send overseas ground forces that they thought they might need for home defence. The Australian Chiefs of Staff noted that only if Japan was friendly could they recommend the dispatch of large numbers of ground troops, an opinion the War Cabinet shared. The War Cabinet also voiced concerns over constraints upon manpower as a reason to limit the nation's level of commitment to a ground expeditionary force. In an analysis prepared in late September, the Military Board recommended the postponement of the formation of the 2nd AIF until after the militia had completed their month-long training periods and until more equipment became available. The Military Board feared that the 2nd AIF would deprive the militia of some of its best leaders and men at a time when the nation most needed their services. It suggested that the government allow the 2nd AIF only to borrow from the militia the equipment it needed for training, and if the force proceeded overseas Britain should provide its weaponry. The Military Board then concluded that the raising of the new force should not prejudice the development of the militia.[14]

Even after agreeing to form the 2nd AIF, the government still hesitated before deciding to send it overseas. In late October, the government informed Britain that the force's period of training in Australia would allow an opportunity for the international position to clarify itself. While visiting London, the Minister for Supply and Development, R.G. Casey, told British authorities that the attitude of Japan determined whether or not the 2nd AIF proceeded to Britain. The British Chiefs of Staff replied by highlighting the manpower advantage Germany enjoyed, and stressed the hope that Australia would not only send the existing division but raise a second. It was not until Menzies received assurances from Winston Churchill, serving as First Lord of the Admiralty, that he allowed the 2nd AIF to go overseas. However, as Australia would discover, Churchill's verbal support was not the same as a commitment. On 29 November, Menzies stated in Parliament that the 2nd AIF would proceed overseas as soon as it had reached a suitable standard of training. Early in January 1940, the first elements of the 2nd AIF embarked for the Middle East for further training before proceeding to France. However, Italy's entry into the war kept the Australians in the Mediterranean.[15]

The last source of official resistance to mobilisation was the Treasury Department. In the official history of the war, Gavin Long wrote that 'Treasury officials seemed resolved that the war should not be an excuse for undue extravagance on the part of the services'. Having been starved for resources throughout the interwar period, the army continued to have difficulty in obtaining the equipment it required during the war's opening months. For example, Treasury initially refused a modest submission from the Minister for Supply and Development for the purchase of 784 vehicles for the 2nd AIF. Additionally, financial considerations were the grounds for the denial of a request to establish a factory to build 25-pounder guns to replace the army's obsolete 18-pounders and build a second plant for the manufacture of munitions. The army eventually got these facilities, but only after some delay.[16]

Raising two armies

The decision to raise the 2nd AIF placed the army in the same situation it faced when it had to form the 1st AIF. The Defence Act limited the employment of the existing military force, both the militia and the permanent forces, to the defence of Australia. The law allowed for conscription, but only for domestic service. If the government wished to dispatch troops overseas, it had to raise a special force of volunteers. In early 1939, the government extended the compulsory territorial obligation of service to include all non-mainland Australian possessions, such as Papua, but empire defence still remained outside the army's mandate. As a result, the army had to again manage two distinct armies, the AIF for overseas service and the permanent forces and the militia for home defence.

While the formation of the 2nd AIF created the same problems for the army's organisation as had the raising of the 1st AIF in World War I, the strategic situation was different and more dangerous, especially after Pearl Harbor. The need to maintain two armies led to an over-expansion of the force's structure, placed an enormous strain upon the provision of equipment, and ultimately helped unbalance the nation's economy. The two-army system also created a legacy of poor relations between the members of the 2nd AIF and the militia, which carried over into the present, and tarnished the post-war structure of what was to become the Australian Regular Army (ARA) and the Citizen Military Force (CMF). During the interwar period, the army had suggested to the government that it change the Defence Act in order to prevent a recurrence of the two-army system. However, the subject of army effectiveness almost never roused the interwar governments to action. In addition, the issue was fraught with political danger, which reinforced the politicians' preference to avoid military matters. Instead of necessary reform, the government preferred to ignore one of the most important and obvious lessons of World War I, and instead chose to maintain the status quo. The government's inability to act doomed the military to a repetition of the two-army system. As a result, its failure to change the Defence Act was one of the great mistakes of interwar defence policy.[17]

The outbreak of the war also led to a modification in the terms which the army employed to identify its branches. The army began the war using the term 'militia' for its volunteer non-permanent forces. Gradually a new designator emerged for this body, the 'Citizen Military Forces' or CMF. The exact date of the transition is not known. Well into 1940, the correct term was militia, but by 1942 CMF had entered into general usage. Till the war's end, militia remained acceptable and understood, although by 1945 CMF was the preferred term. When the army reraised its forces after the war, it gave the new force the title 'Citizen Military Forces'. Since the government did not merge the AIF into the home army (the permanent forces and the CMF) after its return to Australia in 1942, it was necessary to develop a new term that encompassed all the branches of the force. Consequently, the army introduced the designation Australian Military Forces or AMF. It allowed the army to include within a single institution all of its various categories of service: AIF, CMF, and Permanent Forces.

As in World War I, Australia initially suggested to Britain a force of 20,000 men, again organised into an infantry division and a cavalry brigade. The War Office accepted both, although Australia subsequently withdrew the offer of a mounted unit and focused its attention on the infantry.[18] The army raised the infantry division on a regional basis and designated it the 6th, since there were already five, or equivalent, militia infantry divisions in existence. Victoria and New South Wales each contributed a brigade group, while the remaining states combined to provide the third brigade. The government had intended to recruit approximately half of the 6th Division's personnel from the militia, but lack of government enthusiasm and a hesitancy by militia officers to leave the nation unprotected resulted in the majority of the ranks being filled from elsewhere. The Military Board decided to utilise the identification number of a militia battalion from each region in which the division recruited in order to maintain a link to the local unit and to the AIF of World War I. To distinguish the AIF from the militia, every expeditionary unit that duplicated a militia unit received as a prefix the number '2' identifying it as part of the 2nd AIF. The army later extended this to all AIF units. The sharing of titles was destined to be the only connection between the militia and the AIF, and henceforth the two organisations developed as completely separate entities. Table 5.3 outlines the order of battle of the major AIF formations as they existed in 1941.[19]

Table 5.3 Organisation of the 2nd AIF: major formations, 1941

Division	Brigades
6th Division	16th, 17th, 19th Brigades
7th Division	18th, 21st, 25th Brigades
8th Division	22nd, 23rd, 27th Brigades
9th Division	20th, 24th, 26th Brigades

One of the principles of interwar defence policy had been the desire to establish uniform standards in order to promote inter-operability between formations of the different members of the empire. In practice, this meant that the member states of the empire tended to adopt the British organisation. However, when the army organised the 6th Division, it did so on the Australian standard, which was largely unchanged since World War I. Unfortunately, there were a number of significant differences between the British and Australian structures. Most importantly, the Australian infantry brigade once again had four battalions, whereas the British version contained only three. The 6th Division's artillery establishment included three field brigades, each containing three batteries of four 18-pounder guns and one battery of four 4.5-inch howitzers, while a British division had three field regiments, each containing two batteries of twelve 25-pounder guns. The British division's 72 modern dual-purpose weapons represented considerably greater firepower than the Australian version of 48 obsolete weapons. Additionally, the British structure contained a number of units that did not appear on the Australian table of organisation, for example, a motorised reconnaissance regiment, a machine-gun battalion, an anti-tank regiment, and numerous light aid detachments. Also of consequence was the fact that the Australian formation contained a higher number of infantry and service personnel, so that it had a strength approximately 25 per cent higher than that of a British division. Table 5.4 compares the establishments of the Australian and British divisional structures.

Table 5.4 Comparison of Australian and British divisional structures for the 6th Division[20]

Arm or formation	Strength: Australian standard	Strength: British standard	Deficit (−) Surplus (+)
Headquarters	159	184	−25
Reconnaissance Regt.	440	444	−4
Infantry	9,621	6,417	+3,204
Artillery	2,345	2,374	−29
Engineers	910	933	−23
Signals	534	491	+43
Army Service Corps	1,576	1,183	+393
Miscellaneous	943	941	−2
Total	*16,528*	*12,967*	*+3,561*

The two armies also organised their infantry battalions on different standards. In the Australian Army, each infantry battalion consisted of a headquarters company, three rifle companies (including Lewis guns), and a support company of machine-guns and 3-inch mortars. The British equivalent contained four smaller rifle companies (including Bren guns and 2-inch mortars), but a larger and more powerful headquarters company consisting of seven platoons (signals, mortar, carrier, pioneer, anti-aircraft, transport, and administrative). The British model was more mobile, and possessed an abundance of firepower, in the form of 52 Bren guns and increased mortar support, despite having fewer troops. An Australian battalion had nearly 800 officers and men, while a British battalion's strength was less than 700.[21]

In March 1939, Squires had suggested that the Australian Army should change its battalion organisation to the imperial establishment, but nothing came of his idea. While the 6th Division remained in Australia the difference in organisation did not matter, and it made more sense for the AIF to have the same structure as the militia. However, with the decision to move the AIF overseas, it proved necessary to reorganise the 6th Division formation and to raise subsequent AIF divisions on the British standard. Consequently, each Australian brigade lost a battalion, the three surplus becoming part of the 7th Division. The battalions also had to reconfigure their companies to the British arrangement and give up some of their personnel. The artillery also switched to the regiment pattern of two 12-gun batteries, but Australia was unable to provide any 25-pounders. Instead the batteries of the 6th Division each contained eight 18-pounders and four 4.5-inch howitzers, at least until re-equipped.[22]

Besides two reorganisations, the 6th Australian Division faced daunting material shortages, a legacy of the government's unwillingness to provide sufficient stockpiles of equipment. Additionally, the government had never purchased most of the non-divisional equipment that the Senior Officers Conference had recommended. Therefore, many of the AIF's non-divisional and corps formations were dependent on equipment transfers from Britain. Exacerbating the situation was the fact that the government made no provision in the army's reserve stocks for the creation of additional divisions, even though the Defence Act implied the possibility of this requirement, since the militia could not serve overseas.

In November 1939, Squires, now serving as CGS, cabled Major-General John Northcott, who was in London accompanying the Minister for Supply and Development. The CGS sent Northcott a long list of deficiencies in 6th Division equipment. Squires wanted to know what items Britain could supply. He noted that, if the division was to sail in a timely manner, it would do so without approximately two-thirds of its motor transport and with none of its carriers. He mentioned to Northcott the substitution of 1,500 horses for divisional transport, but advised against this measure, hoping that the War Office could provide sufficient vehicles. As for weapons, the division would have no 25-pound guns, 2-pound anti-tank guns, anti-tank rifles, or 2-inch mortars. Australia could provide plenty of rifles, and the required 48 Vickers guns for the machine-gun battalion, but the militia would need the Lewis guns back once Britain had issued Bren guns to the division. The formation did not have much of its signal and engineering stores, and even basic items such as tents would have to come from Britain.[23]

The 6th Division was only the first of several AIF formations. Australia would announce the raising of the 7th Division on 28 February 1940, the 8th Division on 22

May 1940, the 9th Division in early June 1940, and the 1st Armoured Division on 1 January 1941. The 6th, 7th, and 9th Divisions served in the Mediterranean theatre until their return to Australia to fight the Japanese. The 8th Division lost two of its brigades in the doomed defence of Malaya and Singapore, and most of its other elements surrendered to the Japanese on Timor, Ambon, and New Britain. 1st Armoured Division spent most of the war performing garrison duties in Western Australia, although some of its units served in the island campaigns. The army also raised a number of minor AIF formations, such as the independent companies, which served in Timor, New Guinea, and New Caledonia, as well as considerable numbers of corps, support, and service units.

In March 1940, Menzies announced Australia's intention to provide a corps headquarters and corps troops to support the AIF in the Mediterranean. This was a substantial undertaking, as a British corps had an establishment of more than 16,000, over

1st Armoured Division at Puckapunyal, 1942, parading with General Grant M3 Medium Tanks. (AWM 012691)

and above the men in the divisions allocated to the corps. However, a corps would significantly enhance the combat capability of the AIF, as it contained a number of powerful units. To establish the corps, the army had to raise for the AIF two medium artillery regiments, a survey regiment, three anti-aircraft regiments, three machine-gun battalions, and three pioneer battalions. The corps also contained numerous support units, such as light aid detachments, casualty clearing stations, workshops, signal units, and supply detachments.[24] In mid 1941, the War Office approached the Australian Government regarding the possibility of the Commonwealth providing a second corps headquarters and support units for the Mediterranean. The two corps would consist of the three Australian infantry divisions and the New Zealand Division. Britain also sought additional formations, such as an Army tank brigade and a greater flow of replacements. The War Cabinet reviewed the suggestion and concluded that Australia did not have the manpower to meet all these requests. Australia agreed to provide an army tank brigade and more replacements, but the War Cabinet concluded that a second corps establishment was beyond the nation's means. Australia, at least for the distant campaign in the Middle East, had reached the limit of its manpower.[25]

The effect on the home army of the raising of the 2nd AIF repeated many of the difficulties that had occurred during World War I. The governments of both conflicts professed the same intention—that the raising of an expeditionary force was not to impede the development of the home army. One of the reasons for Menzies' and the army's reluctance to dispatch troops overseas, in the face of unclear Japanese intentions, was the realisation that an overcommitment to the AIF could have a detrimental effect upon the militia. During the 'phoney war' the government remained averse to the removal overseas of equipment from the militia, and even demanded the return to the home army of some items on loan to the AIF.[26] In January 1940, Squires asked the Military Board if it intended to maintain the current organisation of the army—five infantry and two mounted divisions.[27] The Military Board affirmed the existing structure, explaining that 'it is essential to maintain the present organization of the Militia in order to provide for a minimum basis for mobilization of the Army, if required for co-operation in the defence of the Commonwealth'. The Military Board also recommended that the army try to retain as many of its officers, non-commissioned officers, and specialists as possible, as it needed them to train the universal enlistees.[28]

However, in both world wars, the demands of the active theatre naturally took priority. As the AIF grew, it attracted personnel away from the militia. For example, in September 1940 the AIF had a strength of over 114,000, of which 84,000 were undergoing training in Australia. The CMF, by contrast, had only 80,000 soldiers, of which only half were actually under arms.[29] In June 1940, after the debacle in France, the government decided to increase the size of the forces maintained at home to 75,000. However, only 22,000 of these were on full-time duty, while conscripts undergoing training made up the remainder.[30] Shortly after the expansion of the war to the Pacific, the home army had an available strength of only 73.9 per cent of its war establishment. Table 5.5 compares the establishment and available strength of the CMF in early 1942. Japan's attack also found the army short of training facilities, equipment, and instructors, which further delayed the development of the CMF.

Table 5.5 Comparison of CMF field force war establishment and available strength, early 1942[31]

Region	War establishment	In camp or full-time deployment
Northern Command	16,940	12,071
Eastern Command	56,263	34,625
Southern Command	58,980	51,323
Western Command	9,295	8,186
7th Military District	8,190	7,075
8th Military District	5,181	3,246
Total	*152,849*	*116,526*

By July 1940, the militia was still far from the desired standard of efficiency. In a message to Stanley Bruce, the High Commissioner in London, Menzies complained, 'we [Australia] would not relish having to defend ourselves against even a minor attack from Japan in less than a year from now.'[32] Even after the militia had completed its cycle of three months' training, the Department of Defence noted, 'the amount of training carried out by the Militia during the year 1939–40 was not sufficient to enable them to reach a standard which would fit them for active service, but was a valuable contribution towards that objective.'[33] On the eve of Pearl Harbor, serious deficiencies remained, and one historian considered the army's state of readiness to be only 40 per cent.[34] At any one time, only 30 per cent of units were on full-time duty, while most of the force remained on a rotation of three-month camps that, a battalion history suggests, provided little continuity and, at best, fragmentary and inadequate training.[35] Immediately after the Japanese intervention, the Chiefs of Staff signalled their recognition of the unpreparedness of the militia when they recommended to the government that the time had now come for the nation to establish and train the forces it would require to prevent invasion. Horner has sarcastically noted, 'one would have thought that this would have been an admirable aim a year earlier.'[36] Instead, during 1940–41, the AIF became a veteran organisation, while the CMF remained a part-time army of green troops who were expected to take the field only if Japan attacked. In the opinion of one militia unit, the militia had become little more than training cadres for the AIF.[37] It is not surprising, therefore, that the AIF emerged as the more important of the two forces.

If the home army's condition was still less than efficient, the state of its equipment only served to compound the problem. Despite two years of war the CMF remained poorly armed, and one senior general noted that if the government called up the entire militia it would be impossible to equip them as well as the AIF remaining in Australia. An inventory of equipment compiled at the end of November 1941 showed the army under establishment in nearly all categories. Some, such as tanks, were virtually non-existent, while others, namely anti-tank guns and anti-aircraft guns, were at approximately 50 per cent of requirements. The munitions industry was unable even to keep up with the call on basic items, such as rifles and grenades, which were at 73 per cent and 31 per cent of demand. Mechanical transport was also under strength, as the army had only 16 per cent of its motorcycles, 47 per cent of its light and medium trucks, and 13 per cent of its heavy trucks. The field artillery was at establishment, but only if it included the obsolete 18-pounders and 4.5-inch howitzers. Ammunition stockpiles were also well below establishment. The army had only 25 per cent of its requirements for the field artillery, 15 per cent for its 3.7-inch anti-aircraft guns, and only a mere 1 per cent for the 2-pound anti-tank gun.[38]

Exacerbating the growing differences between the AIF and the CMF was the fact that the overseas force had evolved into a completely separate institution from that of the home army. The AIF had its own seniority list (at least until 1942) and its own establishment, and would develop its own *esprit de corps*. While in Australia, the AIF trained in camps separate from the CMF. Administratively the AIF was also kept independent from the Army's normal chain of command and its commander, General Sir Thomas Blamey, reported directly to the Minister for the Army instead of the Military Board.[39] An additional source of tension within Australia's military forces was the conflict between the Staff Corps and the militia officers regarding command appointments in the AIF, a legacy of interwar grievances.[40]

As long as the AIF remained an expeditionary force, the effects of the two-army system, while debilitating, did not directly affect the organisation of the army in Australia. This changed when Japan entered the war and the AIF returned home. Part of the

General Sir Thomas Blamey. (AWM 141838)

problem was that the two forces did not have the same establishment. The army had reorganised the AIF onto the British standard, while the militia units remained on the pre-war Australian establishment. Although the differences were not large, it would require an enormous reposting of men and equipment to standardise the force.[41]

The CMF also experienced a continual drain of manpower as soldiers volunteered for the AIF. For a brief period the government prohibited militiamen from joining the AIF, but it soon removed this restriction. Even when in effect, it only applied to the actual posting of the soldier, since militiamen remained able to volunteer for the AIF on the condition that they remain with their CMF units, on an AIF reserve list, until required elsewhere. Despite the government's stated policy of maintaining the strength of the CMF, it was soon encouraging CMF officers and men to join the AIF. As early as February 1940, Southern Command actively sought militia officers for the 6th Australian Division's reinforcement contingent. The army also called upon the CMF to provide the manpower needed to create the AIF training establishment. After the entry of Japan, volunteers swamped the AIF recruiting stations far in excess of its requirements. The army enrolled these soldiers as part of the AIF, but posted the excess to CMF formations. Since the sole purpose of the CMF had always been the defence of Australia, perhaps it would have been more appropriate for these soldiers to have either joined or remained in the militia. However, the status of the AIF was such that the threat of invasion became an occasion to further weaken the CMF while enhancing the AIF.[42]

Despite the pressure on the CMF, during the war's early years the army largely succeeded in maintaining the force's organisation. While the army merged a few battalions and unlinked others because of fluctuations in strength, from the war's beginning up to Japan's intervention the divisions continued to resemble the organisation that the army had raised in 1920. However, after the Japanese thrust southwards, the army could no longer retain the prewar system, and instead the CMF followed an unstable existence of frequent reorganisation. In a race to provide a force capable of defending the continent, the army swapped formations and units throughout the force, assigning the most combat-ready units to the most critical areas. This meant that prewar brigades and battalions were broken up and redistributed to other divisional headquarters according to training and equipment standards. The AIF divisions were also affected by structural changes, but their reorganisations were never as frequent or as determined as those experienced by the CMF.

Even after the immediate threat of invasion passed, land headquarters continued to transfer CMF brigades and battalions freely among its divisions. Partially this was a result of the need to balance the field command structure and declining manpower levels with operational requirements. But more importantly, the lack of stability in CMF formations was also a legacy of the force's neglect during the interwar period. When Australia met the Japanese challenge in New Guinea, there was no CMF division that was fully ready for the challenge. Instead, the army assigned elements as they were available. In effect, CMF divisional headquarters were administrative and command holding cells that controlled a shifting array of units. As a consequence, the pre-war order of battle was virtually unrecognisable by mid 1943. It was not until after the army's adoption of the jungle division standard that the CMF achieved a degree of stability, and then only for the three divisions that the force converted. The remaining non-jungle standard divisions continued to change to the war's end as the army responded to contracting personnel establishments. Therefore, for much of the war the CMF was an unstable institution whose structure constantly changed in pursuit of shifting organisational policies.

The radical changes this policy caused in the organisation of the 3rd Division provides some idea of how frequently the army moved formations and units among its CMF divisions headquarters. Table 5.6 outlines the organisation of the 3rd Division in September 1939.

Table 5.6 Organisation of the 3rd Division, September 1939[43]

Formation	Battalions
HQ 4th Infantry Brigade	14th, 22nd, 29th, 46th Battalions
HQ 10th Infantry Brigade	24th/39th, 37th, 52nd Battalions
HQ 15th Infantry Brigade	57th/60th, 58th, 59th Battalions

After the 3rd Division moved to Queensland in 1942, it broke up the 10th Brigade in an effort to bring the rest of its units up to strength. When the division transferred to New Guinea for the Salamaua Campaign in 1943, it had under its command the 15th Brigade, 29th Brigade (15th, 42nd, and 47th Battalions) and the 17th Brigade AIF (2/5th, 2/6th, 2/7th Battalions). This represented one of the few occasions when a CMF headquarters commanded an AIF formation. Towards the end of the campaign, the Headquarters 5th Division took over and the Headquarters 3rd Division rotated back to Australia. The 3rd Division's troops remained in New Guinea, but served under a different headquarters. In 1944, the 3rd Division was reconstituted in Australia as a jungle division but without the AIF troops. When it deployed to Bougainville in early 1945, it retained the 15th and 29th Brigades and gained the 7th

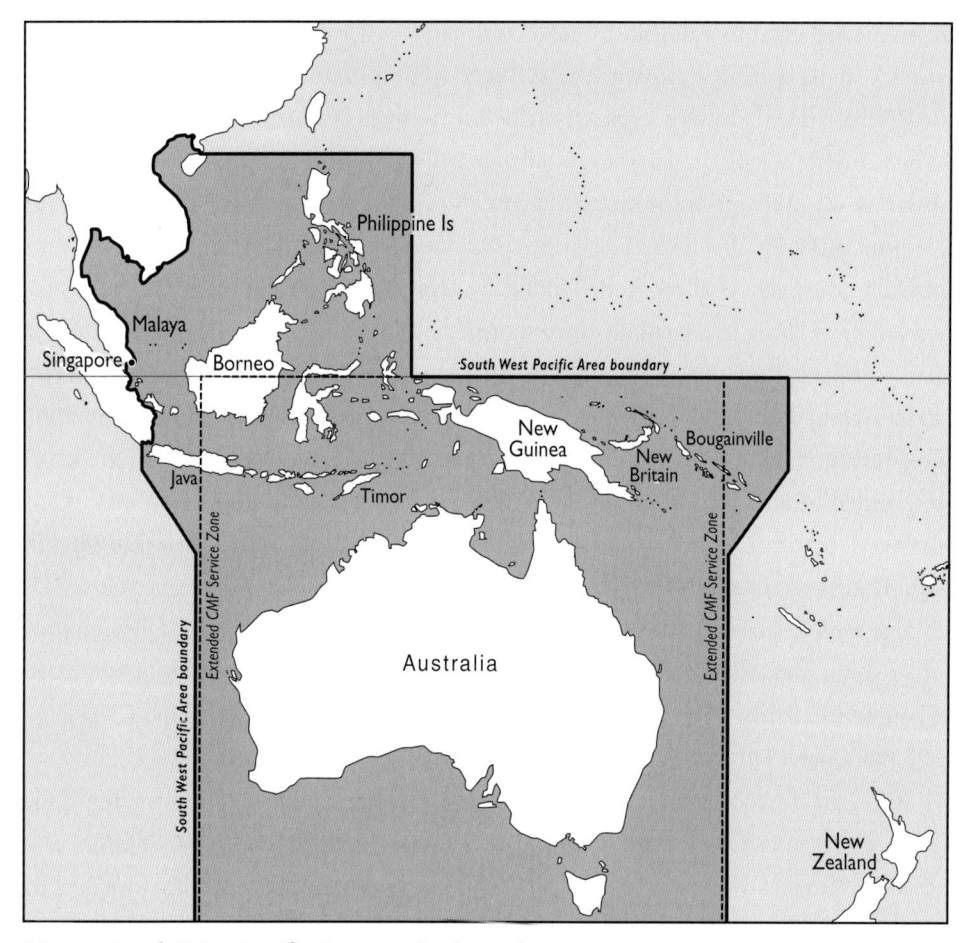

Map 6 South-West Pacific Area service boundary

Brigade (9th, 25th, 61st Battalions). The 3rd Division was actually one of the more stable CMF formations, and it survived to the war's end. Other CMF formations simply disappeared, either through amalgamation or disbandment.

Of the army's main branches, the AIF also became the larger. For example, by September 1943 it had over 265,000 members, while the CMF's establishment was only slightly more than 117,000. Over the course of the war, over 206,000 personnel opted to transfer out of the militia into the AIF. The army also allowed militia formations to become AIF units if 65 per cent of the war establishment voted to join the expeditionary force. When this happened, however, it sometimes resulted in the shake-up of an established unit as the Adjutant-General reassigned those who refused to volunteer and replaced them with transferees from within the AIF establishment. For example, the army had to replace 617 men of the 39th Infantry Brigade when it became an AIF formation. As a consequence, the army was frequently in a state of flux, with soldiers and units changing organisations as they moved from CMF to AIF status.[44]

The soldiers of the two forces also enlisted under different terms of service. The AIF could be sent anywhere, while under the Defence Act the CMF had to serve in either Australia or its territories. On 19 February 1943, the government of John Curtin, who had become Prime Minister in October 1941, extended the territorial obligation of the militiamen to most of the South-West Pacific Area. However, the effective removal of the territorial limitation was politically impossible.[45] Despite now having the ability to serve outside Australian territory, few CMF soldiers did. Australia continued to maintain two distinct armies, and defined their area of operations by the type of troops. The CMF fought the Japanese, but almost entirely in territories that met the definition of the traditional terms of service. The only significant citizen soldier body to serve outside Commonwealth territory was the 11th Brigade, which garrisoned Merauke in Dutch New Guinea, less than 50 miles from Australian Papua. When the war moved on, it was the AIF that landed in Borneo while the CMF remained in the war's backwaters, fighting isolated enemy garrisons in New Guinea, New Britain, and Bougainville, all mandated territories. Lastly, if the invasion of Japan proved necessary, Australia planned to use the AIF. Map 6 illustrates the CMF service boundary within the South-West Pacific Area.

If the AIF and the CMF spent the war largely as separate branches of the army, the one area of shared interest was the army's school organisation. The mobilisation and enormous growth of the army during World War II greatly increased the force's need for trained leaders, staff officers, and specialists. Unfortunately, because of the government's fiscal policy, the army's schools had languished throughout the interwar period. Most schools spent the years between the wars either dormant, for example, the Central Training Depot, or listed on the force's order of battle as not maintained in peace, for example, the gas school. Except for the Royal Military College and the artillery school, most army schools passed the interwar period in, at best, a notional existence. Thus the army had to create an educational system virtually in its entirety.

By early 1944, the army possessed an extensive educational system providing technical training in all aspects of the waging of a modern war. Table 5.7 (p. 154) provides an outline of the army's school organisation.

By the end of the war the Australian Army had an extensive and well-defined training and educational organisation. More importantly, most of it survived into the postwar period. Thus, the wartime expansion of the school organisation laid an enduring foundation for the continued training and professional development of army personnel to the present.

Table 5.7 Organisation of the army's school system, February 1944[46]

School	Location	Student capacity	
Royal Military College	Duntroon, ACT	93	
Staff School	Duntroon, ACT	16	Senior Wing,
		56	Junior Wing
Tactical School	Beenleigh, QLD	24	Senior Wing,
		28	Junior Wing,
		28	Jungle Defence Wing
Armoured Fighting Vehicle School	Puckapunyal, VIC	90	
School of Artillery (Field)	Holsworthy, NSW	139	
School of Artillery (AA)	Randwick, NSW	324	
School of Searchlights	Middle Head, NSW	66	
School of Radio Physics	Sydney, NSW	60	
School of Military Engineering	Liverpool, NSW	487	
Camouflage Development and Training Centre	St Georges Heights, NSW	21	
School of Signals	Bonegilla, VIC	95	
Small Arms School	Bonegilla, VIC	120	
Officer Cadet Training Unit	Woodside, SA	250	
School of Mechanisation	Seymour, VIC	130	
AASC School	North Geelong, VIC	166	
AAOC School	Broadmeadows, VIC	135	
E&ME School	Ingleburn, NSW	350	
AAMC School	Ivanhoe, VIC	26	
School of Tropical Medicine	Sydney, NSW	34	
Gas School	Cabarlah, QLD	80	
School of Military Intelligence	Southport, NSW	102	
School of Physical Training	Frankston, VIC	60	
School of Army Cooperation	Canberra, ACT	15	
School of Hygiene & Sanitation	Sydney, NSW	30	
Army Women's Service Officers' School	Melbourne, VIC	60	
School of Army Education	Glenfield, NSW	40	
School of Army Cooking and Catering	Chermside, QLD	30	
Provost Training School	Darley, VIC	60	
School of Malaria Control	Brisbane, QLD	16	
School of Military Law	as arranged	30	
LHQ Army Women's Services Adm. (Officers) School	Melbourne, VIC	24	
School of Army Education (Women's Service)	Keilor, VIC	30	
Army Women's Service's Supervisory Personnel Course	Darley, VIC	40	
Australian Army Medical Women's Service Training School	Darley, VIC	120	

Expansion of the coastal defence, anti-aircraft, and support organisation

Although the Australian Government began the modernisation of the coastal defence organisation in 1933, the purchase of essential equipment was so slow that the onset of war six years later found much of the work still unfinished. The army lacked all of the guns it required, some which it did have were not mounted, and the gunners had not received much of their essential technical equipment. Therefore, upon declaration of war the army had to accelerate work at a number of locations in order to bring as many batteries as possible into service. By early November it had completed the mounting of a 6-inch battery at Sydney's South Head and had temporarily placed 6-inch batteries at Port Kembla and Bribie Island near Brisbane. In addition, work was continuing on the 9.2-inch battery at Newcastle and the 6-inch and 4.7-inch batteries protecting Hobart. Preliminary work also began on a 6-inch battery for Port Moresby.[47]

After the fall of France, the increasing likelihood of Japanese intervention led to further increases in the coastal defence organisation. The coastal gunners were, in fact, the nation's first line of defence against invasion. Progressively, the army expanded its

Coastal Artillery gunners manning a 4-inch gun, Fort Pierson, Hobart. (AWM 051471)

defences at existing fortresses and began new works at other ports. Townsville, Cairns, Portland Roads, Rabaul, and the Torres Strait all received coastal defences. The government even considered installing 6-inch guns on Nauru and Ocean Islands, but decided that it could not spare the required weapons from the defence of the mainland. The limiting factor on the build-up of the coastal defences remained the supply of guns. No Australian armoury could produce 6-inch guns, and the Commonwealth had to obtain them from Britain, which could only supply them in limited numbers.

As late as April 1942, Major-General J.S. Whitelaw, the Major-General Royal Artillery, concluded that most Australian ports required additional defences, including important centres such as Sydney, Brisbane, Fremantle, and Darwin. To meet this need, General Douglas MacArthur, the American commander, arranged for the shipment from the United States of a number of 155-mm mobile gun batteries, with necessary searchlights and fire control equipment. The Australian Army received sufficient guns to raise eight heavy batteries, which it designated with a letter, A through H Battery. Eventually, the army formed a further 11 letter batteries. Although they employed American equipment, the Australian Army staffed and commanded these batteries. Initially, the army assigned them to mainland defence, but as the Japanese threat receded, the letter batteries moved forward to defend harbours in New Guinea. Map 7 illustrates Australia's coastal defence system at its peak in 1944.[48]

In addition to the improvement of the coastal defence organisation, the army also had to devote considerable resources to providing the nation's cities with a viable air defence capability. Coastal and air defence were actually two aspects of the same problem, the protection of the Commonwealth from invasion, as an air attack would precede a landing. In fact, until November 1941 anti-aircraft batteries were under the command of the local coastal fortress headquarters. Unfortunately, by the end of the interwar period the army had only just begun to address its air defence requirements, and when the war began, Australia possessed only a rudimentary anti-aircraft organisation. The expansion of the aerial defence system was, therefore, a high priority.

The biggest impediment to the growth of the anti-aircraft organisation was the shortage of guns and supporting equipment. Australia had limited production capacity for the 3.7-inch anti-aircraft gun, but most of the other requirements had to come from Britain. By the end of 1941, Australian factories had completed 165 3.7-inch anti-aircraft guns, and the army had raised 17 anti-aircraft batteries. Plans called for the construction of a further 135 guns during 1942. However, it was not until 1942 that Australia gained the ability to manufacture predictors. Without this piece of equipment, anti-aircraft fire was largely ineffective. After Japan's entry into the war,

WORLD WAR II

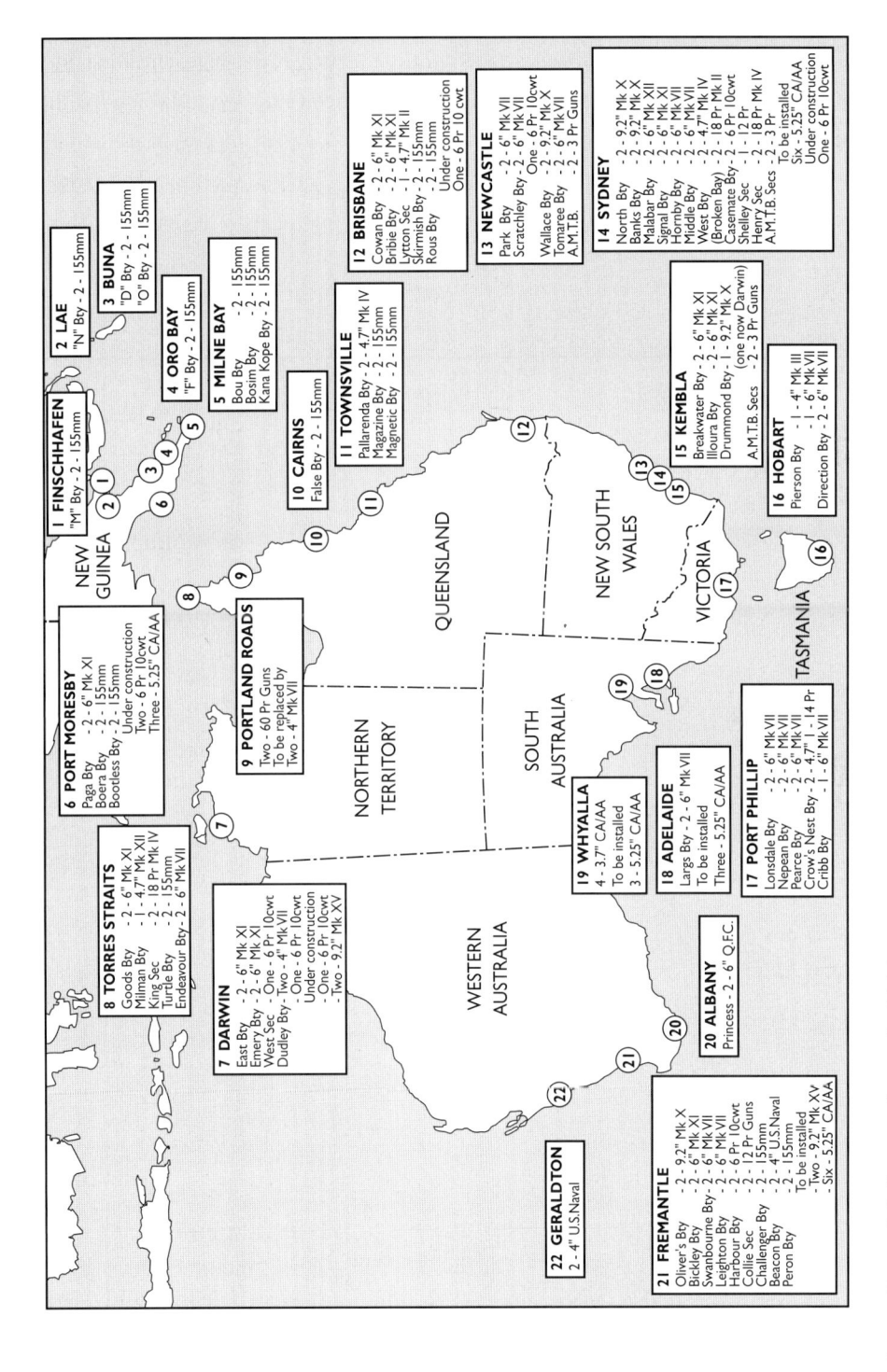

1 FINSCHHAFEN
"M" Bty - 2 - 155mm

2 LAE
"N" Bty - 2 - 155mm

3 BUNA
"D" Bty - 2 - 155mm
"O" Bty - 2 - 155mm

4 ORO BAY
"F" Bty - 2 - 155mm

5 MILNE BAY
Bou Bty - 2 - 155mm
Bosim Bty - 2 - 155mm
Kana Kope Bty - 2 - 155mm

6 PORT MORESBY
Paga Bty - 2 - 6" Mk XI
Boera Bty - 2 - 155mm
Bootless Bty - 2 - 155mm
Under construction
Two - 6 Pr 10cwt
Three - 5.25" CA/AA

7 DARWIN
East Bty - 2 - 6" Mk XI
Emery Bty - 2 - 6" Mk XI
West Sec - One - 6 Pr 10cwt
Dudley Bty - Two - 4" Mk VII
Under construction
One - 6 Pr 10cwt
Two - 9.2" Mk XV

8 TORRES STRAITS
Goods Bty - 2 - 6" Mk XI
Milman Bty - 1 - 4.7" Mk XII
King Sec - 2 - 18 Pr Mk IV
Turtle Bty - 2 - 155mm
Endeavour Bty - 2 - 6" Mk VII

9 PORTLAND ROADS
Two - 60 Pr Guns
To be replaced by
Two - 4" Mk VII

10 CAIRNS
False Bty - 2 - 155mm

11 TOWNSVILLE
Pallarenda Bty - 2 - 4.7" Mk IV
Magazine Bty - 2 - 155mm
Magnetic Bty - 2 - 155mm

12 BRISBANE
Cowan Bty - 2 - 6" Mk XI
Bribie Bty - 2 - 6" Mk XI
Skirmish Bty - 1 - 4.7" Mk II
Lytton Sec - 2 - 155mm
Rous Bty - 2 - 155mm
Under construction
One - 6 Pr 10 cwt

13 NEWCASTLE
Park Bty - 2 - 6" Mk VII
Scratchley Bty - 2 - 6" Mk VII
Wallace Bty - 2 - 9.2" Mk VII
Tomaree Bty - 2 - 6" Mk VII
A.M.T.B. - 2 - 3 Pr Guns

14 SYDNEY
North Bty - 2 - 9.2" Mk X
Banks Bty - 2 - 9.2" Mk X
Malabar Bty - 2 - 6" Mk XI
Signal Bty - 2 - 6" Mk VII
Hornby Bty - 2 - 4.7" Mk VII
Middle Bty - 2 - 18 Pr Mk II
West Bty
(Broken Bay) - 2 - 6 Pr 10cwt
Casemate Bty - 1 - 12 Pr
Shelley Sec - 2 - 18 Pr Mk IV
Henry Sec - 2 - 3 Pr
A.M.T.B. Secs
To be installed
Six - 5.25" CA/AA
One - 6 Pr 10cwt

15 KEMBLA
Breakwater Bty - 2 - 6" Mk XI
Illoura Bty - 2 - 6" Mk XI
Drummond Bty - 1 - 9.2" Mk X
(one now Darwin)
A.M.T.B. Secs - 2 - 3 Pr Guns

16 HOBART
Pierson Bty - 1 - 4" Mk III
Direction Bty - 2 - 6" Mk VII

17 PORT PHILLIP
Lonsdale Bty - 2 - 6" Mk VII
Nepean Bty - 2 - 6" Mk VII
Pearce Bty - 2 - 6" Mk VII
Crow's Nest Bty - 2 - 4.7" - 1 - 4 Pr
Cribb Bty - 1 - 6" Mk VII

18 ADELAIDE
Largs Bty - 2 - 6" Mk VII
To be installed
Three - 5.25" CA/AA

19 WHYALLA
4 - 3.7" CA/AA
To be installed
3 - 5.25" CA/AA

20 ALBANY
Princess - 2 - 6" Q.F.C.

21 FREMANTLE
Oliver's Bty - 2 - 9.2" Mk X
Bickley Bty - 2 - 6" Mk XI
Swanbourne Bty - 2 - 6" Mk VII
Leighton Bty - 2 - 6" Mk VII
Harbour Bty - 2 - 6 Pr 10cwt
Collie Sec - 2 - 12 Pr
Challenger Bty - 2 - 4" U.S. Naval
Beacon Bty - 2 - 155mm
Perron Bty
To be installed
Two - 9.2" Mk XV
Six - 5.25" CA/AA

22 GERALDTON
2 - 4" U.S. Naval

Map 7 Coastal defence at its peak, 1944

Britain released to Australia 120 Bofors guns for low-level anti-aircraft defence, and by April 1942 the United States Army had six anti-aircraft battalions in Australia. The Americans helped protect the sky above Fremantle, Darwin, Townsville, and Brisbane. In November 1941, the army reorganised its fixed defence structure and removed the anti-aircraft batteries from the control of the fortress command and placed them under the control of the line of communication areas.[49] Table 5.8 outlines the army's anti-aircraft organisation as it existed in late 1942.

Table 5.8 Anti-aircraft organisation, late 1942[50]

L of C Area	Formation	Establishment
NSW L of C Area	Sydney AA Group	103rd HAA Regt
		108th, 110th, 111th LAA Regts
		1st, 7th, 9th, 15th, 20th, 25th AA Btys
	Newcastle AA Group	3rd, 7th, 18th AA Btys
		222nd LAA Bty
	Kembla AA Group	8th AA Bty
		221st LAA Bty
VIC L of C Area	Melbourne AA Group	112th LAA Regt
		10th, 11th, 30th AA Btys
QLD L of C Area	South Queensland AA Group	2/2nd HAA Regt
		113th, 114th LAA Regts
		6th, 38th AA Btys
	North Queensland AA Group	34th, 35th, 36th, 37th AA Btys
		223rd, 224th, 226th LAA Btys
SA L of C Area		12th, 26th AA Batteries
WA L of C Area	Fremantle AA Group	2/3rd, 109th, 116th LAA Regts
		4th, 5th, 29th AA Btys
TAS L of C Area		13th AA Bty
NT Force	Darwin AA Group	2/1st LAA Regt
		2nd, 14th, 22nd AA Btys
		225th, 233rd LAA Btys
NG Force	Port Moresby AA Group	23rd, 32nd AA Btys
		2/4th HAA Bty
		2/7th, 234th, 156th LAA Btys
	Milne Bay AA Group	33rd, 23rd (det) AA Btys

If the expansion of the army's coastal and aerial defence structure was great, the growth of its support establishment was even more dramatic. The commencement of the Pacific phase of World War II shifted Australia's attention to the island barrier to the country's north. In New Guinea, Australian and American troops would wage a desperate battle to halt the Japanese advance, then drive them back. The proximity of these efforts to Australia meant that the nation's homeland had to serve as the army's base and support line of communication. In the Middle East, the 2nd AIF had relied on British forces for its base logistic and line of communication maintenance. After Pearl Harbor, Australian resources would have to fulfil this role.

The successful sustainment of Australian armed forces across the remote top of the country, and the support of operations in New Guinea and the adjacent islands, required a tremendous logistical effort, a role for which the army was not designed. Traditionally, the army had relied on a major power to provide this function while Australia emphasised combat units at the expense of the logistical arms. As a consequence, the army's support components were relatively underdeveloped. Now, faced with the Japanese crisis, the army had to expand its rear elements rapidly if its combat units were to remain effective. The army required a host of units that it had either never supported or only minimally supported in the past. They included petroleum units for the storage and distribution of fuels and lubricants, terminal units for the handling of cargo in ports, and refrigeration units for the field storage of perishable foods. The army even developed farm, dairy, and fish units in forward areas in order to provide the troops with fresh food while also reducing the strain on the force's limited transportation capacity.

Since Australia's base area was around the major cities of the south-east while the field force's areas of operation were along the northern coast or in New Guinea, the army had to expend considerable effort in expanding its transportation capabilities. The Darwin base was a particularly difficult area to reach, since ships could not safely make the passage, and the rail line from South Australia only went as far north as Alice Springs. Although isolated, Darwin rapidly developed into a major military and aviation base. To sustain the war effort in the Northern Territory, the army had to rely on convoys of trucks making the passage over unsealed roads from the railheads at Alice Springs or Mt Isa. The road from Alice Springs was not sealed until early 1944. During the effort, 17 transport companies serviced Darwin, and to keep the trucks rolling the army also had to establish workshops for maintenance, petroleum depots for fuel, and even field bakeries and farms to provide fresh food for the drivers. Over the course of the effort, transport companies carried nearly 500,000 tons of supplies and nearly 200,000 troops.

Darwin Mobile Force during anti-gas drill. (AWM P1449/41)

Another support area that underwent rapid expansion was water transportation. Normally this should have been the responsibility of a navy, but the RAN had neither the vessels nor the inclination to support the army in New Guinea or the adjacent islands. In order to provide for the distribution of supplies during these campaigns, it fell to the army to develop its own maritime transport service. The army had already some experience with water transport in Tobruk and Malaya, but the scale of operations in the South-West Pacific area required the raising of an entire new arm. Consequently, in September 1942 the army raised a Directorate of Water Transport (Small Craft), and gave the task of water distribution to the engineers. Before the war, the Royal Australian Engineers had employed small boats to help maintain the coastal forts, and was the only branch of the army with any experience with watercraft. In addition, the Australian Army was following British practice. In the British Army, it was the Royal Engineers who controlled water transportation. At its peak, the Royal Australian Engineers operated more than 1,900 watercraft, ranging in size from small launches to 300-ton cargo ships. The types of vessels included ambulance boats, amphibians, landing craft, work boats, lighters, tugs, and ocean-going ships. After the war, water transportation became the responsibility of Royal Australian Engineers—Transportation Service.[51]

In order to dispatch urgently needed supplies to places inaccessible by sea or isolated by the rough terrain of New Guinea, the army developed its own air transport organisation. The RAAF or the American Army Air Corps operated the planes, but Australian Army troops prepared the cargo for aerial delivery and dispatched it over

Army Boat 442 *Frances Peat* at Lae, New Guinea. (AWM P1568.029)

the drop zone. The first air drops took place in July 1942 during the Kokoda campaign. During World War II, the army raised three air dispatch units, called 1st, 2nd, and 3rd Air Maintenance Companies. After the war's conclusion, the army continued to maintain an air-dispatch capability, as well as a training establishment, in association with the RAAF.[52]

As Australia gained experience in amphibious operations in New Guinea, the need for specialised units to support the landing became increasingly apparent. As a result, in 1944, the army raised the 1st and 2nd Beach Group, each with an establishment of approximately 1,800 personnel. The duty of the beach groups was to organise the landing of troops and stores, establish dumps, and assist in the provision of support within the maintenance area. Each beach group was meant to support a divisional size landing.[53]

Higher direction of the war

Over the course of the war, the army significantly modified its arrangements for the higher direction of the force, including changes in its command and administration structures. In part, these adjustments represented the different management requirements of a small peacetime institution versus the much greater needs of an army in the midst of a desperate struggle for national survival. However, the evolution of the higher direction structure also reflected the need to compensate for years of neglect. Last, these changes reflected the nation's place as a minor power that had no choice but to cede much of its control over strategy, war aims, and military operations to its senior allies.

After the start of the war, Menzies implemented a number of changes at the political level in order to improve the government's ability to manage the nation's efforts. These included the creation of the War Cabinet on 15 September and, on 13 November, the division of the Department for Defence into four related ministries, the Ministry for Defence Coordination and three service ministries, one each for the RAN, Army, and RAAF. At the same time as he set up the War Cabinet, Menzies also established the Chiefs of Staff Committee. It was composed of the three service heads: the CGS for the army, the Chief of Naval Staff for the RAN, and the Chief of the Air Staff for the RAAF. The purpose of the Chiefs of Staff Committee was to provide advice to the War Cabinet on military matters.[54]

The first change to the army's hierarchy was not actually a result of the war but was a belated implementation of the reform Squires had proposed in his report as Inspector-General. This was the army's conversion to a regional command structure. Before Japan's entry into the war, the only substantial modification to Squires' scheme was the activation of the 8th Military District in Port Moresby to control Australian forces in Papua. Map 8 illustrates the regional arrangement for the army's administration in 1939.

As long as the war's focus remained overseas, the command system met the army's needs. However, as the potential for hostilities in the Pacific increased, the headquarters of the commands and military districts gradually came under greater administrative pressure. This was a result not only of the raising of the AIF but also the expansion of the CMF. The CMF's activation to full-time duty after Japan's attack compounded the difficulties the commands and military districts faced. In addition, Army Headquarters also had a considerably greater workload than it had had before the war. The CGS's burden, in particular, had increased to include the command and administration of the home army as well as meeting the domestic needs of the AIF. To ease the situation, the government created the position of General Officer Commanding-in-Chief Home Forces (GOC-in-C Home Forces). Lieutenant-General Iven Mackay received the appointment on 4 August 1941, effective 1 September. Chart 5 (p. 165) illustrates the army's higher direction in August 1941.

Mackay's primary responsibility was to prepare the army for a potential invasion of Australia by Japan. His position was of equal rank to the CGS, but was subject to the direction of the latter. However, the GOC-in-C Home Forces had the right of direct

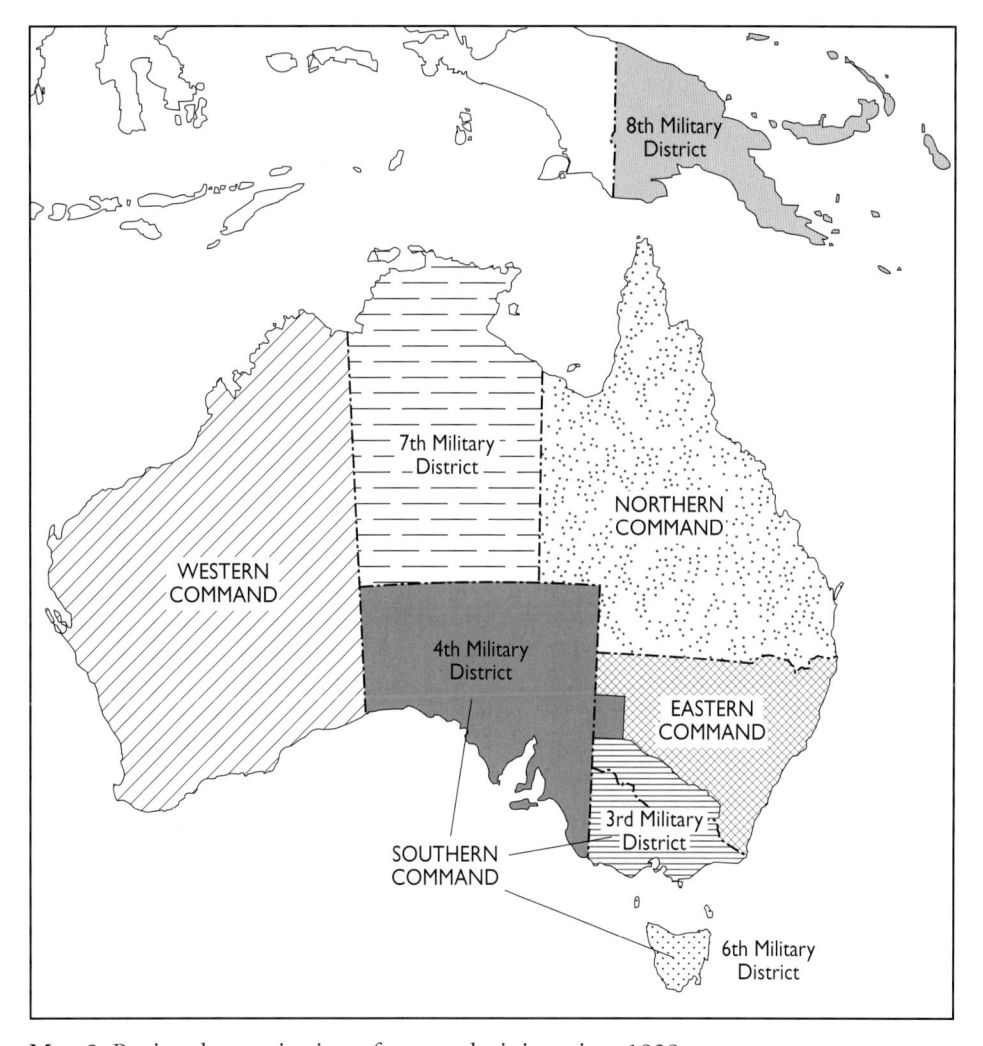

Map 8 Regional organisation of army administration, 1939

access to the minister. Mackay initially commanded all army field forces in Australia, except those specifically withdrawn from his control, such as the AIF. The administrative control of the formations under his command continued, as before, through the command and military districts headquarters. With Mackay's appointment the army could now create, for the first time, a single headquarters for the command of its field force, responsible for the defence of the nation. In addition, Mackay's appointment lightened the workload of Army Headquarters. After Japan's entry into the war, the Military Board decided to further modify the army's command structure. It narrowed Mackay's territorial responsibilities in order for him to concentrate his efforts on Australia's most critical areas. Consequently, Mackay retained command of field forces

Lieutenant-General Sir Iven Mackay (left) as GOC 6th Division with some of his officers. (AWM 002211)

in the Northern, Eastern, and Southern Commands, while control of forces in Western Command and the 7th and 8th Military Districts reverted to Army Headquarters.

Additionally, in order to allow the commanders of the Northern, Eastern, and Southern Commands to focus more clearly on defensive preparations, the army created a base headquarters in each of these areas. This change was an attempt to correct one of the problems that the Squires reform had created, the combination of command and administrative duties in a single office. The base commandants assumed responsibility for the administrative requirements of their areas, freeing the command headquarters to concentrate on operational tasks. While the base commandant was subordinate to the General Officer Commanding Command, he had his own headquarters and staff. In the smaller regions, administrative matters remained the responsibility of the command or military district headquarters. Chart 6 (p. 166) outlines the organisation of the army's higher direction after Japan's declaration of war.[55]

Mackay's appointment as GOC-in-C Home Forces proved shortlived. So far, Australia had responded in an *ad hoc* manner to the increasing demands the war had placed upon its management hierarchy. The army had largely continued the peacetime structure of its management, and in the process had created several parallel chains of

WORLD WAR II

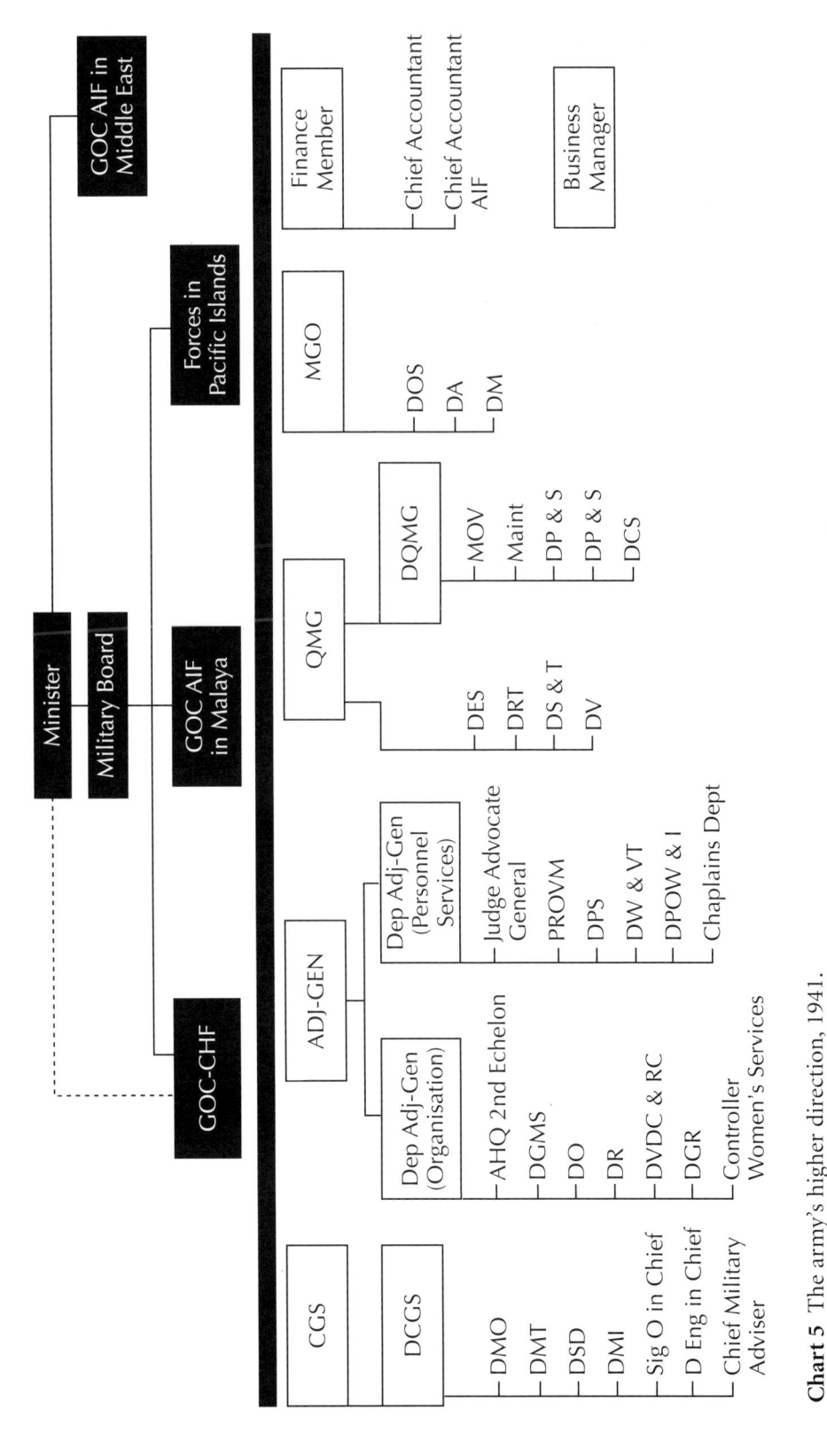

Chart 5 The army's higher direction, 1941.
(Source: 'Organisation of AHQ', 1942, AWM 113, item MH 1/110)

Chart 6 The army's higher direction within Australia after Japan's entry, 1942.
(Source: 'Organisation: N, E, S, Commands', 17 December 1941, AA (Vic), MP 508/1, item 240/701/120)

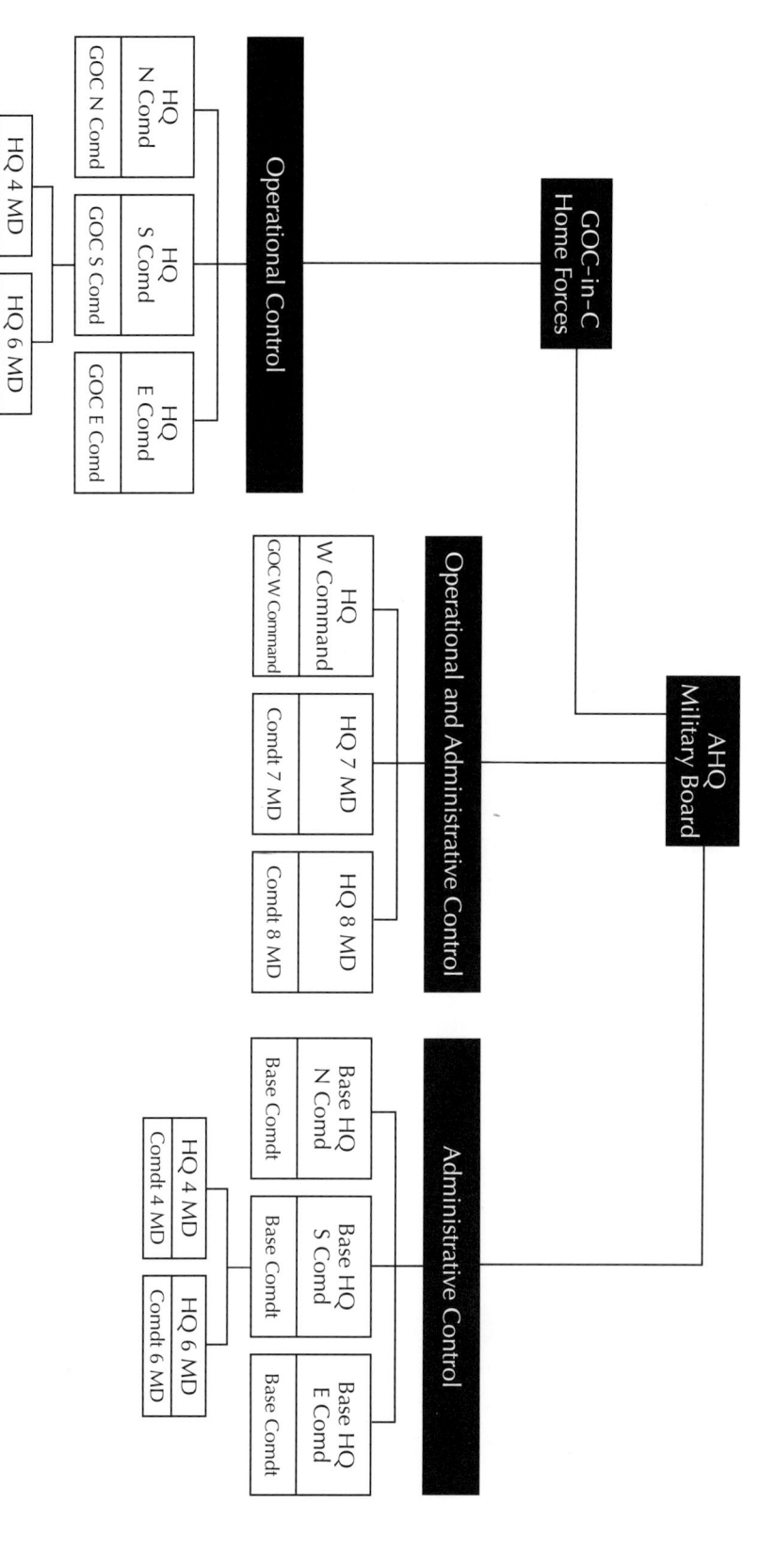

command. Operational matters were the provenance of the GOC-in-C Home Forces, as long as they involved the units of the three eastern commands. Elsewhere in Australia, Army Headquarters controlled the forces. Mackay also answered to a committee, the Military Board. Administrative duties were the responsibility of the base headquarters, except in Western Australia, where it was the responsibility of Headquarters Western Command, and in the 7th and 8th Military Districts, which answered directly to Army Headquarters. None of these institutions had any control over the AIF in the Middle East. This was under Blamey's command, and he reported directly to the minister. What the army lacked was a single commander who could direct and coordinate all aspects of the nation's military defence.

With the Commonwealth directly under threat after Japan's entry into the war, the government returned the AIF to Australia and reorganised the higher direction of the army on military command lines. At the same time, the government appointed a single officer to command all of the nation's military forces. In March, Blamey returned and took up the job of Commander-in-Chief Australian Military Forces (C-in-C AMF). Despite his appointment, however, the army did not replace the two-army system. Instead, both organisations existed side by side, linked by their common commander. On 9 April 1942, Blamey issued orders that reorganised the Australian territory from its peacetime regional administrative structure to a system based on operational headquarters. In doing so, the headquarters command, base commands, and military districts ceased to function. The Military Board also went into abeyance, and its responsibilities became part of the C-in-C AMF's duties. Blamey established field commands to control army forces in the following areas of operation:

- Headquarters 1st Army: New South Wales and Queensland (from Northern and Eastern Commands)
- Headquarters 2nd Army: Victoria, South Australia, Tasmania (from Southern Command)
- Headquarters III Corps: Western Australia (from Western Command)
- Headquarters Northern Territory Force: Darwin (from 7th Military District)
- Headquarters New Guinea Force: Port Moresby (from 8th Military District).

After the call-up of the CMF to full-time duty, the support and administrative functions of the army increased tremendously. To manage the greater workload, and to alleviate the field commanders of an administrative burden, Blamey also raised a headquarters lines of communication area in each of the former commands and military districts. Their duties included matters such as the management of prisoner-of-war camps, oversight of recruitment efforts, the operation of training establishments, and the command of static coast and anti-aircraft defences. In the Northern Territory

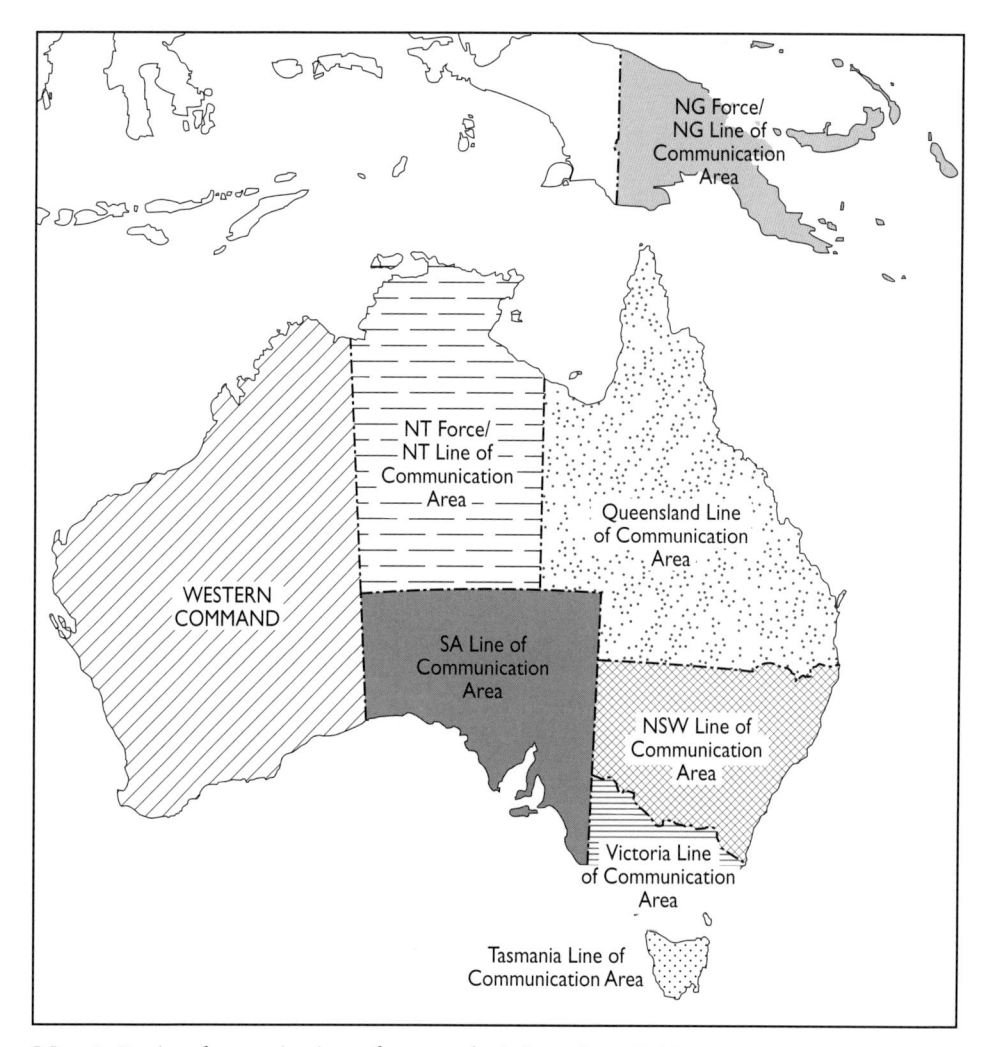

Map 9 Regional organisation of army administration, 1944

and New Guinea, the army did not raise a separate headquarters line of communication area, but combined the function with the operational headquarters. On 16 June 1944, since Western Australia now contained relatively few troops and installations, Blamey reraised Western Command, merging both III Corps and Western Australia Line of Communication Area into a single headquarters. Map 9 illustrates the regional organisation of the army's administration as it existed in 1944.

The staff for the 1st Army came from the Australian I Corps staff, who had also returned from the Middle East, while Mackay's headquarters provided the personnel for the 2nd Army. Blamey designated his headquarters General Headquarters, although he soon changed the name to Land Headquarters. As a result of this reorganisation, the government abolished Mackay's position and appointed him to command 2nd Army.[56] Chart 7 outlines Blamey's administrative control of the army

WORLD WAR II

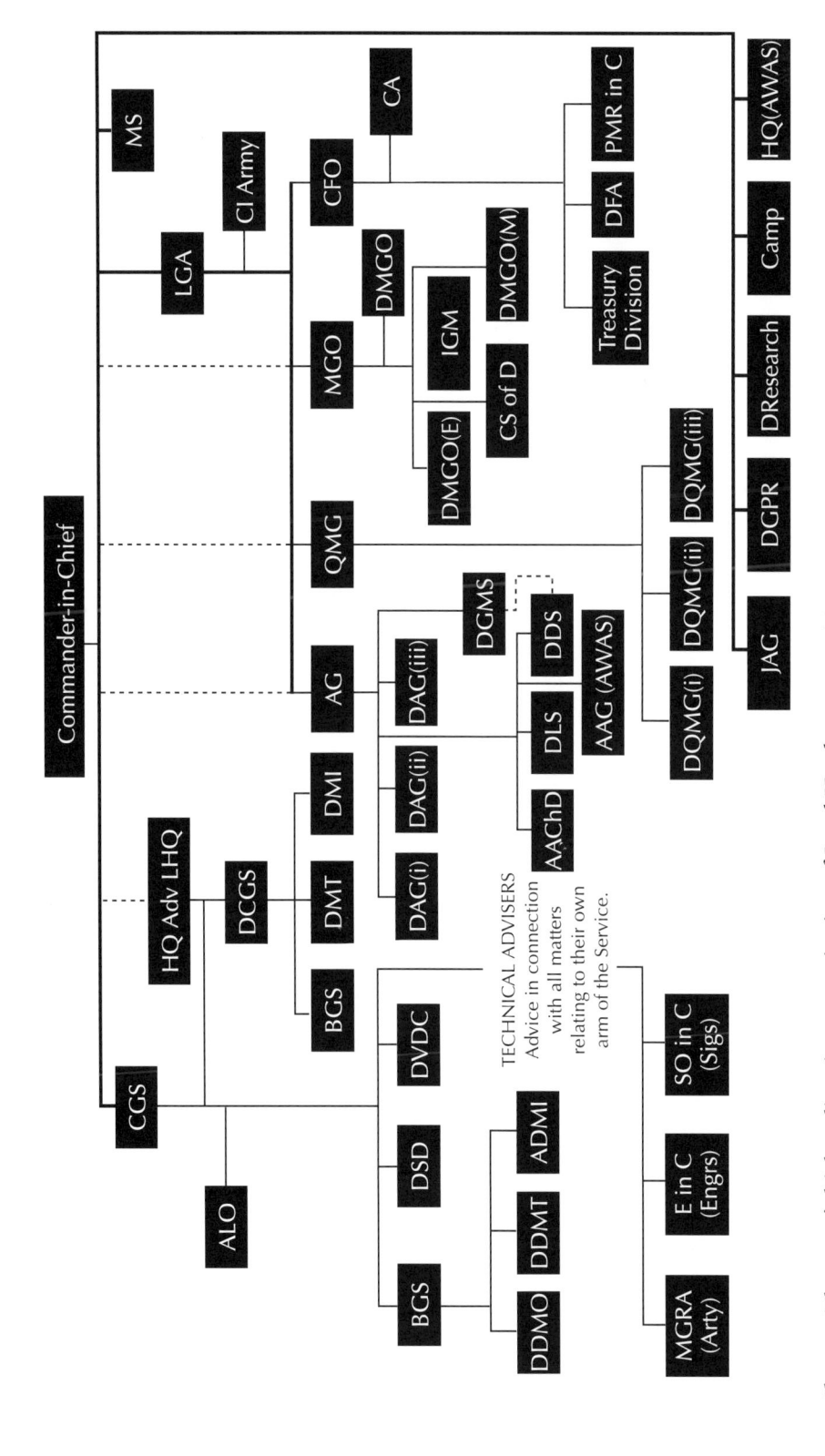

Chart 7 The army's higher direction: organisation of Land Headquarters, 1944. (Source: *Army War Effort*, February 1944, ADFA 254612)

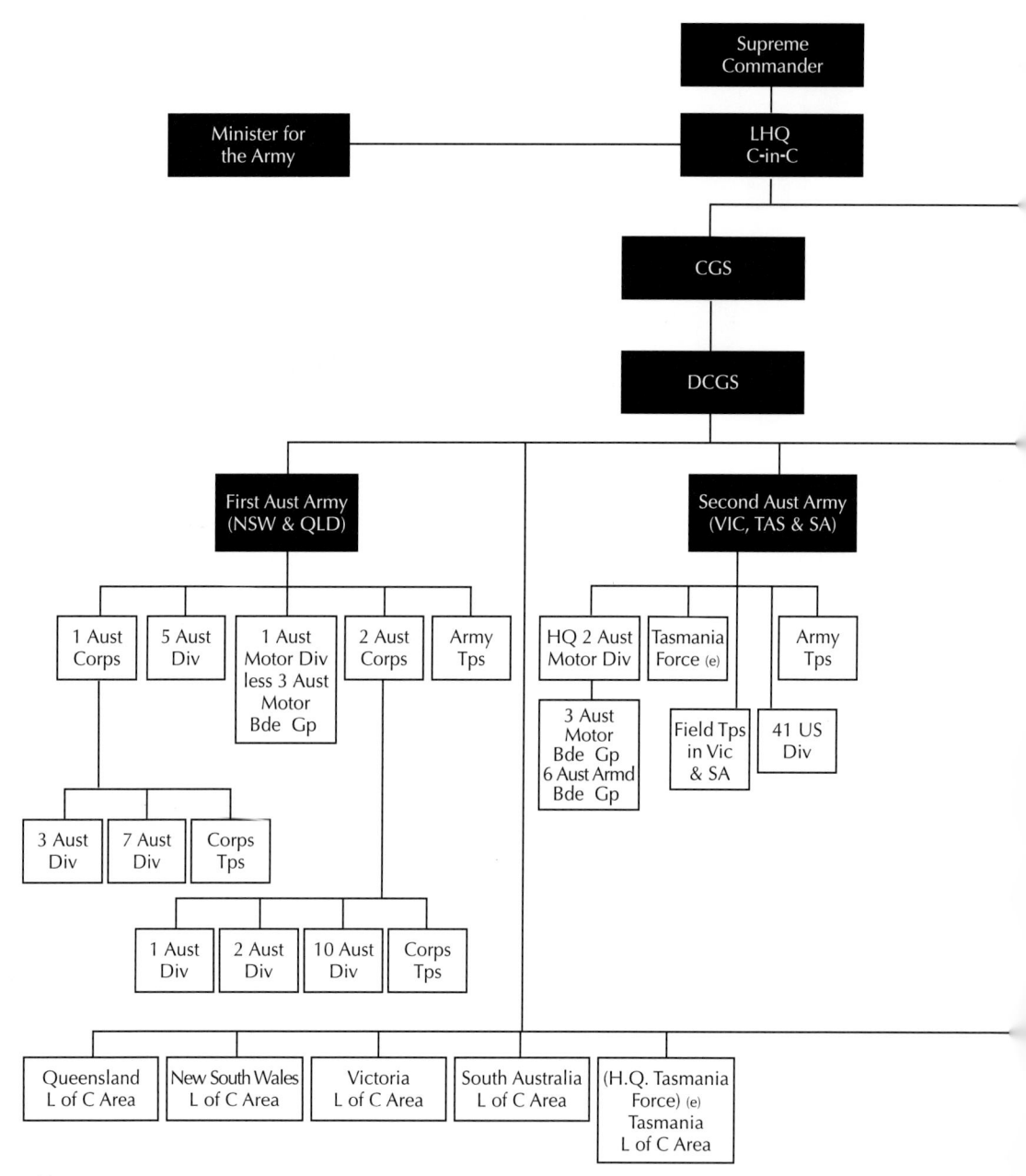

THE AUSTRALIAN ARMY

```
                                          ┌──────────────┐
                                          │   Supreme    │
                                          │  Commander   │
                                          └──────┬───────┘
          ┌──────────────┐                ┌──────┴───────┐
          │ Minister for │────────────────│     LHQ      │
          │  the Army    │                │    C-in-C    │
          └──────────────┘                └──────┬───────┘
                                                 │
                                          ┌──────┴───────┐
                                          │     CGS      │
                                          └──────┬───────┘
                                                 │
                                          ┌──────┴───────┐
                                          │    DCGS      │
                                          └──────┬───────┘
                         ┌───────────────────────┴───────────────────────┐
                  ┌──────┴───────┐                               ┌───────┴──────┐
                  │ First Aust Army│                             │Second Aust Army│
                  │  (NSW & QLD)  │                              │ (VIC, TAS & SA)│
                  └──────────────┘                               └──────────────┘
```

1 Aust Corps	5 Aust Div	1 Aust Motor Div less 3 Aust Motor Bde Gp	2 Aust Corps	Army Tps		HQ 2 Aust Motor Div	Tasmania Force (e)		Army Tps
						3 Aust Motor Bde Gp 6 Aust Armd Bde Gp	Field Tps in Vic & SA	41 US Div	

3 Aust Div	7 Aust Div	Corps Tps

1 Aust Div	2 Aust Div	10 Aust Div	Corps Tps

Queensland L of C Area	New South Wales L of C Area	Victoria L of C Area	South Australia L of C Area	(H.Q. Tasmania Force) (e) Tasmania L of C Area

Notes
(a) Except in the cases of New Guinea Force and Northern Territory Force fixed coast defences, A.A. Units and Grn. Bns. allotted for close defence of L of C Areas are under Comd. their respective HQ L of C Area. Emergency roles will be allotted by operational comds.
(b) All troops in NT, NG and Tas are under Comd NTF, NGF and TF respectively.
(c) Control of policy and general direction of the Branches of AG, QMG, MGO, and CFO will be exercised by the LGA.

Chart 8A Distribution of the Australian Army, May 1942.

(Source: AA (Vic), MP729/6, item 37/401/759)

WORLD WAR II

```
LGA (c)
├── AG (d)
├── QMG (d)
├── MGO (d)
├── CFO (d)
├── CMA
└── Administrative Planning Section
```

- **3 Aust Corps (WA)**
  - Field Tps in WA
    - 4 Aust Div
  - Corps Tps
- **Northern Territory Force**
  - 19 Aust Bde Gp
  - Fd Tps in NT
    - NT L of C Area
      - Fixed Coast Defences AA Units & Grn Bns
- **New Guinea Force**
  - Fd Tps in NG
    - Fixed Coast Defences AA Units & Grn Bns
- **LHQ Reserve**
  - 1 Aust Armd Div
    - 3 Aust Army Tk Bde
- **LHQ Tps**
  - 2/2 Aust Pnr Bn
  - 2/1 Aust MG Bn
- **AIF (Overseas)**
  - AIF in Australia not allotted to Field Army

- Western Australia L of C Area
- New Guinea L of C Area

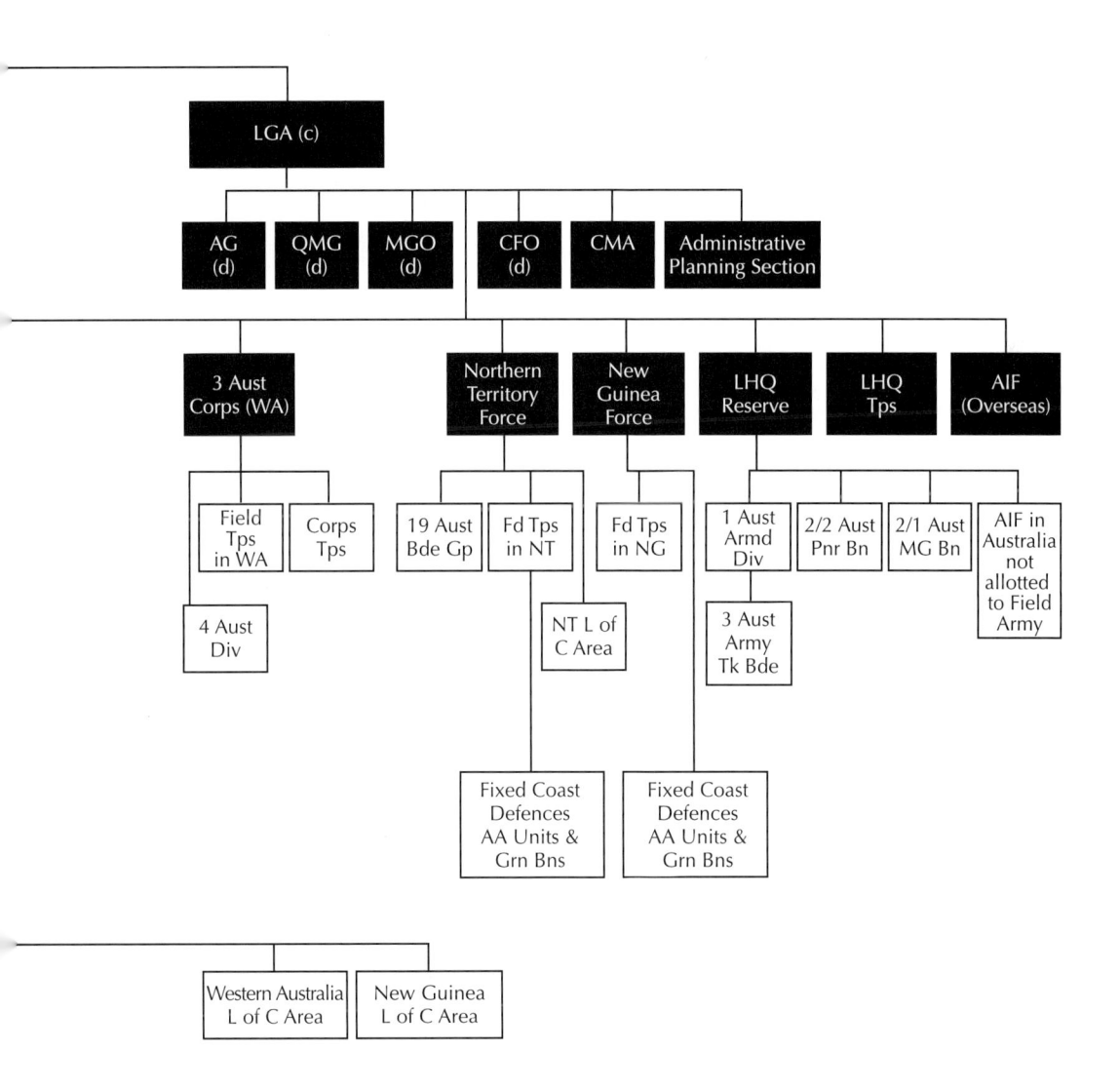

(d) In regard to matters on which it is convenient or expedient the AG, QMG, MGO and CFO will deal direct with the C–in–C and will keep the LGA informed of any policy matters which arise and of any decisions given which affect policy.

(e) Commander, Tasmania Force is under command GOC–in–C Second Aust Army for operations only and is responsible direct to LHQ for all other matters.

through land headquarters. Chart 8A illustrates the operational structure under land headquarters, with major units under command as it existed in May 1942.

While Blamey was technically in control of all Australian military forces, the arrival of the American supreme commander, General Douglas MacArthur, soon eclipsed his authority. The American President, Franklin D. Roosevelt, had ordered MacArthur to leave the Philippines and take command of all United States forces in Australia. Roosevelt had decided to make Australia a major base against Japan, much to the relief of the Curtin Government who, fearing invasion, had desperately sought help from the Americans. On 9 March, Roosevelt proposed to Churchill that they divide the world into three strategic planning regions. The two major allies shared control of the Atlantic theatre, the United States had exclusive jurisdiction in the Pacific, and Britain took charge in the Indian Ocean and the Middle East. The scheme placed Australia within the Pacific Zone, and its war planning henceforth became subject to the strategic dictates of Washington. Neither Roosevelt nor Churchill had consulted the Australian Government on these arrangements, and the Commonwealth had little choice in its acceptance of them. By this act, the last vestiges of imperial responsibility for Australia passed, and the Commonwealth's defence became an American duty.[57]

On 17 March 1942, MacArthur arrived in Australia. Curtin welcomed him warmly, along with the assurance of American protection that he represented. However, his presence, and the build-up of American forces, came at a price. Australia would have to give up almost all control over its forces and the direction of the war in the region. Shortly afterwards, Curtin subordinated control of all Australian military assets to MacArthur's headquarters. On 18 April, MacArthur activated his command, the South-West Pacific Area, and Australian forces came under his operational control. Since, at this time, Australia provided the majority of the ground combat troops in the South-West Pacific Area, MacArthur designated Blamey as Commander, Allied Land Forces. Despite Blamey's title, MacArthur effectively limited his colleague's mandate to the Australian forces, especially as the United States Army grew in strength. In the war's later stages, MacArthur confined the Commonwealth's divisions to backwaters and sideshows while the American Army led their commander back to the Philippines.[58]

Manpower

In 1920, the army's senior officers estimated that Australia could support a maximum force of five infantry and two cavalry divisions in a major war. In addition, they believed that the army could only sustain these divisions in the field with the help of

General Douglas MacArthur. (AWM 013423)

a major power, which would provide for much of the force's support requirements. However, the government's decision to raise the AIF, in addition to the home army, meant that the nation had accepted a policy that would inevitably create a force greater than that which the senior officers had believed feasible. Soon after Menzies announced the decision to form the 6th Division, the Chiefs of Staff Committee reminded the government that the army had already expanded beyond the estimates of a sustainable force.[59] However, after Japan's thrust southward, the need to defend the continent overtook any debate over manpower allocation. The Curtin Government decided that Australia required 25 divisions to save it from the invasion, of which 12 would be Australian with the remainder coming from the United States.[60] Curtin also called for a considerable increase in the size of the RAAF and a more modest expansion by the RAN. By 1942, the army had an establishment of 14 divisions, not including the lost 8th—eleven infantry and three armoured—twice as many as the senior officers had believed possible. The rapid growth of the field force, as well as the need to develop Australia into a base against Japan, also led to the enormous expansion of the force's support and service elements. Although the United States provided considerable logistical assistance, the ground campaigns of the South-West Pacific Area represented the first time in the Australian Army's history that it had to rely largely on its own resources for its support.

The senior officers, however, were correct. Australia did not have the manpower to maintain a field force and logistic structure on such a large scale, at least not without damaging the economy, falling short of its commitments to the Empire Air Training Scheme, and failing to provide food and supplies to Britain and to American forces in the region. To sustain the three services at the level Curtin proposed required a monthly intake of 24,000 men and 11,000 women. By late 1942, it was clear that the services could expect only 5,000 men and 5,000 women each month. As early as June, Blamey informed the War Cabinet that it was not possible to maintain the army at its current size, and he recommended the elimination of one division from the order of battle. He also warned that the disbandment of another division was likely.[61] Furthermore, while the army had on paper an order of battle of 14 divisions, in reality, many of the formations were greatly under strength, especially in the CMF. For example, in July 1943 the eight CMF divisions contained only 18 CMF brigades, with a total of 51 battalions. This was considerably less than the 24 brigades and 72 battalions that a force of such a size normally had.[62] Manpower proved one of the greatest constraints on the Australian war effort, and its allocation determined the shape of the army in the second half of the war.

With the passing of the threat of Japanese invasion in mid 1943, the government turned its attention to the reduction of the army and the provision of additional labour to the civilian economy.[63] Japan had been beaten back in New Guinea, and Curtin considered invasion unlikely. The government now believed that it could safely decrease its military commitments and thereby release workers to other areas of the war economy or the civilian sector. Consequently, on 1 October the government informed the army that it would have to discharge 20,000 soldiers to industry by the following June. The government also informed the munitions industry that it would have to release a similar number. This was the first of a series of reductions that would remove over 100,000 men from the army.[64]

To determine the army's future personnel requirements, defence planners sought to clarify the nature of Australia's participation in the war. In September 1943, the Defence Committee presented the findings of its inquiry into the basis of the army's establishment. The review highlighted the organisational objectives of the army as the maintenance of a force which was sufficient to provide the following:

a   a striking force for offensive operations

b   sufficient forces suitable for and capable of relieving the forces mentioned in (a) after the operations have been completed to hold the areas seized

c   essential garrisons of the mainland and New Guinea

d   anti-aircraft and fixed defences, lines of communication and administrative units essential for the maintenance of the above forces.[65]

By March 1944, Lieutenant-General John Northcott, the CGS, had identified the war establishment needed to meet these objectives. Table 5.9 outlines his findings according to the tasks listed above. In addition to these requirements, the army also had on its order of battle 28,500 troops in the replacement pool and 33,000 personnel listed as non-effective. Last, the army could call upon 40,000 members of the Volunteer Defence Corps to assist with home defence.

Table 5.9 War establishment requirements of the army, September 1943[66]

	Requirement	War establishment
a	Strike force for operations in South-West Pacific Area to consist of three divisions on the jungle standard, an armoured brigade, corps, and line of communication troops	88,700
b	Follow-up force to consist of three divisions, corps and line of communication troops	66,800
c	Defence of mainland and New Guinea garrisons	106,300
d	Administrative units	108,500
	Total war establishment	*370,300*

Lieutenant-General John Northcott, CGS 1942–45. (AWM 107728)

In February 1944, the strength of the army was over 464,000, although this included only 338,000 'A'-class males, the rest being 98,000 'B'-class or lower, and more than 28,000 females. Northcott had identified a sizeable difference between the army's requirements and its current staffing levels, which suggested the possibility for the discharge of some personnel. However, the CGS warned that if the current monthly intake remained at 1,500 per month, and if the discharge rate remained at 4,000 per month, and if the army did not release more than 20,000 men to industry, the force could sustain its order of battle through the end of 1944. Beyond that point, without an increase in the recruitment rate, the army would have to contract.[67]

The need to divert army manpower to other uses forced the War Cabinet to outline the military's future role in the nation's war effort. By the end of 1943, Curtin had determined that Australia's war effort would consist of:

a   The maintenance of six divisions and two armoured brigades for active operations.
b   The maintenance of the RAN at present strength, plus construction programme.
c   The maintenance of the RAAF at a strength of fifty-three squadrons.[68]

In seeking the agreement of Britain and the United States to this proposal, Curtin also guaranteed that Australia would continue to supply food and other materials to Britain and India as well as the forces of the United States in the South-West Pacific Area. The War Cabinet also saw a need for the government to give greater attention to the satisfaction of essential civilian needs. As a result of these decisions, the War Cabinet decided upon a further cull of the army. On 23 August 1944, the government ordered the army to reduce its establishment by a further 30,000 men, over and above normal discharges, in order to increase the labour pool in agriculture and other areas of the economy. The RAAF was to lose 15,000. However, despite these releases, the government still foresaw a shortage of at least 37,000 men and 11,000 women in non-armed forces employment. The government ordered the final wartime reductions in June 1945, when it commanded the release of 50,000 personnel, a figure later raised to 64,000.[69]

Faced with demands for his troops, Blamey had little choice but to steer the army's contraction. In early 1943, in order to provide the army with nine full-strength infantry divisions, Blamey undertook a major reshuffling of the force. In the process it proved necessary to disband the 4th Division and the 14th Brigade as well as several additional battalions. In addition, Blamey shifted other formations and units among the divisions. For example, the Headquarters 11th Brigade, with the 26th and 31st/52nd Battalions, transferred from the 5th to the 3rd Division. Tasmania lost its infantry garrison, as its battalions moved to the 3rd Division, while the 28th Brigade gave up the 19th Battalion to the 6th Brigade. The Army also reduced the establishment of the Armoured Corps and lowered its commitment to coastal defence by 3,600 men. The army hoped to free up an additional 8,000 soldiers by replacing them with Volunteer Defence Corps or Australian Women's Army Service personnel. The army next streamlined its administrative structure by placing the control of the lines of communication areas directly under the command of the 1st and 2nd Armies.[70] Later in the year, Blamey informed the

War Cabinet that the army would have to eliminate a further infantry brigade, and amalgamate the 1st Motorised Brigade into the 7th Division.[71]

From 1944 to the end of the war, Australia managed to maintain a force of six infantry divisions—three AIF and three CMF—for operations in the South-West Pacific Area. However, the establishment of units within Australia continued to decline. In mid 1945, the government decided that, because of the course of the war, a further contraction in the army's offensive formations was possible. Consequently, the government planned to reduce the army to three divisions once the CMF had wound up its campaign against the Japanese garrisons in New Guinea, New Britain, and Bougainville. Furthermore, after the conclusion of the Borneo offensive the army anticipated another opportunity for rationalisation. For the war's final phases the army would have fewer than two divisions to occupy territory stretching from Bougainville to Borneo, and would provide, at most, a brigade group to assist Britain in the recovery of its South-east Asian colonies. The army's last division, an AIF formation, would participate in the conquest of the Japanese mainland. Japan's surrender overtook these final reductions and, instead of planning further campaigns, the army addressed the more palatable exercise of demobilisation. Charts 8B, 8C, and 8D illustrate the progressive decline of the army as Blamey managed its contraction.[72]

Mechanisation policy

The speed with which Germany overran Poland and defeated France convinced Australian defence planners of the importance of armoured fighting vehicles in modern warfare. To date, Australia had sent only infantry divisions to the Middle East, and depended on the British Army for tank support. Australian planners believed that the provision of an armoured division was a top priority, both to protect the infantry from enemy armoured assaults and to provide the AIF with a more powerful attack. Related to this was the belated recognition that mounted troops had little utility in mechanised war. As the army developed its armoured forces, it also took the opportunity to reorganise the CMF cavalry divisions onto a mechanised basis.[73]

The army had undertaken some mechanisation development work during the interwar period, but because of the army's impoverishment, progress had barely gone beyond the experimental stage.[74] The army established its first tank unit (militia) in 1930, and by the end of the fiscal year it had a roster of 35 officers and men. Pearce called for the manufacture of an Australian-designed armoured car during his 1933 address on Australian defence, the following year the Munitions Supply Board

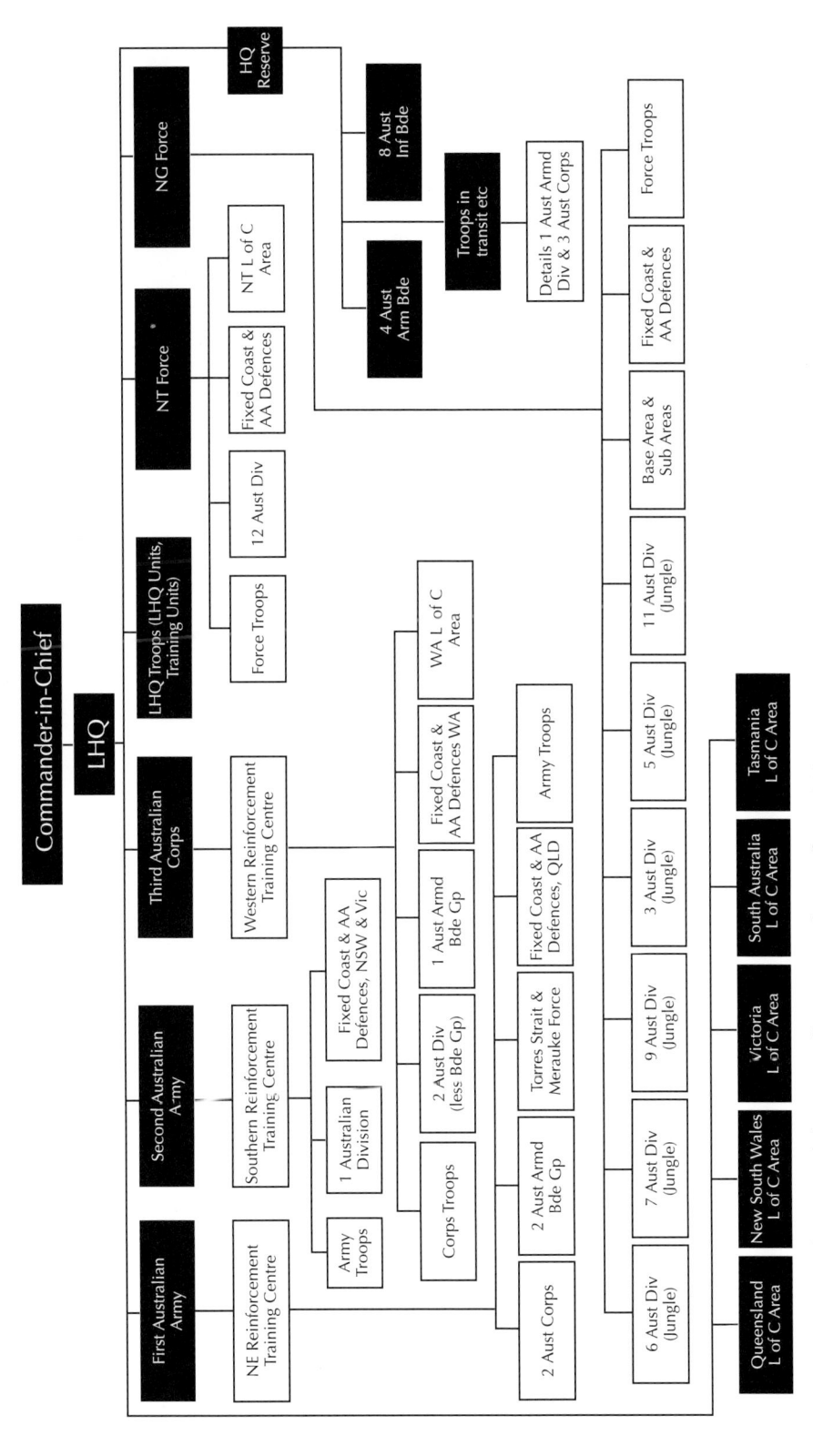

Chart 8B Distribution of the Australian Army, September 1943.
(Source: Blamey Collection, 3 DRL6643, AWM)

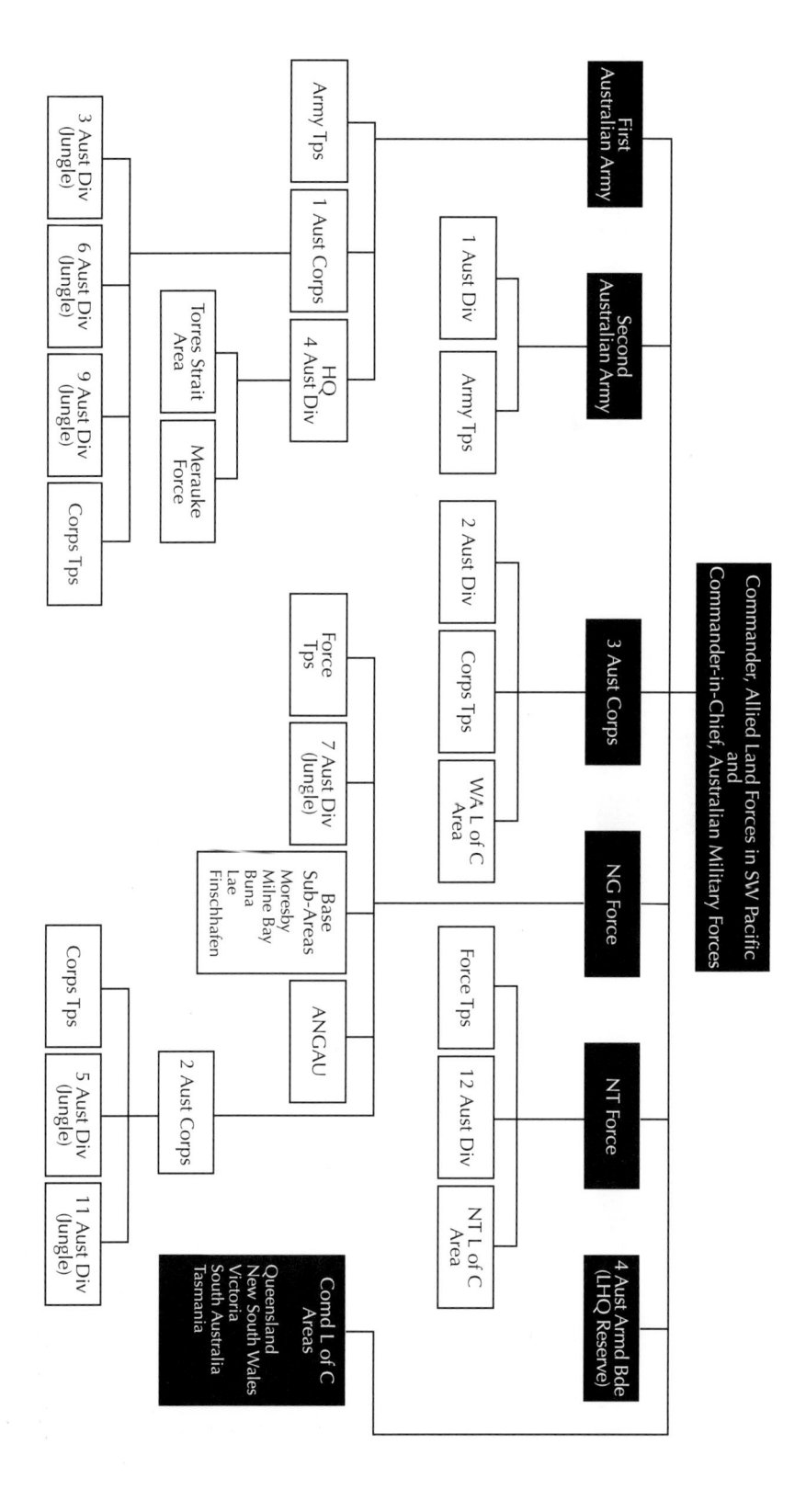

Chart 8C Distribution of the Australian Army, February 1944.
(Source: *Army War Effort*, February 1944, ADFA 254612)

WORLD WAR II

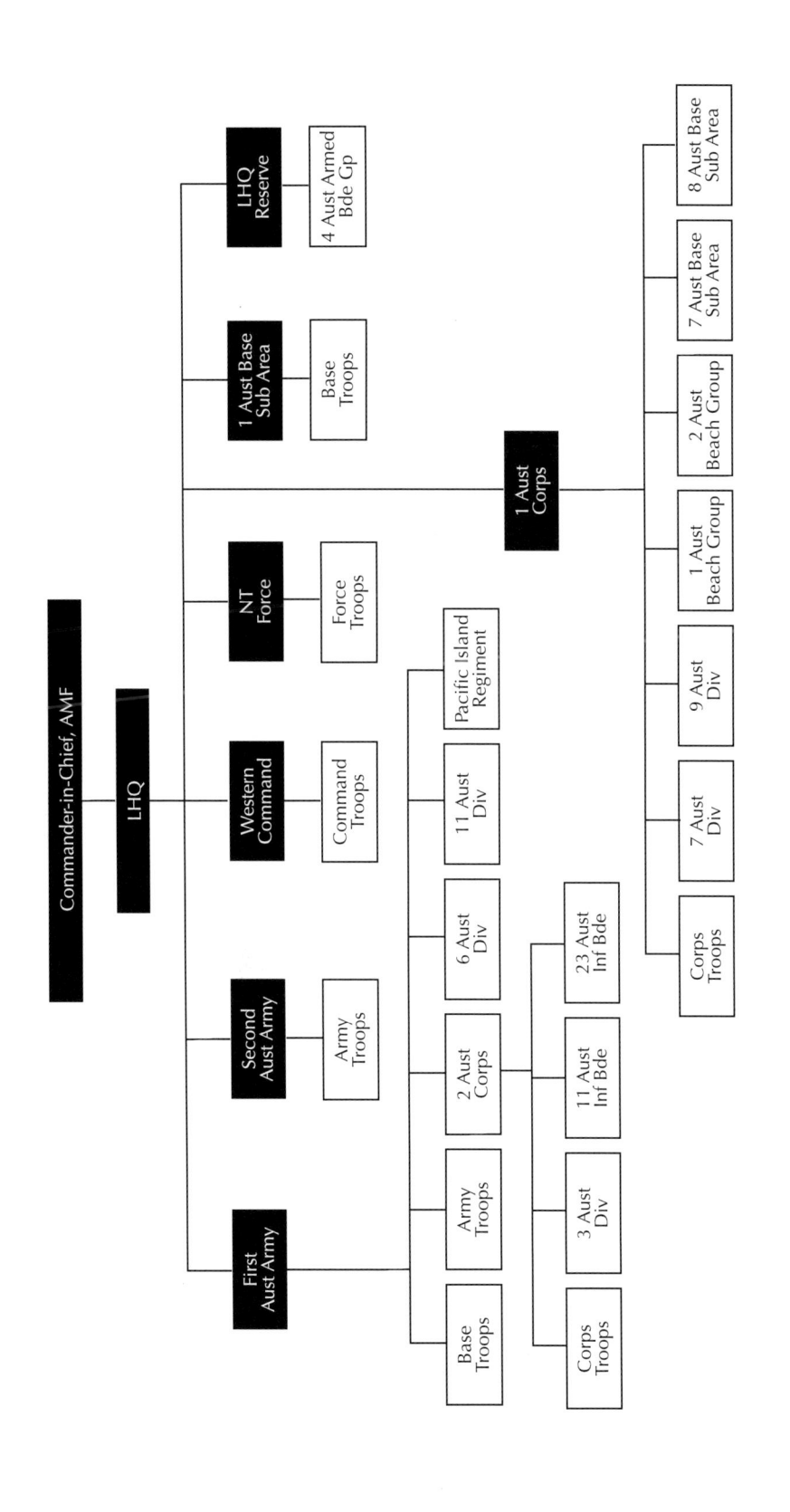

Chart 8D Distribution of the Australian Army, August 1945.
(Source: *Army War Effort*, August 1945, AWM 113, item MH1/170)

delivered a few trial vehicles, and the army raised the 1st Armoured Car Regiment the next year. The only interwar success of major note regarding mechanisation was the replacement of horses by motor vehicles in the Australian Army Service Corps, and even this must be qualified, as it was done on the peacetime establishment rather than at the much higher wartime requirement.[75]

The government accepted the army's arguments, and agreed on 1 January 1941 to the raising of an armoured division for the AIF. This was the army's second mechanised formation, as the government had also acceded to the war office's request for a corps-level tank brigade. The government originally intended to send these formations to the Middle East, but with Japan's intervention they remained in Australia, and spent most of the war on garrison duty. In the end, only a few small tank units went overseas, and then only as far as the jungles to the north. To support its armoured establishment, the army also created a Directorate of Armoured Fighting Vehicles in December 1941. Training schools were also soon underway, as well as tank-gunnery ranges at Singleton, New South Wales, and Puckapunyal, Victoria.

In May 1942, Blamey turned his attention to improving the capability of the CMF's light horse. During the course of the war, the army had converted them into motorised or mechanised units, but retained the cavalry division organisation. This meant that they were about 8,000 troops smaller than an infantry division, and lacked the combat support and service arms needed to maximise their combat potential. Blamey considered them valueless for operational purposes, and decided to reorganise them into proper divisions, with appropriate support units, including an armoured component. His decision led to the raising of the 1st and 2nd Australian Motor Divisions, the 1st containing two motor brigades, while the 2nd had a motor brigade and an armoured brigade. Blamey improved the motor divisions later in the year when he replaced one of the 1st Australian Motor Division's motor brigades with an armoured brigade. Land headquarters also redesignated the motor divisions as armoured divisions, the 1st Australian Motor Division becoming the 3rd Australian Armoured Division and the 2nd Australian Motor Division becoming the 2nd Australian Armoured Division.[76]

These divisions, along with the 3rd Australian Army Tank Brigade, represented the high point of Australia's armour development. However, beginning in 1943, the deterioration of the army's manpower position led to its gradual disbandment. In February, the army reduced the armour establishment by eliminating the 2nd Australian Armoured Division, leaving the 1st and 3rd Australian Armoured Divisions, the newly formed 4th Armoured Brigade, and the 3rd Australian Army Tank Brigade. In July, the army broke up the 3rd Australian Army Tank Brigade and reorganised it into two tank battalion groups. September brought further reductions, including the replacement of the 1st Australian Armoured Division by the 1st Australian Armoured Brigade Group. The 3rd Australian Armoured Division also lost its motor brigade in September, and in the following month the army broke up the rest of the division.[77]

The pattern continued throughout 1944, with additional units being disbanded and the personnel used as reinforcement for other formations. By August, the armoured forces consisted only of the 1st Australian Armoured Brigade Group and the 4th Australian Armoured Brigade. However, the former would go in September, and only the 4th, renamed the 4th Australian Armoured Brigade Group, survived until the Japanese surrender.[78]

Jungle divisions

The expansion of the war to the jungles of New Guinea created an interesting organisation dilemma for the Australian Army. As it returned to Australia, the AIF remained organised on a pattern that the British had designed for combat in Europe. The CMF, who had stayed behind, still followed the old imperial standard, which was suitable for the open spaces of Australia. The army fought its first campaigns in New Guinea using forces organised either on the British or imperial standards. One of the lessons of the battles for Buna, Gona, and the other 1942 battles was the army's need for a divisional organisation specifically designed for the conditions in which it fought. The recognition of this requirement led to the reorganisation of the force onto a new pattern, the jungle division.

In February 1943, land headquarters issued a directive identifying a need for three types of divisions.[79] They were armoured divisions, standard infantry divisions and jungle infantry divisions. The army planned to use the armoured and standard divisions in Australia, while it designated the jungle division for the tropics. The army initially planned to convert five infantry divisions to jungle status, but actually organised six. Those converted were the three AIF Infantry Divisions (6th, 7th, and 9th) and three of the CMF Divisions (3rd, 5th, and 11th). This meant that all six divisions that Curtin had agreed to provide for operational purposes were jungle divisions. The implication of this decision was that the government had limited the use of its offensive capable forces to tropical areas. Any redeployment to a non-tropical theatre required significant readjustment of the divisional standard.

The principal differences between the standard and jungle organisations was that the jungle division was a lighter formation. It required, therefore, a lower level of maintenance, an important feature because of the army's deficiency in support arms. The jungle division had fewer artillery pieces, as these had proved extremely difficult to manoeuvre in the New Guinea interior. The reorganised formation also had considerably fewer motor vehicles and maintenance personnel, and smaller infantry battalions, compared with those found in a standard division. The infantry battalion headquarters lost its anti-aircraft and carrier platoons, which were vehicle-dependent units, but gained an extra platoon of medium machine-guns. The division retained some carriers in a divisional-headquarters-controlled company that the commander could allocate as needed. The army also eliminated as many administrative personnel as possible, since experience demonstrated that they tended to congregate in base areas and increase the formation's maintenance requirement. The jungle division did have less firepower than the standard division, but its design was better suited for the projection of its power in the tropics. With an establishment of 13,118, a jungle division had approximately 4,000 fewer men than the standard division.[80]

The greatest problem the army had faced in New Guinea was logistical support. The island lacked roads and port facilities, and the interior's terrain was among the most difficult in the world. Away from the coast, walking was the main means of movement. Native porters were essential for the transport of supplies and the portage of the wounded. Wherever possible, the army supplemented its ground-based logistical network with air transport and supply dropping. However, inadequate numbers of planes, coupled with difficult flying conditions, placed severe limits on the amount of cargo the RAAF could move. The standard division also contained a large number of motorbikes, trucks, and mechanised vehicles, which were imperative in conditions such as the Australian bush but of limited use in the rugged, roadless jungles of the South-West Pacific Area. Instead, jungle divisions required large numbers of jeeps, and a few tanks, carriers, and tractors for combat support and movement over muddy tracks. Fewer vehicles also meant a lower requirement for maintenance personnel and reduced the amount of supplies the division needed, thereby lowering the strain on Australia's limited logistical support.

The creation of jungle divisions was significant for the army because it represented the first time it had developed on its own an organisation expressly for conditions in which its forces would fight. In the past, imperial authorities had designed the organisations that the Australian Army had utilised. Consequently, previous formations satisfied more the needs of London than Canberra. Australia's decision to develop a local organisation also reflected the growing maturity of its commanders and a willingness to decrease their association with the imperial army.

Table 5.10 provides a comparison of the principal elements of a standard and a jungle division.

Table 5.10 Comparison of standard and jungle division organisations[81]

Type	Standard division organisation	Jungle division organisation
Infantry	3 infantry brigades, each with three battalions	3 infantry brigades, each with three battalions less transport elements
		1 division carrier company
RAA	HQ RAA	HQ RAA
	3 field regiments, each with three batteries	1 field regiment
	1 anti-tank regiment	1 light anti-aircraft battery (airborne)
	1 light anti-aircraft regiment	
	1 survey battery	
RAE	HQ RAE	HQ RAE
	1 field park company	1 field park company
	3 field companies	3 field companies
	Camouflage training unit	Camouflage training unit
Signals	3 companies	3 companies
AASC	HQ AASC	HQ AASC
	3 companies	Supply depot company
		General transport company
AAMC	3 field ambulance companies	3 field ambulance companies
ORD	3 brigade ordnance field parks	3 brigade ordnance field parks
	Mobile laundry and decontamination unit	
AEME	10 light aid detachments	6 light aid detachments
	3 brigade workshops	3 brigade workshops
	Light anti-aircraft regiment workshop	
Misc.	Provost company	Provost company
	Divisional postal unit	Divisional postal unit
	Field cash office	Field cash office
	Divisional salvage unit	Divisional salvage unit
	Divisional reception camp	Divisional reception camp
	Divisional concert party	

The reorganisation also meant that the army had adopted a two-tier structure, however. Formations that the army had not designated for jungle status remained on a different standard. While this did mean that their structure was better suited for the Australian continent, it also meant that they were no longer first-rank formations that could participate in the war against Japan. The brunt of the combat, therefore, fell on a select number of formations for the rest of the war, while the remainder of the army declined ever more into a garrison state. To some extent this was inevitable because of the nation's limitation on manpower. The army concentrated its offensive power in the jungle divisions, while the forces in Australia survived with troops who were not fit for overseas service.

The Volunteer Defence Corps and women at war

During the war, a number of private- or government-sponsored movements emerged to assist the war effort. Some, such as the Australian Red Cross or the Salvation Army, had peacetime functions, which these organisations redefined as wartime aid to the nation's service men and women. Others were new entities, for example, the Australian Women's Land Army. The body that had the greatest effect upon the organisation of the army was the Volunteer Defence Corps. It was inaugurated on 15 July 1940 under the auspices of the Returned Sailors', Soldiers', and Airmen's Imperial League of Australia. Its founding principle was to provide a means by which ex-servicemen could make a contribution to the defence of their communities. In May 1941, the Volunteer Defence Corps became part of the army. The following year, it became a corps of the CMF. Once it was under the government's control, the government expanded its membership in order to allow fit males who were in reserved occupations the opportunity to perform some military duty. By September 1942, only 20 per cent of the Volunteer Defence Corps had seen previous service.[82]

The army defined the objective of the Volunteer Defence Corps as to 'augment the local defences of the State by providing static defence of localities and the protection of vulnerable points and by giving timely information regarding enemy movements to superior military organizations'.[83] More succinctly, its purpose was to 'Deny, Delay, and Protect'.[84] Some of the particular missions for which the Volunteer Defence Corps prepared included the construction of road blocks, demolition of bridges and piers, protection of airbases, industrial sites, and vulnerable points, coastwatching, and village and guerrilla warfare. When workers joined the organisation, they often provided for the defence of their plants. For example, protecting the BHP steel works at Newcastle were three Volunteer Defence Corps battalions, each representing an eight-hour shift. When the manpower situation became difficult, the Volunteer Defence Corps expanded its role, especially in the manning of anti-aircraft batteries and coast defence fortifications.[85]

So that the Volunteer Defence Corps could achieve its mission, the army organised it geographically to correspond to the line of communication areas. In each line of communication area, the army appointed a Volunteer Defence Corps commander. It then subdivided each line of communication area into Volunteer Defence Corps groups, each holding several battalions. The army abolished the group level in 1944. A typical battalion held approximately 400 men, organised into companies, platoons, and sections. However, the Volunteer Defence Corps did not have any fixed establishment, as the operational task determined the shape of a particular unit. The commander of the Volunteer Defence Corps was a director who held the equivalent rank of a brigadier. Blamey attached the position to his staff at land headquarters. The Volunteer Defence Corps was responsible for its own administration and training, but for operational matters it fell under the control of the officer commanding the line of communication area to which it belonged.[86]

At each command level, down to the battalion, the Volunteer Defence Corps contained a handful of full-time staff to manage administrative and training matters. Most volunteers served on a part-time basis, reporting for duty for only about six hours a week. Later in the war, the army did authorise the recruitment of up to 5,000 Volunteer Defence Corps members for full-time duty to perform tasks such as coastwatching and the guarding of vulnerable points, but the number serving continuously never exceeded 3,000. Part-time and full-time serving volunteers did, however, allow the army to divert substantial line of communication area troops to other duties. In 1944, the army had replaced over 6,000 army personnel with Volunteer Defence Corps staff.[87]

In fact, the Volunteer Defence Corps was so popular that it attracted far more members than the army believed could be profitably employed, and its establishment was as much a product of individual demand and political advantage as military requirement. When first absorbed by the army, the Volunteer Defence Corps had an establishment set at 50,000. Within two months, recruits oversubscribed the ranks to such an extent that the government raised the limit to 80,000. This was still insufficient, and the Volunteer Defence Corps carried a further 18,000 as supernumeraries. The government approached Blamey with the idea of increasing the limit further, but he objected, basing his argument on the absence of a military need. However, Blamey's words had little effect on Francis Forde, who had become Minister for the

Army in October 1941. In December 1942, Forde authorised additional expenditure in order to equip a volunteer force of up to 100,000 men.[88]

While the formation of the Volunteer Defence Corps provided the army with additional resources for local defence, especially during the fearful first half of 1942, it did create some problems for the army. The most serious was the provision of uniforms and equipment, as the CMF was desperately short of these items itself. The army attempted to maintain a policy of issuing materials to the Volunteer Defence Corps only once it had satisfied the CMF's demand. However, the government found this policy politically unsustainable, and capitulated to demands for more resources for the volunteers. An appeal from the Coogee–Randwick Area Returned Sailors', Soldiers', and Airmen's Imperial League of Australia in September 1940 for uniforms, arms, and equipment was a typical effort by the volunteers for better access to war goods. In this letter the Coogee–Randwick veterans noted that their desire was for sufficient arms so that they might constitute a real fighting force that was able to serve Australia in case of invasion. The Minister for the Army at the time, Spender, had difficulty rejecting such requests, and instead required the army to provide the volunteers with greater access to rifles. However, the issuance of other weapons, such as mortars and grenades, had to wait until the army had satisfied the demands of higher priority formations. Consequently, in 1944, when the nation's need for them was clearly in decline, active-duty Volunteer Defence Corps battalions were only then reaching an average of approximately 75 per cent of an infantry battalion's equipment establishment.[89]

Like the rest of the army, the Volunteer Defence Corps began to contract in 1943. By December 1943, its strength was down to under 86,000. In July 1944, the army undertook a major reorganisation of the volunteers. The army placed more than half of its membership on reserve status. In October 1944, the 1st Army placed 15 Volunteer Defence Corps battalions onto reserve status and disbanded several other units entirely. The only formation remaining on active status in the Brisbane area was the 10th Australian Anti-Aircraft Group, which contained three static heavy anti-aircraft batteries. Shortly after the end of the war, the army demobilised the entire Volunteer Defence Corps.[90] Table 5.11 outlines the organisation of the Volunteer Defence Corps as it existed in August 1944.

During the war, the role of women in the services expanded greatly, both in terms of the number of females in uniform and the jobs they performed. Before World War II, the only women serving in the army were the members of the Australian Army Nursing Service. The Australian Army Nursing Service had long been a part of the force as it had been established in 1902 as a reserve voluntary organisation. With the commencement of the Great War, the Australian Army Nursing Service switched to active status and its members accompanied the AIF to Egypt, then France. Upon demobilisation, the organisation again reverted to reserve status, but with the onset of the next great war, there was no question whether nurses would accompany the 2nd AIF. During World War II, Australian Army Nursing Service personnel served in Egypt, Libya, Greece, Crete, Syria, Malaya, Singapore, and throughout the South-West Pacific Area.[91]

Table 5.11 Organisation of Volunteer Defence Corps, 1944[92]

Line of communication area	No. of VDC battalions	Full-time personnel	Part-time personnel: active	Part-time personnel: reserve	Total personnel
Queensland	23	547	4,008	8,053	12,608
New South Wales	33	498	11,472	10,730	22,970
Victoria	24	154	5,444	13,585	19,183
South Australia	10	68	2,983	4,194	7,245
Western Australia	16	130	5,037	4,343	9,510
Tasmania	5	88	1,222	2,348	3,658
Total	*111*	*1,485*	*30,166*	*43,253*	*75,174*

The demand for wartime labour led to the formation of two other women's organisation by the army. They were the Australian Army Medical Women's Service and the Australian Women's Army Service. The Australian Army Medical Women's Service grew out of the Voluntary Aid Detachment system, whose origins lay in the Australian Red Cross and the Order of Saint John. They performed unpaid voluntary duties in the military hospital system. In March 1942, the army brought Voluntary Aid Detachments under the Army Medical Service for full-time service, and in December 1942 it established it as a branch of the CMF. The Voluntary Aid Detachment system began as a means to provide extra medical comforts to soldiers, but with its takeover by the army it took on the extra purpose of freeing up male hospital staff for other duties. They worked as, among other things, occupational therapists, dietitians, laboratory assistants, and operating theatre assistants. They also took over from men many administrative, cooking, and laundry responsibilities. The army established a training school for the Australian Army Medical Women's Service, while those aspiring to become officers or non-commissioned officers could attend Australian Women's Army Service schools. Some Voluntary Aid Detachment personnel saw service in the Middle East before their formal incorporation into the army. With the reorientation of the war effort to the Pacific, staff of the Australian Army Medical Women's Service served throughout Australia and the South-West Pacific Area.[93]

The Australian Women's Army Service developed out of a similar need to replace male soldiers with female personnel in order to maximise the strength of the fighting units. On 13 August 1941, the War Cabinet authorised the creation of the Australian Women's Army Service. Female soldiers filled various positions, including wireless operators, draughtswomen, photographers, signal operators, dispatch riders, mechanics, and storekeepers. They also replaced men in static coastal and aerial defence positions as searchlight operators, radar operators, predictor operators in anti-aircraft batteries, and plotters in battery plotting rooms. They also filled many administrative and clerical positions. The Australian Women's Army Service served throughout Australia, and late in the war the army sent a contingent to New Guinea.[94]

The government did not object to the service of female personnel overseas if they performed medical duties. Nurses sailed with the 6th Division to Egypt and, along with the Australian Army Medical Women's Service, could be found in all theatres of the war. Curtin, however, was much more hesitant to send overseas the women of the Australian Women's Army Service, as the government considered the duties they performed non-traditional. In February 1941, the war cabinet refused Blamey's request for a limited number of women to serve in canteens in the Middle East in order to free up men for the front. In December, the war cabinet again rejected Blamey's bid, this time for 500 women to take up cipher, stenographic, clerical, and canteen positions.[95] Blamey also had to argue strenuously to get the Australian Women's Army Service overseas in the Pacific. As the front moved forward, Blamey redeployed his advance land headquarters into New Guinea. Since by this stage female personnel had replaced male staff in critical cipher and signal positions in his headquarters, Blamey either had to have the women or find men with whom to replace them. Forde wrote to Blamey to express his opposition to the Australian Women's Army Service leaving Australia. Blamey eventually received the government's sanction, but for not more than 500 personnel. These women served mainly in Lae in the Headquarters 1st Australian Army, while a limited number got as far forward as Hollandia.[96]

With the end of the war, as part of the demobilisation process the government gradually eliminated the Australian Women's Army Service. Its fate became clear in April 1946, when the army excluded its remaining members from participating in a survey of serving personnel regarding their interest in a further two-year enlistment with the post-war forces.[97] On 30 June 1947, its disbandment became effective.

The medical women's service survived in the post-war army. The Australian Army Nursing Service received its 'Royal' designation in November 1948, and in July 1949 it became a part of the Regular Army. In 1951 it became a corps. The Australian Army Medical Women's Service continued as a part of the CMF until its disbandment in 1951.

As the invasion of Japan neared, Australian decision-makers assessed the role of their forces in the final battle. Although the sudden surrender of Japan, following the atomic bombing of two of its cities and Russian intervention in Manchuria, obviated the need for an amphibious assault upon the enemy's homeland, the Australian Government had planned for the AIF to assist in the conquest of the Japanese mainland. However, the army's leaders accepted that a commitment of its forces, at such a great distance from Australian territory, would be heavily dependent for its maintenance and support on the United States. Therefore, if Australians were to participate, the designated units would have to undergo a major reorganisation in order to make them compatible with the American order of battle and logistic requirements. A report prepared in May 1945 did suggest the possibility of the participation of up to two infantry divisions in the campaign in Japan. The report recommended that if this occurred, the division's personnel establishment should mirror that of the United States Army and that Australia should re-equip the formations with American equipment and weapon systems. Australia, in fact, would have provided troops with little more than their uniforms and personal weapons. The report also recommended cooperation with Britain in the reconquest of its colonies in South-East Asia, but noted that this required the retention of units either on the Jungle Standard or their conversion back to the British model.[98]

The conclusion of the war brought all thoughts of further offensive operations to a halt. Instead, the War Cabinet turned its attention to the issues of demobilisation and of Australia's contribution to an occupation force for Japan. The army, the largest military force the nation had ever raised, quickly dissolved as the soldiers of the AIF and CMF once again became civilians.

6
POST-WAR REORGANISATION AND THE KOREAN WAR

All will agree that the great lesson of the war was our national unpreparedness ... and our greatest trust in the future should be never to revert to such a state again.

Francis M. Forde[1]

The victorious conclusion to World War II did not end Australia's need to deploy military forces overseas. As the Commonwealth began the process of demobilisation, it also had to find troops willing to fulfil the nation's post-war military responsibilities. These duties included the acceptance of the surrender of over 300,000 Japanese military personnel and their maintenance until repatriation, the provision of assistance to the British and Dutch governments and the restoration of their colonial authority, and the recovery from overseas and storage or sale in Australia of large quantities of equipment. The government's desire to claim a role in the Pacific settlement reinforced the need to maintain an overseas presence, including the dispatch of more than 10,000 troops to help occupy Japan.[2] While all these measures were finite in terms of commitment, the emergence of the Soviet Union and the spectre of world communism assured that the Australian Army that did develop after the war would be significantly different from that which had existed in the past.

In addition, the ease with which Japan had overturned the edifice of Australia's interwar security arrangements galvanised the post-war governments of Chifley and Menzies to seek a more active Australian voice in the formulation of defence plans for the Western Pacific.[3] One of the lessons of the Singapore fallacy was that Australian decision-makers could no longer passively rely upon the kind words of imperial authorities when considering the Commonwealth's national security. As a consequence, Australia had to pursue a broader-based national security strategy. While post-war defence planning continued to foresee a role for the empire, decision-makers also emphasised the collective security capability of the United Nations and sought a continuing American presence in the region. The ultimate achievement of these policies was Australia's entry, with New Zealand, into a regional security pact with the United States. ANZUS, as the agreement became known, became the keystone of Australian security, and the pact continues to affect the Commonwealth's defence decision-making and force structure organisation to the present.

Defining the post-war security environment

The course of World War II reinforced the correctly held belief of defence strategists that Australia could not defend itself, on its own, against an assault by a great power. During the war, after Britain had failed to either deter or contain Japan, the responsibility for Australian defence passed to the United States. Although the Commonwealth did commit significant, even critical, resources to the allied effort, it was the United States that ultimately bore the principal burden. Consequently, Australian decision-makers understood that the nation would have a similar post-war security need, namely, the Commonwealth would have to create an environment in which a major friendly power, or powers, undertook to safeguard the continent. While Australian leaders accepted that the nation would have to assume a greater share of the nation's defence than it had had to in the past, it was also clear that outside assistance was a prerequisite for true security.

The government's first steps towards this goal were undertaken well before the end of the war, even before it had identified any particular post-war responsibilities or assessed the nature and level of threats that might exist. Since Australia, standing alone, was indefensible, the accuracy of threat definition was not critical. Rather, it was more important for the government to begin establishing the international relationships upon which Australia would base its security in the post-war world. The Curtin Government outlined the principles of its intended policies in 1943, and subsequent administrations largely adhered to them. In August 1943, Curtin told the Defence Committee that the key to Australia's post-war defence was its participation in a system of collective security.[4] By January 1944, the government had identified the essential post-war defence requirements as local defence, participation in collective security, cooperation in empire defence, and the policing of the World War II peace treaties.[5] Of course, empire defence and the guaranteeing of the peace treaties were themselves other aspects of collective security. The following March, Curtin continued this theme in his instructions to his Minister for Post-War Reconstruction, J.B. Chifley. He requested that the minister should consider post-war defence policy from the perspective of:

1 The experience of this war in relation to the principles of Australian and Empire defence, and to the nature, strength and organisation of the Australian forces.
2 As and when any progress is made in regard to the principles and nature of the collective system, either on a world or regional basis, their implications in regard to Australian defence should be considered.[6]

By 1946, the Council of Defence undertook its deliberations on the basis that collective security was the critical factor in post-war defence planning.[7]

The principles of Australian security, therefore, had quickly reduced themselves to two core interrelated elements, greater attention to the requirements of local defence and the nation's participation in collective security systems. For the Commonwealth, the latter initially took the form of a renewed interest in imperial security and support for the United Nations. John Dedman, the Minister for Defence, made this point at a meeting of the Council of Defence in 1947. He identified the basis of Australian security as resting upon a 'blending of the collective security provided by the United Nations and the British Commonwealth, and of the forces to be maintained for . . . self-defence'.[8] Dedman reiterated his remarks the following year in a policy address. He announced that there were four roles for which the government expected the army to prepare, and for which it was to organise its forces. They were:

1 Commitment to the United Nations.
2 Cooperation in British Commonwealth Defence.
3 Local Defence.
4 Provision for expansion in war.[9]

Taking into account the government's policy outline and the post-war strategic environment, the army's leaders proposed a radical new organisation for the force, including both permanent and CMF field force units, which laid the foundation of the Australian Regular Army (ARA). It received Chifley's approval in June 1947, and is discussed in full below.

The renewal of defence participation interests with Britain, despite the Singapore debacle, is not surprising, and both the Chifley and Menzies governments believed the 'mother country' still had an important role to play in South-East Asia. However, the proposals advanced by Australia at the 1947 Prime Ministers' Conference did not suggest a security relationship on the same order of magnitude that had existed previously. Replacing the Royal Navy's pledge of maritime supremacy was an arrangement based upon individual responsibility and collective defence. Members of the Commonwealth were to develop the defences of their support area, accept joint responsibility for the protection of the lines of communication linking the support areas, and agree that it was in every nation's strategic interests to maintain the empire's position in those areas that directly affected the security of their territory and communications.

Australia's place within this collective security system received a clearer explanation in the government's 1950 defence review. The review examined the nation's security policy from the perspective of the Commonwealth's place within a system of defence that aimed to contain the Soviet Union. It defined Australia's responsibility as the need to join with other Commonwealth countries, the United States, and the countries of Western Europe in organising deterrent forces and developing defence plans with which to contain communist aggression. If war did occur, Australia's role would be to assist the British in the defence of the Middle East, especially the critical air bases from which the allies would launch a strategic air offensive against the Soviet Union, and the army drew up plans for the dispatch of a force of up to three divisions, with supporting corps and army troops. Australian intervention would have once again resulted in the raising of an expeditionary force for the Middle East. Since, during this period, the Soviet Union could not project military power over the vastness of the Pacific, Australia's territorial defence was left to the United States Navy.[10]

Despite these arrangements, Australian policy-makers considered the renewed ties with Britain to be a stopgap measure, and the commitment to the Middle East would prove temporary. Australia's joining with Britain and New Zealand in the ANZAM agreement in 1949 signalled the true location of the Commonwealth's future interests. In addition, in order for Australia to attain real security, its arrangements had to include a major power of sufficient strength to offset any potential hostile opponent. Although Britain retained considerable military potential, its strength had declined relatively, and the 'mother country' itself had to seek allies to offset the threat of the Soviet Union to Western Europe. The only nation with interests in the Pacific that could provide the level of absolute protection that the Commonwealth desired was the United States. As a result, both Herbert Evatt and Percy Spender, the Ministers for External Affairs in the Chifley and Menzies governments respectively, sought to secure American assistance.[11] Under the direction of these ministers, Australia pursued an ambitious and eventually successful foreign policy agenda aimed at ensuring an ongoing American commitment to the South-West Pacific region. At the 1946 meeting of the Commonwealth prime ministers, Chifley had announced that he believed in the need to involve the United States in the security preparations for the South-West Pacific Region.[12] The following year, the Chiefs of Staff Committee argued in their strategic review that 'it is ... in Australia's strategic interest to support any measures designed to perpetuate the United States of America's influence in the Western Pacific'.[13]

The Americans, however, were reluctant to maintain a presence in the area, a fact the United States demonstrated by its transfer to Australia of the huge Manus base. Millar has observed that the United States believed that, with Japan defeated and with the restoration of the colonial powers in South-East Asia, it had 'no further military need of Australia or of bases in her vicinity'.[14] This attitude tended to reinforce the renewal of Australian ties with Britain, especially because of the 'mother country's' presence in Malaya. Yet the commitment to the empire did not lessen Australia's desire to reach an agreement with the United States. During talks with John Foster Dulles, the American negotiator, Spender used to advantage the good relations Australia enjoyed with the United States because of its participation in the Korean War, and the increasing concern of the Truman administration over the spread of communism. He informed Dulles that a security treaty between the two countries was a condition for Australia to accept the American-brokered peace treaty with Japan. Overcoming Dulles's reluctance to provide a security guarantee, Spender succeeded in laying the groundwork for additional discussions, which led to the signing of the ANZUS Treaty in 1951.[15]

The ANZUS Treaty never became the NATO Treaty for the Pacific, and the United States did try to minimise its responsibilities in the region until the Vietnam War. Nor did the agreement offer the unquestionable security that American military power provided to Canada. However, its signing represented a major step forward in securing the assistance of a great power for the protection of Australia. ANZUS did not immediately replace the role of Britain in Australian security arrangements, but it did suggest that a realignment in the region's defence had begun, thereby lessening the significance of the empire's eventual retreat from the South-West Pacific.

The Interim Army

At the conclusion of World War II, as had happened at the end of World War I, the government discarded the existing army organisation in order to build a new structure. In both world wars, the inherent liabilities of the two-army system mandated such a step. The armistice provided the army and the government with the opportunity to craft a new structure based on the lessons of the recently concluded conflict, and the requirements of post-war defence planning. In 1920, the army's first attempt at this type of reform had largely failed, as the military's unpreparedness in 1939 demonstrated. However, post-war ministers had learned from the disaster that so nearly befell Australia after the entry of Japan into World War II. As a result, political leaders understood that they could no longer completely abrogate the responsibility for their nation's defence to decision-makers in London. Consequently, the post-World War II defence assessment would be more successful than the previous exercise, although it too would fall short of the desires of the army's leaders.

Complicating the process of designing the army's new organisation were several significant post-war responsibilities that the Australian Government had undertaken, and which required the commitment of considerable military forces. As a result, the army could not completely dissolve itself, as it had at the end of World War I. Instead, it was necessary to 'create a temporary military organisation to manage immediate post-war duties, while at the same time identifying the needs of a permanent institution to meet ongoing responsibilities. These included necessary steps, such as demobilisation, participation in the occupation of Japan, repatriation of prisoners of war and internees, maintenance of a military presence in occupied areas until the restoration of civil rule, and the removal to Australia of large quantities of military equipment and either their disposal as surplus or their transfer to storage.

In February 1945, planners serving on the Demobilisation Committee decided to call the organisation that would fulfil the Commonwealth's immediate post-war commitments the 'interim forces'. With the establishment of this temporary entity, the army suspended the organisation of the CMF and halted recruitment into the AMF. The government began recruitment for the interim forces in February 1946 on the basis of a two-year term of service. The restoration of the CMF had to await the determination of the requirements of the permanent army organisation.[16] From 'interim forces' would evolve the name 'Interim Army', which the military would employ to describe all the forces under its command until the army readopted a permanent structure.[17]

In May 1946, the Military Board modified the definition of the Interim Army to include anyone who joined the service after the conclusion of the war and any new units the military might raise. The Adjutant-General's proposal for a new definition was 'all members of the AMF serving on continuous full-time duty on 1 October 1945 and personnel who joined the AMF on continuous full-time duty after that date'.[18] The

Adjutant-General had carefully selected his words to provide a definition that included all current serving members of the AMF. In this way he avoided the possibility of once again creating more than one army. The use of the phrase 'full-time duty' was not yet a concern, as the army did not reraise its part-time forces until 1948.[19]

While the government demobilised the AMF as rapidly as possible, it did not finish the task until February 1947, because of the vast scale of the process and the need to retain some troops for post-war responsibilities. As the army underwent a massive contraction, the occupation of Japan required it to raise a new force specifically for that duty. The allied occupation forces were to oversee the surrender of the Japanese homeland and the implementation of the peace treaty, when signed. Based upon the ferocity of the enemy's resistance during the war, it was unclear how cooperative the Japanese government and people would be in the acceptance of their defeat. While the other various post-war duties of the Interim Army were short-term, winding-down operations, the occupation of Japan was of greater significance and undefined duration. In the end, the Japanese people proved remarkably cooperative, and after a relatively brief period of weapon collection, Australian troops settled down into a role more similar to that of a garrison than an occupation. However, even allowing for the Korean War, Australia's contribution to the occupation force lasted a surprisingly long time, and some troops remained in Japan into the 1950s.

As a result of the government's determination that Australia should have a greater say in the Japanese settlement, Chifley approached the Americans with the suggestion that the Commonwealth's contingent should form an independent force subject directly to the Supreme Allied Commander (MacArthur). Furthermore, he had rebuffed a British request seeking Australia's participation in an imperial organisation. However, the British wanted to present a united imperial front in order to maximise their role in the settlement with Japan and reexert their influence in the Pacific. As an inducement, Clement Attlee, the British prime minister, suggested to Chifley the formation of a British Commonwealth Occupation Force that would have an Australian as its commander. Australians would also fill the majority of headquarters staff positions. Chifley agreed because he saw it as an opportunity to enhance Australian prestige and bring the Australian commander into closer contact with the Americans in MacArthur's Tokyo headquarters. The government initially gave the appointment of Commander-in-Chief British Commonwealth Occupation Force to Lieutenant-General John Northcott until his replacement by Lieutenant-General Horace Robertson, who served until nearly the end of the British Commonwealth Occupation Force's existence.[20]

Lieutenant-General J. Northcott inspecting Australian troops in Kure, Japan.
(AWM 129250)

The Australian Government agreed to provide for the occupation of Japan a brigade group, with supporting headquarters and base troops. The Australian component numbered about 10,000 personnel out of an establishment of approximately 37,000, the rest of the force consisting of British, Indian, and New Zealand troops. Australia raised its component from soldiers in Australia and from those still scattered across the South-West Pacific, from Bougainville to Borneo. Because of the requirements of the Defence Act, everyone who served in Japan was a volunteer and had to

Lieutenant-Colonel F. S. Walsh (3 RAR, BCOF), receives the Gloucester Cup from Lieutenant-General H. C. H. Robertson. (AWM 146375)

attest specifically for occupation duty. The army raised three new battalions, numbered 65 through 67, and these formed the main element of 34th Australian Infantry Brigade. The major units of brigade were:

- Headquarters 34th Infantry Brigade
- 1st Armoured Car Squadron
- 'A' Field Battery
- 28th Field Company
- 34th Brigade Signal Section
- 65th, 66th, 67th Infantry Battalions
- 168th General Transport Company
- 20th Field Ambulance
- 140th Brigade Ordnance Field Park
- 140th Brigade Workshop.

In addition, small detachments of other corps also belonged to the brigade. These troops, especially the infantry, represented the core units of the future ARA.

Australia also made a sizeable contribution to the British Commonwealth Occupation Force's headquarters, force support, and base establishments. This included units such as the 13th Movement Control Group, 14th Workshop and Park Company, 21st and 22nd Line Maintenance Sections, 41st Advanced Supply Depot, 47th Field Baking Platoon, 20th Field Butchery Platoon, 1st Transport Company, 6th Refrigeration Plant Operating Platoon, 130th General Hospital, 334th Light Aid Detachment, and 8th Base Postal Unit. While the occupation of Japan was largely an American effort, within the British Commonwealth Occupation Force Zone it was Australian units that provided for the majority of the organisation's support at all levels. In fact, the British Commonwealth Occupation Force represented the first time in the army's history in which Australian forces served in the dominant role in an operation, particularly in the provision of support. While this development represented a new stage in maturity of the army, it was short-lived, and limited to the relatively simple task of garrisoning Japan. When the army next went to war, in Korea and the conflicts in South-East Asia, it again assumed a subservient role as the junior partner to a major power. Map 10 (p. 202) illustrates the region of Japan in which the British Commonwealth Occupation Force operated.[21]

By 1948, it was clear that the occupation force had fulfilled most of its goals. The Council of Defence therefore decided to reduce the nation's commitment to the occupation to a battalion group. Accordingly, by the end of the year only the 67th Infantry Battalion and supporting units remained, with an establishment of less than 2,400. In early 1950, Menzies announced his intention to withdraw the rest of the force. The army required these experienced soldiers at home to serve as instructors in the government's new Universal Training Scheme. However, the North Korean invasion of South Korea prolonged the overseas commitment of the 67th Battalion, now called 3 RAR. Instead of returning home, it joined the United Nations' force in Korea.[22]

Although the Adjutant-General's May 1946 definition of the Interim Army had been inclusive, it did not alter the fact that the army contained soldiers who served under a multitude of different terms of engagement. These include soldiers who were members of the pre-war PMF and CMF, had volunteered for the AIF or CMF after the war began, or who had been conscripted into the CMF. Many of these awaited demobilisation, which the army did not conclude until February 1947. The service categories also included members who after the end of the war had joined the Interim Army on two-year terms of engagement, or who served with the British Commonwealth Occupation Force. The reraising of the nation's permanent forces in mid 1947 added a further category of troops. The resumption of enlistment in the CMF on 1 July 1948 also brought the part-time soldiers back into the fold.

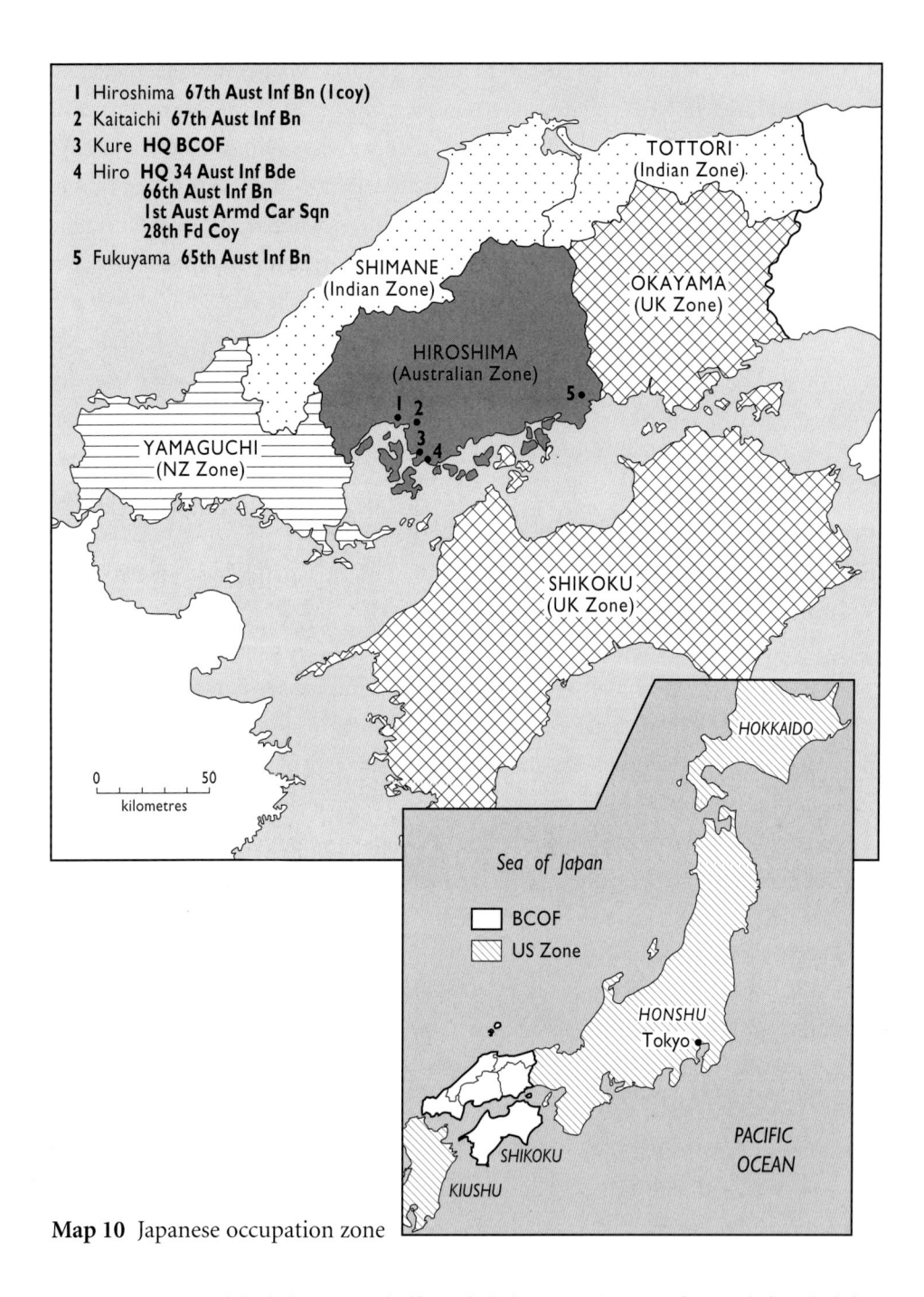

1 Hiroshima 67th Aust Inf Bn (1 coy)
2 Kaitaichi 67th Aust Inf Bn
3 Kure HQ BCOF
4 Hiro HQ 34 Aust Inf Bde
        66th Aust Inf Bn
        1st Aust Armd Car Sqn
        28th Fd Coy
5 Fukuyama 65th Aust Inf Bn

Map 10 Japanese occupation zone

The army simplified this state of affairs slightly in June 1947, when it disbanded the AIF and transferred its remaining members to the Interim Army. However, far too many service conditions still remained. In 1948, the Military Board proposed a rationalisation of the army's service conditions into two categories of permanent soldiers in addition to the CMF. It required any soldiers serving in the Interim Army, or on a short-term engagement, to transfer to the permanent forces or the army would discharge them after they completed their present service obligation. The Military Board also offered anyone who had enlisted under a wartime engagement the option of either re-enlisting in the permanent forces or receiving a discharge on 1 December 1948. By these means, the Interim Army faded away, and the force gradually reorganised onto a more durable basis.[23]

The re-forming of the Australian Army

Australian defence planners had always intended that the Interim Army would gradually fade away, and that they would supplant it with a revived permanent and citizen force structure. The transition began almost as soon as the war came to an end. In early 1946, Lieutenant-General Sydney Rowell, as Vice-Chief of the General Staff (VCGS), presented the army's first policy paper on the nature of the post-war army. Rowell noted that the only threat that Australia faced was from the Soviet Union. Australia, he wrote, could not rely for its defence upon its isolation from the rest of the world. Instead, it must be ready to help friendly powers to deter or defeat the Soviet Union. As a consequence, Rowell believed that the army had to organise its forces on the basis of overseas service, and that Australia's participation in the United Nations and its ties to Britain and the United States would assure its protection. Rowell concluded that Australia had to prepare its forces for battle against the Soviets, and that they had to be able to serve overseas in order to assist other regions that were under direct threat of aggression, particularly Britain and Europe. Last, he warned that it would take the combined might of the United States and the British Empire to assure victory against the Soviet Union.[24]

Rowell's analysis was prescient in its prediction of the coming alignments and tensions of the Cold War. He ignored the potential threat posed by China, since it was in the midst of a civil war, but this would become a greater concern during the Menzies era. To counter the Soviet Union, and to provide a force for overseas deployment, Rowell proposed a force of five division groups. Permanent forces would make up the first echelon of one division group, while citizen soldiers would form most of the next two contingents of two divisions each. The permanent forces were to be ready to deploy within three months, while the CMF was to have its final contributions ready within nine to 12 months. Permanent troops would compose the first division, while the second contingent was to have a high proportion of professional soldiers to enable

Lieutenant-General S. Rowell, CGS 1950–54, inspecting Australian troops in Korea. (AWM 157576)

its rapid deployment. Rowell believed that universal training was an essential component of the scheme, as the army needed a pool of experienced men from which to draw the personnel needed to fill out the later deployments.[25]

Rowell's policy paper was a theoretical draft intended for internal consideration. As the VCGS admitted in the introduction, he had drawn up the assessment without any consideration of the costs involved, a fatal flaw in any Australian security proposal. However, he did identify some of the army's ideas for its post-war forces. These included the need for standing combat formations, an establishment with a higher percentage of regular soldiers than in the past, a need for conscription with a lengthy training period, and an expectation that the army's operational theatre was overseas. Although the government rebuffed Rowell, his ideas would eventually come to pass.

In late 1946, the Defence Committee presented to the Council of Defence a proposal that had a greater chance of success, although it too required considerable trimming before gaining the government's agreement. It called for the three services to have a force of approximately 117,000 personnel, divided into 74,000 permanent and 43,000 citizen. The Defence Committee proposed that the army's share would be 33,600 regulars and

42,400 citizen soldiers. The proposal also called for the reintroduction of universal training, with a period of four months' continuous training. Additionally, the Defence Committee sought the amendment of the Defence Act in order that service in the army include a liability for overseas deployment. If approved, this would eliminate the need for the two-army system that had proved so inefficient in both world wars. Furthermore, if the government amended the Defence Act, it would simplify the army's training, administration, and command structure, because the force could employ the same structure for peace and war.

The Council of Defence reviewed the recommendations in March 1947, but Chifley considered its £90 million cost unacceptable. Instead, he insisted that the services had to fit their requirements into a defence vote of approximately £50 million. Furthermore, he continued, this figure also included the administrative expenses of the Department of Defence and the Department of Munitions Supply and Shipping. The Prime Minister also urged the Defence Committee to give priority to scientific research, and ordered that it provide funds for the newly established Joint Intelligence Organisation, the Scientific Advisory Committee, and the New Weapons and Equipment Development Committee from the defence vote. The Council of Defence allocated the defence estimate as: RAN: £15 million; RAAF: £12.5 million; and Army: £12.5 million. Scientific research received £6.7 million; munitions, £3.5 million; and defence administration, £650,000. The army's share over the five-year aggregate was £62.5 million. The government did not apply the British Commonwealth Occupation Force charges to the services' vote, as those costs came out of a separate estimate.[26]

Once again, the driving force behind the shaping of the army was fiscal expediency, not security concerns, and the government again signalled that it had higher priorities than force development. The prime minister observed at a meeting of the Council of Defence that the proportion of the national income that the government believed it could devote to defence would determine the strength of the armed forces. Security requirements were less important inputs in determining the defence estimate.[27] The Military Board, therefore, had to reconcile the amount provided with the cost of maintaining a force of the size and quality necessary to carry out the role of the post-war army. Chifley did honour the government's pledge that it would commit greater resources to local defence in the post-war world. However, his definition of defence extended to programs designed to improve the capabilities of the nation's military and industrial infrastructure without directly improving the operational capabilities of the armed forces. The Council of Defence's decisions also meant that the organisation of the army and the effectiveness of the force structure were not the government's highest priority. To some extent, there was an acceptance that the army could compensate for any shortfall by relying on surplus equipment and the enormous pool of demobilised veterans. However, it also meant that in the future, as the army expended its reserves of equipment and ex-soldiers aged, the force had either to find more resources or accept a period of decline.[28]

The Council of Defence refused several other recommendations by the Defence Committee. It mandated that the army would raise its permanent and citizen forces on a voluntary basis, as the government had no desire to reimplement a universal training scheme. Despite the obvious problems of the wartime two-army system, the government also refused to modify the Defence Act section requiring army personnel to agree voluntarily to serve overseas. Thus the army remained the only service lacking the freedom to deploy its forces, as they existed in peace, on operations outside Australia. The Council of Defence also rejected the four-month-long period of training that the Defence Committee had suggested for CMF recruits. Instead, it recommended only 24 days home training and 14-day camps of continuous instruction. Although the nation had a large pool of experienced soldiers, and accepting that training periods were now longer than before the war, the relatively brief obligation hampered the army's ability to create an effective CMF. By rejecting the army's suggestions, the government revealed how little it had learned from the crisis of 1939.[29]

Within its fiscal mandate the army proposed a force structure consisting of:

- A Permanent Field Force of one Independent Brigade Group. This would include three Infantry Battalions, an armoured unit, plus necessary supporting artillery, engineer, signal and administrative units.
- A Citizen Field Force of two Infantry Divisions, an Infantry Brigade Group, an Armoured Brigade Group and select corps units.
- Necessary fixed establishments to command, administer, and maintain the Army including personnel for fixed defences, training establishments and base and administrative troops.[30]

The army had an overall strength of 69,000, divided as 19,000 PMF and 50,000 CMF.[31] Table 6.1 outlines the distribution of personnel between the PMF and the CMF allocated to the field forces. The army did not have to raise most of the permanent field force from scratch, as the forces serving with the British Commonwealth Occupation Force fulfilled this role. Thus, when the permanent field force came into existence, its units were already on overseas service, and there would be no permanent combat troops in Australia until they returned.

*Table 6.1 Distribution of field force personnel
in the post-war army, 1947*

Field Forces	PMF	CMF
PMF field force	4,470	
PMF cadres for CMF field force	1,150	
CMF field force		48,850
Total field force	*5,620*	*48,850*

*Table 6.2 Distribution of fixed establishment personnel
in the post-war army, 1947*

Fixed establishments	PMF	CMF
Fixed defences	482	1,150
Base and administrative troops	10,398	
Training establishments	2,500	
Total fixed establishments	*13,380*	*1,150*

Table 6.2 outlines the distribution of personnel between the PMF and CMF allocated to fixed establishments. The army assigned a relatively high proportion of its regular troops to fixed establishments in order to maintain the extensive network of educational and training facilities it had formed during World War II.

On 3 June 1947, the cabinet approved the post-war organisation of the army as outlined above. The army planned that after its return from Japan, the PMF infantry brigade headquarters would be located in Melbourne and one of its battalions would be placed in each of the main States. In November 1948, the army redesignated the 65th, 66th, and 67th Battalions the 1st, 2nd, and 3rd Battalions of the Australian Regiment (Royal Australian Regiment after 10 March 1949). This was the first time Australia had employed a regimental system to designate its infantry battalions. The 65th Battalion became 1 RAR and took up residence in Ingleburn, New South Wales, while the 66th Battalion became 2 RAR and made its home in Puckapunyal, Victoria. The 67th Battalion, which became 3 RAR, remained in Japan and then Korea, but when it eventually returned to Australia it settled into Enoggera, Queensland. Puckapunyal also became the location of the PMF's armoured components. Table 6.3 (p. 208) outlines the order of battle of the PMF's field force units.

The army centred one CMF division—the 2nd—on Sydney, with units in New South Wales and Queensland. The other CMF division—the 3rd—had its headquarters in Melbourne, with units across Victoria, South Australia, and Tasmania. The army based the CMF Independent Brigade, numbered 13th, on Perth. The army stationed one armoured brigade in New South Wales, with a second in Victoria. The only troops located in the Northern Territory were those required to man the fixed defences. Additional post-war forces included the Pacific Islands Regiment, for the protection of Australia's territories in Papua and New Guinea.[32] Table 6.4 (pp. 209–10) outlines the order of battle of the CMF Field Force.

Table 6.3 Order of battle of PMF field force units[33]

Corps	Unit	Location
Armour	27th Armoured Regiment	Victoria
Artillery	1st Field Regiment	New South Wales
	4th Anti-Tank Battery	Victoria
	5th Light Anti-Aircraft Battery	New South Wales
Engineers	1st Field Regiment	New South Wales
Signals	27th Armoured Regiment Signal Troop	Victoria
	1st Field Regiment Signal Troop	New South Wales
	1st Engineer Signal Troop	New South Wales
	34th Infantry Brigade Signal Troop	Victoria
Infantry	HQ 34th Infantry Brigade	New South Wales
	65th Infantry Battalion	Queensland
	66th Infantry Battalion	New South Wales
	67th Infantry Battalion	Victoria
Supply and transport	1st Transport Company	Victoria
Medical	20th Field Ambulance	Victoria
Ordnance	34th Inf. Bde Ord. Field Park	New South Wales
Electrical and mechanical	3 Workshops and four Light Aid Detachments	New South Wales and Victoria

The CMF also fielded a considerable array of corps troops. These included units such as 2nd Medium Regiment, 1st Heavy Anti-Aircraft Regiment, 16th Construction Squadron, 2nd Medium Regiment Signal Troop and the 12th Field Ambulance.

After the conclusion of the war, the army also reorganised and reduced its coastal and aerial defence network. Table 6.5 (p. 211) outlines the structure of the nation's remaining fixed defences.

Table 6.4 Order of battle of the CMF field force[34]

Formation	Corps	Units
HQ 2nd Division	Armour	7/21st Recce. Regt
	Artillery	5th, 7th, 11th Fd Regts
		3rd Anti-Tank Regt
		1st LAA Regt
		2nd Div. Locating Bty
	Engineers	2nd Fd Eng. Regt
	Signals	2nd Div. Signal Regt
	Infantry	HQs 5th, 7th, 8th Inf. Bdes
		2nd, 3rd, 9th, 17/18th, 25th, 30th, 31st, 41st, 42nd, 45th Bns
	Supply and transport	2nd, 3rd, 4th, 5th Tpt Coys
	Medical	5th, 8th, 11th Fd Amb.
	Ordnance	2nd Div Ord. Fd Park
	Electrical and mechanical engineers	102nd, 103rd, 104th Inf. Wksp
		1st, 2nd, 5th, 9th, 10th, 11th, 19th, 20th, 21st, 28th, 30th LAD
		2nd LAA Wksp
	Postal	2nd Div. Postal Unit
	Provost	2nd Div. Provost Coy
HQ 3rd Division	Armour	3rd Recce. Regt
	Artillery	2nd, 10th, 13th Fd Regts
		6th Anti-Tank Regt
		2nd LAA Regt
		3rd Div. Locating Bty
	Engineers	3rd Fd Eng. Regt
	Signals	3rd Div. Signal Regt
	Infantry	HQs 4th, 6th, 9th Inf. Bdes
		5th, 6th, 8/7th, 10th, 12/40th, 27th, 38th, 58/32nd Bns
	Supply and transport	6th, 7th, 8th, 9th Tpt Coys
	Medical	3rd, 4th, 6th Fd Amb.
	Ordnance	3rd Div. Ord. Fd Park
	Electrical and mechanical engineers	105th, 106th, 107th Inf. Wksp
		3rd, 4th, 12th, 13th, 14th, 22nd, 23rd, 24th, 29th, 31st LAD
		3rd LAA Wksp

Formation	Corps	Units
	Postal	3rd Div. Postal Unit
	Provost	3rd Div. Provost Coy
1st Independent Armoured Bde Group	Armour	HQs 1st, 2nd Armd Bdes
		1st, 12/16th, 8/13th, 4/19th Armd Regts
	Artillery	22nd Fd Regt
	Engineers	10th Ind. Fd Sqn
	Signals	1st, 2nd Armd Bde Sig. Sqn
		22nd Fd. Regt Sig. Tp
	Infantry	6th Motor Regt
	Supply and transport	1st Armd Bde Coy
	Medical	1st Fd Amb.
	Ordnance	1st, 2nd Armd Bde Ord. Fd Pk
	Electrical and mechanical engineers	2nd Armd Wksp
		1st Med. Wksp
		6th, 7th, 16th, 26th, 32nd, 33rd, 34th, 35th LAD
	Postal	2nd Armoured Bde Postal Sec.
	Provost	2nd Armoured Bde Provost Det
HQ 13 Infantry Bde	Artillery	3rd Fd Regt
	Engineers	13th Fd Sqn
	Signals	13th Inf. Bde Sig. Tp
		3rd Fd Regt Sig. Tp
	Infantry	16th/28th, 11/44th Bns
	Supply and transport	10th Tpt Coy
	Medical	7/13th Fd Amb.
	Electrical and mechanical engineers	15th, 25th LAD

The army's fixed defence system enjoyed a precarious existence, especially since the success of air power during the war and the dawning of the missile age suggested that the utility of coastal defence was in decline. However, at least for the time being, coastal defence remained an army responsibility, and the fixed defence network continued to serve as part of the nation's invasion deterrence capability.

The decision to create standing units of infantry and armour did create a legal problem for the government. Section 31 of the Defence Act prohibited the formation of infantry and armoured units, in time of peace, in the permanent forces. By statute only the CMF could raise these types. It is for this reason that, when the army established the Darwin Mobile Force in 1939, it enlisted the unit's members as gunners or engineers, despite the fact that most performed infantry duties. To legitimise the formation of the PMF Brigade Group, the government exploited a loophole in the Defence Act. Technically, Australia was still in a state of war, despite the end of hostilities, because the Governor-General had not yet revoked the 'Time of War' proclamation that he had issued in 1939. While it remained in effect, the government could maintain any type of military forces it saw fit. It was not until 1950 that Menzies removed the restriction from the Defence Act, thereby ensuring the legal standing of the full-time serving combat forces. The Governor-General did not revoke his proclamation until 1952.[35]

Table 6.5 Organisation of fixed defences[36]

Region	Establishment
Eastern Command	HQ 1st Fixed Defence Brigade
	5th CA Regiment
	1st Static AA Regiment
	1st, 2nd CA Batteries
Western Command	HQ 3rd Fixed Defence Brigade
	7th CA Regiment
	5th Static AA Regiment
	6th, 11th CA Batteries
4th Military District	cadre
6th Military District	cadre
7th Military District	8th, 9th CA Batteries

Note: 4th and 6th Military Districts staffed on care and maintenance basis.

Another complicating legal problem for the post-war army was the requirement in Section 148 of the Defence Act that all officers of the permanent forces had to graduate from the Royal Military College unless they served in non-combatant branches. Traditionally, this meant that in order to serve in the Staff Corps, Instructional Corps, or the Royal Australian Artillery, an officer had to pass through the Royal Military College. Historically, the army had suffered from a shortage of permanent officers ever since the expansion of the military after Kitchener's inspection in 1911. Since the planned post-war establishment of the PMF was approximately ten times the size of the interwar PMF, it threatened to exacerbate the army's long-standing difficulty in meeting its officer requirements. To alleviate this problem, the army undertook steps to accelerate the production of Royal Military College graduates. Undermining the intent of the Defence Act, but not its legality, the army offered 'Royal Military College Wings', short courses in Australia and Japan in order that officers received the necessary accreditation. The government amended Section 148 in 1952, and created the Officer Cadet School thereby, providing another source of trained officers for the army.[37]

Recruiting for the PMF began on 1 August 1947, and for the CMF on 1 July 1948. Both branches of the army were bidding for labour in a buoyant economy and from among a population that was tired of war. As a consequence, the rate of enlistment fell far below projections, and by April 1948 the permanent forces had only 5,411 members. Over the next year the situation worsened, and recruitment could not keep up with discharges as soldiers opted to leave the Interim Army rather than committing themselves to a six-year term of service with the regulars. In February 1949, the permanent forces had only 4,031 personnel, and the government had agreed to include 3,500 civilians in non-combatant positions within the target establishment of 19,000. Especially affected were the combat units. In late 1949, the army had only a thousand regular infantrymen, including those in Japan, out of the goal of 3,000. When the 65th and 66th Battalions left Japan, many of their members transferred to the remaining 67th Battalion in order to bring that unit up to strength. Both battalions returned to Australia at little more than company strength.[38]

By the end of 1947, it had become clear that the flow of recruits into the permanent forces was insufficient. In an effort to promote recruitment, Cyril Chambers, the Minister for the Army, authorised a name change for the PMF. On 13 September 1947, he agreed that the PMF would henceforth be known as the Regular Army. The new designation also brought the name of the army's permanent forces into line with the United Kingdom, which had recently made a similar change. Shortly thereafter the Military Board modified the name to the Australian Regular Army (ARA). For the next 25 years the army was to consist of two branches, the ARA and the CMF.

Enlistment rates became so dire that in order to stimulate recruitment the army had little choice but to create a second, less demanding category of service, the Regular Army Supplementary Reserve. Enlistment in the Regular Army Supplementary Reserve was open only to serving soldiers who were ineligible for the ARA, for example, because of marginal medical disqualification, or who found its six-year terms of service unattractive. The Adjutant-General hoped that the new reserve scheme would allow the army to retain soldiers who had essential skills, such as tradesmen, but who were not necessarily combat troops. Members of the Regular Army Supplementary

Reserve served on three-year terms of engagement. Moreover, to encourage recruitment, the army set the maximum age for enlistment in the Regular Army Supplementary Reserve at 57, with retirement at 60. The recruitment period ran from April to October 1948, during which the army attracted over 5,300 personnel.[39]

After a year of recruitment, the personnel situation of the CMF was equally desperate. By August 1949, the CMF had only 14,178 officers and men out of its establishment of 50,000. By June 1951, the figure was still below 21,000. The army did introduce a number of incentive schemes to attract men, but they had only a marginal affect. To encourage enlistment, the government granted public servants leave with pay to attend citizen soldier camps of continuous training. In October 1948, a Military Board directive authorised the reimbursement of fares to CMF members who required public transport to attend parades. The Military Board proposed a number of incentives, such as tax-free service pay and an efficiency bonus, but Chifley rejected them because of Treasury concerns. Government-enforced frugality, in a tight employment market, ensured that the citizen force was unable to attract enough recruits for the force to attain its goal. Ultimately, the CMF had to rely on conscription, which Menzies reintroduced in 1950, to fill out its ranks.[40]

The army's difficulty in finding recruits also led to the re-establishment of a women's service. The outbreak of the Korean War further exacerbated the shortage of male personnel and added impetus for an increase in women serving in the army. In early 1950, in a minute to the Military Board, Rowell requested the re-establishment of the Australian Women's Army Service, which the army had disbanded in 1947. In particular, he pointed out that there was an acute need for skilled female personnel in signals, where there was a deficiency of 360 of all ranks. John Dedman, the Minister for Defence, approved the appointment of just three female officers and 77 other ranks. This, however, was only the beginning. In December 1950, the army raised the Women's Australian Army Corps. The Crown granted the royal prefix the following year, creating the Women's Royal Australian Army Corps. In late 1951, the army authorised the raising of a CMF arm of the new women's corps, and the Military Board set its establishment at 3,000 officers and other ranks. The army organised the women into companies and attached them to command headquarters. The Women's Royal Australian Army Corps survived until its effective disbandment in 1984, by which time the army had integrated nearly all of its personnel into other corps.[41]

The army had not disbanded its two women's medical services after the completion of demobilisation, and these personnel continued to serve in the army's hospitals. The Australian Army Nursing Service gained its royal prefix in 1948 to become known as the Royal Australian Army Nursing Service. In July 1949, Dedman approved the Nursing Service, as well as the Australian Army Medical Women's Service, as part of the ARA. The nurses continued their integration into the force's organisation when, in 1951, the army reconstituted them as a corps known as the Royal Australian Army Nursing Corps. Also in 1951, the Military Board authorised the establishment of a CMF nursing arm, with an establishment of 900 officers and other ranks. The Australian Army Medical Women's Service survived until 1951, when the Military Board approved its disbandment, incorporating its duties into the Royal Australian Army Nursing Corps. In addition to providing medical assistance in the army's hospitals in Australia, detachments of the Australian Army Medical Women's Service and the Royal Australian Army Nursing Corps served with the British Commonwealth Occupation Force, while some nurses saw duty on the Korean peninsula. The Royal Australian Army Nursing Corps continues to serve the army to the present.[42]

In 1948, the government established a further category of CMF units, which became known as the Supplementary Reserve. In that year, the Institution of Engineers Australia put forward a proposal to raise a reserve of specialist engineering units. A similar program existed already in the British and American armies. These units were to be composed of engineers, tradesmen, or technical specialists who had corresponding responsibilities in their civilian occupations. In addition, a government agency or private company sponsored each unit. For example, the army raised railway units from all the State government railways, with the exception of Tasmania, whose government refused to authorise time off for training. The army also raised other units with specialised skills, such as quarrying, lumbering, power generation, and road construction. The sponsoring agency was responsible for recruitment, and had to agree to allow leave for training and to make the supplementary reservist available upon mobilisation. The army obligated the members of the CMF Supplementary Reserve to attend an annual 14-day camp, but they did no mandatory home training.[43] Table 6.6 lists the units that made up the CMF Supplementary Reserve.

In determining the shape of the post-war army, Australian decision-makers did not take into account to any appreciable degree the role of atomic weapons in their deliberations. Although the Chifley Government showed an interest in the development of modern weapons through the creation of a number of scientific and weapons advisory panels, there is little evidence that these advances had any effect upon the structure of the post-war army at this stage. Australia was privy to some American studies regarding

Table 6.6 Order of battle, CMF Supplementary Reserve[44]

Command	Unit	Sponsoring agency
Eastern	109th Construction Sqn	Snowy Mountains Hydro-Electricity Authority
	HQ 21st Construction Regt	Department of Main Roads
	101st Construction Sqn	Department of Main Roads
	102nd Construction Sqn	Department of Public Works
	108th Plant Sqn	Metropolitan Water Sewerage and Drainage Board, Department of Public Works, Department of Main Roads
	103rd Construction Sqn	Metropolitan Water Sewerage and Drainage Board
	5th, 6th, 7th, 8th Port Construction and Repair Teams	Maritime Services Board
	HQ 8th Railway Group	New South Wales Government Railways
	53rd Railway Sqn	New South Wales Government Railways
Southern	107th Plant Sqn	State River and Water Supply Commission
	HQ 16th Construction Regt	State Electricity Commission
	99th Construction Regt	State Electricity Commission
	HQ 22nd Construction Regt	Country Roads Board
	104th Construction Sqn	Country Roads Board
	105th Construction Sqn	State River and Water Supply Commission
	91st Forestry Sqn	Victorian Forestry Commission
	80th Quarrying Sqn	State Electricity Commission
	1 Tp 39th E and M Sqn	State Electricity Commission
	203rd Works Section	State Electricity Commission
	41st Railway Sqn	Victorian Railways
Northern	42nd Railway Sqn	Queensland Railways
Central	43rd Railway Sqn	South Australian Railways
Western	44th Railway Sqn	Western Australian Railways

the effect of atomic weapons on force structure, but the resulting Australian organisation closely resembled that which had existed before the war, and which was most suited for a conflict employing conventional weapons and tactics. In part, the Soviet Union's lack of atomic capability might have deterred the army from considering an organisation for waging nuclear war. Fiscal control, however, was also a factor, as the army did not have the monies to re-equip the force along nuclear lines, especially since the atomic era was only just beginning and its effect on the nature of war was unclear. Instead, the army had to make do with materials left over from the war. Therefore, the army again followed Britain's lead in structuring its forces, from divisions to sections, including the adoption of London's weapon and personnel establishments.[45]

The army also revived the pre-war practice of numbering infantry battalions and cavalry regiments (now armoured formations) in descent from the 1st AIF order of battle, in order to provide continuity of tradition and *esprit de corps*. This exercise, however, was somewhat forced, as during the war there had been 36 2nd AIF and 61 CMF battalions, but the post-war army had room for only 21 citizen and three regular battalions. Some veterans used their political influence to assure the continuation of their battalion's name. For example, the members of the 42nd Battalion Association, a battalion that had served in both world wars, lobbied the Minister for the Army to have the unit raised in central Queensland designated the 42nd. Their efforts proved successful. The Post-War Army Planning Committee had considered the implementation of a regimental system, but the weight of opinion was in preference for the recreation of World War I titles, even if this required numerous battalion linkages. The army announced the names of those regiments that survived into the new structure in February 1948, a few months before CMF recruitment began.[46]

In the return to the pre-war pattern, the army's experiment with jungle divisions also disappeared. The army defined the force's most likely deployment options not as the tropics but as either European or desert theatres. The only consideration given to jungle warfare was the Chiefs of Staff Committee's recommendation that units be capable of conversion to a tropical standard, although, as World War II demonstrated, such a reorganisation was a major undertaking. In the resulting organisation, the only significant departure from the pre-World War II structure was the creation of the Australian Armoured Corps and the permanent presence of armour on the force's order of battle. The reconstructed force included several permanent and CMF armoured units.[47]

The army continued to support the Commonwealth Cadet Corps, and in 1948 the force had 226 training units organised into 23 cadet battalions. Table 6.7 outlines the cadet corps order of battle.

Table 6.7 Cadet corps order of battle, 1948

State	Battalions
Queensland	1st, 2nd, 3rd, 4th Battalions
New South Wales	7th, 8th, 9th, 10th, 11th, 12th, 13th, 14th, 15th, 16th, 17th Battalions
Victoria	20th, 21st, 22nd, 23rd Battalions
South Australia	27th Battalion
Western Australia	30th, 31st Battalions
Tasmania	33rd, 34th Battalions

Despite the cadet movement's renewal, the army no longer had any illusions that the training of boys provided a short cut to the creation of efficient adult soldiers. Southern Command's rejection of a request from the cadet corps that it provide affiliation with local CMF units was a reflection of the army's changed attitude and reduced expectations. Instead of valuing the partnership, Southern Command headquarters believed that there was no practical advantage to be gained from having cadets parade with the CMF.[48] Instead, the cadet corps had a more limited objective. It served as a way to introduce boys to military activities, promote recruiting, and identify future leaders. The army noted the purpose of cadet training as being to:

a   Give them a foundation of military knowledge and discipline

b   Develop them mentally and physically.

c   Provide future leaders …

d   Develop a sense of citizenship and patriotism.[49]

In 1951, the army changed the cadet corps' name to Australian Cadet Corps.

Korea and the restoration of national service

Australia's participation in the Korean War did not have a significant effect on the army's organisation. Also, it did not lead to any significant expansion in the number of units or personnel on the ARA or the CMF establishment. From the Commonwealth's perspective, Korea was a limited conflict, and the achievement of Australian objectives did not warrant the raising of a mass army. Instead, the Korean War highlighted the continuing deficiencies in the army's readiness and the difficulties that it had in maintaining its in-theatre forces, even at the nation's token level of commitment. Furthermore, Robert O'Neill, the Australian official historian of the war, believes that the government decided to commit forces to the conflict purely out of a desire to enhance the Commonwealth's relationship with the United States.[50] Therefore, the lasting achievements of the war, from the Australian perspective, were diplomatic. Spender used Australia's show of support in his negotiations with the United States for a security pact, resulting in the ANZUS Treaty. During the conflict, the government did undertake other military initiatives, such as the introduction of a revised national service scheme. However, these were not a direct result of the war, but reflected the government's wider fear of the spread of communism.

Shortly after North Korea's invasion of South Korea on 25 June 1950, the United States called upon the Australian Government to contribute its military and naval resources to the United Nations Command. Menzies quickly agreed to RAN and RAAF assistance, and assets of those services soon found themselves at war. The decision to commit ground forces, however, was taken more slowly. The initial contribution was 3 RAR, which had been Australia's principal combat element in the British Commonwealth Occupation Force. Keeping its forces to the minimal level that was diplomatically possible, Australia did not commit a second battalion until April 1952.

In late July 1950, at the height of the Pusan crisis, the Australian Government received a formal request from MacArthur for the deployment of ground forces to Korea. On 26 July, Menzies assented and offered the services of 3 RAR, which was stationed in Japan. However, the battalion was not combat ready, as it was greatly under strength and had been engaged in occupation duties for four years. Furthermore, the troops' enlistment terms specified service in Japan. The government could not order them to Korea without first obtaining their agreement to serve on the peninsula. Fortunately, out of a strength of 550 men, 524 volunteered for Korea.[51]

The Regular Army was so under strength that it did not have enough available manpower to bring 3 RAR up to establishment. Instead, the government authorised a special recruitment drive to attract the 1,000 volunteers required either immediately or as replacements. To expedite deployment, they had to have had previous military experience. The army airlifted the first batch to Japan at the end of August, and the battalion moved to Korea at the end of September. Over the course of the commitment, the ARA was unable to provide sufficient replacements from within its organisation, and had to resort to a series of special enlistments. Ultimately, these *ad hoc* measures raised nearly 3,400 men. The personnel situation only grew worse after a second battalion's commitment in April 1952. The army had already cannibalised the chosen unit, 1 RAR, in an effort to support 3 RAR. The army now had to draw down 2 RAR to build up 1 RAR before the unit could move overseas.[52]

O'Neill has commented on this state of affairs in his official history. He points out the irony of a situation in which the nation had such difficulty supporting a few battalions in Korea, whereas a few years ago it was able to maintain a force of more than six divisions on active operations. The circumstances were so bad that the army estimated it would take five months to bring 1 RAR up to strength in preparation for its deployment. Moreover, Australia had to refuse Britain's request for assistance in Malaya because of a lack of resources. At the time, the government considered Malaya a strategic interest, but all Rowell believed he could spare was a handful of officers and 2,000 Owen guns. O'Neill explains that operations were not a priority for the army at this time. Instead, it was in the midst of a long-term development program. Thus, Korea actually retarded the military's advancement towards its goal of raising division-sized units, particularly because it took ARA soldiers away from national service training duties. In addition, O'Neill noted, the principal guidelines for the armed forces remained fiscal, not strategic, and as a consequence the army had little capacity to provide combat forces at short notice.[53]

While the battalions of the RAR earned an enviable reputation in Korea and won the regiment's first battle honours, the army at home underwent important changes under the Menzies Government's direction. In September 1950, Menzies announced that the government would re-implement a national service scheme, change the army's condition of overseas service, and expand the ARA.[54] As a consequence, the army's share of the defence expenditure rose from £26.2 million in fiscal year 1950–51 to £91.5 million in fiscal year 1952–53. Some of this increase was a result of costs involving the Korean commitment, but much of it was to support the national service scheme. When taking these steps, Menzies was not motivated by any particular problem that the participation in the Korean War had revealed. Rather, his decisions derived from a fear of communism, particularly the regional threat of China and the global threat of the Soviet Union.

The failure of voluntarism to bring forth enough recruits for the CMF was also a motivating factor for Menzies. Under the national service scheme, each conscript underwent 98 days of continuous training in national service training battalions in the first year, followed by 14 days' camp and 12 days' home training with the CMF for the next three years. This provided a total of 176 days of training. Upon the completion of this obligation, the soldier passed into the reserves for an additional five years. The army transferred the national serviceman, after the first year's training, to a CMF unit. The army determined the particular CMF unit through a combination of the trainee's preference, unit requirement, and regional convenience. In addition to joining the reserves upon completion of his training, a national serviceman could continue to practise with the CMF, transferring to the national service voluntary training list. However, if he preferred, he could join the national service inactive list, and thereby incur no further training obligation. In addition to conscription, soldiers could still join the CMF by voluntary enlistment.

Through this scheme, national servicemen became a source of members for the CMF. As a consequence, the strength of the citizen force rose sharply. However, there were some negative consequences. The army implemented the scheme with three training cycles in a year. Therefore, with the arrival of each batch of recruits, a CMF unit had to return to elementary training in order to integrate the new arrivals into the unit. The CMF also lost many of its ARA cadres to the national service training battalions, thereby throwing additional administrative and training duties onto the part-time officers and non-commissioned officers. The scheme also swamped the ARA, which had to provide camps and instructors for the national servicemen as they underwent their 98-day training period. As originally designed, the government had proposed an annual quota of 15,000 conscripts in three lots of 5,000. Two months after Menzies' announcement, the government reduced the quota to 10,000 in three lots of 3,300. The army accordingly made its arrangements on this basis. The government then unexpectedly reversed direction in March 1951, and increased the quota to 29,250 in three lots of 9,750. Despite these handicaps, the army was ready. On 6 August 1951, the scheme commenced.[55]

Another change Menzies made was to modify the government's policy towards the limitation on service outside Australia. Menzies decided to amend the terms of service for both the ARA and CMF to include a soldier's attestment to serve anywhere overseas at the government's discretion. The government intended to ask existing personnel to agree to the new service condition, while for new recruits their acceptance of overseas service was a condition of their enlistment. National servicemen, however, remained exempt from this obligation.

While the changes in overseas service conditions that Menzies introduced were significant, they also introduced new problems, which would have prevented the army from obtaining their full benefit if mobilisation had ever occurred. The government could now order any CMF unit overseas as it saw fit without having to seek the agreement of the unit's enlisted members. Theoretically, this meant that the government now had the ability to project its military power quickly without having to undergo the lengthy process of finding troops who were willing to serve. Moreover, the modification brought the army's terms of enlistment into agreement with those of the RAN or RAAF, whose members the government already had the power to dispatch anywhere in the world. However, the exclusion of national servicemen from the new service condition effectively negated any gains that the army obtained. National servicemen represented a significant percentage of CMF strength, and the requirement to get the permission of conscripted soldiers before their deployment overseas meant that Menzies' changes were cosmetic, and failed to address the force's requirements for the dispatch of forces overseas. If mobilisation did occur, the army would once again be unable to respond with the present force, and instead have to either reorganise existing units or raise a new force, as it had done twice before.[56]

Menzies also addressed the organisation of the ARA. He believed that the Regular Army was too small, and that the military should raise a second permanent brigade group. The prime minister foresaw one brigade serving as a mobile strike force, which the army would maintain at a high level of readiness in order to facilitate its rapid deployment. The second brigade would become a depot for units posted overseas. Menzies also realised that both brigades could act as cadres for divisions in case of a major war.

As so often in the past, however, a reversal of government policy prevented the army from achieving the promise of Menzies' proposals. For fiscal year 1953–54, he halted the expansion of the military vote and imposed a crushing change in direction. Instead of the £91.5 million that the government had provided in the previous year, it would now provide only £64.3 million. As a consequence, the army abandoned its plans to raise a second ARA brigade. It also cut the national servicemen's training obligation from 176 to 140 days.[57]

Higher direction of the army

After Japan's surrender and the return to peace, the army put in place a command structure that was nearly identical to that which had existed before the war. When Blamey took control of the nation's military forces and converted the commands and the Military Board into operational headquarters, in his reforms of April 1942, he had swept away the army's hierarchy for its higher direction. Blamey, who retired shortly after the end of the war, had little role in redefining the army's higher direction. After the surrender of Japan he submitted his resignation. Joseph Chifley, who became prime minister after Curtin's death, initially rejected Blamey's request, but suddenly, in early November, the government informed him that it no longer required his services. Lieutenant-General Vernon Sturdee became acting C-in-C AMF until his

Lieutenant-General V. A. H. Sturdee, CGS 1946–50. (AWM 145063)

appointment as CGS on 1 March 1946. It would fall to Sturdee to re-establish the army's administration at its highest levels.

Sturdee's first step was to recreate the command structure that Squires had recommended in 1938. Sturdee noted in January 1946 that he believed this command system 'is the most suitable organisation for the control of demobilisation, and the Interim Army, and forms a sound basis on which the Post War Army Organisation can be built, no matter what form such organisation may eventually take'.[58] Sturdee took the first step towards its re-establishment when he abolished 2nd Army at the end of 1945 and transferred its functions to the line of communication areas. In effect, each headquarters line of communication area acted as a headquarters command. All that remained was to change their names. He then proposed the following:

- Queensland Line of Communication Area to become Northern Command
- New South Wales Line of Communication Area to become Eastern Command
- Victoria Line of Communication Area to become Southern Command
- South Australian Line of Communication Area to become 4th Military District under control of Southern Command
- Tasmania Line of Communication Area to become 6th Military District under control of Southern Command
- Headquarters First Army to be replaced by Headquarters 8th Military District.[59]

As Western Command already existed, Sturdee did not have to make any changes in Western Australia. The CGS's plan received the minister's approval on 23 February 1946. Map 11 illustrates the army's regional administration in 1946.[60]

At the end of 1949, the army slightly modified its command organisation further. Sturdee proposed that the Military Board should establish the 4th and 6th Military Districts as commands in their own right, rather than continuing their subordination to Southern Command. He believed that this would increase the army's identity in both States. The governments of South Australia and Tasmania had also objected to their inclusion in Southern Command, and to the control of their military forces from Melbourne. Accordingly, the Military Board agreed to a reorganisation, resulting in

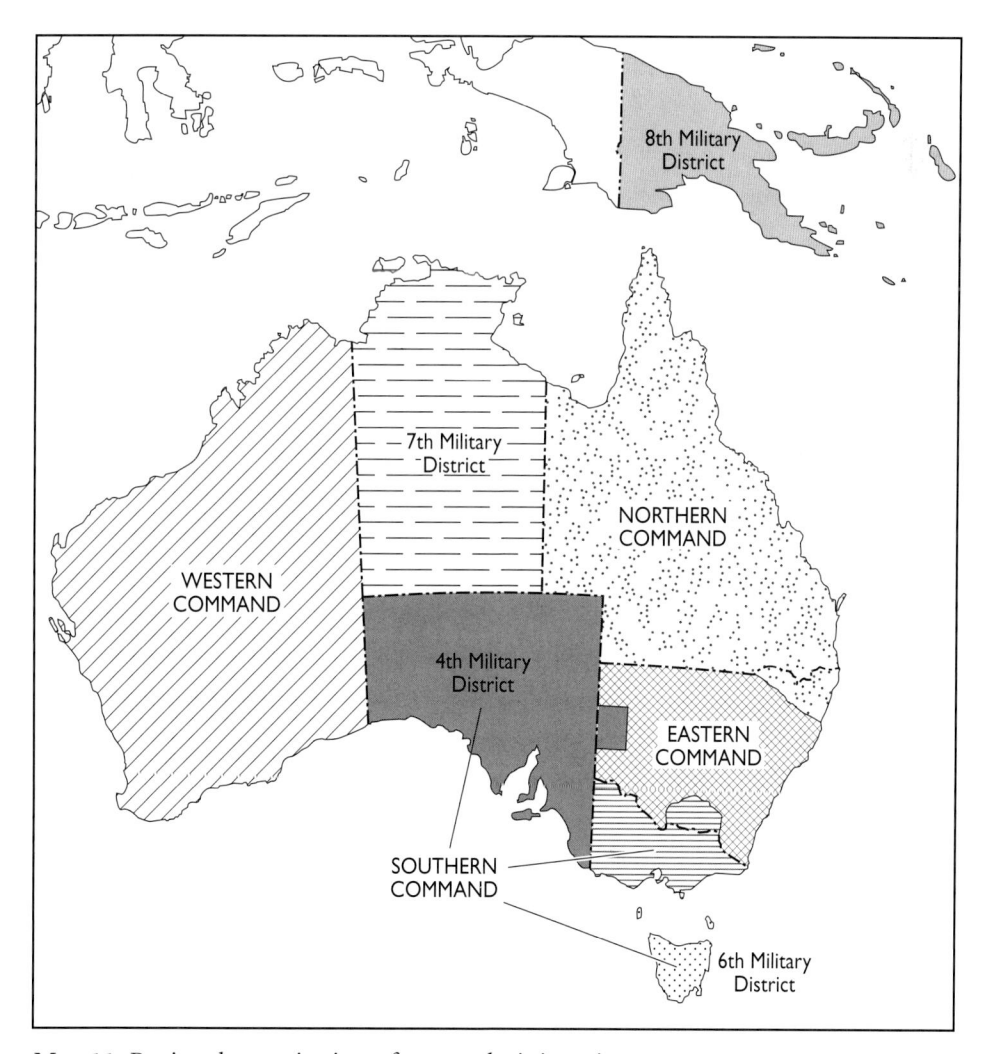

Map 11 Regional organisation of army administration, 1946

the formation of Central Command for South Australia and Tasmania Command for Tasmania. These modifications went into effect on 1 January 1950. Map 12 illustrates the army's regional administration after the 1950 changes.[61]

The government recreated the Military Board in early 1946 after its abolition by Blamey in 1942. It met for the first time on 30 April 1946. The government slightly altered its membership by the addition of the recently formed office of VCGS as a full voting member. Its members were:
- President: Minister for the Army, Francis Forde
- CGS: Lieutenant-General V.A.H. Sturdee
- VCGS: Lieutenant-General Sydney Rowell

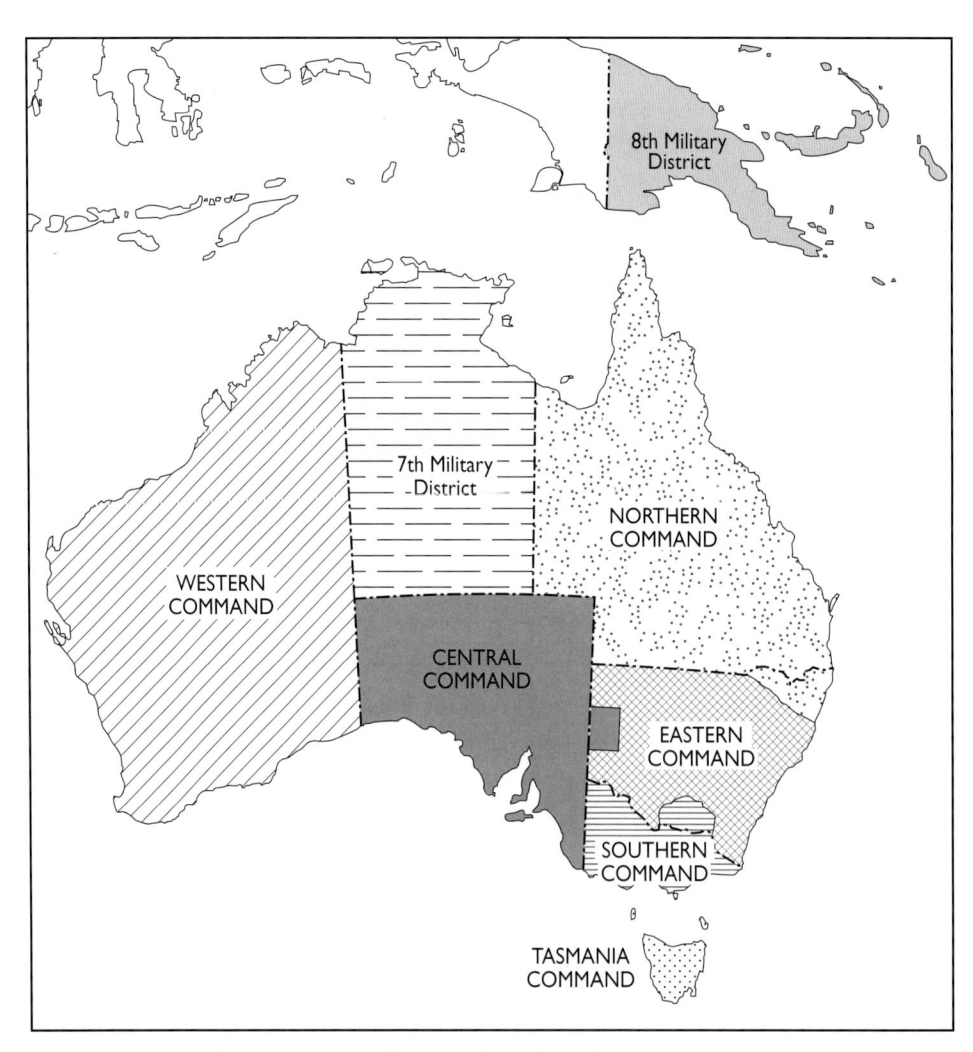

Map 12 Regional organisation of army administration, 1950

- Adjutant-General: Major-General C.A. Clowes
- Quartermaster-General: Major-General W. Bridgeford
- Master-General of the Ordnance: Major-General L. Beavis.

The Military Board also included a finance member and a business member. Although the government re-established the Military Board, it left the office of the Inspector-General vacant, and no one served in that capacity until the position's revitalisation in 1987.[62]

The VCGS was a post-war creation. The years immediately after the end of World War II were complex ones, as the army had to manage considerable post-war responsibilities while also laying the foundation for its future organisation. To facilitate the administrative control of these two separate functions, the CGS divided the duties of his office between the already existing position of the Deputy Chief of the General Staff (DCGS) and the new office of the VCGS. Sturdee gave responsibility for matters relating to the British Commonwealth Occupation Force, the Interim Army, and coordination of staff procedures at Army Headquarters to the Deputy Chief of the General Staff. The VCGS was responsible for matters relating to the future of the armed services and for briefing the CGS on inter-service situations. The VCGS held a seat on the Military Board in his own right, whereas the DCGS only attended in the CGS's absence. Chart 9 (p. 226) outlines the restructured Army Headquarters.[63]

In 1948, the Military Board expanded its membership to include a CMF officer as a full member. Previously, the Military Board had sought citizen soldier advice only on a consultative basis. Sturdee resisted the appointment, arguing that it was unnecessary, as he believed that the army already adequately managed CMF affairs through existing administrative channels. The CGS also opposed the appointment, on the grounds that a CMF member of the Military Board would need the right of direct access to citizen units and, if the appointee abused this right, it could have an adverse effect upon the army's normal chain of command. Additionally, in Sturdee's objections, there was the suggestion of a lingering staff corps–CMF rivalry, and that the CGS did not want to risk the dilution of permanent officer influence on the Military Board by the advancement of a militiaman. In any case, the CGS had to give way, and on 11 March 1948 John Dedman, the Minister for Defence, announced the appointment of Major-General G.F. Wootten as CMF member of the Military Board.[64]

The years immediately following World War II bore a number of similarities to the national security agenda which existed during the interwar period. Although more cognisant of national security concerns, and despite showing a greater acceptance of

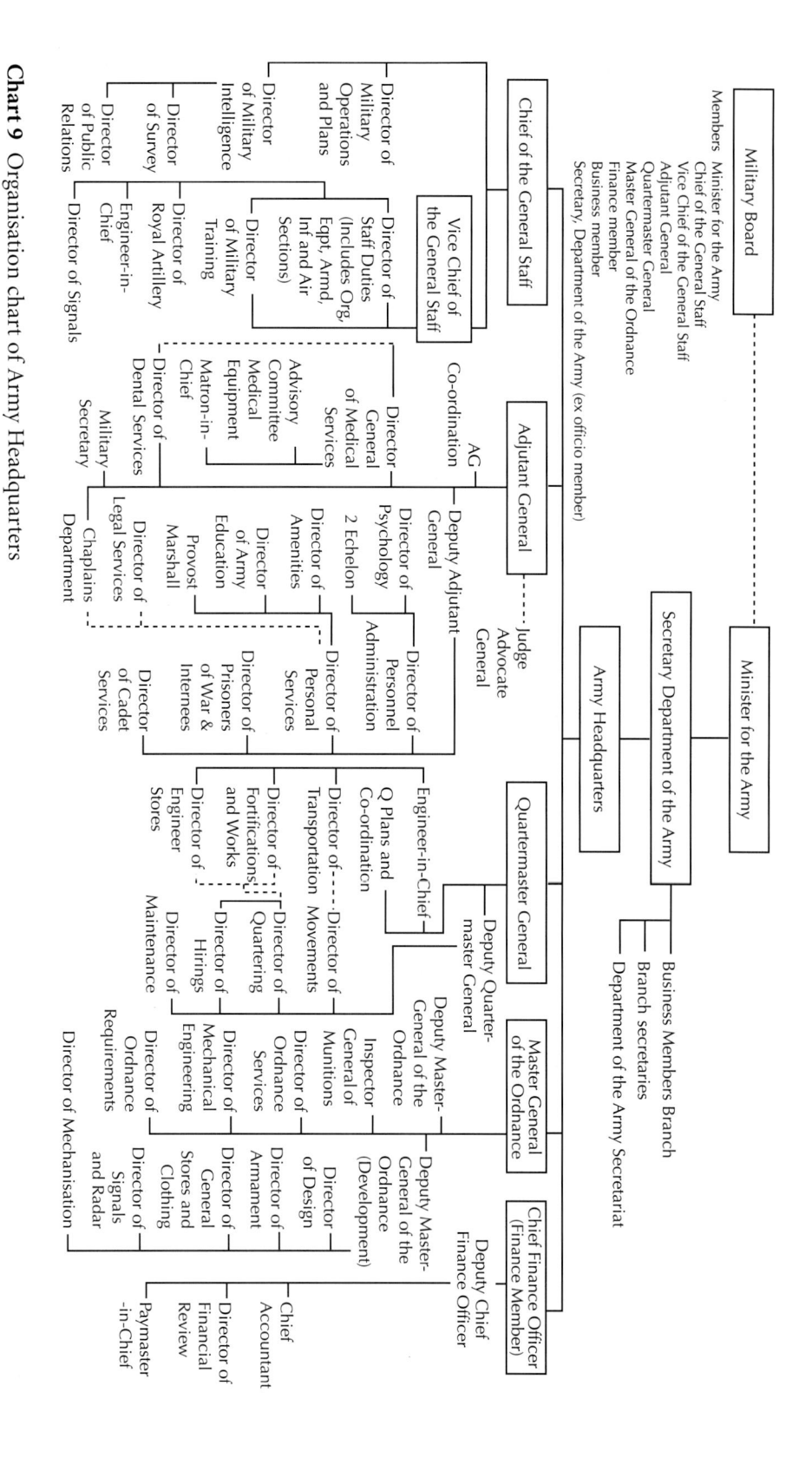

Chart 9 Organisation chart of Army Headquarters
(Source: 'Organisation of Army Headquarters', 1 October 1947, AA (Vic), MP742/1, item 240/1/2766)

Major-General George F. Wootten. (AWM 016069)

the principle that Australia should bear a larger share of the cost of its own defence, the governments of Chifley and Menzies continued to see advantage in allowing other countries to carry as much as possible of Australia's defence burden. Both parties actively pursued a collective security agenda, and sought an American commitment to the region, not only as a means to assure survival in a major war but also as a way to minimise the military estimate. Both parties planned to make the major focus of their policies the economic development of the nation. This strategy did incur obligations, as Australia's affirmative response to the United States' request for a Korean contribution suggests, but the security it provided outweighed the price. However, post-war comparisons with the Commonwealth's servility to London during the interwar period should not be overstated. Australia had matured as a sovereign state during World War II, and its governments were no longer captives to an overseas security policy, but rather were active participants in the shaping of a collective response that reflected their own national interests.

The organisation that the army developed in support of the government's strategic policy also contained elements that paralleled the interwar period. Although it now possessed a regular field force, most of the army's military power remained centred on the CMF. To a great extent, the ARA existed to provide for the administrative and training requirements of the CMF, and it was the citizen soldier, not the regular, who remained the bulwark of the army's forces in case of another major war. The introduction of the national service scheme only served to buttress the importance of the CMF in the nation's defence. However, this too can be overstated. In reality, the CMF's post-war apogee was all too brief. Within a few years it became clear that the nation's future military emphasis had shifted to the regulars and that the influence of the citizen soldier had begun to wane.

As in 1918, the post-war security environment had not been immediately clear, and it took the nation's defence planners a few years to ascertain the true nature and degree of threat that Australia was likely to face. The initial response was to create a force structure that was similar to that which had existed before the war, albeit smaller. The commencement of the Cold War and the rise of Communist China called into question the post-war organisation of the army, and the relationship between the ARA and the CMF. The post-war structure that the army created in 1948 proved a temporary expedient, and by the end of the Korean War it had become clear that the army's organisational work had only just begun.

7

THE RISE OF THE AUSTRALIAN REGULAR ARMY

In future, the Regular Army will be supported by the non-regular forces and not the reverse as at present.

Ragnar Garrett[1]

In the aftermath of the Korean War, Australia entered a period of security policy dominated by the concept of 'forward defence'. However, while the era was one of unprecedented deployment overseas of Australian military forces, from the perspective of the army and the evolution of its organisation, the period is more noted for two related developments—the increased professionalism of the institution and the emergence of the ARA as the dominant branch of the army. In the previous five decades, the defence of the Commonwealth had relied ultimately upon the citizen soldier, and the nation's small cadre of professional soldiers served principally in a support capacity to the CMF. Even the AIFs that fought the world wars were largely volunteer citizen organisations, although in the second great conflict some conscripted troops also fought overseas. Furthermore, after the armistices, both AIFs melted away as the temporary soldiers returned to their civilian occupations. In both of these instances, the nation's security reverted largely to a citizen basis, while the professional soldiers attempted to redefine the organisation of the army in light of the changes in the international security picture that the wars had wrought. Even after World War II, when the army established an ARA field force, the CMF remained the principal representative of Australian defence.

With the commencement of the Cold War, Australia entered a new era in defence planning, which relaid the foundation of the army's organisation. In particular, during the years of continuity afforded by the lengthy leadership of Menzies, the government perceived the post-World War II environment as a hostile, potentially violent confrontation between the nations of the democratic and communist camps. This ongoing fear of communist aggression, and the government's acceptance of the necessity to assist the other democracies in its deterrence, manifested itself in Australia by heightened concerns over national security, a determined quest for allied assistance in the region, a greater willingness to undertake overseas commitments in both war and peace, and an increased awareness of defence responsibility within a collective system. Australian resources dedicated to defence continued to be relatively minor, both compared to the efforts of Britain and the United States and as a measurement of domestic gross national product, but the Commonwealth's effort was a sustained one and far greater than any previous undertaking.

The interpretations drawn by political and military decision-makers regarding the Cold War security environment provided the rationale and the impetus for the switching of the nation's military defence from its traditional reliance on the citizen soldier to one based on the regular. Although it never operated as a field force, the raising of a regular infantry brigade in 1948 was the first step in the creation of an institution whose primary purpose was to support the permanent soldiers, supplemented by the CMF, if necessary. Furthermore, in case of global war, the ARA, rather than the CMF, became the template for the army's expansion, complemented by regular support and administrative arms. The transformation was gradual. The army commenced the process with its 1957 reorganisation, and did not complete the task until the implementation of the Millar reforms of the early 1970s. Although a gradual undertaking, it was a relentless process, and it occurred over the objections of the citizen soldiers. By the end of the period, Australia's citizen soldier tradition had come to an end, and the nation's remaining part-time soldiers now served in the Army Reserve, a body specifically designed and raised to support the ARA.

The strategic environment

While the transformation of the army into a force dominated by the regular soldier was a painful process for the CMF, it was not the result of a conspiracy to degrade the place of the citizen soldier in the nation's military hierarchy. Instead, it was the logical outcome of national security policies that aimed to achieve a higher degree of defence readiness in the face of Cold War realities. The issue that dominated the security policy agenda, throughout the two decades following the Korean War, was the threat of communist expansion. Although this had world-wide implications, the principal focus of the Australian Government's concern was the danger communism posed to its own territory and to the colonial and post-colonial states of South-East Asia.

The Australian Government, largely under Menzies' guidance, implemented policies and set objectives through which it hoped to secure the nation against communist aggression. Although Australian security thinkers paid greater attention to self-reliance, they did not believe that the nation could defend itself. Instead they sought to secure Australia's defence within a collective system, and their efforts to enhance the army's effectiveness was a function of this objective.[2] In April 1957, Menzies formalised these principles in an address to parliament. He stated that:

> It is of immense importance to us that the free nations of South-East Asia should not fall one by one to Communist aggression. Security in the area must, therefore, be a collective concept. We believe that participation in regional arrangements for collective defence is the most effective method of securing the safety of Australia.

He continued that Australia 'cannot expect the defensive assistance of the great democratic powers unless we are prepared to take a proper part in the common defence'.[3] Security policy, therefore, evolved along two related lines. First, there was the necessity to engage other nations who might have an interest in the area and to develop a strong alliance system to protect Australian territory. Second, it was essential to develop a force structure that was capable of protecting Australia while also being able to join in an allied effort to deter regional communist movements.

Because of its colonies and interests in South-East Asia, Britain continued to play an important role in Australian security considerations. Although Britain maintained significant military resources in the region, the course of World War II had demonstrated that it was no longer a power of the first rank, and its relative loss of strength limited its ability to project power, deter communist aggression, and safeguard Australia's security. The 1956 Suez Canal fiasco illustrated the limits of British power and influence. Therefore, Australian governments, from Curtin forward, followed a policy of engagement with the United States, the only nation in the world capable of providing for Australia's security in the potentially hostile world that Menzies had envisaged.

By the end of the Korean War, Australia had already joined in two formal security arrangements, in addition to its ongoing participation in the United Nations. The ANZAM agreement created a framework for an Anglo-Australian–New Zealand defence relationship regarding the Malayan peninsula and Singapore, an area that Australian defence planners recognised as critical if they were to safeguard the mainland from communist aggression. The ANZUS Treaty established a tripartite security arrangement with the United States and New Zealand. It became the mainstay of Australian defence planning and the mechanism through which the Commonwealth fostered close ties with the United States. In 1954, Australia joined the United States, Britain, France, New Zealand, Pakistan, Thailand, and the Philippines to form the South-East Asia Treaty Organisation (SEATO). This agreement established a consultative framework for security matters in the region and provided for military assistance between members and protocol states—South Vietnam, Laos, and Cambodia—under certain conditions. The organisation had a combined headquarters, which oversaw contingency planning and coordinated exercises between the military forces of member states. Australia used SEATO as an additional mechanism to foster ties with the United States, and Menzies employed it to justify Australian intervention in Vietnam.

After Malaya became independent in 1957, it became necessary to modify ANZAM in order for the government of Malaya to become a direct participant. In September 1957, the controlling document became the Anglo-Malayan Defence Agreement. This was, in fact, a bilateral agreement between Britain and Malaya, but Australia associated itself with the treaty and continued to base troops on the peninsula and participate in the strategic reserve organisation. In 1971, the Five Power Defence Arrangements between Britain, Australia, New Zealand, Malaysia, and Singapore succeeded the Anglo-Malayan Defence Agreement. Although not a formal treaty, the Five Power Defence Arrangements provided the means to administer the Commonwealth's military forces in the region.[4]

Successful collective security arrangements are not without cost, as they are dependent upon all member states sharing the burden of defence preparation and, when necessary, combat risk. Therefore, to assure the viability of Australia's security provisions, especially the critical agreements with the United States, and to play its part in the deterrence of communism, the Australian Government had to participate in the region's limited wars and counter-insurgency campaigns. Furthermore, the government also accepted that it was strategically wiser to wage these conflicts as far away from Australian soil as possible, thus establishing the policy of 'forward defence'. Menzies explained these points to the nation in 1955 when he announced that Australia would provide forces for the ANZAM area strategic reserve. He hoped that 'Australians [would] … realise the basic truth … that if there is to be a war for our existence, it should be carried on by us as far from our soil as possible'.[5]

As a consequence of this policy, Australia dispatched its military forces to help its partners in three regional conflicts—the Malayan Emergency, Confrontation with Indonesia, and the Vietnam War—as well as minor preventive deployments to areas such as Thailand. Millar has rightly described these commitments as the premium on an insurance policy, which a minor nation pays to help assure the willingness of a great partner to assume responsibility for its defence in a major war. He wrote that the main purpose of Australian involvement in Vietnam was

> to show the United States that Australia was a willing ally, one that stood up to be counted and thus deserved to be stood up for if necessary, as well as to encourage the United States to remain committed to the defence of Australia's South East Asian neighbourhood against militant communist action.[6]

Australia, therefore, was never an unwilling participant in these overseas engagements, as they helped to advance the most critical objective of Australian foreign policy and national security planning, namely encouraging the United States to maintain an interest in the region. As Coral Bell concludes, 'the Australian government's wish to have Americans in Vietnam was undoubtedly much stronger than the American government's wish to have Australians there.'[7] Australia, she continued, was not dragooned into Vietnam. Rather the nation's involvement came about as a direct result of the government's policy of seeking favour with the United States.[8] Related to this objective was the government's acquiescence to American requests to build satellite-tracking and submarine communication facilities on Australian soil.

Menzies believed that a future war against a communist opponent could occur on a number of different levels. In its security analysis, the government defined the nature of the potential threat as consisting of three possible contingencies. They were global war, limited war, and the undermining of states through subversion and infiltration. Menzies considered global war unlikely because of the nuclear deterrent, but he believed that the other forms of conflict, such as another Korean War, were likely to occur. Furthermore, government planners assumed that a limited war could break out with little warning, and that the most critical period would be the early phase, as the democratic nations marshalled their forces to stem the communist onslaught.[9]

In the past, Commonwealth defence planning had assumed that a lengthy warning period would precede the onset of war, and that in the meantime the maritime resources of the Royal Navy would safeguard Australia's shores until the CMF had mobilised. The failure of the Singapore Strategy had exposed the limitations of such assumptions, and the experience derived from the preparation of the AIFs also suggested that the length of time required to prepare the CMF was far too long under the conditions of modern war. Furthermore, the necessity of preventing the smaller nations of the Pacific Basin from falling under the communist banner, and thereby shifting the global balance against the democracies, meant that Australia required the capacity to assist its allies with greater speed than was possible in the past. To meet this requirement, Menzies determined that Australia had to have a standing force that the government could dispatch to the threatened point early enough in the conflict to prevent the enemy from gaining a decisive advantage. The implementation of this plan underlay the gradual advancement of the regular soldier and the development of the ARA into the army's dominant branch.

As the previous chapter discussed, post-war planners had initially foreseen the Middle East as the primary area of interest. They anticipated that in a major war Australia would send an expeditionary force to help protect the line of communication through the Suez Canal and the region's air bases. In late 1951, Menzies formalised Australia's commitment by agreeing to participate in the Middle East Defence Command with Britain, France, Turkey, and the United States. As a result, the RAAF sent two of its squadrons to Malta. However, by mid 1952 the government's interest in the Middle East had begun to fade as a result of the ongoing Malayan Emergency, the worsening French position in Indo-China and the growing strength of mainland China. A 1952 order of battle, drawn up by the Director of Staff Duties, illustrates the transitional nature of Australian thinking. His main plan outlined the dispatch of an expeditionary force to the Middle East. However, he also included a variant that identified the procedure for converting a desert-scale formation to a standard more suitable for service in the tropics.[10]

The stability of the Malayan Peninsula was of particular concern to Commonwealth decision-makers, as they considered this area the nation's last barrier against a thrust from the north. Although the 1953 strategic review largely reaffirmed the 1950 strategic review's principles, and while it officially retained Australia's military commitment to the Middle East, the new study placed greater stress on the defence of South-East Asia. Defence thinkers considered the retention of Malaya in non-communist hands essential if Commonwealth territory were to remain out of the range of an enemy's ability to project power against the Australian littoral.[11] The 1953 strategic review stated that, in the event of global war, it was the government's view that one of the aims of the allies should be to ensure the retention of Malaya. It defined the probable role of Australia's forces as:

- the defence of Australia
- the provision of Australia's share in the defence of the ANZAM region
- the provision of an appropriate contribution to the vital overseas theatres.

Thus, while the 1953 strategic review did not end Australia's Middle Eastern role, it did make it clear that the dispatch of an expeditionary force to Egypt was contingent on the security of South-East Asia.[12]

The Commonwealth's concerns over Malaya received further consideration at a meeting between the Australian Defence Committee, the New Zealand Chiefs of Staff, and the Chief of the Imperial General Staff, Field Marshal Sir John Harding, in Melbourne in October 1953. Harding proposed the establishment of a Far East Strategic Reserve, whose purpose was to deter Chinese aggression. He suggested a brigade-size organisation. Australia's contribution would be a battalion group, as well as air and naval assets.[13] Harding's suggestion developed slowly, and it was not until February 1955, at a meeting with Churchill in London, that Menzies accepted the recommendations of the Melbourne conference. The prime minister insisted that in a general war the primary objective of Australian policy was the security of South-East Asia, and that defence planning should aim at the rapid deployment of forces to that area. Subsequently, Menzies announced his decision to participate in the Far East Strategic Reserve and base Australian forces in the Malayan region. In his address, he also stated that, although the force's primary purpose was the deterrence of communist aggression against South-East Asia, it would also be available to undertake anti-terrorist operations against the insurgents in Malaya. After the conclusion of the Emergency, Australian troops continued to serve in Malaya. The government also employed them in a combat role during the Confrontation with Indonesia.[14]

In late 1956, the Defence Committee updated its report on the strategic basis of Australia's defence policy. This report continued to identify communism as the essential threat. It emphatically stated that the 'ultimate aim of the communists is a communist dominated world'.[15] However, unlike the 1953 edition, this version signalled that a major policy change, away from the security priorities that defence planners had established in the 1950 study, had occurred. The Defence Committee noted that 'due to her geographical position and proximity to South East Asia, it is this area which is of great strategic importance to Australia, and her primary role should be directed to that area in cold, limited and global war'.[16] The Defence Committee admitted that Australia could not secure this area on its own. The report therefore concluded that it was essential to coordinate Australian planning for South-East Asia, including ANZAM arrangements, with the United States.

To fulfil its role in South-East Asia, and thereby provide for Australian defence, the Defence Committee concluded that the nation's military requirements would be best met with hard-hitting, flexible, mobile, and readily available forces. It continued that to meet these requirements the army required two types of forces. First, the army had to have immediately available a body of regular troops that the government could deploy at the onset of a conflict. Second, the army had to have subsequent forces that could either follow up the regular troops or provide for the defence of the north-west approaches to Australia in the event that South-East Asia fell to communist conquest.[17]

If the 1956 strategic policy review marked the formal end to Australia's commitment to the Middle East, it also had the effect of raising the status of the ANZAM agreement in the Commonwealth's planning. Furthermore, it rationalised political and military decision-making so that planners could narrow future defence analysis to the immediate vicinity of Australia. For the army's leaders, the switching of defence focus to South-East Asia meant that they could now make the tropics the central focus of their organisational, training, and doctrinal preparations instead of also having to consider desert requirements.[18] Another aspect of government policy found within the Far East Strategic Reserve commitment was the recognition of a need to have a standing force readily available for commitment overseas.

In the 1960s, the government's concern over communist aggression in South-East Asia and the Indian Ocean Basin was complicated by the growth of the Indonesian nationalist movement, and Jakarta's ability to destabilise the region.[19] The aggressive posturing of the Sukarno regime, its policy of confrontation with Malaysia, and its accompanying build-up of naval and military assets concerned Canberra. Furthermore, Australian planners worried that the Indonesians might implement a campaign, similar to confrontation, along its border with the Australian half of New Guinea and thereby destabilise the territory. These uncertainties regarding Jakarta's intentions provided another reason for Australian planners to maintain American interest in South-East Asia and develop and sustain the army's permanent forces at a higher level of readiness than it had before World War II.

Subsequent studies refined the policies set out by the 1956 strategic review, but its basic premises remain unaltered until the post-Vietnam War period. A 1966 Defence Committee policy paper confirmed the belief that the best strategic concept for Australia was 'the continued participation with our allies in the maintenance of a forward defence policy of holding mainland South East Asia against communist expansion'. The report also noted a need to have the ability to respond to aggressive Indonesian nationalism.[20] The Defence Committee listed several short-of-war situations that might require Australian troops, including:

  a The support of Malaysia and Singapore against a resurgence of Indonesian confrontation or communist terrorist activities
  b The support of SEATO counter-insurgency plans
  c Bilateral military assistance in mainland South East Asia such as to South Vietnam and Thailand

d Internally or externally inspired subversion or insurgency or possibly civil disorder in Papua/New Guinea; and

　　e United Nations peace-keeping task.[21]

The Defence Committee identified limited war situations requiring Australian intervention as:

　　a Communist aggression in mainland South East Asia covered by SEATO plans or alternative plans developed in concert with the United States or other allies.

　　b Indonesian aggression against Malaysia and Singapore or interference with our bases or sea and air communications; and

　　c Open hostilities later in the period with Indonesia over Papua/New Guinea.

Although the potential scenarios had evolved, the basic requirements for the army's organisation had stayed the same. The government remained committed to a policy of forward defence, and to having military forces capable of 'making a prompt and sustained contribution to Allied forces in South East Asia in a wide range of situations'.[22]

The army post Korea

The commencement of national service in 1951 swelled the ranks of the CMF so that by 1953 it had a strength of more than 80,000, organised into two infantry divisions, three infantry brigades that could form a third division, and two armoured brigades. More importantly, most units were at full strength. The CMF hit its peak strength in 1955, when it numbered over 85,000 personnel, with a further 44,000 on the inactive list.[23] Table 7.1 (p. 238) outlines the distribution of the CMF's major combat formations as of April 1953.

　Perhaps the main beneficiary of the expansion were the gunners, whose number of regiments increased greatly. In 1947, there were only three artillery regiments on the army's establishment as corps troops—2nd Medium Regiment, 3rd Composite Anti-Aircraft Regiment, and 1st Heavy Anti-Aircraft Regiment. By 1953 there were 16 more, mostly organised into formations termed Army Group Royal Artillery. The army had no trouble creating these units, as it could draw upon its large store of surplus guns.[24] However, while the expansion appeared a sensible move, since the troops and guns were freely available, it contained the seeds of its own destruction. The army artillery establishment was now greatly in excess of the CMF's field force requirements. With only three divisions, the CMF was essentially a corps-size force, but it

Table 7.1 Distribution of major CMF combat formations, April 1953

Command	Formation
Northern	7th Infantry Brigade
	11th Infantry Brigade
	HQ 5th Army Group Royal Artillery (Field)
Eastern	HQ 2nd Infantry Division
	5th Infantry Brigade
	8th Infantry Brigade
	14th Infantry Brigade
	1st Armoured Brigade
	HQ 1st Army Group Royal Artillery (Anti-Aircraft)
Southern	HQ 3rd Infantry Division
	4th Infantry Brigade
	6th Infantry Brigade
	2nd Armoured Brigade
	HQ 2nd Army Group Royal Artillery (Field)
	HQ 4th Army Group Royal Artillery (Anti-Aircraft)
Central	9th Infantry Brigade
Western	13th Infantry Brigade

now had enough artillery regiments to support several corps. In contrast to the past, when the army had to rely on an ally for much of its non-divisional artillery needs, the CMF now had more firepower than it could profitably employ. In addition, as the guns inevitably wore out, the army would not be able to justify their replacement on a similar scale. In fact, the mid 1950s was the heyday of the army's peacetime artillery, and it proved an unsustainable aberration.

Perversely, the influx of national servicemen did little to improve the army's combat capability. In fact, the strain of maintaining the scheme probably had a negative effect on the readiness of the force, as it required the army to assign ARA personnel as instructors to national service training units from its already over-extended combat elements. The ARA also gained little from the national service scheme, as the conscripts served in the CMF after the completion of their basic training. Also, the scheme's terms of service did not include a mandate requiring national servicemen to serve overseas. The government did offer a £10 allowance to national servicemen who attested for overseas service, but in 1952 only 25 per cent had done so.[25] The CMF did contain a core of volunteers, which the Defence Act obligated to serve overseas, but these were scattered throughout the organisation, so that there were no units capable of overseas deployment without considerable reorganisation.[26] Complicating the situation further was the fact that national servicemen who, after the completion of their training obligation, had volunteered for the CMF could still request an immediate transfer to the inactive list if they wanted to avoid overseas services.[27]

While the CMF grew, the ARA remained under establishment throughout the 1950s. This was largely a result of the difficulty of recruiting in an economy that offered full employment, although unappealing service conditions were also a factor. As a result, the ARA was under considerable strain to meet its responsibilities. As the previous chapter related, the army had to employ *ad hoc* methods to attract volunteers throughout the Korean War. The most the army could support in Korea was two battalions, a marked contrast to the force the nation had mobilised during World War II. When the conflict ended, the Commonwealth agreed to the request of the United States that it keep its forces in Korea in order to enforce the peace treaty. Only after American troop reduction began did Australia begin a phased withdrawal of its own forces. One battalion (3 RAR) returned to Australia in November 1954, while the second (1 RAR) remained in Korea until early 1956.[28] When the regulars did return, the army used them to administer the national service training brigade and battalion structure or to serve as instructors.

The need to provide a battalion group for the Far East Strategic Reserve only complicated the situation further. In 1955, the ARA had an establishment of only about 23,000 from which to form a field force, as well as to provide assistance to the CMF, the national service scheme, and the cadets. In addition, the ARA also had to provide personnel to staff the army's command, fixed defences, support, and maintenance infrastructure. As a result, many regulars who should have been in the field force actually had other duties. Millar's comment that in 1957 the army 'had so much tail that the dog was scarcely visible' was not far from the truth.[29] Therefore, as currently constituted, neither the ARA nor the CMF was able to provide the government with the military capability it desired. While the CMF could eventually mobilise an expeditionary force, neither the citizen nor regular branches had sufficient standing troops to fulfil either deterrence or ready reaction roles.

Although it was only a battalion group, the Commonwealth's commitment to the Far East Strategic Reserve represented a major dedication of resources for the ARA. Britain approached the Australian Government for assistance early in the Malayan Emergency, but the army, already fully engaged in Korea, could not support multiple commitments. Until 1955, Australia's role in Malaya was almost exclusively sea or air based. The initial Australian Army contingent to the Far East Strategic Reserve consisted of a force of approximately 1,500 officers and men, allocated as follows:

- one infantry battalion
- one field battery
- one field troop
- one transport platoon
- one section of field ambulance
- one section provost
- detachments of brigade headquarters, brigade signal troops, headquarters transport company, infantry workshops, and field regiment light aid detachment.[30]

In September 1955, the forward element of 2 RAR took up residence in Penang, and within a few months its men were hunting communist insurgents in the Malayan interior. In addition, to provide training and support for Australia's return to tropical warfare, the army reopened its Jungle Training School at Canungra.

The 1957 reorganisation

In 1956, the army began to address the recommendations of a recently completed defence review. The Defence Committee, in 'The Strategic Basis of Australian Defence Policy', highlighted the discrepancy between the government's assessment of the threat environment with the capability of the army. As suggested above, the disparity between the roles that the government anticipated for the army and the resources with which the army could respond was considerable. Therefore a reorganisation of the army, with the aim of creating a regular field force with a higher degree of readiness, and a CMF whose structure was more suited to the provision of an expeditionary or follow-up force, was necessary in order to improve the correlation between military requirements and capabilities.

An additional impetus for reform was the Menzies Government's insistence that the armed forces had to improve their effectiveness while also contracting their budgets. The army's vote for 1956–57 was £1 million less than the previous year, and the government cut a further £3 million from the 1957–58 estimate. By adjusting manpower priorities, the army's leaders hoped to create a more combat-ready force at a lower cost.[31]

At a conference in Melbourne in May 1957, Lieutenant-General Henry Wells, the CGS, explained that one of the objectives for the army was to have some ARA forces immediately available for operations within Australia or overseas. However, he observed that this was not possible at present because the level of support provided to the CMF and national service absorbed too great a proportion of regular personnel.[32] Wells believed it was essential for the army to improve its reaction capability if it was to meet its Cold War obligations. The objective of what became known as the 1957 reorganisation was to reallocate resources and manpower in such a way that it produced an ARA field force that met the government's Cold War requirements. The cabinet highlighted this demand when in February 1957 it instructed John Cramer, the Minister for the Army, to give absolute priority to the build-up, equipping, and maintenance of a regular field force.[33] This reorganisation is significant because it was the first in a series of adjustments to the army's structure and hierarchy that gradually shifted the balance within the force from the CMF to the ARA.

The force level that the army's leaders projected to meet the nation's potential commitments under SEATO and/or ANZAM consisted of the following:

a one Australian battle group, as part of the Commonwealth Far East Strategic Reserve, available for operations at call
b a regular force, of up to one division, that could be available for operations within three months
c one CMF division, with supporting units, deployed in operations by the earliest practicable date
d one CMF division, with appropriate supporting units to be available to:
   i   reinforce as necessary the forces involved in SEATO operations, or
   ii meet the requirements of an ANZAM contingency plan
e one CMF division, with appropriate supporting units, to be maintained in Australia as a regional reserve and as a basis for expansion.

To achieve this goal, the army proposed two alternative programs:[34]

- Plan A called for a regular field force of two brigade groups and an armoured regiment, in addition to the battalion group committed to the Far East Strategic Reserve
- Plan B called for a regular field force of only one brigade group and an armoured regiment, in addition to the battalion group committed to the Far East Strategic Reserve.

Each plan advanced the same proposals for the CMF. The CMF retained its basic structure of three divisions, but its establishment declined from the current level of approximately 82,000 to about 51,000. While the CMF retained its key combat formations, it lost some support units. In addition, the army planned to lower the citizen formations' posting strength to approximately 66 per cent of war establishment. The reduction in the CMF's establishment would allow the army to transfer resources to the ARA.

The plans also formally divided the army into two categories of readiness. Category A consisted of those forces, maintained on a regular basis in peace, that either formed part of the regular field force, provided administrative, maintenance, and training units to support the regular field force, or provided necessary support in peace to the Category B forces. Category B consisted of those forces necessary to follow up the regular field force in limited or global war, provide for home defence, or effect the expansion of the military forces in an emergency. This included the CMF field force. The army planned to raise the remainder of its proposed wartime order of battle as needed.

Category A consisted almost exclusively of the ARA, except for those citizen-soldier units that the army considered essential for the support of the regular field force. The plan allocated most CMF units to Category B, and their role was to provide follow-up or support units for the ARA. The only exception was the case of the massive expansion of the army for a major war. In such an eventuality, the CMF provided the template for the nation's military mobilisation. Defence planners considered such an event highly unlikely, however.

Plan A—the two-brigade regular field force—provided greater potential for the ARA, but also required a much broader reorganisation of the army and a more emphatic shifting of the demarcation between the ARA and the CMF. Plan A assumed that the regular field force was the priority, and to achieve this goal planners believed that it was necessary to reduce the ARA's commitments towards the CMF and national service. Table 7.2 outlines the ARA personnel required to implement a Plan A field force.

Table 7.2 Establishment of Plan A field force

Units	Officers	Other ranks	Total
Independent Brigade Group	254	4,685	4,939
Independent Brigade Group	254	4,685	4,939
Armoured Regiment, including Signal and LAD detachment	35	457	492
Total	543	9,827	10,370

However, the ARA had available only 95 officers and 1,921 other ranks (2,016 in total) to staff the proposed units of the Plan A field force. Although these figures did not include personnel serving with the Far East Strategic Reserve and the small amount of infantry undergoing training at the Infantry Training Depot at Ingleburn, it is clear that the army faced a massive shortfall in field-force-capable troops.[35]

To provide the required personnel, the army proposed a modification in the service obligation under the national service scheme to require that some of the trainees serve full time in the ARA. The army also planned to reallocate many of the ARA personnel currently assisting the CMF to regular units, since a smaller citizen force required

fewer instructors. The army believed that the following arrangement satisfied its personnel requirements:
- available in Australia: 2,016
- allotted from other ARA categories: 1,400
- allotted from national service intake: 7,000.

By this method the army could raise slightly more than the 10,370 men it needed to staff the Plan A field force.

The army proposed to divide the national service intake into two streams. The revised scheme would see approximately 4,200 conscripts per year serving in the ARA for a two-year period of full-time duty. After the completion of this obligation, the national servicemen were liable for a further three years on the inactive service, but they incurred no further training requirement unless mobilised. To reduce the CMF to 51,000, the army proposed an annual intake of just 12,000. To lighten further the burden on the ARA, national servicemen would train for only 77 days. To compensate, however, the army increased its service obligation from two years to three, at a rate of 21 days' service per year, thus maintaining the overall training period at 140 days. To speed up the CMF contraction, the army planned to move to the inactive list any national servicemen currently serving in units identified for disbandment. The army estimated that approximately 10,000 national servicemen fell into this category. Under this scheme, therefore, the army proposed a peacetime establishment for both the ARA and the CMF of over 81,000, although both branches remained well short of their war strengths.

Although Plan A was the most attractive from the ARA's perspective, and even though it most fully provided for the force's structural requirements as dictated by the government's strategic assessment, it did have serious political ramifications that made it unacceptable to the government. Its implementation required the government to amend the Defence Act in order that able-bodied males become liable for conscription into the full-time army in peace for the first time in the Commonwealth's history. Furthermore, the Defence Act obligated those selected for the ARA to serve overseas at the government's desire, a feature that had generated considerable political debate in the world wars. In addition, some defence planners objected to the proposal because it eliminated the universality of the current national service scheme. Major-General Ivan Dougherty, the CMF member of the Military Board, believed that the movement to a selective service system was undemocratic, and that it could deny the CMF personnel who might make good leaders.[36] Instead Plan B, which did not have these liabilities, received the government's approval.

Table 7.3 Composition of the army: Plan A

Category	Forces	Peace establishment	Allocation of present strength	Required in war
A	1 Inf. Bn Gp in FESR	1,430	1,430	1,430
A	2 Inf. Bde Gps, 1 Arm. Regt	13,022	11,584	13,200
A	Pacific Islands Regiment	850	646	2,550
A	Total all other ARA units	17,698	16,277	17,698
	Total category A	**33,000**	**29,937**	**34,878**
B	Three Inf. Divs with supporting units	76,000	51,500	114,000
B	Home Defence	incl. in above	nil	14,150
B	Base administrative and training units	nil	nil	35,000
B	Reinforcement in training	nil	nil	24,500
	Total Category B	**76,000**	**51,500**	**187,650**
	Total	*109,000*	*81,437*	*222,528*

Table 7.3 outlines the composition of the army under proposed Plan A.

Plan B called for a regular brigade group in addition to the battalion group allocated to Far East Strategic Reserve. This plan's emphasis was not on the use of conscripts in the ARA but on the modification of the army's existing responsibilities in order to make better use of existing resources. Therefore, like Plan A, it limited the CMF's establishment to 51,000. This permitted a reduction in the national service intake to 12,000 trainees a year, from the current level of 29,250. In addition, they would train for an initial period of only 77 days. Once the national serviceman was in the CMF, his terms of engagement were the same as for Plan A. Table 7.4 outlines the composition of the army under proposed Plan B.

A comparison between Tables 7.3 and 7.4 illustrates one of the ongoing problems facing the Australian Regular Army since its formation after World War II. Even though Plan B provided a field force of half the size of that proposed in Plan A, there was no corresponding reduction in the personnel requirements of the army's management, training, and maintenance. Under both plans, the army's non-field force establishments required more than 17,500 personnel. Under Plan A, the field force represented 46.3 per cent of the army's strength, compared to 31.1 per cent under Plan B, but this was only because of the higher overall establishment, not because of any personnel savings in support areas.

Table 7.4 Composition of the army: Plan B

Category	Forces	Peace establishment	Allocation of present strength	Required in war
A	1 Inf. Bn. Gp in FESR	1,430	1,430	1,430
A	1 Inf. Bde Gp, 1 Arm. Regt	5,800	4,439	6,262
A	Pacific Islands Regiment	850	646	2,550
A	Total all other ARA units	17,920	16,420	18,321
	Total Category A	26,000	22,935	28,563
B	Three Inf. Divs with supporting units	76,000	51,500	114,000
B	Home Defence	incl. in above	nil	14,150
B	Base administrative and training units	nil	nil	35,000
B	Reinforcement in training	nil	nil	24,500
	Total Category B	76,000	51,500	187,650
	Total	102,000	74,435	216,213

In 1957 the army began a three-year reorganisation based on Plan B. It called for an ARA of:

- one brigade group immediately available
- one battalion group as part of the Far East Strategic Reserve
- administration, maintenance, and training units to support the field force and the remainder of the army.

As a part of this reorganisation, the army also raised a Special Air Service company. The rationale for this new unit was the success the British Special Air Service forces had enjoyed in counter-insurgency operations during the Malayan Emergency. The army believed that it should have a similar capability in case of a deployment to South-East Asia.[37]

The reorganisation envisaged a CMF composed of:

- one division ready for deployment at earliest date possible
- one division to be available to reinforce forces involved in operations
- one division to remain in Australia as a regional reserve and to provide a basis for further expansion
- support, security, and administrative units as required.[38]

Table 7.5 (p. 246) outlines the theoretical structure for a brigade group under the 1957 reorganisation. Table 7.6 (p. 246) outlines the theoretical organisation of a battalion group under the 1957 reorganisation. Both organisations also had their own logistical support force. Table 7.7 outlines the organisation of the logistical support force for a brigade group. Table 7.8 outlines the organisation of the logistical support force for a battalion group. However, it soon became apparent that the reform would not provide the army with the up-to-strength regular field force that it intended. Table 7.9 (p. 248) outlines the establishment objectives and shortfall of personnel at the beginning of the reorganisation.

Table 7.5 Organisation of ARA brigade group, 1957 [39]

Unit Type	Composition
Brigade headquarters	HQ Inf. Bde; Inf. Bde LAD
Armour	Armd Regt; Armd Regt Sig. Tp; Armd Regt LAD
Artillery	Fd Regt (less 1 battery); Bty Lt Regt; Fd Regt Sig. Tp; Fd Regt LAD; LAA Bty; LAA Bty LAD
Engineers	Fd Sqn, Fd Sqn LAD
Signals	Inf. Bde Sig. Sqn
Infantry	2 Infantry Bns; SAS Coy
Intelligence	Fd Security Section (–); APIS (–)
Support	Transport Coy; Transport Coy LAD
Medical	Fd Ambulance
Dental	Dental Unit
Ordnance	Ordnance Fd Pk
Electrical & mechanical	Inf. Wksp; Inf. Wksp Stores Sec.
Pay	Fd Cash Office
Provost	Inf. Bde Provost Unit
Postal	Postal Unit

Table 7.6 Organisation of ARA battalion group, 1957 [40]

Unit type	Composition
Artillery	Field Battery
Engineers	Field Tp
Signals	Inf. Bde Gp Sig. Sqn (det.)
Infantry	Infantry Battalion; SAS Coy
Intelligence	Field Security Sec.; APIS Sec.
Medical	Field Ambulance (–)

Table 7.7 Organisation of ARA brigade group: logistical support force[41]

Unit type	Composition
Headquarters	HQ Aust. Force; Movement Control Group (det.); HQ Aust. Force LAD; Adv. Records Office (det.)
Engineers	Const. Regt (less one squadron); Engr Stores Sec. Bde Sp. Unit; Small Ships (det.); Port Operating Squadron
Signals	L of C Sig. Regt
Support	Composite Coy RAASC
Medical	Fd Hyg. Sec.; Casualty Clearing Station; General Hospital; Medical Platoon (det.); Laundry Platoon
Dental	Dental Unit (det.)
Ordnance	Composite Ord. Coy; Med. Wksp Special Stores Sec.; Tpt Coy Wksp Stores Sec.
Electrical and mechanical	Tpt Coy Wksp; Med. Wksp
Provost	Force Provost Platoon
Psych.	Psych. Unit
Pay	Fd Cash Office; Base Cash Office
Postal	Base Postal Unit
Miscellaneous	Graves Registration Unit; Amenities Unit (det.)

Table 7.8 Organisation of ARA battalion group: logistical support force[42]

Unit type	Composition
Headquarters	Adv. part HQ Inf. Bde
Engineers	Construction Tp; Det. RAE (incl Plant Tp and Stores Sec.); MC Unit (det.)
Signals	L of C Signal Regt (det.)
Support	Transport Platoon, Supply Platoon (det.)
Medical	Fd Hygiene Sec. (det.)
Dental	Dental Unit (det.)
Ordnance	Ordnance Fd Pk (det.)
Electrical and mechanical	Battalion Gp LAD
Provost	Sec. Provost Coy
Pay	Fd Cash Office
Postal	Postal Unit

Table 7.9 Composition of ARA, 1956–57 [43]

Forces	Requirement	Present strength
1 Inf. Bn Gp for FESR	1,430	1,430
1 Inf. Bde Gp	5,800	2,283
Pacific Islands Regiment	850	646
All other ARA units	20,630	18,391
Total personnel of ARA	*28,710*	*22,750*

The army's establishment was nearly 6,000 under strength. Furthermore, as Cramer pointed out, the ARA had actually declined in strength for the last few years, and if this trend continued it would put even more pressure on the force's ability to raise an infantry brigade group.[44] In fact, this is precisely what happened. In 1958, the ARA's strength had sunk to 20,771. It did begin to recover the next year, but by 1960 it still stood at only 21,843, only 76 per cent of the goal.[45]

In a series of studies, the Adjutant-General examined the problem. He reported in May 1957 that of the 1,200 ARA personnel freed up by the reduction in the national service intake, only 500 were suitable for service with the field force. He anticipated that the army could expect to transfer only a further 500 from training and maintenance categories, thus leaving the brigade group well short of its goal.[46] The tropical establishment of the brigade group—not including the armoured brigade or logistical support units—was 4,644 (257 officers and 4,387 other ranks). By mid 1958 the army had assigned 3,635 personnel to the formation, but of these, over 700 were ineligible for service overseas because of being over age, under age, medically unfit, or due for discharge. Thus the brigade group was still considerably under strength. In order to raise the strength of the regular field force, he suggested, it should receive the entire year's intake of recruits as well as stripping the rest of the force of all suitable men. He believed that by this method he could raise the strength of the formation to over 4,000—still more than 600 short of establishment but a major improvement. However, the Adjutant-General pointed out, the policy would affect the raising of the brigade group's logistical support force. The logistical support force had an establishment of over 2,100 and, except for the assignment of a few headquarters and administrative staff, the army had not yet had the opportunity or the manpower to raise the formation. Additionally, the Adjutant-General anticipated that, because of the reallocation of their personnel to the field force, some areas of the army's command, maintenance, training, or support sections would collapse under the strain of operating with too low a level of staffing.[47]

As a compromise, the Adjutant-General said, it was possible for the army to provide a battalion group for overseas service by the end of the year without any damage to the rest of the force. However, he felt compelled to warn that any effort to form such a battalion group before 31 December—the end of the recruit cycle—would require crossposting from other infantry units to fill out the battalion group. He noted that 1 RAR and 2 RAR were both at 75 per cent of strength, and that it was possible to cannibalise one of the battalions to bring the other up to strength, but that both could not go overseas. In neither scenario did the Adjutant-General include the requirements for first and second reinforcements in his figures.[48]

The pentropic reorganisation

Even before the army had fully implemented the 1957 reorganisation, it became clear that the reform would not produce an order of battle that would allow the army to fulfil its missions as required by the 1956 strategic review. The army had to allocate manpower to too many responsibilities, and this inhibited the rationalisation of the force structure and the creation of the desired hard-hitting, mobile, and readily available regular field force. The army had simply found it impossible to recruit enough soldiers to bring its units up to the required strength. Table 7.10 (p. 250) illustrates the continuing shortfall in the ARA's brigade group establishment. It now appeared more likely than ever that the army would have to find the required troops from within the service.

To this end, the army embarked on the most radical, and ultimately ill-conceived, reorganisation of its history—the pentropic division. The pentropic division was, as the name implies, a five-sided structure, rather than the triangular system that the army had traditionally used for its divisions. The pentropic division was built around five infantry battalions, each of which had a capacity for limited independent operations. The pentropic infantry battalion was approximately 50 per cent larger in personnel and fielded twice as much firepower as a tropical establishment battalion. The pentropic battalion was composed of five rifle companies, plus an administrative and a support company. Supporting the division's five infantry battalions were five field regiments of artillery and five field squadrons of engineers. The pentropic division included an armoured regiment, but this contained only three squadrons of tanks, unlike the heavier American pentomic version, which had five tank units. Making up the rest of the division's components were signals, transport, medical, ordnance, electrical and mechanical, pay, provost, and postal elements. The division also included an aviation regiment, an innovation in an Australian division. The division had an establishment of 14,045 officers and men.[50]

Table 7.10 Manpower deficiency in ARA brigade group, 31 July 1958[49]

Unit	Required establishment	Actual strength	Deficiency
HQ Inf. Bde	90	41	49
Inf. Bde LAD	20	nil	20 (not raised)
Armd Regt	402	391	11
Armd Regt Sig. Tp	12	11	1
Armd Regt LAD	89	73	16
Fd Regt (less one battery) and Bty Lt Regt	540	464	76
Fd Regt Sig. Tp	48	38	10
Fd Regt LAD	33	28	5
LAA Bty	174	163	11
LAA Bty LAD	7	8	+1
Ind. Fd Sqn	295	274	21
Independent Fd Sqn LAD	5	5	–
Independent Inf. Bde Sig. Sqn	117	90	27
Inf. Bn	848	616	232
Inf. Bn	848	605	243
SAS Coy	220	160	60
FS Sec. (–)	10	9	1
APIS (–)	3	3	–
Tpt Coy	311	282	29
Tpt Coy LAD	24	18	6
Fd Amb.	245	88	157
Dent. Unit	41	23	18
Inf. Ordnance Fd Pk	37	38	+1
Inf. Wksp	163	153	10
Inf. Wksp Store Sec. (type C)	3	3	–
Independent Inf. Bde Pro. Unit	41	34	7
Postal Unit (Type A)	4	4	–
Total	4,644	3,635	1,009

The adoption of the pentropic division also required the army to amend its use of terms. The basic infantry formation remained the battalion. However, in the pentropic context, when supporting arms and service came under the control of the battalion headquarters, the army referred to the larger formation as a battle group. If the divisional commander placed two or more battle groups under a single command, the combined organisation was known as a task force. Brigade, the headquarters traditionally subordinate to the division, disappeared from the army's lexicon. The reason for the abandonment of brigade designation was that it implied a fixed organisation of a constant size, whereas task force suggested a more fluid command structure, whose components divisional headquarters allocated according to mission requirements.[51]

The United States Army had itself recently reorganised its infantry divisions onto a pentanna organisation called the pentomic division. To a limited extent, therefore, a part of the decision to adopt a similar divisional structure came from the desire to reconfigure the Australian field force onto a basis which provided compatibility with the Commonwealth's most important ally. However, this rationale is easily overstated. A more important factor was the fiscal imperative, which also played a part in the decision to address reorganisation. Despite the greater focus on defence issues under Menzies, the government still followed a policy of providing for defence in the cheapest manner possible. By 1960, the army's equipment was still largely surplus from World War II, and was becoming increasingly worn-out and obsolete. A reorganisation that created a more efficient force structure promised to free up monies that the force could apply to capital purchases.[52]

However, the most important motivation for undertaking pentropic was that the army's leaders simply believed that some form of reorganisation was essential. The army continued to suffer from significant structural problems, so the real question facing the senior officers was not whether to reorganise but what type of organisation to adopt.[53] The current structure simply provided insufficient numbers of units readily available and properly equipped for operations at short notice.[54] In outlining the reasons for the reorganisation, the Headquarters Southern Command explained that the aim was to create

a   An effective regular force which will be properly equipped and readily available to move to any conflict in which Australia may be involved; and

b   A CMF volunteer force adequately trained and equipped to provide a follow-up force and a basis for further expansion.[55]

In announcing the decision to adopt the pentropic structure, Athol Townley, the Minister for Defence, stressed the importance of the army having a force that was available for an immediate contribution. He stated that the improvements to the Regular Army included:
- increasing the strength of the field force
- reorganising the field force to improve its tactical flexibility

- raising a logistical support group
- improving mobility by the provision of fixed and rotary aircraft
- providing additional types of modern equipment.[56]

The objective of the reorganisation was to acquire a readily available expeditionary force, a capability that had so far eluded the army. Furthermore, all field force units would be either a part of the pentropic division or designed for its support. To further assure the achievement of this goal, the army also intended to raise the field force's essential logistical and combat support elements.[57]

The reorganisation process began in late 1958 when the Director of Staff Duties requested the branches and directorates of Army Headquarters to study the application of the American pentomic division to Australian requirements and determine whether the army should adopt the structure, or a similar one modified to meet local conditions.[58] Concurrently with its study of the pentanna structure, Army Headquarters also decided to investigate the possibility of reforming its system for its higher direction. One option was to switch from the present geographic-based chain of command to one determined by function. The initial proposal was for three functional establishments—command, training, and administrative support—instead of the current system of seven State- and Territory-based commands.

The army expended considerable effort in assessing the functional system, but the DCGS's prediction that two reorganisations would be too difficult proved correct in the end. Instead, the army implemented, as detailed below, a quasi-functional system within Headquarters 1st Division, but fundamental changes to the army's system of higher direction had to wait until the Hassett reforms of the early 1970s.[59]

By late 1959, the army had gained the government's assent to the pentropic proposal, and began the process of developing new establishments and reorganising units.[60] The army's proposed order of battle included:

- a Far East Strategic Reserve
- Expeditionary Forces Priority I and Priority II, comprising:
  — 1st Division (including ARA Task Forces)
  — 1st Combat Support Group and Communication Zone Units (including an ARA Logistical Support Force for the ARA Task Forces)
- Expeditionary Forces, Priority III, and basis for expansion comprising:
  — 3rd Division
  — 3rd Division Support Group
  — Home Defence Units.[61]

Within this organisation, the field force structure that the army intended to develop for the ARA consisted of:
- Australian contribution to the Far East Strategic Reserve
- a task force of two battle groups
- one battalion of the Pacific Islands Regiment
- reduced headquarters, administrative staff, maintenance, and training units.

The total strength of the ARA was to be 21,000. The principal elements of the CMF's contribution to the field force was:
- three battle groups to join the two ARA battle groups to form the 1st Division
- five battle groups, restricted in strength, as the basis for expansion (3rd Division)
- Communication Zone units required to support the above forces (on a restricted basis).

The army also raised combat, logistical, and administrative units as needed for the support of the field force, but on a restricted basis. The total strength of the CMF was 30,000, providing an army of 51,000.[62]

Table 7.11 outlines the changes the pentropic system required in the Australian Regular Army's order of battle. Table 7.12 (p. 254) outlines the changes the army proposed for the existing CMF order of battle in order to adapt the structure to the pentropic system.

Table 7.11 Comparison of existing order of battle with proposed pentropic order of battle: ARA formations[63]

Existing order of battle	Proposed pentropic order of battle
Australian component FESR, including 1 infantry battalion group	Australian component FESR, including one reduced battle group
1 infantry brigade group with two battalions (at restricted establishment)	A task force of two battle groups
Logistic support force for the brigade group (mainly shadow posted)	Combat and logistic support for the task force (raised in peace but with some elements still shadowed posted)
1 battalion of the Pacific Islands Regiment	1 battalion of the Pacific Islands Regiment
Headquarters and administrative staffs, maintenance, training, and miscellaneous units	Reduced headquarters and administrative staffs, maintenance, training, and miscellaneous units (no national service staffs)

Table 7.12 Comparison of existing order of battle with proposed pentropic order of battle: CMF formations[64]

Existing order of battle	Proposed pentropic order of battle
2 divisions on a reduced basis	3 battle groups (which, married to the two ARA battle groups above, make up 1st Pentropic Division) available within 3–4 months
1 skeleton division as a basis for expansion	A division of 5 battle groups restricted in strength, as a basis for expansion
Communications Zone units on a restricted basis	Communication Zone and Combat Support Group units required to support the above forces in the theatre of operations, to be raised on a restricted basis, primarily for the support of one division
Total CMF strength of 50,194, of whom 30,812 are national servicemen and 19,382 are volunteers	Total CMF strength of 30,000 (all volunteers)

The priority levels associated with the ARA and CMF field force units were meant to indicate their level of readiness and capability to undertake operations. This step was essential, because the army did not have the resources to maintain all units at the same equipment and readiness level. Therefore, the army planned to place the emphasis on the regular forces in order to have some units operational in the shortest period possible. The time frame of the priority levels were:

- Priority I: readily available for operations: the ARA field force
- Priority II: available for operations within three to four months: the CMF follow-up force
- Priority III: available for operations within six months: the CMF basis for expansion.[65]

By January 1962, the army planners expected to have the ability to maintain one ARA battle group, with logistical support elements, at a 14-day warning level. They expected to be able to have an entire task force ready for operations, including its combat support and logistical support forces, within 30 days of activation.[66] Major-General I.T. Murdoch, the DCGS, believed that the only way to maintain CMF units at a level of readiness higher than Priority II was if the establishments of select citizen force units contained a substantial leavening of ARA personnel. Murdoch estimated that to improve the readiness of the lower-priority formations required the allocation of approximately 2,200 regular soldiers. This, he considered, was not the optimal use of such strength, and the army would be better off if it guaranteed that Priority I units achieved their assigned establishment.[67]

In late 1959, the army issued the planned allocation of strength for the ARA. This was a key step, because at its core the pentropic reorganisation was essentially a rationalisation of the ARA, and the army intended to find the personnel for its expanded field force from internal sources, not by recruiting towards a higher establishment. In fact, the army had proposed a reduction in the establishment of the ARA from the current ceiling of 26,000 to only 21,000. The reduction was actually less severe than the ceiling adjustment suggests, as the army was more than 4,000 under establishment when the reorganisation began. Table 7.13 (p. 256) compares the allocation of personnel under the existing tropical establishment system with the pentropic organisation.

As Table 7.13 illustrates, the troops allocated to the operational forces increased by 4,544, despite the ceiling reduction. To find these soldiers, the army had to reduce the number of personnel serving in support, administrative, and training areas by a corresponding amount, and end the ARA's involvement with national service. The instructions prepared by Headquarters Western Command to implement the pentropic reorganisation illustrates how the army defined its manpower policy. It noted that the army would post field force units to full establishment. The remainder of the force—the command, administrative, and training structure and the ARA cadres with CMF units—the army intended to underpost by the number by which the overall total establishment exceeded the approved ceiling of 21,000. These instructions make it clear that the field force would have the first pick of manpower and the rest of the army would make do with what was left. The army planned to find further savings in its estimate by reducing its civilian work force by more than a thousand.[68]

The decision to implement the pentropic structure was not without trauma or disagreement. The army had done only minimal preliminary testing of the concept before deciding to undertake the reorganisation. While it is true, as Millar has observed, that the army did not have the strength to set aside a division for experimentation, it certainly should have conducted a battalion-level test.[69] In fact, the first full strength test by a battalion group would not occur until October 1962, in a exercise entitled 'Nutcracker'.[70] As a result, the army leaped into a major reshuffle without adequate preparation or understanding of the operational complexities of the pentropic organisation. Once the reorganisation was underway, Australian commanders found the size of the formations too large to control at the battalion level, while the absence of a mid-level command headquarters—the brigade—placed far too great a

Table 7.13 Current and planned allocation of strength in the ARA[71]

Category	Strength as of 31 Oct 1959	Allocation of strength 1961–62
Operational forces		
1 ARA field force		
a One Inf. Bn GP (−) and other elements of FESR	1,351	1,299
b One infantry brigade group (2 BG TFs)	4,051	5,890
c 1 combat support group	nil	401
2 Logistic support force	nil	2,260
3 Home defence		
a Pacific Islands Regiment	611	660
b 25 FS Sec.	2	7
c Signals Intelligence Unit	132	174
Total operational forces	6,147	10,691
CMF field force (Priority II and III) ARA cadres	1,759	1,227
Training installations		
1 Training installations staffs	2,042	1,600
2 Trainees	2,014	1,710
3 National service staffs	1,178	nil
Total training installations	5,234	3,310
Headquarters, communications, operational support and maintenance units, etc.	7,893	5,098
Miscellaneous	693	674
Total	21,726	21,000

burden on the divisional headquarters. Furthermore, the increased size of the formations proved unwieldy, particularly for counter-insurgency operations in the tropics. The American Army's abandonment of its pentomic structure in 1961 also removed the rationale of alliance compatibility. After the American renunciation of the pentanna system, the Australian DCGS, Major-General T.S. Taylor, announced that the army continued to consider pentropic to be the best divisional structure for Australia, and that no major changes were under consideration.[72] However, despite Taylor's enthusiasm, the pentropic experiment would fail, and by 1964 the army would begin the process of reconversion back to a more traditional organisation.

The main beneficiary of the pentropic reorganisation was of course the ARA, and its adoption greatly strengthened the position of the regulars. By comparison, the effect on the CMF was devastating.[73] The extent to which the regulars gained from the experiment was such that some have described its introduction as a plot against the CMF. Certainly, 'plot', as McCarthy states in *Once and Future Army*, is too strong a word. But the ARA must have had some degree of appreciation for the effect the pentropic implementation would have on the CMF.[74] The first blow to the CMF was the cabinet's approval of the Military Board's recommendation to suspend the national service scheme. Townley stated that the army no longer required national service, since the possibility of global war was now remote, and since conscripts were not eligible for overseas service they were not useful for the build-up of the regular field force.[75] While not concurrent with the pentropic reorganisation, the ending of national service was an essential prerequisite if the ARA were to find the personnel it needed for the field force and release funds for other uses. The ARA had nearly 1,200 soldiers working as national service instructors, and the scheme's termination freed these troops for other duties. Although the government had reduced the CMF's intake of national servicemen from nearly 30,000 to only 12,000 per year in 1957, they still represented the dominant category of service in the citizen forces. In addition, since conscripts incurred a three-year training obligation, the ending of national service effectively cost the CMF about 35,000 personnel. Volunteers made up the rest of the CMF establishment.

The sudden elimination of future intakes of national servicemen, combined with the discharge of most of the serving conscripts, dramatically reduced the size of the CMF. Also affecting the CMF was the closure of many of the army's regional training centres, which denied the force access to rural volunteers. As a result, the CMF quickly declined from a strength of approximately 51,000 to only about 20,000, well below its new manpower ceiling of 30,000. At that level, and to fit within the army's new order of battle, the CMF had to disband many units. It lost 30 infantry battalions, more than half of its artillery, and all of its infantry brigade, armoured, and artillery headquarters. Furthermore, citizen-soldier morale plummeted, and throughout the 1960s the CMF suffered from high wastage and low enlistment.[76]

The CMF also lost two of its divisional headquarters. The 2nd Division disappeared, while the 1st Division became a regular formation. The 3rd Division Headquarters remained under CMF control, but existed on a restricted basis and at the lowest priority level. Furthermore, the army limited its function to that of an expansion base. Thus, any expeditionary force was by necessity centred on 1st Division and the regulars. In effect, this meant that the CMF had become a supplement to the ARA. This was a significant change of national policy, as until this point the basis of expeditionary force structure had rested with the CMF. One Member of Parliament commented that the new organisation meant 'the disappearance of the CMF as a competent fighting force in the community' and that the 'CMF had been given its death warrant'.[77]

Perhaps the greatest blow to the CMF was the modification of the regional system, which closely tied a citizen soldier to the local community. The relationship between the community and the citizen soldier was the essence of the CMF tradition. As a result of the pentropic reorganisation, the CMF underwent a painful contraction, which resulted in the disbandment of many units and the restructuring of the rest. Few, if any, units escaped some degree of change. Even more disturbing was the loss of the traditional unit titles of its infantry battalions. CMF battalions included in their ancestry units that had served with the 1st AIF or had won a place of honour in World War II. Names such as the Capricornia Regiment (42nd Infantry Battalion) or the Ballarat Regiment (8th Infantry Battalion) disappeared from the army's order of battle. In their place, the army raised State-based CMF infantry regiments, for which it had secured the 'royal designation'. For example, the army amalgamated all the infantry battalions in Victoria into two pentropic battalions—1 RVR and 2 RVR. The entire CMF infantry order of battle contained only nine battalions, namely 1 and 2 RQR, 2 and 3 RNSWR, 1 and 2 RVR, 1 RTR, 1 RSAR, and 1 RWAR. As a concession to the preservation of the traditions of the CMF, the Director of Staff Duties, Brigadier A.L. MacDonald, assigned the former battalion names to pentropic companies. Thus, A Company 1 RVR was called the Scottish Company (formally 5th Battalion, the Victorian Scottish), and D Company 1 RQR was known as the Wide Bay Company (formally 47th Battalion, the Wide Bay Regiment). However, a company lacked the same degree of status as a battalion, and a State-based regiment could never promote allegiances to the community to the same extent as the regional regiments had once done. The army formed the CMF State regiments on 1 July 1960.[78] Table 7.14 outlines the new CMF battalion structure.

The CMF retained its university regiments. However, these became exclusively officer training units. Consequently, the army narrowed their focus to infantry training and deleted other corps subunits from their establishment. In 1960, the university regiments were the Queensland University Regiment, Sydney University Regiment, University of New South Wales Regiment, Melbourne University Regiment, Adelaide University Regiment, and the Western Australian University Regiment.[79]

The reduction in the establishment of the CMF and the disbandment of many of its units meant that there was now a shortage of positions for many citizen force officers who desired to continue their military careers. To alleviate this problem, and to absorb the surplus CMF officers, the army created in each command an organisation called the Officer Staff Group. The purpose of this body was to:

Table 7.14 Redesignation of CMF battalions as pentropic companies[80]

Pentropic battalion	CMF source battalions	Pentropic rifle company designations
1 RQR	9th Bn (The Moreton Regt)	A Coy: The Moreton Coy
	25th Bn (The Darling Downs Regt)	B Coy: The Darling Downs Coy
	47th Bn (The Wide Bay Regt)	C Coy: not available
	41st Bn (The Byron Scottish Regt)	D Coy: The Wide Bay Coy
		E Coy: The Byron Scottish Coy
2 RQR	51st Bn (The Far North Queensland Regt)	A and B Coys: The Far North Queensland Coy
	31st Bn (The Kennedy Regt)	C Coy: The Kennedy Coy
	42nd Bn (The Capricornia Regt)	D and E Coys: The Capricornia Coy
2 RNSWR	30th Bn (The New South Wales Scottish Regt)	A Coy: The New South Wales Scottish Coy
	17th/18th Bn (The North Shore Regt)	B Coy: The North Shore Coy
	2nd Bn (The City of Newcastle Regt)	C Coy: The City of Newcastle Coy
	13th Bn (The Macquarie Regt)	D Coy: The Macquarie Coy
	6th Bn (New South Wales Mounted Rifles)	E Coy: The Mounted Rifles Coy Support Coy: The Kuring Gai Coy
3 RNSWR	45th Bn (The St George Regt)	A Coy: The St George Coy
	34th Bn (The Illawarra Regt)	B Coy: The Illawarra Coy
	3rd Bn (The Werriwa Regt)	C Coy: The Werriwa Coy
	4th Bn (The Australian Rifles)	D Coy: The Australian Rifles Coy
		E Coy: The Riverina Coy
		Support Coy: The St George Coy
1 RVR	5th Bn (The Victorian Scottish Regt)	A Coy: The Scottish Coy
		B Coy: The Merri Coy
	6th Bn (The Royal Melbourne Regt)	C Coy: The Melbourne Coy
	58th/32nd Bn (The City of Essendon Regt)	D Coy: The Essendon Coy
		E Coy: The Footscray Coy
2 RVR	8th/7th Bn (The North Western Victorian Regt)	A Coy: The Geelong Coy
		B Coy: The Ballarat Coy
	38th Bn (The Northern Victorian Regt)	C Coy: The Sunraysia Coy
		D Coy: The Bendigo Coy
	59th Bn (The Hume Regt)	E Coy: The Goulburn Valley Coy
1 RTR	12th Bn (The Launceston Regt)	A Coy: The Launceston Coy
	40th Bn (The Derwent Regt)	B Coy: The Derwent Coy
1 RSAR	27th Bn (The South Australian Scottish Regt)	A Coy: The South-East Coy
		B Coy: The River Coy
	43rd/48th Bn (The Hindmarsh Regt)	C Coy: The Mid-North Coy
	10th Bn (The Adelaide Rifles)	D Coy: The Adelaide Coy
		E Coy: The Port Adelaide Coy
1 RWAR	11th/44th Bn (The City of Perth Regt)	A Coy: The City of Perth Coy
		B Coy: The Cameron Coy
	16th Bn (The Cameron Highlanders of Western Australia)	C Coy: The Swan Coy
		D Coy: The West Australian Rifles Coy
	28th Bn (The Swan Regt)	E Coy: The North Coast Coy

- train CMF officers in the regimental and staff skills appropriate to their rank
- prepare CMF officers for promotion by instruction at coaching courses
- study special projects, including aspects related to combat development
- assist in the control and umpiring of field exercises and in the conduct of CMF annual camps
- ensure the availability of officers to replace, temporarily, unit officers who are absent from their units at critical periods, e.g. annual camps
- assist headquarters of cadet brigades and battalions.[81]

However, to prevent the Officer Staff Group from becoming a potential drain on ARA resources, Taylor noted that no regular personnel could serve in these units. CMF personnel could remain in an Officer Staff Group for a maximum of four years, after which an officer either had to return to regimental duty or had to go on the inactive list. Each command created its own, and the army set the total establishment at 1,041 officers. The Officer Staff Group concept evolved into an organisation of considerable size. In effect, it became a reserve force that allowed the CMF to retain more officers than its organisation would normally require. By 1962, its name had become command and staff training units.[82]

Although the army's leaders quickly abandoned the idea of reorganising the command system from a geographical to a functional basis, they did implement some minor reforms to the service's higher direction structure. One change in place by the end of 1959 was the redesignation of Headquarters 7th Military District as Headquarters Northern Territory Command. Another reform was the redesignation of Headquarters Tasmania Command as the Headquarters Tasmania Regiment and its placement under the control of Headquarters Southern Command in July 1960. Therefore, Hobart had once again reverted to the control of Melbourne. The demotion of Tasmania Command, however, would prove temporary, and by the 1964 reorganisation it had regained its independence.[83]

More significant was the attempt to implement a *de facto* functional command arrangement within the existing geographic command system. First the army divided the force structure into five groups, which in turn formed two functionally effective divisions. The five parts were:
- 1st and 3rd Divisions
- Combat Support Group
- Communication Zone Group
- Command, Administration, and Training
- Home Defence.

The infantry component of the 1st Division was the two ARA battle groups, 1 RQR, 2 RNSWR, and 3 RNSWR, while the 3rd Division included 2 RQR, 1 RVR, 2 RVR, 1 RSAR, and 1 RWAR. The army defined the combat support group as those combat and support units that could be allotted to a division if required, while the communication zone contained those elements necessary to maintain the rear area of an operational theatre. The first three parts made up the field force, while the fourth represented the Australian support area.[84]

Table 7.15 identifies the major elements of the 1st Division. Table 7.16 (p. 262) identifies the major elements of the 3rd Division. Table 7.17 (p. 262) identifies the major elements of the 1st Division combat support group.

Table 7.15 Main elements of 1st Division (pentropic)[85]

Type	Units
Armoured	1st Armoured Regt.
	A Sqn 4th/19th PWLH
Artillery	HQ RAA 1st Division
	1st, 4th, 5th,* 7th,* 23rd* Fd Regts
	131st Div. Loc. Bty*
Engineers	HQ 1st Fd Regt
	1st, 4th,* 5th,* 6th,* 7th Fd Sqns
Signals	1st Div. Sig. Regt
Infantry	1 RAR, 3 RAR, 1 RQR,* 2 RNSWR,* 3 RNSWR*
Intelligence	1st Div. Int. Unit
Aviation	16th Army Lt AC Sqn
Supply	HQ CRAASC 1st Div.
	1st, 2nd,* 3rd* Transport Coys
Medical	1st,* 2nd, 5th* Fd Amb.
Ordnance	HQ CRAAOC 1st Div.
	1st Div. Ord. Coy
	101st, 103rd,* 104th* Inf. Wksp Stores Sec.
Electrical and mechanical	HQ CRAEME 1st Div.
	1st Armd Regt LAD
	1st, 4th, 5th,* 7th,* 23rd* Fd Regt LAD
	101st, 103rd,* 104th* Inf. Wksp
Pay	1st Div. Cash Office
Provost	1st Div. Pro. Coy

* Units made up mainly of CMF with ARA elements.

Table 7.16 Main elements of 3rd Division (pentropic)[86]

Type	Unit
Armoured	1st/15th RNSWL
	A Sqn 10th LH
Artillery	HQ RAA 3rd Div.
	2nd, 3rd, 11th, 13th, 15th Fd Regts
	132nd Div. Loc. Bty
Engineers	3rd, 11th, 12th, 13th, 14th Fd. Sqns
Signals	3rd Div. Sig. Regt
Infantry	2 RQR, 1 RVR, 2 RVR, 1 RSAR, 1 RWAR
Intelligence	3rd Div. Int. Unit
Supply	HQ CRAASC 3rd Div.
	10th Transport Coy
Medical	4th, 6th, 9th Fd Amb.
Ordnance	3rd Div. Ord. Coy
	105th, 107th, 113th Inf. Wksp Stores Sec.
Electrical and mechanical	HQ CRAEME 3rd Div.
	1st/15th RNSWL LAD
	2nd, 3rd, 11th, 15th LAD
	3rd Div. Sig. Regt LAD
	105th, 107th Inf. Wksp
Pay	3rd Div. Cash Office
Provost	3rd Div. Pro. Coy

Table 7.17 Main elements of combat support group for 1st Division (pentropic)[87]

Type	Unit
Armoured	4th/19th PWLH* (less A Sqn), 12th/16th HRL,* 2nd/14th QMI*
Artillery	10th Med. Regt*
	18th LAA Regt*
	130th Corps Loc. Regt*
Engineers	HQ 3rd Fd Eng. Regt*
	2nd,* 8th,* 10th,* 16th* 38th* Fd Sqn
	15th Corps Fd Pk Sqn*
Infantry	1st SAS Coy
	1st RNSWR (Cdo)*
Supply	7th,* 33rd,* 36th* Transport Coy
Electrical and mechanical	4th/19th PWLH,* 12th/16th HRL,* 2nd/14th QMI* LAD
	10th Med. Regt Wksp*
	18th LAA Wksp*
	7th,* 33rd,* 36th* Coy Wksp

* Units made up mainly of CMF with ARA elements.

*Table 7.18 Main elements of combat support group for
3rd Division (pentropic)*[88]

Type	Unit
Armoured	10th LH (less A Sqn), 8th/13th VMR, 3rd/9th SAMR
Artillery	112th Fd Bty
Engineers	34th Fd Sqn
Infantry	1st RTR (2 coys)
	2nd Cdo Coy
Electrical and mechanical	10th LH, 8th/13th VMR, 3rd/9th SAMR LAD

Table 7.18 identifies the major elements of the 3rd Division combat support group. Although the army's order of battle lists more units than presented in the table, most were not raised in peacetime.

The communication zone group consisted largely of engineering, signal, and supply units such as the 16th and 21st Construction Regiments, 11th Port Regiment, 8th Railway Group, 11th Movement Control Group, 3rd Line of Communication Signal Regiment, and 7th Supply Group. The main units of the home defence category were those associated with coast defence, communication, and intelligence. Examples of these are the 113th, 121st, and 125th Coast Batteries, 9th HAA Regiment, 101st Wireless Regiment, and 8th through 13th Field Security Sections.[89]

Although the units that made up these categories existed throughout Australia, the army put into effect a chain of command that cut across geographical boundaries. Eastern Command became the key headquarters, with responsibilities far greater than those of the other commands. It was the superior headquarters for the 1st Division, which in turn contained the core of the Priority I field force units. Headquarters 1st Division exerted command over its designated subunits, irrespective of location, in all matters except for local administration, which remained the responsibility of the local command headquarters. Furthermore, Headquarters 1st Division exerted command over the units of the formation's logistic support force and combat support group, except where the army had specifically allocated them to another headquarters. Headquarters 1st Division thus commanded all the units that formed the field force, whatever their physical location.[90]

Eastern Command, however, set the policies that the 1st Division implemented, and, in effect, acted as a corps headquarters. It formulated the training policy for all units under the command of the 1st Division. It also set the training policy for field force units, including the combat support group and the logistical support force, which were not under the direct command of the 1st Division or had been loaned back to another headquarters. Headquarters Eastern Command was also responsible for the planning and preparation for the dispatch of an expeditionary force. By these measures, Eastern Command's responsibilities were far greater than any other command, and in effect it combined its command function with that of an operational field force headquarters.

The army's leaders viewed the steps taken to centralise the control of field force units under Headquarters 1st Division and Eastern Command as interim measures in the evolution of a functional system. The broad direction in which they hoped to develop the concept was that Army Headquarters would become a body whose sole purpose was policy-making. Below this level, the army would create two command headquarters, which would exercise command over the force's units. The army planned to create one to command the field force and the other to manage the force's logistical requirements. One of these commands, as yet undesignated, would also have been responsible for training. The plan also included a provision to downgrade the existing regional command headquarters to administrative districts. At this stage, however, the army went no further with its experiments with functional administration. Instead, the demise of the pentropic structure and the ensuing reorganisation postponed further considerations of command reform.[92]

If the ramifications of the pentropic organisation upon the CMF were not a cause of concern to the army's leadership, its effect upon some sections of the ARA's structure was worrisome. In order to fill out the field force within a reduced establishment, as well as raising the combat support and logistical support formations, the army had to reduce the number of personnel in the army's non-operational areas severely. Accordingly, the Australian Support Area suffered a 20 per cent across-the-board cut in establishment. The origins of the term Australian Support Area are not clear, but it was in use by the pentropic period. Essentially, the Australian Support Area included all units that were not a part of the field force, or were not logistical or combat support units whose purpose was to support the field force. Thus, it contained those units that fulfilled the army's administrative, training, technical services, and educational requirements. While perhaps mundane, its work was essential for the smooth and efficient performance of the army. After its reduction in 1960, it became apparent that the army had created an impossible situation for the Australian Support Area, which it could only rectify with more manpower. Within the 21,000 ceiling, however, this was impossible without taking resources back from the operational organisation. Instead, the army had to bring in additional civilian staff and increase its use of Women's Royal

Australian Army Corps personnel, but essentially the Australian Support Area had to survive as best as it could until the restoration of its strength later in this period.[93]

The other area of difficulty with the pentropic structure was that the Commonwealth's units were now incompatible with its other major ally, the United Kingdom. Since 1955, Australian units had been operating with British formations in the Far East Strategic Reserve. This commitment did not stop with the independence of Malaya, the ending of the Emergency, or the formation of Malaysia. As a result, whenever an RAR battalion rotated to Malaya, the army had to reorganise it from its larger pentropic establishment to the smaller tropical establishment. Furthermore, at the completion of its tour overseas, the army had to expand it back up to pentropic strength. Therefore, the army was in the position of periodically having to reorganise its battalions so that they could fulfil an operational requirement. To alleviate this problem, the army raised 4 RAR at Woodside, South Australia, in 1964. However, the decision to raise 4 RAR placed the Regular Army in the strange situation of having to maintain two different battalion establishments in a force of only four battalions. In addition, throughout the pentropic experiment, the army had retained the Pacific Islands Regiment on the tropical establishment.[94]

The end of pentropic

In 1962, the Defence Committee submitted to Athol Townley, the Minister for Defence, an assessment that identified a considerable worsening in the nation's strategic situation in the last few years. The committee opined that there was a 'clear requirement for a progressive expansion of the defence program that will increase the level of Australian military capability and preparedness …'.[95] In response, the cabinet requested a full report on the strategic situation, which the Defence Committee presented in February 1963. This document stressed not only the danger to the region posed by Soviet and Chinese communist aggression, but also the threat of Indonesian nationalism. The Defence Committee also pointed out that, since the planned Australian contribution to various SEATO contingencies was rather small, the Commonwealth was under growing pressure from the United States to increase its military resources. The strategic review concluded that, as a result of the more alarming threat environment, Australia needed to improve its military capability.[96]

Instead of immediately acting upon these reports, Townley requested a study detailing the army's deficiencies. More specifically, he requested recommendations on the aspects of the current three-year program that the government could accelerate, and sought an outline of long-term objectives for completion by 1972. The army replied in a document called *The Army Outlook to 1972*, and phrased its responses from the perspective of the pentropic structure. The paper noted that the army's condition in 1963 allowed it to provide no more than the battalion group in Malaya and one battle group, with supporting units, for deployment in Cold War operations. At present, the army had too many deficiencies in logistical support to allow for the provision of a task force of two battle groups. It concluded that by 1967 it would be possible to provide a third regular battle group on a reduced scale, restructure the Regular Army Reserve, build up the strength of existing CMF units, and increase the Pacific Islands Regiment to two battalions. In addition, the paper recommended the provision of equipment and war reserves for one complete division, with support units, and an increase in the scale of the army's aviation assets. The army thought that by 1972 it would be possible to provide enough additional regular units, particularly logistical, to ensure the effectiveness of the three ARA battle groups. Additional goals were to improve the CMF through the provision of some new equipment for the second citizen force division, add a third battalion and some support units to the Pacific Islands Regiment, and continue to purchase further stores of equipment, especially helicopters. The army believed it was essential to raise a third regular battle group in order to be able to supply a task force to SEATO, while maintaining a reserve for the defence of Australia, New Guinea, or Malaysia.[97]

Although the paper included recommendations for the CMF, its primary thrust was the advancement of the ARA. The report assumed that the government would have to raise the ARA establishment ceiling, and suggested that the level should be 28,000 by June 1967 and over 34,000 by 1972. The current strength of the Regular Army was less than 22,000, with a forecast membership of 24,500 by mid 1965. To reach these goals, the army suggested the reimplementation of national service, although conscripts would now serve in the ARA, not the CMF. *The Army Outlook* also considered the Australian Cadet Corps, and advanced the idea of an increase in its ceiling from the current level of 40,000 to 45,000 by 1972. However, the paper pointedly noted that this increase should not involve the allocation of any additional ARA personnel, and that the cadet corps remained the lowest priority among all the army's tasks.[98]

The Army Outlook also revealed that, despite the implementation of the pentropic organisation, the army's structure still fell short of meeting the force's strategic obligations. The army had converted its forces onto the pentropic basis in order to obtain greater combat effectiveness from within a smaller establishment, hence the reduction of the size of the ARA and the increase in the proportion of personnel allocated to field force units. *The Army Outlook* revealed that this had not eventuated. Instead, the ARA still required a considerable increase in its establishment if it were to field more than a single operational battle group in addition to the Malayan battalion group. In fact, the army and the government had already recognised this problem, and the 1962–63 three-year program had raised the pentropic personnel ceiling from 21,000 to 24,500. The proposals outlined in *The Army Outlook* required the allocation of an even greater share of the army's resources to the ARA.[99]

As a result of these assessments, Menzies decided to increase the budgets of the three services. The army's estimate rose from £67.8 million in the fiscal year 1962–63 to £79 million for the following year.[100] The increase allowed the army to expand the ARA to three battle groups, in addition to the battalion in the Far East Strategic Reserve, reconstitute the regular reserve, double the size of the Pacific Islands Regiment, and enlarge the CMF. The government also raised the establishment ceiling of the ARA from 21,000 to 28,000 by 1967, with the eventual target set at 33,000. In November 1964, Menzies announced the restoration of national service on a selective basis. Those chosen incurred a two-year full-time obligation in the ARA, followed by three years in the regular reserve, rather than service in the CMF, as in the past. In May 1965, the government amended the legislation in order to make those conscripted liable for overseas service. The government did provide those eligible for selection for national service the option to volunteer for the CMF for a six-year period of service. However, a candidate had to take up this option before national service selection occurred.[101] The design of this national service scheme was a turning point in the provision of manpower to the army. For the first time, the government had implemented conscription for the benefit of the permanent forces, and this ensured that everyone who served in the ARA was eligible for overseas service, thereby obviating the restrictive and unpredictable necessity of securing volunteers, as in the past. Thus, not only would the ARA become larger, but it would also achieve its allotted establishment and strategic requirements by the addition of as many national servicemen as required.

The period in which the government made these decisions was one of great turmoil in the South-East Asian region, and this underscored the inadequacy of Australia's military preparations to meet its potential obligations. The regional disturbances facing the government included Burma teetering on the edge of internal unrest, Laos in the midst of a civil war, the Viet Cong posing an increasing threat to South Vietnam, and the government of the Philippines contending with the Huk rebellion. Of more importance, and of greater concern to the Australian Government, was Indonesian assertiveness and its policy of confrontation over the incorporation of the British colonies in Borneo into a Malaysian state, as well as its conflict with the Netherlands over the fate of the western half of New Guinea. In a few years Vietnam became Menzies' principal concern, but during the first years of the 1960s Indonesian nationalism appeared the more immediate threat.[102]

In early 1962, considering the worsening situation in Vietnam, the cabinet had designated the battalion in Malaya as the Australian contribution to SEATO. Unfortunately, the government had already reserved this battalion for possible deployment to Laos, and both of these commitments were in addition to its existing Commonwealth responsibilities in the Far East Strategic Reserve. Thus, the government had tasked one battalion to three separate theatres. Moreover, had the army ever been required to provide a brigade group for SEATO, it would have had to allocate virtually every infantryman in the regular force, which would have left nothing further for Malaya, New Guinea, or even for the defence of Australia itself.[103]

Faced with this multitude of possible conflict points, the Australian Army had begun the 1960s barely able to maintain its contribution to the Far East Strategic Reserve. However, within a few years, as a result of this build-up and the reimplementation of national service, the nation would finally have an army that was capable of undertaking multiple commitments. In 1965, this gave the government the ability to dispatch troops to Borneo and Vietnam in support of its British and American allies.[104]

In January 1963, Lieutenant-General John Wilton became the new CGS, and it fell to him to implement the expansion authorised by the government. At the same time, Wilton had to face the question of what to do with the recently adopted pentropic organisation. The army had completed the reorganisation of its units and writing of new establishments, but the even harder task of implementing a pentropic-based operational doctrine remained. The army, therefore, had only completed its physical adjustments to the pentropic structure. The far more difficult process of training and ethos development still remained. Wilton had never favoured the experiment, and by 1963 it was clear that doubts about the organisation had become widespread. The problems with the pentropic system were numerous, but the most pressing were:

- its lack of compatibility with Australia's major allies
- a span of responsibilities that was too great for a battalion commander
- an overly large battalion, which made manoeuvre and control difficult
- a ponderous battalion headquarters that was designed to deal with a battle group rather than a battalion

- the absence of an intermediate headquarters (brigade), which placed an unacceptable administrative burden on battalion headquarters staff.[105]

Furthermore, the paper *The Army Outlook to 1972* had suggested that the pentropic structure had failed to provide the improved offensive capability, within a reduced establishment, that it had initially promised.[106]

While all these reasons pertained to the internal operations of pentropic formations, the organisation also proved difficult to reconcile with the requirements of Australia's strategic policy. The large size of the pentropic battalion denied the government the strategic flexibility that it could have achieved with a tropical establishment battalion, whose much smaller size allowed the raising of twice as many units. The rigidity of the pentropic organisation would also have proved a disadvantage if Australia had to intervene on its own with a force tailored for particular circumstances, such as in Papua New Guinea. In effect, the pentropic organisation simply provided the army with too few units with which to meet the full range of its potential responsibilities.[107]

Lieutenant-General Sir John Wilton, CGS 1963–66. (AWM DNE/65/0161/VN)

Using the opportunity to re-evaluate the army's order of battle in light of the planned expansion, Wilton suggested to the government the scrapping of the pentropic organisation in favour of a return to a more traditional tropical establishment. The government, he wrote, gave its swift approval, thus bringing the pentropic experiment to an end and launching the army upon another major reconfiguration of its units. However, the primary focus of this reorganisation, like the one conducted in 1960, was the ARA, not the CMF. Army planners concentrated their attention on the requirements for establishing and maintaining a field force centred on an ARA division. Thus, the 1964 reorganisation gave the ARA the opportunity to define the requirements of a divisional-size field force more specifically and set up command relationships that would support its management and deployment. Significantly, the body that would plan the reorganisation was given the title 'Committee to Review the Organisation of the Division and Combat Support Group' and its chairman was Brigadier K. Mackay, the Director of Military Operations and Plans. The place of the CMF was to conform to the needs of the ARA.[108]

In late 1964, Mackay presented his interim report to Wilton. The CGS had provided the committee with planning parameters which included the following:

a ... the need to plan for the Regular Field Force to operate in at least two areas, e.g., South East Asia and Papua/New Guinea and to provide for a reserve.
b In a limited war the initial contribution will be provided by the Regular Field Force which must be capable of rapid build up by the CMF ...
c In cold war the necessary flexibility to provide from the Field Force any particular grouping based on smaller battalions to meet likely situations.
d Manpower—maximum conservation and utilisation.
e ABCA standardisation.
f ... maximum flexibility within the divisional organisation, and an ability to group into three task forces which would be tailored as required ...
g As far as practicable the whole force must be air portable ... both for strategic and tactical movement.
h Units not essential to the functioning of the division, but required in part or in whole to support it should be included in the Combat Support Group.
i All scalings and holdings [must be] consistent with the 'light' concept in both equipment and mobility.[109]

The criteria advanced by Wilton were based upon those first put forth in 1957, but with some modifications. He again highlighted the army's regional commitments, the need for a readily available regular field force, and the importance of maximising the combat potential of the force. Wilton also observed that conflicts on the level of confrontation suggested the need for a greater capacity in counter-insurgency warfare. Therefore, the army required forces that not only could combine into a field force but which were also light, flexible, air mobile, and able to operate as small groups.

The committee proposals continued to define the army's structure from the perspective of the division, including necessary combat support and logistical support groups. For example, the divisional organisation that Mackay presented included:
- nine infantry battalions
- three close support artillery regiments
- one location battery
- three field squadrons
- one cavalry regiment of two cavalry squadrons and one anti-tank squadron
- one aviation regiment of three task force squadrons and a division headquarters squadron.[110]

The committee also identified the units that, while not integral to the division's organisation, were essential for its support. They included:
- one armoured regiment of two squadrons
- an armoured personnel carrier squadron capable of lifting one battalion
- one general support medium regiment of three batteries
- one general support field regiment of three batteries
- one light air defence regiment
- two construction squadrons
- one bridge troop
- one infantry battalion.[111]

The committee requested the tenth battalion in order to have an infantry force for the defence of the support area.

The army had considered reintroducing the term brigade in the new tropical establishment division, but decided to retain the task force designation. The Director of Military Training recommended the reforming of brigades and argued that, in current military usage, the term was taken to mean a flexible organisation of battalions or equivalent units controlled by a common headquarters. He also pointed out that the British and American armies employed the term *brigade*.[112] However, the army appears to have made its decision on the basis of public relations. A Military Board assessment noted that, by using the term *task force*, the army could 'avoid criticism on the grounds that [it] has not been able to make up its mind and that the change was a retrograde step'.[113]

On 20 December 1964, the Minister for the Army, Alexander J. Forbes, announced the abandonment of the pentropic system and the reorganisation of the army.[114] Under the new organisation, the Australian Army consisted of a field force of three divisions, with supporting army and communication zone troops and an Australian Support Area organisation, comprising regional and area commands, training centres, communication centres, depots and workshops, and CMF and cadet cadres.[115] The ARA component consisted of:

  a Divisional troops amounting to almost one division.
  b Part of the Army troops which might be expected to support one division.
  c Communication Zone units for the support of about one task force including certain units and sub units required to ensure that up to date operational techniques continue to be developed.
  d Australian Support Area units sufficient to support the field forces raised in peace and to provide an adequate basis for expansion in war.[116]

Army troops were those units that headquarters had previously called the combat support group, and whose name it changed in August 1965.[117] The ARA also included a task force of Pacific Island units. The CMF consisted of:

  a Divisional units amounting to approximately two divisions.
  b Army troops for the support of three divisions less those provided by the regular component.
  c Communication Zone units for support of three divisions less those provided by the regular component.
  d Elements for supplementing the Australian Support Area organisation in an emergency.[118]

On 23 December, Army Headquarters issued a priority list for the reorganisation of the ARA and the CMF. It was:

  a infantry battalions,
  b supporting arms within the division,
  c services within the division,
  d combat support group units [Army Troops], and
  e communication zone units.[119]

Regular battalions commenced the process in early 1965, while the CMF started in the middle of the year. The army reorganised the existing ARA battalions into eight tropical establishment battalions of 35 officers and 749 OR. The army also slightly restricted the battalion establishment by not raising the surveillance platoon until acquisition of equipment, and by allocating only nine infantrymen to a section, one less than required. Each battalion had only four companies, instead of five in a pentropic unit, as well as an administrative and support company. By this procedure, the ARA activated four new battalions numbered 5 RAR through 8 RAR. The raising of 9 RAR had to await the army's expansion during the Vietnam War.[120]

The CMF expanded from eight pentropic battalions to 15 tropical establishment battalions. Although the army retained the State regimental system, it did acknowledge CMF sensitivities and permitted the designation of the reformed battalions with traditional numbers. The disposition of the CMF infantry was now:

- Northern Command: 1 RQR, 2 RQR, 51 RQR, 41 RNSWR
- Eastern Command: 2 RNSWR, 3 RNSWR, 4 RNSWR, 17 RNSWR
- Southern Command: 1 RVR, 2 RVR, 5 RVR, 6 RVR
- Central Command: 1 RSAR
- Western Command: 1 RWAR
- Tasmania Command: 1 RTR.[121]

The reform also permitted the re-establishment of the 2nd Division based in New South Wales and Queensland, thereby providing the CMF with two divisions. In addition, Southern Command raised an Independent CMF Rifle Company at Mildura.

To help control its units, the army created a system of intermediary headquarters immediately below the level of the commands. Intermediary headquarters came in three types—ARA task force headquarters, CMF task force headquarters, and area headquarters. The responsibility of the ARA task force headquarters was to prepare the units under its command for dispatch overseas as part of a field force. It was thus responsible for the training of these units. However, the ARA task force headquarters did not provide for the local administration of units under its command. This was the duty of the area headquarters. A CMF task force headquarters performed a similar function for CMF field force units to that which the ARA task force headquarters performed for regular units. The army assigned citizen force units to a particular CMF task force headquarters in peace, on the basis of geographic convenience. However, should the army deploy a CMF task force headquarters overseas, it planned to select the component units on the basis of readiness and their suitability for the mission rather than despatching an existing organisation.

Area headquarters existed for the purpose of providing administrative assistance to the ARA and CMF task force headquarters. Australian Support Area units were also to come under the command of the local area headquarters. The aim of the area headquarters was to relieve the task force commanding officer of as many of his administrative duties as possible in order to enable him to concentrate on the preparation of his units for operations. Some of the duties of the area headquarters were provision of assistance to state authorities in a civil emergency, supervision of user trials, conduct of training courses and promotional examinations, area security, control and allocation of accommodations, and numerous other tasks that were essential to the maintenance of the army but inappropriate undertakings for the commander of field force units. If no area headquarters existed in the region to assist a task force headquarters, a headquarters command fulfilled area duties.[122]

In the major commands, the army created a network of area headquarters. For example, in Northern Command the army established Headquarters North Queensland Area, which provided administrative assistance to the field force units of 3rd Task Force Headquarters (ARA), and in Eastern Command, Liverpool Area relieved the Headquarters 1st Division of much of its local administration. Below the level of area headquarters, the army also set up subareas in order to perform local area tasks and provide additional administrative assistance to nearby ARA units. For example, within the North Queensland Area, the army established a subarea in Townsville. Some area headquarters could have fairly narrow responsibilities; in Southern Command, Headquarters Puckapunyal Area's sole task was to provide administrative relief to the 1st Armoured Regiment and associated units of the armour establishment.[123]

The creation of Headquarters 6th Task Force in December 1966 illustrates the task force concept. This ARA task force commanded all the elements that made up a field force, including its support units. Thus Headquarters 6th Task Force controlled not only infantry battalions but also all the myriad support units it required on deployment. The units under its command were:
- B Squadron 1st Cavalry Regiment
- 4th Field Regiment
- 7th Field Squadron
- 22nd Engineer Support Troop
- 104th Signal Squadron
- 2 RAR
- 8 RAR
- 3rd Transport Platoon
- 6th Ordnance Field Park
- 6th Task Force Headquarters Light Aid Detachment

- Squadron Section 1st Cavalry Regiment Light Aid Detachment
- 4th Field Regiment Light Aid Detachment
- 7th Field Squadron Workshop.[124]

In 1965, the army formed three headquarters task forces for the ARA (1st, 3rd, and 6th) and five for the CMF (2nd, 4th, 5th, 7th, and 9th), and area headquarters and subareas as needed. Chart 10 (p. 276) outlines the restructured army after the implementation of the post-pentropic reorganisation.[125]

It was also possible for the army to vest the functions of a task force headquarters and an area headquarters in the same office. For example, in Northern Command in 1970, the intermediary headquarters consisted of Headquarters 3 Task Force/North Queensland Area, Headquarters 6 Task Force/South Queensland Area, and Headquarters Central Queensland Area. The first two headquarters were dual task force and area headquarters, and their commanding officer was considered a formation commander, whereas the headquarters for Central Queensland was only an area headquarters. Consequently, the General Officer Commanding Northern Command exercised command over units in the Central Queensland Area. However, whenever the army established dual headquarters, it was with the understanding that the command and administrative functions remained separate. In the examples provided above, in the early 1970s the army eventually separated both dual headquarters.[126]

Since the 1957 reorganisation, the plight of the CMF had steadily worsened, as the government valued, in the army's hierarchy, the regular soldier more highly than the citizen soldier. In 1966, J.M. (Malcolm) Fraser, then Minister for the Army, reiterated the policy that the CMF existed to provide a back-up in a defence emergency to the ARA and national servicemen, and that the citizen force's primary mission was to serve as a basis for expansion in case of a major war.[127] Despite this trend, after the end of pentropic era, the army did make some effort to improve the CMF. In 1965, the army investigated the possibility of raising CMF battalions in remote country areas where the force no longer had a presence. The primary motivation was that, because of the withdrawal of the CMF from rural Australia, young men of military age residing in these areas were unable to opt to join the citizen forces in lieu of conscription into the ARA. The reestablishment of a CMF presence in these areas would provide country residents with the same opportunities enjoyed by those who lived in urban centres. In addition, the creation of units with terms of service suitable for remote areas would allow the CMF to regain contact with the Australian bush and allow its inhabitants to participate in the nation's citizen soldier tradition.[128]

THE AUSTRALIAN ARMY

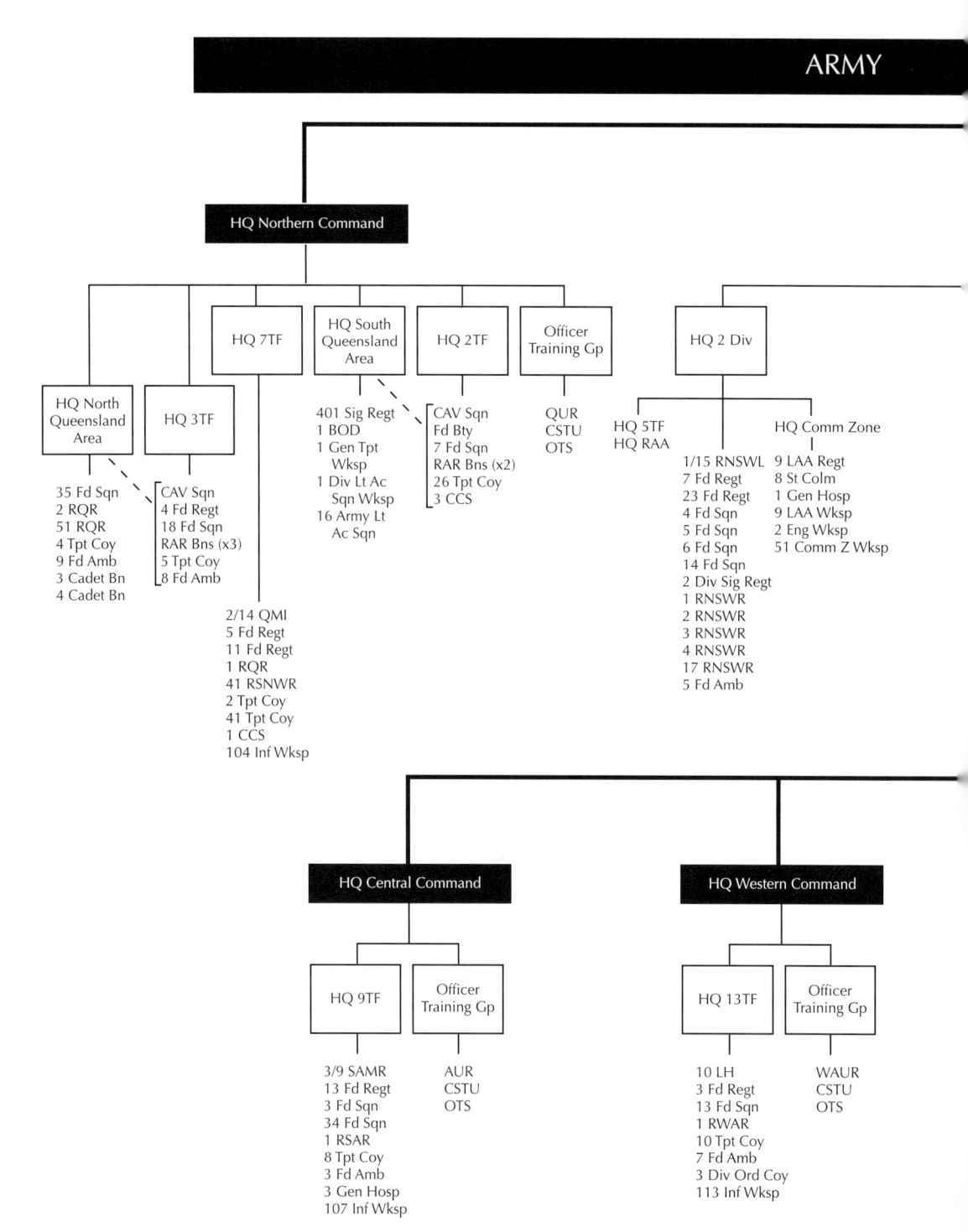

ARMY

- **HQ Northern Command**
  - **HQ 7TF**
    - **HQ North Queensland Area**
      - 35 Fd Sqn
      - 2 RQR
      - 51 RQR
      - 4 Tpt Coy
      - 9 Fd Amb
      - 3 Cadet Bn
      - 4 Cadet Bn
    - **HQ 3TF**
      - CAV Sqn
      - 4 Fd Regt
      - 18 Fd Sqn
      - RAR Bns (x3)
      - 5 Tpt Coy
      - 8 Fd Amb
    - 2/14 QMI
    - 5 Fd Regt
    - 11 Fd Regt
    - 1 RQR
    - 41 RSNWR
    - 2 Tpt Coy
    - 41 Tpt Coy
    - 1 CCS
    - 104 Inf Wksp
  - **HQ South Queensland Area**
    - 401 Sig Regt
    - 1 BOD
    - 1 Gen Tpt Wksp
    - 1 Div Lt Ac Sqn Wksp
    - 16 Army Lt Ac Sqn
  - **HQ 2TF**
    - CAV Sqn
    - Fd Bty
    - 7 Fd Sqn
    - RAR Bns (x2)
    - 26 Tpt Coy
    - 3 CCS
  - **Officer Training Gp**
    - QUR
    - CSTU
    - OTS
  - **HQ 2 Div**
    - HQ 5TF
    - HQ RAA
    - **HQ Comm Zone**
      - 1/15 RNSWL
      - 7 Fd Regt
      - 23 Fd Regt
      - 4 Fd Sqn
      - 5 Fd Sqn
      - 6 Fd Sqn
      - 14 Fd Sqn
      - 2 Div Sig Regt
      - 1 RNSWR
      - 2 RNSWR
      - 3 RNSWR
      - 4 RNSWR
      - 17 RNSWR
      - 5 Fd Amb
      - 9 LAA Regt
      - 8 St Colm
      - 1 Gen Hosp
      - 9 LAA Wksp
      - 2 Eng Wksp
      - 51 Comm Z Wksp

- **HQ Central Command**
  - **HQ 9TF**
    - 3/9 SAMR
    - 13 Fd Regt
    - 3 Fd Sqn
    - 34 Fd Sqn
    - 1 RSAR
    - 8 Tpt Coy
    - 3 Fd Amb
    - 3 Gen Hosp
    - 107 Inf Wksp
  - **Officer Training Gp**
    - AUR
    - CSTU
    - OTS

- **HQ Western Command**
  - **HQ 13TF**
    - 10 LH
    - 3 Fd Regt
    - 13 Fd Sqn
    - 1 RWAR
    - 10 Tpt Coy
    - 7 Fd Amb
    - 3 Div Ord Coy
    - 113 Inf Wksp
  - **Officer Training Gp**
    - WAUR
    - CSTU
    - OTS

Chart 10 Army post-pentropic organisation, 1965.
(Source: 'Allocation of Major Units to Formations', AA (ACT), A6922/1, item 1/29)

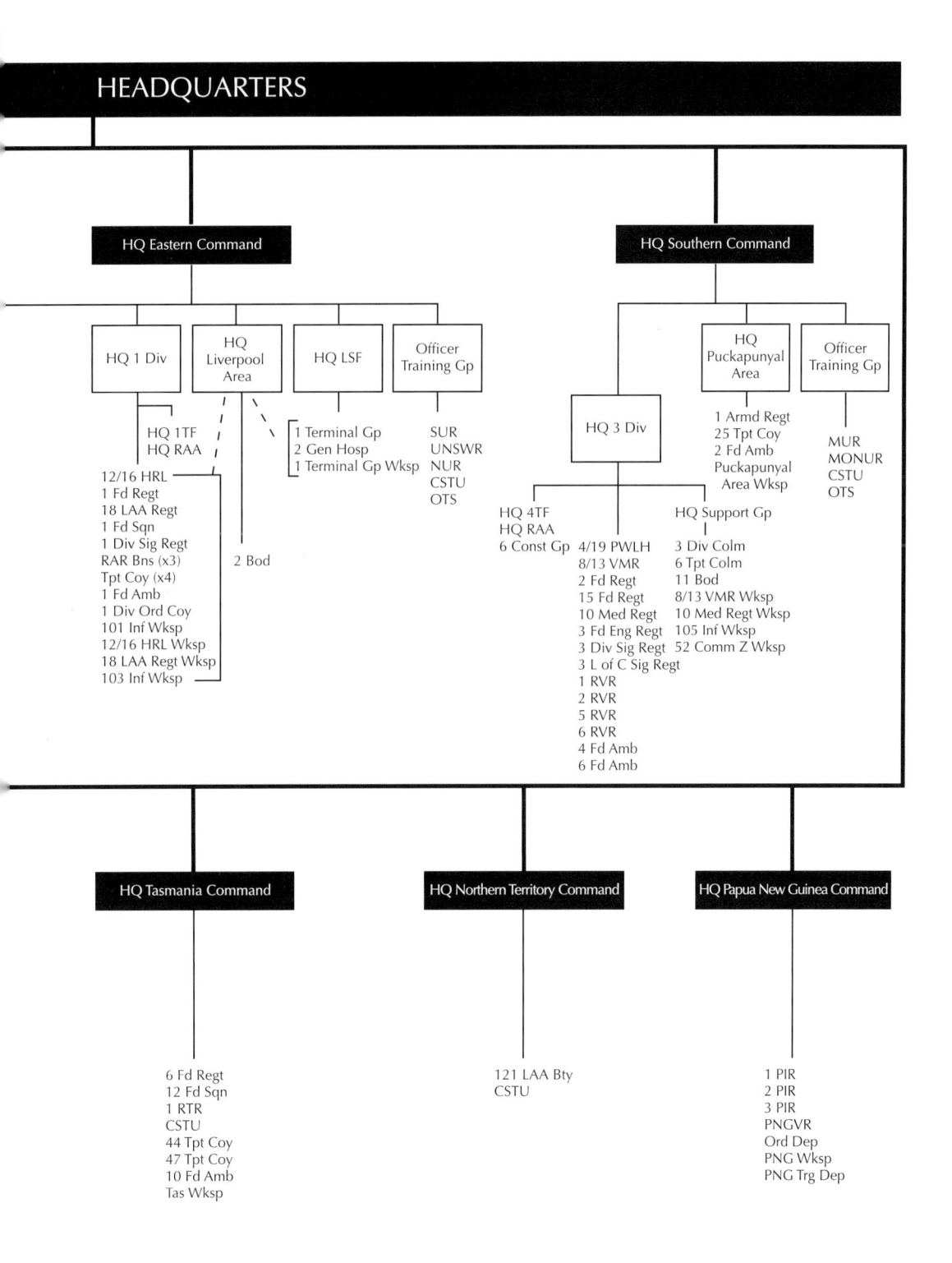

HEADQUARTERS

HQ Eastern Command

- **HQ 1 Div**
  - HQ 1TF
  - HQ RAA
  - 12/16 HRL
  - 1 Fd Regt
  - 18 LAA Regt
  - 1 Fd Sqn
  - 1 Div Sig Regt
  - RAR Bns (x3)
  - Tpt Coy (x4)
  - 1 Fd Amb
  - 1 Div Ord Coy
  - 101 Inf Wksp
  - 12/16 HRL Wksp
  - 18 LAA Regt Wksp
  - 103 Inf Wksp
- **HQ Liverpool Area**
  - 2 Bod
- **HQ LSF**
  - 1 Terminal Gp
  - 2 Gen Hosp
  - 1 Terminal Gp Wksp
- **Officer Training Gp**
  - SUR
  - UNSWR
  - NUR
  - CSTU
  - OTS

HQ Southern Command

- **HQ 3 Div**
  - HQ 4TF
  - HQ RAA
  - 6 Const Gp
  - 4/19 PWLH
  - 8/13 VMR
  - 2 Fd Regt
  - 15 Fd Regt
  - 10 Med Regt
  - 3 Fd Eng Regt
  - 3 Div Sig Regt
  - 3 L of C Sig Regt
  - 1 RVR
  - 2 RVR
  - 5 RVR
  - 6 RVR
  - 4 Fd Amb
  - 6 Fd Amb
  - HQ Support Gp
  - 3 Div Colm
  - 6 Tpt Colm
  - 11 Bod
  - 8/13 VMR Wksp
  - 10 Med Regt Wksp
  - 105 Inf Wksp
  - 52 Comm Z Wksp
- **HQ Puckapunyal Area**
  - 1 Armd Regt
  - 25 Tpt Coy
  - 2 Fd Amb
  - Puckapunyal Area Wksp
- **Officer Training Gp**
  - MUR
  - MONUR
  - CSTU
  - OTS

HQ Tasmania Command

- 6 Fd Regt
- 12 Fd Sqn
- 1 RTR
- CSTU
- 44 Tpt Coy
- 47 Tpt Coy
- 10 Fd Amb
- Tas Wksp

HQ Northern Territory Command

- 121 LAA Bty
- CSTU

HQ Papua New Guinea Command

- 1 PIR
- 2 PIR
- 3 PIR
- PNGVR
- Ord Dep
- PNG Wksp
- PNG Trg Dep

Although the report's conclusions were not overly enthusiastic, they resulted in the raising of special CMF units, which became known as 'special condition battalions' or the 'Bushmen's Rifles'. In 1966, the army authorised the formation of one special condition battalion in each command. Their designations were:

- Northern Command: 49 RQR
- Eastern Command: 19 RNSWR
- Southern Command: 22 RVR
- Central Command: 43 RSAR
- Western Command: 28 RWAR
- Tasmanian Command: 50 RTR.

The units drew their personnel from throughout the State, and did not have any particular local affiliation. The army did not require the members of these units to attend night parades or weekend bivouacs. Instead, the service condition provided concentrated training in either in a single 33-day camp or two camps of 16 and 17 days. This training cycle removed the need for a recruit to live near a CMF centre, and thereby made citizen force membership again possible for those who lived in the country's more remote areas. Tasmanian Command never raised its battalion, although it did enlist approximately 60 special-condition soldiers. Instead of serving with 50 RTR, the Tasmanians were allocated by the army to 22 RVR.[129]

The 1964 reorganisation also provided the army with the opportunity to review its reserve system. Although at this time the army had several reserve bodies, none of them provided the ARA with an immediate source of personnel to bring its units up to strength, and they could not serve as first reinforcements. The ARA reserves consisted of the Regular Army Reserve and the retired list, neither of which had a training obligation. The enrolment of the Regular Army Reserve in 1964 was nearly 4,000. Yet before the army could call upon these former regular soldiers, the men would have to undergo a medical examination and refresher training. Thus, the army did not consider them an immediate source of reinforcements. The CMF had maintained its own list of inactive officers since 1948—the Reserve CMF—but, like the ARA reserves, it did not have a training obligation. The Reserve CMF was most suited as a source of officers in case of general mobilisation. In 1970, this body had over 2,700 members. Construction engineering units made up the CMF Supplementary Reserve. This meant that these troops were best suited for service in the communication zone rather than with an ARA task force. While government policy now defined the purpose of the entire CMF as the support of the ARA, it was not a reserve organisation, but consisted of formed units that had a designated place in the army's order of battle.

Neither regular nor citizen soldier leaders planned to break up CMF units to provide drafts for the ARA.[130]

To address this manpower deficiency, Wilton sought the government's permission to raise a new back-up force, which the army would maintain at a higher level of readiness than its other reserve bodies. In 1964, his initiative led to the formation of the Regular Army Emergency Reserve. The Defence Act allowed the government to call out the Regular Army Emergency Reserve in time of operational necessity, either by proclamation of the Governor-General or by notice in the *Gazette*, a much lower threshold than a declaration of war or defence emergency. The Regular Army Emergency Reserve consisted of former male soldiers of the ARA or Regular Army Supplementary Reserve. The regulations excluded former CMF soldiers from the new reserve body, because the army did not believe that citizen soldiers could have obtained the high degree of training required for an immediate reserve. The obligations on members of the Regular Army Emergency Reserve included an annual medical examination, 14 days' full-time training per year, and a liability for overseas service. The army set the reserve's recruitment goal at 3,600, the number of troops it needed to complete the deployment of two battle groups.[131]

When Townley announced the formation of the Regular Army Emergency Reserve, he stated that it provided for the expansion of the army in time of emergency. In particular, he identified its role as being to bring units of the field force up to full strength and provide first reinforcements. For example, it was the army's policy to maintain infantry sections with nine rather than the ten soldiers called for on the establishment. Regular Army Emergency Reserve personnel could provide the tenth man. In addition, before sending a field force overseas, the army had to replace personnel who were unfit for deployment because of age, medical condition, or immediacy of discharge.

However, as a result of the Vietnam expansion, the Regular Army Emergency Reserve did not develop in the anticipated manner. By 1970, its primary role was to supply a reserve of non-commissioned officers, warrant officers, and select tradesmen for support units rather than the infantry. Throughout this period, the army placed its priority upon the maintenance of the combat units, and it was the rear area units which had the greater need for an immediate intake of personnel in case of mobilisation.[132]

The end of pentropic also led to some modifications to the CMF's officer staff group (command and staff training unit) concept. The CMF now had an organisation called the Officer Training Group attached to each command headquarters. This body administered CMF officers who were surplus to regimental establishment, and oversaw CMF officer training. It contained the command and staff training unit as well as an officer cadet training unit. It also commanded the university regiments in their respective commands. In 1969, the army redesignated the officer training groups as the command training groups.[133]

In 1968, the army again considered its reserve forces, when it addressed the future of the CMF supplementary reserve scheme. The army concluded that these units, with the exception of the railway and some port repair units, still served an important function. The army went so far as to suggest the raising of additional types, including works sections and airfield specialists, although ultimately this expansion did not occur. The army also decided not to merge the supplementary reserve into the CMF proper because it did not want to alienate the unit sponsors, especially since they bore nearly all the scheme's expense. However, in 1969 the army did disband the supplementary reserve's railway units. When they were originally raised, the army had envisaged their function as part of a Middle East expeditionary force. The shift in security focus to South-East Asia left them with little scope for employment, although the potential for their use within Australia appears to have been overlooked.[134]

Vietnam considerations

The dual commitment of field force units to Borneo and Vietnam in 1965 had little effect upon the organisation of the army other than its expansion along existing lines. Despite the redesignation of the SAS Company as a regiment in August 1964, and the raising of 9 RAR in November 1967, the army remained essentially on the same model established by the 1964 reorganisation. By 1966, the strength of the ARA had reached 41,000, and by 1970 it totalled about 44,500. The CMF also grew larger, and, partially as a result of the attractiveness of the alternative service option to national service, in 1968 it reached nearly 36,000 personnel, although this was still far below the levels of the 1950s. While it had little effect on the army's organisation, the Vietnam War represented a major allocation of the force's resources. During the conflict, more than 50,000 Australians served in Vietnam, and the army's contribution peaked at approximately 8,300 soldiers in 1968. Table 7.19 outlines the establishment of the Australian Task Force, as it existed in 1970.[135]

Supporting the Australian Task Force was the Australian Logistic Support Group. It contained additional construction, transport, medical, and repair units, including 17th Construction Squadron, 30th Terminal Squadron, 11th Movement Control Group, 26th Transport Squadron, 1st Australian Field Hospital, and 17th Construction Squadron Workshop.

Table 7.19 Australian Task Force order of battle, 1970: main units[136]

Type	Units
Armour	A Sqn 1st Armoured Regt
	B Sqn 3rd Cavalry Regt
Artillery	4th Fd Regt
	131st Div. Loc. Bty (det.)
Engineers	1st Fd Sqn
	21st Engineer Sp. Tp
Survey	1st Topo. Svy Tp (–)
Signals	104th Sig. Sqn
Infantry	2 RAR
	7 RAR
	1st SAS Sqn
Aviation	161st Indep. Recce. Flt
Supply	5th Tpt Coy
	8th Petroleum Pl.
	176th Air Dispatch Coy
Medical	8th Fd Amb.
	33rd Dental Unit
Electrical and mechanical	102nd Fd Wksp Stores Sec.
	106th Fd Wksp Stores Sec.
	131st Div. Loc. Bty Wksp
	1st Fd Sqn Wksp
	102nd Fd Wksp
	106th Fd Wksp
	5th Tpt Coy Wksp
	1st TF HQ LAD
	A Sqn 1st Armd Regt LAD
	B Sqn 3rd Cav. Regt LAD
	4th Fd Regt LAD

If the organisation of the army changed little during this period, the relationship between the force's two branches also remained largely constant, and there was little opportunity for the CMF to arrest its decline. Fraser, the Minister for the Army, did not believe that the CMF had a place on active operations, such as the Vietnam War, which he accepted was the purpose of the ARA.[137] Major-General P.A. Cullen, the CMF member of the Military Board, attempted to find a role for the CMF in Vietnam, but the rest of the Military Board rebuffed his suggestion for the deployment of a composite citizen soldier battalion.[138] The Australian Army's contribution to the Vietnam conflict was provided by the regulars and national servicemen, and no CMF unit served in South-East Asia. The only means for CMF personnel to gain combat experience was to either enlist in the ARA or participate in a training scheme that permitted a small number of officers to spend their annual camp in Vietnam attached to a regular unit.

The national service scheme's option of joining the CMF for six years instead of serving two in the Regular Army also did little to raise the status of the citizen forces. In fact, it had the opposite effect. The feature created the impression that the CMF was a haven for draft dodgers. The legislation even contained a loophole that allowed someone to select for the CMF, then, if his birth date was not chosen, to effectively terminate his military responsibilities by failing to attend parades and camps. Eventually, his CMF unit issued a discharge and the individual incurred no further obligation for service.[139]

The army's leaders realised that when the Vietnam War did end the army would inevitably undergo a contraction that might even include the suspension of the national service program. In 1969, the army undertook a study to evaluate the force's manpower requirements post Vietnam. Presented in August 1969 and entitled *Review of the Size and Shape of the Army Post Vietnam*, the report forecast an establishment of approximately 28,000.[140] The report's primary purpose was to determine how large a field force a regular army of such a size could support. It concluded that with such an establishment the army would have a fixed manpower requirement in the Australian Support Area of 16,965, leaving just 11,035 for the field force. These figures did cause some concern, because they represented a higher proportion of Australian Support Area personnel to field force personnel, as a percentage of total establishment, than had existed in 1964. In that year, the field force had represented over 47 per cent of the army, whereas the report anticipated that in a future army it would be difficult to maintain a field force at greater than 30 per cent of the army's establishment. Even more worrying was, the report noted, Australian Support Area units had operated with inadequate staff for years, and were only able to function through a system of lending back personnel whose primary assignment was with the field force.

Major-General S.C. Graham, the DCGS, also prepared a paper. It argued for the retention of national service and the expansion, rather than contraction, of the army's establishment. He believed that the army was currently under strength, since it could only support overseas a task force in Vietnam and the battalion group in Malaysia. Graham thought it was essential for the ARA to expand from its current level of 44,000 to the range of between 55,000 and 60,000. He did not explain the rationale

Table 7.20 Comparison of 1964 army manpower allocation with estimated post-Vietnam requirements[142]

Classification	Manpower allocation 1964	Estimated requirements 1969
Australian support area	8,076	11,750
Overseas staffs	137	154
ARA cadres with CMF	837	1,276
Cadet staffs	266	324
Papua New Guinea	193	641
Manpower not related to establishment (trainees, etc.)	2,349	2,820
Available for field force	10,750	11,035
Total	*22,608*	*28,000*

behind the selection of this figure, but this was the minimum strength necessary to deploy and maintain an ARA field force of a division. Since the ARA had only 28,000 volunteers in its ranks in 1970, the rest being national servicemen, he did not think that the army could reach the desired size without the use of conscription. Therefore, Graham not only wanted to retain national service but also sought to broaden its reach in order to bring into the ARA a larger number of conscripts.[141]

Table 7.20 compares the manpower allocation of the 1964 army with that of a post-Vietnam army with an estimated strength of 28,000.

The report justified the need for a larger Australian Support Area component because of the additional maintenance requirements resulting from the acquisition of new installations, a higher level of capital expenditures on items such as armoured personnel carriers, artillery, and radios, and the expansion of army aviation. The growing independence of the Australian Army from the British and American armies also brought with it a greater requirement for internally written doctrine and an increased commitment to army schools. The report, therefore, highlighted a correlation between that of a maturing professional army and the need for a greater allocation of troop strength to rear area activities. The post-war army that emerged after the withdrawal from Vietnam mirrored, to a fair degree, the judgments presented in this report.

The reforms of the early 1970s

The early 1970s were tumultuous years for the army, as it underwent a series of reforms at both the organisational and command levels. As anticipated, the withdrawal from Vietnam in 1972 brought about a reduction in the strength of the

ARA, a situation compounded by the abolition of national service by the incoming Labor government of E.G. Whitlam. As its numbers contracted, the army also began to act upon the recommendations of two major inquiries—the Army Review Committee's investigation into the force's command arrangements and the Millar Committee's review of the CMF. Also during this period, the army began to address the implications of the Tange reforms, although they are properly the subject of the next chapter.

The Australian contribution to the Vietnam War peaked in 1968 as a task force of three infantry battalions with an overall strength of more than 8,000. In 1970, a gradual withdrawal began, and the army did not replace 8 RAR when it came home. The remaining two battalions returned to Australia in 1971, leaving only a few support units, which left early the following year. Within a few days of his election on 5 December 1972, Whitlam ordered home the last service personnel, the 128 members of the Australian Army Training Team Vietnam, bringing Australia's participation in the conflict to a quick conclusion. Also in early December, Whitlam suspended national service and ended conscription into the army. Furthermore, he announced that currently serving national servicemen and CMF optees could seek their discharge.[143]

The immediate task facing the army's leaders was to prevent a disintegration of the force while preserving its operational capability. The CGS, Lieutenant-General F.G. Hassett, believed that the minimum strength to which the government should allow the army to fall was 34,000, and that its planning establishment should be 36,000. In a letter to Lance Barnard, the Minister for Defence, he insisted that any shortfall in personnel should be considered only a temporary measure.[144] Hassett also strongly believed in the retention of the regular division. He informed Barnard that the division was the 'lowest level at which experience in higher command can be gained and almost all of the military skills, techniques and disciplines inherent in modern warfare are represented'. The CGS also noted that the division was the minimal level at which the army could be seen as providing a credible deterrent, and that its structure remained essential for the development of doctrine and the conduct of operations.[145]

The initial design of the post-Vietnam army came out of a report entitled *The Future Shape of the ARA*, issued just after the government's suspension of national service. The report did not address the CMF, confining its comments to the ARA. It anticipated that the field force units would feel the greatest effect of the loss of the conscripts. It did, however, suggest the retention of all nine battalions, but on reduced or even cadre establishments. The objective was to retain the organisation of the ARA field force, with the flexibility that nine battalions provided, in order to permit its rapid expansion in case of threat. Clearly, the army viewed the post-war establishments as a temporary measure pending the re-expansion of the units to something nearing their full strength. Nine battalions also served to justify the retention of the traditional divisional structure. *The Future Shape of the ARA* proposed the following establishments for the infantry battalions:

- manning level of 600: 1 RAR, 2 RAR, 4 RAR
- manning level of 500: 6 RAR
- manning level of 375: 8 RAR
- manning level of 200: 3 RAR, 5 RAR, 7 RAR, 9 RAR.

The report noted that the army would continue to support the majority of the other ARA units, but suggested their merger or maintenance on a cadre level as required. Last, the report anticipated a greater role for the Women's Royal Australian Army Corps in the Australian Support Area in order to make up for the shortfall in male personnel.[146]

The army did not adopt the proposals as outlined in *The Future Shape of the ARA*, however. As the report concluded, its design was meant to create an all-volunteer ARA on an expansion basis. This, of course, was the CMF's function. Thus, under this formula, the Commonwealth would have two military bodies whose primary role in peacetime was expansion to operational size when required. Even if the army maintained the redesigned ARA at a higher level of readiness than the CMF, it would not fulfil the requirement of an immediately available force that the nation's strategic obligations required.

Instead, the army had to adopt a different program, which not only maintained the divisional hierarchy but also kept the field force at a size more suitable for operational deployment. The army accepted that its ultimate establishment was 36,000, of which the Australian Support Area would require 21,500. This left a field force of 14,500. The army linked six of its ARA battalions and reorganised the division onto a six-battalion basis in three task forces. The linked battalions were 2/4 RAR, 5/7 RAR, and 8/9 RAR. In June 1973, the field force had a strength of slightly more than 9,700 personnel. The army assumed that its strength would grow by approximately a thousand per year, and that it would reach its operational establishment in 1976.[147] Table 7.21 outlines the field force's allocation of personnel in June 1973 and the objective for 1976. The six-battalion division would remain the basis for the organisation of the ARA into the 1990s.

Table 7.21 Allocation of field force strength in June 1973 compared with 1976 goal[148]

Formation	Strength June 1973 (officers/other ranks)	Goal 1976 (officers/other ranks)
3rd Task Force	172/1,748	221/2,627
6th Task Force	154/2,029	229/2,699
1st Task Force	155/1,959	228/2,752
Division troops	154/1,048	182/1,880
Force troops	221/2,084	270/2,906

At the same time that the army dealt with the post-Vietnam contraction, it also implemented the findings of the Hassett Report. In March 1970, the Minister for the Army, Andrew Peacock, announced the appointment of then Major-General F.G. Hassett as chairman of the Army Review Committee. This body was responsible for an investigation into the army's existing system for its higher direction. Its report, *The Command and Organizational Structure of the Army in Australia*, included far-reaching recommendations that aimed to create a command structure that could serve both in peace and war, and allow Army Headquarters to distance itself from its existing command role in order to concentrate on policy-making.[149]

The main problem with the geographical command system was that it did not lend itself to a state of war. Hassett noted that the current arrangement fragmented the field force among seven commanders in various States and Territories. He observed sarcastically that it was unlikely that Australia would have to defend itself on a State basis. In addition, in case of mobilisation the army did not presently have the means to ensure the inculcation of a uniform doctrine because training, within its own boundaries, was the responsibility of each individual command. Hassett also pointed out that the army required a centralised logistical system for its maintenance. When overseas, in the past, the army enjoyed the luxury of being able to rely on a major ally for support. In 1970, it was no longer clear that this would be a viable option in the future, and Australia might have to maintain its forces on its own. A senior headquarters dedicated to logistics would provide the army with a pool of officers who had obtained the practical experience and doctrinal understanding necessary for the support of the force. The army also remained the only one of the three services that had not switched to a functional basis, and such a reform would, therefore, ease interservice communication.

Under the geographic command system, the army did not contain a single headquarters, below the level of Army Headquarters, that controlled any one complete function. Under the current system, field force units, training procedures, and logistical maintenance were under the responsibility of the seven regional commands. Blamey had temporarily overcome this situation during World War II by the raising of army and lines of communication headquarters, but during the post-war reorganisation the army reverted to its traditional regional pattern. This occurred because the geographic system, despite its limitations during war, had proven an extremely useful mechanism for command and administration during peacetime, especially when the CMF was the force's dominant branch. The army had always organised, recruited, trained, administered, and maintained its CMF elements on a geographic basis. The cadet corps also benefited from the geographical approach. However, as a result of the growing importance of the ARA, the geographic command system lost one of its prime advantages. A functional command system, therefore, was a reform that offered greater benefit to the ARA than to the CMF.

The committee's second area of concern was the need to improve the ability of Army Headquarters to focus on matters of policy. This was a serious problem, because in 1970 Army Headquarters held direct command over approximately 140 units representing about 14,000 personnel. As a result, its staff spent most of their time addressing issues of detail rather than those of executive coordination. Moreover, Hassett pointed out that, in case of mobilisation, Army Headquarters would have to manage the massive expansion of the army while also coordinating the army's role in the war effort with the other services and government departments. The committee believed that directing policy was the primary duty of the army's most senior officers, and, consequently, it was essential to limit the duties of Army Headquarters in order to allow its members to focus upon that task.

Ten years earlier, the Military Board had considered the functional command concept but, after considerable review, had declined its implementation in order to concentrate on the pentropic reorganisation. However, the army did attempt to establish a transitional functional command system by placing most field force units under the control of Headquarters 1st Division. Only for administrative purposes did such units remain under the dictates of their regional command headquarters. This arrangement proved awkward, as it was not possible to restrict sufficiently the responsibilities of commands for units in their region. In a further attempt to streamline the control of logistical support units, the army had established special headquarters for their command. For example, 3rd Division raised a headquarters support group and the 2nd Division controlled a headquarters communications zone. While these steps did provide for a degree of rationalisation according to function, they were, at best, half-way measures that imposed two potentially conflicting command systems within a single institution.[150]

The present structure for the army's higher direction included under Army Headquarters the seven command headquarters whose jurisdictions roughly correlated with the State and Territory boundaries. They were Northern (Queensland), Eastern (New South Wales), Southern (Victoria), Western (Western Australia), Central (South Australia), Tasmania, and Northern Territory. Hassett proposed their replacement with three commands, whose responsibilities the army defined not by geography but by function. They were Field Force Command (subsequently Land Command) and Training Command, both located in Sydney, and Logistic Command (subsequently Support Command), centred in Melbourne. The army allocated all of its units, including the CMF, to one of these commands.

Field Force Command contained all field force units in Australia except for certain communication zone logistic units on loan to Logistic Command. It had the equivalent of three divisions—one ARA (1st Division) and two CMF (2nd and 3rd Divisions)—and its headquarters had the responsibilities of a corps. On mobilisation, depending upon its extent, Field Force Command might evolve into a field army headquarters that would create secondary headquarters as needed. Hassett identified the primary responsibilities of the Field Force Command as:

a in peace, command of all ARA and CMF Field Force formations and independent units within Australia except certain ARA communications zone units;

b the responsibility for operational readiness of all formations and units in the field force … ;

c in war, command of the land forces of Australia … for the defence of Australia and its Territories;

d development of detailed Army contingency plans for the defence of Australia and its Territories and for the dispatch of an Army expeditionary force to an overseas theatre;

e provision of a field force structure which is capable of the expansion necessary on mobilisation;

f in peace, command of New South Wales District.[151]

The 1st Division, largely composed of ARA units, remained the most important formation in the field force. It would, however, move its headquarters from its current location in the former Eastern Command to Queensland.

Logistic Command 'comprise[d] all functional Australian Support Area units concerned with the principal tasks of transport, supply and maintenance engineering, the fixed signal network, the procurement and trials organization and in peace some ARA communications zone logistical units'.[152] Logistic Command also controlled, on a loan-back basis, certain communication zone logistic units that belonged to Field Force Command. The duties of Logistic Command included:

a   command of all ARA non divisional logistic units in Australia, except Royal Australian Engineers, Royal Australian Army Medical Corps and Royal Australian Army Dental Corps;

b   operational readiness of units under its command ... ;

c   control of materiel, movement and maintenance engineering requirements of the Army ... ;

d   control of reserve stocks and development of plans for an expansion to meet the needs of mobilization;

e   provision of a structure which is capable of the expansion necessary on mobilization;

f   command of all units concerned with the design, research and development of material required by the Army;

g   command of fixed signal units; and

h   in peace, command of Victoria District.[153]

Simultaneously with the raising of Logistic Command, Hassett also recommended a reorganisation of the army's logistic corps. The army divided its logistic services among three corps: the Royal Australian Army Ordnance Corps, the Royal Australian Army Service Corps, and the Royal Australian Electrical and Mechanical Engineers. The Royal Australian Engineers also had some support functions, principally the provision of water transportation and movement control. Hassett recommended that the army reconfigure the establishments and duties of the support corps along functional lines, namely transport, supply, and repair. The primary effect of this decision was the disbandment of the Royal Australian Army Service Corps. Hassett allocated its supply responsibilities to the Royal Australian Army Ordnance Corps and its transport duties to the newly raised Royal Australian Corps of Transport. The army decided to create the Royal Australian Corps of Transport in order to concentrate control over all transportation tasks in a single organisation. In addition to receiving ground and amphibian transportation, aerial delivery, and postal tasks from the Royal Australian Army Service Corps, the Royal Australian Corps of Transport also absorbed the water transportation and movement control capabilities of the Royal Australian Engineers. The Royal Australian Electrical and Mechanical Engineers remained largely unaffected by these developments.[154]

Training Command had responsibility for all schools and training units, including those belonging to the cadet corps. Hassett defined the responsibilities of Training Command as:

   a   command of all Army Schools and training centres;
   b   command of the Australian Cadet Corps;
   c   development of training policy and doctrine ... ;
   d   provision of a structure which is capable of the expansion necessary for mobilization;
   e   civil education of members of the ARA, and CMF where appropriate;
   f   conduct of ... promotion and educational examination system; and
   g   production of major AHQ exercises ... [155]

The main exception to Training Command's oversight was the Royal Military College. It continued to report directly to the CGS.[156]

Based upon the order of battle as it existed in 1970, Hassett determined that Field Force Command would contain 23,668 ARA and 30,899 CMF personnel, Logistic Command would have 12,459 ARA and 7,968 CMF personnel, and Training Command's establishment would consist of over 12,500 ARA and CMF personnel. In addition, Training Command's responsibilities included the provision of support to over 41,000 cadets. The figures for Field Force Command and Logistic Command included troops then serving in Vietnam and Malaysia.

The replacement of the seven regional commands, however, did not eliminate all local responsibilities that these headquarters had formerly performed. There remained numerous minor matters which, Hassett believed, were best served at the local level. These included coordination with local and State governments, recruiting, disaster assistance, and the provision of common housekeeping functions. Despite the adoption of the functional system, therefore, the army still needed to maintain some administrative presence in each State and Territory. To fulfil this function, Hassett proposed the reestablishment of headquarters military districts in all the States and the Northern Territory. They would not have the same range of duties that their namesakes had enjoyed. Instead, they were relatively small entities with minor command functions and responsibilities limited to regional matters. Typical units assigned to a military district included bands, amenities units, signal troops, recruiting units, district support units, and military hospitals. It was possible to colocate a headquarters military district within that of the local field force intermediate level headquarters (task force, for example), but if this were done, the functions of the two headquarters were to remain completely separate.[157]

The reorganisation of the army's command relationship onto a functional basis also permitted adjustments to the structure of army headquarters. Army Headquarters had had a traditional organisation, with responsibilities divided among four branches: operations, personnel, supply, and materiel. The main problem with the existing structure was that staff had too many command responsibilities and were unable to concentrate on policy issues. Therefore, the reorganisation provided army headquarters with the opportunity to delegate a large amount of executive detail permanently to the command headquarters. In addition, Hassett believed that there was an overlapping of responsibility between the four existing branches of Army Headquarters, especially concerning equipment and logistical matters. His proposal for the reform of Army Headquarters, therefore, was sweeping.

Hassett outlined the rationalisation of responsibilities between the branches of Army Headquarters as a three-stage process. The first stage saw the elevation of the office of the CGS as an executive office above the other branches of the headquarters. The CGS received a subordinate, the VCGS, who would oversee the reform as well as the day-to-day management of the army. The CGS's planning role was taken over by the Operations Branch. These changes freed the CGS to focus on his task as commander of the army and principal adviser to the Minister for Defence. At this time the army retitled the other branches of headquarters. The office of the Adjutant-General became Personnel Branch, the office of the Quartermaster becoming Logistics Branch, and the office of the Master General of the Ordnance becoming Materiel Branch. The titles authorised for the heads of these offices became Chief of Operations, Chief of Personnel, Chief of Logistics, and Chief of Materiel.

Hassett's second stage in the reform process was when the reorganised Army Headquarters supervised the raising of the functional commands. The final stage saw the reallocation of responsibilities between the branches of Army Headquarters and the functional commands. For example, the Logistics Branch split off a number of its directorates—those dealing with supply, transport, and maintenance engineering—to Logistic Command. The Operations Branch reduced its interest in training and the Directorate of Cadets and Directorate of Army Education relocated to Training Command. The directorates concerned with the combat corps moved from Operations Branch to Field Force Command. At this point, Hassett also recommended the consolidation of the four Army Headquarters branches to three, with the abolition of the Materiel Branch and the transfer of most of its functions to a Deputy Chief of Staff (Logistics Branch). However, this final step did not take place, and the army continued to maintain four branches in its headquarters. In addition, the office of the CMF member remained attached to Army Headquarters.[158]

Hassett also suggested the replacement of the Military Board by a four-member committee—the Minister, Secretary, CGS, and VCGS—but except for the addition of the VCGS to its members, the Military Board decided instead to maintain the existing structure. Despite joining the Military Board, the office of the VCGS once again enjoyed a temporary existence. After the completion of the implementation of the Hassett reforms its necessity passed, and the army was unable to sustain the appointment. The army again abolished the position, and the DCGS reverted to the second officer within the CGS Executive.[159]

Hassett believed that the implementation of these recommendations would create an army headquarters with greater ability to focus on policy development rather than command of units. For example, Hassett identified the possible duties of the reconfigured Operations Branch as 'the development of concepts in tactical doctrine, the formulation of equipment objectives, the determination of overall organizations for the field force and for policy aspects of military training'. In addition, the new Operations Branch would oversee the standardisation aspects of the ABCA Agreement and manage the Directorate of Combat Development.[160]

The Military Board approved Hassett's recommendations, and in 1971 their implementation commenced. To create the new command headquarters, the army drew upon its existing structure. Headquarters Eastern Command became Headquarters Field Force Command; Headquarters Southern Command became Headquarters Logistic Command; Headquarters 1st Division became Headquarters Training Command; and Headquarters Northern Command became Headquarters 1st Division. In June 1973, the Military Board reported that reorganisation of Army Headquarters was nearing completion. The functional command system was operational, and it had assigned the army's units to their appropriate command. In addition, the Military Board noted that it had approved the establishments for the military districts. The army anticipated the completion of the functional reorganisation by November 1973.[161] Chart 11 outlines the reformed Army Headquarters.

The next major reform that the army embarked upon was a product of T.B. Millar's examination into the CMF. Millar took up this task in April 1973 at the request of Lance Barnard, the Minister for Defence. The *Report of the Committee of Inquiry into the Citizen Military Forces* (the Millar Report) was the most sweeping appraisal of citizen forces that the Australian Government had ever conducted. It was also the last. As a result of the committee's findings the army abolished the CMF, at least in the form in which it had existed since the nation's founding. In its place, the army created a new reserve organisation that was a component of the ARA and whose sole purpose was to support the regulars.

Army higher direction, Hassett reforms, 1973

Military Board
- CGS
- Executive Office VCGS

Army Headquarters
- Operations Branch
- Personnel Branch
- Materiel Branch
- Reserve Branch
- Office of the Citizen Military Forces Member/Inspector General of the Army Reserve
- Logistics Branch

Functional Commands
- Field Force Command
- Logistic Command
- Training Command

Military Districts
- 1st Military District
- 2nd Military District
- 3rd Military District
- 4th Military District
- 5th Military District
- 6th Military District
- 7th Military District

– – – – Military Board Representation

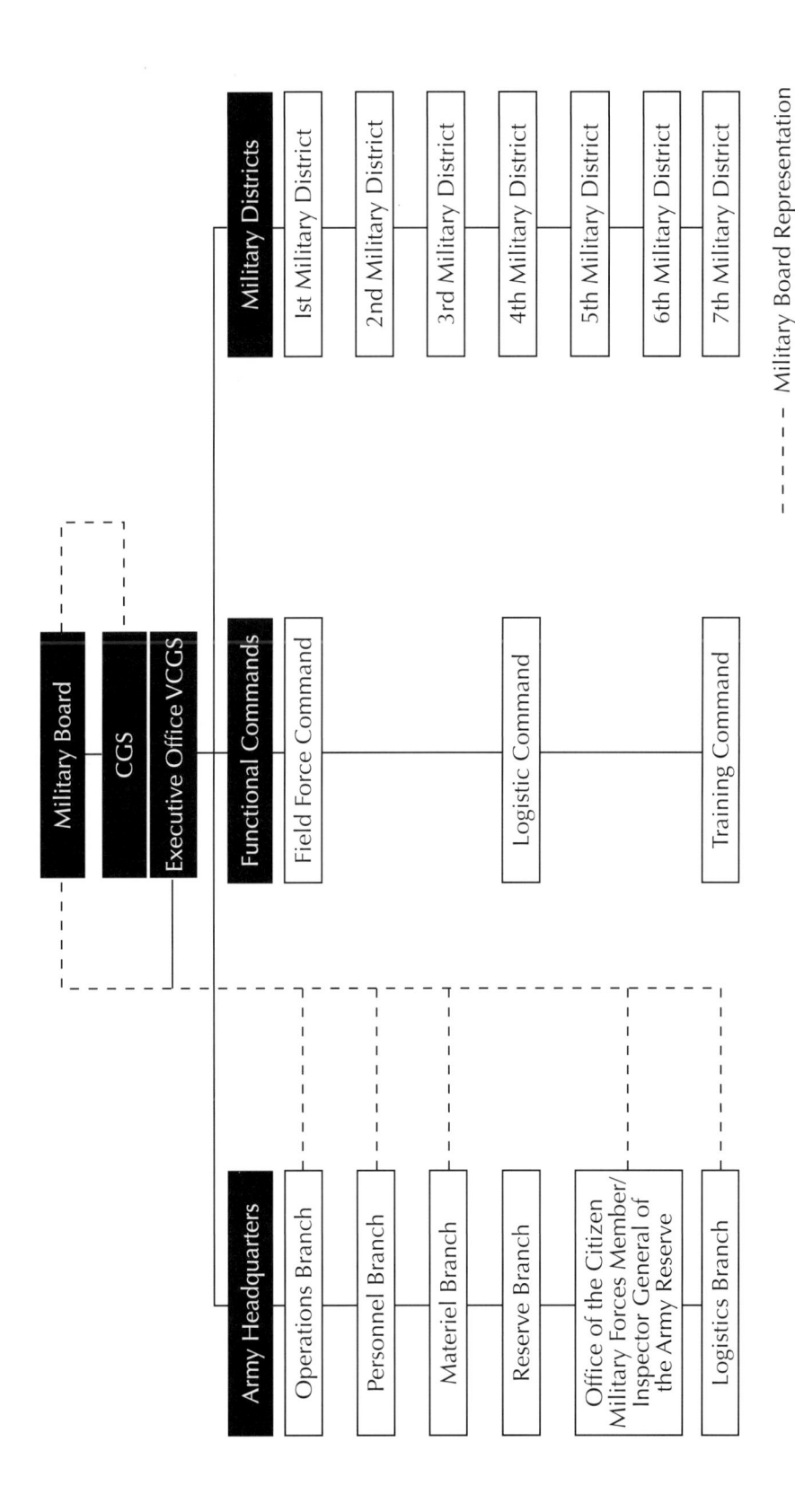

Chart 11 Army higher direction, Hassett reforms, 1973.
(Source: AA (ACT), A6839/1, item 76/54)

By 1970 it had become clear that the CMF was in deep trouble. It suffered from a number of problems, including poor morale, difficulties with recruitment and retention of its members, unacceptably low levels of unit establishment and readiness, and a force structure that was top heavy with officers and non-commissioned officers. For the last few years, the strength of the CMF had spiralled downward from a post-pentropic peak of nearly 36,000, which it had reached in 1967. By March 1970, the authorised establishment for the CMF remained set at 60,000, but its actual strength was less than 32,000. In fact, few CMF units enjoyed posted strengths that were greater than 50 per cent of establishment. Table 7.22 summarises the CMF manpower situation by category.

Table 7.22 CMF strength, March 1970[162]

Category	Authorised establishment	Posted establishment	Posted establishment as percentage of authorised establishment
Headquarters	1,284	541	42.1%
Training groups	1,288	968	75.2%
Armour	4,123	2,107	51.1%
Artillery	5,974	2,889	48.4%
Engineers	7,417	3,214	43.3%
Survey	55	0	–
Signals	3,457	999	28.9%
Infantry	22,278	14,497	65.1%
Intelligence	332	192	57.8%
Supply	5,897	2,693	45.7%
Medical and dental	2,294	1,128	49.2%
Ordnance	1,483	423	28.5%
Electrical and mechanical	1,894	877	46.3%
Pay	170	154	90.6%
Provost	409	221	54.0%
Psychology	263	179	54.0%
Bands	93	60	64.5%
Nursing	506	156	30.8%
WRAAC	564	325	57.7%
MC Training Gp	220	169	76.8%
Total	*60,001*	*31,802*	*53.0%*

Making the CMF's situation even worse was the inclusion within its ranks of large numbers of national service optees, many of whom might immediately resign if conscription ended. In fact, this is precisely what happened. After Whitlam's suspension of national service in late 1972, the CMF's establishment declined rapidly. By early 1974 it was under 20,000, although in addition to the loss of the optees there was also a steep decline in enlistments. More significantly, Major-General A.V. Murchison, the CMF member of the Military Board, pointed out that most of the losses had occurred in the ranks of private through sergeant, which further increased the oversupply of officers. As McCarthy has observed, in 1965 the CMF could have provided a battalion for Vietnam; by the early 1970s this was no longer possible.[163]

The CMF's senior officers were aware of the strain under which the institution operated, and did make a number of suggestions that they hoped would rectify the situation. In late 1971, Cullen, a former CMF member of the Military Board, proposed that the army establish a CMF Ready Reaction Force. Cullen defined the purpose of this force as being to 'improve the CMF's capability of contributing quickly in response to any situation of defence emergency'. His scheme called for the army to provide units designated for the ready reaction force with greater access to training facilities and equipment than was normal for CMF units. Peacock, then serving as Minister for the Army, encouraged the concept despite the belief of Lieutenant-General M. Brogan, the CGS, that it had little strategic or operational merit. Brogan maintained that the ARA was better placed than the CMF to fulfil this type of mission. In 1973, he wrote to Barnard, the Minister for Defence, suggesting the scrapping of the idea, especially in light of the investigations now underway by the Millar Committee.[164]

Previously, in 1970, Cullen had advanced another scheme for the improvement of the CMF. In response to a request from Hassett for ideas on how to stem the fall in the CMF's numbers, Cullen submitted a paper to the Army Review Committee. Hassett had warned that without a change in the downward personnel trend it might be necessary to reduce the CMF to one division or replace it with an officer and non-commissioned officer training organisation.[165] Cullen's proposal was ambitious, as it outlined a program to improve the size, efficiency, and morale of the CMF, and had as its objective nothing less than to restore the citizen soldiers to their place as the nation's primary military force. To achieve this he suggested the extension of the existing national service scheme to include the CMF. In the previous national service scheme, which had ended in 1960, conscripts served with CMF units, whereas under the current system the citizen forces only received optees who were determined to avoid a commitment in the Regular Army. Under

Cullen's proposal, conscripts would either serve two years full time in the ARA or five years part time in the CMF. National servicemen in the CMF would incur a greater training obligation, and would serve under conditions similar to the 'Bushmen's Rifles', which Cullen considered among the best-trained citizen soldier infantry battalions. In addition, he recommended that the army provide in each command a CMF camp centre where citizen force units could train. The army would also outfit these centres to the same standard enjoyed by ARA training establishments. Cullen expected that under this scheme it would be possible to expand the CMF to five divisions, and that by 1975 it would have a strength of approximately 200,000. The acceptance of Cullen's proposal would have required a complete reordering of the army. In effect, Cullen was trying to return the army to the period in which the ARA served to support the CMF. It was no surprise that the government failed to act upon his submission.[166]

Major-General N.A. Vickery, another CMF member of the Military Board, provided his own submission to the Army Review Committee. His submission was not nearly as ambitious as Cullen's, but it, too, was based on the belief that an opportunity still existed to reinvigorate the CMF. Vickery believed that it was necessary to make CMF enlistment more attractive to the nation's young men. While he did not propose changes in the structure of the institution, Vickery saw great scope for significant and cumulative improvements in service conditions. These included more realistic and adventurous training activities, greater access to state-of-the-art equipment, improved uniforms and modernised depots, a pension scheme to encourage long service, and an increase in the number of CMF personnel allowed to attend army schools. He also recommended a public relations campaign to dispel the suggestion that the CMF was filled with draft dodgers.[167]

As the Millar inquiry got underway, Murchison began his own investigation into the CMF and sought the opinion of his senior officers. Their responses were highly positive, and they did not doubt their ability to fix the CMF. Most of his respondents framed their comments from the perspective of improvements in existing service conditions. They addressed the need to enhance service pay, improve the attractiveness of training depots, broaden the availability of army schools, instructors, and modern equipment, and increase the provision of ARA cadre staff. One officer made the point that casual kitchen labourers hired to serve meals at a camp received pay more than double the salary of the soldiers. Others welcomed, although cautiously, the idea that Women's Royal Australian Army Corps personnel could serve in citizen force field force units, a provision the CMF implemented in early 1974. Once again, therefore, the army accepted female personnel as a means to fill gaps in its male ranks.[168]

One officer, Major-General J.M. McNeill, General Officer Commanding 3rd Division, went further and made detailed suggestions aimed more at reanimating the role of the CMF than merely improving its service conditions. He recognised that the nation required the regular soldiers, but he believed the balance had shifted too far in favour of the ARA. To rectify this, McNeill wanted the army to maintain some CMF units at a high enough level of readiness to enable them to reinforce an expeditionary force quickly. He also believed it was necessary for the army to create a separate CMF command, at the same level as the army's functional commands, which was directly responsible to Army Headquarters. The CMF Command would support a decentralised structure, where the emphasis would be on the maintenance of local units wherever a community expressed interest in the citizen soldiery. Such an arrangement would also permit the CMF to maintain its geographically orientated organisation, reinforce the citizen soldier's connection to the community, and permit the maximum participation possible by the nation's young men and women. Lastly, McNeill saw the CMF, not the ARA, as the proper basis of expansion in case of mobilisation for a major war. In addition to these papers, Murchison prepared his own submissions to the Millar Committee, as did a number of other senior CMF officers.[169]

The CMF's fate rested ultimately in the hands of the Millar Committee, however. In 1970 it was a large, diverse, if understrength, institution, divided into two categories. The Active CMF was the force's principal body. Its purpose was to back up the regulars in a defence emergency, and to provide a framework for expansion in case of mobilisation. It was itself subdivided into four subcategories based on training obligations. These were normal units, special condition battalions (Bushmen's Rifles), supplementary reserve units, and units of a specialist nature, including the university regiments, commando units, and command training groups. In 1970, the Active CMF contained over 350 units, many with detached subunits. The CMF's other branch was less significant. The Reserve CMF was little more than a list of inactive officers who had no service obligation. In its analysis, the Millar Inquiry investigated both CMF bodies as well as the ARA's reserve bodies, namely the Regular Army Reserve, Regular Army Emergency Reserve, and the retired list.[170]

The terms of reference of the Millar Inquiry gave the committee wide latitude in its judgments. Barnard instructed Millar to 'report on the role of the Citizen Military Forces as part of the Australian Army in the strategic circumstances of the 1970s and 1980s'.[171] More specifically, the committee was to determine the type of support that the CMF could provide to the ARA and the effectiveness of the citizen forces as presently constituted. The Millar Inquiry was also to review the steps the army could take to improve the CMF, enhance its role, and make it more attractive to recruits. The Millar Inquiry began with great hope that it might provide the vision by which the CMF could reanimate itself. Instead, it proved the final step in the assertion of the ARA's dominance. By the time the army had completed the Millar reform, the CMF was gone. In its place, the army raised a new reserve organisation, which existed solely and undisputedly to assist the ARA.

The key recommendations put forth by the Millar Inquiry focused on the purpose of a reserve system. Instead of a force in its own right, the CMF was to become part of the ARA's reserve structure. The goal, Millar believed, was to create a single army or, to use his term, a 'total force'. Thus, while remaining cognisant of the different service conditions of part-time and full-time soldiers, the institution was to promote, within a single force structure, better coordination, training, planning, and mutual activities between its components than had been possible in the past. In case of mobilisation, expansion would no longer occur along CMF lines but instead would follow the structure and requirements of the regular force. Even the name of the CMF would change, and it would be replaced by the title 'Army Reserve'. This left little doubt of the nature of the relationship between the ARA and the units that had formerly belonged to the citizen forces.[172]

Millar also recommended the amalgamation of the CMF with the existing ARA reserve bodies, namely the Regular Army Reserve and the Regular Army Emergency Reserve, thereby creating a single and simplified reserve structure. In effect, reserve units would no longer be representative of a region or a community but would have to fit into the army's field force, logistical support, or training establishments. Therefore, Army Headquarters assigned each former CMF unit to one of the army's functional commands. Although Millar did recommend the creation of a Reserve Branch, under the command of a Major-General Chief of Reserves, and the establishment of a position called Inspector-General Army Reserve, there would be no headquarters CMF command. He also advised the creation of a reserve command and staff college, but this was one of the few recommendations upon which the army failed to act.

The tone of the recommendations that the Millar Inquiry presented made it clear that the members of the committee no longer regarded the CMF as an independent force upon which the defence of the nation rested. The committee saw little to distinguish the CMF from the ARA's reserve bodies. Certainly, the ethos of the citizen soldier had little influence in their deliberations, and it is clear from the recommendations the committee put forth that it viewed the regulars as the rightful inheritors of the Australian military tradition. The Millar Inquiry made a number of suggestions to improve the lot of the reserve (CMF) soldier, including equalisation of pay between regulars and reserves, standardisation of uniforms between the two branches, and the introduction of a housing loan scheme for reservists. Yet none of these proposals were from the perspective of maintaining the CMF as a viable institution within the nation's defence structure.

Of particular sensitivity to CMF officers was the maintenance of the name Citizen Military Force to denote the army branch to which they belonged. Millar recommended a change to either the 'Australian Army Reserve' or, more simply, the 'Army Reserve'. One senior CMF officer reported that he and his staff considered it ill advised to change the name of the CMF because of the public recognition it already enjoyed. Another suggestion was that the army adopt the term 'Australian National Defence Force' in order that the new term should reflect the traditions of the CMF. However, in the end the army took up Millar's suggestion of 'Army Reserve', to which Barnard gave his assent.[173]

The recommendation that had the most dramatic effect on the CMF's order of battle was Millar's suggestion that Army Headquarters reorganise reserve units 'in such a way as to bring them and their sub-units to a minimum 70 per cent of establishment'.[174] This requirement, as well as the allocation of units to the functional commands, caused the greatest structural upheaval ever experienced by the CMF, and led to a painful, massive contraction of the organisation's order of battle. The situation was not helped by the army's continued difficulty in attracting recruits. The CGS wrote to the Minister in April 1975 and pointed out that although the army, to date, had enlisted 5,000 reservists in the period 1974–75, the situation of the reserve forces remained grave, with many units well under strength. The problem was that discharges from the reserves remained high, and the intake had little effect on the overall establishment. In fact, for the near future, the combined Active CMF and Regular Army Emergency Reserve strength remained at only about 21,000.[175]

Throughout 1975 the army addressed the reserve's reorganisation. At the higher level it resulted in the disbandment of Headquarters 3rd Division and its replacement with Headquarters 3rd Divisional Field Force Group (a proper divisional headquarters would be reraised in 1984).[176] However, the real trauma occurred at the unit level. Since so many citizen units were severely under strength when Millar began his inquiry, the use of a 70 per cent threshold of establishment as the definition of effectiveness proved fatal for much of the former CMF. By 30 June 1975, the army had either disbanded or amalgamated 17 major and 224 minor units that had failed to meet the cut-off.[177] Table 7.23 outlines the fate of a number of major CMF units.

Table 7.23 Amalgamation and disbandment of CMF units, 1974: major units[178]

State	Unit strength	Establishment strength	Posted	Fate
Queensland	5th Fd Regt	475	115	linked to form 5th/11th Fd Regt
	11th Fd Regt	475	123	linked to form 5th/11th Fd Regt
New South Wales	9th LAA Regt	484	8	disbanded
	18th LAA Regt	484	22	disbanded
Victoria	2nd Fd Regt	475	85	amalgamated as 2nd/15th Fd Regt
	15th Fd Regt	475	121	amalgamated as 2nd/15th Fd Regt
	1st RVR	792	158	amalgamated as 1st RVR
	5th RVR	792	161	amalgamated as 1st RVR
	6th RVR	792	91	amalgamated as 1st RVR
	2nd RVR	792	183	amalgamated as 2nd RVR
	22nd RVR	792	90	amalgamated as 2nd RVR
	1st Independent Rifle Coy RVR	259	49	amalgamated as 2nd RVR
South Australia	3rd/9th SAMR	513	175	reduced to cavalry squadron, A Sqn 3rd/9th SAMR
	13th Fd Regt	475	71	reduced to fd bty, 48th Fd Bty
Western Australia	3rd Fd Regt	475	60	reduced to fd bty, 7th Fd Bty
Tasmania	12th RTR	792	192	reduced to 12th Independent Rifle Coy RTR
	40th RTR	792	165	reduced to 40th Independent Rifle Coy RTR

The extremely low posted strengths for these units suggests that the CGS (Hassett) was correct to conclude that many CMF units would be unable to reach Millar's 70 per cent threshold any time in the near future. Furthermore, if the army were to have an efficient reserve, there was little choice but to take the steps outlined in table 7.23. However, the fate of these units also suggests how quickly the CMF had lost personnel in the early 1970s. Even the unit with the worst establishment listed above, 9th LAA Regiment, with a posted strength of just eight, had 155 officers and men in 1970. Other units showed a similar dramatic decline. In 1970, the 2nd Field Regiment had 204 officers and men, 2nd RVR had 345 officers and men, and 22nd RVR had 451 officers and men. At the beginning of the decade, the 1st Independent Rifle Company, RVR, had an establishment of 201 officers and men, which would have met the mandatory 70 per cent of establishment cut-off, but by 1974 it could only muster 49 personnel (19 per cent of establishment) and, as a result, it was amalgamated.[179]

Some units that the army thought could meet the 70 per cent cut-off through recruitment were given a chance to attract more members. However, if they failed to meet the threshold quickly, their disbandment or amalgamation was certain. For example, the army gave the three CMF infantry battalions in South Australia (10th RSAR, 27th RSAR, and 43rd RSAR) a chance to improve their strength, but they remained too feeble to serve individually as efficient units. Hassett then recommended their amalgamation into a single battalion—10th RSAR. Similarly, Army Headquarters gave the 6th Field Regiment in Tasmania a chance to improve its numbers, but it too failed, and the army reorganised it as 16th Field Battery.[180] Sometimes a unit did manage to save itself. Lieutenant-General Donald Dunstan, the CGS in 1977, had slated 25th RQR for disbandment. However, he reversed his decision, and authorised the unit's retention on the order of battle when an influx of recruits brought its establishment up to the required level.[181]

If Millar's 70 per cent target was not already a difficult enough barrier, the army also changed its policy towards CMF establishments, which made the task of survival virtually impossible for much of the citizen soldier order of battle. Traditionally, CMF units had a lower establishment than comparable ARA units. Now, however, the army insisted that reserve and regular units had to have the same establishments. This change, in effect, raised the threshold for survival. For example, in 1970 the fixed establishment of the various battalions of the RVR varied from a low of 538 officers and men (2nd RVR) to a high of 661 officers and men (6th RVR). In the aftermath of the Millar Inquiry, the army set the establishment for all CMF infantry battalions at the same level as the regulars—792 officers and men. This also occurred in the other corps. For example, in 1970 a CMF field regiment had an establishment of 362, whereas after the Millar Inquiry the army increased its staffing goal to 475. To remain on the order of battle, therefore, CMF units now had to meet a higher standard than that which the army had considered acceptable before the commencement of the reorganisation.[182]

Army Headquarters moved quickly to implement Millar's recommendations. By the end of June 1975 Hassett reported the completion of the first phase, including the reorganisation of most of the former CMF. He also noted that the allocation of the remaining units to the appropriate commands was well under way, with the transfer of the training groups to Training Command being the last step. The CGS also informed Millar that of his committee's twenty-nine recommendations, the army had already put nineteen into effect or were in the midst of their implementation, and that it would resolve a further four shortly. The remaining six, Hassett noted, were outside the army's direct control, and required the government's assistance. In slightly more than a year, the army had removed the last traces of the citizen soldier tradition from the army and thereby completed the trend that had begun after the Korean War and which was to assure the dominant position of the regulars in the nation's defence.[183]

In addition to these major reforms, the achieving of independence by Papua New Guinea in 1975 also had an effect on the organisation of the army, although the ramifications were relatively minor. In 1972, the army established a joint force headquarters to provide the basis for the future assumption of control over the defence force by the Papua New Guinea Government. By the following year, the army had identified the units it would transfer to the Papua New Guinea Defence Force and those that would stay a part of the Australian Army but remain overseas. Only a handful of support units stayed under Australian control, while the bulk of the army's forces in the former territory transferred to the control of the new government. Some longstanding Australian units did not survive the transition, for example, the Papua and New Guinea Volunteer Rifles. Upon independence in 1975, the two battalions of the Pacific Islands Regiment, as well as the units making up the region's administrative and support infrastructure, ceased to be part of the Australian Army's order of battle. Table 7.24 lists the units that became part of the Papua New Guinea Defence Force, and Table 7.25 contains those that remained part of the Australian Army but continued to serve in the former colony's territory.[184]

Table 7.24 Units transferred to the Papua New Guinea Defence Force upon independence of PNG[185]

HQ PNGDF	HQ Murray Bks Area	HQ Taurama Bks Area
HQ Lae Area	HQ Wewak Area	PNG Recruiting Team
PNG Construction Sqn	PNG Sig. Sqn	1st Pacific Islands Regiment
2nd Pacific Islands Regiment	PNG Int. Sect.	PNG Tpt Pl.
PNG Mov. Unit	PNG Trn. Sqn	Taurama Med. Centre
PNG Dental Unit	PNG Engr. Stores Tp	PNG Sup. Pl.
PNG Ord. Dep.	PNG Wksp	PNG Pro. Unit
PNG Mil. Cadet School	PNG Trg. Dep.	
PNG Med. and Dent. Equip. Dep.		

Table 7.25 Australian army units remaining in Papua New Guinea upon independence of PNG[186]

Aust Def. Asst Gp, PNG	Dist. Engr. Office	8th Fd Svy Sqn
183rd Recce. Sqn	PNG Det. 1st ACU	183rd Recce. Sqn Wksp
19th Psych. Unit		

Artillery, aviation, and transport developments

Advances in military technology and changes in strategic requirements resulted in a number of modifications in the army's capabilities, and affected its relationship with the other services. The principal areas where this occurred were coastal defence, air defence, aviation, and maritime transportation. Each of these cases required the RAN, army, and RAAF to reconsider the demarcation of responsibility for the provision of these tasks.

Coastal defence was one of the army's original responsibilities. Since Federation, the army had garrisoned fortresses around Australia in order to deter the landing of hostile troops or bombardment by surface vessels. The heyday of the coastal defence duty was during World War II, when batteries defended every port or strategic place around the coast. Since that point, the coastal defence system had declined, and in 1962 there were just three coast artillery units, the 113th, 114th, and 125th Batteries guarding Newcastle, Sydney, and Fremantle respectively. Part of the reason for this contraction was the normal reduction in forces that followed the victory over Japan.

However, the success of carrier- and land-based aviation during World War II, the development of jet-powered planes, and advances in rocketry meant that an attacker no longer had to approach the coast in order to attack Australia. As technology changed, Australia's gun-based coastal defences became increasingly obsolete. In addition, the government's emphasis on forward defence meant that the army's primary role was to defend Australia in the islands to the north, not off Sydney Harbour. In 1962, the Chiefs of Staff Committee decided that there was no longer a requirement for fixed coastal artillery, and ordered the disbandment of the army's three remaining batteries. In the future, coastal defence would be the responsibility of the RAN and the RAAF, whose ability to project power out into the air–sea gap would deter enemy warships or planes from coming within striking range of the Australian coast.[187]

Advances in missile and aviation technology also mandated changes in the organisation of the nation's anti-aircraft defence. At the end of World War II, the army controlled both fixed and mobile forces capable of firing upon low- and high-level aircraft. Post-war improvements in aircraft, especially the development of high-speed jets, meant that anti-aircraft guns no longer had the capability of effectively attacking these planes. To solve this problem, the Americans and British investigated the use of missiles and deployed a number of systems. In 1957, the Menzies Government announced that it would acquire the surface-to-air Bloodhound Missile from Britain. However, instead of giving these weapons to the army the government awarded them to the RAAF, and gave the air force the responsibility for air defence above 15,000 feet. Although, up to this point, only the army had had experience in the operation of ground-based anti-aircraft weapons, the government chose to allocate this task to the RAAF. In effect, the decision limited the army's anti-aircraft defence role to low-altitude weapons. The army did not acquire surface-to-air missiles until the purchase of the Redeye in 1970, followed by the Rapier in 1975. However, both systems were designed for low-level defence, and their arrival did not represent a regaining of capability.[188]

If this decision by Menzies cost the army part of its anti-aircraft capability, another of his choices led to the establishment of army aviation on a secure basis. Until 1957, army aviation led a precarious existence under the control of the RAAF. The army maintained a small number of pilots for artillery observation, but they served in RAAF units under the command of the air force. This began to change in 1957, when the government authorised the raising of the ARA's first aviation unit, 1st Army Aviation Company. Since the concept was an experiment, the unit did not own its light planes but leased them from the private sector. In 1960, army aviation gained a more favourable status with the raising of 16th Army Light Aircraft Squadron, although the unit remained under the control of the RAAF. It flew both light fixed-wing and rotor-wing craft which, in this case, the army owned. Further advances followed, including the raising of 1st Aviation Regiment and the transfer of command over army aviation from the RAAF to the army in 1964. In 1968, army aviation gained the status of a corps with the formation of the Australian Army Aviation Corps. The army's establishment also gained its own aviation school, and in 1969 the RAAF transferred to the army control of the Oakey Aerodrome. Today, Oakey remains the home of 1st Aviation Regiment as well as the School of Army Aviation.

The last major capability adjustment during this period affected the army's blue-water fleet. Since World War II, the Royal Australian Engineers Transportation Service had maintained a squadron of ocean-going transport vessels, in addition to its considerable coastal and river water-transport assets. Throughout the South-East Asian conflicts, the army's LSMs (landing ship medium) and the Army Ship *John Monash* of 32nd Small Ship Squadron helped to sustain the commitments to Vietnam, Malaya, and Borneo. By the late 1960s, these vessels were nearing the end of their serviceable life and, in anticipation of their retirement, the army had begun the construction of a new LCH (landing craft heavy) class of eight ocean-going vessels. The first of these, Army Ship *Balikpapan*, joined the order of battle in 1971. It, however, would be the only LCH to sail under the army's command. In 1970, Fraser, now serving as Minister for Defence, approved a Chiefs of Staff Committee's recommendation to revise the division of maritime responsibility between the army and the RAN. In the new agreement, the navy received responsibility for all ocean-going vessels. The decision also limited the army's future maritime transportation role to coastal and river waters only. As a result, the army had to transfer the *Balikpapan*, and its sister ships still under construction, to the RAN.

At this time, the army also nearly lost part of its remaining coastal maritime transport responsibility. In 1971, Admiral Victor Smith, Chairman, Chiefs of Staff Committee, had initially decided to transfer the army's LCM8s to the RAN. If implemented, it meant that the only watercraft remaining on the army's establishment were its obsolete DUKWs, which it was withdrawing from service, and their replacement, the LARC-Vs. However, later in the year, Smith advised the services that for the time being the army would retain operational control of the LCM8s for a further three years. In addition, he recommended that the two services review the timing of the landing-craft transfer within the next two years. It is not clear if such a review took place, but the army continues to command these craft.[189]

Although the transfer of the LCHs to the RAN represented a loss of capability for the army, it was the right decision. The agreement did protect the army's needs by the inclusion of a clause that identified the primary function of these vessels as the support of the army. While maritime soldiering had appeal for some parts of the army, the force's fleet was too small to provide an adequate career path for those who served on these vessels. A sea-going fleet was a specialty that the army could not really afford, and, although it meant a loss of assets for the army, the RAN was the more appropriate service to provide this function. However, the army's role on the high seas did not come totally to an end. The RAN's major transport vessels—HMA Ships *Tobruk*, *Kanimbla*, *Manoora*, and *Jervis Bay*—have on board, as one of their departments, a ship army detachment of army personnel who are responsible for the loading and unloading of army stores and personnel. The RAN commands and operates the vessels, but soldiers continue to be responsible for the army's cargo.[190]

For much of Australia's history, the nation had maintained a policy of two armies. After World War II the government raised the ARA, which served alongside the CMF. In both world wars the government raised specially enlisted AIFs, while a separate home army remained behind to guard the nation. The course of World War II should have driven home the inefficiency of this practice. While it did have benefits, such as allowing the government to provide cheaply for defence, and although it closely connected the citizen soldier to the community, it proved a difficult means by which to project and sustain military power. With the onset of the Cold War and the growing menace of communist and, later, Indonesian aggression in South-East Asia, the strategic wisdom of the two-army policy became increasingly hard to justify.

As recently as 1971, the Military Board had defined a role for the CMF which, although limited and subservient, still provided the citizen soldier with an important function. Its purpose was

   a to augment the Regular Army in time of war and in time of defence emergency; and
   b with the Regular Army, to provide the basis for the expansion of the whole Army upon general mobilisation.[191]

The Millar Inquiry revealed how fragile even this level of responsibility had become. Throughout the post-Korea period, the CMF relentlessly declined in importance and status in the nation's defence hierarchy relative to the ARA. The overall trend, even if its numbers temporarily rose, was a gradual diminution of relevance.

The determination of the regulars to prevent a repetition of the amateurish nature of interwar preparations, as well as an ongoing staff–militia rivalry, certainly contributed to the demise of the CMF and the rise of the ARA. However, two other points that helped shape this transition also stand out. The first is that defence decision-makers were correct in their analysis that the post-World War II strategic environment mandated a greater reliance by the Australian Government on the regular soldier. The CMF simply could not match the response capability that a properly established regular field force offered. Although the ARA managed to maintain itself during the Korean War only by the narrowest of margins, after the 1960 and 1964 reorganisations the regulars had evolved into a professional military force that was able to meet its strategic requirements. The second point is harder to justify by recourse to national need. There is little doubt that CMF officers felt betrayed by their regular counterparts. While there is no suggestion that the ARA engineered its rise with the express purpose of ridding the army of the CMF, it is certainly true that the process occurred with little regard to the sensibilities of the citizen soldier. The Military Board and a series of senior ARA officers undertook a number of reorganisations and implemented policies with a callous indifference to their effect on their CMF counterparts. The end result of these judgments was the destruction of the CMF and with it the loss of an ethos and institutional memory that stretched back to the founding of the nation.

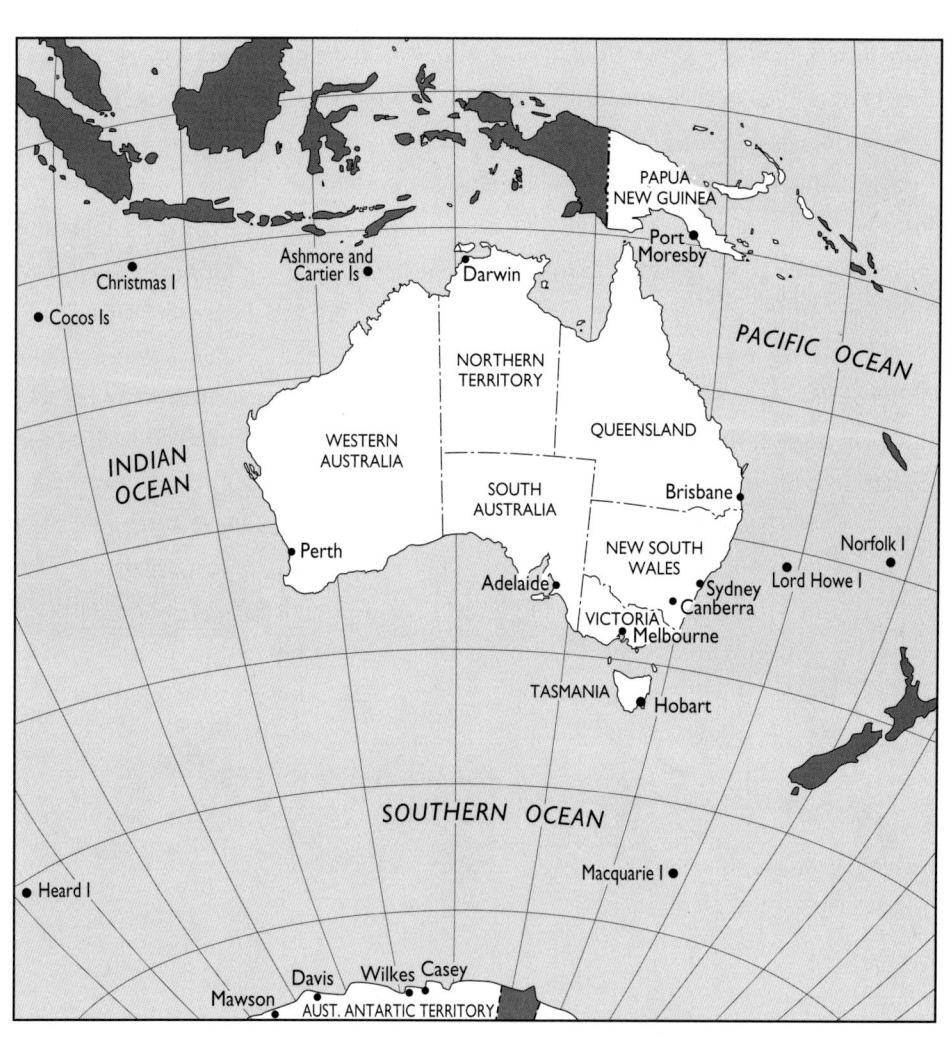

Map 13 Australian territory, 1975

8
THE DEFENCE OF AUSTRALIA

Even though our security may be ultimately dependent upon US support, we owe it to ourselves to be able to mount a national defence effort that would maximise the risks and costs of aggression.[1]

While the first half of the 1970s had been a turbulent time for the organisation of the Australian Army, the middle of the decade would usher in a period of comparative tranquillity. By 1975, the definition and construction of the modern Australian Army—its force and command structure and the relationship between the ARA and the reserves—had largely been finalised. Further organisational review would take place, especially at the ministerial and joint force levels, but the resulting modifications appear comparatively minor and tangential when compared to the transformation in the army that the preceding period had wrought. However, what was about to change significantly was the definition of the strategic environment in which the army operated, and military leaders would have to redefine the force's organisation in light of the government's new security policy. The redirection of national defence priorities would complicate and overshadow the institutionalisation of further evolution in the army's organisation.

Since the embarkation of 34th Brigade in 1946 for service with the British Commonwealth Occupation Force, the pattern for the army had been for the ARA to operate overseas in fulfilment of the government's policy of forward defence. In 1975, after the government withdrew from Malaysia the last infantry battalion deployed overseas, the army entered a period during which the emphasis would be on domestic service. This did not exclude overseas service, as the army has built up an impressive record of participation in United Nations peace-keeping missions in places such as Cambodia, Somalia, Rwanda, and East Timor. However, except for the participation of a tiny number of troops in the Persian Gulf War, between 1975 and 1999 the army served in peace and largely at home.

If the post-1975 changes have been of a lesser order of magnitude than those that had occurred previously, they were not of lesser importance or difficulty. The abandonment of the forward defence, and its replacement by continental defence, required government decision-makers and military leaders to re-evaluate the army's role within the Commonwealth's security hierarchy, and to redefine the purpose and objectives of the nation's ground forces. This process was not always easy, and army leaders did have difficulty in identifying a force structure that appropriately supported the strategic situation. Accompanying these developments was the emergence of a number of other long-term trends. These included a reduction in the army's dependence on Australia's allies, with a commensurate increase in reliance on and integration with the RAN and RAAF, the emergence of a new joint force command system between the level of the heads of service and that of the Minister for Defence, the acceptance of the need to relocate the bulk of the army's combat formations to the north of the country away from their traditional bases in the south, and the necessity of re-examining the role of female soldiers within the force's operations.

Self-reliance

Since the arrival of the First Fleet in 1788, the burden of Australia's ultimate defence has rested on the armed forces of overseas allies. Throughout the colonial period, and for much of the post-Federation era, the Royal Navy served as the guarantor of Commonwealth security. During World War II the United States took up this duty, and Australia has remained closely allied with America ever since. Britain re-exerted its influence in the region after the defeat of Japan, especially in Malaya, but, while the return of the British was useful, there was no suggestion that Australia's former protector could again play the principal role in the Commonwealth's security as it had done in the past. Successive Australian governments, therefore, have continued to cultivate the American relationship and have made it the central element of their national security policy. In the aftermath of its defeat in the Vietnam War, the United States made it clear that its allies would have to do more to secure their defence, however. The American alliance remained, but the Commonwealth could no longer abdicate its sovereign responsibilities to the extent that it had done in the past, and the government now had to provide for a greater share of the country's defence from its own resources.

In November 1976 the Minister for Defence, D. James Killen, presented to parliament a White Paper that confirmed that the nation was to become more self-reliant. The White Paper maintained that in the future it would be up to Australia to provide its own credible defence effort with which to deter potential aggressors. At the same time, Killen confirmed the end of the policy of forward defence. He noted that the government would no longer base its security policy on the expectation that its forces would serve overseas in support of another nation's military effort. He did not rule out such participation, but instead believed that Australia could make a greater contribution to the Western defence system by reducing its dependence on allies and accepting more responsibility for the security of its own region. Although the White Paper continued to recognise the importance of Australia's alliance with the United States, it also warned that American assistance would probably not be forthcoming in any situation short of a threat to the nation's survival.[2]

In reality, Killen's White Paper merely confirmed a shift in national defence policy that had been underway since the government of John Gorton, and the 1976 White Paper was just the latest of a series of reviews that pointed to fundamental changes in the region's strategic environment.[3] The Defence Committee's 1971 *Strategic Basis* paper showed an early awareness of this trend when it commented on the Australian–American relationship. It noted that the keystone of Australia's forward defence policy was the willingness of the United States to maintain a presence in South-East Asia. Australia did not have the capability to play a forward defence role on its own, since the maintenance of its forces in Vietnam and Malaysia depended on the United States and Britain respectively. Without such assistance, Australia's commitment to forward defence was unsustainable. A related document, 'The Environment of Future Australian Military Operations', outlined the implications of the allied withdrawal more directly. It concluded that it was unlikely that the Commonwealth would again deploy troops to South-East Asia, and instead the primary area of operations would be the Australian mainland and adjacent territories.[4]

The Defence Committee also observed that the United States had indicated its intentions in 1969 when Richard Nixon advanced the Guam Doctrine. In his speech, the American president called upon his country's allies to make greater efforts to provide for their own defence. Since Australian forces were deeply involved in Vietnam, Nixon's announcement did not cause an immediate reordering of the nation's security policy. However, the government did not miss the serious implications the Guam Doctrine posed for the future security of the Commonwealth, and the 1971 *Strategic Basis* anticipated an 'increased emphasis on the defence of Australia'.[5] Of lesser importance to the reshaping of Australia's security policy, although still of significance, was Britain's announcement that it would withdraw from east of Suez, thereby ending its military presence in Malaysia. Australia's two strongest allies, then, were intent on reducing their influence in the region. The abandonment of SEATO in 1975 only served to underscore the non-viability of that treaty. Faced with these changes in the strategic fabric, the Defence Committee concluded that Australia's future military credibility depended upon its capability to defend itself.[6]

The Defence Committee's 1973 assessment reached a similar but more focused conclusion. This report advised the government that Australia must assume the primary responsibility for its defence against a regional threat and, as a consequence, the services must develop capabilities, such as logistical support, which in the past an ally had provided. A defence review that the Department of Defence prepared the previous year again asserted that in any situation less than a major war involving the great powers the Commonwealth must place greater emphasis on self-reliance. The report also assumed that self-reliance would become the central feature of Australian defence policy in the future. The 1975 *Defence Report* echoed this theme, but instead of self-reliance employed the term 'continental defence', one of a number of euphemisms the armed forces and the government would employ to denote a defence policy that aimed to provide Australia with the ability to defend itself against a regional threat on its own.[7]

Despite the Guam Doctrine, Australian leaders continued to perceive the United States, and the ANZUS treaty, as fundamental components of the Commonwealth's security policy. The government interpreted Nixon's words as having two meanings. First, they were a warning to America's allies that the United States expected regional powers to take on a greater share of the defence burden of the Western Alliance. Second, they were an effort to reassure these same allies that America would honour its existing treaty obligations. Security assessments, however, warned that the nature of an American reaction to a threat to Australia's security might depend on the extent to which the Commonwealth had prepared itself in peace.[8]

If Australia was now to provide for a larger share of its defence, it had to do so in an environment complicated by the absence of an easily discernible threat. Security assessments suggested that for the foreseeable future there was little likelihood of danger to Australian territory. The Defence Committee also considered a general war unlikely because of the deterrent effect of mutually assured destruction. Instead, the government accepted that global stability, the avoidance of general war, and the control of local conflicts would be the normal pattern of future security affairs.[9] In 1975, the annual defence report concluded that the 'prospect of direct strategic pressure against

Australian interests by a major power remains remote'. Furthermore, the report continued, no regional power presently had the capability to threaten Australia.[10]

After the 1979 Soviet invasion of Afghanistan, the Fraser Government increased its anti-communist rhetoric and strengthened the RAN's presence in the Indian Ocean, but its internal security assessments did not note any appreciable increase in risk.[11] Paul Dibb's influential 1986 study reiterated the belief that Australia did not face any identifiable direct military threat and the expectation that this security environment would continue.[12] With the collapse of the Soviet Union and the end of the Cold War, Australian defence planners anticipated that a greater degree of fluidity in the international arena would occur, but the Commonwealth's position and perception of threat remained largely unaffected. In reviewing the post-Cold War situation, the 1993 strategic assessment counselled caution, but saw reason neither to assume that a worse threat environment would eventuate nor to note a heightening of contingencies against which Australia's armed forces should plan. There have been some exceptions to these generally positive interpretations of the threat environment, but most defence analysts continue to advance a fairly confident picture of the state of Australia's security, both in the present and for the foreseeable future.[13]

In addition to a stable threat environment, the change from a bipolar to a multipolar world order has not affected Australia's relationship with the United States. The defence links between the two nations remain strong, and ANZUS continues to serve as the cornerstone of the Commonwealth's security policy. Furthermore, nothing has occurred since the end of the Cold War to cause the government to challenge its belief that sufficient warning, allowing for the timely expansion of the army, would precede any adverse change in the defence environment. The government, therefore, continues the policy established in the early 1970s, of making force structure plans and procurement priorities on the basis that for the foreseeable future the level of threat is not more than the lowest contingency, and that the possibility of a major confrontation with a hostile force on Australian territory remains remote.

Since 1973 the army has enjoyed an era of sustained peace. The defining characteristics of this period have been a virtually non-existent level of threat, contingency planning aimed at the lowest level of armed confrontation, and continued good, though varying, relations with the United States. Australia's strategic interests have also remained focused on the immediate vicinity and the territory from which a hostile country could project military power against Australian territory, maritime resources, and lines of communication. Geography still dictates that the critical area of focus remains the immediate north. Despite such favourable factors—stability, strategic situation, and the lack of a threat—the development of an appropriate organisation for the army has not become any easier, and some aspects of structural design have actually become harder. In fact, budgetary shortfalls resulting from the low-threat situation have had serious consequences for the development of the army. Furthermore, the absence of a clear threat has made contingency planning and its coordination with force capabilities an extremely difficult task.

The Tange reform

Before the army could evolve an appropriate organisation for the new strategic situation, it had to respond to the far-reaching reforms that were about to cascade through the Department of Defence and the service ministries. Although only tangentially related to the organisation of the army, the Tange Reform, named for Sir Arthur Tange, the Secretary of the Department of Defence who was responsible for its development, had important ramifications for the Commonwealth's armed forces, especially at the highest levels of command. As a result of Tange's efforts, the government amalgamated the existing three service ministries (Army, Navy, and Air) and parts of the Department of Supply into the Department of Defence. This undertaking actually

Russell Office Complex, headquarters of the Department of Defence. (National Archives of Australia, A6135, K7/2/92/13)

Lieutenant-General Sir Leslie Morshead. (AWM 052619)

re-created the pattern of defence organisation that had existed from Federation until World War II, when the government created the service ministries in response to wartime expansion.[14]

The government had begun its investigation into the reorganisation of the Defence Group in 1972, but did not finalise the issue until the passage of the Defence Force Reorganisation Bill in September 1975. Tange's program was not the first time the government had considered a reform of such magnitude. In 1957, Lieutenant-General Sir Leslie Morshead had recommended a similar consolidation of the defence-related ministers to the Menzies Government. However, in order to minimise political risk, the Prime Minister ignored Morshead's most sweeping proposals and countenanced only the relatively uncomplicated incorporation of the Department of Defence Production into the Department of Supply. As a result, the government retained five ministries within the Defence Group, namely Defence, Army, Navy, Air, and Supply.[15]

In addition to the creation of a single Department of Defence, Tange's report contained two other major recommendations that affected the command and organisation of the army more directly. The Defence Secretary also suggested that the government create the position of the Chief of Defence Force Staff (CDFS), and abolish the Military Board (as well as the boards for the RAN and RAAF). The CDFS would command Australia's defence forces, and be the senior officer of the Commonwealth's armed forces. The chiefs of staff of the services, namely the Chief of Naval Staff, Chief of the Air Staff, and the CGS, would continue to command their respective services, but would do so under the CDFS. Under the new organisation, the CDFS became the principle military adviser to the minister, although the chiefs of staff also retained the right to comment on matters relating to their responsibilities.[16] In 1976, the government adopted the title Defence Force to describe the three services, and to suggest their unity under the person of the CDFS. The term 'Defence Force' gradually evolved into Australian Defence Force, achieving official status in 1985–86 when it appeared in the annual *Defence Report* for the first time. The following year, the *Defence Report* employed the abbreviation 'ADF'.[17] The use of 'Defence Force' and 'ADF' also reinforced the sense of subservience of the heads of the RAN, Army, and RAAF to the CDFS. In 1984, the government simplified the title of the Chief of the Defence Force Staff to Chief of the Defence Force (CDF) in order to reflect the position's command responsibilities more accurately.

Tange's suggestion for a CDFS was not without precedent. In his 1957 report, Morshead had made a similar, though not as far-reaching, proposal to Menzies, which led to the creation of the position of Chairman of the Chiefs of Staff. However, as established, the Chairman of the Chiefs of Staff lacked strong statutory authority. Furthermore, the office had neither the right to command the formations and units of the three services nor the administrative power to mandate greater coordination among the armed forces. As a consequence, the power and influence of the office varied greatly, depending upon the strength of the individual. Tange's proposal eliminated these difficulties by clearly establishing that the chain of command flowed downward from the CDFS and that the chiefs of staff were subordinate.[18]

The effect of the appointment of a CDFS, however, was more than just the elevation of a single officer to the position of commander of the three services. Once implemented, these changes forced the army to reassess the relationship between the head of the service and the minister, the chain of command and the status of the CGS. Tange's reforms also facilitated the advancement of the concept of 'jointness' and thereby helped to improve cooperation and coordination between the different branches of the armed forces. Tange also believed that, by having a single commander, the Department of Defence would benefit through better fiscal management, coordination of acquisition, and the adoption of uniform standards and procedures for functions common to all service. Thus the reform also contained an aspect of fiscal efficiency as motivation for its adoption.

While Tange's proposals were therefore sweeping, perhaps their most important ramification was not fully appreciated when the Minister for Defence appointed General Sir Francis Hassett as the first CDFS on 9 February 1976. The previous day, Hassett had been serving as the Chairman of the Chiefs of Staff Committee, and his acquisition of a new title seemed to suggest that there were more similarities than differences between the two offices. However, this was not to prove the case. The CDFS's staff gradually evolved into the Headquarters ADF and absorbed many of the functions that the three services had previously performed individually, thus downgrading the responsibilities of Army Headquarters. In fact, the duties of the CGS and Army Headquarters have slowly declined, and now they oversee only the raising, training, equipping, and maintenance of the force, while operational command is vested in joint headquarters.[19]

The elimination of the Military Board also had major ramifications for the army at the command level. While there had been some modifications in the organisation of the Military Board since its establishment in 1905, the responsibilities of its core members had not changed greatly. By the time of the Tange reforms, the office of the CGS had evolved into the effective commander of the Australian Army. The position was the force's most senior, and since 1939 it had warranted three stars. The offices of the Chief of Personnel, Chief of Logistics, and the Chief of Materiel (until 1973 Adjutant-General, Quartermaster, and Master-General of the Ordnance respectively) were two-star positions, and subordinated to the CGS. However, the holders of these positions also had, as military members of the Military Board, the right of access to the Minister for Defence and equal statutory responsibility for the functions of their offices, while also being junior to the CGS in the army's chain of command. The office of the CMF member of the Military Board (subsequently titled Inspector-General of the Army Reserve) also had a similar dual relationship with the CGS. In the aftermath of the Military Board's abolition the Chief of Personnel, Chief of Logistics, Chief of Materiel, as well as the Chief of Operations became principal staff officers to the CGS. They also serve on the CGS Advisory Committee.

On the eve of the Tange reform, the internal command and control structure of the army contained three main elements: Army Headquarters, functional commands, and the military districts. Each element reported to the office of the CGS although, as noted above, some branches also had independent representation on the Military Board. With the implementation of the Tange proposals, the army was able to simplify this structure. Below the CGS there would now be two command paths. The first was Army Headquarters, which was responsible for the force's administrative control. It would include the DCGS as well as offices for operations, personnel, materials, logistics, and reserves. The other path was responsible for the operational control of the army's commands. It included the headquarters for Field Force Command, Logistic Command, and Training Command, as well as the military districts. The Tange reforms maintained the distinction in the army, put in place by Hassett, between command of units and the conduct of administration and policy development.

One final change made by Tange was the redesignation of Army Headquarters as Army Office. The use of the word 'headquarters' had the connotation that it was the final service authority in the army's organisation. This, of course, was no longer the case. Furthermore, the switch to 'Army Office' helped to emphasise the CGS's subordination. Last, as Chart 12 illustrates, it was no longer possible to describe the higher direction of the army solely from the prospective of the army. Instead, the army's higher direction could now be viewed only from the context of its place within the higher direction of the Department of Defence.[20]

Jointness

The Tange reforms would have another important flow-on effect, which held even greater implications for the operational control and capabilities of the ADF. One of the objectives behind the creation of a CDFS with real powers was to improve the service's ability to undertake joint operations. Traditionally the RAN, Australian Army, and RAAF had had little to do with each other, and the conduct of joint operations was one of the areas in which there was great potential for the ADF to improve its effectiveness. In the past, each service had tended to undertake combined or joint operations with the equivalent branch of allied armed forces. In some cases, the affiliation with another country's forces was the preferred operational choice. The most extreme example was the institutional loyalty of the RAN to the Royal Navy. From Federation through to the end of World War II, Australia's warships were little more

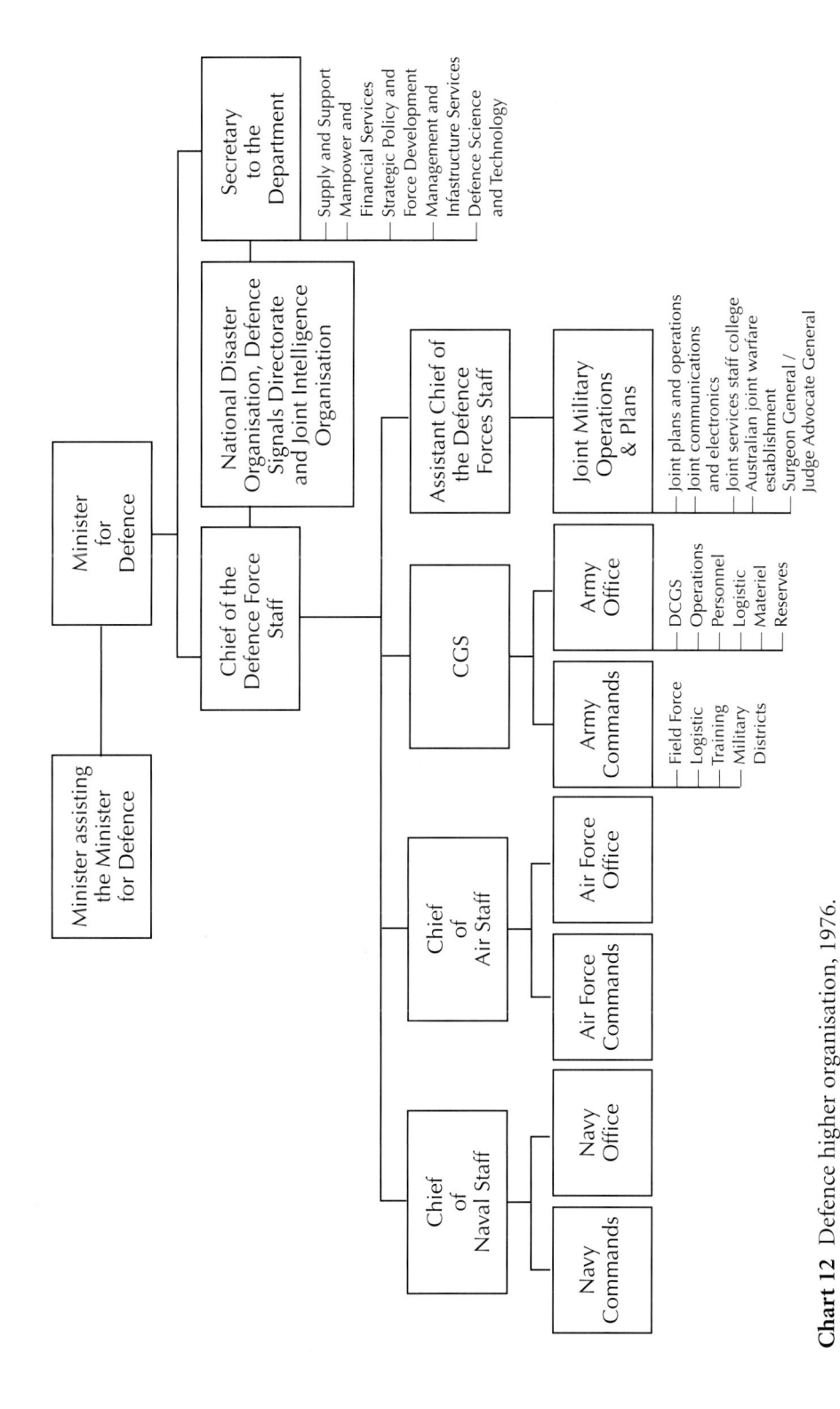

Chart 12 Defence higher organisation, 1976.
(Source: 'Defence Higher Organisation', AA (ACT), A3688/25, item 586/R3/15)

than a subunit of the imperial fleet. Furthermore, up to the early 1950s, the RAN, and to a lesser extent the RAAF, often had a British officer as its head of service. This did happen in the army, but never to such an extent as in the navy, and the most recent occurrence was the brief tenure of Squires as CGS in 1939. Although the army's relationship with allied forces never reached the degree of subservience accepted by the RAN, weaknesses in the Commonwealth's ground troop organisation, particularly in logistics, assured considerable dependence upon others for much of its maintenance and combat support. Thus it was only natural for the Australian Army to have more in common with, for example, the American ground structure in Vietnam than with the RAN or RAAF.

The government's adoption of a policy of self-reliance, coupled with a reduction in American and British interest in South-East Asia, therefore had important ramifications for the ADF. Unable to depend upon their opposites in allied forces as they had done in the past, the Australian services had no choice but to strengthen their reliance on each other. Reflecting this, the 1971 strategic assessment concluded that, with greater focus on the defence of Australia, there was a greater requirement for the three services to complement each other and operate as a joint force.[21] Of course, Australia's armed forces have always maintained a degree of interoperability. It is simply that, in the past, joint operations were a lower priority than that of achieving compatibility with the corresponding service of an ally. In early 1974, in anticipation of the need for greater interaction between Australia's ground, air, and maritime forces, Hassett wrote to Admiral Victor Smith, Chairman of the Chiefs of Staff Committee, to express his agreement that the services should begin to study in detail the requirements of joint operations. He also proposed that the army's exercises planned for August in the Kimberley region should also include elements of the RAN and the RAAF.[22]

While improved coordination between the armed forces made operational sense, the government also expected it to improve the effectiveness of the ADF while at the same time lowering expenses through the rationalisation of common functions. The 1979 establishment of a joint communications network, in place of one for each service, was just one example.[23] It was, however, only the beginning. Gradually the ADF has built up an infrastructure that exists solely for the purpose of facilitating jointness. For example, in 1996 the Department of Defence amalgamated the movements organisations of the three services into a new entity called the 1st Joint Movements Group. This created a single agency responsible for the provision of all operational movement support to the ADF. Thus, instead of having to coordinate the actions of several movement organisations, for example, in order to transport an army unit by RAAF plane, commanders now consult a single jointly staffed agency.[24]

In 1985 Kim Beazley, the Minister for Defence, authorised the creation of a joint force headquarters called Maritime Command. The following year, he announced the addition of a Land Command and an Air Command. These new headquarters were created out of three service command headquarters, namely, Fleet Headquarters, Field Force Command Headquarters, and RAAF Operational Command Headquarters. To reflect these developments, the army soon changed the title of Field Force Command to Land Command. The creation of these headquarters gave the CDF a non-service-based chain of command through which to command the ADF's forces. In addition, their orientation was environmental. While the maritime headquarters largely controlled RAN assets, it could also command RAAF or army units, as assigned, in order to meet mission objectives. Thus, joint operations was the natural operational context of an environmental headquarters. Gradually the operational command of army formations and units passed from the control of Field Force Command to the ADF's joint force organisation. In addition, the CDF received a Vice-Chief of the Defence Force, who had responsibility for the day-to-day administration of the growing Headquarters ADF. Chart 13 (p. 322) outlines the place of the army within the defence structure as it existed in 1988.[25]

On 1 July 1988, the CDF, General P.C. Gration, authorised the raising of a joint force headquarters in Darwin. Beazley had given his approval the preceding March. Termed Northern Command (NORCOM), it was given the responsibility of planning for operations in the defence of Northern Australia. Gration also expected Headquarters NORCOM to be capable of expansion in order that it could command and control significant additional forces in case of a major deployment to the north. He designated the position for an army brigadier, and subordinated NORCOM to headquarters land force. To manage the ground force component of NORCOM, the army raised a Headquarters Land Component NORCOM.[26]

In 1996, General J.S. Baker, serving as CDF, implemented the next major reform of the ADF's command organisation when he created a single joint commander called Commander Australian Theatre. He had recognised the need for this headquarters as a result of coordination difficulties that occurred between NORCOM and Maritime Command during the Kangaroo 95 exercise. The headquarters for Maritime Command, Land Command, and Air Command now fell under the control of Commander Australian Theatre. In addition, Baker also decided to bring the single service chiefs of staff back into the Headquarters ADF, although only at

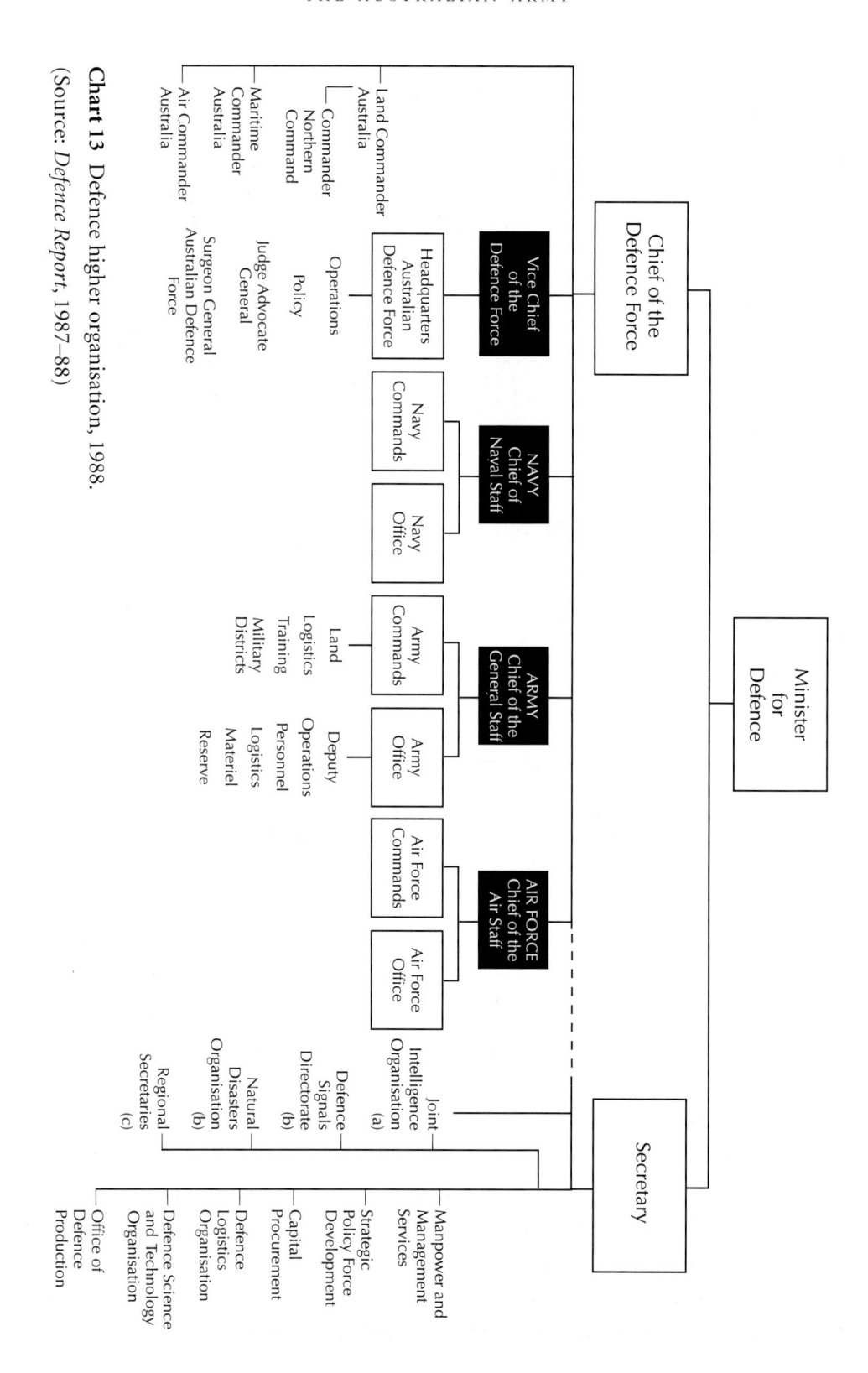

Chart 13 Defence higher organisation, 1988.
(Source: *Defence Report, 1987–88*)

Lieutenant-General Peter Gration (left), CGS 1984–87. (AWM P01748.001)

the strategic level. As a result, he redesignated the title CGS as Chief of Army. The Chief of Naval Staff became Chief of Navy and the Chief of Air Staff became Chief of Air Force.

An event that confirmed the importance of jointness to the future of the ADF was the opening of the Australian Defence Force Academy in 1986. Up to that point, each service had maintained its own academy for the training of new officers. However, the Australian Defence Force Academy provides its cadets with a university education in a triservice environment. Besides the cost-saving possibilities of having a centralised education system, the government also established the Australian Defence Force Academy as a long-term experiment and commitment to the advancement of jointness. Theoretically, as its graduates participate in joint training exercises or when they obtain appointments at the joint command level, the commonality of experience at the Australian Defence Force Academy will have a positive effect in reducing rivalry and promoting an understanding of the purpose and capabilities of the services other than one's own. The introduction of triservice training, however, has not been without trauma or resistance. For example, in 1999 the RAN introduced a policy of sending part of their incoming cadet class to sea first in order to inculcate some naval values before exposure to the Australian Defence Force Academy.

The question of jointness has had great implications for the nature and function of the army. In the past, the army's leaders naturally interpreted the army's strategic purpose from the perspective of land warfare and have, therefore, perceived its role in terms of continental defence employing traditional organisations. This occurs despite the fact that divisions or brigades, with their accompanying heavy support, might be more suited for operations in overseas theatres under the umbrella of an ally's support than in the defence of the Australian mainland. As early as 1991, Woodman and Horner pointed out that Australia's contemporary defence posture was perhaps best interpreted as a maritime strategy, and they believed the army should design itself to fit within that framework. They go on to suggest that joint operations must be the central mechanism by which the army will determine its force structure and doctrine in order that it can define an appropriate role within the government's strategic vision. Consequently, they conclude that if the army is to find appropriate missions for which it is to tailor its organisation and equipment priorities, it must do so within the context of its ongoing participation in joint operations.[27]

Core force

The end of forward defence meant that the army now had to reconsider the force's organisation in light of the requirements for continental defence. In many ways this proved much harder to accomplish than reorganisations in the past. In earlier periods, the sense of a perceived danger, such as Japanese expansionism or communist aggression, was more obvious, and this made the framework of a suitable response more readily deducible, even if resources were not available for its full implementation. The absence of a clear threat during the 1970s acted as an inhibiting factor in the clarification of the army's requirements. In fact, a number of observers have rightly commented that for more than a decade there was a lack of coordination between the government's policy of self-reliance and the organisation of the army.[28] One scholar has gone so far as to declare that by 1979 the government had failed to achieve its goal of self-reliance and that the policy was in disarray.[29]

However, while part of the problem was the absence of a known threat against which to plan, there were a number of other elements that also influenced the inability of the military decision-makers to coordinate government security policy with the army's organisation. The most significant factor was that after the government abandoned forward defence it failed to clearly enunciate a successor policy. The details of self-reliance, especially from the army's perspective, remained largely undefined, and the government did not replace diffuse rhetoric with concrete details until well into the 1980s. This left army planners in the position of having to make judgments on organisation, establishment, doctrine, training, and expenditure without a clear idea whether their efforts met the government's expectation. For example, in late 1976 the Fraser Government outlined the capabilities it desired:

- The possession of a force in being capable of dealing with short term contingencies and foreseeable tasks.
- The force in being should possess or have under development the structure, equipment and professional skills necessary for timely expansion against a range of contingencies.
- The force in being should have substantial capability for independent operations.
- The force in being should have the ability to absorb high tech equipment.
- The force in being should retain the capacity to operate effectively with the United States.[30]

However, the report failed to identify the nature of the contingencies, the required rate of expansion, the nature of the independent operations, the type of high-tech equipment, or the purpose of operations with the Americans.

Instead of preparing for a specific contingency, or series of contingencies, defence planning occurred around the concept of 'core force'. Killen advanced the idea in his 1976 White Paper, although the origin of the policy is outlined in slightly different terms in the 1971 and 1973 *Strategic Basis* papers.[31] The government defined the term 'core force' as the possession of a force that was capable of handling local situations but was also capable of timely expansion in case of the emergence of a major threat to Australian security.[32] The core force idea therefore contained two elements. First, it recognised that even in a no-threat environment it was possible for a hostile power to undertake low-level military operations against Australian territory with little or no warning. Second, it assumed that the nation's intelligence agencies would be able to alert the government to the emergence of a major security threat in a timely manner, thereby providing sufficient warning for the expansion of the defence forces. The government expected a two-tier defence response from the army: ready-reaction troops to deter low-level incursion, and the ability to expand into a force designed to fight against a major threat.

The government also observed that, since the capabilities of the RAN and the RAAF were largely dependent upon the units already on their establishments, because of the long lead times necessary to acquire more equipment, the provision of an expansion capability was realistically only applicable to the army. Although the navy and air force had some ability to increase their strength by bringing mothballed units back into service, this had limitations, and they would probably have to fight with the forces they already had. The army was different. For the ground troops it was possible to build up the stores of most types of armaments relatively rapidly, either through domestic production or by purchase from friendly overseas suppliers. Therefore, for the army, the establishment of existing equipment was not the determinant of the force's ultimate size. Rather, the key factor was its maintenance in peacetime of the necessary range of military skills, tactics, command and control, and operational procedures that the force would require for a major conflict. The ability of the force to retain its existing knowledge base and to absorb advances in the military art were the primary controlling factors in the army's expansion plans.[33]

However, the interpretation of how the army was to achieve the objectives of a core force was largely left to the force's leaders. From the beginning, military decision-makers placed the emphasis on the expansion base necessary to protect the Commonwealth in a major war against a future developing threat. This policy assumption took precedence over the other half of the core force policy, the ability to react to local situations that might develop with little warning. The rationale for this decision is readily apparent. Like their interwar predecessors, the army's leaders saw the threat of invasion as being far more dangerous than that of raids, and they sought to construct a force structure that was more suited for high-intensity warfare than for low-level operations. Moreover, they believed that only the divisional formation provided the army with the combination of skills and firepower that it would need on the modern battlefield. Furthermore, if the army were to incorporate all the skills necessary to wage a major conflict, it required a divisional structure in which it could gain the experience that rapid expansion demanded. Last, there was a sense within the army that it would be far easier to form smaller units from larger formations than to engineer the reverse. As a result, the retention of the divisional structure and the creation of an infrastructure for its support in the field became the army's priority.

In 1974, Hassett, as CGS, wrote to the Minister for Defence, Lance Barnard, and noted that a properly founded field force had to be 'based on a divisional structure in order to give the maximum return in firepower and mobility in relation to the manpower employed'.[34] A few years later, Lieutenant-General Donald Dunstan, also as CGS, expressed concern to the CDFS over whether the army was giving sufficient attention to the maintenance of skills needed for a major conflict. He went on to note that, while the army had to pay some attention to the demands of shorter-term requirements, it was necessary to devote a substantial part of the defence force to the expansion base and develop the capabilities required for more serious threats.[35] In 1982, these ideas gained greater weight when the army outlined its planning philosophy in a booklet meant for public distribution. In it the army argued that for the immediate future

> the division, which is internationally accepted as the basic self-contained organization on which all modern armies are structured and defence credibility assessed, will continue to be the Australian Army's organizational basis for combat in war and training in peace. It is the lowest level formation in which all combat arms and supporting services are represented.[36]

Over the next decade, the army spent considerable effort in maintaining and refining its divisional organisation in order that it could serve as the basis of expansion in case of the emergence of a major threat.

Although RAR's reduction from nine to six battalions left the force with only two-thirds of the infantry complement normally found in a division, the maintenance of a regular division was a high priority for the army. During this period, the structure of 1st Division (an ARA formation) underwent two major reorganisations. The first was a review of the tropical warfare division that the army had used during the era of forward defence, when it assumed that its theatre of operations would be the jungles to the north. With the onset of continental defence, the army had to modify the division's establishments in order for it to be more suitable for operations in Australian conditions. The objective was to have a force capable of initially deploying light mobile forces, which could be followed up by heavier formations as needed. The division was to have a flexible structure in order that it could operate in a dispersed mode for low-intensity conflict, but also be able to concentrate its strength for higher levels of confrontation. In addition, it was to have the capability to create task forces designed for specific missions. Training Command codified the new organisation in its doctrine publication *Training Information Bulletin* no. 28. By the end of 1976, the army had completed the review process and had begun the process of changing over to the new establishments.[37]

The new divisional structure lasted only a few years, however, before it was overtaken by another reform. Dunstan, the CGS, believed that 1st Division had become too heavy, and as a standard infantry formation, it lacked the diversification in organisation that would facilitate the learning of multiple skills. While the 1975 division was an improvement over the tropical division in regard to continental operations, it did not provide the army with a mechanism by which to test a wide variety of operational possibilities. Dunstan believed that, in an organisation as small as the ARA, it was a liability to have three task forces with identical organisations and roles, as this limited the army's ability to develop the full range of skills it might require for expansion. He therefore proposed to the CDFS changes that would permit the army to restructure the division into a formation that contained units orientated around different specialties. The scheme still allowed the division to fight as a whole, but would permit it to gain additional capabilities that would be of benefit in case of expansion against a major threat.[38]

In 1979, Dunstan proposed the following specialisations for the task forces of 1st Division:

- 1st Task Force was to focus on mobile operations and prepare for tasks in conjunction with the 1st Armoured Regiment
- 3rd Task Force was to be reorganised onto light scales, and it was to concentrate its training on air-portable and air-mobile operations as well as warfare in tropical areas
- 6th Task Force was to remain a standard infantry task force, focusing its training on conventional operations in open country.[39]

In order to gain experience at even more techniques, Dunstan assigned secondary training objectives to each task force. For example, 1st Task Force was also to develop a capability for amphibious deployment, 3rd Task Force was to gain an ability to operate under jungle conditions, and 6th Task Force was given secondary specialisations in urban warfare and amphibious deployment. In addition, each task force was to retain the ability to fight as a standard infantry formation. The reserve elements also received a degree of specialisation. For example, reserve units in North Queensland were to adopt the organisation and training of 3rd Task Force. The government accepted Dunstan's proposals, and Killen announced the changes in early 1980.[40]

Dunstan's reorganisation of the division also allowed the army to secure, on a permanent basis, two new capabilities that it had been trying to develop. Dunstan believed that one of the lessons of the Vietnam War was that the infantry needed an organic mobility capability instead of having to rely on *ad hoc* arrangements. In 1976, the army began a mechanisation experiment with 5/7 RAR that saw the entire battalion gradually mounted in armoured personnel carriers. The next year, the battalion held a highly successful exercise as a mobile infantry unit in a battle group which also contained tanks. However, the cost of maintaining an entire unit on a mechanised basis caused some concern in Army Office, and Dunstan was only able to continue by limiting the experiment to one mounted company in the battalion. However, with the adoption of specialised

An armoured personnel carrier of 5/7 RAR during Exercise Crocodile 99 West. (Department of Defence, D99031-26)

task forces in 1980, the army required 1st Task Force to develop skills for mobile war. Consequently, the army authorised the mounting of all of 5/7 RAR in armoured personnel carriers, giving the force a permanent mechanised infantry capability.[41]

Similarly, Dunstan's plan of allocating specific skills to the task forces also led to the army gaining a parachute-capable battalion. As early as 1974, 6 RAR had converted one of its companies into an airborne company. At this time, however, it was not possible to extend the capability to the rest of the unit, and most of 6 RAR remained a standard infantry battalion. In 1980, 6 RAR conducted its first parachute exercise. The success of the operation led Killen to state that airborne operations were a requirement of a mobile land force. In 1981, Dunstan was able to advance the concept, and authorised the development of a full parachute-capable battalion. Since his division of skills between the task forces allocated air mobile operations to 3rd Task Force, Dunstan gave 3 RAR the assignment. In 1983, 3 RAR received the title of parachute infantry battalion. This achievement meant that for the first time since World War II the army's order of battle contained a battalion of paratroops.[42]

Having secured a divisional structure that provided a broad base of skills for expansion, the army then developed the Army Force Structure Plan, which orientated the force's organisation even further towards the higher end of conflict intensity. In 1984, the army began to consider the Army Force Structure Plan, and a related document, *The Army Development Guide*, even as it was becoming increasingly clear that the government wanted greater capability against low-level threats. The government would shortly authorise the Dibb Review, and the army feared that its findings might negate the objectives of the Army Force Structure Plan. There is some evidence that the military was aware of the government's reluctance to sanction any further capability development against a major threat, and that the army's leaders attempted to hide the full implications of the *Army Development Guide* and the Army Force Structure Plan from their political masters.[43]

Both documents aimed to define a structure that would support a force shaped for medium-level operations.[44] Writing to the CGS, Major-General A. Clunies-Ross noted that the emphasis of the proposed structure was to mould a force in being that could rapidly expand itself for a major conflict, and that its philosophy would be to subordinate speed of reaction to combat power.[45] Thus the proposed organisation was not suitable for a small ready reaction force, but rather for the deployment of division or corps-level formations. Although the army had no intention of forming a corps headquarters, one of Headquarters Field Force Command's tasks was to plan for its future raising.[46]

The Army Force Structure Plan sought to combine a reorganisation of 1st Division with an improvement in the effectiveness of reserve units in order to give the army the capability of fielding three divisions, including a mechanised division. Through this process, it would also improve the integration of the ARA and the Army Reserve, and thereby help to advance the objective of a 'total army'. The ARA division was to lose 1st Brigade, which would move to Puckapunyal in order to incorporate reserve armoured units into its establishment. In 1984, the army had returned to using the term 'brigade' instead of 'task force' to describe its intermediary formation. 3rd Division, centred on Victoria, would consist of 1st Brigade and the reserve 4th Brigade, and would gradually evolve into a mechanised division. 1st Division would remain in Queensland, where it would contain the army's ready reaction force (the recently raised Operational Deployment Force), and would also incorporate reserve battalions into its brigades. 2nd Division would remain a standard infantry formation. The army also intended to integrate divisional troops whenever possible. In addition, it planned to improve the readiness of some corps-level units.[47]

While the army placed its priorities on the division, some effort was made to improve the force's ability to cope with a low-level incursion, either on the Australian mainland or in the surrounding region. In 1981, the government announced the creation of a high-readiness formation called the Operational Deployment Force. Its combat element consisted of 3rd Task Force (Brigade), located in Townsville. One of the key units it could draw upon was Sydney-based 3 RAR, whose newly gained parachute skills would give the Operational Deployment Force the critical dimension of airborne insertion. The Operational Deployment Force was to maintain itself at a readiness level capable of deploying a company group within seven days, and the full brigade within 28 days, of initial warning. In addition, the army designated the 2nd Field Logistic Battalion, also in Townsville, as the Operational Deployment Force's logistical support group. The Operational Deployment Force passed its first test when it successfully deployed a company group to RAN fleet units near Fiji after a coup overthrew the government in May 1987. However, the Operational Deployment Force remained under strength during the entire core-force era. In 1984, instead of being the intended brigade group, it still only had two battalions and limited air transport, although it could call on 3 RAR to make three battalions if necessary.[48]

The army also raised three Regional Force Surveillance units to help patrol the far north, provide surveillance and reconnaissance, and serve as the first line of contact with any hostile landing. Each unit belonged to the reserves, and the army drew many of its members from local residents who were extremely familiar with the operational environment. The units and their point of concentration were North-west Mobile Force (Darwin), 51st Battalion Far North Queensland Regiment (Cairns), and the Pilbara Regiment (Port Hedland). Since these units were responsible for security over a vast area of operations, they combined the traditional company/platoon structure with a decentralised patrol system. For example, the 51st Far North Queensland Regiment contained four companies, but its operational element was 41 patrols, each based on a local community. The strength of a patrol was a sergeant and six other ranks.[49]

In the end, the core-force concept fell far short of providing the nation with the army it required to fulfil the government's policy of self-reliance. The key problem was that the army was unable to balance the two different capabilities that core force required. For the core force to have worked, the army needed an immediately ready reaction force while simultaneously catering for the requirements of an expansion base. It did not help the situation that the army's leaders greatly preferred the expansion base option, and that they made its pursuit their priority. This allowed the army to maintain on its order of battle a large number of specialised units whose mission was essentially the retention of the skills required for expansion. However, the consequence was that the army did not have the resources to support a large standing force,

Members of a Regional Force Surveillance unit on a tracking exercise. (Department of Defence, MSU K95 1099-20)

and had to spread its strength too thinly, with the result that many units were under strength. Instead of paying close attention to the requirements of low-intensity warfare, the army's leaders trusted that the two purposes of core force were complementary, and that from the expansion base for medium-level war they would be able to extrapolate a low-level force, as needed, for minor operations. This attitude failed to recognise that the defeat of minor incursions would require specialised equipment, training, and doctrine, not necessarily compatible with an organisation designed for higher levels of warfare.[50]

Ultimately, however, the problem with the core force was that the government failed to define the term adequately and to set priorities.[51] This in turn let military leaders maintain an organisation best suited for a major conflict in a fiscal environment that could not support an expansion base on the necessary scale. The resulting force structure was ill prepared to respond to a low-level emergency, and it did not possess the depth needed to maintain an effective expansion capability. In fact, the army was a hollow organisation, with most of its units below strength, inadequately equipped, and poorly prepared. In addition, the army had failed to develop the infrastructure it would require to maintain itself without the aid of an ally. A 1984 assessment noted:

> while the framework for a corps of three divisions exists, the divisions are in skeletal form and are significantly deficient in logistics and supporting elements ... Even if all our resources were concentrated in one division it would still be inadequately equipped, lacking in logistic capability and at a low level of training.[52]

Complicating the situation was that the government consistently failed to provide the resources needed to bring the army up to the targeted strength. In 1976, Killen had announced the government's intention to increase the army's establishment from 31,500 to 34,000 by 1981 in order that the force would have the manpower it required to maintain the expansion base. Four years later, the government stated its intention to bring the two battalions of the Operational Deployment Force up to strength, and add 5,000 regulars to the personnel of the ARA by 1986. In 1982, Killen conceded defeat. Instead of meeting impossible recruiting targets, the force would have to emphasise the acquisition of manpower skills. In fact, the ARA's establishment barely budged from the level of 1975, and the force remained well below its goal.[53]

During this period, the army also reconsidered the role of the Australian Cadet Corps. In 1974, Millar had presented to the government a report on the cadets, in addition to his review of the CMF.[54] Despite Millar's recommendation that the army retain the cadets, although with some modifications, the Whitlam Government decided to abolish the scheme. The army did not mourn its loss, as the cadet corps no longer served an essential function, and was a drain upon resources without sufficient compensating benefit. In 1974, the Military Board concluded that 'the costs and effectiveness of cadet training cannot be justified from the viewpoint of its contribution to the defence of Australia'.[55] Its only tangible use for the army was that it might play a role in the identification of future leaders. The cadet corps' disbandment released 335 ARA personnel for other duty, a relief to the force, since it was chronically under establishment.[56]

After the change of government in 1976, Fraser reversed the previous administration's decision and reactivated the cadet corps, although he did reduce its dependence on the army. The army now had to assign only 141 regulars to the scheme, and cadet corps units depended more than ever on their sponsoring schools for their administration and management. The government limited the army's responsibilities to the provision of instructors, medical staff, and support personnel for the cadets' seven-day annual camp. Still the scheme remained popular, and in 1977 had a triservice membership of over 25,000, of which the vast majority belonged to the army.[57]

In the mid 1970s, the status of the army's female personnel again came under scrutiny, with the result that women soldiers gradually gained a greater role in the force. Except in traditional professions, such as nursing, women, in the view of the army, were merely a useful supplement to its establishment when it was unable to recruit sufficient numbers of male personnel. During World War II, women were allowed to serve in a wide array of positions, since this freed up men for other duties. After the war, the army re-established the Women's Royal Australian Army Corps because it was unable to recruit enough men. However, regulations limited its members to non-combat positions and heavily restricted their career opportunities.

In 1975, the Military Board expanded the range of positions in which women could serve, and only forbade their assignment to units that might be involved in close combat. Lieutenant-General A.L. MacDonald, the CGS, expressed some reluctance over this change, and had a number of reservations. He believed that in the ARA women should not serve in any divisional or corps unit—other than field hospitals—since this might limit the action of a commanding officer, or require the reformation of a unit, if the army were to deploy it on a mission that might involve close combat. He did accept that women could play a larger role in the Army Reserve, especially since the army continued to have difficulty attracting sufficient numbers of reservists.[58]

The following year, however, a government report opined that there was a need for women to have greater job opportunities in the services, and that there should be closer equality between male and female personnel in conditions of service. The report went on to suggest that women might serve in areas in which hostilities were in progress, but not as combatants. This was the beginning of a continuing debate over the extent to which women might participate in the military. The armed forces were not alone in this re-evaluation of women's roles, and the struggle within the army was only a reflection of a broader discussion within Australian society. On 1 July 1984, the army effectively disbanded the Women's Royal Australian Army Corps and transferred its personnel to the corps to which they were currently affiliated. A few officers for whom no place could be found in other corps continued to belong to the Women's Royal Australian Army Corps, but as they left the service the corps gradually faded away. The following year, girls became eligible to participate in the cadet corps for the first time. In 1984, a further expansion of opportunity for female personnel occurred when the services fell subject to the recently enacted *Sex Discrimination Act*. When the Australian Defence Force Academy opened in 1986, 52 of the 325 incoming officer cadets were female.[59]

The trend towards greater career opportunities has accelerated in the 1990s. In May 1990, the CDF announced that women would be allowed into all positions defined as combat related. This included tasks such as transport, communications, and intelligence. In the army, women remained excluded only from the armour, artillery, infantry, and combat engineers. As a result, the range of army positions in which female personnel could serve rose from 19 per cent to over 55 per cent. By the mid 1990s, the proportion of eligible positions had reached two-thirds, and the share of the army's personnel who were female had climbed to about 10 per cent. The spread of women throughout the RAN has been even more pronounced. Women have also increased their presence at the Australian Defence Force Academy, and now represent 26 per cent of the officer cadet population. Although women in the army have moved into areas of greater responsibility, the issue of their role in combat units, which will affect their ability to reach the highest levels of command, awaits further resolution.[60]

The campus of the Australian Defence Force Academy. (ADFA)

The move north

In February 1985, Kim Beazley, the Minister for Defence, asked Paul Dibb to undertake a review of the state of Australia's defence capabilities. The minister instructed Dibb to comment on the structure and appropriateness of the ADF, and to make recommendations regarding the future direction of the armed forces. The government was well aware that there was a lack of coordination between the ADF's establishment and the government's strategic priorities. A 1984 parliamentary report made this point quite clearly. It, too, placed the blame for the divergence between the ADF's organisation and policy requirements on the failure of the government to provide defence planners with sufficient guidance in order to develop appropriate force structures.[61] Dibb also made this point in his report. He commented that the Department of Defence and the ADF had different interpretations of the strategic environment, and that this handicapped the service's preparations. In fact, of the three services, it was the army that had the greatest difficulty in coordinating its force structure with the strategic requirement. One of Dibb's aims, therefore, was to suggest ways that would bring the armed forces into closer agreement with the government's security policy.[62]

Beazley accepted Dibb's findings, and in 1987 incorporated them into his new White Paper, *The Defence of Australia*. The White Paper expanded upon Dibb's findings, and set the basis for the development of the army for the next decade. While neither Dibb's nor *The Defence of Australia*'s findings resulted in massive changes to the army's force structure, they led to a change in planning focus that switched the emphasis from the expansion-base model to one better suited for low-intensity conflict. The expansion of the army remained an important consideration, but the military's ability to react to and repel small-scale incursions now had a higher priority than it had had since the establishment of the core-force concept in 1976.[63]

The changes in the army's orientation that followed meant that the force's organisation moved gradually from the idea of a core force and evolved into what has become known as the terminal force concept. The difference between the two terms is that under the conditions of a terminal force the government expected the army, like the RAN and the RAAF, to be able to engage the enemy successfully with existing forces only, and not to rely on the expansion base for operations. It also confirmed that preparation for operations above the level of low intensity was no longer a priority. Thus, a terminal-force orientation had major implications for how the army allocated its resources, since it would require combat and support units to exist at a higher level of readiness than under a core-force strategy.[64]

However, this shift in organisational philosophy did not result solely from a stronger focus on low-level operations. Rather, it also came about through refinements in how the government measured, assessed, and projected risks to the nation's security. Under the core-force concept, the government had not been terribly specific about the kinds of dangers against which the ADF should prepare. The government judged threat assessments in the traditional context of either raids or invasion instead of correlating these assessments with the capabilities of potentially hostile nations, although it employed the terms 'low-intensity' or 'medium-intensity' conflict. Under core force, the army had focused its efforts on corps-level operations despite the absence of such a capability by any other country in the region. In addition, the government did not foresee any nearby nation as being able to gain such skills for at least 10 to 15 years. Moreover, it believed that it would receive sufficient warning if such a threat did begin to emerge. Certainly, the Soviet Union could project such power, but the possibility was remote, and such an eventuality would guarantee American involvement.

The government's new method of determining risk involved the identification of what security analysts have termed credible contingencies. Under this system, risk management required decision-makers to take into account the capabilities of potentially hostile nations before deciding the level of threat the nation faced or the dangers against which the ADF should prepare. This process allowed the government to enunciate the missions and capabilities for which it expected its armed forces to plan and train more clearly. This, in turn, provided defence planners with a better mechanism by which to determine the appropriateness of the Commonwealth's force structures. The result has been an improvement in the coordination of the organisation of the army with the missions anticipated for its employment by the government.[65]

Dibb believed that Australia required an army capable of containing and defeating incursions or raids close to their landing area. He noted that the organisation's emphasis would have to be on the more credible threat of low-level conflicts, and that hostilities of a more serious nature were not feasible, at this time, given the military effectiveness of the other nations in the region. In addition, he thought it was necessary for the army to have as one of its missions the protection of the military installations and civil infrastructure upon which the nation's air and maritime defence depended. Dibb concluded that the threat could only come from the north, and he recommended that the army increase its presence in the region of Australia closest to the risk. This would allow the army to gain a greater familiarity with its most likely area of operations and improve its ability to respond rapidly to hostile action. The first step, he believed, was to base a regular reconnaissance unit in the Northern

Territory, with the eventual goal being a brigade group. Since the army already maintained the Operational Deployment Force in Townsville, the transfer of a brigade group to Darwin meant that more than half of the ARA's combat capability would be in the north. Dibb also rejected the suggestion that the army required more tanks. He believed that the army's existing tank establishment was orientated towards conventional warfare, and was not appropriate for low-level incursions. Consequently, he maintained that the army should reduce the size of the 1st Armoured Regiment and make it into an integrated (ARA/reserve) unit. His opinions assured that the proposal in the Army Force Structure Plan for the mechanisation of the 3rd Division would fail. Dibb also questioned the army's artillery component. Since targets in a low-level conflict would be rare, he thought there was no place for the army's medium guns, except in the expansion base. Dibb also recommended a greater role for helicopters, since they would provide the force with flexibility and mobility while still being able to project firepower against dispersed targets.[66]

Beazley's 1987 White Paper, *The Defence of Australia*, took up Dibb's themes and, in particular, reiterated the importance of achieving self-reliance. The White Paper especially stressed the need to gain exercise experience in the far north. It recommended the transfer of the 2nd Cavalry Regiment to Darwin to help support the regional force surveillance units. In addition, *The Defence of Australia* suggested that the army consider basing a brigade group in the north. The White Paper also insisted that the army include on its order of battle highly mobile forces that were capable of responding rapidly to a range of northern contingencies. Furthermore, the report required the army to designate those units it would assign to the defence of vital military installations and civilian infrastructure. *The Defence of Australia* also envisaged that the army would orientate its capabilities around the requirements of an increasing scale of operations. The army would require an air-portable ready reaction force that would serve as the initial deployment, either to contain the enemy or secure an entry point for additional forces. The organisation was also to contain elements with greater firepower, which were to be available for a follow-up deployment. *The Defence of Australia* confirmed that the army was to continue to support an expansion base, but at a lower priority.[67]

To improve the mobility of the ground forces, Beazley approved the transfer of control over battlefield helicopters from the RAAF to the army. The control of light air assets had always been a contentious issue between the two services. While the army received command of its light fixed and rotor-wing artillery observation and transport craft in 1964, heavier helicopters still remained on the RAAF's order of battle. In *The Defence of Australia*, Beazley announced that battlefield helicopters would now

Army aviation: a Blackhawk helicopter discharging troops. (Department of Defence, TOWD 96088-11)

belong to the army because of the need to enhance its capability for reconnaissance, tactical mobility, fire support, and logistic support. In addition, the possession of battlefield helicopters would improve the army's ability to operate in a dispersed setting, the most likely operational environment for the defence of north Australia. Initially the army received 14 Blackhawks, with more on order. On 20 November 1986, the army expanded its aviation assets, with the raising of 5th Aviation Regiment in Townsville as its battlefield helicopter unit. 5th Aviation regiment also operates Chinook transport helicopters for heavy-lift tasks. The army's acquisition of battlefield helicopters is one of the few examples in which the force obtained a new capability during this period. It was an important development, as it has allowed the army to improve its flexibility not only for conventional operations but also to support low-level actions, for example, those conducted by the Special Air Service Regiment.[68]

Except for during World War II, the Northern Territory had always been a relatively minor military installation for the three services. A 1961 study revealed that the army had no plans in existence for the deployment of large numbers of units to the

The SAS on patrol. (Department of Defence, SASRLRPV)

Northern Territory during periods of tension with Australia's neighbours or during the early stages of a limited war. It only noted that in a prolonged war the build-up of forces would be similar to that which had occurred in 1942–45. Northern Territory's command duties were also fairly modest. The study identified them as being to care for the area facilities, supply local RAAF and RAN units, maintain the link in the communication chain, and provide staging accommodation for up to 350 troops in transit to South-East Asia. Thus, the army's responsibilities in the Northern Territory neither were onerous nor required a significant commitment of ARA resources.[69]

The importance of the Northern Territory in the hierarchy of the army's command structure now changed in light of *The Defence of Australia*'s recommendation to transfer a brigade to the north. In addition, as a result of the region's growing importance, it gained its own joint force headquarters—NORCOM. The army's leaders, however, were not overly enthusiastic at the prospect of sending so many troops to Darwin, and did make some efforts to satisfy the intent of the White Paper without actually having to station a brigade there. They authorised psychologial studies, which concluded that long-term service in the tropics would have a negative effect on service personnel and their dependants. Senior officers feared that the shift north would lead to a rise in discharges as experienced soldiers decided against re-enlistment, and that recruitment would suffer, since anyone joining the army could now expect to spend a considerable part of his or her career in the tropics, rather than the more salubrious south.

The army accepted the necessity of redeploying the 2nd Cavalry Regiment to Darwin, but, to avoid or delay the transfer of the entire brigade group, the army presented a number of other options.[70] The *Report of the Study into the Provision of an Appropriate Army Presence in Northern Australia* provided four:

a   permanently basing an existing or newly raised brigade in Darwin;
b   permanently basing a lesser formation than a brigade, based on 2nd Cav. Regt. and a second major combat unit, with limited arms and services support;
c   conducting regular collective training throughout the north, with the permanent basing of additional minor units in the north, in addition to NORCOM, RFSUs and 2nd Cav. Regt;
d   rotation of units through permanent bases.[71]

The army's preferred option was (c). This was because it represented the lowest cost and had the least impact on the existing force structure. The report also stated that option (c) minimised the effect upon 1st Division. In its argument, the army noted the extra expenses that the movement of a brigade group to Darwin entailed. Constructing the required infrastructure would cost an additional $795 million, whereas the training option, with only a few minor units moved to the north, would cost only $120 million. Option (c) also had significantly lower continuing annual operating costs, that is, $4.1 million versus $35.6 million for option (a).[72]

The Chiefs of Staff Committee, however, disagreed with the report's findings. While they accepted that in the short term it might prove necessary to rely upon option (c), the committee was unwilling to accept this as a permanent solution. Instead, it noted that this suggestion would not meet the strategic intentions of the government's plan. The committee then recommended that the army undertake a further study into how it would fulfil the requirement of substantially increasing its presence in the north. The Chiefs of Staff Committee also requested that the army draw up a plan, on a priority basis, outlining the infrastructure development a brigade group would require to support its operations in northern Australia.[73]

Unable to persuade the Chiefs of Staff Committee, the army now had little choice but to make plans for the transfer of 1st Brigade to Darwin. In May 1990, the army's establishment in Darwin consisted of Headquarters 7th Military District and Headquarters Land Component NORCOM. Both formations had a total establishment of

124 ARA and 71 reserve personnel. In addition, the region supported NORFORCE, the regional force surveillance unit that was responsible for patrolling the Northern Territory and the Kimberley region of Western Australia. Now the army was to commit a significant amount of its combat and logistical resources to the defence in depth of Australia.[74] Table 8.1 outlines the incremental movement of 1st Brigade to Darwin, and the establishment of the required support units, as planned in mid 1993. While

Table 8.1 *Movement plan for the increased army presence in northern Australia, 1991–92 to 2000–01*[75]

Fiscal year	Units moving to the north	Approximate ARA numbers	Progressive total
91–92	7th Log. Coy	38	47
	DSU NA (ACS elm.)	1	
	HQ LCN	8	
92–93	2nd Cav. Regt	410	490
	7th Log. Coy	33	
93–94	1st Armd Regt (–)	26	573
	7th Log. Coy/1st BASB (fwd)	42	
	7th Training Group	5	
	HQ 1st Bde (fwd)/HQ LCN	6	
	7th Int. Coy	4	
94–95	2nd Cav. Regt	52	782
	161st Recce. Sqn	107	
	1st BASB (fwd)/7th log. Coy	50	
95–96	2nd Cav. Regt	44	1,062
	1st Armd Regt (–)	204	
	DSU NA (ACS elm.)	2	
	104th Sig. Sqn	30	
96–97	HQ 1st Bde	30	1,122
	104th Sig. Sqn	30	
97–98	HQ 1st Bde	25	1,327
	104th Sig. Sqn	34	
	1st BASB (7th Log. Coy)	146	
98–99	5/7 RAR (Mechanised)	540	1,867
99–00	Combat Engr Regt	220	2,087
00–01	103rd Medium Bty	135	2,222
	Total		*2,222*

there were some modifications to this schedule, by late 2000 all of 1st Brigade had completed the move to Darwin.

The movement of additional combat elements to the north has had an obvious effect on the distribution of the army. Traditionally, the army had based most of its units in the Commonwealth's most densely populated region, the coastal crescent from Brisbane to Adelaide. However, in 2001 a regular soldier must expect to spend a significant part of his or her career in the far north of the country. Table 8.2 outlines the gradual change in the concentration of the army's combat elements as a result of the move north.

Table 8.2 confirms that as 1st Brigade moved to Darwin and the army's establishment contracted, the percentage of combat troops based in the north has soared. In 1991, only 22 per cent of the ARA's fighting troops were in the tropics, but by the turn of the century the army projected that the figure would rise to 60 per cent. The percentage of reservists in the north has also increased, but much more modestly, from 12 per cent to 15.7 per cent.

Table 8.2 Projected share of combat force soldiers in the north of Australia, 1991–92 to 2000–01[76]

Year	ARA northern based	ARA total force	Reserve northern based	Reserve total force
1991–92	3,173	14,440	2,789	23,000
1996–97	4,741	12,210	3,271	21,500
2000–01	6,615	11,110	3,302	21,000

While Land Command managed the move northwards of a major share of its organisation, Logistic Command also began a review of its own structure. The objective was to achieve savings through the elimination of administrative overhead, and improve efficiency by the consolidation of operations, especially at the level of base support. In fact, such a reform was overdue, because the Australian Support Area contained an overabundance of small headquarters, numerous minor units, and an excess of manpower. In 1988, Logistic Command began to raise composite logistical battalions and companies through the amalgamation of units under its control. For example, it formed the Puckapunyal Logistic Battalion by merging the Puckapunyal Movement and Transport Unit, 331st Supply Company, and the Puckapunyal Workshops Company into a single entity. Further to the north, the Albury Transport Unit, 31st Supply Battalion, and Albury Base Workshop Battalion joined to form the Bandiana Logistic Group. With a smaller order of battle, Logistic Command no longer needed as many intermediate headquarters to oversee its units. For example, it had supported a network of headquarters movement and transport staffs, one in each military district, but had disbanded them by 1990.

By 1990, Logistic Command had lowered the number of units under its command from 55 to 27 and reduced its establishment by approximately 1,400 service personnel. Besides freeing up soldiers for other tasks, the formation of these units had another important benefit. Composite logistic units were not single corps structures but contained members from all the support services. The establishment of the Puckapunyal Logistic Battalion included assets of the Royal Australian Corps of Transport, Royal Australian Army Ordnance Corps, and the Royal Australian Electrical and Mechanical Engineers. By cutting across corps boundaries, Logistic Command hoped to build a force that addressed problems of support from the perspective of logisticians rather than the narrow perspective of a single culture. Table 8.3 outlines Logistic Command's order of battle after the formation of composite units.[77]

Although *The Defence of Australia* did not have a major effect on the army's field force order of battle, it did cause military planners to rethink how they would organise it into operational packages. The army continued to maintain its formations according to the traditional designation of divisions and brigades, but now superimposed upon this structure mission responsibilities that allocated the units to different categories and levels of readiness. By 1989, the army had identified six force element groups that served to divide the combat forces into distinct roles. They were:

- a Land Headquarters, which was responsible for command and control of units at the operational level, including NORCOM
- the Ready Deployment Force, which contained those elements the army required for contingencies that emerged suddenly. Within this force element group were the Operational Deployment Force, Regional Force Surveillance Units, and Logistical Support Force
- a Ready Deployment Force Augmentation, which was designed to provide additional capabilities that might be required by the Ready Deployment Force
- a Manoeuvre Force, drawn primarily from 1st Division, which was designed to assist the Ready Deployment Force, if required
- a Follow-on Force, which was based on 2nd Division and would deploy after 1st Division in case of escalation
- a Logistic Force Group, which was meant to support deployed forces from outside the area of operations.[78]

Table 8.3 Logistic Command order of battle, 1991[79]

Location	Unit
Melbourne, Victoria	HQ Logistic Command
1st Military District	Ashgrove Log. Coy
	Townsville Log. Coy
	Brisbane Log. Bn
	1st Movement Control Unit
	Wallangarra Sup. Coy
	Spt. Area Wksp Bn
	Oakey Wksp Bn
2nd Military District	Moorebank Log. Gp
	Bogan Gate Sup. Coy
	Myambat Sup. Coy
	Marrangaroo Sup. Coy
	Randwick Sup. Coy
	Sydney Wksp Coy
	Singleton Log. Coy
	ACT Wksp Pl.
3rd Military District	Bandiana Log. Gp
	Broadmeadows Log. Bn
	Puckapunyal Log. Bn
	P&EE Graytown
	3rd Movement Control Unit
4th Military District	Adelaide Log. Bn
	P&EE Port Wakefield
	4th Movement Control Unit
5th Military District	Perth Log. Bn
	5th Movement Control Unit
6th Military District	Hobart Log. Coy
	6th Movement Control Unit

By 1991, the army had further refined the force element groups system and identified roles for surveillance and protective forces. The surveillance forces were the regional force surveillance units that were formally classified as part of the ready deployment force. The protective forces contained the reserve elements that were responsible for the defence of installations.

The army also assigned to each force element group a level of preparedness that corresponded with the force's readiness. In a sense, the preparedness level served as an indicator of the force element group's place on the army's mobilisation schedule. Low-preparedness units required at least six months to achieve deployment capability, and their availability was, therefore, predicated on the government having received sufficient warning of an escalation in the threat environment. Table 8.4 outlines the strength of the force element groups and their level of readiness. Table 8.4 also demonstrates that the army remained considerably below its approved establishment and was, in fact, only at 84 per cent of strength.

Table 8.4 Force element groups: levels of personnel and preparedness, 1990–91[80]

Force element group	Authorised establishment	Actual establishment	Preparedness level
Command and control	1,519	1,206	High
Ready deployment force	4,040	3,721	High
RDF augmentation	579	383	Medium
Surveillance forces	1,549	1,512	High
Manoeuvre forces	11,428	9,912	Medium
Follow-on forces	6,021	5,071	Low
Protective forces	9,418	7,601	Low
Logistics forces	3,335	2,790	Low to medium
Total	*37,889*	*32,196*	

Defence efficiency

For most of the 1990s, the objectives the government assigned to the ADF remained similar to the ones that *The Defence of Australia*, the 1976 White Paper, and even the 1971 *Strategic Basis* Paper, had established. Lieutenant-General John Coates, a former CGS, has observed that the government of Paul Keating carried forward the policies of his predecessors with remarkable consistency.[81] Until nearly the end of this period, the government's interpretive framework still rested on the idea of self-reliance, continental defence, jointness, and the absence of a threat for the foreseeable future. In addition, Australia's treaty with the United States remained a critical element of defence policy.

Only in the decade's final years did the nation's security policy change. In 1997, the Howard Government released two White Papers concerned with strategic policy, *Australia's Strategic Policy* from the Department of Defence, and *In the National*

Interest from the Department of Foreign Affairs and Trade.[82] While these reviews affirmed the importance of the defence of the Australian mainland, they also sought a broader vision and advocated a greater capability for the Commonwealth's armed forces in the region. Instead of a narrow continental-based interpretation of defence needs, the White Papers believed that it was necessary for Australia to adopt a more outward-looking maritime strategy, which fostered greater connections between the nation's foreign and defence policies. In addition, these reviews recognised the importance of overseas peace-keeping operations, and saw a continuing need for this type of deployment. The shift in policy represented neither a return to forward defence nor a downgrade of the importance of the defence of Australian mainland. Rather, it added a new responsibility that increased the ADF's planning priority for regional intervention. The government's 1997 adoption of a maritime-based strategy meant that after 25 years of continental defence the army would have to address a new strategic concept and define new roles for the force.

The 1990s were a tumultuous time for those responsible for the organisation of the army. Ironically, this upheaval was not a result of the collapse of the Soviet Union, the ending of the Cold War, or even Australia's 1997 shift in strategic direction. Rather, the single greatest factor in the shaping of the army and the ADF during the decade was the fiscal imperative of Treasury. While monetary concerns have always been a factor in military funding, especially in a democracy during peacetime, in Australia it has not been since the interwar period that Treasury concerns have wielded such influence over the organisation of the Australian Army. The decade's theme was neither military effectiveness nor even strategic capability. Instead, it was the efficiency with which the armed forces provide their capabilities. Moreover, the decade's governments were reluctant to sanction greater overall expenditure, even for new programs or capital purchases. In effect, recent government fiscal policy has required the ADF to provide for government-sanctioned capability enhancements, largely through the cannibalisation of existing resources instead of through supplemental appropriations. There is little doubt that there was waste and opportunity for the redirection of assets in the army of 1990. However, the quest for efficiency within defence no longer had a basis in strategic realities, but instead became a governmental mantra-like response to current problems and an automatic solution for future expenditure requirements.

In *The Defence of Australia*, the government accepted the need to modernise the equipment of the armed forces, both to replace worn-out systems and to maintain a technological edge over the Commonwealth's neighbours. Force modernisation required the government to commit to a number of expensive capital initiatives, including the over-the-horizon radar project, the RAN's submarine and frigate programs, the update of the RAAF's F-111s, the purchase of helicopters, and the re-equipment of the army with modern vehicles. In addition, the expansion of HMAS *Stirling* on the west coast of Australia, the construction of new airfields for the RAAF in the north, and the infrastructure development associated with the movement of 1st Brigade to Darwin added further to Defence's capital expenditure. The ADF's acquisition programs, as anticipated in 1987, required the defence budget to increase by 3 per cent per year in real terms, if there were to be no effect on other areas of the armed forces. Unfortunately, between 1987 and 1992 the defence estimate experienced no real growth. Furthermore, a report prepared in 1991 did not expect the situation to change, and concluded that the army would have to make do with little or zero growth in its budget for the foreseeable future. This, in fact, is precisely what happened. In fiscal year 1992–93 the Commonwealth allocated approximately 2.4 per cent of the nation's Gross Domestic Product to defence. Within a few years, the rate had declined to 1.9 per cent, and has remained below 2 per cent ever since.[83]

Although the bulk of the capital improvements that triggered the fiscal crisis belonged to RAN, and to a lesser extent RAAF, it was the army that bore the brunt of the necessary cutbacks. Partially, this was because the navy and the air force had been able to define for themselves more obvious roles in continental and maritime defence than the army, but differences in the nature of the services' structures were also a factor. Armies are labour-intensive institutions, whereas the other services have more inflexible personnel levels because of their dependence on expensive weapons platforms. *The Defence of Australia* called for an increase in RAN and RAAF capability that necessitated the retention, refurbishment, or expansion of the number of ships and planes they maintained. In the army, however, units of people was the critical factor. Therefore, for the army the first efficiency review of the decade, the 1991 Force Structure Review, was an exercise in achieving economies through reorganisation in order to create a force that possessed the same degree of combat efficiency but with a smaller establishment and at a lower cost.[84]

As a result of the 1991 Force Structure Review, the Department of Defence had to shed nearly 10,500 uniform and almost 4,000 civilian positions. Of this, the army's share was 5,220 military personnel from its regular establishment. Robert Ray, the Minister for Defence, expected the army to find the required savings by reducing the number of personnel employed in its headquarters and base support functions. To offset some of the effect from these losses, the army created a new reserve scheme called the Ready Reserves. Its purpose was to provide the army's combat force with a substantial body of reasonably well-trained part-time soldiers, but at a cost considerably less than that required to prepare a similar number of regulars.

In addition to personnel redundancies, the government wanted the armed forces to find further savings by making use of the newly developed Commercial Support Program. A.K. Wrigley had proposed this idea in his recent report, *The Defence Force and the Community: A Partnership in Australia's Defence*. Wrigley suggested that the ADF could improve its fiscal accountability by transferring much of its administrative and maintenance tasks to the private sector, when a contractor could provide the same capability at a lower cost. While allowing the armed forces to transfer responsibility of non-core functions to cheaper operators, Wrigley believed the scheme would have a further benefit by broadening Defence's support base within the civilian community. The final area that the three services were to explore was the reorganisation of those functions, which they all currently provided, on a joint, single ADF, basis.[85]

In order to preserve the force's combat capability, the army decided to direct the majority of its cuts at its logistic and support areas. Despite this, Force Structure Review requirements still mandated a reduction in Land Command's authorised establishment of regular soldiers from 13,319 to 11,110. To offset these losses, Lieutenant-General John Coates, the CGS, set the recruitment goal for the new Ready Reserve scheme at 3,200 part-time soldiers. When the Ready Reserve figures are added to that of the regulars in Land Command, the size of the army's operational force actually increased. The establishment of the rest of the reserves, now termed the General Reserve, remained approximately the same, and contributed a further 22,000 part-time troops to land command. The army subsequently lowered the General Reserve establishment to 21,400.[86] Table 8.5 (p. 350) outlines the distribution of personnel in Land Command after the full implementation of the Force Structure Review.

After the Force Structure Review reorganisation, the army had two ARA brigades, with a total of four battalions; one Ready Reserve brigade with three battalions; and seven General Reserve brigades, with a total of 14 battalions. The ARA retained its parachute capability in 3 RAR, and 5/7 RAR continued as a mechanised unit. The Logistic Support Group commanded a variety of engineering, supply, transport, medical, provost, and other support units. Its purpose was either to augment the logistic capability of support units already attached to a force element group or to provide force-level support during a deployment.

In addition, the army reconfigured Headquarters 1st Division into a deployable joint force headquarters. In this role, it could serve either as a headquarters for controlling operations offshore or as a supplement to Headquarters Army Component

Table 8.5 Planned distribution of personnel in Land Command after implementation of Force Structure Review[87]

Formation	ARA	General reserve	Ready reserve	Total
Surveillance forces	104	1,210	–	1,314
Ready force troops	1,108	562	–	1,670
Ready deployment force (3rd Bde)	3,728	19	–	3,747
Darwin Bde (1st Bde)	2,148	177	63	2,388
Ready Reserve Bde (6th Bde)	707	–	3,012	3,719
HQ 2nd Div. and Div. Troops	80	1,110	–	1,190
5th Bde	81	2,195	–	2,276
8th Bde	89	2,019	–	2,108
4th Bde	99	2,188	–	2,287
7th Bde	114	2,648	–	2,762
11th Bde	87	1,984	–	2,071
9th Bde	108	2,367	–	2,475
13th Bde	103	2,185	–	2,288
Logistic Support Group	696	66	–	762
Force troops	1,803	3,355	125	5,283
CH47 increment	55	–	–	55
Total	11,110	22,085	3,200	36,395

NORCOM as required. The army did retain Headquarters 2nd Division, but limited its function to the development of the skills and doctrine required for conventional divisional operations. Headquarters 3rd Division in Melbourne was disbanded, bringing to an end the army's longest-serving division. Coates selected 6th Brigade in Brisbane, which had been an ARA formation, for conversion into the Ready Reserve brigade.[88]

For the first time since World War I, the Australian Army no longer had a division on its establishment. Headquarters 2nd Division remained on the order of battle, but was purely a planning staff and made no pretence of being a field formation. The army's highest operational headquarters was now the brigade. While this represented a break with tradition, it also was a long-overdue recognition that divisions had no place in the current strategic requirement. Divisions were a legacy of the Cold War and the expansion-base army. The vastness of Australia's north required a smaller structure as well as formations capable of independent operations. On the basis of currently authorised establishments, projected area of operations, and national strategic requirements, the brigade was an improvement over the more unwieldy division. Table 8.6 outlines Land Command's order of battle as a result of the Force Structure Review.

Table 8.6 Land Command order of battle, June 1991[89]

Formation	Units
Surveillance Forces	NORFORCE
	Pilbara Regt
	51st FNQR Regt
Ready Force Troops	Ready Force HQ
	131st Div. Loc. Bty
	1st Signal Regt plus Wksp
	1st Div. Int. Coy
	5th Avn Regt plus Wksp
	11th MC Gp
	1st MP Coy
Ready Deployment Force Bde	HQ 3rd Brigade
	103rd Sig. Sqn
	B Sqn 3rd/4th Cav. Regt
	1 RAR
	2/4 RAR
	3 RAR
	4th Fd Regt
	3rd Cbt Engr Regt plus Wksp
	162nd Recce. Sqn plus Wksp
	3rd BASB
Darwin Brigade	HQ LCN
	HQ 1st Bde
	104th Sig. Sqn
	1st Armd Regt (−)
	2nd Cav. Regt
	5/7 RAR
	103rd Mdm Bty
	1st Cbt Engr Regt
	161st Recce. Sqn plus Wksp
	7th Int. Coy
	1 BASB
Ready Reserve Brigade	HQ 6th Bde
	139th Sig. Sqn
	A Sqn 4th Cav. Regt
	6 RAR
	8/9 RAR
	49 RQR
	1st Fd Regt

Formation	Units
	6th Cbt Engr Regt
	6th BASB
HQ 2nd Division and Div. Troops	HQ 2nd Div.
	8th Sig. Regt
	2nd Div. Int. Coy
	RACT Pipes and Drums
5th Brigade	HQ 5th Bde
	1/19 RNSWR
	4/3 RNSWR
	23rd Fd Regt
	5th Fd Sqn
	BASB (to be raised)
8th Brigade	HQ 8th Bde
	2/17 RNSWR
	41 RNSWR
	7th Fd Regt
	14th Fd Sqn
	BASB (to be raised)
4th Brigade	HQ 4th Bde
	108th Sig. Sqn
	5/6 RVR
	8/7 RVR
	2nd/10th Mdm Regt
	10th Fd Sqn
	BASB (to be raised)
7th Brigade	HQ 7th Bde
	140th Sig. Sqn
	A Sqn. 2nd/14th QMI
	9 RQR
	25 RQR
	5th Fd Regt
	11th Fd Sqn
	BASB (to be raised)
11th Brigade	HQ 11th Bde
	141st Sig. Sqn
	31 RQR
	42 RQR
	11th Fd Regt
	35th Fd Sqn
	BASB (to be raised)

Formation	Units
9th Brigade	HQ 9th Bde
	144th Sig. Sqn
	A Sqn 3rd/9th SAMR
	10/27 RSAR
	12/40 RTR
	6th/13th Fd Regt
	3rd Fd Sqn
	BASB (to be raised)
13th Brigade	HQ 13th Bde
	109th Sig. Sqn
	A Sqn 10th LH
	11/28 RWAR
	16 RWAR
	3rd Fd Regt
	13th Fd Sqn
	BASB (to be raised)
Logistic Support Group (major units)	HQ 1st LSG
	LSG Sig. Sqn
	17th Const. Sqn plus Wksp
	26th Tpt Sqn
	1st Fd Hosp.
	2nd Fd Sup. Bn
Force troops (major units)	LHQ
	4th/19th PWLH
	1st/15th RNSWL
	7th Sig. Regt
	1st Avn Regt plus Wksp
	173rd Gen. Spt Sqn plus Wksp
	16th AD Regt
	21st Const. Sqn plus Wksp
	21st Const. Regt
	22nd Const. Regt
	7th Engr Spt Regt
	2nd Fd Hosp.
	3rd Fwd Gen. Hosp.
	10th Terminal Regt
	9th Tpt Regt
	1st Petrol Coy
	3rd Recovery Coy

One of the key components of the Force Structure Review was the Ready Reserve program. This scheme was a balanced attempt to improve the readiness of the army while avoiding the great expense of more regular personnel. The army estimated that a Ready Reserve soldier cost only 42 per cent as much as a regular. The Ready Reserve's service obligation was one year's full-time duty followed by five years' part-time duty, consisting of 50 days per year, including two periods of two weeks' continuous service. Because of the extent of this training, Coates believed that a ready reservist formation could serve either as an initial expansion or as a rotation force for the ARA. If the scale of operations required additional troops, they would come from the General Reserve brigades. Not only were Ready Reserve training requirements considerably greater than those incurred by the General Reserve but they were also much more than the training undertaken by the ARA's previous expansion force, the Regular Army Emergency Reserve. Therefore, the program promised to provide Land Command with a body of troops who had a significantly greater degree of preparation than was typical of Australian reserve organisations. Strengthening the Ready Reserve's experience base was the fact that it was also open to regular soldiers who opted not to re-enlist in the ARA but who wanted to retain an association with the army on a part-time basis. Women could also join the Ready Reserve, and enjoyed the same opportunities that the Department of Defence accorded to full-time service personnel. Most ready reservists served in 6th Brigade, but 1st Armoured Regiment and 16th Air Defence Regiment also had a few on their establishments. Although the Ready Reserve program did not fully achieve its recruitment objectives, its contribution to the army's capabilities was potentially significant, and a 1995 review believed the experiment to be a success.

However, the Ready Reserve concept did not prove durable. After the 1996 election, the Howard Government summarily terminated the scheme. In effect, the army not only gave up the regulars from the combat arms called for in the 1991 Force Structure Review reduction but now also lost the compensatory reserve organisation. This was a double blow, which would have to be made up from other areas of the organisation.[90]

In order to sustain the capability of the combat arms, Coates and his successor, Lieutenant-General J.C. Grey, maintained the pressure on the army's support elements. Under their tenure, not only did the rationalisation of Logistic Command continue but Land Command also began to address the structure of the support forces under its control, in a further effort to shift resources to the fighting units. The first area to come under review was the brigade support area, also known as formation level support. In a sense, the situation of the army's formation level support was similar to that which used to exist in Logistic Command. Land Command contained myriad small support units, which provided for a brigade's supply, transport, repair, and medical requirements. Each of these units had its own headquarters, administrative staff, and equipment establishment. As with Logistic Command, therefore, Land Command's formation level support system contained an excessive amount of overhead, which the army could no longer tolerate under the pressure of the Force Structure Review. The solution was a reorganisation program that was also similar to that implemented by Logistic Command; the army would raise composite support units for Land Command's formation-level support area.

In 1991, Coates authorised the trial of an experimental unit called a brigade administrative support battalion. The headquarters of this unit functioned as an umbrella under which Land Command could attach various units tailored to the support requirements of the parent brigade. Thus, following the army's program of increasing its flexibility, the brigade administrative support battalion controlled a variety of elements capable of performing the entire range of support tasks. Obviously, the unit was not corps specific, but rather brought together under one agency a number of logistic functions. In July 1991, the army formed the trial unit in 3rd Brigade and designated it 3rd Brigade Administrative Support Battalion. It was an amalgamation of 9th Transport Squadron, 102nd Field Workshop, 3rd Field Supply Company, 2nd Field Ambulance, and 16th Field Dental Unit. The trial was deemed a success, and soon the army would raise a brigade administrative support battalion for each of its brigades. Table 8.7 (p. 356) outlines the units that Land Command amalgamated to raise brigade administrative support battalions.

The army subsequently modified several brigade administrative support battalions in order to create what it called a combat service support battalion. However, there was no difference in the tasks this variation performed, and the army only undertook the redesignation in order to associate the combat service support battalion name with a task force rather than a brigade. The 1st Combat Service Support Battalion was raised by the renaming of 1st Brigade Administrative Support Battalion, and 7th Combat Service Support Battalion was created by an amalgamation of the 6th and 7th Brigade Administrative Support Battalions.[91]

The concept of a formation-level composite logistic unit was not new, as the army had first studied the idea in 1980. Ultimately, however, it took the financial pressure of the Force Structure Review to serve as the catalyst for their raising. The army did not bother to conduct an exhaustive trial of 3rd Brigade Administrative Support Battalion, as it was essential that Land Command do something quickly in order to meet its Force Structure Review target. The creation of composite logistic units at the

Table 8.7 *Raising of brigade administrative support battalions*[92]

Brigade administrative support battalion	Amalgamated units
1st BASB (1st Brigade)	7th Log. Bn, 5th Tpt Sqn, 11th Fd Amb., 35th Fd Dent. Unit, 1st Fd Sup. Coy, 101st Fd Wksp, LCM8 det., Tk Tpt det.
3rd BASB (3rd Brigade)	5th Tpt Sqn, 11th Fd Amb., 33rd Fd Dent. Unit, 6th Fd Sup. Coy, 106th Fd Wksp
4th BASB (4th Brigade)	7th Tpt Sqn, 6th Fd Amb., 3rd Fd Dent. Unit, 4th Fd Sup. Coy, 105th Fd Wksp
5th BASB (5th Brigade)	3rd Tpt Sqn, 5th Fd Amb., 2nd Fd Dent. Unit, 5th Fd Sup. Coy, 103rd Fd Wksp
6th BASB (6th Brigade)	5th Tpt Sqn, 11th Fd Amb., 33rd Fd Dent. Unit, 6th Fd Sup. Coy, 106th Fd Wksp
7th BASB (7th Brigade)	2nd Tpt Sqn, 10th Fd Amb., 1st Fd Dent. Unit, 101st Fd Sup. Coy, 104th Fd Wksp
8th BASB (8th Brigade)	16th Tpt Sqn, 1st Fd Amb., 6th Fd Dent. Unit, 8th Fd Sup. Coy, 111th Fd Wksp
9th BASB (9th Brigade)	8th Tpt Sqn, 3rd Fd Amb., 4th Fd Dent. Unit, 9th Fd Sup. Coy, 107th Fd Wksp
11th BASB (11th Brigade)	4th Tpt Sqn, 9th Fd Amb., 15th Fd Dent. Unit, 108th Fd Wksp
13th BASB (13th Brigade)	10th Tpt Sqn, 7th Fd Amb., 5th Fd Dent. Unit, 13th Fd Sup. Coy, 113th Fd Wksp

formation level allowed the army to consolidate a host of minor support units into nine composite battalions. The reduction in administrative requirements thereby freed up positions that Army Office could reallocate to combat units. While principally a result of fiscal necessity, the brigade administrative support battalions did provide an operational benefit besides the streamlining of a formation's support area. In the past, a brigade's rear zone typically contained a number of task-specific units, each with its own headquarters and chain of command. The range of units made it difficult for the brigade headquarters to control and secure its own rear area. Under the new arrangement, the headquarters of a brigade administrative support battalion became responsible for the control of its parent brigade's support area. This established a clear chain of command in the support area, and released the brigade commander and staff to focus on operational matters.

With the rationalisation of its formation support area under way, Land Command also began to address the structure of the logistic units under its command that operated further back in the force support area. Continued pressure on personnel numbers and resources made the reorganisation of this zone inevitable, as the priority was to maintain the strength of the army's combat arm. Consequently, in December 1992, Land Command disbanded 1st Air Transport Support Regiment, grouping its surviving elements into 176th Air Dispatch Squadron. It then reorganised 10th Terminal Regiment and disbanded two of its squadrons. These steps helped Land Command to meet its Force Structure Review cutbacks, while also retaining the force's important air dispatch and water transport capabilities, albeit on a reduced scale.[93]

More dramatic developments soon followed this relatively modest reorganisation of the air and water transport regiments, leading to the extension of the composite logistic concept to the entire force support area. Throughout the 1990s pressure on the army was relentless, and the force continued to shed personnel. In 1995, Land Command began to consider the raising of a composite logistic battalion for its force support area, which it called a force support battalion, but it was not until 1998 that further strain on personnel establishments forced the issue. As a result, the army raised three force support battalions. The first formed was 10th Force Support Battalion, which came about through an amalgamation of 2nd Field Logistic Battalion and 1st Division Postal Unit with the remains of 10th Terminal Regiment. Land Command then redesignated 9th Transport Regiment as 9th Force Support Battalion and consolidated under its command a diverse selection of units including 15th and 26th Transport Squadrons; Ship Army Detachments Kanimbla, Manoora, and Tobruk; 176th Air Dispatch Squadron; 4th Military Police Company; 1st Financial Services Unit; and the Deployed Forces Support Unit. The army also formed 2nd Force Support Battalion as a reserve unit, and incorporated into it 44th Transport Squadron, 10th Field Ambulance, 111th Combat Support Platoon, Logistical Support Force Workshop, and 46th Military Police Platoon. To reflect the changing terminology and to better identify its role in force support, Headquarters Logistic Support Group became Headquarters Logistic Support Force.[94]

The rationalisation of the support elements reached the point at which the army even considered amalgamating its three logistic corps into a single entity. The British had recently done this with the raising of the Royal Logistic Corps. In 1993, Brigadier Paul O'Sullivan presented a report that advanced the benefits of a similar move by the Australian Army. Since composite units already perform most logistic functions, or would do so within a few years, there were compelling reasons to link the three affected corps—the Royal Australian Corps of Transport, Royal Australian Army Ordnance Corps, and Royal Australian Electrical and Mechanical Engineers—into a single institution. However, Grey, the CGS, rejected this reform for two reasons. First, he believed that the army was already in the midst of too many changes, and feared the effect on morale of a corps-level consolidation. Second, he thought that the amalgamation of the logistic corps would lead to demands for a similar economy from the combat corps. As a result the logistic corps remained independent.[95]

Despite the amalgamations and personnel reductions, the savings obtained proved inadequate. An internal report anticipated shortfalls in the army's budget, and warned of underfunding in salary and operating costs. It also projected rising operating and maintenance costs as the force received new vehicles, helicopters, and night vision devices, for which the Department of Defence had made no provision. Another analysis noted that because of the limitations of the budget, the army was unable to meet its training requirements. Moreover, future projections remained grim, as the Department of Defence would have to find resources for the replacement of major weapons platforms early in the next century. This included a new tank for the army, strike aircraft and a new trainer for the RAAF, and a new class of patrol boats for the RAN.[96]

In 1994, the Keating Government released a new White Paper called *Defending Australia*. While it reaffirmed the army's role in the defence of northern Australia, it also outlined the future direction of the Department of Defence. The three services, and the civilian areas of the Department of Defence, would have to continue to maximise combat effectiveness by reducing the number of service personnel involved in administrative and support functions. The White Paper emphasised the need for the Defence Group to act as 'one organisation' by eliminating any duplication of function that existed in the three service, as well as civilian, structures. The goal was for the Department of Defence to seek further efficiencies from within its existing structure in order to increase the fighting power of the ADF, including the strengthening of the army's combat arms. For the army, the expectation was further initiatives in jointness, greater commercialisation of logistic functions, relentless downward drift in personnel numbers, and an ongoing rationalisation of its order of battle as it reallocated resources from logistical elements to combat units.[97]

The consequences of this course of action, however, were potentially serious. As the army hollowed out its logistic arms, it lessened its ability to sustain itself on operations, a dangerous development in an era in which the force might not have the recourse of an ally's assistance. In effect, the government was following a policy that enhanced the fighting power of the army but only at the expense of its ability to sustain itself. This practice was creating an army that focused all its effort on the initial stage of an operation, but with the result that a prolonged or widespread campaign would be extremely challenging. *Defending Australia* explained that the government regarded the development of the logistic arms, beyond the minimal level, as a drain on the force's combat capability, and that the infantry and the other combat arms had first priority. The government was unwilling to provide sufficient resources to enhance both branches of the army. This trend has not abated. A recent statement by the Department of Defence set for the army the objective of having 65 per cent of its regular personnel in the combat force. This is an astonishingly high objective for a modern, technology-dependent army.[98]

After its election, the Howard Government renewed the call for economy from within the Defence Group. In October 1996, Ian McLachlan, the Minister for Defence, appointed a committee to investigate the Department of Defence once again, with the objective of securing major new savings. The committee submitted its report, which was to be known as the Defence Efficiency Review, early the following year.[99]

The emphasis of the review was on the management of defence, including determining whether the organisation's administrative and financial procedures were of the highest effectiveness. The Defence Efficiency Review also considered duplication of functions between the armed forces and advised on the possibility of their merger into a single program. For example, it recommended the establishment of a single agency to administer property, whereas till then each service had maintained its own property management operation. Logistic support and equipment maintenance was another area in which the review believed Defence could achieve substantial economies through greater coordination and joint management. In addition, the review required the armed forces to examine all of their functions in order to distinguish between core and non-core operations. The services were then to submit non-core tasks to tender in order to find contractors who were able to provide the service more cheaply. The ultimate goal was the privatisation of all defence functions for which there existed a less expensive contractor. The Defence Efficiency Review, therefore, was an intensification of Wrigley's Commercial Support Program.

In one sense, the objective of the Defence Efficiency Review was to treat the armed forces as businesses that were accountable to shareholders—the citizens of Australia—and apply commercial practices and techniques to the act of waging war. While this was not a new objective, its development under the Howard Government was an exacerbation and regimentation of policies presented in previous efficiency reviews. In fact, the Defence Efficiency Review, with its requirement of privatising as much of the defence establishment as possible, placed the highest value on the principles of economic rationalisation rather than operational concerns.

Another indication of the creeping redefinition of the Department of Defence as a commercial, rather than military, organisation is found in the language of its annual reports. Since the start of the decade, the defence report has identified the services as programs and their operations as subprograms and referred to the chiefs of services as program managers. Military functions and language have disappeared from view.

The Defence Efficiency Review's developers projected that the implementation of their findings would result in an estimated savings of over $500 million as a one off, and annual savings of between nearly $800 million and $1,000 million per year. However, much of these savings would come about through personnel reductions. Defence would have to lose approximately 4,700 military personnel and 3,100 civilians. In addition, the review anticipated a further redundancy of 7,000 military and 5,900 civilian personnel if the services achieved their projected privatisation objectives.[100] The army had already lost approximately 6,000 personnel as a result of the Force Structure Review. By mid 1994 the worst of these redundancies appeared to be over and the force's establishment enjoyed a degree of stability for a few years. However, the implementation of the Defence Efficiency Review's recommendations renewed the army's downward spiral. Table 8.8 illustrates the effect of these reviews on the army's strength throughout the 1990s. From a 1991 peak of 57,628, the army declined to a strength of just 45,865 at the decade's end. This represented a loss of 11,763 personnel, of whom 7,237 were regular and 4,526 reserve soldiers.

Table 8.8 Army personnel levels, 1990s[101]

Year	Regular establishment	General Reserve establishment	Ready Reserve establishment	Total
1990	30,333	25,136		55,469
1991	31,143	26,485		57,628
1992	30,157	25,104	973	56,234
1993	28,054	23,956	2,124	54,134
1994	26,347	22,842	2,462	51,651
1996	25,964	22,274	3,116	51,354
1997	25,885	24,880		50,765
1998	24,940	24,837		49,777
1999	23,906	21,959		45,865

In 1999, the army had yet to feel the full effect of the Defence Efficiency Review, although it had implemented a number of changes. Logistic Command was particularly hard hit, and had to close down or consolidate units in order to achieve the required economies. Eventually, the army lost Logistic Command in its entirety. In its place, Defence raised a new joint Support Command Australia, under which it grouped the logistical organisations of the three services. Formed on 1 July 1997, its purpose was to provide logistics on a joint basis across the whole of the ADF. The commander of Support Command Australia reported directly to the CDF, although the position was responsive to each service chief. Support Command Army, the successor to the army's Logistic Command, reported directly to the Commander Support Australia and was, therefore, outside the army's direct chain of command. Support Commander Navy and Support Commander Air Force were the terms given to the components of the other services which were under Support Command Australia.

Although the raising of Support Command Australia was itself a major adjustment, it would soon be overtaken by further changes in the joint hierarchy of the Department of Defence. In mid 2000, Moore announced a further rationalisation of the administration of support to the three services. The result was a merger of the logistic and maintenance duties of Support Command Australia with the acquisition responsibilities of the Defence Acquisition Organisation, creating a new structure called Defence Materiel Organisation. Within the Defence Materiel Organisation, the army's support interests were represented by two areas. Supply requirements for the three services were given to the new Joint Logistics Command. Maintenance was separated from supply and is now collocated with acquisition. Each service has a separate division to coordinate its acquisition and maintenance needs. The army's is called 'Land Systems Division'. The cumulative result of all these changes to the army's logistic systems is that the force no longer has a base logistic order of battle, and these functions are now performed either on a joint basis or by private companies. In fact, the management of the force's logistics is now so far removed from the army's direct control that its location on a Department of Defence organisational chart is no longer obvious. The army's remaining logistic responsibilities are still critical, but they are limited to operational support at the unit, formation, and force levels.

Training Command also had to rationalise the army's school system, and the army's logisticians would suffer another loss with the closing of their corps-based schools. Each corps had maintained its own school. For example, the Royal Australian Corps of Transport ran the Army School of Transport, at which it provided driver, transport, and movement training. At the end of 1995, Training Command raised the

Army Logistic Training Centre in Bandiana. Into the new centre it consolidated the Army School of Transport, the Royal Australian Electrical and Mechanical Training Centre, the Royal Australian Army Ordnance Corps Centre, Army Catering School, Army College of TAFE, School of Army Health, and the Chaplaincy Centre. While the catalyst for the merger was in part financial, the move did make sense. Most of the army's logisticians now served in composite units, which provided for a multitude of support tasks instead of a narrow corps specialty. The creation of the Army Logistic Training Centre only brought the school system into alignment with what was the reality in the field.[102] After the Army Logistic Training Centre's successful establishment, Army Office extended the policy of integrating all corps training and education to the combat arms. In 1998, at Puckapunyal, it created the Combat Arms Training Centre through an amalgamation of the Schools of Armour, Artillery, Infantry, and Military Engineering.

In a related economy, a few years later, the support arms also lost their independent museums. In 1997, the army merged them into a single institution called the Army Museum, which it located next to the Army Logistic Training Centre. To improve the army's combat effectiveness, Training Command opened the Combined Arms Training and Development Centre.

One of the other objectives of the Defence Efficiency Review was to streamline the service's headquarters staffs, and Army Office had to eliminate approximately 100 positions. To reach this goal, the army opted to disband the corps directorates. Each corps had maintained a director and staff who advised army office on matters relating to their specialty, as well as overseeing the writing of doctrine and equipment specifications and the management of career development. By this time, other agencies had taken over many of the directorates' traditional functions; for example, the Directorate of Officer Career Management now oversaw posting and promotion recommendations and the Combined Arms Training and Development Centre prepared the force's doctrine. Consequently, in 1997 Army Office shut the corps directorates. In their place, the corps' senior officer would also serve as an Honorary Head of Corps, in addition to his or her other duties. During this period, the army also disbanded its headquarters military districts in order to release additional personnel from administrative duties.[103]

At the same time as the army managed its contraction, it also sought to reshape itself in order to realise greater effectiveness in its combat ability. The 1994 White Paper had called for a reassessment of the land force structure. In 1996, Lieutenant-General J.M. Sanderson presented the results of the army's study in a report called *An*

Major-General John Sanderson, CGS 1995–98. (AWM CANA89/076/03)

Australian Army for the 21st Century.[104] Army 21, as the report was known, aimed at 'examining the number and readiness of infantry units, the benefits of additional ground reconnaissance units, the balance between Regular and Reserve elements and the resource implications required for further change'.[105]

Sanderson also saw Army 21 as an opportunity to define a more significant role for the army in the nation's defence, and to correlate its organisation more closely with the probable nature of operations in the country's far north. Since the onset of the continental defence security policy, the army had struggled to find an appropriate place in the defence hierarchy. Neither the government nor the army had substantively identified the force's task, and previous reviews did little more than modify the terminology. For example, the 1994 White Paper used the phrases 'short warning conflict' and 'major conflict' in lieu of the 1987 White Paper's 'low-level conflict', 'escalated low-level conflict', and 'substantial conflict'. In fact, the ground forces typically came last in the government's priorities, as the RAN and RAAF took advantage of their ability to engage the enemy in the maritime environment to the north and secured for themselves a more prominent role. Instead of developing an offshore capability of its own, the army's function within the defence of Australia became limited to taking action after the enemy stepped ashore. Except for the guarding of installations which the other services required for operations, the army did not have a major mission, short of repelling an actual invasion.

Moreover, the army had not helped its position by its continued reliance on major formations. The situation was somewhat reminiscent of the interwar period, when the army had insisted on maintaining divisions for invasion defence when the government desired a first line component to fight raids, although the modern force's leaders never sought to undermine the nation's security agenda as their predecessors had attempted to do. On a number of occasions, the army had stressed the need to improve the flexibility of its formations, but always within the division or brigade structure. The army only abandoned the division in 1991, but its brigades still provided concentrations of firepower that were in excess of requirements for dispersed operations in the Australian outback. In effect, throughout the era of self-reliance, the army continued to favour preparation for major operations, and sustained a structure for expansion in case of a major threat.

Sanderson called for the reorganisation of the army into a highly mobile, powerful, yet self-reliant force that was capable of operating against a number of opponents over a widely dispersed battlefield. His objective was to reshape the army in order to fulfil its short-warning conflict strategic guidance rather than that of a higher-level conflict. The key element of the Army 21 idea was a radically new concept called the enhanced combat force. Instead of following the traditional corps pattern for the organisation of military forces, the enhanced combat force built its structure around five characteristics—command and control, detection, response, protection, and support. To meet the requirements of these characteristics, Army 21 saw the need for a new type of all-arms unit that would have all the required elements embedded within its organisation. The enhanced combat force would employ a task-force structure, and have under its direct command a variety of infantry, armour, artillery, engineer, and support assets, thereby creating a force that was flexible and largely self-contained. Army 21 would also minimise the division of the army into regular and reserve components by their integration throughout the enhanced combat force. This would increase the number of units capable of some degree of ready response, allowing the army to deploy forces concurrently to a number of threatened areas. In fact, all units would contain some reserve personnel. In addition, reservists would now have ongoing exposure to the army's most up-to-date equipment. Another vital feature of Army 21 was the proposed increase in the force's motorisation and mechanisation, including the purchase of light armoured vehicles, Bushranger infantry vehicles, and additional helicopters. As a result, for the first time in the army's history, units would have their own integral transportation. The army also planned to replace its air defence systems with modern mobile batteries of surface-to-air missiles. Since the task forces were to have the capability to operate in a dispersed mode, Sanderson also called for considerable improvement in the force's command, control, and intelligence systems, including the incorporation of civilian computerisation, communication, and remote-sensing technologies.[106]

In early 1997, Ian McLachlan, the Minister for Defence, issued a follow-up report to Army 21, called *Restructuring the Australian Army*, which largely reiterated Sanderson's recommendations. Curiously, however, while McLachlan confirmed the importance of the defence of Australia as the army's primary duty, his report also contained the statement that 'the Land Force must be capable of conducting offshore operations, either unilaterally or as part of a coalition. The present Land Force structure is inadequate to meet the demands of widespread concurrent operations on Australian soil or to

Australian light armoured vehicles. (Department of Defence, DARD96/0046-07)

sustain operations offshore.'[107] The implications of McLachlan's observation did not become clear until later in the year, when the government issued its new defence White Paper, *Australia's Strategic Policy 1997*.

With the publication of *Australia's Strategic Policy*, as well as the companion Department of Foreign Affairs and Trade's White Paper *In the National Interest*, the Howard Government suddenly swept away the foundation of 25 years of national security policy. This new strategic review shifted the nation's defence policy from one focused nearly exclusively on continental defence to one that saw more opportunity for the attainment of the Commonwealth's security through greater engagement with the Asia–Pacific region. The review defined three basic tasks for the ADF, 'defeating attacks on Australia, defending our regional interests, and supporting our global interests'.[108] The White Paper continued that 'preparedness levels will be determined more by the requirements of regional operations and deployment in support of global interests ... than by the needs of defeating attacks on Australia'.[109] The Commonwealth was not returning to the era of forward defence, but the Howard Government was announcing its intention to redefine national security in terms of a maritime rather than a continental concept of strategy, and signalling the possibility of Australia assuming a more assertive role in the region.

The Army 21 program was soon in tatters. Its most important principle, the need for the army to prepare for low-level, dispersed, continental contingencies in Australia's north, was suddenly invalid. Instead, *Australia's Strategic Policy* meant that the army now required a force structure that could react to a wider range of conflicts, including overseas deployments. It fell to Lieutenant-General Frank Hickling, the new Chief of Army, to make the necessary adjustments. In October 1998, he announced that the 'Army would embrace a maritime concept of strategy'.[110] After 25 years of continental defence, the army would have to shift its focus to offshore operations and learn how to project power across the sea–air gap to the north of Australia. Reflecting this change in focus, when the army issued its new doctrine manual, it described the force's primary role from the perspective of a maritime strategy.[111]

East Timor

Before the army had time to adjust fully to the Howard Government's new maritime-based strategic policy, it received its first test. After the collapse of the Suharto regime, Indonesia teetered on the brink of violent implosion. The situation in East Timor was particularly tense as the Timorese people pressed for their independence, after 24 years of occupation. In early 1999, B.J. Habibie, the new Indonesian president, agreed to allow the East Timorese to decide their own future. After an overwhelming vote for independence, Jakarta-backed militia groups commenced a campaign of violence and destruction against those who had dared to seek separation from Indonesia. The United Nations called for the restoration of peace and security to East Timor, and the Commonwealth soon found itself playing a leading role in the crisis. It became clear that outside military intervention was necessary in order to stop militia attacks. This led to the forming of the United Nations authorised peace-enforcement mission called International Force East Timor (INTERFET), to which Australia provided the majority of troops and leadership. The position of commander INTERFET fell to Major-General Peter Cosgrove. The ADF's designation for the army's participation was Operation Stabilise. While it is difficult to comment on such a recent and ongoing event, some observations can be made.

As events unfolded in Dili, the Australian Government took the precautionary step of improving the readiness of 1st and 3rd Brigades. In August, army units began to receive their warning orders, and from this point on events moved rapidly. On 20 September, soldiers from 2 RAR, SAS, and B Squadron 3rd/4th Cavalry Regiment landed at Comoro Airfield outside Dili. The next day, 3 RAR and C Squadron 2nd Cavalry Regiment came ashore at Dili harbour. The deployment of these units marked the beginning of the Australian Army's largest overseas operation since the end of the Vietnam War. At its peak, Operation Stabilise involved over 7,500 ADF personnel serving either in East Timor or in support of the deployment from the Australian base. Of this figure, the army's share was approximately 5,300 troops. After INTERFET ended in February 2000, the army continued to maintain a battalion group in East Timor, and will do so for the foreseeable future.

It is ironic that, despite the army's near-exclusive focus on continental defence from the end of the Vietnam War up to the publication of *Australia's Strategic Policy* in 1997, East Timor was essentially a ground operation. Throughout all those years, it was the RAN and the RAAF who received the greater part of the defence vote because of their presumed ability to project power over the maritime environment to Australia's north. However, when a crisis did occur, it was the army that was at the forefront of the ADF's response. Certainly, the army required the help of the RAN and RAAF to cross the air–sea gap, but INTERFET was only able to fulfil its mission because of the deployment and success of the ground troops.

This reality showed the fallacy of so much of the government's previous strategic guidance regarding the organisation of the army. The direct defence of the Commonwealth's territory must be the ADF's primary objective, but the interpretation that limited the army's role purely to continental defence inhibited the capabilities of the force and allowed the other services to starve the ground troops of resources. The army must itself share part of the blame for this situation because of the fact that its leaders were content with a close defence of Australia role rather than pushing for a more dynamic policy. All parties appear to have forgotten the fact that all previous overseas deployments of Australian military forces, with only a few minor exceptions, were ground force intensive, and that the other services played only minor roles. It is to be hoped that the critical part the army played in INTERFET's success will lead to greater integration of the army into a maritime-based defence policy and justify the provision of additional resources to the force.

Despite Operation Stabilise's success, a number of shortcomings were apparent, especially in the support and reserve areas. The various efficiency reviews of the 1990s had scaled back the depth of the army's logistic forces, leaving them with insufficient manpower and gaps in their capability. Operation Stabilise proved the short-sighted nature of this policy, and it was only by a dangerously narrow margin that the support element was able to sustain the deployment for the duration of the mission. Initially, 3rd Brigade Administrative Support Battalion provided formation-level support to the deployed force. As the operation grew in scale, the battalion's resources proved inadequate for the task, and the army had to supplement it with additional assets. As a result, 1st Combat Service Support Battalion, which was preparing to deploy as the rotation force, dispatched early to Dili part of its establishment, which it designated 1st Combat Service Support Team.

The support elements available at the force level were even more acute than those that existed at the force level. The unit responsible for formation support during Operation Stabilise was 10th Force Support Battalion. While its water-transport assets were adequate for its duties, other areas of its establishment had critical shortages, and it had to secure additional assets from its sister unit, 9th Force Support Battalion. The area in most dire need was terminal workers, which, ironically, was one of the trades most heavily cut back during the rationalisations of the 1990s. Without additional staff, cargo would inevitably build up in Dili port, impairing the efficiency of the entire line of communications. When the army reduced its terminal establishment, the expectation had been that if any shortages occurred the force could employ contractors to fill the gaps. However, what might have been good practice domestically now imperilled the operation. Unfortunately, in Dili the militia had damaged the port's cargo-handling infrastructure, and there were no commercial vendors in existence to tender for the job. The army's existing terminal troops had to do the work on their own for the foreseeable future. The logisticians avoided disaster only by supplementing the terminal ranks with a detachment of air dispatchers from 176th Air Dispatch Squadron, a unit of 9th Force Support Battalion. Air dispatchers were familiar with cargo-handling procedures because of their own work in loading transport planes. In addition to its air dispatchers, 9th Force Support Battalion also had to dispatch to East Timor a truck troop to further augment the deployment's force-level support.

The army's need to supplement the establishment of deployed support units with other assets did create an awkward situation. When 9th Force Support Battalion dispatched its drivers and air dispatchers to Dili, the battalion was already fully committed in Darwin to supporting the Australian end of Operation Stabilise's line of communication. In addition, 9th Force Support Battalion was in the midst of readying itself for deployment to East Timor in February 2000 as part of the rotation force. 1st Combat Service Support Battalion was in a similar situation. It was the formation support unit for the rotation force, but it had already dispatched part of its unit to help the deployment force. In February, 2 RAR and 3 RAR rotated home, but the lack of depth in the support ranks meant that for the logisticians there would be no rest. Having already worked hard in Darwin, 9th Force Support Battalion moved to Dili for its turn at supporting the deployment.

Making the task even harder for the logisticians was the fact that a number of nations that contributed ground troops to the operation failed to provide for their support. As the mission's leaders, this responsibility then fell to the Australian Army's already strained logistic team. For example, the 240-person Kenyan contingent arrived with virtually no integral logistic capability, and was entirely dependent on 1st Combat Service Support Team for its maintenance. In fact, the degree to which Australia provided assistance to its allies was without precedent in the army's history. Traditionally, the Australian Army was the one that relied on an ally for much of its support when overseas. In East Timor, this role was reversed, and Australia, as the largest contingent, found itself in the unique position of having to help the units of other nations. If Australia is to continue to take the lead in regional intervention, as suggested by the 1997 White Paper, then force planners must recognise when determining support arm establishments that the army may need logistic resources above its own requirements in order to help sustain junior coalition partners.

Bringing the initial deployment force up to strength was a difficult task, but not nearly as daunting as it was to find the soldiers for the rotation force. In a situation reminiscent of the personnel problems of the Korean commitment, the army had to be imaginative in securing the assistance of recently discharged soldiers or in inducing reservists to take up short-term engagements within the regular forces. Since the support forces had relatively less depth than the combat arms, the challenge for the logisticians was even greater. For example, in order to bring 26th Transport Squadron up to strength for its transfer to Dili, it absorbed 66 reservists from 12 other units.

What made the rotation possible was the willingness of the army's reserve ranks to serve in East Timor. As so often in the past, the Defence Act did not give the government the authority to compel reserve soldiers to serve in East Timor. Instead, the army had to secure each soldier's permission individually. This also meant that in the army's integrated regular/reserve elements, only part of a unit was eligible for service overseas, and, as a result, before any commitment a reorganisation was necessary. The army did not employ any reserve units in East Timor, despite their presence on the order of battle. This created the situation in which the army had to bring its regular order of battle up to strength by running down the reserves. Such a fact must raise, once again, the question of the ultimate purpose and utility of the reserve organisation.

The last 25 years have been difficult ones for the Australian Army. While the situation has never approached the grim times of the interwar period, the ground troops did not do well in the competition for resources and missions when compared to the other services. Broadly, this situation came about because of the failure of the government and the military leaders to identify adequately a role for the army in the nation's defence policy. For too many years the army continued to place its emphasis on an expansion force while government interests suggested a focus on smaller levels of operations. In the aftermath of the withdrawal from Vietnam, the army also failed to make a case for offshore operations to complement the RAN and RAAF's plan to project power over the air–sea gap to the nation's north. Only gradually did the army evolve, yet it still did not abandon the division until 1991, and did not seek to accommodate the national security agenda until the Sanderson era. Ironically, it was then that the government once again changed the direction of its defence policy, catching the army in transition to a now unsustainable structure.

One other comparison with the interwar period is compelling. Between the world wars, the government based the nation's security on the Royal Navy's promise to deter or defeat Japan, against the considerable opposition of its military leaders. This policy was essentially a maritime strategy in which the army had only two limited roles, raid defence and installation security. However, once World War II began, especially after Japan's entry, the manifest failure of the British fleet, along with the RAN, to meet the Commonwealth's security requirements became evident. Instead, it was the army that had to secure the safety of the continent. Although the situation that Australia faced in East Timor was not remotely as serious as that which existed after December 1941, there are some similarities. Since the replacement of forward defence with continental defence in the early 1970s, the RAN, and to a lesser extent the RAAF, have done well relative to the army in garnering support from the government. In East Timor, however, despite the army's lesser station in the nation's security hierarchy, it was the ground troops upon whom the success of the operation depended. Once again, it has proved that maritime strategy must not mean an exclusive focus on the water, but must also include the surrounding land. Only when the nation possesses the ability to project and sustain ground forces into this more broadly defined maritime environment will Australia have a viable maritime-based security policy.

The Australian Army's professionalism, effectiveness, and accomplishments in East Timor did warrant the praise generated by the operation's success. However, this adulation conveniently ignores the fact that the deployment could have easily become a disaster, largely as a result of limitations in the army's support arms. Fortunately for Australia, INTERFET remained a peace-enforcement mission. Had it escalated, even marginally, in order that the logistical element had to add ammunition replacement and casualty removal to their tasks, the operation would have been seriously compromised. The army had little depth and, moreover, little room for expansion of its support capability in the short term. East Timor revealed that, while Australia could project a brigade group overseas, it did not have the ability to support such a deployment under war requirements. This situation is a result of a more-than-decade-long relentless focus on the combat arms at the expense of the support arms. While it is no doubt important to field as many battalions as possible, the army will only compromise their utility if it does not have the ability to sustain them on operations. Moreover, the achievement of budgetary efficiency is an illusory gain if it compromises military effectiveness. At present, the consequence of the Force Structure Review, the Defence Efficiency Review, and the commercialisation of defence operations is the creation of an unbalanced force that overly favours the combat arms. The government has already announced an enhancement of the army's regular infantry battalion order of battle. Moore instructed the army to bring 4 RAR (Cdo) to full strength. The army had separated the unit from 2 RAR in February 1995, but had not had the resources to complete its staffing. In addition, the Minister for Defence ordered the conversion of 6 RAR into a regular unit. This battalion had been a Ready Reserve unit, but with that scheme's abandonment, the army had filled its ranks largely with general reservists. Now it was to resume its place as a regular battalion. It is to be hoped that the support services will receive similar treatment soon.

9

THE FUTURE OF ARMY ORGANISATION

It would require major changes in the international system for war to break out among major powers in our region. But history shows that such major changes are not impossible.[1]

In the aftermath of the ADF's participation in the East Timor crisis, the Howard Government began to prepare a new White Paper on the Commonwealth's strategic policy and defence requirements. In June 2000, the Department of Defence issued a preliminary report called *Defence Review 2000: Our Future Defence Force (A Public Discussion Paper)*. It was a result of a nationwide community consultation led by Andrew Peacock, and its undertaking was to allow public input into the White Paper's development. The emphasis in *A Public Discussion Paper* demonstrated that the government intends to move further down the path it first outlined in its previous White Paper, *Australia's Strategic Policy, 1997*. The report identified three main requirements for the ADF's organisation, namely, the need to provide:

- forces for defeating attacks on Australia
- forces structured for regional security
- forces for military operations other than war (peace-keeping).[2]

Thus, for the foreseeable future the capability for regional deployments will remain one of the army's core tasks. Unfortunately, as so often in the past, the government's report did not specify particular requirements, identify mandatory assets, or suggest any organisational changes that the army would have to implement in order to obtain these capabilities. Without such guidance, finding methods to reconcile the different needs of continental defence with overseas deployment and peace-keeping while continuing to meet government demands for greater efficiency may prove to be the army's next great challenge.

Prime Minister Howard has acknowledged that the government will have to provide additional resources to the Defence Group, but *A Public Discussion Paper* identified neither the amount of any increase nor its allocation among the services. Thus the preliminary report contained the ominous statements that 'the Government is determined to increase Defence's efficiency further to give value to taxpayers. The next series of reforms and efficiency measures need to be bold.'[3] Elsewhere, the report states that the government's ongoing quest for efficiency will 'go some way to providing capability in future years'.[4] Missing one of the biggest lessons of the East Timor operation, the army's lack of depth in its support arms, the report then calls for a renewed redirection of funds to combat capabilities.[5] While it is likely that the army will receive additional monies, it still appears that any enhancement of capability will also have to rely on the internal shifting of resources. Thus the turmoil of the 1990s, resulting from the Force Structure Review and the Defence Efficiency Review, among others, is set to continue.

Another lesson of East Timor for the army was that as presently constituted it can only undertake operations on such a scale by denuding other areas of the force of personnel. It is now clear that the contraction of the 1990s resulted in a force that lacks the depth needed to meet all its obligations. The Howard Government's renewed enthusiasm for regional intervention and operations other than war is therefore worrying, as these deployments will most likely be personnel intensive. In addressing this concern, the Joint Standing Committee on Foreign Affairs, Defence, and Trade has called for a near doubling of the ARA's capability by the creation of four ready brigades. In addition, the committee believes that the army must have the ability to expand to 12 brigades within a reasonable warning period.[6] The committee's suggestions appear somewhat unrealistic, especially in an already difficult recruiting environment, and John Moore, the Minister for Defence, lost no time in labelling the proposal implausible. While any conclusion must be tentative, it does appear unlikely that the army will receive a major increase in its personnel.[7]

Despite the vital role the Army Reserve played in Operation Stabilise, the difficulty of its employment has once again led to a reconsideration of its members' service obligation. Under the existing provisions of the Defence Act, the government can call out the reserve only when Australia is under direct threat. As a consequence, the army was unable to utilise any reserve units in East Timor, and those reservists who did serve had to volunteer specifically for the operation. The greatest stumbling block is probably the Defence Act's lack of an employment guarantee for called-up reservists. In the aftermath of East Timor, Moore moved to amend the Defence Act. Hopefully, when realised, this will provide the army with a truly useful reserve force.[8]

THE FUTURE OF ARMY ORGANISATION

While the East Timor deployment has brought forth debate on a number of army-related issues, these are overshadowed by an even greater problem, the effect of which the government is only now beginning to consider, but which will reach crisis proportions over the course of the decade. The ADF is faced with the obsolescence of a number of major weapon systems, including the RAN's guided missile frigates and patrol boats, and the RAAF's F-111 strike and F/A-18 air combat capabilities. Allan Hawke, the Secretary of the Department of Defence, has noted that, at its current level of funding, the ADF would be unable to manage the replacement of these systems, and that the forces are facing what he called a tsunami of unfunded, but approved, defence projects. Although none of the major platforms belong to the army, the fact is that in the past the ground troops have suffered disproportionate budget cutbacks in order to provide resources for the rearmament of the other services.[9]

In December 2000, the government released its White Paper. *Defence 2000: Our Future Defence Force* was issued as this book was nearing completion.[10] While it is too soon to observe the effect its recommendations will have on the army's role and organisation, some observations are possible. The White Paper confirms the organisation of the ARA on a six-battalion basis, thus making permanent Moore's temporary

An armoured personnel carrier on Exercise K95. (Department of Defence MSU K95/C99-20)

Lieutenant-General Peter Cosgrove, CGS from 2000. (Department of Defence)

increase in the army's establishment in the aftermath of the East Timor intervention. This assures the existence of 4 RAR (Cdo) and 6 RAR as full-strength regular battalions. In addition, the White Paper promises the addition of two squadrons of armed reconnaissance helicopters, which represents a considerable enhancement of the army's aviation assets. The army will also receive new guided weapons, air defence missiles, body armour, night vision equipment, and communication systems. In addition, the force will be able to modernise its armoured personnel carriers, although no improvement in the army's tank force is anticipated. *Defence 2000: Our Future Defence Force* fortunately also proposes improvements for the logistic support force, including replacement of the army's medium landing craft and the increased readiness of individual units. Responsibility for implementing changes to the army's organisation required by the White Paper belongs to Lieutenant-General Peter Cosgrove, Hickling's successor as Chief of Army.

For the three services, the White Paper also reverses the Howard Government's contraction of defence spending and proposes to provide an additional $24 billion over 10 years. Despite this large sum, however, the allocation of resources to defence as a factor of gross domestic product will barely change, and it is projected to remain at less than 2 per cent per year.

The White Paper also announced significant changes in the role of the Army Reserve. Instead of acting as a mobilisation base, reserve units are to support and sustain the regular force. To make this possible, the government has amended the call-out restrictions of the Defence Act, and has provided a degree of employment protection for reserve soldiers. These changes were enacted in March 2001. It is too early to judge their effect on the army, but it is a welcome development.

Despite the promise of *Defence 2000: Our Future Defence Force*, what the army requires more than anything else is a period of stable security policy direction and funding, during which it can institutionalise any gains it realises from the latest White Paper. The army's past is littered with changes in national security direction and broken funding promises that have repeatedly undermined the development of the force and its ability to fulfil its role in the defence hierarchy. It is far too early to tell whether the Howard Government initiative will follow a similar path, but for the sake of the nation's security it is hoped that the programs outlined in *Defence 2000: Our Future Defence Force* eventuate and ongoing resources are provided by which to maintain the force at the desired level of readiness.

As the army celebrates its 100th anniversary, its organisation contains both similarities and differences to that which Hutton envisaged at its founding. The army is again structured around the brigade, although not to ease incorporation into an imperial division but because it is the formation which makes the most sense for Australia's present strategic objectives. If the nature of battle continues to emphasise the traditional arms of infantry, artillery, and armour (the modern conception of the light horse), the army's ranks now also include the highly technological arms of modern war, such as aviation and missile air defence. Moreover, the importance of communication is evident in the large number of signals units on the order of battle. One legacy that the army has been unable to change, however, is the service's traditional focus on combat troops rather than on creating a balanced force. For much of its history, Australia has allocated a disproportionate percentage of its strength to the battalions, squadrons, batteries, and field companies of the combat arms because an ally has provided for much of its support. The reductions in strength of the 1990s have seen a resumption of this tendency, although which power would now provide for the force's sustainment in a major conflict is not altogether clear. Table 9.1 outlines the army's order of battle as it existed in 1999.

As a result of the commercialisation of the army's support establishment, it is no longer necessary to provide an order of battle for the force's base logistic organisation. In 1999, the ADF sought tenders for its defence integrated distribution system. This proposal is the latest evolution in the commercialisation and triservice integration of the ADF's base logistic support structure. When it is fully operational in mid 2001, civilian staff will undertake virtually all of the ADF's base logistic tasks, and Support Command will have reassigned nearly all the few remaining uniform personnel to other duties. In 1901, most of the army's base logistic systems existed offshore, under the control of the imperial government in London. Today, it is the infrastructure of the Australian nation that largely fulfils this function.

One of the most significant changes of the past century has been the growth in professionalism of the Australian Army. During its early period, the army relied on British schools and manuals for nearly all of its intellectual development, doctrine, and training guidance. Some schools did exist within Australia, such as the Royal Military College, but they were few in number and frequently moribund. During World War II, the army established the full range of schools required for the waging of war. Fortunately, after the conclusion of hostilities the army preserved these institutions, and most remain on the order of battle today. Furthermore, advances in technology have been met with the creation of the necessary instructional institutions. For example, the army's takeover of the battlefield helicopter capability led to the formation of the School of Army Aviation. Listed below is Training Command's school system as it existed in 1999.

- Command and Staff College
- Royal Military College
- Army Recruit Training Centre
- Combat Arms Training Centre
- Army Logistic Training Centre
- Army Financial Services Unit
- Army Promotion Training Centre
- Army Adventurous Training Centre

Table 9.1 Army's combat order of battle, 1999: major elements[11]

Type	Formations and units
Headquarters	Land Headquarters
	Deployable joint force headquarters
	2nd Division
	7th Task Force
	1st, 3rd, 4th, 5th, 8th, 9th, 11th, 13th Brigades
	Headquarters Logistical Support Force
Armoured	1st Armoured Regiment
	2nd Cavalry Regiment
	1st/15th RNSWL, 4th/19th PWLH, 2nd/14th QMI, 12th/16th HRL,
	B Squadron 3rd/4th Cavalry, 10th LH, 3rd/9th SAMR
Artillery	8th/12th, 2nd/10th Medium Regiments
	1st, 4th, 7th, 23rd Field Regiments
	16th Air Defence Regiment
	7th, 16th, 48th Field Batteries
	131st Locating Battery
Engineers	1st, 2nd, 3rd, 4th, 5th, 8th Combat Engineer Regiments
	21st, 22nd Construction Regiments
	3rd, 13th, 35th Field Squadrons
	17th, 21st Construction Squadrons
	12th, 19th Chief Engineer Works
	1st Topographic Survey Squadron
Signal	7th, 8th Signal Regiments
	103rd, 108th, 109th, 110th, 141st, 142nd, 144th, 145th Signal Squadrons
	126th Commando Signal Squadron
Infantry	1st, 2nd, 3rd, 4th (Cdo), 5th/7th, 6th RAR
	9th, 25th/49th, 31st, 42nd RQR
	1st/19th, 2nd/17th, 4th/3rd, 41st RNSWR
	5th/6th, 8th/7th RVR
	10th/27th RSAR
	11th/28th, 16th RWAR
	12th/40th RTR
	Special Air Service Regiment
	1st Commando Regiment
	Norforce, Pilbara Regiment, 51st FNQR
Aviation	1st, 5th Aviation Regiments
Intelligence	1st Intelligence Battalion
	1st Intelligence Company
	2nd Division Intelligence Company
Support	1st, 7th Combat Service Support Battalions
	3rd, 4th, 5th, 8th, 9th, 11th, 13th Brigade Administrative Support Battalions
	2nd, 9th, 10th Force Support Battalions
Medical	3rd Forward General Hospital
	1st, 2nd Field Hospitals
	2nd, 3rd, 4th Preventive Medicine Companies
Provost	2nd, 3rd, 4th Military Police Companies
Psychological	1st Psychological Unit

- Parachute Training School
- Army Communications Training Centre
- Special Forces Training Centre
- ADF Helicopter School
- School of Army Aviation
- Defence Intelligence Training Centre
- Royal Australian Electrical and Mechanical Engineers Aircraft Maintenance School
- School of Army Education
- Army Military Police Training Centre
- Combined Arms Training and Development Centre.

Under the direction of the Royal Military College, the army maintains seven university-based officer cadet training regiments. They are Queensland University Rifles, Sydney University Rifles, University of New South Wales Rifles, Monash University Rifles, Melbourne University Rifles, Adelaide University Rifles, and Western Australian University Rifles. In 1998, Training Command also began to establish a network of regional training centres. Their purpose is to provide individual and collective training for regular and reserve soldiers. The army also continues to conduct officer cadet training at the triservice Australian Defence Force Academy.[12]

The ADF continues to advance the concept of jointness, and the army exists within the broader framework of the Department of Defence. Chart 14 (p. 382) outlines Australia's defence structure as it existed at the end of 1999.

At the end of this first century of its existence, a number of conclusions can be made on the organisation of the Australian Army. At its beginning, the army was little more than groups of ill-trained colonial soldiers, supported by a handful of professionals, forcibly united into a single institution upon the nation's Federation, and lacking all the prerequisites required for an effective, capable fighting force. Across the new nation there was an almost total absence of modern equipment, trained men, efficient officers, and institutional culture and memory. Amateurism was the hallmark of the force. A hundred years later, one must employ the opposite terms to convey the nature of the present Australian Army. It has become a force composed of skilled, well-armed and -led professionals, and an institution possessing a rich tradition of battle honour and excellence.

If the Australian Army today is a highly competent force, it has achieved this condition in an environment of seemingly constant organisational change. Since its creation, the army has enjoyed few periods of stability. Rather, the pattern has been that every few years defence decision-makers have reviewed the existing structure, in the light of modifications in the nature of war or government policy, and made changes in the army's organisation. Sometimes the changes have been relatively minor, such as those proposed by Hamilton in 1914. At other times they have been quite dramatic, for example the massive reconfiguration of the army during the pentropic era. While perhaps unsettling to participants in these changes, this pattern is the correct one. War is a dynamic forum of innovation and adaptation to advances in weaponry, operations, and technology, as well as modifications in the strategic environment. There are exceptions in the army's history when the organisation changed little, the interwar period being the prime case. Not coincidentally, the interwar period also represented the nadir of the army's competence. The ensuing difficulties that the army experienced in World War II, as it recovered from the stagnation of the interwar period, suggests the detrimental effect that the lack of innovation and adaptation can have on military effectiveness.

Chapter 1 identified three primary national characteristics that have helped to define the shape of the army's organisation. They are:
- the government's frequent change in the direction of national security policy
- the periodic resistance of army leaders to conforming to strategic guidance
- the nation's dependence on a major ally for its ultimate defence.

Of the three, the first has been the most influential. The establishment of security policy is rightly the prerogative of the government, although, obviously, input from the services is important. Unfortunately, Australian governments have not always carried out this mandate as skilfully as they might. While military institutions must periodically adapt themselves to changes in the art of war, all too often the Australian pattern has been one of frequent change in defence direction, and this has resulted in a lack of focus and coordination between the organisation of the army and its strategic guidance. Even worse, on other occasions the nation's political leaders have abdicated responsibility to others, usually imperial leaders in London, and have accepted their security promises at face value. The best example is the government's unquestioning faith in the Singapore Strategy, even in the face of overwhelming evidence of its inability to deter or contain Japanese aggression. When gaps between directed policy and organisational reality have developed, the government has been slow to bring the two into alignment. For much of the era of continental defence, the army sustained an organisation best suited for a middle-level conflict, while the government anticipated only low-level incursions.

Although government consultation with its military advisers should occur during the formulation of security policy, the fact remains that on many occasions the government has made its determination with little or no advice or notice to the armed

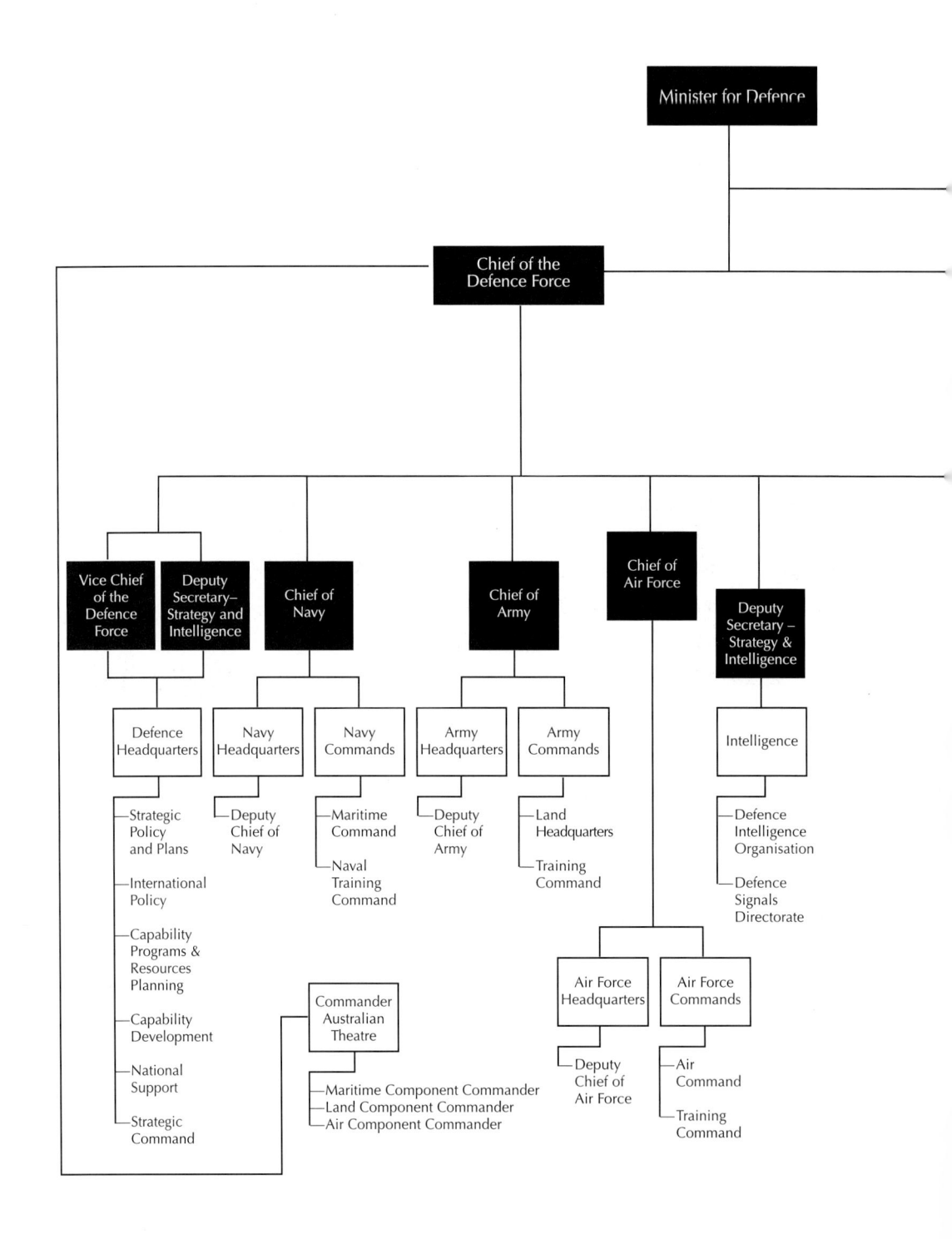

Chart 14 Defence higher organisation, 1999.
(Source: *Defence Annual Report*, 1998–99)

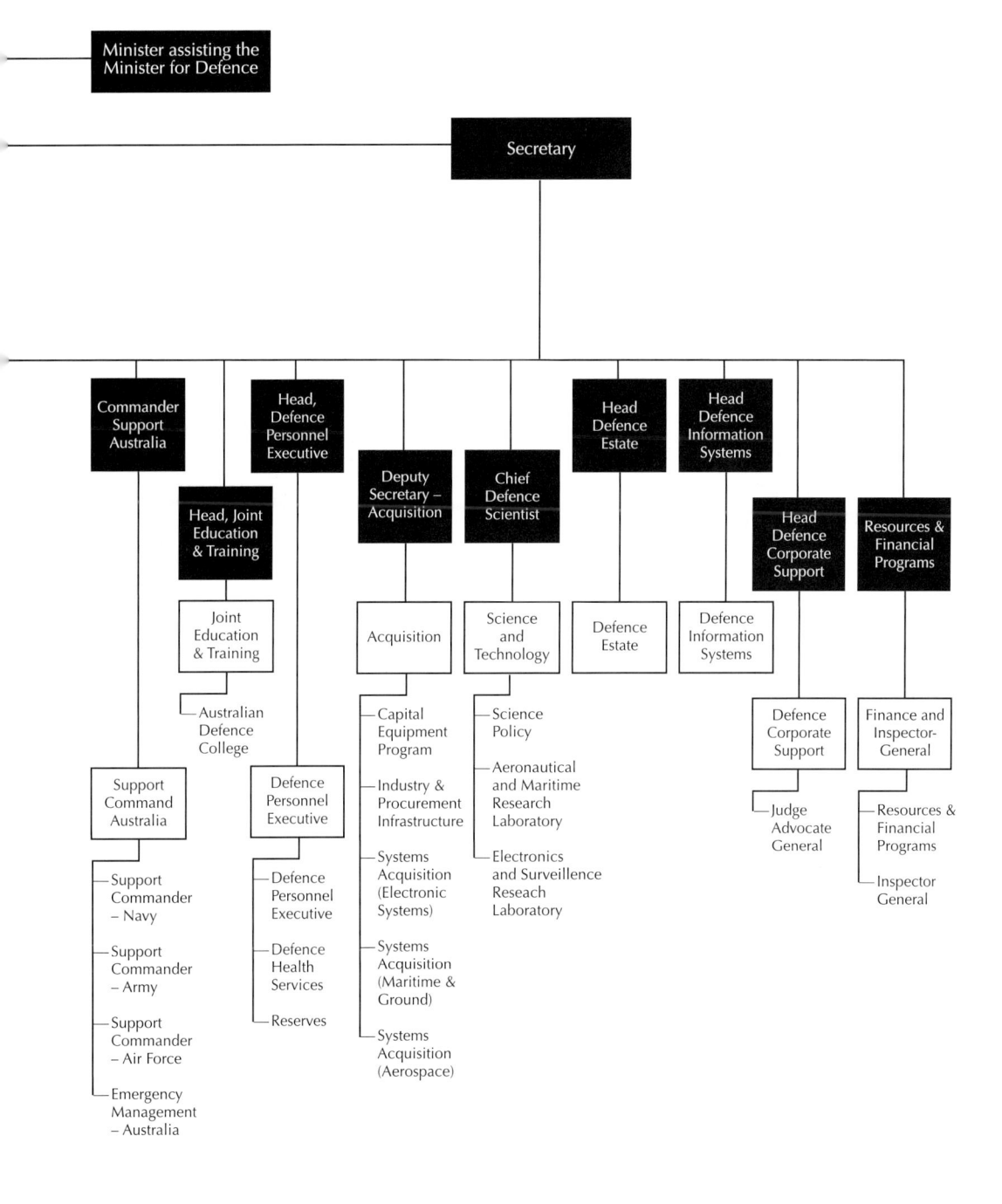

THE FUTURE OF ARMY ORGANISATION

Minister assisting the Minister for Defence

Secretary

- **Commander Support Australia**
  - Support Command Australia
    - Support Commander – Navy
    - Support Commander – Army
    - Support Commander – Air Force
    - Emergency Management – Australia

- **Head, Defence Personnel Executive**
  - **Head, Joint Education & Training**
    - Joint Education & Training
      - Australian Defence College
  - Defence Personnel Executive
    - Defence Personnel Executive
    - Defence Health Services
    - Reserves

- **Deputy Secretary – Acquisition**
  - Acquisition
    - Capital Equipment Program
    - Industry & Procurement Infrastructure
    - Systems Acquisition (Electronic Systems)
    - Systems Acquisition (Maritime & Ground)
    - Systems Acquisition (Aerospace)

- **Chief Defence Scientist**
  - Science and Technology
    - Science Policy
    - Aeronautical and Maritime Research Laboratory
    - Electronics and Surveillance Reseach Laboratory

- **Head Defence Estate**
  - Defence Estate

- **Head Defence Information Systems**
  - Defence Information Systems

- **Head Defence Corporate Support**
  - Defence Corporate Support
    - Judge Advocate General

- **Resources & Financial Programs**
  - Finance and Inspector-General
    - Resources & Financial Programs
    - Inspector General

forces. In the nation's early period, the government much preferred the opinions of London decision-makers to those of its own senior officers. Even in the modern period, the army's leaders have not always been given the opportunity to present their views before the government has announced significant changes in defence policy. For example, Whitlam's summary suspension of national service and Howard's unexpected shift towards greater regional engagement caught the army unprepared, and caused great difficulty within the force as it redesigned itself to accommodate the new policy.

More worrying is the fact that many of the government's frequent changes in strategic direction have come about not because of legitimate reassessments of the security picture but because of the demands of fiscal policy. Fiscal responsibility is, of course, an obligation that a government owes its people. However, the reality is that the demands of the Australian Treasury have all too often taken precedence over assessments of the strategic environment in the determination of the army's organisation. During the interwar period, the army was almost starved out of existence by the lack of funds. More recently, the government has insisted on making the ADF more fiscally accountable, in line with current thinking in the private sector. There is a degree of validity to this demand, but political decision-makers do not appear cognisant of the fact that military organisations are unique institutions that have roles not duplicated in the commercial world. While it may be useful to think about the army from the perspective of corporatisation, civilian leaders must never forget that the military is not composed of managers but of warriors. The painful reorganisation brought about by the fiscal rationalism of the 1990s suggests that the government prefers to measure military success in terms of efficiency rather than effectiveness. Surely, this is the wrong standard upon which to base the nation's survival.

Overall, the government's role in guiding the organisation of the army has not been as positive as it should have been. In too many instances, the army has had to react to government-imposed cutbacks or changes in strategic direction that are not the product of a legitimate and well-thought-through analysis of the nation's security environment. The result has been a higher than necessary frequency of change, including on occasion the complete reversal of direction, and relatively brief windows of stability. For example, Menzies initiated an expansion of the army in 1951 with the objective of increasing the strength and reaction capability of the ARA. However, only two years later he slashed the force's budget by a third, forcing the army to abandon the new program. While military institutions must avoid stagnation, it is also essential that they enjoy periods of tranquillity during which they can perfect their operations. All too often, the Australian Government's abrupt changes in direction have made this task far more difficult than necessary.

Given the government's exacting concern with the cost of defence from Federation to the present, it is ironic that so many changes of organisation have occurred. Each change in direction comes at a cost, both compromising effectiveness and budget, as the army abandons old policies and diverts energies to implement new objectives. What the army requires from its political masters is greater clarity and consistency of vision. If this were provided, the burden facing the army's leaders would be lighter to bear and the goals of defence easier to achieve.

On occasion, the army's own leaders have also made the task facing their service harder through an unwillingness to conform to the government's strategic guidelines. Sometimes there has been a vast gulf between what the government expected the army to provide in order to meet the nation's security policy and what military leaders in fact decided to maintain. The most dramatic example of an imbalance between force design and strategic requirement was the period between the two world wars. For much of the interwar period, the army insisted on preparing to defend against invasion while the government wanted it to employ its forces to repel raids. Even when required by Pearce, the Minister for Defence, to create an anti-raid first line component, successive CGSs avoided the issue, and continued to seek a revision of the government's strategic policy. The difference of opinion between the two sides was huge, and remained so until the mobilisation for World War II. Although the army's appreciation of the threat environment proved more astute than the government's insouciant transfer of responsibility to London, it still represented a failure in civil–military relations, and was an inappropriate response by officers who were accountable to a properly elected civilian leadership.

If the army's leaders were sometimes complicit in failing to meet the force's strategic guidance, the nation's political leaders must also share part of the blame. After all, throughout the interwar period a succession of Ministers for Defence signally failed to impose their will upon their senior officers. In fact, the government had so little interest in security matters and was so eager to accept imperial guarantees that no Minister for Defence made a serious attempt to address the near insubordination of his senior officers. On other occasions, however, the divergence between the army's organisation and security policy came out as a result of the government's failure to articulate clearly the desired capabilities and roles expected of the military. For much of the era of continental defence, the army continued to shape its structure around an expansion base simply because the government had not adequately defined the force's requirements. In a properly functioning civil–military relationship, both parties have vital roles to play in the design of an army's organisation. On the civilian side of the equation, it is essential that the government state its expectations in order that the military can translate these desires into an effective force. On the other hand, military leaders are required to provide their civilian masters with the force they expect. Only when both sides properly fulfil these tasks can they bring about an alignment between the requirements of security environment and the organisation of the army.

The inability of its relatively small population to defend its vast territory has meant that for its entire history Australia has had to rely on a major power for its ultimate defence. Britain fulfilled this role for the colonial period and the first part of the twentieth century. During World War II the Americans took up the responsibility, and Australia's alliance with the United States remains the cornerstone of its security policy to the present. Periodically, Australia has had to pay the premium for this insurance by its participation as a junior partner in a coalition led by its protector. Although not as influential as the first two national characteristics, this dependency on a great power has had some effect on the organisation of the Australian Army.

At times in its history, the army has had to conform the establishment of its formations and units to the imperial standard. When Australia raised the 2nd AIF, it followed the Australian practice of four battalion brigades, only to have to reorganise the 6th Division into the British three battalion brigade once it arrived in Egypt. This resulted in the situation in which the relatively small Australian Army had to maintain two different divisional organisations, one for the AIF and the other for the CMF at home. After the victory over Japan, Australia abandoned its jungle division standard, which had proved so effective in the tropics to Australia's north, for the restoration of the British pattern in case it had to send another expeditionary force to the Middle East. The need to accept the major partner's structure remained after the United States entered the war, although to a lesser extent. As the end of the war in the Pacific neared, Australia planned to participate in the invasion of the Japanese home islands. However, since the United States would dominate the operation, any Australian contribution would have to conform to the American division standard, necessitating another reorganisation had it eventuated.

During the brief pentropic era, the army's organisation on the five-sided principle at times seemed almost comical, particularly when it participated in operations with an ally. Every time Australia deployed a battalion to Malaya it had to reorganise the unit onto the imperial standard. Then, at the completion of the battalion's tour of duty, the unit had to again reorganise back to its pentropic establishment. In the end, the army opted to maintain two battalion standards, pentropic for home duty and imperial for service in the Far East. Of course, when it first considered the pentropic system, the army had given as one of the rationales for its adoption the fact that the Americans were implementing a similar organisation. After the United States Army abandoned the experiment, Australia attempted to maintain the system on its own. However, having an organisation that matched neither of its main allies was not sustainable, and this was one of the reasons for Wilton's reorganisation of the army onto traditional lines in 1965.

While not affecting the organisation of the army directly, the need to find a place within a major-power-led coalition also placed pressure on Australia to adopt the other force's equipment standard. This was most prevalent during the period of British leadership, but has also had some effect under the guardianship of the United States. During the interwar and early World War II years, Australia's association with Britain placed it at quite a disadvantage because of the imperial army's failure to invest in modern weapons and commence rearmament despite the rising German and Japanese menace.

Perhaps the greatest, and most dangerous, result of this dependency occurred during the interwar period, when it encouraged government complacency towards the assessment of threat facing the nation, and exacerbated a reliance on London for military advice rather than domestic sources. The government's faith in the Singapore Strategy was total, especially since this allowed it to claim the ability to provide security at virtually no cost. In the end, British protection proved almost worthless, and Curtin greeted the arrival of American troops as salvation from the nation's most dire moment. Throughout the interwar period, the army's senior officers had attempted to influence security policy, but were constantly rebuffed by the government's preference for the seemingly more expert opinions emanating from London. It was not until after the conclusion of World War II that Australian officers became the government's true advisers on military affairs, an example of the force's growing professionalism.

As the Australian Army begins its second century, its past can help illuminate its path forward. One of the most important issues facing the army will be the need to continue to create an organisation that meets the force's mission and capability requirements as defined by the government's strategic guidance. At the moment, the army's organisation and role in the nation's defence hierarchy is in flux as it strives to meet the requirements of the ADF's emerging maritime concept of strategy. Despite the nation's lack of a significant threat at present, the only certain question is not whether this will change but when. Military and government decision-makers therefore have a responsibility to continue to address the issue of the army's organisation and to implement modifications they believe will best ensure the nation's security. The Australian Army must never sink into complacency or stagnation. If there is any lesson to be learned from the first hundred years, it is that the willingness to seek and implement change is essential.

Abbreviations

AA	Anti-aircraft
AA (ACT)	Australian Archives, Canberra
AAC	Australian Armoured Corps
AAChD	Assistant, Chaplain Department
AAG (AWAS)	Assistant Adjutant-General, Australian Women's Army Service
AAMC	Australian Army Medical Corps
AAMWS	Australian Army Medical Women's Service
AANS	Australian Army Nursing Service
AA (NSW)	Australian Archives, Sydney
AAOC	Australian Army Ordnance Corps
AASC	Australian Army Service Corps
AAVC	Australian Army Veterinary Corps
AA (VIC)	Australian Archives, Melbourne
ABCA	America, Britain, Canada, and Australia
AC	aircraft
AD	Air Defence or Air Dispatch
ADF	Australian Defence Force
ADFA	Australian Defence Force Academy
ADG	Army Development Guide
ADMI	Assistant Director Military Intelligence
AFSP	Army Force Structure Plan
AFV	Armoured Fighting Vehicle

ABBREVIATIONS

AG	Adjutant-General
AGA	Australian Garrison Artillery
AGPS	Australian Government Printing Service
AHQ	Army Headquarters
AIC	Australian Instructional Corps
AIF	Australian Imperial Force
ALO	Army Liaison Officer
ALTC	Army Logistic Training Centre
Amb.	Ambulance
AMDA	Anglo-Malayan Defence Agreement
AMF	Australian Military Force
AN&MEF	Australian Naval and Military Expeditionary Force
ANZAC	Australia and New Zealand Army Corps
ANZAM	Australia, New Zealand, and Malaya
ANZUS	Australia, New Zealand, and United States Security Treaty
APC	Armoured Personnel Carrier
APIN	army presence in Northern Australia
APIS	Aerial Photographic Interpretation Section
ARA	Australian Regular Army
ARes	Army Reserve
Armd	armoured
Art.	artillery
ASA	Australian Support Area
Asst.	Assistance
Avn	Aviation
AWAS	Australian Women's Army Service
AWM	Australian War Memorial
BASB	Brigade Administrative Support Battalion
BCFESR	British Commonwealth Far East Strategic Reserve
Bde	Brigade
BGS	Brigadier-General Staff
Bks	barracks
Bn	battalion
Bty	battery
CA	coast artillery
Cav.	cavalry
Cbt	combat
CDC	Colonial Defence Committee

ABBREVIATIONS

CDF	Chief of Defence Force
CDFS	Chief of Defence Force Staff
Cdo	commando
CFO	Chief Financial Officer
CGS	Chief of the General Staff
CID	Committee of Imperial Defence
C-in-C AMF	Commander-in-Chief Australian Military Forces
CMF	Citizen Military Force
CO	Commanding Officer
Const.	construction
COSC	Chief of Staff Committee
Coy	company
CPD	Commonwealth Parliamentary Debates
CPP	Commonwealth Parliamentary Papers
CQ	Central Queensland
CRAAOC	Commander Royal Australian Army Ordnance Corps
CRAASC	Commander Royal Australian Army Service Corps
CRAEME	Commander Royal Australian Electrical and Mechanical Engineers
DAG	Deputy Adjutant-General
DCGS	Deputy Chief of the General Staff
DCR	Defence Central Registry
DDMO	Deputy Director of Military Operations
DDMT	Deputy Director of Military Training
DDS	Director Dental Service
DGMS	Director General Medical Service
DGPR	Director General Public Relations
Dent.	dental
Dep.	depot
Det	detachment
DI (A)	Defence Instruction Army
Dist	district
Div.	division
DLS	Director Legal Service
DMGO	Deputy Master-General of the Ordnance
DMI	Director of Military Intelligence
DMT	Director of Military Training
DOA	Defence of Australia
DQMG	Deputy Quartermaster-General

ABBREVIATIONS

DResearch	Directorate of Research
DSD	Director of Staff Duties
DSU	Defence Support Unit
DVDC	Director of Volunteer Defence Corps
E in C	Engineer in Chief
EME	Electrical and Mechanical Engineers
Engr	engineer
Equip.	equipment
FA	Field Artillery
Fd	field
FEG	force element group
FESR	Far East Strategic Reserve
FF	field force
Flt	flight
FNQR	Far North Queensland Regiment
FS	field security
FSB	force support battalion
FSR	Force Structure Review
Fwd	forward
FY	fiscal year
GOC	General Officer Commanding
GOC-in-C Home Forces	General Officer Commanding-in-Chief Home Forces
Gp	group
GPS	Government Printing Service
GRes	General Reserves
GS	General Staff
HAA	Heavy Anti-Aircraft
HMAS	His/Her Majesty's Australian Ship
Hosp.	hospital
HQ	headquarters
HRL	Hunter River Lancers
HTM	heavy trench mortar
Hyg.	hygiene
IDC	Imperial Defence Committee
IG	Inspector-General
IGM	Inspector-General, Munitions
IGS	Imperial General Staff (Australian Section)
Inf.	infantry

ABBREVIATIONS

Int.	intelligence
INTERFET	International Force East Timor
JAG	Judge Advocate-General
LAA	Light Anti-Aircraft
LAD	light aid detachment
LARC-5	Lighter Amphibious Resupply Cargo, 5 ton
LCH	landing craft heavy
LCM	landing craft mechanised
LH	light horse
LHQ	land headquarters
Loc.	locating
L of C	line of communication
Log.	logistic
LSF	logistical support force
LSG	logistical support group
LSM	landing ship medium
Lt.	light
LTM	light trench mortar
MB	Military Board
MBI	Military Board Instruction
MC	movement control
MD	military district
Mdm	medium
Med.	medical
MG	machine-gun
MGO	Master-General of the Ordnance
MGRA	Master-General Royal Artillery
Mil.	military
Mov.	movement
MP	military police; Member of Parliament
MS	Military Secretary
NARA	National Archives and Records Administration at College Park
NCO	non-commissioned officer
NLA	National Library of Australia
NORCOM	Northern Command
NQ	North Queensland
NSW	New South Wales
NZ	New Zealand

ABBREVIATIONS

ODF	operational deployment force
ORBAT	order of battle
Ord.	ordnance
PIR	Pacific Islands Regiment
Pk	park
Pl.	platoon
PM	Prime Minister
PMF	Permanent Military Force
PNG	Papua New Guinea
PNGDF	Papua New Guinea Defence Force
Pr	pounder
Pro.	provost
Psych.	psychological
PWLH	Prince of Wales Light Horse
QLD	Queensland
QMI	Queensland Mounted Infantry
QMG	Quartermaster-General
RAA	Royal Australian Artillery
RAAC	Royal Australian Armoured Corps
RAAF	Royal Australian Air Force
RAANC	Royal Australian Army Nursing Corps
RACT	Royal Australian Corps of Transport
RAE	Royal Australian Engineers
RAER	Regular Army Emergency Reserve
RAFA	Royal Australian Field Artillery
RAGA	Royal Australian Garrison Artillery
RAN	Royal Australian Navy
RAR	Royal Australia Regiment
RASR	Regular Army Supplementary Reserve
Recce	reconnaissance
Regt	regiment
RFSU	Regional Force Surveillance Unit
RMC	Royal Military College
RN	Royal Navy
RNSWL	Royal New South Wales Lancers
RNSWR	Royal New South Wales Regiment
RQR	Royal Queensland Regiment
RRes	Ready Reserve

ABBREVIATIONS

RSAR	Royal South Australian Regiment
RSL	Returned Sailors', Soldiers', and Airmen's Imperial League of Australia
RTR	Royal Tasmania Regiment
RVR	Royal Victoria Regiment
RWAR	Royal Western Australian Regiment
SA	South Australia
SAMR	South Australian Mounted Rifles
SAS	Special Air Service Regiment
SB	special battalion
SEATO	South-East Asia Treaty Organisation
Sec.	section
Sig.	signals
SO-in-C	Signal Officer-in-Chief
Spt	support
SQ	South Queensland
Sqn	squadron
SR	supplementary reserve
Sup.	supply
Svy	survey
SWPA	South-West Pacific Area
TAS	Tasmania
TE	tropical establishment
TF	task force
Tk	tank
Topo.	topographical
Tp	troop
Tpt	transport
Trn.	training
VCGS	Vice-Chief of the General Staff
VDC	Volunteer Defence Corps
VIC	Victoria
VMR	Victoria Mounted Rifles
WA	Western Australia
WAAAF	Women's Australian Auxiliary Air Force
Wksp	workshop
WRAAC	Women's Royal Australian Army Corps
WRANS	Women's Royal Australian Naval Service

NOTES

1 The origins of army organisation

1 *Report and Summary of Proceedings together with Appendices and Minutes of the Federal Military Conference Assembled in Sydney, New South Wales, to Consider a General Scheme of Military Defence Applicable to the Australian Colonies and Tasmania*, Government Printer, Sydney, 1894, p. 5.
2 Information for this table and the rest of this section is taken from *Reader's Digest Atlas of Australia*, Readers' Digest, Sydney, 1994, p. 8; *Year Book Australia 1997*, Australian Bureau of Statistics, Canberra, 1997, pp. 74–9; J.C.R. Camm & J. McQuilton (eds), *Australians: A Historical Atlas*, Syme & Weldon, Sydney, 1987, pp. 128–9; and W.G. Coppell, *Australia in Facts and Figures*, Penguin Books, Ringwood, 1994, pp. 4–8.
3 T.B. Millar, *Australia's Defence*, Melbourne University Press, Carlton, 1965, p. 20.
4 John Mordike, *An Army for a Nation: A History of Australian Military Development, 1880–1914*, Allen & Unwin, North Sydney, 1992, pp. 21–2.
5 Ibid., pp. 54–5.
6 Mordike, *An Army for a Nation*, pp. 48–9.
7 Edward Hutton, 'A Co-operative System for the Defence of the Empire', in E. Hutton, *The Defence and Defensive Power of Australia*, Melbourne, 1902, p. 95.
8 Quoted in Hutton, *The Defence and Defensive Power of Australia*, pp. 86–7.
9 *Report and Summary of Proceedings Together with Appendices and Minutes of the Federal Military Conference*, pp. 5–6.
10 Donald C. Gordon, *The Dominion Partnership in Imperial Defence, 1870–1914*, Johns Hopkins Press, Baltimore, 1965, pp. 202–4.

11 'Defence Forces and Defences (Memorandum by Colonial Defence Committee)', in *CPP*, vol. 2, 1901–02 session.
12 Neville Meaney, *The Search for Security in the Pacific, 1901–14*, Sydney University Press, Sydney, 1976, p. 24; Mordike, *An Army for a Nation*, p. 3; and Alan Dupont, *Australia's Threat Perceptions: A Search for Security*, Australian National University, Strategic and Defence Studies Centre, Canberra, 1991, p. 3.
13 Peter Donovan, *Defending the Northern Gateway*, Australian National University, Strategic and Defence Studies Centre, Canberra, 1989, p. 34.
14 Hutton, *The Defence and Defensive Power of Australia*, p. 89.
15 For a discussion of voluntarism see Craig Wilcox, *For Hearths and Homes: Citizen Soldiering in Australia, 1854–1945*, Allen & Unwin, St Leonards, NSW, 1998.
16 For a discussion of this issue see Meaney, *The Search for Security in the Pacific*, p. 266.

2 From Federation to World War I

1 'Hutton to Minister for Defence', 25 April 1902, AA (VIC), B168, item 1902/2688.
2 'A Brief Narrative of the Organization, Strength and Training of the Australian Military Forces Since Federation', Military Board Proceedings, AA (ACT), A2653/1, vol. 1, 1928.
3 The importance of a properly organised military force is discussed in General Staff, *Possibility of Assimilating War Organization Throughout the Empire*, J. Kemp, Melbourne, 1907, p. 12.
4 Data taken from 'Report on the Department of Defence for the Period from 1st March 1901 to 30th June 1906', *CPP*, vol. 2, 1906.
5 Ibid.
6 Data taken from 'Federal Military Committee', n.d., AA (VIC), B168, item 01/4532.
7 Jeffrey Grey, *A Military History of Australia*, Cambridge University Press, Melbourne, 1999, p. 60; and L.M. Field, *The Forgotten War: Australian Involvement in the South African Conflict of 1899–1902*, Melboune University Press, Carlton, 1979, pp. 147–8.
8 Mordike, *An Army for a Nation*, pp. 68–9; *Report of the Military Committee of Inquiry*, Part 1, *General*, n.p., 1901, p. 1; and Colonial Defence Committee, *Memorandum on the Defence Forces and Defences of Australia, 1901*, 1901, p. 7, in AA (ACT), A5954/1, item 1211/2.
9 Edward Hutton, 'Military Forces of the Commonwealth', Melbourne, 1902, p. 5.
10 Mordike, *An Army for a Nation*, p. 68; and 'Western Australia Annual Report, 1901 on Garrison and Defence of King George's Sound', AWM3, item 21.
11 Colonial Defence Committee, *Defence Forces and Defences of Australia, 1901*, pp. 7–9.
12 'Schedule Showing Obsolete RML and Smooth Bore Guns, etc.' and 'Hutton to AAG for Artillery', 28 October 1902, AWM3, item 02/2776; and 'Correspondence Regarding the Updating of a List of Armament—1903', AWM3, item 02/3062.

NOTES (PP. 20–8)

13 Hutton, 'Military Forces of the Commonwealth—1902', pp. 6–7.
14 'AAG for Artillery to the Secretary for Defence', 28 July 1904, AA (VIC), B168/1, item 1902/113.
15 Quoted in Neville Meaney, *The Search for Security in the Pacific*, p. 91.
16 Colonial Defence Committee, *Defence Forces and Defences of Australia, 1901*, p. 3.
17 C. Grimshaw, 'Some Aspects of Australian Attitudes to the Imperial Connection, 1900–1919', Master's Thesis, University of Queensland, 1958, pp. 136–7.
18 Meaney, *The Search for Security in the Pacific*, pp. 40–1; and John Bastock, *Ships on the Australia Station*, Child & Associates, Frenchs Forest, NSW, 1988, pp. 101, 119, and 122.
19 Colonial Defence Committee, *Defence Forces and Defences of Australia, 1901*, p. 3.
20 'Report of the Joint Military and Naval Committee of Defence', 15 April 1901, AA (VIC), B168, item 01/5370.
21 Mordike, *An Army for a Nation*, pp. 111–13; Meaney, *The Search for Security in the Pacific*, p. 40; and Colonial Defence Committee, *Defence Forces and Defences of Australia, 1901*, pp. 10–12.
22 Quoted in Mordike, *An Army for a Nation*, p. 113.
23 Meaney, *The Search for Security in the Pacific*, p. 64.
24 Ibid., p. 42; and R. Norris, *The Emergent Commonwealth: The Australian Federation, Expectations and Fulfilment, 1889–1910*, Melbourne University Press, Carlton, 1975, pp. 119–22.
25 Meaney, *The Search for Security in the Pacific*, pp. 55–7; and 'Further Report of the Federal Military Committee', 12 June 1901, AA (VIC), B168, item 02/113.
26 Meaney, *The Search for Security in the Pacific*, pp. 55–7; and Mordike, *An Army for a Nation*, pp. 71–9.
27 'Hutton to Minister for Defence', 6 July 1903, AWM3, item 03/341.
28 Edward Hutton, 'Military Forces of the Commonwealth—1902', p. 2.
29 'Hutton to Minister for Defence', 6 July 1903, and 'Hutton to Minister for Defence', 13 October 1903, AWM3, item 03/341; and Mordike, *An Army for a Nation*, pp. 124–30.
30 Quoted in Ian D. Rae, 'History of the Australian Army, Part 1: Early History', pp. 13–15.
31 Ibid., p. 6; and David Horner, 'Australian Army Strategic Planning Between the Wars', in Peter Dennis & Jeffrey Grey (eds), *Serving Vital Interests: Australia's Strategic Planning in Peace and War*, ADFA, Canberra, 1996, p. 76.
32 Hutton, 'Military Forces of the Commonwealth—1902', p. 2.
33 Ibid., pp. 1–3.
34 An outline of the organisation of the Australian Military Forces under Hutton's plan can be found in 'Defence Scheme for the Commonwealth of Australia', AWM113, item MH1/3.
35 Hutton, 'Military Forces of the Commonwealth—1902', pp. 2–4; 'Report on the Department of Defence for the Period from 1st March, 1901 to 30th June, 1906', in *CPP*, vol. 2, 1906, p. 10; and Meaney, *The Search for Security in the Pacific, 1901–14*, pp. 64–5.

36 Ibid.

37 Information taken from 'Defence Scheme for the Commonwealth of Australia', AWM113, MH 1/3.

38 Edward Hutton, 'Annual Report Upon the Military Forces of the Commonwealth of Australia', Robt. S. Brain, Melbourne, 1903, p. 12.

39 'Memorandum on Australian Military Defence and its Progress Since Federation', in *CPP*, vol. 2, 1909, p. 7.

40 'Hutton to Acting Minister for Defence', 21 July 1902, AWM3, item 02/1015.

41 Hutton, 'Military Forces of the Commonwealth—1902', p. 4; and Mordike, *An Army for a Nation*, pp. 131–47.

42 Ibid.

43 Edward Hutton, 'Military Forces of the Commonwealth of Australia, Second Annual Report', Robt S. Brain, Melbourne, 1904, p. 9.

44 'Report on the Department of Defence for the Period from 1st March, 1901 to 30th June, 1906'.

45 Information taken from 'Defence Scheme for the Commonwealth of Australia', AWM113, MH 1/3. Totals do not add up exactly, as the table does not include several attached officers, such as the Veterinary Department. The brigades were also not maintained at their peace establishment. 5th Light Horse Brigade's posted strength was only 870.

46 Hutton, 'Military Forces of the Commonwealth—1903', pp. 8–10.

47 Hutton, 'Military Forces of the Commonwealth—1902', pp. 5–6; Hutton, 'Military Forces of the Commonwealth of Australia—1903', p. 20; Hutton, 'Military Forces of the Commonwealth—1904', p. 27; and 'Report on the Department of Defence for the Period from 1st March, 1901 to 30th June, 1906', pp. 10, 13.

48 Hutton, 'Military Forces of the Commonwealth—1902', p. 2.

49 'Hutton to Secretary for Defence', 11 August 1902, AA (VIC), B168, item 1902/2688/folder 2.

50 Quoted in Norris, *The Emergent Commonwealth*, p. 132.

51 'Minister for Defence to Hutton', 24 June 1903, AA (VIC), B168, item 1902/2688/folder 1; 'Hutton to Minister for Defence', 8 July 1903, AA (VIC), B168, item 1902/2688/folder 6; and Mordike, *An Army for a Nation*, pp. 110–11. See also Gordon, *The Dominion Partnership in Imperial Defence*, pp. 202–4.

52 Hutton, 'Military Forces of the Commonwealth—1903', p. 13.

53 Ibid., p. 23; and Hutton, 'Military Forces of the Commonwealth—1904', p. 17; and Meaney, *The Search for Security in the Pacific*, pp. 64–5. See also 'Hutton to Minister for Defence', 8 April 1903, 'Hutton to Assistant Quarter Master General', 8 July 1903, 'Minister for Defence to General Officer Commanding', 1 June 1903, 'Hutton to Minister for Defence', 2 June 1903, and 'Warlike Stores, Summary of Requirements for Peace and War Establishments', 8 April 1903, AWM3, item 03/624.

NOTES (PP. 34–42)

54 Meaney, *The Search for Security in the Pacific*, p. 68; and 'Hutton to Minister for Defence', 26 April 1904, AA (VIC), B168, item 02/867/part 2.
55 'Defence Forces of the Commonwealth: Memorandum by a Committee in Regard to the Command and Administration of the Military and Naval Forces', 18 November 1904, *CPP*, vol. 2, 1904, pp. 1–2.
56 'Defence Forces: Memorandum by the Minister for Defence', 5 November 1904, *CPP*, vol. 2, 1904.
57 Ibid.; and 'Military Board Meeting', 13 April 1905, AA (ACT), A2653/1, item 1905/07.
58 'Memorandum for the Consideration of the Cabinet as to the Future Administration of the Defence Forces of Australia', 15 September 1905, AWM3, item 04/62.
59 'Defences Forces of the Commonwealth: Memorandum by a Committee in Regard to the Command and Administration of the Military and Naval Forces', p. 2.
60 Ibid. For a brief history of the Council of Defence, see Robert Hyslop, 'The Council of Defence, 1905–1939', *Canberra Historical Journal*, vol. 27, March 1991, pp. 40–7.
61 'Memorandum by the Minister for Defence Submitted to the Council of Defence', 12 May 1905, AWM113, item MH1/2.
62 W.R. Creswell, 'Australian Marine Defence', 7 February 1902, *CPP*, vol. 2, 1901–02.
63 'Minutes of the Meeting of the Council of Defence', 12 May 1905, AA (ACT), A9787, item 2.
64 W.R. Creswell, 'Defence of Australia', 1905, AWM113, item MH1/1.
65 'Minutes of the Meeting of the Council of Defence', 12 May 1905, AA (ACT), A9787, item 2.
66 'Answers to question put to the Director of Naval Forces by the Chief of Intelligence', AWM113, item MH1/2; and 'Report of the Committee of Imperial Defence upon a General Scheme of Defence for Australia', 15 August 1906, *CPP*, vol. 2, 1906, p. 12.
67 'Report on the Department of Defence for the Period from 1st March 1901 to 30th June, 1906', pp. 4–5.
68 Hutton, 'Military Forces of the Commonwealth—1904', p. 30.
69 Grimshaw, 'Some Aspects of Australian Attitudes to the Imperial Connection', p. 129; Norris, *The Emergent Commonwealth*, pp. 137, 154; and I.H. Nish, 'Australia and the Anglo-Japanese Alliance, 1901–1911', *Australian Journal of Politics and History*, no. 9, 1963, p. 210.
70 Alfred Deakin, 'The Defence of Australia', 12 June 1905, *CPP*, vol. 2, 1905, p. 315.
71 Ibid., pp. 315–17.
72 'Deakin to G. Sydenham Clark', 3 October 1905, Deakin Papers, 1540, Box 48, Folder 72, NLA.
73 'Bridges to Minister for Defence', 11 October 1905, Deakin Papers, 1540, Box 48, Folder 72, NLA; and 'Australia: Standard of Fixed Defences', 2 November 1905, AA (VIC), B168, item 06/407.
74 'Military Board Meeting', 19 October 1905, AA (ACT), A2653/1, item 1905/07; 'Bridges to Minister for Defence', 11 October 1905, Deakin Papers, 1540, Box 48, Folder 72, NLA; and

J.C. Hoad, *Annual Report for the Year 1907 by the Inspector-General*, J. Kemp, Melbourne, 1908, p. 19.

75 'Deakin to Committee of Imperial Defence', 11 November 1905, Deakin Papers, 1540, Box 48, Folder 72, NLA.

76 'Report of the Committee of Imperial Defence upon a General Scheme of Defence for Australia', 15 August 1906, *CPP*, vol. 2, 1906, pp. 9, 12–14.

77 Ibid., pp. 3–4, 10.

78 'The Strategical Conditions of the Empire from the Military Point of View', and 'Possibility of Assimilating War Organization Throughout the Empire', in *Two Papers Prepared by the General Staff which were Laid Before the Colonial Conference, 1907*, J. Kemp, Melbourne, 1907.

79 'General Scheme of Defence for Australia: Report of Committee of Officers—Organisation', 27 September 1906, *CPP*, vol. 2, 1906, pp. 4–5; and *General Scheme of Defence for Australia: Report of Committee of Officers: Coast Defences*, Government Printer, Melbourne, 1906, p. 9.

80 For Bridges report, see W.T. Bridges, 'Report on the Swiss Military System', *CPP*, vol. 2, 1907.

81 'Memorandum by Thos Ewing, Minister for Defence', 12 November 1908, *CPP*, Miscellananeous Papers, 1907–09, p. 1.

82 Ibid., pp. 1–2; 'Minutes of the Meeting of the Military Board', 10 December 1907, AA (ACT), A2657/T1, vol. 2; and 'A Brief Narrative of the Organization, Strength and Training of the Australian Military Forces Since Federation', Military Board Proceedings, AA (ACT), A2653/1, 1928, vol. 1, Folder 18.

83 'A Brief Narrative of the Organization, Strength and Training of the Australian Military Forces Since Federation', Military Board Proceedings, AA (ACT), A2653/1, 1928, vol. 1, Folder 18.

84 Ibid.

85 Gordon, *The Imperial Partnership in Imperial Defence*, p. 205; and 'Conference with Representatives of the Self-Governing Dominions on the Naval and Military Defence of the Empire', in *CPP*, vol. 2, 1909, p. 28.

86 'Letter from E.W.D. Ward, Under-Secretary of State, Colonial Office', in 'Correspondence Relating to the Creation of an Imperial General Staff for the Services of the Empire as a Whole', AA (ACT), A2657/T1, vol. 2.

87 'Memorandum by the Chief of the General Staff and of the Commonwealth Section of the Imperial General Staff', 11 November 1910, in *CPP*, vol. 2, 1910; and 'Major-General Hoad's Proposals With Regard to an Australian Section of the Imperial General Staff with the Memorandum of the Chief of the General Staff thereon', AA (ACT), A2657/T1, vol. 2.

88 'Report of the Minister for Defence on the Progress of Universal Training', in *CPP*, vol. 2, 1912, pp. 12–13; and 'Minutes of Sub-Conference on Military Defence', in *CPP*, vol. 2, 1909.

89 'Comments by the Minister for Defence on Memorandum of War Office Dated 15 December 1908 on the Subject of Imperial General Staff', and 'Fisher to the Earl of Dudley', 26 March 1909, in 'Correspondence Relating to the Creation of an Imperial General Staff for the Services of the Empire as a Whole', AA (ACT), A2657/T1, vol. 2; and Gordon, *The Dominion Partnership*, p. 275.

90 G.M. Kirkpatrick, *Annual Report of the Inspector-General of the Military Forces*, J. Kemp, Melbourne, 1911, p. 11.

91 'Defence of Australia, Memorandum by Field Marshall Viscount Kitchener of Khartoum', in *CPP*, vol. 2, 1910, p. 5.

92 Ibid., pp. 3–4.

93 Ibid., pp. 6, 16; and 'Report of the Minister for Defence on the Progress of Universal Training', in *CPP*, vol. 2, 1912, p. 6.

94 'Memorandum on the Organization of the New Citizen Forces', 11 July 1911, AA (VIC), B1535, 929/19/566, part 10.

95 Kirkpatrick, *Annual Report of the Inspector-General, 1911*, p. 12.

96 'Memorandum by Kitchener', p. 11.

97 Rae, 'History of the Australian Army, Part 2, 1905–21', p. 15.

98 'Report of the Minister for Defence on the Progress of Universal Training', in *CPP*, vol. 2, 1912, pp. 6, 13.

99 Ian Hamilton, *Report on an Inspection of the Military Forces of the Commonwealth of Australia*, Albert J. Mullett, Melbourne, 1914, p. 14.

100 Data taken from G.M. Kirkpatrick, *Annual Report of the Inspector-General of the Military Forces*, Albert J. Mullett, Melbourne, 1913. The figures for the authorised strength varies slightly from that first proposed by Kitchener.

101 *Committee of Inquiry into the Citizen Military Forces: Report on the Army Cadet Corps* (Millar Report), GPS, Canberra, 1975, p. 5. The story of the cadet corps is told in John Barrett, *Falling In: Australia and Boy Conscription, 1911–1915*, Hale & Iremonger, Sydney, 1979.

102 *Report of the Military Committee of Inquiry, 1901*, Part 1, General, p. 8; 'Cadet Forces of Australia (Scheme of Organization)', in *CPP*, vol. 2, 1904, p. 1; Hutton, 'Military Forces of the Commonwealth, 1903', p. 22; Hutton, 'Military Forces of the Commonwealth, 1902', p. 28; H. Finn, *Report by the Inspector-General of the Commonwealth Military Forces*, J. Kemp, Melbourne, 1906, p. 17; and 'Military Cadet Corps, Report of the Director General', in *CPP*, vol. 2, 1910, pp. 5–6.

103 J. McCay, 'Memorandum on Cadet Training and University Training in Naval and Military Forces', 31 January 1905, AWM3, item 3.

104 Ibid.

105 'Minutes of the Military Board', 20 November 1908, AA (ACT), A2653/1, vol. 2, 1907/1908.

106 'Report of the Minister for Defence on the Progress of Universal Training', p. 5; and Hamilton, *Report on an Inspection of the Military Forces*, p. 14.

107 'Deakin to Sydenham Clarke', 8 January 1906, Deakin Papers, 1540, Box 48, Folder 73, NLA; and 'The Stages in the Application of Universal Training to Australia', 12 May 1909, Pearce Papers, 1927, series 3, NLA; and Hamilton, *Report on an Inspection of the Military Forces*, p. 21.

108 F.B. Smith, *The Conscription Plebiscites in Australia, 1916–17*, Victorian Historical Association, Melbourne, 1966, p. 5; 'Report of the Minister for Defence on the Progress of Universal Training', p. 9; and Hamilton, *Report on an Inspection of the Military Forces*, p. 21.

109 'Defence Scheme for the Commonwealth of Australia', 1913, NLA, MS2553; and 'Some Notes on Staff Tour on Strategic Mobilisation Positions, 1913', AA (VIC), MP826/1, item 3A.

110 'Ultimate Organisation of the Commonwealth Military Forces', presented at the meeting of the Military Board, 1 July 1914, AA (ACT), A2653/1, item 1914.

111 Hamilton, *Report on an Inspection of the Military Forces*, pp. 12, 14–16.

112 Ibid., pp. 11–12.

113 Meaney, *The Search for Security in the Pacific*, pp. 265–6.

114 Defence Department, 'Memorandum on Australian Military Defence and its Progress Since Federation', 8 December 1909, *CPP*, vol. 2, 1909, p. 6.

3 World War I

1 Ernest Scott, *Australia During the War*, Angus & Robertson, Sydney, 1937, p. 22.

2 Ibid., p. 23.

3 'Government Offer of Expeditionary Force', 6 August 1914, and 'Governor General to Minister for Defence', 6 August 1914, AA (ACT), A2657/T1, vol. 2.

4 'Governor-General to Minister for Defence', 6 August 1914, AA (ACT), A2657/T1, vol. 2.

5 Scott, *Australia During the War*, pp. 203–6.

6 'Bridges to Commandants of Military Districts', 10 August 1914, AA (ACT), A2657/T1, vol. 2; and C.E.W. Bean, *The Story of Anzac*, vol. 1, *From the Outbreak of War to the End of the First Phase of the Gallipoli Campaign, May 4, 1915*, University of Queensland Press, St Lucia, 1981, pp. 37–9.

7 'Bridges to Minister for Defence', 8 August 1914, AA (ACT), A2657/T1, vol. 2; 'Protection of Australia', 23 December 1914, AA (VIC), B197, item 1855/1/58; Lloyd Robson, *The First AIF: A Study in its Recruitment, 1914–1918*, Melbourne University Press, Carlton, 1970, pp. 23, 28–9.

8 Grey, *A Military History of Australia*, p. 94.

9 'Minutes of Special Meeting of the Military Board', 22 August 1915, and 'Minutes of Special Meeting of the Military Board', 13 December 1915, AA (ACT), A2653/1, item

1915; and 'Third Military District Commandant to District HQ', 17 August 1915, AA (VIC), B539, item 264/1/28.

10 Information taken from 'Australian Imperial Force, Units and Formations of the AIF Serving Abroad', AA (VIC), MP367/1, item 469/2/418.

11 Bean, *The Story of Anzac*, vol. 1, p. 119; and *Report upon the Department of Defence From the First of July, 1914 until the Thirtieth of June, 1917*, Albert J. Mullett, Melbourne, 1917, p. 51.

12 Smith, *The Conscription Plebiscites in Australia*, p. 9; and Grey, *A Military History of Australia*, pp. 112–13.

13 Craig Wilcox, 'False Start: The Mobilisation of Australia's Citizen Army, 1914,' *Journal of the Australian War Memorial*, no. 26, April 1995, pp. 4–9.

14 Ibid.; Scott, *Australia During the War*, pp. 197–8; and David Horner, *The Gunners: A History of Australian Artillery*, Allen & Unwin, St Leonards, NSW, 1996, pp. 81–2.

15 'Meeting of the Military Board', 5 September 1914, AA (ACT), A2653/1, item 1914.

16 'Statement for the Minister', 23 November 1914, AA (VIC), B539, item 112/2/218; 'Protection of Australia', 23 December 1914, AA (VIC), B197, item 1855/1/58; and 'Minutes of the Military Board', 30 July 1915, AA (ACT), A2653/1, item 1915.

17 'Minutes of the Military Board', 4 June 1915, 22 June 1915, and 9 November 1915, AA (ACT), A2653/1, item 1915; and 'Minutes of the Military Board', 3 July 1917, AA (ACT), A2653/1, item 1917.

18 'Report by Inspector-General, Australian Imperial Force', 30 December 1915, AA (VIC), B539, item 212/1/22.

19 Ibid.

20 'Adjutant General's Comments on the Report of the Inspector-General, AIF', 12 January 1916, AA (VIC), B539, item 212/1/22.

21 Ibid., and 'Minute Paper Re: Inspector General's Report: AIF Training', 17 January 1916, AA (VIC), B539, item 212/1/22.

22 'Meeting of the Military Board', 10 March 1916, AA (ACT), A2653/1, item 1916; and 'Meeting of the Military Board', 27 February 1918, AA (ACT), A2653/1, item 1918.

23 'Meeting of the Military Board', 30 August 1915 and 11 September 1915, AA (ACT), A2653/1, item 1915.

24 'Meeting of the Military Board', 23 May 1916, AA (ACT), A2653/1, item 1916.

25 'Meeting of the Military Board', 3 July 1917, AA (ACT), A2653/1, item 1917; and 'Memorandum of the Preparation of Australia for Home Defence', 15 June 1917, AA (VIC), B197, item 1856/4/392.

26 'Proposals of the Government for Home Defence of Australia', 12 June 1918, in *CPP*, vol. 4, 1917–19.

27 'Meeting of the Military Board', 11 January 1917, AA (ACT), A2653/1, item 1917.

28 Ibid.

29 'Meeting of the Military Board', 24 August 1917, AA (ACT), A2653/1, item 1917.
30 'Report of the Swinburne Committee on the Army Reserve', AA (VIC), MP367/1, item 592/2/606; and 'Draft Outline for the Establishment in Australia of an Army Reserve', Mackay Collection, PR87/207, item 17, AWM.
31 'Army Reserve', *Sunday Times*, 19 November 1916.
32 'Meeting of the Military Board', 12 December 1916, AA (ACT) A2653/1, item 1916; and 'Meeting of the Military Board', 19 January 1917, AA (ACT), A2653/1, item 1917.
33 'Number of Enlistments in the Australian Army Reserve, November 1919', Mackay Collection, PR 87/207, item 17, AWM; H.G. Chauvel, *Report of the Inspector-General of the Australian Military Forces*, Albert J. Mullett, Melbourne, 1921, pp. 10–11; and H.G. Chauvel, *Report of the Inspector-General of the Australian Military Forces*, Albert J. Mullett, Melbourne, 1924, p. 8.
34 Chauvel, *Report of the Inspector-General*, 1921, p. 11.
35 'Organization for Promoting the Security and Welfare of the Commonwealth of Australia', 5 April 1916, AA (VIC), B197, item 1851/2/260; 'Memorandum Upon the Establishment of a Council of Defence', 1 September 1917 and 15 March 1918, AA (VIC), B197, item 1851/2/46; and Hyslop, 'The Council of Defence', p. 42.
36 'Memorandum Upon the Establishment of a Council of Defence', 15 March 1918, AA (VIC), B197, item 1851/2/46.
37 Ibid.

4 The interwar years

1 'Report on the Military Defence of Australia, by a Conference of Senior Officers of the Australian Military Forces, 1920', vol. 1, p. 6, AWM1, item 20/7.
2 A. Temple Patterson (ed.), *The Jellicoe Papers*, vol. 2, *1916–1935*, Naval Records Society, London, 1968, pp. 346–51, 393.
3 'Report of No. 1 Standing Committee, Council of Defence, Report in Regard to German Possessions in the Pacific', 27 November 1918, AA (VIC), MP1185/6, item 1918/20B.
4 'Imperial Conference 1923, Resolutions Relating to Defence Policy', Council of Defence Agenda, No 1/1935, AA (ACT) A9787/2, item 12.
5 John McCarthy, 'Planning for Future War 1919–1941: The Armed Services and the Imperial Connection', in Peter Dennis (ed.), *Revue Internationale d'Histoire Militaire*, no. 72, Australian Defence Force Academy, Canberra, 1990, pp. 114–15.
6 For a discussion of the implicit obligation to aid Britain, see H.C.H. Robertson, 'The Defence of Australia', *The Army Quarterly*, vol. 30, no. 1, April 1935, pp. 18–19.
7 'Australia's Role in the Pacific Crisis', 4 December 1941, RG165, Entry 79, Box 345, NARA.
8 T.B. Millar, *Australia in Peace and War: External Relations Since 1788*, ANU Press, Botany, NSW, 1991, p. 56.

NOTES (PP. 84–99)

9 Donovan, *Defending the Northern Gateway*, p. 88; and Department of Defence, *Co-operation in Empire Defence*, RAAF Printing Unit, Melbourne, 1945, pp. 7–9.
10 Millar, *Australia's Defence*, p. 20.
11 'Proceedings of the 9th Meeting of the Council of Defence', 15 April 1919, AA (VIC), MP1049/1, item 1919/0106; and 'Notes of Conference Held at Prime Minister's Office Between Members of the Committee Considering Question of Defence and the Acting PM and Acting Minister for Defence', AA (VIC), MP367/1, item 629/1/741.
12 'Meeting of the Military Board', 21 January 1919, and 'Estimated Expenditure of Equipping a Field Force of 300,000 exclusive of Ammunition', 21 January 1919, AA (ACT), A2653/1, item 1919.
13 Data taken from, 'Estimated Expenditure of Equipping a Field Force of 300,000 Exclusive of Ammunition', 21 January 1919, AA (ACT), A2653/1, item 1919.
14 'Swinburne Report', 30 June 1919, AA (VIC), MP367/1, item 629/1/741.
15 Ibid.
16 Ibid.
17 Ibid.
18 Horner, 'Australian Army Strategic Planning Between the Wars', pp. 75–7.
19 Unless otherwise noted, the following section is taken from 'Report on the Military Defence of Australia, by a Conference of Senior Military Officers of the Australian Military Forces', vols. 1 and 2, 1920, AWM1, item 20/7.
20 Information taken from 'Australian Military Forces', AA (VIC), MP153, item 20; and 'Organization, Composition and Distribution of the Australian Army for War', 25 January 1928, AWM113, item MH 1/34.
21 Chauvel, *Report of the Inspector-General of the Australian Military Forces, 1921*, p. 13.
22 'Report on the Military Defence of Australia, by a Conference of Senior Military Officers of the Australian Military Forces', vol. 1, p. 24, AWM1, item 20/7.
23 'Minutes of a Special Meeting of the Council of Defence', 12 April 1920, AA (ACT), A5954/1, items 762/19 and 1209/5; and 'Proceedings of the 9th Meeting of the Council of Defence', 15 April 1919, AA (VIC), MP1049/1, item 1919/0106.
24 'Meeting of the Military Board', 9 June 1920, AA (ACT), A5954/1, item 1209/5.
25 'Memorandum by the Board in Connection with the Estimates for 1920–21', 23 July 1920, AA (ACT), A5954/1, item 1209/5; Chauvel, *Report of the Inspector-General of the Australian Military Forces, 1921*, p. 14; and 'A Brief Narrative of the Organization, Strength and Training of the Australian Military Forces Since Federation', AA (ACT), A2653/1 vol. 1, 1928.
26 'Military Board Agenda, No. 221/20', 17 August 1920, AA (ACT), A5954/1, item 1209/5.
27 Horner, 'Australian Army Strategic Planning Between the Wars', p. 80.
28 'Reorganisation', AA (ACT), A2653/1, item 1920, vol. 2; 'Australian Military Forces', AA

(VIC), MP153, item 20; and 'A Brief Narrative of the Organization, Strength and Training of the Australian Military Forces Since Federation', AA (ACT), A2653/1 vol. 1, 1928. See also 'Military Board Instruction X/G1', 13 October 1920, AA (VIC), B197, item 1937/1/23.

29 'Command and Maintenance of the AMF, War in Australia', October 1941, AA (VIC), MP508/1, item 240/701/190.

30 'Australian Military Forces', AA (VIC), MP153, item 20.

31 'Organization, Composition and Distribution of the Australian Army for War', 25 January 1928, AWM 113, item MH1/134.

32 John McCarthy, *Australia and Imperial Defence 1918–39: A Study in Air and Sea Power*, University of Queensland Press, St Lucia, 1976, p. 11.

33 'Council of Defence: Report of Discussions', 22 March 1923, AA (ACT), A9787, item 3.

34 Ibid., p. 12.

35 Ian Hamill, *The Strategic Illusion: The Singapore Strategy and the Defence of Australia and New Zealand, 1919–1942*, Singapore University Press, Singapore, 1981, pp. 41–2.

36 Figures taken from 'Department of Defence, Estimates of Expenditure, 1922–23', in *CPP*, vol. 2, 1922.

37 Horner, *The Gunners*, p. 192.

38 'CGS Periodical Letter No. 2/1936', AA (ACT), A6828/1, item 2/1936; and 'Summary of Proceedings of Council of Defence', 17 December 1937, AA (ACT), A9787/2, item 41.

39 Figures taken from 'Australian Military Forces', AA (VIC), MP153, item 20. Since the reports were prepared at different times there is a slight difference in the totals for Tables 4.6 and 4.7.

40 Grey, *A Military History of Australia*, pp. 137–8; D.M. Horner, 'Staff Corps Versus Militia: The Australian Experience in World War II', *Defence Force Journal*, no. 26, January–February 1981, p. 15; H.G. Chauvel, *Report of the Inspector-General of the Australian Military Forces*, Albert J. Mullett, Melbourne, 1927, pp. 5–7; and 'First Report by Lieutenant-General E. K. Squires, Inspector-General of the Australian Military Forces', AWM54, item 243/6/58.

41 Ibid., p. 4; H.G. Chauvel, *Report of the Inspector-General of the Australian Military Forces*, Albert J. Mullett, Melbourne, 1922, p. 10; and H.G. Chauvel, *Report of the Inspector-General of the Australian Military Forces*, Albert J. Mullett, Melbourne, 1923, pp. 11, 13.

42 Horner, 'Australian Army Strategic Planning Between the Wars', p. 81.

43 For an example of the role of finances, see the remarks of Prime Minister S.M. Bruce in 'Council of Defence: Report of Discussions', 22 March 1923, AA (ACT), A9787, item 3.

44 Quoted in 'Department of Defence, Estimates of Expenditure, 1922–23', p. 5.

45 Chauvel, *Report of the Inspector-General of the Australian Military Forces, 1924*, p. 8.

46 'Department of Defence, Estimates of Expenditure, 1924–25', in *CPP*, vol. 2, 1924, pp. 2, 6; and 'Minutes of Meeting of Council of Defence', 30 August 1923, AA (ACT), A9787, item 4.

47 'Probable Scale of Attack Against Dominions and Indian Ports, Memorandum by the Overseas Defence Committee: 509', August 1923, AA (ACT), A5954/1, item 1810/10.

48 H.G. Chauvel, *Report for the Inspector-General of the Australian Military Forces*, H.J. Green, Melbourne, 1925, p. 5; and 'Trumble to Military Board', 28 May 1926, AA (VIC), B197, item 1937/1/23.

49 H.G. Chauvel, *Report for the Inspector-General of the Australian Military Forces*, H.J. Green, Melbourne, 1930, pp. 6, 15; and Claude Neumann, 'Australia's Citizen Soldiers, 1919–1939: A Study of Organization, Command, Recruitment, Training and Equipment', thesis for the Degree of Master of Arts, Department of History, UNSW at Duntroon, 1978.

50 Chauvel, *Report for the Inspector-General of the Australian Military Forces, 1930*, pp. 6–7.

51 Ibid., p. 10; 'Organization and Composition of Infantry Brigades', May 1930, and 'Proposed Re-organization 1930/31', 4 April 1930, AA (VIC), B1535, item 849/3/53.

52 'Military Board Agendas 23/32, 24/32, and 25/32', AA (ACT), A2653, item 1932, vol. 1; and 'Circular Letter to Military Districts', 11 March 1932 and 6 April 1932, AA (VIC), B1535, item 849/3/165.

53 Horner, 'Australian Army Strategic Planning Between the Wars', p. 89; and 'Department of Defence, Estimates of Expenditures, 1932–33', AA (ACT), A2653, 1932, vol. 2, Estimates.

54 Chauvel, *Report for the Inspector-General of the Australian Military Forces, 1930*, p. 12.

55 'Minutes of Meeting of Council of Defence', 30 August 1923, AA (ACT), A9787, item 4.

56 Neumann, 'Australia's Citizen Soldiers', pp. 48, 93.

57 'Australian Army Organisation', 3 May 1935, AA (ACT), A9787/2, item 12.

58 Ibid.

59 'Composition, Organization and Distribution of the First Line Component of the Australian Army for War', 1 December 1937, AA (VIC), MP826/1, item 62.

60 Ibid.

61 George Pearce, 'Statement of the Government's Policy Regarding the Defence of Australia', 25 September 1933, pp. 3–4, in Pearce Papers, 1827, series 1, item 1, NLA.

62 Ibid., pp. 1–9.

63 Horner, 'Australian Army Strategic Planning Between the Wars', p. 92.

64 Horner, *The Gunners*, p. 207.

65 'Review of Defence Preparations: The Army', AA (VIC), MP726/6, item 15/401/59; 'CGS Periodical Letter No. 4/1935', AA (ACT), A6828/1, item 4/1935; 'CGS Periodical Letter No. 1/1936', AA (ACT), A6828/1, item 1/1936; 'CGS Periodical Letter No. 4/1937', AA (ACT), A6828/1, item 4/1937; and Horner, *The Gunners*, pp. 203–5.

66 Information taken from 'Order of Battle, Limited Mobilization', 31 August 1939, AA (VIC), MP 826/1, item 41.

67 Horner, *The Gunners*, pp. 210–11.

68 Information taken from 'Order of Battle, Limited Mobilization', 31 August 1939, AA (VIC), MP 826/1, item 41.

69 'Appreciation of Australia's Position in Case of War in the Pacific', 23 March 1932, pp. 1–2, AWM54, item 910/2/4.

70 Ibid., p. 2.
71 Ibid., pp. 2–3.
72 'Australian Coast Defence: Comments by Chief of the General Staff for Representation to the Council', June 1935, p. 2, AA (VIC), MP826, item 39. Interestingly, the report included a notice of disassociation from these opinions by the naval representative.
73 Ibid.
74 Ibid., p. 5.
75 'Memorandum by The Chief of the General Staff on Report on Certain Aspects of Australian Defence by Sir Maurice Hankey', 5 March 1935, Hankey Collection, ADFA, 180391. For Hankey's report, see 'Australian Defence', Hankey Collection, ADFA, 180391.
76 'Reconsideration of Revise of CID Paper 249C: Memo by CGS', 26 June 1935, AA (VIC), MP826, item 39.
77 'Memorandum by Lavarack on Report on Certain Aspects of Australian Defence by Sir Maurice Hankey', Hankey Collection, ADFA, 180391.
78 'A Common Doctrine on the Organisation and Employment of the A.M.F.', AA (VIC), MP826/1, item 14.
79 'CGS Periodical Letter No. 1/1936', AA (ACT), A6828/1, item 1/1936.
80 'The Composition, Organisation and Distribution of the First Line Component of the Australian Army for War', 1 December 1937, AA (VIC), MP826/1, item 62.
81 'Strategic Concentration Outline Plan', 4 June 1937, AA (VIC), MP826/1, item 19.
82 'Infantry Battalions of the Australian Military Forces', August 1936, AA (VIC), B1535, item 849/3/435.
83 'A Common Doctrine', p. 26, AA (VIC), MP826/1, item 14.
84 Ibid.
85 Ibid., pp. 49–51.
86 Ibid., p. 51.
87 Archdale Parkhill, *The Defence of Australia: What the Lyons Government Has Done*, H.J. Green, Melbourne, 1936, pp. 7, 13; and 'Appreciation: The Concentration of the Australian Land Forces in Time of War', AA (VIC), MP826/1, item 43.
88 'First Report by Lieutenant-General E.K. Squires, Inspector-General of the Australian Military Forces', December, 1938, AWM54, item 243/6/58.
89 Ibid; and 'Infantry Battalions of the Australian Military Forces', August 1936, AA (VIC), B1535, item 849/3/435.
90 'First Line Component: Funds Needed to Complete Requirements: Weapons', 1 February 1939, AA (VIC), MP826/1, item 46.
91 'Squires Report', AWM54, item 243/6/58; and 'Defence Requirements: Army: Modified Proposals: Fixed Coast Defences: Statement of Shortage of Personnel of the PMF', 11 March 1938, AA (VIC), MP726/6, item 15/401/59.

92 'Squires Report', AWM54, item 243/6/58.
93 G.A. Street, *Statement by the Hon. G.A. Street, MC, MP, Minister for Defence, on the First Report by Lieutenant-General E.K. Squires*, Melbourne, 1939, p. 5.
94 'Minute: Regular Units: Organisation and Recruiting', 4 May 1939, AA (VIC), B1535, item 849/2/32; 'CGS Periodical Letter No. 3/1939', AA (ACT), A6828/1, item 3/1939; 'Raising of a Permanent Force', AA (VIC), B1535, item 849/2/39; and 'Defence Development Program, 1937/38 to 1940/41: Report on Progress to 30 June 1939', AA (ACT), A9787/2, item 107.
95 Horner, *The Gunners*, p. 212; and 'CGS Periodical Letter No. 4/1938', AA (ACT), A6828/1, item 4/1938.
96 'Squires Report', AWM54, item 243/6/58.
97 Street, *Statement by Street on Squires Report*, pp. 5–7; and '7th Military District: Constitution and Organisation', 8 March 1939, AA (VIC), MP385/3, item 106/5/189.
98 'Command and Maintenance of the AMF, War in Australia', October 1941, AA (VIC), MP508/1, item 240/701/190.
99 'Council of Defence, Summary of Proceedings', 5 July 1939, AA (ACT), A9787/2, item 110; 'CGS Periodical Letter No. 4/1938', AA (ACT), A6828/1, item 4/1938; and 'Defence Development Programme, 1937–38 to 1940–41: Report on Progress to 30th June 1939', AA (ACT), A9787/2, item 107.
100 'Defence Development Program, 1937/38 to 1940/41: Report on Progress to 30 June 1939', AA (ACT), A9787/2, item 107; and 'Council of Defence, Outline of Procedure', 18 March 1938, AA (ACT), A9787/2, item 49.
101 'Defence Development Program, 1937–38 to 1940–41: Report on Progress to 30 June 1939', AA (ACT), A9787/2, item 107; and 'Council of Defence, Notes by Chief of the General Staff', 24 February 1938, AA (VIC), MP726/6, item 15/401/59.
102 'Board Minute on Agenda No. 191/1939', 17 September 1939, AA (VIC), B1535, item 929/19/1148.
103 'Attendance of Militia Personnel at Continuous Courses', 12 September 1939, and 'Minute by the Minister G.A. Street', 16 December 1939, AA (VIC), B1535, item 929/19/1148.
104 Quoted in Donovan, *Defending the Northern Gateway*, pp. 95–6.
105 'Council of Defence, Notes by Chief of the General Staff', 24 February 1938, AA (VIC), MP726/6, item 15/401/59.
106 For example, see 'General Staff Memorandum on the Policy Regarding the Preparation of War Plans', 12 November 1937, AWM54, item 243/6/11.
107 'CGS Periodical Letter No. 2/1936', AA (ACT), A6828/1, item 2/1936; and 'CGS Periodical Letter No. 3/1936', AA (ACT), A6828/1, item 3/1936.
108 'Extracts From Defence Schemes of the Various States', 1901, Deakin Papers, 1540, series 14, box 38, item 534, NLA.

5 World War II

1. Quoted in Paul Hasluck, *The Government and the People, 1939–1941*, Australian War Memorial, Canberra, 1965, p. 152.
2. Quoted in John Robertson, *Australia at War, 1939–1945*, William Heinemann, Melbourne, 1981, p. 6.
3. Ian Hamill, 'An Expeditionary Force Mentality? The Despatch of Australian Troops to the Middle East, 1939–1940', *Australian Outlook*, vol. 31, no. 2, August 1977, p. 320.
4. Quoted in John McCarthy, 'Australian Responses to the European War, 1939–41', *The Australian Journal of Defence Studies*, vol. 1, no. 2, October 1977, p. 151.
5. Gavin Long, *To Benghazi*, Australian War Memorial, Canberra, 1952, pp. 33–5; Hasluck, *The Government and the People, 1939–1941*, pp. 149–51; and 'Statement of Emergency Action Taken by the Defence Services', 28 August 1939, AA (ACT), A5954/69, item 582/1.
6. 'CGS Periodical Letter No. 4/1939', AA (ACT), A6828/1, item 4/1939; and 'Australian War Effort: Basis of Preparation by the Service', 11 September 1939, AA (ACT), A2671/1, item 6/1939.
7. Data taken from 'War Measures Instituted Since the Outbreak of War', 4 November 1939, AA (ACT), A981/1, DEF 59, part 1.
8. Long, *To Benghazi*, p. 35; and 'Order of Battle: Limited Mobilisation', 31 August 1939, AA (VIC), MP826/1, item 41.
9. Data taken from 'Strength and Present Dispositions of the Force to Meet Scales of Attack', AA (ACT), A2671/1, item 418/1941.
10. 'Military Board Memorandum on Immediate Military Requirements', 9 September 1939, AA (ACT), A2653/1, 1939, vol. 3.
11. Long, *To Benghazi*, p. 39.
12. 'Announcement by Menzies Regarding . . . the Reintroduction of Compulsory Military Service', 20 October 1939, and 'Removal of Suspension of Universal Training', 26 October 1939, AA (VIC), B1535, item 929/19/1158; 'Broadcast by Menzies', 6 March 1940, and 'War Measures Instituted Since the Outbreak of War', 4 November 1939, AA (ACT), A981/1, DEF 59, part 1; 'Policy to be Adopted for the Future Training of the Militia', 5 February 1940, AA (ACT), A2653/1, 1940, vol. 1; and R.M. Bennett, *Expansion of the Australian Army (World War 2): The Raising of the 2nd AIF*, Department of Defence, Canberra, 1974, p. 30.
13. 'Minute Paper', 23 October 1939, AA (VIC), B1535, item 929/19/1158; and 'Broadcast by Menzies', 6 March 1940, AA (ACT), A981/1, DEF 59, part 1.
14. 'Report by the Military Board on the Raising of a Special Force for Continuous Service Either in Australia or Overseas', 13 September 1939, AA (ACT), A2653/1, 1939, vol. 3; 'Australia's War Effort: Basis of Preparations by the Services', 11 September 1939, AA (ACT), A2671/1, item 6/1939; 'Despatch of Forces Overseas: Draft War Cabinet Decision',

AA (ACT), A5954/69, item 582/2; and 'Australian Cooperation in Empire Defence', AA (ACT), A5954/69, item 582/9. See also, 'The War Situation from the Australian Viewpoint', 23 March 1942, AA (ACT), A5954/1, item 587/5.

15 Hasluck, *The Government and the People, 1939–1941*, p. 168; McCarthy, 'Australian Responses to the European War, 1939–41', pp. 152–4; 'Despatch of Forces Overseas: Draft War Cabinet Decision', AA (ACT), A5954/69, item 582/2; and 'Statement by Prime Minister in House of Representatives', 29 November 1939, AA (ACT), A816/1, item 52/302/135.

16 Long, *To Benghazi*, p. 41.

17 See also Horner, 'Staff Corps versus Militia', p. 13.

18 'Cable to Secretary of State for Dominion Affairs', 6 April 1940, AA (ACT), A1608/1, item B/45/2/1.

19 'Report by the Military Board on the Raising of a Special Force for Continuous Service Either in Australia or Overseas', 13 September 1939, and 'Formation, Designation and Organization of the Special Force', 28 September 1939, AA (ACT), A2653/1, 1939, vol. 3.

20 'Numbers Required for an Australian Corps of Two Divisions, Corps Troops, and Line of Communication Units: British Organisation, War Cabinet Agendum No. 22/1940', 10 February 1940, AA (ACT), A2671/1, item 22/1940.

21 'The New Infantry Organization, Lecture by Lt.-Col. J.C.W. Baillon', December 1939, AWM54, item 923/1/6; and 'Organization and War Establishments 2nd AIF, War Cabinet Agendum 22/1940', 11 March 1940, AA (ACT), A2671/1, item 22/1940.

22 Long, *To Benghazi*, pp. 51–3; 'Cypher Telegram, Squires to London House', 21 November 1939, AA (ACT), A5954/69, item 582/2; and 'Minute by Squires re: Organization of Battalion', 8 March 1939, AA (VIC), B1535, item 849/2/25.

23 'Cypher Telegram, Squires to Northcott', 21 November 1939, AA (ACT), A5954/69, item 582/2; 'Report by the Military Board on the Raising of a Special Force for Continuous Service Either in Australia or Overseas', 13 September 1939, AA (ACT), A2653/1, 1939, vol. 3.

24 'Organization and War Establishments AIF, War Cabinet Agendum No. 22/40, supplement No. 4', AA (ACT), A2671/1, item 22/1940; and 'Australia and the War: The Future Programme', 6 March 1940, AA (ACT), A981/1, DEF 59, part 1.

25 'Future Establishment and Organization of AIF, War Cabinet Agendum No. 197/1941, Supplement No. 1', 13 August 1941, Blamey Collection, 3DRL6643, item 4/15, AWM.

26 'Department of Defence Co-ordination to Bruce', 4 January 1940, AA (ACT), A1608/1, item B/45/2/1.

27 'Military Board Agenda Item 29/1940', 23 January 1940, AA (ACT), A2653/1, 1940, vol. 1.

28 'Policy to be Adopted for the Future Training of the Militia', 5 February 1940, AA (ACT), A2653/1, 1940, vol. 1.

29 'Summary of Camp Strength by Camps of AIF and Militia Forces', 21 September 1940, AA (ACT), A816/1, item 52/302/50.

30 David Horner, *Crisis of Command: Australian Generalship and the Japanese Threat, 1941–1943*, Australian National University Press, Canberra, 1978, pp. 16 18.

31 Figures taken from 'Strength and Present Dispositions of the Forces to Meet Scales of Attack', AA (ACT), A2671/1, item 418/1941.

32 Quoted in John McCarthy, 'The Imperial Commitment, 1939–41', *Australian Journal of Politics and History*, vol. 23, no. 2, August 1977, p. 181.

33 Bennett, *Expansion of the Australian Army*, p. 29.

34 McCarthy, 'The Imperial Commitment', p. 181.

35 F.M. Budden, *That Mob: The Story of the 55/53rd Australian Infantry Battalion, AIF*, Budden, Ashfield, 1973, pp. 1–2.

36 Horner, *Crisis of Command*, p. 33.

37 Russell Mathews, *Militia Battalion at War: The History of the 58/59th Australian Infantry Battalion in the Second World War*, 58/59th Battalion Association, Sydney, 1961, p. 1.

38 Ibid., p. 21; 'An Appreciation of the Situation on the Defence of Southern Australia by Senior Staff Officers of Southern Command', 15 October 1941, AWM54, item 243/6/13; and 'Statement Showing Requirements of Initial (Fighting), Training and 6 Months Reserve of Certain Items of Equipment Together With Stocks Available and Percentage of those Stocks in Relation to the Initial (Fighting) Requirements for AMF (Order of Battle) Mobilization, AIF in Australia and Armoured Division (AIF)', 30 November 1941, AA (ACT) A2671/1, item 418/1941.

39 Horner, *Crisis of Command*, p. 14, and 'Raising of Training Units and Reinforcements AIF and AMF', AA (VIC), MP729/6, item 37/401/660.

40 For a discussion of this see Horner, 'Staff Corps versus Militia: The Australian Experience in World War II'.

41 'Conversion of Infantry From AMF to AIF War Establishment', 1 April 1942, Blamey Collection, 3DRL6643, item 2/85.22, AWM.

42 'War Cabinet Agendum 197/1942, Future Policy of AIF', AA (ACT), A5954/69, item 261/6; 'Formation of Training Units: Reinforcement 2nd AIF', 16 February 1940 and 'Reinforcement Officers: 2nd AIF', 27 February 1940, AWM49, item 40; and 'AMF Southern Command: Recruiting Corps Troops and 7th Division AIF', 2 May 1940, AWM49, item 43. See also, Bennett, *Expansion of the Australian Army*, p. 22.

43 Information taken from 'Order of Battle, Limited Mobilisation', 31 August 1939, AA (VIC), MP826/1, item 41.

44 'C-in-C to DSD', 4 May 1943, and 'C-in-C to CGS', 31 December 1942, Blamey Collection, 3DRL6643, item 2/85.22, AWM; and Bennett, *Expansion of the Australian Army*, p. 34.

45 'Extended Area for Use of Conscripts', 19 February 1943, RG165, Entry 77, File 6000, NARA.

46 Information taken from 'Army War Effort', February 1944, ADFA, item 254612.

NOTES (PP. 155–75)

47 'War Measures Instituted Since the Outbreak of War', 4 November 1939, AA (ACT), A981/1, DEF 59, part 1; and 'Australian War Efforts: Basis of Preparation by the Service', 11 September 1939, AA (ACT), A2671/1, item 6/1939.

48 Horner, *The Gunners*, pp. 318–19; see also Reg Kidd and Ray Neal, *The History of the Letter Batteries in World War II*, Castlecrag, 1998.

49 Horner, *The Gunners*, pp. 238, 316–17.

50 Information taken from ibid., 316–17.

51 Ronald McNicoll, *The Royal Australian Engineers 1919 to 1945: Teeth and Tail*, Corps Committee of the Royal Australian Engineers, Canberra, 1982, pp. 299–303.

52 176 Air Dispatch Company, *Unit History*, 176 Air Dispatch Company, Richmond, NSW, 1999.

53 'Army War Effort', August 1944, Blamey Collection, 3DRL6643, item 3/8, AWM.

54 David Horner, *Inside the War Cabinet: Directing Australia's War Effort 1939–45*, Allen & Unwin, St Leonards, NSW, 1996, pp. 3–5.

55 'Modification in Operational Control of GOC Home Forces', 5 February 1942, RG165, Entry 77, File 6000, NARA; 'Organization: Northern, Eastern and Southern Commands', 27 January 1942, AWM54, item 721/12/25; and 'The Army War Effort', August 1944, Blamey Collection, 3DRL6643, item 3/8, AWM.

56 Horner, *Crisis of Command*, p. 66; and 'The Army War Effort', August 1944, Blamey Collection, 3DRL6643, item 3/8, AWM.

57 Robertson, *Australia at War*, pp. 111, 114; and 'History of the Establishment of the SWPA', AA (ACT), A5954/69, item 649/5.

58 'The Army War Effort', August 1944, Blamey Collection, 3DRL6643, item 3/8, AWM.

59 'Australian Cooperation in Empire Defence', 26 September 1939, AA (ACT), A5954/69, item 582/9.

60 Robertson, *Australia at War*, p. 100; and 'Summary of Recent Appreciation of Defence in Australia by the Australian Chiefs of Staff', RG165, Entry 421, File ABC381 Australia, NARA.

61 Robertson, *Australia at War*, p. 194; and 'War Cabinet Minute, Agendum No. 281/1942: Re-organization of the Army in Australia', 30 June 1942, Blamey Collection, 3DRL6643, item 4/15, AWM.

62 Bennett, *Expansion of the Australian Army*, pp. 28–9.

63 For a discussion of the government's desire to balance the war effort, see Paul Hasluck, *The Government and the People, 1942–1945*, Australian War Memorial, Canberra, 1970, pp. 371–442; and Horner, *Inside the War Cabinet*, pp. 150–63.

64 Robertson, *Australia at War*, pp. 159–60.

65 'Review of the War Effort of the Services in the Light of the Present Situation With Particular Reference to the Provision Being Made for the Defence of the Mainland', March 1944, AA (ACT), A5954/1, item 309/2.

NOTES (PP. 177–86)

66 Data taken from ibid.
67 Ibid.
68 'The Maintenance of a Balanced Australian War Effort While Providing for United States and United Kingdom Needs', January 1945, AA (ACT), A5954/1, item 309/4.
69 Ibid.; and 'The Australian Direct War Effort', 14 June 1945, Blamey Collection, 3DRL6643, item 2/23.12, AWM.
70 'Outline of Re-organizational Changes to Effect A Reduction of the Order of Battle', 12 April 1943, AA (ACT), A5954/69, item 261/1; 'Existing and New Organizations of Infantry Divisions', and 'Reorganization of Infantry Divisions,' 9 March 1943, AWM54, item 721/2/11, part 2; and 'Reorganization of L of C Areas in Relation to Armies', 17 February 1943, AWM54, item 721/12/25.
71 'Blamey to CGS', 3 September 1943, Blamey Collection, 3DRL6643, item 2/23.72, AWM.
72 Robertson, *Australia at War*, p. 196; and 'The Australian Direct War Effort', 14 June 1945, Blamey Collection, 3DRL6643, item 2/23.12, AWM.
73 'The Formation of an Armoured Division', 13 November 1940, AA(VIC), MP729/6, item 37/401/228; and 'War Cabinet Agendum: Conversion of AMF Cavalry Units', AA (VIC), MP729/6, item 37/401/759.
74 The origins of Australian mechanisation is told in R.N.L. Hopkins, *Australian Armour: A History of the Royal Australian Armoured Corps, 1927–1972*.
75 Chauvel, *Report of the Inspector General, 1930*, p. 11; 'Statement of the Government's Policy Regarding the Defence of Australia', 25 September 1933, Pearce Papers, 1827, series 1, item 1, NLA; 'CGS Periodical Letter, No. 1/1934', AA (ACT), A6828, item 1/1934; 'CGS Periodical Letter, No. 3/1934', AA (ACT), A6828, item 3/1934; and 'CGS Periodical Letter, No. 1/1935', AA (ACT), A6828, item 1/1935.
76 'Blamey to Minister for Defence', 1 May 1942, AA (VIC), MP729/6, item 37/401/759; 'The Army War Effort', August 1944, Blamey Collection, 3DRL6643, item 3/8, AWM; and Hopkins, *Australian Armour*, pp. 325–30.
77 'The Army War Effort', August 1944, Blamey Collection, 3DRL6643, item 3/8, AWM; and Hopkins, *Australian Armour*, pp. 325–30.
78 Ibid.
79 Unless otherwise noted this section is taken from 'Re-organization of Infantry Formations in the A.M.F.', 13 February 1943, AWM54, item 721/2/11, part 2.
80 'Basic Staff Table of Units of a Jungle Division', 21 November 1943, AWM54, item 905/25/57.
81 Data taken from organisational charts of Jungle and Standard Divisions in AWM54, item 721/2/11, part 3.
82 'The Army War Effort', February, 1944, Blamey Collection, 3DRL6643, item 3/7, AWM; 'Citizen Militia Force Known as Volunteer Defence Corps', 30 September 1942, RG 165, Entry 77, File 6020, NARA.

83 'S. Comd. Operation Instruction No. 4, For VDC', 14 March 1941, AA (VIC), MP729/6, item 37/401/505.

84 'Citizen Militia Force Known as Volunteer Defence Corps', 30 September 1942, RG 165, Entry 77, File 6020, NARA.

85 Ibid.; and 'The Army War Effort', February, 1944, Blamey Collection, 3DRL6643, item 3/7, AWM.

86 'The Army War Effort', August 1944, Blamey Collection, 3DRL6643, item 3/8, AWM.

87 Ibid.; and 'Australian War Effort', February, 1944, Blamey Collection, 3DRL6643, item 3/7, AWM.

88 'CGS to C in C', 9 October 1942, and 'C in C to Minister for Army', 13 October 1942, Blamey Collection, 3DRL6643, item 2/35, AWM; and 'Australian War Effort', February 1944, Blamey Collection, 3DRL6643, item 3/7, AWM.

89 'CGS to Spender', 2 August 1941, and 'Spender to Adjutant-General', 27 August 1941, AA (VIC), MP729/6, item 37/401/574; and 'OC Coogee–Randwick Area RSL Defence Corps to the Prime Minister', 3 September 1940, A1608/1, F/45/1/2, part 1.

90 'Future Policy of the VDC', 7 May 1944, AA (ACT) A5954/69, item 268/2; 'VDC Establishment', 31 August 1944, Blamey Collection, 3DRL6643, item 2/35, AWM; and 'Rear Echelon First Army', October 1944, AWM54, item 243/6/32.

91 For the story of the Australian Army Nursing Service, see Jan Bassett, *Guns and Brooches: Australian Army Nursing from the Boer War to the Gulf War*, Oxford University Press, Melbourne, 1992. See also '2nd AIF: Summary War Establishment', AA (ACT), A5954/69, item 261/7.

92 'Army War Effort', August 1944, p. 33, Blamey Collection, 3DRL6643, item 3/8, AWM.

93 'Australian War Effort', February, 1944, Blamey Collection, 3DRL6643, item 3/7, AWM; and *Argus*, 26 July 1941.

94 'Australian War Effort', February, 1944, Blamey Collection, 3DRL6643, item 3/7, AWM.

95 'War Cabinet Minutes', 4 February 1941, and 30 December 1941, and 'War Cabinet Agendum No. 444/1941', 29 December 1941, AA (ACT), A5954/69, item 741/7.

96 *Argus*, 15 May 1945; 'Blamey to Forde', 17 July 1945 and 25 July 1945, Blamey Collection, 3DRL6643, item 2/34.2, AWM.

97 'Recruiting for the Interim Army', 13 April 1946, AWM54, item 834/1/2.

98 'Organisation of AIF Formations for Offensive Operations After Conclusion of OBOE Series', 10 May 1945, Blamey Collection, 3DRL6643, item 2/23.12, AWM.

6 Post-war reorganisation and the Korean War

1 'Summary of Proceedings of the Inaugural General Meeting of the Military Board', 28 February 1946, AA (ACT), A816/1, item 31/301/407.

2 Graeme Sligo, 'The Development of the Australian Regular Army, 1944–1952', in Peter Dennis & Jeffrey Grey (eds), *The Second Fifty Years: The Australian Army, 1947–1997*, University College, University of New South Wales, ADFA, Canberra, 1997, p. 47.

3 An example of Australia taking a leading role in the shaping of its defence relationships is the Canberra Pact between the Commonwealth and New Zealand. See T.B. Millar, 'Anglo-Australian Partnership in Defence of the Malaysian Area', in A.F. Madden & W.H. Morris Jones (eds), *Australia and Britain: Studies in a Changing Relationship*, Sydney University Press, Sydney, 1980, p. 71.

4 Noted in 'Minute: Post War Defence Policy', 7 February 1944, AA (ACT), A816/1, item 14/301/275.

5 'Post War Defence Policy', 7 January 1944, Blamey Collection, 3DRL6643, item 2/27, AWM.

6 'Curtin to Chifley', 2 March 1944, AA (ACT), A816/1, item 14/301/274.

7 'Minutes of Council of Defence Meeting', 12 March 1947, AA (ACT), A9787/2, item 111.

8 Ibid.

9 'The Progress of the Five Years Defence Programme and Higher Defence Machinery', 29 April 1948, p. 8, AA (ACT), A5954/69, item 98/10.

10 Defence Committee, 'A Strategic Basis of Australian Defence Policy', 8 January 1953, AA (ACT), A1209/23, item 1957/4152; and 'Organisation of Australian Expeditionary Force', 23 July 1952, AA (ACT), A6922/1, item 1/05.

11 'Minutes of Council of Defence Meeting', 12 March 1947, AA (ACT), A9787/2, item 111; and Robert O'Neill, *Australia in the Korean War, 1950–53*, vol. 1, *Strategy and Diplomacy*, Australian War Memorial and AGPS, Canberra, 1981, p. 21.

12 Millar, 'Anglo-Australian Partnership in Defence of the Malaysian Area', p. 72.

13 'An Appreciation by the Chiefs of Staff of the Strategical Position of Australia', September 1947, AA (ACT), A816/1, item 14/301/321.

14 Millar, *Australia in Peace and War*, pp. 156, 160.

15 Coral Bell, *Dependent Ally: A Study in Australian Foreign Policy*, Oxford University Press, Melbourne, 1988, pp. 48–9; and O'Neill, *Australia in the Korean War*, vol. 1, p. 188.

16 'Outline Plan for Demobilisation of the Australian Defence Forces', February 1945, AA (VIC), MP742/1, item 284/1/325.

17 'Plans for Demobilisation of the Australian Defence Forces', May 1945, AA (VIC), MP742/1, item 284/1/305.

18 'Adjutant-General to Military Board', 29 April 1946, AA (VIC), MP742/1, item 240/1/2317.

19 'Military Board Minute, Agendum 16/1946', 3 May 1946, AA (VIC), MP742/1, item 240/1/2317.

20 Peter Bates, *Japan and the British Commonwealth Occupation Force, 1946–52*, Brassey's, London, 1993, pp. 13–16.

21 J.E. Murphy, 'History of the Post-War Army', pp. 23–4, 168, ADFA, 146233; and 'Plan for a British Commonwealth Force to Participate in the Occupation of Japan', 15 May 1946, AWM114, item 130/2/43, part 5.

22 J.E. Murphy, 'History of the Post-War Army', p. 26; and Robert O'Neill, *Australia in the Korean War*, vol. 1, pp. 36–7.

23 'Board Minute on Military Board Agendum 141/1947', 27 August 1947, AA (VIC), MP742/1, item 240/1/2785; 'Military Board Instruction No. 191', 7 November 1947, AA (ACT), A2653/1, 1947, volume 4; 'Supplement No. 1 to Military Board Agendum 7/1948', and 'Chifley to Minister for the Army', 31 March 1948, AA (ACT), A2653/1, 1948, vol. 1. See also Sligo, 'The Development of the Australian Regular Army', p. 39.

24 'The Post-War Army: Policy Paper No. 1', 6 March 1946, AA (ACT), A816/1, item 52/301/245.

25 Ibid.

26 'Minute by Defence Committee', 4 May 1945, AA (ACT), A5954/1, item 1645/1; 'Notes of Meeting of Ministers on Council of Defence', 6 March 1947, 'Minutes of Council of Defence Meeting', 12 March 1947, and 'Minutes of Council of Defence', 30 May 1947, AA (ACT), A9787/2, item 111. See also O'Neill, *Australia in the Korean War*, vol. 1, pp. 23–5.

27 'Notes of Meeting of Ministers on Council of Defence', 6 March 1947, AA (ACT), A9787/2, item 111.

28 Murphy, 'History of the Post-War Army', p. 27, ADFA, 146233.

29 'Council of Defence Agendum, 2/1947: Post-War Policy and Allocation of the Vote', 27 May 1947, AA (ACT), A816/1, item 14/301/294A; and 'Army Post War Plan', March 1947, AA (ACT), A816/1, item 521/301/245.

30 'Army Post War Plan', March 1947, AA (ACT), A816/1, item 521/301/245.

31 Murphy, 'History of the Post-War Army', p. 41, ADFA, 146233.

32 'Post War Army: PMF Brigade Group', 29 August 1947, AA (VIC), MP724/1, item 240/1/2781; and 'Chief of the General Staff Branch, Army Organisation', AA (VIC), MP742/1, item 240/1/3118. See also David Horner (ed.), *Duty First: The Royal Australian Regiment in War and Peace*, Allen & Unwin, North Sydney, 1990, p. 54; and Bates, *Japan and the British Commonwealth Occupation Force*, p. 187.

33 Information taken from 'Post War Army Organisation', AWM51, item 146.

34 Ibid.

35 'Minute: Short Term Service in PMF', 23 April 1946, AA (ACT), A2653/1, 1945, vol. 8; and Sligo, 'The Development of the Australian Regular Army', p. 43.

36 Information taken from 'Post War Army Organisation', AWM51, item 146.

37 Sligo, 'The Development of the Australian Regular Army', pp. 43–4.

38 'Parliamentary Questions', 22 April 1948 and 23 February 1949, AA (ACT), A5954/69, item 98/12. See also Murphy, 'History of the Post-War Army', pp. 65–6, Horner (ed.), *Duty First*, p. 54, and O'Neill, *Australia in the Korean War*, vol. 1, p. 31.

39 'Post-War Army Organisation and Activities: Demobilisation 1939–45 War', AA (VIC), MP742/1, item 240/1/3118; and Adjutant-General, 'Means of Improving Recruiting', 14 January 1948, and 'Special Enlistment in the ARA of Serving Other Rank Personnel', 21 January 1948, AA (ACT), A2653/1, 1948, vol. 1.

40 D.S. McCarthy, 'The Once and Future Army: An Organizational, Political and Social History of the Citizen Military Forces, 1947–1974', thesis submitted for the degree of Doctor of Philosophy in the School of History, University College, Australian Defence Force Academy, University of New South Wales, 1997, pp. 30–3.

41 'Manning of Service Signal Stations', 16 February 1950, AA (ACT), A2653/1, 1949, vol. 1; and 'Women's Services', 12 May 1950, and 'Cabinet Minute, Decision No. 269', 6 December 1951, AA (ACT), A2653/1, 1949, vol. 3.

42 'RAANS and AAMWS in the ARA', 7 July 1949, and 'Cabinet Minute, Decision No. 269', 6 December 1951, AA (ACT), A2653/1, 1949, vol. 3; and Bassett, *Guns and Brooches*, pp. 182–3.

43 'The Supplementary Reserve', AA (ACT), A3688/26, item 729/R1/20; and 'Outline of Actions Leading to the Raising of the SR Railway Units', 31 December 1968, AA (ACT), A3688/25, item 579/R6/12.

44 Information taken from 'Supplementary Reserve on the AMF ORBAT of E and S Comd as of 26 October 1967', AA (ACT), A3688/26, item 729/R1/20.

45 'Post-War Army Establishment on Which CMF Units are to be Raised', 21 October 1947, AA(ACT), A2653/1, 1947, vol. 3; and 'An Appreciation by the Chiefs of Staff on the Strategical Position of Australia', September 1947, p. 36, AA (ACT), A816/1, item 14/301/321. For the American source, see 'Disclosure of Contents of British Crossroads Report to Service Chiefs of Canada, Australia and New Zealand', 5 June 1947, RG165, Entry 421, File 471.6 Atom, 17 August 1945, section 1, NARA.

46 'Designation of Units, Military Board Agendum 131/1947', 20 August 1947, and 'Designation of Units of the Post War Army', 26 February 1948, AA (ACT), A2653/1, 1947, vol. 4. For the 42nd Battalion Association campaign see AA (VIC), MP742/1, item 240/1/2886.

47 Murphy, 'History of the Post-War Army', pp. 7, 168; and 'An Appreciation by the Chiefs of Staff on the Strategical Position of Australia', September 1947, p. 35, AA (ACT), A816/1, item 14/301/321.

48 'Affiliation of School Cadet Units with CMF Battalions', 30 August 1948, AA (ACT), A2653/1, 1948, vol. 1; and 'Post War Army Organisation', AWM51, item 146.

49 'The Australian Cadet Corps', AA (VIC), MP742/1, item 240/1/3118.

50 O'Neill, *Australia in the Korean War*, vol. 1, p. 76.

51 Robert O'Neill, *Australia in the Korean War, 1950–53*, vol. 2, *Combat Operations*, Australian War Memorial and AGPS, Canberra, 1985, pp. 9–10.

52 Murphy, 'History of the Post-War Army', pp. 57–8, 78–9, 173.

53 O'Neill, *Australia in the Korean War*, vol. 1, pp. 33–4, 106, 251.

54 See Robert Menzies, 'The Defence Call to the Nation', *Current Notes on International Affairs*, vol. 21, no. 9, September 1950, pp. 658–69.

55 Murphy, 'History of the Post-War Army', pp. 66–75, 167–8.

56 Menzies, 'The Defence Call to the Nation', pp. 664–5; and Murphy, 'History of the Post-War Army', pp. 66–7.

57 Murphy, 'History of the Post-War Army', pp. 74, 87, 92.

58 'Machinery for Higher Direction of the Army', 15 January 1946, AA (ACT), A2653/1, 1945, vol. 7.

59 Ibid.

60 'Reinstitution of Command Organisation', 23 February 1946, AA (ACT), A2653/1, 1945, vol. 8.

61 'Reorganisation of 4th and 6th Military Districts', 17 November 1949, and 'Reorganisation of Southern Command', 5 December 1949, AA (ACT), A2653/1, 1949, vol. 1.

62 'Reconstitution of the Military Board', 9 July 1946, AA (ACT), A2653/1, 1945, vol. 7.

63 'General Staff Branch Instruction No. 1', 8 March 1946, AA (ACT), A2653/1, 1946, vol. 1.

64 'Sturdee to Minister for Defence', 20 January 1948, and 'Appointment of CMF Member to the Military Board', 11 March 1949, AA (ACT), A2653/1, 1947, vol. 1.

7 The rise of the Australian Regular Army

1 'The Reorganisation of the AMF 1959/60–1961/62: General Staff Instruction No. 1', 22 December 1959, AA (ACT), A6059/2, item 41/441/69a.

2 Thomas-Durrell Young, *Assessing the 1987 Australian Defence White Paper in the Light of Domestic Political and Allied Influences on the Objective of Defence Self-Reliance*, Research School of Pacific Studies, Australian National University, Canberra, 1988, pp. 2–3.

3 *CPD*, 4 April 1957, p. 572.

4 For a summary of the agreements governing the strategic reserve, see David Hawkins, *The Defence of Malaysia and Singapore: From AMDA to ANZUK*, Royal United Service Institute, London, 1972.

5 Quoted in Dupont, *Australia's Threat Perceptions*, pp. 48–9.

6 Millar, *Australia in War and Peace*, p. 175.

7 Bell, *Dependent Ally*, p. 76.

8 Ibid., pp. 69–79.

9 *CPD*, 4 April 1957, pp. 571–2.

10 'Organisation of Australian Expeditionary Forces', 23 July 1952, AA (ACT), A6922/1, item 1/05.

11 Stewart Woodman and David Horner, 'Land Forces in the Defence of Australia', in David Horner (ed.), *Reshaping the Australian Army: Changes for the 1990s*, Australian National University, Canberra, 1991, p. 10.

12 Defence Committee, 'A Strategic Basis of Australian Defence Policy', 8 January 1953, AA (ACT), A1209/23, item 1957/4152.
13 Peter Edwards, *Crises and Commitments: The Politics and Diplomacy of Australia's Involvement in South East Asian Conflicts, 1948–1965*, Allen & Unwin, North Sydney, 1992, pp. 110, 163.
14 Ibid., pp. 167–9, 170, 175–8.
15 Defence Committee, 'The Strategic Basis of Australian Defence Policy', October 1956, AA (ACT), A1196/7, item 15/501/378.
16 Ibid.
17 Ibid.
18 Peter Dennis & Jeffrey Grey, *Emergency and Confrontation: Australian Military Operations in Malaya and Borneo, 1950–1966*, Allen & Unwin, St Leonards, 1996, p. 71.
19 Edwards, *Crises and Commitments*, p. 114.
20 'Review of the Tasks, Capabilities and Structure of the Australian Defence Forces, Chief of Staff Agendum No. 89/1966, Appendix 1: Extract From Interim Review of the Strategic Basis of Australian Defence Policy', 1 December 1966, AA (ACT), A6922/1, item 2/09.
21 Ibid.
22 Ibid.
23 McCarthy, 'The Once and Future Army', pp. 74, 81.
24 'Post War Organisation', AWM113, item MH1/175; and Horner, *The Gunners*, pp. 438–41.
25 McCarthy, 'The Once and Future Army', pp. 55–6.
26 Ibid., p. 65.
27 Ibid., p. 69.
28 Horner, *Duty First*, pp. 93–4; and Grey, *A Military History of Australia*, p. 215.
29 T.B. Millar, 'Australian Defence, 1945–1965', in Gordon Greenwood & Norman Harper (eds), *Australia in World Affairs, 1961–1965*, F.W. Cheshire, Melbourne, 1968, p. 274.
30 'British Commonwealth FESR: General Directive', 1955, AA (ACT), A6059/2, item 41/441/82.
31 Figures quoted in Troy Ramage, 'In Search of Security: Australian Strategic Planning and the Army, 1945–1964', thesis submitted in part fulfilment of the requirements for the degree of Bachelor of Arts (Honours), School of History, University College, Australian Defence Force Academy, University of New South Wales, 1997, p. 70.
32 'Minutes of Conference Held at Victoria Barracks', 31 May 1957, AA (ACT), A6059/2, item 41/441/47.
33 McCarthy, 'The Once and Future Army', p. 69.
34 Unless otherwise noted, the information from this section is taken from: 'The Composition of the Army: Appendix A to Supplement No. 4 to Military Board Agendum No. 43/1956'; 'Reorganisation of the Australian Army: Proposal for Two Full Years Full Time National

Service: Annex B to Supplement No. 3 to Agendum No. 43/1956'; and John Cramer, 'Reorganisation of the Australian Army', 1956, all in AA (ACT), A6059/2, item 41/441/18.

35 After the implementation of the 1957 reorganisation, the actual establishment for the regular Infantry Brigade Group was slightly smaller than that considered in 1956. Its establishment was 257 officers and 4,387 other ranks, for a total of 4,644 personnel. See 'Present Strength: 1 Inf Bde Gp', AA (ACT), A6059/2, item 41/441/60.
36 'Dougherty to DCGS', 25 June 1956, AA (ACT), A6059/2, item 65/441/19.
37 David Horner, *SAS: Phantoms of the Jungle, A History of the Australian Special Air Service*, Allen & Unwin, Sydney, 1989, pp. 33–4.
38 'Three Year Army Programme, 1957–58 to 1959–60', AA (ACT), A6059/2, item 23/441/19.
39 'Staff Table: 1 Inf. Bde Gp.: Personnel', AA (ACT), A6059/2, item 41/441/60.
40 'Composition of Battalion Group and an Appropriate Logistic Support Element', AA (ACT), A6059/2, item 41/441/60.
41 'Infantry Brigade Group: Logistic Support Units', AA (ACT), A6059/2, item 41/441/60.
42 'Composition of Battalion Group and an Appropriate Logistic Support Element', AA (ACT), A6059/2, item 41/441/60.
43 Data taken from 'Composition of the Regular Army: By Categories Based on Strengths in Army Programme for 1956–7', AA (ACT), A6059/2, item 41/441/18.
44 Cramer, 'Reorganisation of the Australian Army', AA (ACT), A6059/2, item 41/441/18.
45 Establishment figures quoted in Ramage, 'In Search of Security', p. 71.
46 'Minutes of Conference Held at Victoria Barracks', 31 May 1957, AA (ACT), A6059/2, item 15/441/23.
47 'Manpower Problems and Implications in the Despatch of Infantry Brigade Group Overseas', 20 August 1958, and 'Infantry Brigade Group: Logistic Support Units', 1957, AA (ACT), A6059/2, item 41/441/60.
48 Ibid; and 'Implications of Build Up of BN Group to TE', 1958, AA (ACT), A6059/2, item 41/441/60.
49 Data taken from 'Present Strength: 1 Inf. Bde Gp.', AA (ACT), A6059/2, item 41/441/60.
50 *The Australian Army Journal* dedicated an issue to the pentropic organisation. It includes an outline of the formation, and provides establishments of its subunits. See 'The Pentropic Division', *Australian Army Journal*, no. 129, February 1960. See also, Millar, *Australia's Defence*, p. 128.
51 'Conference Notes, CGS Conference', 1–3 December 1959, AA (ACT), A6059/2, item 41/441/69, part 1.
52 'Minutes of Reorganisation Conference', 12 March 1959, AA (ACT), A6922/1, item 1/14.
53 Ibid.
54 'The Reorganisation of the AMF 1959/60–1961/62: General Staff Instruction No. 1', 22 December 1959, AA (ACT), A6059/2, item 41/441/69a.

55 'Reorganisation of the AMF 1960–61: Southern Command General Instructions', 21 March 1960, AA (ACT), A6922/1, item 1/20.
56 'Defence Review: Statement by Athol Townley to the House of Representatives', 27 March 1960, AA (ACT), A6059/2, item 41/441/88.
57 Ibid; and 'Reorganisation of the AMF: Command Relationships', 14 November 1960, AA (ACT), A6059/2, item 41/441/69, part 2.
58 'Director of Staff Duties to Branches and Directorates', 15 December 1958, AA (ACT), A6059/2, item 41/441/70.
59 'DCGS to Army HQ', 10 March 1959, AA (ACT), A6059/2, item 41/441/70; and 'Minutes of Reorganisation Conference', 12 March 1959, AA (ACT), A6922/1, item 1/14.
60 See 'Composition of the Australian Defence Forces: Cabinet Decisions, November 1959', AA (ACT), A1209/23, item 57/4311.
61 'The Reorganisation of the AMF 1959/60–1961/62: General Staff Instruction No. 1', 22 December 1959, AA (ACT), A6059/2, item 41/441/69a.
62 'Reorganisation of the AMF 1960–61: Southern Command General Instructions', 21 March 1960, AA (ACT), A6922/1, item 1/20; and 'Provisional Allocation of Strengths by Commands', 27 December 1959, AA (ACT), A6059/2, item 41/441/69, part 1. See also 'Composition of the Forces', 22 December 1959, AA (ACT), A6059/2, item 41/441/69a.
63 From 'The Reorganisation of the AMF 1959/60–1961/62: General Staff Instruction No. 1', 22 December 1959, AA (ACT), A6059/2, item 41/441/69a.
64 From Ibid.
65 'Composition of the Forces', 22 December 1959, AA (ACT), A6059/2, item 41/441/69, part 1; 'DCGS to AHQ', 10 March 1959, AA (ACT), A6059/2, item 41/441/70; and 'The Reorganisation of the AMF 1959/60–1961/62: General Staff Instruction No. 1', 22 December 1959, AA(ACT), A6059/2, item 41/441/69a.
66 'The Reorganisation of the AMF 1959/60–1961/62: General Staff Instruction No. 1', 22 December 1959, AA (ACT), A6059/2, item 41/441/69a.
67 'DCGS to AHQ', 10 March 1959, AA (ACT), A6059/2, item 41/441/70.
68 'Re-organization of the AMF: Western Command, Instruction No. 1', 7 April 1960, AA (ACT), A6922/1, item 1/23.
69 Millar, *Australia's Defence*, p. 129.
70 'Wilton Diary, 1963', 76, ADFA, 222709, box 2 folder 6.
71 Data taken from 'Current and Planned Allocation of Strengths, Australian Regular Army and Civilians', 21 December 1959, AA (ACT), A6059/2, item 41/441/69, part 1. The Miscellaneous category includes personnel on duties such as overseas staffs, officers on interchange, and cadet staffs.
72 'Minute by Maj.-Gen. T. S. Taylor, DCGS', 20 June 1961, AA (ACT), A6059/2, item 41/441/152.

73 J.C. Blaxland, *Organising an Army: The Australian Experience, 1957–1965*, Strategic and Defence Studies Centre, Australian National University, Canberra, 1989, p. 48.

74 McCarthy, 'The Once and Future Army', p. 196.

75 'Defence Review: Statement by Athol Townley to the House of Representatives', 27 March 1960, AA (ACT), A6059/2, item 41/441/88.

76 Blaxland, *Organising an Army*, p. 64: O'Neill, *Australia in the Korean War*, vol. 2, p. 271.

77 Quoted in McCarthy, 'The Once and Future Army', pp. 149–50, 153.

78 'Territorial Titles for Infantry Companies', 19 July 1960, AA (ACT), A6059/2, item 41/441/69c; and 'Conference Notes: CGS Conference', 1–3 December 1959, AA (ACT), A6059/2, item 41/441/69, part 1.

79 'University Regiments, DMT', 7 Janaury 1960, AA (ACT), A6059/2, item 41/441/69, part 1.

80 Information taken from AA (ACT), A6059/2, item 41/441/69, part 2.

81 'Command and Staff Training Units', 1 September 1962, A3688/25, item 605/R2124/1.

82 'DCGS to AHQ, Re: Officer Staff Groups', n.d., A6059/2, item 41/441/69, part 2.

83 'Reorganisation of the AMF 1960–61: Southern Command General Instructions', 21 March 1960, A6922/1, item 1/20.

84 'GOC Eastern Command to AHQ: Proposal for a New Establishment for Headquarters Eastern Command', 15 May 1961, AA (ACT), A6922/1, item 1/15; and McCarthy, 'The Once and Future Army', p. 144.

85 'The Reorganisation of the AMF 1959–62, Planning Order of Battle', 15 November 1960, AA (ACT), A6922/1, item 1/14.

86 Ibid.

87 Ibid.

88 Ibid.

89 Ibid.

90 'Reorganisation of the AMF Command Relationship Affecting 1st Division, 1st Division Combat Support Group and The Logistic Support Group', AA (ACT), A6059/2, item 41/441/70.

91 'Reorganisation of the AMF–Command Relationships', 14 November 1960, AA (ACT), A6059/2, item 41/441/69, part 2.

92 'Examination of Systems for the Command and Control of the Australian Army', September 1960, and 'Re-organization Study of the AMF Command, Administrative and Training Structure: Basic Assumptions', AA (ACT), A6059/2, item 41/441/70.

93 'Review of the Size and Shape of the Army Post-Vietnam, Appendix 1 to Annex C: Comparison of 1964 Manpower for a 22,700 Army with Estimated Need of a 28,000 Army in 1969', 14 August 1969, AA (ACT), A6840/1, item 51.

94 Horner, *Duty First*, p. 142; and 'The Reorganisation of the AMF 1959/60–1961/62: General Staff Instruction No. 1', 22 December 1959, AA (ACT), A6059/2, item 41/441/69a.

95 'Minute by Townley Re: Australia's Strategic Position', 6 February 1963, DCR, A3688, item 256/R1/3.
96 'Australia's Strategic Position, Report by the Defence Committee', 6 February 1963, DCR, A3688, item 256/R1/3.
97 'The Army Outlook to 1972, Part II: Considerations', DCR, A3688, item 256/R1/3.
98 Ibid.
99 Ibid.
100 Figures quoted in Troy Ramage, 'In Search of Security', p. 70.
101 Edwards, *Crises and Commitments*, pp. 271–2, 329.
102 Ibid., p. 329; and 'Wilton Diary, 1963', p. 74, ADFA, 222709, box 2, folder 6. See also 'Vietnam Interview', Wilton Collection, ADFA, 222709, box 4, folder 25.
103 Ibid., p. 228; and Millar, *Australia's Defence*, p. 127.
104 Millar, 'Australian Defence, 1945–1965', p. 296.
105 'Committee to Review the Organisation of the Division and Combat Support Group: Interim Report, Vol. 2', 18 December 1964, AA (ACT), A6922/1, item 1/29.
106 'The Army Outlook to 1972, Part II: Considerations', DCR, A3688, item 256/R1/3.
107 'Committee to Review the Organisation of the Division and Combat Support Group: Interim Report, Vol. 2', 18 December 1964, AA (ACT), A6922/1, item 1/29. See also, Blaxland, *Organising an Army*, pp. 98–9.
108 'Wilton Diary, 1963', p. 74, ADFA, 222709, box 2, folder 6.
109 'Committee to Review the Organisation of the Division and Combat Support Group: Interim Report, Vol. 1', 18 December 1964, AA (ACT), A6922/1, item 1/29.
110 Ibid.
111 Ibid.
112 DMT, 'Comments on Interim Report on the Re-organisation of the Division and Combat Support Group', 5 January 1965, AA (ACT), A6922/1, item 1/29.
113 Quoted in Blaxland, *Organising an Army*, p. 108.
114 'New Organisation for the Australian Army: Statement by Minister for the Army, Dr. the Hon. A.J. Forbes', 20 December 1964, AA (ACT), A6922/1, item 1/29.
115 'AMF Engineer ORBAT', 9 December 1965, AA (ACT), A3688/26, item 603/R11/6.
116 Ibid.
117 'Reorganisation: Royal Australian Engineers, HQ Northern Command', 26 August 1965, AA (ACT), A3688/26, item 603/R11/6.
118 'AMF Engineer ORBAT', 9 December 1965, AA (ACT), A3688/26, item 603/R11/6.
119 'Reorganisation of the Field Force', 23 December 1964, AA (ACT), A6922/1, item 1/29.
120 Ibid.; 'Committee to Review the Organisation of the Division and Combat Support Group: Interim Report, Vol. 2', 18 December 1964; 'Re-organisation of the CMF', 24 December 1964; and 'Infantry Battalion (TE) Outline Organisation', all in AA (ACT), A6922/1, item 1/29.

NOTES (PP. 273—80)

121 'Re-organisation of the CMF', AA (ACT), A6922/1, item 1/29.
122 'MBI No. 1–4: Intermediate HQ: Function', November 1965, AA (ACT), A3688/25, item 605/R2122/2; and 'Reorganisation: Intermediate Headquarters', AA (ACT), A6922/1, item 1/29.
123 'Area Reorganisation Instruction No. 49', 31 July 1973, AA (ACT), A3688/25, item 586/R3/15; and 'Allocation of Major Units to Formations', January 1965, AA (ACT), A6922/1, item 1/29.
124 'Grouping of Units Under Command HQ 6 TF', 14 November 1966, AA (ACT), A3688/24, item 605/R1508/4.
125 The Army reserved 8th TF for the CMF. See 'DSD to HQ Commands: Reorganisation of Intermediate HQ', 21 June 1965, AA (ACT), A3688/24, item 605/R1507/2.
126 'GS Instructions 28, Command Relationships and Responsibilities of Task Force/Area Headquarters in Northern Command', AA (ACT), A3688/25, item 605/R2122/2; and 'Raising/Reorganisation Instruction 11/69', 30 April 1969, AA (ACT), A3688/24, item 605/R1507/2.
127 McCarthy, 'The Once and Future Army', pp. 224–5.
128 'CMF Service for Persons in Remote Country Areas', 13 October 1965, AA (VIC), B420/1, item R579/2/17.
129 'CMF Service Under Special Conditions', 20 July 1966; 'CMF Service Under Special Conditions: Numerical Designation of New Battalions', 14 July 1966; and 'Transfer of Officers, NCOs, and Specialists to 22 RVR', all in AA (VIC), B420/1, item R579/2/17. See also Neil Leckie, *Bushmen's Rifles: A History of the 22nd Battalion The Royal Victoria Regiment*, Ex 22 Bn RVR Association, Mulgrave, 1999.
130 'Citizen and Reserve Forces', AA (ACT), A1945/39, item 206/3/18; 'Reserve Citizen Military Forces', AA (ACT), A3688/26, item 174/R1/98; and 'The Supplementary Reserve', AA (ACT), A3688/26, item 729/R1/20.
131 'Defence Forces: Emergency Reserves, Cabinet Submission No. 214', May 1964; and 'Defence Forces: Emergency Reserves: Notes on Cabinet Submissions', AA (ACT), A1945/39, item 206/3/18.
132 'Defence Forces: Emergency Reserves: Notes on Cabinet Submissions', AA (ACT), A1945/39, item 206/3/18; and 'Regular Army Emergency Reserve (RAER)', AA (ACT), A3688/26, item 174/R1/98.
133 'Review of Officer Training Groups', 20 August 1969, AA (ACT) A3688/25, item 605/R2124/1; 'AHQ to Central Command: Raising/Disbanding Officer Training Group, Central Command', 23 December 1965, AA (ACT) A6922/1, item 1/31; and 'Military Board Minute No. 56/64, Reorganisation of the CMF', 30 October 1964, DCR, A3688, item 582/R1/20.
134 'Outline of Actions Leading to the Raising of SR Railway Units', 31 December 1968; and 'Supplementary Reserve Units', 23 May 1968, AA (ACT), A3688/25, item 579/R6/12.

135 Horner, *Duty First*, pp. 186–7; and Grey, *A Military History of Australia*, p. 237.
136 Army Review Committee 1970, 'The Command and Organizational Structure of the Army in Australia', 1 January 1971.
137 McCarthy, 'Once and Future Army', pp. 224–5.
138 Ibid., pp. 226–7.
139 Grey, *A Military History of Australia*, p. 231.
140 See 'Review of the Size and Shape of the Army Post-Vietnam', 14 August 1969, AA (ACT), A6840/1, item 51.
141 'National Service', 16 September 1970, DCR, A3688, item 582/R1/20.
142 Data taken from 'Review of the Size and Shape of the Army Post-Vietnam', 14 August 1969, AA (ACT), A6840/1, item 51.
143 Peter Edwards, *A Nation at War: Australian Politics, Society, and Diplomacy during the Vietnam War, 1965–1975*, Allen & Unwin, St Leonards, 1997, pp. 319–20; and Grey, *A Military History of Australia*, pp. 235–6.
144 'CGS to Minister for Defence', CGS No. 382/1973, 27 December 1973, AA (ACT), A6835/1, item 55.
145 Ibid.
146 'Future Shape of the ARA', 7 December 1972, AA (ACT), A3688/24, item 584/R1/4.
147 'Reshaping the Regular Army: ASA Aspects', 20 June 1973, AA (ACT), A3688/26, item 581/R1/74.
148 Data Taken From 'Chart on the Growth of the Field Force, June 1973 to 1976', AA (ACT), A6922/1, item 1/29.
149 For this section, unless otherwise noted, see Report of the Army Review Committee 1970, 'The Command and Organizational Structure of the Army'. See also 'Statement by the Minister for Army, Hon. A.S. Peacock MP on the Army Review Committee', 12 March 1970, DCR, A3688, item 581/R1/15.
150 'Allocation of Major Units to Formations', January 1965, AA (ACT), A6922/1, item 1/29.
151 Report of the Army Review Committee 'The Command and Organizational Structure of the Army', p. 31.
152 Ibid., p. 37.
153 Ibid., p. 38.
154 'Summary of Decisions by the Military Board on the Conclusions of the Report of the Army Review Committee 1970', DCR, A3688, item 581/R1/15.
155 Report of the Army Review Committee, 'The Command and Organizational Structure of the Army', p. 43.
156 *DI(A), Admin. 10–1, Amendment No. 1*, 1981, p. 5.
157 'Army Command Arrangements in SA, WA, TAS', 26 November 1974, AA (ACT), A6835, item 5.

158 'Summary of Decisions by the Military Board on the Conclusions of the Report of the Army Review Committee 1970', DCR, A3688, item 581/R1/15; and 'Army Reorganization', *Army Journal*, no. 274, March 1972, pp. 3–33.

159 Ibid.; and 'CGS to All Military Board Members, CGS No. 89/1971', DCR, A3688, item 581/R1/15.

160 Report of the Army Review Committee, 'The Command and Organizational Structure of the Army', pp. 93–4.

161 'MB Minute 325/1973: Reorganization of the Army, Introduction of the Functional Command System', 27 June 1973, and 'Initial Allocation of Formations and Units to Command, Military Districts and AHQ', n.d., both in AA (ACT), A3688/25, item 122/R2/7; and 'The Reorganisation of Army Headquarters: Timetable for Implementation', 21 October 1971, DCR, A3688, item 581/R1/15.

162 'CMF Units in Being', 25 March 1970, AA (ACT), A3688/26, item 174/R1/98. It should be noted that the Authorised and Posted Establishment columns actually total 59,996 and 31,792. The original document does not provide an explanation for the discrepancy.

163 'CMF Member's Liaison Letter: 1/1974', 15 March 1974, AA (ACT), A3688/24, item 186/R1/238; and *Committee of Inquiry into the Citizen Military Forces*, March 1974, B-2 (hereafter cited as Millar Report). See also McCarthy, 'Once and Future Army', p. 241.

164 'CGS to Minister for Defence, CGS no. 185/1973', June 1973, AA (ACT), A6835/1, item 4.

165 'Hassett to Maj.-Gen. N.A. Vickery, CMF Member', 8 June 1970, DCR, A3688, item 582/R1/20.

166 'Army Review Committee: Submission by Major-General P.A. Cullen Re Citizen Military Forces', 5 May 1970, DCR, A3688, item 582/R1/20.

167 N.A. Vickery, 'Decline in Strength of the CMF', 30 September 1970, DCR, A3688, item 582/R1/20.

168 'Comments on the CMF Member's Paper Improvements in the CMF', AA (VIC), B420/1, item R174/1/7; and 'CMF Member's Liaison Letter: 1/1974', 15 March 1974, AA (ACT), A3688/24, item 186/R1/238.

169 'Comments on the CMF Member's Paper Improvements in the CMF', AA (VIC), B420/1, item R174/1/7.

170 DCGS, 'CMF and Reserves', n.d., DCR, A3688, item 582/R1/20; and 'Review of CMF and Reserves', December 1970, AA (ACT), A3688/26, item 174/R1/98.

171 Millar Report, p. ix.

172 The recommendations are found in ibid., pp. 130–2.

173 McCarthy, 'The Once and Future Army', p. 280; 'DAAG to GSO, Re: Renaming of CMF', February 1973, and 'Green to Murchison', 28 February 1973, AA (VIC), B420/1, item R174/1/6.

174 Millar Report, p. 130.

175 'CGS to Minister for Defence, CGS No. 140/175', AA (ACT), A6835, item 6; and *Defence Report, 1977*, AGPS, Canberra, 1977, p. 53. The Regular Army Emergency Reserve represented a relatively minor part of the new reserve organisation. In November 1974 it could only muster 460 other ranks. See 'Role of the Australian Army Reserve', 12 November 1974, AA (ACT), A3688/24, item 186/R1/238.

176 'CGS to Minister for Defence, CGS No. 10/1976', 22 January 1976, AA (ACT), A6835, item 7.

177 'CGS to Millar, CGS No. 492/1975', 25 September 1975, AA (ACT), A6835, item 6.

178 Data taken from 'CGS to the Minister, CGS No. 366/1974', AA (ACT), A6835/1, item 5.

179 Ibid.; and 'CMF Units in Being', 25 March 1970, AA (ACT), A3688/26, item 174/R1/98.

180 'CGS to Minister for Defence, CGS No. 113/1975', AA (ACT), A6835, item 6; and 'CGS to Minister for Defence, CGS No. 230/1975', 1 July 1975, AA (ACT), A6835, item 7.

181 'CGS to Minister for Defence, CGS No. 674/1977', 5 August 1977, AA (ACT), A6835, item 10.

182 'CGS to the Minister, CGS No. 366/1974', AA (ACT), A6835/1, item 5; and 'CMF Units in Being', 25 March 1970, AA (ACT), A3688/26, item 174/R1/98.

183 'CGS to Millar, CGS No. 492/1975', 25 September 1975, AA (ACT), A6835, item 6.

184 'PNG and Australian Units Serving in PNG', 27 February 1973, AA (ACT), A3688/24, item 579/R4/42; and Department of Defence, *Australian Defence Review*, AGPS, Canberra, 1972, p. 29.

185 'PNG and Australian Units Serving in PNG', 27 February 1975, AA (ACT), A3688/24, item 579/R4/42.

186 Ibid.

187 Horner, *The Gunners*, pp. 446–8.

188 Ibid., pp. 442–6, 506–7.

189 'Department of Supply and Transport Information Newsletter No. 3', 27 September 1971, AWM98, Box 4, item NN-DAQMG (MOV).

190 'Small Vessels and Craft: Division of Operational and Administrative Responsibility Between the Services', 18 December 1970, Army Museum; and Brian Alsop, *Australian Army Watercraft, The Unknown Fleet: From the Second World War to the Present Day*, Australian Water Transportation Association, Marrickville, 1996, pp. 13, 64–5.

191 'Role of the Australian Army Reserve', 12 November 1974, AA (ACT), A3688/24, item 186/R1/238.

8 The defence of Australia

1 *Australian Defence*, Acting Commonwealth Government Printer, Canberra, 1977, p. 10.

2 Ibid., pp. 10–11.

3 Dupont, *Australia's Threat Perceptions*, p. 67.

4 Graeme Cheeseman, *The Search for Self-Reliance: Australian Defence Since Vietnam*, Longman Cheshire, Melbourne, 1993, pp. 3–4; and Defence Committee, 'Strategic Basis of Australian Defence Policy', 1971, p. 1.

5 Defence Committee, 'Strategic Basis of Australian Defence Policy', 1971, p. 68.

6 Ibid., pp. 7–8; Grey, *Military History of Australia*, p. 249; and Millar, *Australia in Peace and War*, pp. 217, 435. See also Ross Babbage, 'Australian Defence Planning, Force Structure and Equipment: The American Effect', *Australian Outlook*, vol. 38, no. 3, December 1984, p. 165.

7 Defence Committee, 'Strategic Basis of Australian Defence Policy', 1973, p. 18; Department of Defence, *Australian Defence Review*, AGPS, Canberra, 1972, pp. 11, 27; and *Defence Report, 1975*, AGPS, Canberra, 1975, p. 5.

8 Defence Committee, 'Strategic Basis of Australian Defence Policy', 1971, pp. 8–9.

9 Ibid., pp. 5–6; and Defence Committee, 'Strategic Basis of Australian Defence Policy', 1973, p. 1.

10 *Defence Report, 1975*, p. 5.

11 Dupont, *Australia's Threat Perceptions*, p. 81.

12 Paul Dibb, *Review of Australia's Defence Capabilities*, AGPS, Canberra, 1986, p. 1.

13 *Strategic Review, 1993*, Canberra, 1993, pp. 5, 14, 37. For an example of an argument that Australia's threat environment is more dangerous than generally acknowledged, see David Evans, *A Fatal Rivalry: Australia's Defence at Risk*, Macmillan, Melbourne, 1990.

14 For his recommendations, see Arthur Tange, *Australian Defence: Report on the Reorganisation of the Defence Group of Departments*, 1973.

15 'Reorganization of Australian Defence Establishment', 21 March 1958, NARA, RG59, Box 3226, File 743.56. See also Grey, *Military History of Australia*, p. 220; and Millar, *Australia's Defence*, pp. 94–5.

16 *Defence Report, 1975*, p. 34.

17 Joan Beaumont, *The Australian Centenary History of Defence*, vol. 5, *Australian Defence: Sources and Statistics*, Oxford University Press, Melbourne, 2001, p. 251.

18 Grey, *Military History of Australia*, p. 221.

19 Peter Dennis et al., *The Oxford Companion to Australian Military History*, Oxford University Press, Melbourne, 1997, p. 145.

20 'Army Command and Control Structure', 15 January 1975, AA (ACT), A6839/1, item 76/54; and 'Defence Higher Organisation', AA (ACT), A3688/225, item 586/R3/15.

21 Defence Committee, 'Strategic Basis of Australian Defence Policy, 1971', p. 68.

22 'CGS to Admiral Victor Smith, Chairman, Chiefs of Staffs Committee, CGS no. 2/1974', 29 January 1974, AA (ACT), A6835, item 5.

23 For an example of the effect on communications, see 'CGS to the Minister for Defence, CGS no. 853/1979', 27 September 1979, AA (ACT), A6835, item 14.

24 *1st Joint Movements Group: Corporate Plan, 1997–2000*, Headquarters 1st Joint Movements Group, Sydney, 1999.

25 *Defence Report, 1985–86*, AGPS, Canberra, 1986, p. 5; and 'Report of the Army Review Committee 1988: The Organization for Command of the Australian Army', 1 November 1988, AA (ACT), A6721, item A88–17134, part 1.

26 'Directive by the Chief of the Defence Force to Commander Northern Command (COMNORCOM)', 22 October 1990, DCR, A6721, item A90–2829, part 4.

27 Woodman & Horner, 'Land Forces in the Defence of Australia', pp. 25–6.

28 For examples of these types of comments, see Grey, *Military History of Australia*, p. 252; and Dibb, *Review of Australia's Defence Capabilities*, p. vi.

29 B.D. Beddie, 'The Australian Armed Forces in Transition', *Armed Forces and Society*, vol. 5, no. 3, Spring 1979, p. 427.

30 *Australian Defence*, p. 13.

31 Defence Committee, 'Strategic Basis of Australian Defence Policy', 1971, p. 67; and Defence Committee, 'Strategic Basis of Australian Defence Policy', 1973, p. 18.

32 *Defence Report, 1975*, p. 5.

33 *Australian Defence*, p. 31.

34 'CGS to Minister for Defence, CGS No. 194/1974', 24 July 1974, AA (ACT), A6835, item 5.

35 'CGS to CDFS, CGS no. 913/1979', 22 October 1979, AA (ACT), A6839/1, item 79/100.

36 *The Army in the 1980s*, Canberra, 1982, p. 7.

37 Headquarters Training Command, *Training Information Bulletin*, no. 28, *The Infantry Division*, HQ Training Command, Sydney, 1975, pp. 1-1 to 1-3; Michael Evans, *Forward From the Past: The Development of Australian Army Doctrine, 1972–Present*, Land Warfare Studies Centre, Canberra, 1999, pp. 13–14; and 'CGS to CDFS, CGS no. 157/1976', 2 April 1976, AA (ACT), A6839/1, item 77/29.

38 'D.B. Dunstan: Minute Paper: Army Development, Proposed Changes in the Field Force', 17 September 1979, AA (ACT), A6834, item 14.

39 Ibid.; and 'Press Statement by Minister for Defence D.J. Killen', 21 February 1980, AA (ACT), A3688/24, item 586/R3/20.

40 Ibid.; and *Defence Report, 1976*, AGPS, Canberra, 1976, pp. 9–10, 37. See also *The Army in the 1980s*, pp. 8–9.

41 Horner, *Duty First*, pp. 294–7, 310.

42 Ibid., pp. 324–7.

43 'CGS to CDF, CGS no. 30/1985', 8 January 1985, 'Secretary Department of Defence to CGS', 24 December 1984; 'Brief for CGS: Army Force Structure Plan Proposals For Increased Integration', 31 January 1985; and 'DGOP-A to DCOPS', 19 July 1985, all in DCR, A6721, item A84-21619, part 1.

44 'The Army Development Guide (ADG) (Provisional) vol. 1: part 6: Force Structure of ASA Elements', DCR, A6721, item A85–5350, part 1.

45 'Maj.-Gen. A. Clunies-Ross to CGS', February 1986, DCR, A6721, item A86–4932, part 1.

46 'Senior Commanders' Conference: The Army Force Structure Plan, Outline Proposals', 14 August 1984, DCR, A6721, item A84–21619, part 1.

47 Ibid.

48 *Defence Report, 1981*, AGPS, Canberra, 1981, pp. 11, 40; and Joint Committee on Foreign Affairs and Defence, *The Australian Defence Force: Its Structure and Capabilities*, AGPS, Canberra, 1984, pp. 50, 109.

49 Parliamentary Standing Committee on Public Works, *Report Relating to the Proposed Redevelopment of Facilities for 51st Battalion Far North Queensland Regiment Throughout Far North Queensland and the Torres Strait*, AGPS, Canberra, 1997, pp. 5–6; and *Defence Report, 1981*, p. 42.

50 'The Army Development Guide (ADG) (Provisional), vol. 1, part 6: Force Structure of the ASA Element', DCR, A6721, item A85–5350, part 1; and *The Australian Defence Force: Its Structure and Capabilities*, pp. 108–9.

51 *The Australian Defence Force: Its Structure and Capabilities*, pp. 57–8.

52 Ibid., p. 111.

53 *Australian Defence*, p. 32; *Defence Report, 1980*, AGPS, Canberra, 1980, p. 11; and D.J. Killen, 'The Government's View', in Robert O'Neill & D.M. Horner (eds), *Australian Defence Policy for the 1980s*, University of Queensland Press, St Lucia, 1982, p. 31. For the establishment of the Army, see Department of the Parliamentary Library, *Australian Defence Statistics 1972–1992*, Department of the Parliamentary Library, Canberra, 1992, p. 19.

54 See *Committee of Inquiry into the Citizen Military Forces, Report on the Army Cadet Corps*.

55 Quoted in 'A New System of Service Cadets, CGS No. 166/1976', 6 April 1976, AA (ACT), A6835, item 7.

56 *Defence Report, 1975*, p. 22.

57 'CGS to CRES, CGS No. 565/1977', 28 June 1977, AA (ACT), A6835, item 10. See also *Defence Report, 1976*, p. 22; and *Defence Report, 1981*, p. 23.

58 'CGS to DCOS, Re: Employment of Women, CGS No. 161/1976', and 'Employment of Service Women in the Army', CGS No. 439/1976, AA (ACT), A6835, item 7.

59 'Disbandment of Women's Royal Australian Army Corps', 25 March 1980, AA (ACT), A3688/24, item 584/R1/4; *Australian Defence*, p. 32; *Defence Report, 1981*, p. 25; and *Defence Report, 1983–84*, AGPS, Canberra, 1984, p. 62.

60 Hugh Smith, 'Women in the Australian Defence Force: In Line for the Front Line?', *The Australian Quarterly*, vol. 62, no. 2, Winter 1990, pp. 125–6; *Defence Annual Report, 1997–98*, Commonwealth of Australia, Canberra, 1998, p. 233; and *Defending Australia: Defence White Paper, 1994*, AGPS, Canberra, 1994, p. 65. See also Allan Shephard, *A Compendium of Australian Defence Statistics*, Australian Defence Studies Centre, Canberra, 1995, pp. 24–5.

61 *The Australian Defence Force: Its Structure and Capabilities*, pp. 57–8.

62 Dibb, *Review of Australia's Defence Capabilities*, p. vi.

63 See Department of Defence, *The Defence of Australia*, AGPS, Canberra, 1987.
64 Woodman & Horner, 'Land Forces in the Defence of Australia', pp. 82–3.
65 Thomas-Durrell Young, *Threat-Ambiguous Defence Planning: The Australian Experience*, Strategic Studies Institute, Carlisle Barracks, PA, 1993, p. 4.
66 Dibb, *Review of Australia's Defence Capabilities*, pp. 3, 9–13.
67 Department of Defence, *The Defence of Australia*, pp. 53, 57–9.
68 Ibid., p. 57; and 5th Aviation Regiment, 'Unit History', HQ 5th Aviation Regiment, Townsville, n.d.
69 'Conference Notes: Operational Requirements in Northern Territory Command', 9 November 1961, AA (ACT), A6059/2, item 41/441/149.
70 Department of Defence, *The Defence of Australia*, p. 56.
71 Quoted in 'Chief of the General Staff Directive to Commanders of Functional Commands, Military Districts, and Land Component Norcom for an Appropriate Army Presence in Northern Australia', December 1990, DCR, A6721, item A90-2829, part 4.
72 'Report of the Study into the Provisions of an Appropriate Army presence in Northern Australia', September 1989, DCR, A6721, item A90–2829, part 1.
73 'Chiefs of Staff Committee, Minutes of Meeting on 30 January & 1 February 1990 Re: Appropriate Army Presence in Northern Australia', and 'DGCO 106/90: Strategic Guidance for Infrastructure Development in the North', 9 March 1990, DCR, A6721, item A90–2829, part 1.
74 'DCGS 487/90, An Appropriate Army Presence in Northern Australia', 3 May 1990, DCR, A6721, item A90–2829, part 2.
75 Data taken from 'Movement Plan for the Increased Army Presence in Northern Australia', 28 July 1993, DCR, A6721, item A90–2829, part 22.
76 Data taken from 'Distribution of Army Combat Force, DPA-A No. 2014/91', 26 June 1991, DCR, A6721, item A90–2829, part 10.
77 'Corps Conference Briefing Notes: Logistic Command Restructuring Update', ALTC, 206/1/6, part 1.
78 'Organisation and Structure of the Army Reserve', DCR, A6721, item A89–35896, part 1.
79 'The Order of Battle for the Army', 6 June 1991, DCR, A6721, item A89–1189, part 1.
80 Data taken from *Defence Report, 1990–91*, AGPS, Canberra, 1991, p. 65.
81 John Coates, 'The Army and the White Paper', in Jenelle Bonnor & Gary Brown (eds), *Security for the Twenty-First Century? Australia's 1994 Defence White Paper*, Australian Defence Studies Centre, Canberra, 1995, p. 137.
82 See *Australia's Strategic Policy*, Department of Defence, Canberra, 1997; and *In the National Interest*, Department of Foreign Affairs and Trade, Canberra, 1997.
83 'AFS Review: Final Report, 1991', DCR, A6721, item A97–39009, part 1; and Graeme Cheeseman, 'Australia's Force Structure Review: The 1987 White Paper Revisited', in

Robert A. Hall (ed.), *The New Look Defence Force: Perspectives on the Force Structure Review*, Australian Defence Studies Centre, Canberra, 1992, p. 29. Figures taken from *Defence Review 2000: Our Future Defence Force (A Public Discussion Paper)*, Department of Defence, Canberra, 2000, p. 48.

84 For this review, see *Force Structure Review, 1991*, AGPS, Canberra, 1991.

85 See *Report of the Interdepartmental Committee (IDC) on the Wrigley Review: The Defence Force and the Community*, AGPS, Canberra, 1991, pp. 4–8.

86 'AFS Review: Final Report, 1991', DCR, A6721, item A97–39009, part 1; 'Force Structure Review: Land Command Implementation Plan Update: Annex A, Land Command FSR: Manpower', 17 March 1992, DCR, A6721, item A92–6467, part 1; and 'Force Structure Review: Land Command Draft Outline Implementation Plan', 11 July 1991, DCR, A6721, item A90–2829, part 9.

87 Data taken from 'Force Structure Review: Land Command Draft Outline Implementation Plan', 11 July 1991, DCR, A6721, item A90–2829, part 9.

88 'AFS Review: Final Report, 1991', DCR, A6721, A97–39009, part 1; and 'Army's Report to COSC on Progress on Force Structure Review Implementation as at 1 November 1991', DCR, A6721, item A90–2829, part 14.

89 'Land Command Force Structure Review', 27 June 1991, DCR, item A6721, A90–2829, part 8.

90 *Ready Reserve Program, 1991*, AGPS, Canberra, 1991; and 'AFS Review: Final Report, 1991', DCR, A6721, item A97–39009, part 1. See Also John Coates & Hugh Smith, *Review of the Ready Reserve Scheme*, University College, UNSW, Canberra, 1995.

91 'CGS Exercise 91, Log Div/LHQ Presentation: Brigade Administrative Support Battalion', 28 May 1991, ALTC.

92 'Land Command Force Structure Review', 27 June 1991, DCR, item A6721, A90–2829, part 8.

93 'Developments in the Royal Australian Corps of Transport: Introduction', ALTC; and 'Plan for the Downsizing of 10 Terminal Regiment to its Force Structure Review Establishment', 20 September 1993, AA (NSW), C3650/1, item 624/1/11.

94 Headquarters 9th Transport Regiment, 'Unit History', 1999; *10th Terminal Regiment History*, 10th Terminal Regiment, Mosman, 1998; and 'Land Command Update: Royal Australian Corps of Transport Technical Advisory Committee Conference', 12 May 1995, ALTC.

95 Director of Movement and Transport, 'Presentation at Royal Australian Corps of Transport Technical Advisory Committee Meeting', 8 November 1994, ALTC, 206-1-6, part 4.

96 'Army's Report to COSC on Progress on Force Structure Review Implementation as at 1 November 1991', DCR, A6721, item A90–2829, part 14; and Cheeseman, 'Australia's Force Structure Review', p. 30. See also *Defending Australia, Defence White Paper, 1994*, pp. 42–51.

97 *Defending Australia, Defence White Paper, 1994*, pp. 59–61, 118–19.

98 Ibid., pp. 52–3.
99 See *Future Directions for the Management of Australia's Defence: Report of the Defence Efficiency Review*, Department of Defence, Canberra, 1997.
100 Ibid., pp. 53–4.
101 Figures compiled from *Defence Annual Reports* for the years 1989–90, 1990–91, 1991–92, 1992–93, 1993–94, 1995–96, 1996–97, 1997–98, 1998–99.
102 Training Command, *Army Logistic Training Centre: Handbook, 1999/00*, Army Logistic Training Centre, Bandiana, 1999, pp. 7–8.
103 *Defence Annual Report, 1997–1998*, pp. 223–4.
104 See Department of Defence, *An Australian Army for the 21st Century*, Commonwealth of Australia, Canberra, 1996.
105 Greg de Somer, *The Capacity of the Australian Army to Conduct and Sustain Land Force Operations*, Land Warfare Studies Centre, Canberra, 1999, p. 68.
106 *An Australian Army for the 21st Century: Restructuring The Australian Army*, Canberra, 1997, p. 13; and Evans, *Forward From the Past*, pp. 44–5.
107 *Restructuring the Australian Army*, p. 3.
108 *Australia's Strategic Policy, 1997*, p. 29.
109 Ibid., p. 41.
110 de Somer, *The Capacity of the Australian Army to Conduct and Sustain Land Force Operations*, p. 72.
111 Ibid., pp. 72–5. See *Land Warfare Doctrine 1: The Fundamentals of Land Warfare*, Doctrine Wing, CATDC, 1998.

9 The future of army organisation

1 *Defence Review 2000: Our Future Defence Force (A Public Discussion Paper)*, p. 4.
2 'Defence Review 2000: Public Discussion Paper, Executive Summary', *Australian Defence Force Journal*, no. 143, July–August 2000, p. 7.
3 *Defence Review 2000: Our Future Defence Force*, p. x.
4 Ibid., p. 53.
5 Ibid.
6 Joint Standing Committee on Foreign Affairs, Defence and Trade, *From Phantom to Force: Towards a More Efficient and Effective Army*, Commonwealth of Australia, Canberra, 2000, p. ix.
7 *Canberra Times*, 5 September 2000.
8 *Australian*, 23 December 1999.
9 *Australian Financial Review*, 28 April 2000.
10 See *Defence Review 2000: Our Future Defence Force*.

11 *Defence Annual Report, 1998–1999*, Commonwealth of Australia, Canberra, 1999, pp. 43–5.
12 Ibid., pp. 45–6. Note: in early 2001 the ADF amalgamated the Command and Staff College with the other service staff colleges to form the Australian Command and Staff Course. It is located at Weston, ACT, and forms a part of the Australian Defence College.

Bibliography

Primary sources: manuscript

Army Logistic Training Centre, Bandiana

The Royal Australian Corps of Transport Directorate Files

Army Museum, Bandiana

The Royal Australian Corps of Transport Collection

Australian Archives, Canberra

A816	Department of Defence, Correspondence Files, 1935–57
A981	Department of External Affairs, Correspondence Files, 1927–42
A1196	Department of Air, Correspondence Files, 1935–60
A1209	Prime Minister's Department, Correspondence Files, 1957
A1608	Prime Minister's Department, Correspondence Files, 1939–46
A1945	Department of Defence, Correspondence Files, 1957–74
A2031	Defence Committee Minutes
A2653	Volumes of the Military Board Proceedings, 1905–76
A2657	Volumes of Papers of Historical Interest, 1909
A2671	War Cabinet Agenda Files, 1939–46
A3688	Department of the Army, Correspondence Files, 1946–79
A5954	Shedden Collection, 1937–71
A6059	Department of the Army, Correspondence Files, 1956–64

BIBLIOGRAPHY

A6828	CGS Periodical Letters, 1933–40
A6835	CGS Outward Correspondence, 1963–74
A6839	Policy and Working Files of the Office of the CGS, 1973–79
A6840	Non-file Records of the CGS
A6922	Policy and Working Files of the Directorate of Staff Duties of AHQ, 1939–73
A9787	Council of Defence Minutes and Agenda Papers, 1905–50

Australian Archives, Melbourne

B168	Department of Defence, Correspondence Files, 1901–06
B197	Department of Defence, Correspondence Files, 1906–36
B420	HQ 3rd Division, Correspondence Files, 1966–91
B539	AIF, Correspondence Files, 1914–17
B1535	Department of the Army, Correspondence Files, 1930–39
B3756	Department of Defence, Victoria, 1885–1901
MP153	Defence Papers
MP367	Department of Defence, Correspondence Files, 1917–29
MP726	Department of Civil Aviation, Correspondence Files, 1953–61
MP729	Defence Army Series, 1936–45
MP742	Department of Army, Correspondence Files, 1943–51
MP826	Defence Schemes, 1906–38
MP1049	Department of the Navy, Correspondence Files, 1911–59
MP1185	Department of the Navy, Correspondence Files

Australian Archives, Sydney

| C3650 | Headquarters 10th Terminal Regiment, Correspondence Files, 1976–98 |

Australian Defence Force Academy Library

Hankey Papers

Wilton Papers

Australian War Memorial

AWM1	Pre-Federation and Commonwealth Records
AWM3	Records of the Department of Defence, Central Registry, 1900–38
AWM49	Interwar Army Records, 1920–42
AWM54	Written Records, 1939–45 War
AWM98	Vietnam War Records
AWM113	Records of the Military History Section (Army), 1940–61

Blamey Papers

Mackay Papers

Department of Defence Central Registry

A3688   Department of Army, Correspondence Files, 1946–79

A4090   Department of Defence, Correspondence Files, 1974–85

A6721   Department of Defence, Year and Single File Series, 1985–present

Headquarters Fifth Aviation Regiment, Townsville

Unit History

Headquarters 9th Transport Regiment, Sydney

Unit History

National Archives and Records Administration, College Park

RG59   General Records of the Department of State

RG165   Records of the War Department General and Special Staffs

National Library of Australia

Deakin Papers

Pearce Papers

MS2553

Primary sources: official publications

The Army in the 1980s, Canberra, 1982.

Australian Defence, Acting Commonwealth Government Printer, Canberra, 1977.

Australia's Strategic Policy, Department of Defence, Canberra, 1997.

Chauvel, H.G., *Report of the Inspector-General of the Australian Military Forces*, Albert J. Mullett, Melbourne, 1921.

—— *Report of the Inspector-General of the Australian Military Forces*, Albert J. Mullett, Melbourne, 1922.

—— *Report of the Inspector-General of the Australian Military Forces*, Albert J. Mullett, Melbourne, 1923.

—— *Report of the Inspector-General of the Australian Military Forces*, Albert J. Mullett, Melbourne, 1924.

—— *Report of the Inspector-General of the Australian Military Forces*, H.J. Green, Melbourne, 1925.

—— *Report of the Inspector-General of the Australian Military Forces*, H.J. Green, Melbourne, 1930.

Colonial Defence Committee, *Memorandum on the Defence Forces and Defences of Australia*, 1901.

BIBLIOGRAPHY

Committee of Inquiry into the Citizen Military Forces (Millar Report), 1974.

Committee of Inquiry into the Citizen Military Forces: Report on the Army Cadet Corps (Millar Report), 1974.

Commonwealth Parliamentary Debates (CPD)

Commonwealth Parliamentary Papers (CPP)

Defence Annual Report, 1993–1994, Department of Defence, Canberra, 1994.

Defence Annual Report, 1995–1996, Department of Defence, Canberra, 1996.

Defence Annual Report, 1996–1997, Department of Defence, Canberra, 1997.

Defence Annual Report, 1997–1998, Department of Defence, Canberra, 1998.

Defence Annual Report, 1998–1999, Department of Defence, Canberra, 1999.

Defence Report, 1975, AGPS, Canberra, 1975.

Defence Report, 1976, AGPS, Canberra, 1976.

Defence Report, 1977, AGPS, Canberra, 1977.

Defence Report, 1981, AGPS, Canberra, 1981.

Defence Report, 1983–84, AGPS, Canberra, 1983.

Defence Report, 1985–86, AGPS, Canberra, 1986.

Defence Report, 1989–90, AGPS, Canberra, 1990.

Defence Report, 1990–91, AGPS, Canberra, 1991.

Defence Report, 1991–92, AGPS, Canberra, 1992.

Defence Report, 1992–93, AGPS, Canberra, 1993.

Defence Review 2000: Our Future Defence Force, Department of Defence, Canberra, 2000.

Defence Review 2000: Our Future Defence Force (A Public Discussion Paper), Department of Defence, Canberra, 2000.

Defending Australia: Defence White Paper, 1994, AGPS, Canberra, 1994.

Department of Defence, *An Australian Army for the 21st Century*, Commonwealth of Australia, Canberra, 1996.

—— *Australian Defence Review*, AGPS, Canberra, 1972.

—— *Co-operation in Empire Defence*, RAAF Printing Unit, Melbourne, 1945.

—— *The Defence of Australia*, AGPS, Canberra, 1987.

Department of the Parliamentary Library, *Australian Defence Statistics 1972–1992*, Department of the Parliamentary Library, Canberra, 1992.

DI(A), Admin 10–1, Amendment No. 1, 1981.

Dibb, Paul, *Review of Australia's Defence Capabilities*, AGPS, Canberra, 1986.

Finn, H., *Report by the Inspector-General of the Commonwealth Military Forces*, J. Kemp, Melbourne, 1906.

1st Joint Movements Group: Corporate Plan, 1997–2000, Headquarters 1st Joint Movements Group, Sydney, 1999.

Force Structure Review, 1991, AGPS, Canberra, 1991.

Future Directions for the Management of Australia's Defence: Report of the Defence Efficiency Review, Department of Defence, Canberra, 1997.

General Scheme of Defence for Australia: Report of Committee of Officers: Organisation, Government Printer, Melbourne, 1906.

General Staff, *Possibility of Assimilating War Organization Throughout the Empire*, J. Kemp, Melbourne, 1907.

Hamilton, Ian, *Report on an Inspection of the Military Forces of the Commonwealth of Australia*, Albert J. Mullett, Melbourne, 1913.

Headquarters Training Command, *Training Information Bulletin*, no. 28, *The Infantry Division*, HQ Training Command, Sydney, 1975.

Hoad, J.C., *Annual Report for the Year 1907 by the Inspector-General*, J. Kemp, Melbourne, 1908.

Hutton, Edward, *Military Forces of the Commonwealth*, Melbourne, 1902.

—— *Annual Report upon the Military Forces of the Commonwealth of Australia*, Robt S. Brain, Melbourne, 1903.

—— *Military Forces of the Commonwealth of Australia: Second Annual Report*, Robt S. Brain, Melbourne 1904.

In the National Interest, Department of Foreign Affairs and Trade, Canberra, 1997.

Joint Committee on Foreign Affairs and Defence, *The Australian Defence Force: Its Structure and Capabilities*, AGPS, Canberra, 1984.

Joint Standing Committee on Foreign Affairs, Defence and Trade, *From Phantom to Force: Towards a More Efficient and Effective Army*, Commonwealth of Australia, Canberra, 2000.

Kirkpatrick, G.M., *Annual Report of the Inspector-General of the Military Forces*, J. Kemp, Melbourne, 1911.

—— *Annual Report of the Inspector-General of the Military Forces*, Albert J. Mullett, Melbourne, 1913.

Land Warfare Doctrine 1: The Fundamentals of Land Warfare, Doctrine Wing, CATDC, 1998.

Parliamentary Standing Committee on Public Works, *Report Relating to the Proposed Redevelopment of Facilities for 51st Battalion Far North Queensland Regiment Throughout Far North Queensland and the Torres Strait*, AGPS, Canberra, 1997.

Patterson, A. Temple (ed.), *The Jellicoe Papers*, vol. 2, *1916–1935*, Naval Records Society, London, 1968.

Ready Reserve Program, 1991, AGPS, Canberra, 1991.

Report and Summary of Proceedings together with Appendices and Minutes of the Federal Military Conference Assembled in Sydney, New South Wales, to Consider a General Scheme of Military Defence Applicable to the Australian Colonies and Tasmania, Government Printer, Sydney, 1894.

Report of the Army Review Committee 1970: The Command and Organizational Structure of the Army in Australia (Hassett Report), 1971.

Report of the Interdepartmental Committee (IDC) on the Wrigley Review: The Defence Force and the Community, AGPS, Canberra, 1991.

Report of the Military Committee of Inquiry, part 1, *General*, 1901.

Report upon the Department of Defence From the First of July, 1914 until the Thirtieth of June, 1917, Albert J. Mullett, Melbourne, 1917.

Restructuring the Australian Army, Canberra, 1997.

Strategic Review, 1993, Canberra, 1993.

Tange, Arthur, *Australian Defence: Report on the Reorganisation of the Defence Group of Departments*, 1973.

Training Command, *Army Logistic Training Centre: Handbook, 1999–2000*, Army Logistic Training Centre, Bandiana, Vic, 1999.

Secondary sources: books

Alsop, Brian, *Australian Army Watercraft, The Unknown Fleet: From the Second World War to the Present Day*, Australian Water Transportation Association, Marrickville, NSW, 1996.

Barrett, John, *Falling In: Australia and Boy Conscription, 1911–1915*, Hale & Iremonger, Sydney, 1979.

Bassett, Jan, *Guns and Brooches: Australian Army Nursing from the Boer War to the Gulf War*, Oxford University Press, Melbourne, 1992.

Bastock, John, *Ships of the Australia Station*, Child & Associates, Frenchs Forest, NSW, 1988.

Bates, Peter, *Japan and the British Commonwealth Occupation Force, 1946–52*, Brasseys, London, 1993.

Bean, C.E.W., *The Story of Anzac*, vol. 1, *From the Outbreak of War to the End of the First Phase of the Gallipoli Campaign, May 4, 1915*, University of Queensland Press, St Lucia, Qld, 1981.

Beaumont, Joan, *The Australian Centenary History of Defence*, vol. 5, *Australian Defence: Sources and Statistics*, Oxford University Press, Melbourne, 2001.

Bell, Coral, *Dependent Ally: A Study in Australian Foreign Policy*, Oxford University Press, Melbourne, 1988.

Bennett, R.M., *Expansion of the Australian Army (World War 2): The Raising of the 2nd AIF*, Department of Defence, Canberra, 1974.

Blaxland, J.C., *Organising an Army: The Australian Experience, 1957–1965*, Strategic and Defence Studies Centre, Australian National University, Canberra, 1989.

Budden, F.M., *That Mob: The Story of the 55/53rd Australian Infantry Battalion, AIF*, Budden, Ashfield, NSW, 1973.

Camm, J.C.R. & McQuilton, John (eds), *Australians: A Historical Atlas*, Syme & Weldon, Sydney, 1987.

BIBLIOGRAPHY

Cheeseman, Graeme, *The Search for Self-Reliance: Australian Defence Since Vietnam*, Longman Cheshire, Melbourne, 1993.

Coates, John, & Smith, Hugh, *Review of the Ready Reserve Scheme*, University College, Canberra, UNSW, 1995.

Coppell, W.G., *Australia in Facts and Figures*, Penguin Books, Ringwood, Vic, 1994.

Dennis, Peter, & Grey, Jeffrey, *Emergency and Confrontation: Australian Military Operations in Malaya and Borneo, 1950–1966*, Allen & Unwin, St Leonards, NSW, 1996.

Dennis, Peter, et al., *The Oxford Companion to Australian Military History*, Oxford University Press, Melbourne, 1997.

Donovan, Peter, *Defending the Northern Gateway*, ANU, Strategic and Defence Studies Centre, Canberra, 1989.

Dupont, Alan, *Australia's Threat Perceptions: A Search for Security*, ANU, Strategic and Defence Studies Centre, Canberra, 1991.

Edwards, Peter, *Crises and Commitments: The Politics and Diplomacy of Australia's Involvement in South East Asian Conflicts, 1948–1965*, Allen & Unwin, North Sydney, 1992.

—— *A Nation at War: Australian Politics, Society, and Diplomacy during the Vietnam War, 1965–1975*, Allen & Unwin, St Leonards, NSW, 1997.

Evans, David, *A Fatal Rivalry: Australia's Defence at Risk*, Macmillan, Melbourne, 1990.

Evans, Michael, *The Role of the Australian Army in a Maritime Concept of Strategy*, Land Warfare Studies Centre, Canberra, 1998.

—— *Forward From the Past: The Development of Australian Army Doctrine, 1972–Present*, Land Warfare Studies Centre, Canberra 1999.

Field, L.M., *The Forgotten War: Australian Involvement in the South African Conflict of 1899–1902*, Melbourne University Press, Carlton, Vic, 1979.

Gordon, Donald C., *The Dominion Partnership in Imperial Defence, 1870–1914*, Johns Hopkins Press, Baltimore, 1965.

Grey, Jeffrey, *A Military History of Australia*, Cambridge University Press, Sydney, 1990.

Hamill, Ian, *The Strategic Illusion: The Singapore Strategy and the Defence of Australia and New Zealand, 1919–1942*, Singapore University Press, Singapore, 1981.

Hasluck, Paul, *The Government and the People, 1939–1941*, AWM, Canberra, 1965.

—— *The Government and the People, 1942–1945*, AWM, Canberra, 1970.

Hawkins, David, *The Defence of Malaysia and Singapore: From AMDA to ANZUK*, Royal United Service Institute, London, 1972.

Hopkins, R.N.L., *Australian Armour: A History of the Royal Australian Armoured Corps, 1927–1972*, AWM and AGPS, Canberra, 1978.

Horner, David, *Crisis of Command: Australian Generalship and the Japanese Threat, 1941–1943*, ANU Press, Canberra, 1978.

—— *SAS: Phantoms of the Jungle, A History of the Australian Special Air Service*, Allen & Unwin, Sydney, 1989.

—— *Duty First: The Royal Australian Regiment in War and Peace*, Allen & Unwin, North Sydney, 1990.

—— *The Gunners: A History of Australian Artillery*, Allen & Unwin, St Leonards, NSW, 1995.

—— *Inside the War Cabinet: Directing Australia's War Effort 1939–45*, Allen & Unwin, St Leonards, NSW, 1996.

Kidd, Reg, & Neal, Ray, *The History of the 'Letter' Batteries in World War II*, Castlecrag, NSW, 1998.

Leckie, Neil, *Bushmen's Rifles: A History of the 22nd Battalion the Royal Victoria Regiment*, Ex 22nd Bn RVR Association, Mulgrave, Vic, 1999.

Long, Gavin, *To Benghazi*, AWM, Canberra, 1965.

McCarthy, John, *Australia and Imperial Defence, 1918–1939: A Study in Air and Sea Power*, University of Queensland Press, St Lucia, Qld, 1976.

McNicoll, Ronald, *The Royal Australian Engineers 1919 to 1945: Teeth and Tail*, Corps Committee of the Royal Australian Engineers, Canberra, 1982.

Mathews, Russell, *Militia Battalion at War: The History of the 58/59th Australian Infantry Battalion in the Second World War*, 58/59th Battalion Association, Sydney, 1961.

Meaney, Neville, *The Search for Security in the Pacific, 1901–1914*, Sydney University Press, Sydney, 1976.

Millar, T.B., *Australia's Defence*, Melbourne University Press, Carlton, Vic, 1965.

—— *Australia in Peace and War: External Relations Since 1788*, ANU Press, Botany, NSW, 1991.

Mordike, John, *An Army for a Nation: A History of Australian Military Development, 1880–1914*, Allen & Unwin, North Sydney, 1992.

1997 Year Book Australia, Australian Bureau of Statistics, Canberra, 1997.

Norris, R., *The Emergent Commonwealth: The Australian Federation, Expectations and Fulfilment, 1889–1910*, Melbourne University Press, Carlton, Vic, 1975.

176 Air Dispatch Company, *Unit History*, 176 Air Dispatch Company, Richmond, NSW, 1999.

O'Neill, Robert, *Australia in the Korea War, 1950–53*, vol. 1, *Strategy and Diplomacy*, AWM and AGPS, Canberra, 1981.

—— *Australia in the Korea War 1950–53*, vol. 2, *Combat Operations*, AWM and AGPS, Canberra, 1985.

Parkhill, Archdale, *The Defence of Australia: What the Lyons Government Has Done*, H.J. Green, Melbourne, 1936.

Reader's Digest, *Atlas of Australia*, Reader's Digest, Sydney, 1994.

Robertson, John, *Australia at War, 1939–1945*, William Heinemann, Melbourne, 1981.

Robson, Lloyd, *The First AIF: A Study in its Recruitment, 1914–1918*, Melbourne University Press, Carlton, Vic, 1970.

Scott, Ernest, *Australia During the War*, Angus & Robertson, Sydney, 1937.

Shephard, Allan, *A Compendium of Australian Defence Statistics*, Australian Defence Forces Studies Centre, Canberra, 1995.

Smith, F.B., *The Conscription Plebiscites in Australia, 1916–17*, Victorian Historical Association, Melbourne, 1966

de Somer, Greg, *The Capacity of the Australian Army to Conduct and Sustain Land Force Operations*, Land Warfare Studies Centre, Canberra, 1999.

Street, G.A., *Statement by the Hon. G.A. Street, MC, MP, Minister for Defence, on the First Report by Lieutenant-General E.K. Squires*, Melbourne, 1939.

10th Terminal Regiment History, 10th Terminal Regiment, Mosman, NSW, 1998.

Young, Thomas-Durrell, *Assessing the 1987 Australian Defence White Paper in the Light of Domestic Political and Allied Influences on the Objective of Defence Self-Reliance*, Research School of Pacific Studies, Australian National University, Canberra, 1988.

—— *Threat-Ambiguous Defence Planning: The Australian Experience*, Strategic Studies Institute, Carlisle Barracks, PA, 1993.

Secondary sources: articles

'Army Reorganization', *Army Journal*, no. 274, March 1972, pp. 3–33.

Babbage, Ross, 'Australian Defence Planning, Force Structure and Equipment: The American Effect', *Australian Outlook*, vol. 38, no. 3, December 1994, pp. 163–8.

Beddie, B.D., 'The Australian Armed Forces in Transition', *Armed Forces and Society*, vol. 5, no. 3, Spring 1977, pp. 414–30.

Cheeseman, Graeme, 'Australia's Force Structure Review: The 1987 White Paper Revisited', in Robert A. Hall (ed.), *The New Look Defence Force: Perspectives on the Force Structure Review*, Australian Defence Studies Centre, Canberra, 1992.

Coates, John, 'The Army and the White Paper', in Jenelle Bonnor & Gary Brown (eds), *Security for the Twenty-First Century? Australia's 1994 Defence White Paper*, Australian Defence Force Studies Centre, Canberra, 1995.

'Defence Review 2000: Public Discussion Paper, Executive Summary', *Australian Defence Force Journal*, no. 143, July–August 2000, pp. 4–7.

Hamill, Ian, 'An Expeditionary Force Mentality? The Despatch of Australian Troops to the Middle East, 1939–1940', *Australian Outlook*, vol. 31, no. 2, August 1977, pp. 319–29.

Horner, David, 'Staff Corps Versus Militia: The Australian Experience in World War II', *Defence Force Journal*, no. 26, January–February 1981, pp. 13–25.

—— 'Australian Army Strategic Planning Between the Wars', in Peter Dennis and Jeffrey Grey (eds), *Serving Vital Interests: Australia's Strategic Planning in Peace and War*, ADFA, Canberra 1996.

Hutton, Edward, 'A Co-operative System for the Defence of the Empire', in Edward Hutton, *The Defence and Defensive Power of Australia*, Melbourne, 1902.

Hyslop, Robert, 'The Council of Defence, 1905–1939', *Canberra Historical Journal*, no. 27, March 1991, pp. 40–7.

Killen, D.J., 'The Government's View', in Robert O'Neill and D.M. Horner (eds), *Australian Defence Policy for the 1980s*, University of Queensland Press, St Lucia, Qld, 1982.

McCarthy, John, 'Australian Responses to the European War, 1939–41', *Australian Journal of Defence Studies*, vol. 1, no. 2, October 1977, pp. 149–57.

—— 'The Imperial Commitment, 1939–41', *Australian Journal of Politics and History*, vol. 23, no. 2, August 1977, pp. 178–81.

—— 'Planning for Future War, 1919–1941: The Armed Services and the Imperial Connection', in Peter Dennis (ed.), *Revue Internationale d'Histoire Militaire*, no. 72, ADFA, Canberra, 1990.

Menzies, Robert, 'The Defence Call to the Nation', *Current Notes on International Affairs*, vol. 21, no. 9, September 1950, pp. 658–69.

Millar, T.B., 'Australian Defence, 1945–1965', in Gordon Greenwood & Norman Harper (eds), *Australia in World Affairs, 1961–1965*, F. W. Cheshire, Melbourne, 1968.

—— 'Anglo-Australian Partnership in Defence of the Malaysian Area', in A.F. Madden and W.H. Morris Jones (eds), *Australia and Britain: Studies in a Changing Relationship*, Sydney University Press, Sydney, 1980.

Nish, I.H., 'Australia and the Anglo-Japanese Alliance, 1901–1911', *Australian Journal of Politics and History*, no. 9, 1963, pp. 201–12.

'The Pentropic Division', *Australian Army Journal*, no. 129, February 1960.

'Possibility of Assimilating War Organization Throughout the Empire', in *Two Papers Prepared by the General Staff Which Were Laid Before the Colonial Conference, 1907*, J. Kemp, Melbourne, 1907.

Robertson, H.C.H., 'The Defence of Australia', *Army Quarterly*, vol. 20, no. 1, April 1935, pp. 15–33.

Sligo, Graeme, 'The Development of the Australian Regular Army, 1944–1952', in Peter Dennis and Jeffrey Grey (eds), *The Second Fifty Years: The Australian Army, 1947–1997*, University College, University of New South Wales, Australian Defence Force Academy, Canberra, 1997.

Smith, Hugh, 'Women in the Australian Defence Force: In Line for the Front Line?', *Australian Quarterly*, vol. 62, no. 2, Winter 1990, pp. 125–44.

'The Strategical Conditions of the Empire from the Military Point of View', in *Two Papers Prepared by the General Staff Which Were Laid Before the Colonial Conference, 1907*, J. Kemp, Melbourne, 1907.

Wilcox, Craig, 'False Start: The Mobilisation of Australia's Citizen Army, 1914', *Journal of the Australian War Memorial*, no. 26, April 1995, pp. 4–9.

Woodman, Stewart, & Horner, David, 'Land Forces in the Defence of Australia,' in David Horner (ed.), *Reshaping the Australian Army: Changes for the 1990s*, Australian National University, 1991, Canberra.

Secondary sources: newspapers

Argus
Australian
Australian Financial Review
Canberra Times
Sunday Times

Secondary sources: theses and unpublished manuscripts

Grimshaw, C., 'Some Aspects of Australian Attitudes to the Imperial Connection, 1900–1919', thesis for the Degree of Master of Arts, Department of History, University of Queensland, 1958.

McCarthy, D.S., 'The Once and Future Army: An Organisational, Political, and Social History of the Citizen Military Forces, 1947–1974', thesis for the degree of Doctor of Philosophy in the School of History, University College, Australian Defence Force Academy, University of New South Wales, 1997.

Murphy, J.E., 'History of the Post-War Army', n.d.

Neumann, Claude, 'Australia's Citizen Soldiers, 1919–1939: A Study of Organization, Command, Recruitment, Training, and Equipment', thesis for the Degree of Master of Arts, Department of History, UNSW at Duntroon, 1978.

Rae, Ian D., 'History of the Australian Army', n.d.

Ramage, Troy, 'In Search of Security: Australian Strategic Planning and the Army, 1945–1964', thesis for the degree of Bachelor of Arts (Honours), School of History, University College, Australian Defence Force Academy, University of New South Wales, 1997.

Index

Australian Army formations and units are listed first, according to the army's order of battle, followed by subjects and organisations. Locators in italics refer to illustrations. Locators suffixed with c, m, and t refer to charts, maps, and tables respectively.

commands 16, 23, 54, 55m, 260
　　Central Command 215t, 224, 238t, 273, 276c, 278, 288; Eastern Command, 128, 137–8t, 147t, 163m, 164, 166c, 167, 211t, 215t, 222, 223–4m, 238t, 263–4, 273, 274, 277c, 278, 288, 292; Field Force Command, 99, 264, 288–91 *passim*, 318, 321, 330; Land Command, 321, 344, 349–57, 358, 379t; Logistic Command, 264, 288–9, 290, 291, 318, 343–6, 354–8; Northern Command, 128, 137t, 138t, 147t, 163m, 164, 166c, 167, 215t, 222, 223–4m, 238t, 273–5 *passim*, 276c, 278, 288, 292 (NORCOM, 321, 340–3); Southern Command, 128, 137, 138t, 147t, 150, 163m, 164, 166c, 167, 215t, 217, 222, 223, 224m, 238t, 251, 260, 273, 274, 277c, 278, 288, 292; Support Command, 361, 378; Tasmania Command, 223–4, 260, 273, 277c, 278; Training Command, 264, 288, 290, 291, 302, 318, 327, 361–2, 378, 380; Western Command, 128, 137t, 138t, 147t, 163m, 164, 166c, 167, 168, 181c, 211t, 215t, 223, 224m, 238t, 255, 273, 276c, 278, 288
military districts:
　　1 MD, 54, 55m, 74, 99, 114; 2 MD, 54, 55m, 74, 99, 111, 114; 3 MD, 54, 55m, 74, 99, 111, 114, 138t, 163m; 4 MD, 54, 55m, 74, 99, 138t, 163m, 166c, 211t, 222, 223; 5 MD, 54, 55m, 99, 223m; 6 MD, 54, 55m, 99, 138t, 163m, 166c, 211t, 222, 223; 7 MD, 128, 137t, 147t, 163m, 164, 166c, 167, 211t, 223m, 224m, 260, 341–1; 8 MD, 147t, 162, 163m, 164, 166c, 167, 222, 223m, 224m
forces:
　　Australian Task Force Vietnam, 280–3, 284; Darwin Mobile Force, 117t, 127, *160*, 211, 331; Deployable Joint Force HQ, 350, 379t; Logistic Support Force (LSF), 246, 247t, 252, 357; NG Force, 158t, 167, 168; NT Force, 158t, 167, 168, 260; Operational Deployment Force (ODF), 330, 331, 333, 338, 344; Ready Deployment Force, 344, 345, 350t, 351t
armies:
　　1 Army, 167, 168, 170c, 177, 179–81c, 188, 190, 222; 2 Army, 167, 168, 170c, 177, 179–81c, 222
lines of communication 91–3 *passim*, 96, 158t, 167–8, 177, 187, 189t, 222
　　Communication Zone, 252, 253, 260, 263, 272, 287
corps:
　　1 Aust Corps, 32, 48, 105t, 154t, 168, 185t; 3 Aust Corps, 167, 168
divisions:
　　1 Armd Div, 145, 183; 3 Armd Div, 273, 287, 288, 330, 344, 379t; 1 Cav Div, 91t, 101; 2 Cav Div, 91t, 101; 1 Div, 65, 66, 91t, 101, 252, 253, 257, 260–4, 274, 287, 288, 292, 327–8, 330, 341, 344, 350; 2 Div, 66, 68, 91t, 101, 114, 182, 183, 209t, 238t, 257, 350,

447

INDEX

352t; 3 Div, 68t, 69, 91t, 101, 121, 151–2, 177, 183, 209t, 238t, 252, 253, 257, 260, 261, 262–3t, 287, 288, 299, 330, 338, 350; 4 Div, 66, 68t, 91t, 101, 177; 5 Div, 66, 68t, 91t, 151, 177, 183; 6 Div, 66, 142–5, 150, *164*, 183, 190; 7 Div, 142t, 144, 145, 178, 183; 8 Div, 142t, 144–5; 9 Div, 142t, 145, 183

brigades:
1 Armd Bde, 183, 238t; 3 Armd Tk Bde, 182; 4 Armd Bde, 182, 183; 4 LH Bde, 31t, 42; 6 LH Bde, 31t, 42; 1 Motorised Bde, 178; 1 AA Bde, 117; 1 Bde, 31t, 91t, 102t, 211, 330, 341–3, 348, 351t, 367; 1 Mixed Bde, 114; 2 Bde, 31t, 91t, 102t; 3 Bde, 31t, 42, 65, 91t, 102t, 351t, 367; 4 Bde, 91t, 102t, 151t, 238t, 330, 350t, 352t; 5 Bde, 91t, 102t, 238t, 350t, 352; 6 Bde, 91t, 102t, 177, 238t, 350, 351t, 354; 7 Bde, 91t, 102t, 151–2, 238t, 350t, 352t; 8 Bde, 91t, 102t, 238t, 350t, 352t; 9 Bde, 91t, 102t, 238t, 353t; 10 Bde, 91t, 102t, 114, 151; 11 Bde, 102t, 153, 177, 238t, 350t, 352t; 11 Mixed Bde, 91t, 101; 12 Mixed Bde, 91t, 101; 13 Bde, 102t, 208, 210t, 238t, 350t, 353t; 13 Mixed Bde, 91t, 101; 14 Bde, 91t, 102t, 177, 238t; 15 Bde, 91t, 102t, 114, 151; 17 Bde, 151; 28 Bde, 177; 29 Bde, 151; 34 Bde, 200, 202m; 39 Bde, 152–3; 1 TF, 275, 286t, 328–9; 2 TF, 275, 328; 3 TF, 274, 275, 286t, 328, 329, 331; 4 TF, 275; 5 TF, 275; 6 TF, 274, 275–6, 286t; 7 TF, 275, 379t; 9 TF, 275; ARA TF, 252

armour   54t, 102t, 106, 138, 178–83, 208–11, 216, 246t, 261–3t, 281t, 294t
1 Armd Regt, 182, 210t, 261t, 274, 281t, 328, 338, 342t, 351t, 354; 1 Cav Regt, 274; 2 Cav Regt, 338, 341, 342t, 351t, 367; 3/4 Cav Regt, 351t, 367; 3/9 SAMR, 263t, 353t; Australian Commonwealth Horse, 17; 4/19 PWLH, 262t, 353t; 2 LH Regt, 28; 11 LH Regt, 114; 13 LH Regt, 31t; 14 LH Regt, 31t; 15 LH Regt, 31t

artillery   54t, 85t, 102t, 108, 118t, 136–7, 138t, 143t, *155*, 158t, 208–11t, 246t, 261t, 262t, 263t, 281t, 294t
Siege Artillery Bde, 71; 2 Mdm Regt, 208, 237; 16 AD Regt, 353t, 354; 1 HAA Regt, 208, 237; 3 Composite AA Regt, 237; 9 HAA Regt, 263; 10 Aust AA Gp, 188; 9 LAA Regt, 300t, 301; 18 LAA Regt, 262, 300t; 2 Fd Regt, 300t, 301; 4 Fd Regt, 274, 351t; 6 Fd Regt, 301; 11 Fd Regt, 262, 300t, 353t

engineers   54t, 85t, 154t, 208t, 209t, 246t, 247t, 261t, 263t, 281t, 294t
16 Const Regt, 215t, 263; 21 Const Regt, 215t, 263, 353t; 22 Const Regt, 215t, 353t; RAE, 105t, 125, 127, 160, 185t, 289, 305

signals   143t, 200, 208–10t, 246t, 247t, 261t, 262t, 274, 281t, 294t, 342t, 351–3t; 101 Wireless Regt, 263
3 L of C Sig Regt, 263; 7 Sig Regt, 353t; 8 Sig Regt, 352t

infantry   54t, 85t, 92t, 102t, 106, 110, 143t, 208–10t, 246t, 261–3t, 294t
2/5th Bn, 151; 2/6th Bn, 151; 2/7th Bn, 151; 11/16 Bn, 124; 1 Bn, 207; 2 Bn, 207, 209t; 30/51 Bn, 124; 31/52 Bn, 177; 3 Bn, 207, 209t, 259t; 8 Bn, 258; 9 Bn, 152, 259t; 15 Bn, 151; 19 Bn, 177; 25 Bn, 114, 152, 259t; 26 Bn, 177; 30 Bn, 124, 259t; 31 Bn, 152, 259t; 42 Bn, 151, 209t, 216, 258, 259t; 47 Bn, 151, 259t; 61 Bn, 152; 65 Bn, 200, 202m, 207, 212; 66 Bn, 200, 202m, 207, 212; 67 Bn, 200, 201, 202m, 207, 212; Australia Regt, 207; Kennedy Regt, 70; 1 RAR, 207, 218–19, 249, 261t, 285, 351t; 2/4 RAR, 285, 351t; 2 RAR, 207, 218, 240, 249, 274, 285, 367, 369, 372; 2 RAR (Cdo), 372; 3 RAR, 201, 207, 218, 261t, 285, 329, 331, 349, 351t, 369; 4 RAR, 265, 285; 5/7 RAR, 285, 328–9, 349, 351t; 5 RAR, 273, 285; 6 RAR, 273, 285, 329, 352t; 7 RAR, 273, 285, 342t; 8/9 RAR, 285, 352t; 8 RAR, 273, 274, 284, 285; 9 RAR, 273, 280, 285; 2 RNSWR, 258, 259t, 261, 273; 3 RNSWR, 258, 259t, 261, 273; 4 RNSWR, 273; 17 RNSWR, 273; 19 RNSWR, 278; 41 RNSWR, 273, 352t; 1 RQR, 258, 259t, 261, 273; 2 RQR, 258, 259t, 261, 273; 25/49 RQR; 25 RQR, 301, 352t; 49 RQR, 278, 352t; 51 RQR, 273; 1 RSAR, 258, 259t, 261, 273; 10 RSAR, 301; 27 RSAR, 301; 43 RSAR, 278, 301; 1 RTR, 258, 259t, 273; 50 RTR, 278; 1 RVR, 258, 259t, 261, 273, 300t; 2 RVR, 258, 259t, 261, 273, 300t, 301; 5 RVR, 273, 300t; 6 RVR, 273, 300t, 301; 22 RVR, 278, 300t, 301; 1 Independent Rifle Coy RVR, 300t, 301; 1 RWAR, 258, 259t, 261, 273; 28 RWAR, 278; SASR, 245, 280, 339, *340*, 367; St George's English Rifle Regt, 28; Pacific Islands Regt (PIR), 208, 248t, 253, 265–7, 272, 302; university regiments, 258; regional force surveillance units (RFSU), 330, 331, *332*, 338, 341, 342, 344; 51 FNQR, 259t, 331, 351t; NORFORCE, 342, 351t; Pilbara Regt, 331, 351t

intelligence   246t, 261t, 262t, 294t, 342t, 351t, 352t
aviation   249, 261t, 281t
1 Army Avn Coy, 304; 1 Avn Regt, 305, 353t; 5 Avn Regt, 339, 351t; 16 Army Lt AC Sqn, 261t, 304–5

logistic units   208–10t, 246t, 247t, 261t, 262t, 281t, 294t, 353t
1 Cbt Service Sup Bn, 355, 368, 369; 2 Fd Log Bn, 331, 357; 2 Force Spt Bn, 357; 9 Force Spt Bn, 357, 368, 369; 10 Force Spt Bn, 357, 368; Bandiana Log Gp, 343, 345t; BASBs, 35t, 342t, 351t, 352t, 355, 356t, 368; Cbt Spt Gp, 260, 270; LSG, 247t, 280, 349, 350t, 353t, 357; Puckapunyal Log Bn, 343–4, 345t

transport:
1 Air Tpt Sup Regt, 357; 9 Tpt Regt, 353t, 357; 10 Terminal Regt, 353t, 357; 11 MC Gp, 263, 280, 351t; 11 Port Regt, 263

postal   209–10t, 246t, 247t
1 Div Postal Unit, 357; 8 Base Postal Unit, 201

medical   85t, 208–10t, 246t, 247t, 261t, 262t, 281t, 294t
1 Aust Fd Hosp, 280; 10 Fd Amb, 357; 12 Fd Amb, 208; 20 Fd Amb, 200; 130 General Hosp, 201

ordnance   96, 208–10t, 246t, 247t, 261t, 262t, 294t
6 Ord Fd Pk, 274; 140 Bde Ord Fd Pk, 200

electrical and mechanical engineers   32, 154t, 208–10t, 246t, 247t, 261t, 262t, 263t, 380, 281t, 294t, 379

INDEX

4 Fd Regt LAD, 275; 6 TF LAD, 274; 334 LAD, 201
pay 246t, 247t, 261t, 262t, 294t
military police (provost) 209–10t, 246t, 247t, 261t, 262t, 294t, 357
training units 121, 87t, 127, 154t, 182, 294t
    ADF Helicopter School, 379, 380; Army Communications Training Centre, 379, 380; Army Logistic Training Centre (ALTC), 362, 378; Army Military Police Training Centre, 379, 380; Army School of Transport, 361, 362; Australian Army Service School, 130; Central Training Depot, 95, 130, 153; Combat Arms Training Centre, 362, 378; Combined Arms Training and Development Centre, 362, 379, 380; Command and Staff College, 378; Command and Staff School, 130; Defence Intelligence Training Centre, 379, 380; Gas School, 153, 154t; Infantry Training Depot, 242; Jungle Training School, 240; Officer Cadet School, 212; Parachute Training School, 379, 380; Royal Australian Army Ordnance Corps Centre, 362; Royal Australian Electrical and Mechanical Engineers Aircraft Maintenance School, 379, 380; Royal Australian Electrical and Mechanical Training Centre, 362; Royal Military College, 378; School of Armour, 362; School of Army Aviation, 305, 379, 380; School of Army Education, 379, 380; School of Army Health, 362; School of Artillery, 153, 362; School of Infantry, 362; School of Military Engineering, 154t; Special Forces Training Centre, 379, 380

Adjutant-General 35, 152, 197–8, 201, 212, 225, 248–9, 291, 317
Afghanistan 313
Air Command 321
air defence 117, 118t, 127, 148, 156–8, 208, 211t, 303, 304
air dispatch 160–1, 184, 357, 369
Anglo-Japanese Pact (1902) 39–40, 81, 90
Anglo-Malayan Defence Agreement 232
Antarctica 5
ANZAM 195, 231, 232, 234, 235, 236, 241
ANZUS 193, 196, 218, 231–2, 312, 313
'Appreciation of Australia's Position in Case of War in the Pacific' (1932) 118–19
ARA–CMF relationship 141, 228, 229–30, 241, 256, 257–8, 266, 285, 296, 298, 302, 307
Arafura Sea 4–5
Army 21 (1996) 363–6
Army Development Guide (ADG) (1984) 330
Army Force Structure Plan (1984) 329–30, 338
Army Headquarters 127–8, 129c, 162–7 *passim*, 182, 225, 226c, 252, 264, 272, 286–8, 291–2, 293c, 299, 317, 318, 362
    LHQ 168, 170–1c, 179c, 182, 183, 190
Army Museum 362
Army Office *see* Army Headquarters
Army Outlook to 1972, The (1972) 266–7, 269
Army Reserve (ARes) 230, 298, 299, 330, 349, 354, 360t, 377
Army Review Committee 295–6
    Hassett Report (1971) 284, 286–92

Attlee, Clement 198
Australia:
    demography 5, 6
    geography 2m, 4–5, 82m, 313
    infrastructure 5–6, 93
    national/cultural characteristics 8–9
    territory 4, 15m, 82–3, 96, 153m, 302, 308m
Australian Armoured Corps (AAC) 216
Australian Army:
    historical overview 380–7
    origins 9–13, 15–20, 380
    planning parameters and principles 3–9, 381
    see also Australian Military Forces (AMF)
Australian Army Aviation Corps 305
Australian Army for the 21st Century, An (Army 21) (1996) 363–6
Australian Army Medical Women's Service (AAMWS) 154t, 189, 190, 191, 214
Australian Army Nursing Service (AANS) *see* Royal Australian Army Nursing Corps (RAANC)
Australian Army Ordnance Corps (AAOC) 126, 154t, 289, 344, 358, 362
Australian Army Reserve 77–8, 92–3, 108, 139, 188
Australian Army Service Corps (AASC) 28, 32, 48, 53, 60, 105t, 126, 143t, 154t, 185t, 261t, 262t, 289
Australian Cadet Corps 45, 55–7
    Federation period 16, 17, 45, 45–6, 50–1, 54–7
    interwar 95, 104t, 106, 108–10 *passim*
    post-WWII 216–17, 266, 283, 290, 291, 333–4
    WWI 71, 74–5
Australian Defence Force (ADF):
    1 Joint Movements Group 320–1
    defence efficiency 346–66, 378
    jointness 317, 318–24, 358, 361, 380
    Tange Reform 314–18
    see also East Timor (INTERFET)
Australian Defence Force Academy (ADFA) 323, 334, 335, 380
Australian Government *see* civil–military relations; defence policy; names of specific governments
Australian Imperial Force (AIF), 1st 189
    and home army 71–6 *passim*
    organisation 62–70, 68t
    post-war 78, 80, 84, 93–4, 105, 137
    unit numbering 75–6, 216
    voluntarism 62, 63, 65, 70, 73–4, 306
Australian Imperial Force (AIF), 2nd 149, 159, 167, 178, 182, 189
    and British model 142–4, 150, 386
    and CMF 146–8, 150–3, 183, 306
    disbandment 191, 202, 229
    mobilisation 138, 139–40
    organisation 141–5, 183, 386
Australian Instructional Corps (AIC) 32, 94–5, 105t, 126, 130, 211
Australian Intelligence Corps 95
Australian Military Forces (AMF):
    'Common Doctrine' 120–3
    designation 141
    service categories 197–8, 201–3
    see also Australian Imperial Force (AIF), 1st; Australian Imperial Force (AIF), 2nd; Australian Regular Army (ARA); Citizen Military Force (CMF); Interim Army; Permanent Military Forces (PMF)

INDEX

Australian Naval and Military Expeditionary Force 63, 80
Australian Red Cross 189
Australian Regular Army (ARA) 282–5, 318, 375–6, 386–7
    1947–50: 212, 218–21, 228; 1957 reorganisation, 240–9; pentropic reorganisation, 249–65; post-Korea, 239–40
    1960s: post-pentropic organisation, 265–80; Vietnam, 280–3
    1970s reforms 283–303, 346, 360–2, 374; capability readjustments, 303–6; Hassett reforms, 286–92, 293c
    1980s: core force concept, 324–35 *passim*; force element group organisation, 344–6
    1990s: defence efficiency, 346–66; *Force Structure Review* reorganisation, 348–53, 378, 379t; northern Australian role, 336–43
    manpower 218–19, 239–40, 243, 244, 248–50, 255, 256t, 266–7, 283, 285–6, 333, 346t, 349, 350, 360–2 *passim*
    national service schemes 219, 220, 238, 242–3, 255, 266, 267, 282–3
    origins 141, 194, 200, 212
    service conditions 212–13, 220, 239, 267
    see also ARA–CMF relationship; Army Reserve (ARes); East Timor (INTERFET); Ready Reserve Scheme (RRes); Regular Army Reserve; Regular Army Supplementary Reserve
Australian Staff Corps 95, 105–6, 130, 148, 211
Australian Support Area (ASA) 261, 264–5, 272, 273, 282, 283t, 285, 288, 343
Australian Women's Army Service (AWAS) 177, 189, 190, 213
Australian Women's Land Army 186
Australia's Strategic Policy (1997) 347, 366, 369, 373
aviation 249, 266, 283, 304–5, 338–9, 376, 378

Baker, Gen J. S. 321
Balikpapan 305
Barnard, Lance 284, 292, 295, 297, 299, 326
Barton, Edmund 15, 17, 20, 23
Beavis, Maj-Gen L. 225
Beazley, Kim 321, 336, 338–9
Beer, Major V. L. 19
Belgium 62
Bell, Coral 233
Bismarck Archipelago 4, 63
Blamey, Gen Sir Thomas 148, *149*, 167–9, 172, 174, 177–8, 182, 187–8, 190, 221, 224, 287
Borneo 153, 178, 268, 269, 280, 305
Bougainville 151, 153, 178
Bridgeford, Maj-Gen W. 225
Bridges, Maj-Gen Sir William T. 35, 42, 44, 46–7, 63–5, 67
Britain *see* Colonial Defence Committee (CDC); Committee of Imperial Defence (CID); empire defence
British Army 1, 10, 34, 43, 67, 133–4, 160, 178, 245, 357
    standards 11, 23, 142–4, 150, 183, 387
British Commonwealth Occupation Force (BCOF) 192, 198–201, 202m, 205, 206, 214, 309
Brogan, Lt-Gen Sir Mervyn 295
Bruce, Stanley 147
Bruche, Maj-Gen Sir Julius 119, *120*
Bushmen's Rifles 278, 296, 297

Canada 46, 196
Casey, R. G. 140
Chamberlain, Joseph 10, 17, 22–3
Chamberlain, Neville 130
Chambers, Cyril 212
Chauvel, Gen Sir H. G. 89, *94*, 106, 108, 111, 112
Chief of Army 323
Chief of Defence Force Staff (CDFS) 316–18, 321
Chief of the General Staff (CGS) 37, 46–7, 47c, 111, 119, 162, 224, 225, 290, 291, 292, 316–18, 323
Chief of Intelligence 35, 37, 46–7
Chief of Logistics 291, 317
Chief of Materiel 291, 317
Chief of Operations 291, 317
Chief of Personnel 291, 317
Chiefs of Staff Committee 139, 147–8, 162, 196, 216, 304, 305, 316, 341
Chifley, J. B. 194, 196, 198, 205, 213, 221
Chifley Government 192, 194–5, 214, 227
China 14, 40, 46, 84, 103, 203, 219, 228, 234, 235, 265
Churchill, Winston 140, 172, 235
Citizen Forces *see* Citizen Military Force (CMF)
Citizen Military Force (CMF) 12–13, 14, 49
    Federation period: Citizen Forces, 26, 45, 49, 50, 51, 54, 56, 59, 61; Militia, 14, 16, 25, 26, 29, 30, 32, 40, 41, 43, 49
    interwar 84–5, 88, 93, 97, 99, 104t, 105, 106, 109–11; Squires scheme, 123–6, 128, 130–1
    post-WWII 212–15, 225, 278–82; 1957 reorganisation, 240–5; decline, 125–6, 228, 230, 256–8, 278–9, 287, 294–5, 306–7; Millar Report (1974), 292, 296–302; national service schemes, 219–21, 228, 237, 238, 284; pentropic reorganisation, 253–4, 256–60, 262t, 263t; post-pentropic reorganisation, 272–3, 275; post-Korea, 237–40, 238t; re-establishment, 197, 201, 206, 207, 209–10t, 213
    service conditions 26, 45, 106, 130, 138–9, 201, 203, 213, 238–9, 296, 299
    strength 16c, 29, 50, 54, 99, 104t, 128, 130, 138, 146–8, 207t, 213, 237, 294t
    WWI 65, 70–5
    WWII 162, 186, 188, 189, 191; mechanisation, 178, 182–3; mobilisation, 138–9; two-army system, 140–2, 146–8, 150–3, 386
    see also ARA–CMF relationship; Army Reserve (ARes); CMF Supplementary Reserve
civil–military relations 3, 8–9, 103, 107, 109, 112–13, 118–23, 131–2, 330, 336, 360, 364, 370, 381, 384–6
Clarke, Sir G. Sydenham 41
Clowes, Maj-Gen C. A. 225
Clunies-Ross, Maj-Gen A. 330
CMF Supplementary Reserve 214, 215t, 278–9, 280
coastal defence 91
    Federation period 13, 19–20, 24, 27, 303
    interwar modernisation 96–8, 115–16, 117t, 123, 125, 132, 155
    post-WWII 208, 210, 211t, 303, 304
    WWI 70, 71, 79
    WWII 117t, 122, 136–8, 155–6, 157m, 303–4
Coates, Lt-Gen John 346, 349, 350, 354, 355

INDEX

Cold War 203, 228, 229–37 *passim*, 241, 306, 313
Colonial Defence Committee (CDC) 10, 12, 17, 19–21, 22, 27, 33, 41, 43, 109
colonial forces 1, 9–13, 15–20
Colonial Office 22
Command and Organizational Structure of the Army in Australia, The (1971) 284, 286–92
command structure *see* higher command; regional command structure
Commander Australian Theatre 321
Commander-in-Chief 24, 35, 37
Commander-in-Chief Australian Military Forces 167
Commercial Support Program 349, 359
Committee of Imperial Defence (CID) 10, 41–4, 43, 109, 119
'Committee to Review the Organisation of the Division and Combat Support Group' (1964) 270
'Common Doctrine on the Organisation and Employment of the AMF' 120–3
Commonwealth Cadet Corps *see* Australian Cadet Corps
communism 192, 195, 196, 218, 219, 229–37 *passim*, 265, 306, 313
Confrontation 7, 232, 235, 236, 268
conscription *see* national service schemes
Cook, Joseph 44–5, 62
core force concept 324–35, 336–8
Cosgrove, Gen P. 367, 377
Council of Defence 25, 34, 37, 78–9, 82–3, 97–9, 107, 110, 112, 194, 201, 204–6
Cramer, John 241, 248
Creswell, Capt W. R. 37–9, 42
Crimean War 12–13
Crocodile 99 West 329
Cullen, Maj-Gen P. A. 281–2, 295–6
Curtin, John 172, 174, 177, 183, 190, 193–4, 387
Curtin Government 153, 172, 174–5, 193–4

Deakin, Alfred 40–4 *passim*, 55, 56–7
Deakin Government 40–1, 44–5, 55
Dedman, John 194, 213–14, 225
Defence 2000 373–7
Defence Acquisition Organisation 361
Defence Act 1903:
    conscription 39, 44–5, 243, 282
    origins 16, 24–5, 32
    permanent combat forces 125–6, 127, 210–11
    permanent officers 211–12
    training 50, 55, 92, 95, 98
    see also overseas service
Defence of Australia (DOA) (1987) 336, 338–41, 344, 346, 347–8, 363–4
Defence Committee 136, 175, 204–6, 235–7, 240, 265
    strategic reports 234, 235–7, 240, 249, 265, 311–13, 320, 325, 346
defence efficiency 278, 346–66, 384
    Commercial Support Program 349
    Defence Efficiency Review (1997) 359–62, 374
    Defence Review 2000 373–7
    Defending Australia (1994) 358–9
    Force Structure Review (1991) 348–51, 355, 360, 374
    logistic support 354–9
    privatisation 349, 359–60, 361, 378, 384
    reserves 349–51, 354
defence expenditure:
    Federation period 3, 8, 23
    interwar 85, 97–8, 101, 104–7, 111, 115–16, 128, 130–2, 384
    post-WWII 205–6, 213, 216, 221, 230, 240, 251, 267, 317, 341, 348, 384–5
    WWII 140
    see also defence efficiency
Defence Force and the Community, The (Wrigley) (1991) 349
Defence Group 314–19, 322c, 359, 382–3c
Defence Materiel Organisation 361
defence policy 7–14
    defence planning principles 7–8
    Federation period: and threat assessment, 7, 8, 20–4, 21–4 *passim*, 26, 27–8; Hamilton review, 59–61; Hutton's planning, 27–34 *passim*; Kitchener's plan, 48–57 *passim*, 60; McCay reforms, 34–9 *passim*; reliance on Royal Navy, 7, 8, 9, 12, 13, 14, 15, 20–7 *passim*, 33–4, 37, 38, 39, 49–50, 58–9
    v. force structure 103, 107, 109, 109–11, 112, 130–1, 131–2, 336, 381, 384–6
    interwar 82, 101, 131–4; international agreements, 83, 84, 103–4, 108–9, 131–3 *passim*; raids v. invasion debate, 108–9, 111–23, 131–2, 134; reliance on Royal Navy, 83–4, 88, 90, 103–4, 107, 111–13, 114–15, 118–19, 123, 131–2, 370–1; Senior Officers' Conference, 88–91, 96, 97, 101; Swinburne report, 86–8, 89, 93, 103
    post-WWII: collective security, 193–6, 203, 227–8, 230–3 *passim*; defence efficiency, 346, 358–60; forward defence, 229, 232–3, 236, 237, 304, 309–11; maritime strategy, 324, 347, 366, 370–1, 387; self-reliance/continental defence, 310–14, 320, 324–5, 331, 338, 371, 373
    see also defence expenditure; empire defence; raids v. invasion; Singapore Strategy; strategic environment; treaties and agreements
Defence Reports 312–13, 316, 360
Defence Review 2000 373–7
'Defence Scheme for the Commonwealth of Australia' (1913) 57
Defending Australia (1994) 358–9, 362–3
de Mesurier, Major Havilland 35
Demobilisation Committee 197
Department of Defence 61, 69, 106, 147, 162, 312, *314*, 315–18, 347, 358–61, 373
Department of Foreign Affairs and Trade 347, 366
Deputy Chief of the General Staff (DCGS) 225, 292, 318
designations and numbering 75–6, 141–2, 156, 207, 212, 216, 250–1, 258, 271, 291–2, 316, 318, 323, 330
Devonshire, Duke of 11
Dibb, Paul 313, 330, 336–8
Director of Military Training (DMT) 47, 271
Director of Staff Duties (DSD) 234, 252, 258
divisional structure 67, 85, 100c, 104, 106, 203, 285
    Army 21 364
    Australian v. British 142–4, 386
    core force concept 326, 327, 330
    Force Structure Review (1991) 350, 351–3t
    jungle division standard 183–6, 386
    mechanisation policy 178, 182–3
    origins 48, 50, 59
    pentropic organisation 249–65, 386–7
    Wilton reorganisation 269–73

INDEX

Dodds, Maj-Gen T. H. 73, 111, 133
Dougherty, Maj-Gen Sir Ivan 243
Dulles, John Foster 196
Dunstan, Lt-Gen Sir Donald 301, 326, 327–9

East Timor (INTERFET) 4, 366–70, 371, 374–7
Empire Air Training Scheme 139, 174
empire defence 1, 386
    Federation period 10–14, 21–7 *passim*, 38, 58, 60, 61, 378, 386; Hutton's scheme, 32–3, 43, 45–6; Kitchener's scheme, 49–50
    interwar 133–4, 135; naval security policy, 83, 84, 90–1, 103–4, 108–9, 131–2, 134, 227–8, 387; raids v. invasion debate, 111–23, 131, 134
    post-WWII 192–7, 198, 203, 216, 233, 286, 310–12
    WWI 62–3, 66–7, 69, 80, 93
    WWII 135–6, 139, 140, 145–7, 172, 177, 371; British standards, 142–4, 150, 183, 387
    see also British Commonwealth Occupation Force (BCOF); Far East Strategic Reserve (FESR); Malayan Emergency; Royal Navy; Singapore Strategy
'Environment of Future Australian Military Operations, The' (1976) 311
equipment:
    Federation period: Hutton's assessment, 19–20, 33–4, 39; standards, 11, 14, 17, 19, 23, 43, 47
    interwar 85, 96, 116, 125, 130; air defence, 117, 127; coastal defence, 115–16, 125, 132; Senior Officers Conference (1920), 96–8, 101
    post-WWII 251, 283; artillery, 303–4, 338; aviation, 304–5, 338–9, 376; mechanisation, 338, 365, *375*, 376; modernisation, 347–8, 358, 365, 375–7; transportation, 305–6, *365*
    WWI 65–7
    WWII 140, 148, 188; air defence, 156, 158, 304; British v. Australian standards, 143–4; coastal defence, 155–6, 303–4; jungle division, 183–4; mechanisation policy, 178, 182–3; transportation, 159–60
    see also guns
Evatt, Herbert 195
Ewing, Thomas 44
expeditionary forces 113, 133–4, 139–40, 142, 153, 252
    see also Australian Naval and Military Expeditionary Force; British Commonwealth Occupation Force (BCOF); Far East Strategic Reserve (FESR)

Far East Strategic Reserve (FESR) 234–6, 238, 239–40, 241, 242, 244, 245, 252, 253, 265, 269
Federal Military Conference (1894) 11
Federation 1, 2, 9–10, 14
Fiji 331
Finn, Maj-Gen H. 37, 39
Fisher, Andrew 45, 62
Fisher Government 44, 45–6
Five Power Defence Arrangements (1971) 232
Five Power treaty (1921) 103
Forbes, Alexander J. 272
force element groups system 344–6
Force Structure Review (1991) 348–51, 355, 360, 374

Forde, Francis M. 187–8, 190, 192, 224
Foreign Office 20
Forrest, John 15–18, 23, 24–5, 33
Four Power Pact 103
France 21, 103, 178, 232, 234
Frances Peat 161
Fraser, Malcolm 275, 281, 305, 333
Fraser Government 313, 325, 333–4
Future Shape of the ARA, The (1972) 284–5

Gallipoli 66, 67
Garrett, Lt-Gen Sir Ragnar 229
General Officer Commanding (GOC) 16, 18, 24–5, 27, 34, 35, 39
General Officer Commanding-in-Chief Home Forces 162–4, 167
General Reserve *see* Army Reserve (ARes)
Germany 4, 8, 21, 40, 46, 62, 63, 70–1, 81–3, 121–2, 131, 136, 137, 140, 178
Gordon, Donald C. 48
Gorton, John 311
Graham, Maj-Gen S. C. 282–3
Gration, Gen P. C. 321, *323*
Great Depression 109–11
Grey, Lt-Gen J. C. 354, 358
Guam Doctrine 311–12
Gulf War 310
guns *49*, *155*
    Federation period 19, 20
    interwar deficiencies 96, 101, 108, 115–17, 125, 127, 130
    standards 20, 143–4
    WWII deficiencies 140, 144, 148, 155, 156

Habibie, B. J. 367
Haldane, Lord 34
Hamilton, Gen Sir Ian 57, 59–60, 381
Hankey, Sir Maurice 119
Harding, FM Sir John 235
Hassett, Gen Sir Francis 252, 284, 286–92, 295, 301, 302, 318, 320, 326
Hassett Report (1971) 284, 286–92
Hawke, Allan 375
Headquarters ADF 317, 321–2
helicopters 338–9, 378
Hickling, Lt-Gen Frank 366
higher command 100c
    Blamey reorganisation, 1941–5: 148, 161–72, 179c, 180c, 181c, 187
    joint force command structure 310, 318–24
    organisation, 1999: 382–3c
    pentropic restructure, 1958–9: 252, 260–1, 263–4
    post-pentropic reorganisation, 1965: 273–7
    reforms, 1970s: 284, 286–92, 293c, 316–18, 319c
    Sturdee reorganisation, 1947: 221–5, 226c
    see also Army Headquarters; Land Command; Military Board (MB); regional command structure
Hoad, Maj-Gen J. C. 35, 41, 43, 47
Hobbs, Lt-Gen Sir J. J. T. 89, *90*
Holmes, Col William 63
Hong Kong 83
Hopetoun, Earl of 23
Horner, David 107, 148, 324
Howard Government 346–7, 354, 359–60, 366, 373–4, 377, 384

INDEX

Howse, Neville 109
Hughes, William 70, 85, 98, 133
Hutton, Gen Sir Edward 10, *18*, 24–6 *passim*, 40, 48, 57, 60, 71, 83, 84, 95, *377*
    defence assets assessment 18–20 *passim*
    profile 18–19, 27
    reorganisation 27–34, 39

Imperial Conference (1897) 10–11
Imperial Conference (1902) 22–3
Imperial Conference (1907) 43
Imperial Conference (1909) 46, 47–8, 57
Imperial Conference (1923) 83, 84, 103, 108–9, 131–2, 133
Imperial Conference (1937) 84, 103
Imperial Defence Committee (IDC) 42
Imperial General Staff 43, 47, 118
Imperial Japanese Navy 103, 117, 119
In the National Interest (1997) 347, 366
Indonesia 4, 237, 265, 306, 366–7
    see also Confrontation with Indonesia; East Timor (INTERFET)
Inspector-General (IG) 35, 37, 111, 225
    see also Squires Report (1938)
Inspector-General of the AIF 72–5
Inspector-General of the Army Reserve 298, 317
Institution of Engineers Australia 214
INTERFET *see* East Timor (INTERFET)
Interim Army 196–203
Italy 103, 140

Japan 8, 43, 70–1, 88, 111, 121–2, 147, 197, 371
    Anglo-Japanese Pact (1902) 39–40, 81, 90
    Federation period 39–40, 43
    interwar 81, 82, 88, 90, 108–9, 112, 122, 134
    Russo-Japanese War 39, 40, 44
    threat 39–40, 43, 82, 88, 90, 108–9, 112, 134, 136, 137
    WWII 81–4 *passim*, 135–40 *passim*, 145, 151, 153, 159, 174, 178, 191, 192, 198
    see also British Commonwealth Occupation Force (BCOF)
Jellicoe, Viscount 82
Jervis Bay 306
Jervois, Col Sir William 12
John Monash 305
joint exercises 320, 321, *329*, *332*, 338
Joint Intelligence Organisation 205
Joint Logistics Command 361
Joint Standing Committee on Foreign Affairs, Defence, and Trade (2000) 374
jointness 310, 317, 318–24, 358, 361, 380
jungle division standard 151, 183–6, 216, 240, 327, 386

Kangaroo 95 (Exercise) 321
Kanimbla 306, 357
Keating Government 346, 358
Killen, James 311, 325, 328, 329, 333
King George's Sound 27, 32, 38
Kitchener, Lord 45, 48–57, 71, 95, 211
Kitchener Plan 48–57, 59, 60, 95
Korean War 201, 214, 217–19, 227, 239

Land Command *see* index of formations and units
Laos 232, 267, 268
Lavarack, Lt-Gen Sir John 115–16, 119–21, 126, 134

League of Nations 4, 81, 85, 88–90, 104, 111
Legge, Maj-Gen J. G. *86*, 87, 89
Limitation of Armaments Conference (1921) 103–4, 107
Logistic Command *see* index of formations and units
logistic support:
    1957 reorganisation 246, 247t, 248
    British Commonwealth Occupation Force (BCOF) 201
    East Timor 369–70, 371
    future 376–7
    Hassett reforms (1970s) 286–9, 290, 291
    interwar 93, 96, 101
    pentropic organisation 264–5
    reorganisations (1990s) 343–6, 349, 354–9, 356t, 361, 378
    WWII 159–61, 167–8, 184
    see also Australian Support Area (ASA); Logistic Command
Logistics Branch 291
Long, Gavin 140
Lyons, Joseph 84, 112–13
Lyons Government 112–13, 126–7

MacArthur, General Douglas 156, 172, *173*, 198, 218
McCarthy, John 103, 104, 257, 295
McCay, Lt-Gen Sir James 34, 35, 37–9, 56, 72, 87, 89
MacDonald, Gen Sir Arthur 258, 334
MacDonald, Ramsay 112
Mackay, Lt-Gen Sir Iven 162–4, 167, 168
Mackay, Brig K. 77, 78, 270–1
McLachlan, Ian 359, 365–6
McNeill, Maj-Gen J. M. 297
Malaya/Malaysia 145, 196, 219, 231, 232, 236, 237, 268
Malayan Emergency 7, 148, 219, 232, 234–5, 239–40, 245, 265, 305, 309, 312, 386
Malta 234
Manchuria 84, 191
Manoora 306, 357
manpower *see under* names of specific bodies
Maritime Command 321
Massey-Greene, Walter 104
Master-General of the Ordnance (MGO) 35, 225, 291, 317
Materiel Branch 291
Meaney, Neville 20, 23
mechanisation 178, 182–3, 328–9, 338, 365, *375*, 376
Mena Army Camp (Egypt) 66
Menzies, Robert G. 128, 130, 135, 137–8, 140, 145–7, 162, 173, 201, 211, 213, 218, 219–21, 229–35 *passim*, 267, 268, 304, 316, 384
Menzies Government 126, 136–40, 192, 194, 195, 227, 240, 251, 304, 315
Middle East 65–6, 67, 69, 140, 146, 159, 167, 172, 178, 190, 195, 234, 236, 280
Military Board (MB):
    Federation period 44, 46, 56; Hutton organisation, 34, 34–7, 36c
    interwar 85, 98–9, 100t, 110, 113
    post-WWII 197, 257, 292, 293c, 295, 306, 307, 333, 334; CMF member, 225, 281–2, 291, 295, 317; post-war army, 202–3, 205, 212, 213–14; restructure, 221, 223–5; Tange Reform, 316, 317, 318
    WWI 71–2, 74–6
    WWII 137–40, 142, 146, 148, 163–7

453

military districts *see* regional command structure
Militia *see* Citizen Military Force (CMF)
Millar, T. B. 8, 84, 196, 232–3, 239, 255, 306, 333
Millar Report (1974) 284, 292, 295–302
Millen, Edward 63, 70
Minister for the Army 148, 224
Minister for Defence 24, 35, 37, 291, 292, 317, 385
Monash, Lt-Gen Sir John 89
Moore, John 361, 371–2, 374, 375–6
Mordike, John 48
Morshead, Lt-Gen Sir Leslie 315–16
munitions industry 20, 117, 130, 140, 148, 156, 175, 178, 182
Munitions Supply Board 178, 182
Murchison, Maj-Gen A. V. 295, 296–7
Murdoch, Maj-Gen I. T. 254–5

national service schemes:
    1911–29 44, 45–6, 49–51, 54–7, 59–60, 71, 77–9
    1939–45 87, 97, 106, 107, 109–10
    1951–57 201, 204, 205, 206, 213, 219–21, 238–9, 242–3, 244, 257
    1965–72 267, 282, 283–4, 295–6, 384
    conscription 69–70, 109–10, 140–1
Naval Agreement with Britain (1903) 21, 41
New Britain 145, 153, 178
New Guinea 4, 40, 63, 190, 208, 236, 237, 268, 302
    WWII 145, 151, 153, 156, 159–61, 168m, 178, 183–4
New Weapons and Equipment Development Committee 205
New Zealand 14, 22, 108, 146, 193, 195, 231, 232, 235
Nine Power Treaty 103
Nixon, Richard 311–12
Norris, Ronald 23
Northcott, Lt-Gen Sir John 144, 175, *176*, 198, *199*
northern Australia 6, 321, 336–43
    transfer of brigade 340–3, 348
nuclear army 101–9, 110, 115, 123, 132–3
Nutcracker exercise 255

Officer Staff Group 258, 260, 279–80
O'Neill, Robert 217–18, 219
Operation Stabilise 366–70, 371, 374–7
Operations Branch 291, 292
O'Sullivan, Brig P. 357–8
Overseas Defence Committee 109
overseas service 22–3, 203, 229
    colonial forces 10–14 *passim*, 16, 17
    Defence Act provisions 24–6 *passim*, 24–7, 32–3, 42, 58, 60, 62, 70, 73–4, 80, 83, 96, 101, 133, 140–1, 144, 153, 205, 206, 219, 220, 238–9, 243, 267, 374
    East Timor 370, 374
    national service scheme 220–1, 238–9, 242–3, 267
    reserves 279, 374, 377
    women 190
    see also expeditionary forces

Pacific region 195–6
    British influence, interwar period 83, 89, 103–4
    WWII 145, 152, 159, 172, 178
Papua New Guinea Defence Force 302, 303t
Parkhill, Archdale 123

Peacock, Andrew 286, 295, 373
Pearce, George 45, 73, 75–9, 86, 88–90 *passim*, 98, 111, 113, 114–15, 118, 120, 178, 385
pentropic reorganisation 249–65, 386–7
    abandonment 269–72
    Australian Support Area 264–5
    and CMF 256–60
    command reform 252, 260–1, 263–4
    formations 252–4
    Officer Staff Group 258, 260, 279–80
    priorities 254–5
    rationale 251–2
Permanent Military Forces (PMF):
    colonial period 12–13
    Federation period 14, 16, 25–6, 28–32, 49, 53, 59
    interwar period 85, 99, 104t, 105–6, 110–11, 125–7, 130
    name change to Australian Regular Army 210–11, 212
    permanent combat units 71, 126, 206, 230
    post-WWII reorganisation 202–4, 206–7, 208t, 210–13
    reserves 77, 212–13
    service conditions 77, 105–6, 111, 202–3, 206, 211–12
    strength 104t, 105t, 110–11, 130, 206–7, 212
    WWI 70, 71, 77
    WWII 136, 139, 141, 202–3, 207
    see also Australian Regular Army (ARA)
Pfalz 70
Philippines 103, 172, 232, 267
Plan 401 133–4
Playford, Thomas 43
Poland 81, 136, 178
Post-War Army Planning Committee 216
Prime Ministers' Conference (1946) 195–6
Prime Ministers' Conference (1947) 194–5
Prince of Wales 13
privatisation 349, 359–60, 378, 384

Quartermaster-General 225, 291, 317

raids v. invasion 21, 22, 23–4, 83, 108–9, 111–23, 131–2, 134, 326, 336, 364
railways 93, 159, 214
Ray, Robert 348–9
Ready Reserve Scheme (RRes) 349–50, 351t, 354, 360t, 372
regional command structure 272–5, 364
    1 AIF 63, 67, 68–9
    disbanded (1997) 362
    v. functional command system 287–91, 298, 299
    Hassett reforms (1970s) 284, 286–92, 293c
    Kitchener plan 52m, 53m, 54, 55m
    origins 16, 36
    pentropic reorganisation 240–65 *passim*
    post-pentropic 270–80, 276–7c, 294t
    reorganisation (1920s) 99, 100t, 101, 102t
    Squires scheme (1930s) 127–8, 129c
    Sturdee's reorganisation (1947) 221–5, 226c
    Tange Reforms 284, 316, 318, 319c
    v. task force system 272–5, 364
    WWII 147t, 162–4, 167, 168m, 170–1c, 179c, 180c, 181c, 287

INDEX

Regular Army Emergency Reserve 278–9, 297, 298, 299, 354
Regular Army Reserve 266, 278, 278–9, 297, 298, 330
Regular Army Supplementary Reserve 212–13, 279
Reid, George 11
Repulse 13
reserve forces 334, 343, 360t
    1948 reorganisation 212–15
    1964 reorganisation 278–80
    1974 Millar Inquiry 297–9, 300t, 301–2
    1996 Army 21 363–5 *passim*
    East Timor 370, 374, 377
    Federation period 16, 26, 27, 28t, 43, 46, 59
    imperial reserve scheme 22–3, 50–1
    interwar reorganisation 92–6 *passim*
    Pearce scheme 77–8
    Volunteer Defence Corps 188–9, 189t
    WWII mobilisation 137–9 *passim*
    see also Army Reserve (ARes); Australian Army Reserve; CMF Supplementary Reserve; Ready Reserve Scheme (RRes); Regular Army Emergency Reserve; Regular Army Reserve; Regular Army Supplementary Reserve
Restructuring the Australian Army (1997) 365–6
Review of the Size and Shape of the Army Post Vietnam (1969) 282
rifle clubs 16, 50, 54, 59, 70, 71, 77, 78, 95–8, 106
roads 5–6, 93, 159
Robertson, Lt-Gen Sir Horace 106, 198, *200*
Roosevelt, Franklin D. 172
Rowell, Lt-Gen Sir Sydney 203–4, 213, 219, 224
Royal Australian Air Force (RAAF) 113, 119, 205, 218, 221, 234, 361, 364, 367, 370, 371, 375
    battlefield helicopters 338–9
    capabilities 303, 304–5, 325–6, 348, 357
    head of service 162, 316, 320, 323
    jointness 310, 318, 320, 321
    WWII 139, 160, 161, 177, 184
Royal Australian Army Dental Corps 289
Royal Australian Army Medical Corps (AAMC) 28, 32, 189, 289
Royal Australian Army Nursing Corps (RAANC) 188–9, 191, 213–14
Royal Australian Artillery (RAA) 28, 31, 32, 105, 125, 127, 185t, 211, 237, 261t, 262t
Royal Australian Corps of Transport (RACT) 289, 344, 358, 361
Royal Australian Electrical and Mechanical Engineers (RAEME) 32, 261t, 289, 344, 358, 362
Royal Australian Engineers (RAE) 105t, 125, 127, 160, 185t, 289, 305
Royal Australian Navy (RAN) 21, 38, 46, 71, 93, 177, 218, 221, 313, 323, 331, 335, 361, 364, 370, 371
    capabilities 160, 303, 304, 305–6, 325–6, 348, 357, 375
    funding 108, 115, 119, 205, 348, 367
    head of service 37, 38–9, 162, 316, 320, 323
    jointness 310, 318, 320, 321, 323
    and Royal Navy 112–13, 115, 122, 131, 139, 318, 320
Royal Military College, Duntroon 57, *58*, 95, 105, 130, 153, 154t, 211–12, 290, 378, 380
Royal Navy (RN) 1, 11–13, 20–4, 26, 27, 29, 37, 38, 40, 41, 42, 44, 46, 50, 83–4, 88, 90, 103–4, 107, 111–15, 118–19, 122, 123, 131–2, 134, 233, 310, 318, 320, 370–1

    see also Singapore Strategy
RSL (Returned Sailors, Soldiers, and Airmen's Imperial League of Australia) 186, 188
Russia 21, 39, 81, 191
Russo-Japanese War 39, 40, 44

St Mark's Collegiate School 55
Salamaua campaign 151
Sanderson, Lt-Gen J. M. 362–5
Scientific Advisory Committee 205
scientific research 205, 214, 216, 304
Scratchley, Lt-Col P. 12
Scullin Government 109–10
SEATO 232, 236, 237, 241, 265, 266, 268, 312
security environment *see* strategic environment
Senior Officers' Conference (1920) 88–101, 103, 106–7, 108, 113, 119, 121, 133, 144
Singapore 145, 231, 232, 236, 237
Singapore Strategy 13, 83–4, 103, 107, 108–9, 111–12, 118–19, 131–2, 134, 136, 192, 233, 381, 387
Smith, Adm Sir Victor 305, 320
South Africa 14, 16–17, 22, 23, 65
South-East Asia 178, 191, 231–7, 267–8, 280, 311, 320
South-West Pacific Area (SWPA) 152m, 153, 159, 160, 172, 177, 178, 184, 190
Soviet Union 192, 195, 203, 216, 219, 265, 313, 337
Spender, Percy 188, 195, 196, 218
Squires, Lt-Gen Ernest K. *124*, 144, 146, 320
Squires Report (1938) 106, 123–8, 129c, 130–1, 162, 164, 222
staff officers 105–6, 128, 146, 148, 211–12
    Officer Staff Group 258, 260, 279–80
    training 95, 97, 107, 109, 126, 130
Stirling (establishment) 348
'Strategic Basis of Australian Defence Policy, The' (1953) 240
Strategic Basis Paper (1971) 311–12, 320, 325, 346
strategic environment:
    Federation period 21, 27, 28, 38–40, 43, 60, 61
    geographic position 2m, 4–6, 82m
    government–army tensions 8–9, 103, 109, 112–13, 118–23, 131–2, 360, 364, 381
    interwar period 81–4, 88–90, 103–4, 108–9, 112, 114–15, 131–2
    post-WWII 225, 226–8, 308m, 370–1, 381, 384–7 *passim*; Cold War, 195, 203, 218–19, 229–37; maritime strategy, 346–7, 371; no-threat environment, 312–13, 324, 325; northern Australia, 336–7; SE Asia, 267–9, 366–7; security environment, 192–6; self-reliance, 310–14
    WWII 135–6, 140
    see also defence policy; Singapore Strategy; treaties and agreements
Strategic Review papers 234, 265
    1956 235–7, 240, 249
Street, G. A. 126, 131, 137
Sturdee, Lt-Gen Sir Vernon 221–3, 224, 225
Sudan 14
Suez Canal 231, 234
Support Command Australia 361
Swinburne, G. 86
Swinburne Report (1919) 86–8, 89, 93, 103

Tange, Sir Arthur 314
Tange Reform (1973) 284, 314–18, 319c

INDEX

tanks 96, 116, *145*, 148, 178, 338, 376
task force concept 272–5
Taylor, Maj-Gen T. S. 256, 260
technology 214, 216, 304, 325, 347–8, 365, 375, 377
Thompson, J. T. 35
Thursday Island 27, 32, 70, 127
Tobruk 306, 357
Townley, Athol 251, 257, 265–6, 279
training 290, 378, 380
    cadets 74–5, 110
    cutbacks 106, 107, 111, 153, 212, 257
    Defence Act provisions 92, 95, 98
    Hassett reforms 289, 290, 291, 302
    jointness 323
    leadership training 95, 107, 109, 115, 123, 133, 211–12
    reorganisation (1990s) 361–2
    Senior Officers' Conference (1920) 93–5, 98, 106–7
    Swinburne report (1919) 87–8, 93
    WWI 65–6, 72, 74–9 *passim*
    WWII 130–1, 137–9 *passim*, 147–8, 153, 154t
    see also national service schemes; Training Command
Training Information Bulletin no. 28 (1975) 327
transport infrastructure 93, 159–61, 184, 288, 304
transportation capability 159–60, 305–6, 365
treaties and agreements:
    interwar 84, 103–4, 108–9
    post-WWII 9, 193, 195, 196, 231–2, 234, 235, 310, 311, 312, 386
    WWII peace treaties 193–4, 196, 198
    see also ANZAM; ANZUS; SEATO
tropical establishment system 253t, 254, 275, 276–7c, 327
Truman administration 196
Tulloch, Maj-Gen A. 10
Turkey 234

United Nations 4, 193, 194, 201, 203, 218, 231, 237, 309, 367
United States 81
    Korean War 218, 227, 239
    security role 9, 103–4, 193, 195–6, 203, 230–3, 234–7 *passim*, 310–13 *passim*, 346, 386
    WWII 156, 158, 159, 172, 174, 177, 191, 198
United States Army 160, 214, 271, 283, 325
    pentomic structure 249, 251, 252, 256, 386–7
United States Navy 103–4
Universal Training Schemes *see* national service schemes
university regiments 258, 280, 380

Vasey, Maj-Gen G. A. 105–6
Versailles Conference 80, 85, 134
Vice-Chief of the Defence Force (VCDF) 321
Vice-Chief of the General Staff (VCGS) 224, 225, 292
Vickery, Maj-Gen M. A. 296
Vietnam War 232, 233, 268, 269, 280–3, 284, 305, 310, 311, 320, 328
Voluntary Aid Detachments 189–90

Volunteer Defence Corps (VDC) 175, 177, 186–8, 189
volunteers 10, 42, 92, 101, 110, 206, 218, 220, 238–9, 374
    AIF, 1st and 2nd 62, 63, 65, 70, 72–5, 80, 141, 150, 152, 199–200
    Federation period 12–13, 16, 17, 25–6, 28, 30, 44, 49, 59–60
    reserve scheme 77–8
    see also Citizen Military Force (CMF); Volunteer Defence Corps

Walsh, Lt-Gen F. S. *200*
War Office 10, 11, 43, 63, 69, 142, 144, 146, 182
Washington Conference (1921) 103–4, 107
water transportation 160, *161*, 288, 304, 305–6, 357, 368–9
weapons technology 214, 216, 304, 357, 365, 375, 377
Wells, Lt-Gen Sir Henry 240–1
White, Lt-Gen Sir C. B. B. 63, 69, 86, 89, 112
White Australia policy 6
White Paper (1976) 311–12, 325, 346
Whitelaw, Maj-Gen J. S. 156
Whitlam, E. G. 284, 295, 384
Whitlam Government 284, 295, 333, 384
Wilton, Gen Sir John 268, 269–71, 279, 387
Wolseley, Lord 10
women:
    post-WWII 213–14, 296, 334–5, 354
    WWII 188–91, 334
Women's Royal Australian Army Corps (WRAAC) 213, 264–5, 285, 296, 334
Woodman, Stewart 324
Wootten, Maj-Gen Sir George 225, *227*
World War I 61, 62–80, 93, 189
    coastal defence 70, 71
    equipment 65–7
    home army 70–6
    lessons 76–80, 85, 87, 96, 99, 141
    readiness 76–80
    see also Australian Imperial Force (AIF), 1st
World War II 201, 386
    anti-aircraft defence 156, 158
    coastal defence 155–6, 157m, 303–4
    equipment 140, 143–4, 148, 155–6, 158, 159–60, 178, 182–4, 188, 303–4
    government role 135–40, 145–6, 162, 172–5 *passim*, 177, 191
    higher direction 148, 161–72, 179c, 180c, 187
    jungle divisions 151, 183–6, 185t, 216
    manpower 172–81
    mechanisation policy 178–83
    mobilisation 136–40
    support organisation 144, 159–61, 167–8, 184, 287
    two armies 140–55, 206, 306
    Volunteer Defence Force 186–8, 189t
    women 188–91, 334
    see also Australian Imperial Force (AIF), 2nd; British Commonwealth Occupation Force (BCOF)